Get Your IT Degree

AND GET AHEAD

Get Your IT Degree

AND GET AHEAD

MARIAH BEAR AND JOHN BEAR
WITH TOM C. HEAD

Osborne/**McGraw-Hill**

Berkeley   New York   St. Louis   San Francisco
Auckland   Bogotá   Hamburg   London   Madrid
Mexico City   Milan   Montreal   New Delhi   Panama City
Paris   São Paulo   Singapore   Sydney   Tokyo   Toronto

Osborne/**McGraw-Hill**
2600 Tenth Street
Berkeley, California 94710
U.S.A.

For information on translations or book distributors outside the U.S.A., or to arrange bulk purchase discounts for sales promotions, premiums, or fund-raisers, please contact Osborne/**McGraw-Hill** at the above address.

Get Your IT Degree and Get Ahead

1234567890 AGM AGM 01987654321

ISBN 0-07-212605-1

Publisher
Brandon A. Nordin

Vice President and Editor-in-Chief
Scott Rogers

Editorial Director
Gareth Hancock

Project Manager
Laurie Stewart

Project Editor
Lisa Theobald

Editorial Assistant
Jessica Wilson

Technical Editor
Rory R. Paredes

Copy Editor
Lunaea Weatherstone

Proofreader
Laurie Stewart

Indexer
Jack Lewis

Computer Designer
Maureen Forys, Happenstance Type-O-Rama

Series Design
Maureen Forys, Happenstance Type-O-Rama

Cover Design
Tisa Lerner

This book was composed with QuarkXPress 4.11.

. . . .

To Joe, as ever

—Mariah

To the memory of Robert S. Carwile
(1907–1998)

—Tom

. . . .

CONTENTS

ACKNOWLEDGMENTS

The authors would like to thank everyone at Osborne/McGraw-Hill, especially Robert Bolick, who had the idea for the book and pulled the team together. Others without whom we quite literally couldn't have done it include Scott Rogers, Gareth Hancock, Jessica Wilson, Laurie Stewart, Rory R. Paredes, Lunaea Weatherstone, Maureen Forys, and Jack Lewis.

Mariah would also like to thank her agent, Laurie Harper, her coworkers at Lonely Planet who put up with her during the writing process, and her long-suffering husband and cats, as well as her father, John Bear, who got her started in this whole wacky educational reference business.

Tom would like to give special thanks to John and Mariah for giving him the privilege of working with them, Hector de Jean at McGraw-Hill and Stacy Short at SolutionCentral for the wonderful marketing help, and Atlantic Records for releasing a double live version of *The Lamb Lies Down on Broadway* just in time for his research. He would also, and especially, like to extend thanks to his family for their support and encouragement.

INTRODUCTION

Congratulations! By buying a copy of this book and sitting down to read it, you've made an important decision. Whether that decision is to pursue a new and lucrative line of work in information technology or to move ahead at your current IT job, the right degree is the way to go. In the opening chapters of this book, you'll find it brought home over and over again how useful and rewarding the pursuit and achievement of an IT degree can be for you. Your IT study will make you more marketable, better prepared for a wide range of higher-level jobs, and in demand no matter what direction the economy heads in tomorrow. And getting that degree will also be a surprising amount of fun. Colleges and universities know they need to compete for enrollments, and that boring doesn't cut it when it comes to luring today's wired students. You'll work hard, you'll stay up late, you'll learn more than you ever thought possible—and you'll have a great time doing it. This book is your first step on that exciting and rewarding journey.

In the pages that follow, you'll find a complete toolbox to assist you on that journey. Whether you need to figure out which IT field is the best for you, determine which degree you should pursue, pick the right school, find financial aid, or get the time off work to go back to school, this book has the help you need. Here's a quick roadmap of what you'll find in the book, and how it will help you attain your ultimate goal—the degree of your dreams.

Chapter 1: An Introduction to the World of IT   So, you know you want to work in the burgeoning information technology field, but you're not sure exactly where. Or you have a decent job and wonder how much the right education could do to further your position. This chapter demystifies the basic jobs and degrees, and helps you figure out which will be right for you.

Chapter 2: Frequently Asked Questions   Are you curious about your job prospects? Wondering about financial aid? Worried you won't fit in in a high-tech environment? Wondering if you can study online without quitting your job? This chapter of FAQs offers answers to the questions prospective IT students and graduates are asking.

Chapter 3: Researching and Applying to an Undergraduate Program   This comprehensive chapter offers a detailed look at IT study, including everything you need to know about starting your first bachelor's degree, whether you're just out of high school or looking to advance after years in the workforce. You'll also find details on how to investigate a school and pick the right one for you, what it will cost, exams you'll need to take, and more.

Chapter 4: Researching and Applying to a Graduate School   If you've already earned a bachelor's degree and are interested in an advanced credential, this chapter has the lowdown on strategies for investigating programs, acing exams, and paying for it all with a minimum of hassle and maximum effect.

Chapter 5: Understanding Degrees and Specializations   Have you found yourself wondering what's the difference between a B.S. in computer science and one in computer engineering? An M.S. in management information systems and a technology-focused M.B.A.? This chapter lists all the degree names you're likely to encounter and explains the differences to help you decide what field will be best for you. The six most popular IT fields are described in depth, as well as common or interesting specializations and concentrations.

Chapter 6: Financial Aid Demystified   Strategies for maximizing the financial aid you get toward your degree, including employee assistance programs, federal grants, and other options available to both recent high school graduates and adults returning to school after an absence of many years. There's a lot of money out there for students of all ages, and this chapter points you in a number of lucrative directions.

Chapter 7: Going Back to School As an Adult   Many midcareer professionals, even very successful ones, want to weigh their options carefully, especially after being away from school for so long. Some even feel intimidated at the thought of facing homework, exams, and other things long left behind. In truth, adult students have many advantages, and this chapter helps you benefit from them and advance your career no matter what your age or experience level. Special hints address balancing school and family, remembering how to learn after years out of a classroom environment, and overcoming common fears and misconceptions.

Chapter 8: Using the Internet to Your Advantage   More and more educational programs are going online, and computer-related study is, not surprisingly, at the head of the pack. If you have a computer and an e-mail account, you can probably find a degree program that will allow you to study with little or no in-person attendance. This also allows students to find the program that's right for them and take advantage of it—even if the school is hundreds or thousands of miles from their home! This chapter also covers other Internet features, such as research tools, online applications, and electronic support groups for students.

Chapter 9: The Importance of Accreditation   Don't be ripped off by slick phonies! Sadly, there are a lot of crooks out there eager to take your money and leave you with nothing but a worthless degree. This chapter tells you how to check out a school, make sure it will serve your needs, and confirm it is fully accredited by the relevant agencies. Step-by-step instructions show you how to verify a school's bona fides if you have any suspicions at all.

Chapter 10: Working with Your Employer   One of the toughest issues successful professionals face is needing a degree to move along in their careers, but not being able to take the time off to get that degree. This chapter helps you strategize for going back to school while staying employed—and even getting your employer to pay for your training. Additional advice focuses on how to parlay your degree into a promotion, a raise, or maybe an entirely new job.

Chapter 11: Credit for Prior Learning   Many good, reputable schools offer college credit for life experience, including computer certifications, military service, and on-the-job training. This chapter shows you how to get the credit you need for the things you've already done.

Chapter 12: The Top 199 IT Schools in the U.S.   This rich compendium offers complete listings for the top 199 schools that award undergraduate and graduate degrees in IT, computer science, specialized engineering, and other relevant fields. Here you will find full information for hundreds of programs, including what they cost, how to contact the people who can get you in, degree requirements, and any innovative study methods available.

Appendices   A range of helpful appendices augment this information, including lists of which schools offer degrees in which subject, a handy glossary of IT and educational terms, and a wealth of other resources to guide you on your way.

In other words, this book offers everything you need to find the degree program that's right for you, figure out the best way to pay for it (or get it paid for!), and move on up into the job of your dreams. There's no excuse for delaying—get started today! Before you know it, you'll be studying for a financially rewarding, intellectually challenging job in the world of IT. As we said above, you've already taken the first, most important step. You've decided to go for the gold in your career, and you've bought this book. All you have to do now is follow through, with this handy guidebook at your side, and you will not only get your IT degree, you *will* get ahead. Now, let's get started!

PART I

What You Need to Know About Your IT Education

In This Part

CHAPTER 1

An Introduction to the World of IT

It's a cliché, but it's true—computers are a part of everyday life and becoming more so each year. Companies around the globe are scrambling to find people to design, build, program, use, and maintain those computers. No longer the realm of techies and hackers (though they're still welcome, have no fear!), the computer industry is now one of the largest segments of the world's economy, and there's no sign that opportunities will be anything but booming in the years to come. In fact, the U.S. government predicts that through the year 2006, employment in technology will grow at a much faster than average rate, with tech jobs being the fastest growing occupations nationwide. We're talking about thousands and thousands of jobs every year, jobs with great salaries and benefits. Right now some 2.1 million people are working in IT-related jobs, and the field is growing five times more quickly than the job market's average. The jobs are out there, the field is exciting, and the IT opportunities are almost limitless.

So What, Exactly, Is IT?

Worried that might sound like a dumb question? It isn't. The exact definition of IT changes almost daily as the fields grow and evolve. In a recent report, the U.S. Office of Technology Policy pointed out that millions of people could be considered to be working in the IT field, including auto mechanics who use diagnostic software, librarians (the original information gatekeepers!), data entry clerks, and so forth. In real life, the definition is a bit more narrow—just because McDonald's uses computerized cash registers, the kid who asks "Want fries with that?" is really not an IT professional. The Information Technology Association of America defines an IT worker as someone involved in the study, design, development, implementation, support, or management of computer-based information systems, particularly software applications and computer hardware.

One useful way of breaking down this broad and all-encompassing field is to make a distinction between jobs that expand the IT tools and jobs that use the tools. Examples of the first sort of job involve hardware and software engineering and systems development. The second sort of job would be IT manager–type functions, dealing with support and planning in various industries. So an IT professional could work at a big computer company developing new technologies, or he (or she) might be the IT manager for a small dance company, helping them figure out what their computer needs are, how to evaluate new database products, and, yes, fixing the laser printer when it jams.

Common job titles include IT manager, MIS manager, network expert, information architect, database designer, e-commerce manager, telecom engineer, and so forth. IT professionals are involved in everything from Hollywood movies to NASA shuttle launches, online book sales to environmental protection. One of the exciting things about this field is that it encompasses so much—and so many possibilities. Indeed, many of today's hottest jobs didn't even exist ten years ago. Ask your parents how many CIOs or network support people they knew when they were little. Think about how many your children will know.

The following section lists some basic job descriptions, adapted from a range of sources, including the U.S. government and industry experts. Chapter 5 discusses these jobs in greater depth, from the standpoint of which education programs will be best for which fields of interest. For a wider view of what sort of jobs an IT education might lead you to, one great source is http://www.monster.com/. While mainly known as a job-hunting site, it also offers a wealth of information on jobs in technology, including a feature wherein a different IT professional is

interviewed every week. The archives are available at http://technology.monster
.com/qanda/, and they really highlight an intriguing range of career opportunities, from the corporate corridors (CTO, research engineer) to the artier fields
(new media designer, lead animator). Another useful resource is the U.S. government's Bureau of Labor Statistics. While their job descriptions can be laughably
dull and stilted (and a bit behind the times, especially in a rapidly changing
field), they do give useful information on where jobs will be opening up and
salaries across the country. Check them out at http://stats.bls.gov/.

Common Job Titles and Skills Needed

As discussed above, IT can be any of a number of things. However, some job titles
and skill sets are more common than others. The list below is a good entrance
point to the world of IT jobs and what's required to do them well.

SYSTEMS ANALYST

This is a hardware-focused, engineering-type field, but it can also have a strong
strategic and financial component that appeals to the management-minded. Systems analysts coordinate the contracting, maintenance, and future growth of a
company's computer and IT systems. They work with all departments and often
report to a financial rather than an operational executive. Successful systems
analysts not only know computers, they know people—how to determine what a
department really needs (as opposed to what they *say* they need), how to work
with a restricted budget to make everyone happy, and how to keep an eye on
forthcoming developments that could revolutionize the industry they're working
in. Key skills include:

▶ People management

▶ Interest in overall systems

▶ Interest in hardware and software

▶ Strategic financial thinking

INFORMATION MANAGER

In some companies, an information manager is really nothing more than a high-
tech librarian, coordinating a company's information resources and making sure
they're properly cataloged and accessible. In other, more tech-savvy organizations,

the information manager may work to administer telecommunications hookups and networks, sometimes serving in a bridge position with network administrators. Key skills include:

▶ Knowledge of information cataloging and delivery systems, including databases, inter- and intranet solutions, telecommunications, and networks

▶ People skills, as the IM is often in constant contact with people who need access to information and are having trouble getting what they need

COMPUTER PROGRAMMER

Simply put, programmers write the code that tells computers what to do. Most programmers specialize in either system code (which tells a computer how to interact with its hardware) or applications code (which tells it how to do specific functions, such as word processing or image manipulation). Large (and these days even small or midsize) companies often have programmers on staff who can help the company achieve its goals. For instance, a publishing company may want to database all of its information and needs a code to turn its books into downloadable Web files. The programmer would meet with the project managers, get an idea of what's needed, let folks know what's possible, and create solutions. Key skills include:

▶ Ability to communicate. It's often said that a programmer who's also a people person can pretty much write his or her own ticket.

▶ Ability to write good code and document it well (not always the same thing).

▶ Multitasking and openness to new things are important—if you're only familiar with C++ and won't touch COBOL, you're a lot less valuable to most organizations.

DIRECTOR OF TECHNOLOGY

Sometimes also known as CTO (chief technology officer), this is a broad-based IT job that also ties into strategic planning. At bigger companies, the DT will be reporting to the CTO, who will be mainly concerned with global development and long-term technology and financial strategy. At smaller companies, the DT or CTO may do hands-on work, coding HTML, deciding on network servers' space allocations, and the like. A frequent complaint is that, at a certain level, technology managers are no longer doing what they are good at—they're spending all their time in strategy meetings and managing personnel issues. However, if you're intrigued by the idea of a position in which you may be helping to determine whether to globally pursue XML training one minute and dealing with an employee who doesn't like his workstation the next, this may be a role for you. One great thing about this job is that almost every company needs a DT, if not also a CTO. So if your real love is environmental activism or filmmaking or just about anything else, you can apply your DT skills to the field you care about. Key skills include:

▶ Broad-based knowledge of hardware and software

▶ Interest in strategic and financial planning

▶ Good people skills

▶ Creative problem-solving

Remember, these are just a few of the many, many jobs out there. The sources given in Appendix D, "Resources," can lead to a wealth of job descriptions and places for finding out more.

The Jobs Are Out There!

Going back to those government studies, experts predict that more than a million new IT professionals will be needed in the next ten years. Right now, a quarter of a million IT jobs are empty because of a lack of trained people. That's about one in ten jobs standing empty in the U.S. alone. And it's a global situation—while America may lead the world in IT jobs, we're not alone in needing trained professionals. A recent Microsoft-funded study projects that European companies will need 1.6 million new IT workers by 2002.

Another exciting thing about the IT jobs available is the sheer diversity. It's pretty much impossible for any organization—from book publishers to pet-food stores to filmmakers—to function without IT professionals. Though the higher-paid jobs will likely remain clustered in the traditional "geek" fields of software and hardware engineering, there's a lot more out there for the trained IT professional. A recent *Computerworld* article highlighted challenging and rewarding IT positions with nonprofit organizations that are dedicated to such causes as helping Third World children, saving endangered species, and battling cancer. In the years to come, it will be increasingly possible to target an area you're interested in (from chip design to saving the bald eagle) and find a rewarding IT job that's a perfect fit.

For examples of what those jobs might be, see the resources listed earlier. One of the truly interesting things about surfing IT job sites and reading interviews such as those posted at Monster.com is the repeated theme that you should find people you like to work with, and then you'll enjoy your job. Although serving as network administrator at a major insurance company might seem like tedium incarnate, the same job at a dynamic, hip advertising agency can be fun and exciting. For some lucky people, just doing a job well is reward enough. For most others, however, their job satisfaction comes not just in the job they're doing, but the environment in which they work and the people they're working with. Almost every company operating today needs at least an IT manager helping them set strategy, buy the right equipment, and support it when it fails. Companies of even moderate size can afford a much more diverse IT workforce, with specialists doing systems planning, Web page design, e-commerce support, digital product management, programming, and more.

These positions generally require a strong base of technical and IT-related skills, but they also require such "soft" skills as management and resource allocation, staff supervision of IT talent, and financial planning. Hiring officers are looking for well-rounded candidates for these positions, and the right degree program is a big step toward proving that you do, indeed, have the right range of "hard" and "soft" skills for the new economy.

And those new-economy jobs are truly *everywhere*. While everyone knows about California's Silicon Valley (and, to be fair, it is still the epicenter of the electronic world in many ways), the wired world of the new millennium is literally everywhere. Little entrepreneurs in the backwoods of Maine are setting up Web sites to sell blueberry preserves...and they need tech support, e-commerce solutions, and other types of IT expertise.

In Austin, Texas, once mainly renowned for its alternative music scene and fabulous city parks, some 20 percent of the workforce is employed in high-tech jobs. Salt Lake City, Utah, has more tech companies than fast-food restaurants. In Cambridgeshire, England, high-tech startups nestle alongside medieval cathedrals in an area now known as Silicon Fen. And so it goes. Whether your heart's desire is to live in the backwoods of the Yukon and freelance from home or to be immersed in the very heart of Seattle's multi-billion-dollar tech economy, there's a position out there for you. All you need is the training to make you attractive to employers and the information on where to get that training. That's what this book is all about.

If There Are So Many Jobs Out There, Do I Really Need a Degree?

We've all heard of those famous success stories—Microsoft founder Bill Gates being the most prominent and the most commonly cited. (Yes, he dropped out of Harvard in his junior year to work as a programmer. Of course, he also went back and got a Ph.D. in artificial intelligence, so he's not exactly the poster boy for lack of education!)

The media loves tales of people who dropped out of college, secured a job in the high-tech world, and became fabulously wealthy and powerful. And it does happen. However, these people are the exception rather than the rule. Much more common are the people who drift into IT jobs with very little training, get some certifications, and make a comfortable living. Most of us know a few of those folks, and they don't generally seem to be hurt by their lack of the "right" degree. So why should you spend four or more years of your life studying IT?

The main reason is that the IT field is evolving—some would say, maturing. What that means, in a nutshell, is that in the early days (and remember, we're talking here about an industry that reinvents itself every couple of years) it was easy to get a good job with little or no training, because there was a lot less competition. Employers snapped up likely hires and trained them on the job. This still happens, but those people are likely to stay in lower-level jobs, while new recruits with the right letters after their names are hired in over them and advance much more quickly. These days, hiring requirements are increasingly complex, and the bar is raised even for entry-level positions. At the managerial level, a degree is quite often a prerequisite.

As one IT professional recently put it in an interview for MSNBC, "Someone with a two-year degree in a technical field can work their way up to senior technologist or supervisor, but they will probably not become the manager or a system architect unless they go back to school."

Hiring managers stress that targeted degrees teach not only useful technical skills, but also such vital higher-level functions as creative problem solving, interpersonal communication, and big-picture thinking. While the stereotype of the sociopathic techie is slowly eroding, managers still find that higher education tends to correlate directly with people skills, which are always in demand at the managerial level. In other words, techies are often perceived as introverts who need management skills and the ability to weigh and present their options to the decision-makers in their organizations. The more broad-based training one has, the more valuable one's perceived contribution to a company.

If your career goal is simply to get a job in the IT field and make some money, you can certainly do that without a college degree. In fact, some industry analysts estimate that as many as half of all IT jobs, especially entry-level ones, could be filled by a person without a four-year degree. "The only problem is, I'm not sure what your job will be after that," says Richard Skinner, president of Clayton College in Morrow, Georgia. "You can enter the field, but you're probably going to have to continue your education." Well, okay, but isn't a college president naturally prejudiced? Possibly. However, a scan of midlevel IT job listings will back this up. It is relatively easy for someone with no degree to get a job doing basic data entry and low-level coding, or repair and installation. However, there's a big jump from that sort of position to one managing people, setting strategy, deciding what computers and software packages will be used, or even directing more artistic aspects of the tech world, such as Web site design or animation. Those higher-level jobs almost always require a degree. None other than Bill Gates recently said on C-SPAN that he'd expect anyone graduating with a four-year degree in computer science to get at least ten good job offers.

In short, if you're looking to move up the career ladder and end up in a leadership position, a degree is virtually a necessity. In addition, the actual training you receive in your IT program is likely to be of a higher caliber than could be found in many certification programs—and you'll be making valuable networking contacts who will help you throughout your career. All these factors come together to make an IT degree a very attractive proposition for anyone who's serious about his or her career.

This is not to imply that people without a degree are not talented or management material. Intelligence, problem-solving skills, and hands-on experience count for a lot. The bottom line will always be whether you can make a system work, fix a glitch, or design an easy-to-use application. When you combine these strengths with formal credentials such as a degree in computer science, and a number of certifications, you have a truly unimpeachable package to take out into the job market.

The Next Step

At this point, you should have a basic feeling for what the IT field has to offer you and how your studies might benefit your career. This chapter has provided a few answers, but almost certainly it has raised as many or more questions. In the next chapter, you'll find a number of the most commonly asked questions answered, and you'll be given resources for how to find out even more.

CHAPTER 2

Frequently Asked Questions

Throughout this book, questions will be asked and answered. Still, there are a number of questions that a lot of students or prospective students ask up front—questions about the workplace, about financial aid, about the IT field in general, and so on. Some of these questions can be answered right here, while others are best addressed by directing you to the appropriate chapter. Either way, this chapter should help clear up some common confusions and misconceptions, sending you on your way to your IT degree and workplace success.

Can I really get a great job fresh out of school?

Yes, you can. Some studies even indicate that fresh out of school may be the best look for a job seeker. According to 1998's IT Workforce Study from Virginia Tech and the Information Technology Association of America, the two most challenging training issues for high-tech companies were the fast pace of changing technology and finding qualified trainers. Companies have not been able to train their workers quickly enough in current technologies, and they're seeking employees—some of them fresh from certification programs and other training programs—with the latest skills.

In fact, your biggest challenge may be staying in school once you get your first great job offer. Pre-graduation recruiting is no longer something only found in the world of pro sports. Just like great pigskin talents, promising IT students are finding themselves offered signing incentives, big salaries, and stock options to jump ship before "Pomp and Circumstance" plays. Is this a smart decision? While it's always hard to turn down money, the answer is generally no. If you're such a hot property before graduation, imagine how much hotter you'll be with those oh-so-important credentials after your name.

How much will a degree cost?

There's a wide, wide range of costs, from the possibility of getting credit for life experience, taking some correspondence courses, and getting a bachelor's degree for a few thousand dollars to the other end of the spectrum, four years at an Ivy League college, which could cost close to $100,000. Most will fall somewhere in between and, thankfully, closer to the lower end of the spectrum.

Many decent state universities have very reasonably priced programs that will run you a few thousand dollars a year. If you get creative with your programs, you can get a degree for a reasonable rate. For example, you can take some classes at a community college (where you might only pay a couple of hundred dollars a year) or look into credit for life-experience learning (see Chapter 11 for details on this little-known and totally legitimate option). If top-notch, name-brand schools are important to you, though, be prepared to spend. The detailed school listings in Chapter 12 give fees, and it's pretty easy to get a feel for the ranges.

But remember: a top-notch school doesn't guarantee you a top-notch job. Yes, employers are impressed when they see Harvard, Stanford, or MIT on your résumé. But they're also pretty savvy and know that you may have learned plenty at a state college, especially if you've got a good résumé and interview well.

Is funding available?

In a word, yes. Chapter 6 demystifies the often confusing and daunting world of financial aid, while Chapter 10 describes ways in which you may be able to get your education funded by your employer. Whether you are looking for scholarships, fellowships, training budgets, or low-interest student loans, the money is out there, and we'll show you how to find it.

Do I really need a degree? Isn't certification enough?

There's no simple answer to this question (see Chapter 1 for a more complete discussion of the issues surrounding it). But, in short, the answer is yes, you *can* get by with only certifications—indeed, you may even do very well. However, if you're looking to advance quickly in your career and/or be considered for higher-level management positions, a focused, career-oriented degree is a big asset. There are a number of reasons for this: a degree helps you to stand out from the crowd, it shows you have a real commitment to the field, and it is an indication of problem-solving skills and an ability to do "big picture" thinking. A degree is the *only* credential that says you have what it takes to meet institutional standards and requirements over a longer time period, which is essential to success in the workplace.

What are the hottest jobs in IT?

One thing you can count on with the high-tech world is that as soon as you make a definitive proclamation, something's going to change. But every indication is that tech jobs are going to be a great growth area, and that the following jobs are likely to be strong for some time. According to *U.S. News and World Report*, two tech professions stand out as fields that will skyrocket over the next five years: systems analyst and computer engineer. Meanwhile, *Working Woman* magazine found that the top salaries right now are going to chief information officers at large corporations. Other top titles include senior software engineer and database administrator.

Managerial jobs that are in demand and hard to fill these days include applications development manager and technical services manager. More and more, the ultimate combination seems to be technical savvy and business know-how. According to David Weldon, senior editor in charge of *Computerworld's* IT career coverage, "Increasingly, computer professionals need to be very good business professionals [as well]." People who have crack technical skills, whether you're talking designing SQL databases or writing Java programs, and also have some business acumen can pretty much write their own tickets.

If the business side of things doesn't grab you, look into network or LAN management, e-commerce development, or telecommunications. All of these areas look to be very popular in the coming years. To stay on top of what's in demand, read industry publications or scan online want ads to see what fields seem to be consistently in demand.

How much money can I expect to make?

Another question with a lot of answers, but the easy one is, probably more than in comparable non-IT-focused jobs. So, for example, a business manager at a non-tech company might make $70,000, whereas an e-commerce manager could make over $120,000, according to a study by the American Electronics Association. William Archey, president and chief executive of that organization, went on to say that all the high-tech jobs surveyed outpaced the private sector wage average, some quite substantially.

Of course, not every computer science graduate is going to step out of college into a six-figure income. But initial offers in the $50,000s, plus stock options, are not at all unusual. Though a computer science or other IT degree is not a license to print money, it's pretty close to a guarantee of employability at a better than average rate. We're not going to promise that you'll never have to say, "Want fries with that?"—but we can say that it's pretty darned unlikely.

Which field should I choose?

The simplest answer to this question is to see Chapter 5, where we discuss the many fields available. As IT is still a growing field, it is often seen to encompass a wide range of subjects. After all, ten years ago, what we call "IT" barely existed. Today, it's very popular, but still not clearly defined. At some companies, the IT manager is the person you go to when you can't get your printer to work. At others, a person with the same title (and probably about twice the salary) is setting information architecture policy, doing global technological business projections, and managing a staff of dozens—some of who are the people you go to when your printer doesn't work.

From a B.S. in computer science to a Ph.D. in computational mathematics, what you'll study and where you'll go are markedly different. In Chapter 5, we explain the different degrees (what's the difference between a B.A. in computer science and a B.S. in the same field, and why do some schools offer both?), the different fields, and the concentrations you may encounter. If you're still not sure what's best for you, some time on the phone or e-mail (or, better yet, face to face if at all possible) with admissions counselors at schools offering the programs that seem best suited to your needs and interests will probably help answer any lingering questions. You're not imposing on admissions counselors or department secretaries when you call to ask about their programs. You may end up paying these people (or at least their schools) thousands and thousands of dollars, and you have a right to all the information you need before making a decision.

Do I have to take entrance exams? How hard are they?

Almost every school, graduate and undergraduate, requires entrance exams. If you're a working adult who's been in the IT field for some years and is looking to enroll in an undergraduate program, you may not need to take any exams. High school students, though, will have to take the Standard Achievement Test (SAT) and/or American College Testing (ACT). Graduate students of any age and experience level will almost certainly need to face the Graduate Record Examination (GRE).

These tests are described in Chapters 3 and 4, (for undergraduate and graduate). The SAT and ACT are not considered particularly difficult, although it never hurts to prepare for them. The GRE can be a bit trickier, and we do recommend finding a test preparation course in your local area before you take this one on. Test-prep courses can range from the modestly priced to the very expensive—look for ones offered by community colleges, adult education programs, and university extension facilities. Those offered by private, for-profit companies can cost up to $1,000 and, while it may be worth it to get a high score, there are probably cheaper options. If you're self-disciplined, you may only need to buy a test-prep book and do all the exercises. If you learn better in a classroom environment, with someone there to help you out, the classes are probably the way to go.

Generally speaking, the more recently you've been in school, the better you'll do on standardized tests. Experts think this is probably just because testing is something you need practice at, and test-prep courses and books can provide that practice.

How important is accreditation? How can I tell if a school is properly accredited?

It is almost impossible to overstate the importance of accreditation. While some good but extremely experimental unaccredited schools do exist, the vast majority of unaccredited schools are slick phonies that exist to take your money and leave you with a worthless piece of paper. If you're interested in a traditional residential school, accreditation really isn't an issue—very few phonies have the resources to fake an entire campus. If, however, you're investigating distance-learning options, you're entering a potential minefield of false claims, shady programs, and broken dreams. A simple Web search for "distance learning + computer science" offers up thousands of options, hundreds of which are fakes. Good, smart, well-meaning people are taken in by these schools, give them money, and get nothing in return. The good news is that it's really not hard to cut through the noise and find out instantly whether or not a school has proper accreditation. Chapter 9 offers expert insight into what to beware of and how to check out any school's claims.

I have a full-time job. How can I take time off to earn a degree?

The easy answer is that you probably don't have to. Of course, you need to evaluate your individual situation and make the decisions that are right for you. But, that said, colleges and universities are filled with what's known as "returning" or "reentry" students—people who have been out in the workforce for a few years and decided to go back to finish (or start) the education they put off to build a career. Many schools offer night and weekend classes, and many structure programs to be done in short intensives rather than the traditional daily courses.

Is it stressful to work full-time and go to school as well? Yes, it can be—we won't lie to you. But thousands of people across the country are doing it, and more often than not, they're finding that the rewards greatly overbalance the stresses. It's absolutely acceptable to do a program on a slightly slower track than full-time students—maybe finishing a bachelor's degree in six years rather than four, or a graduate program in four rather than two. However, adult students also have the advantage of often being able to gain credit for real-life certifications and experiences, which can significantly reduce the actual time spent in classrooms.

If your current job really isn't what you want to be doing, you might also consider looking for enough financial aid to allow you to quit and dedicate yourself to school full-time. That's a scary proposition, but the faster you get through that program, whether graduate or undergraduate, the faster you'll be highly employable in the field of your choice. The money is out there, in both loans and grants. See Chapter 6 for more detailed information on researching, applying for, and winning the financial aid you need.

Am I too old to start on this course of study?

Many years ago, Abigail Van Buren (better known as Dear Abby) ran a letter and response that have become famous in the world of adult education. In essence, someone wrote to her saying that he had always wanted to get an advanced degree, but he was in his 30s and would be 40 years old before the course of study was finished. Dear Abby's response: And how old will you be in four years if you *don't go* to school?

There are several factors at work here. One is the fear of going back to school and being older than everyone else in the classroom. In Chapter 7, on the advantages of midcareer learning, we discuss why this may in fact be an advantage rather than a disadvantage. Adult students are generally seen to be more serious, more dedicated, and more goal-focused than their younger counterparts. Yes, sitting in a classroom full of kids may be disconcerting at first, but once the real work begins, age is fairly irrelevant. Evening and weekend classes tailored to working professionals or reentry students will have a much higher percentage of older students, and age becomes totally irrelevant when studying via distance learning. Unless you choose to tell your online professor and student support group your age, they never need to know.

In the IT field, there is often an additional anxiety about being "too old for computers." It's true that people who grew up using computers may be initially more at home with programming languages and the like, but our files are full of anecdotal tales about grandmothers who take to programming like a fish to water. Senior-citizen advocacy groups such as AARP and SeniorNet tell us there are millions of people over 55 on the Internet, with more coming online every day. As long as you have a genuine interest in learning and an aptitude for math and systematic thinking, you are not too old to learn about computers.

Is IT a "boys' club"? How hard is it for a woman to break in? To succeed?

The short answer is that, although women have made great strides in technical fields and are employed in literally every imaginable realm, they are still a minority by a large margin. The encouraging answer is, this is less and less true every day. Fifteen years ago, it wasn't unusual to hear of women with degrees in computer science answering the phones at technology companies because that was "women's work." According to Carolyn Leighton-Tal, founder of Women in Technology International, the number of women on high-tech fields has increased dramatically over the past ten years—in part because of changing views of women in the workplace and (less charitably) because the shortage of trained professionals means that chauvinistic employers can't afford *not* to hire qualified women. In fact, many Fortune 500 companies now co-sponsor tech groups for women and encourage women's technical education.

Some 28 percent of all bachelor's degrees, 27 percent of master's degrees, and 15 percent of doctorates in IT fields are going to women, and this translates over to the job world, where 29 percent of IT jobs are held by women. This is likely to increase as schools adapt their programs to be more appealing to women. One innovative program is taking place at Smith College in Massachusetts, which has just established the first engineering program at a women's college in the U.S., the Picker Program in Engineering and Technology. Other schools will no doubt follow, with programs specially designed for young women. In a true sign of the times, even the Girl Scouts now have merit badges in the Internet and in technology.

As to whether the IT realm is a boys' club once you've got your degree and are out in the world, company cultures vary, but the stereotypical geeks who haven't ever seen a woman and don't know how to talk to one are increasingly rare. Women may have to put up with some raised eyebrows from older employees who haven't kept up with the times, but one of the nice things about working in a cutting-edge field is that social attitudes tend to change more quickly too. Professional standards are gender-free, and talent will always be appreciated. These days, women are running major corporations and making public policy, not just answering the phones.

I'm physically disabled. Will this affect my ability to get a degree?

Under the Americans with Disabilities Act, signed into law in 1990, all institutions are "required to make reasonable accommodations to the known physical and mental limitations of otherwise qualified individuals with disabilities." As to which schools will be best for you, it's a general rule of thumb that larger state schools and better-funded private schools will have more resources available—more than the minimum required, that is. Most schools will have an ADA-compliance office, and you should contact those offices as part of your pre-application research. Ask what resources are available to disabled students, how many students with disabilities are currently enrolled in the program of your choice, and whether all facilities are accessible or if you'll need to have special accommodations made for you.

If your disability confines you to home, you can still earn your degree through distance learning, and you may well be able to use that training and networking experience to then find IT-related work in a wholly virtual environment. See Chapter 8, on using the Internet, for strategies that will work best for you. As noted below under the FAQ "Can I do my degree online?" it is possible to get a fully accredited degree from a top university without ever leaving your home.

My bachelor's degree is in a nontechnical field. Will that affect my ability to get into a master's program in IT?

In a word, no. As one prominent school says on their Web site, "You do not have to be an undergraduate computer science major to apply, get accepted, or succeed in our graduate department. Frankly, our admissions committee is more impressed by an extraordinary aptitude and knowledge in history, linguistics, or music than by an average knowledge in computer science." Most graduate-level admissions people will tell you they've seen successful students whose undergraduate degrees were in anything from English literature to cognitive psychology. A solid background in math is certainly helpful, and if you haven't taken enough advanced math classes as an undergraduate, you may be asked to take them as a prerequisite to admission—either before enrollment or in your first year of studies, in addition to other core classes. If you're looking to specialize in artificial intelligence, a background in linguistics or psychology is actually considered a big plus.

Good GRE scores are also a big help, especially if your background is nontechnical. Even if the school doesn't require it, consider taking an advanced GRE exam in math and/or computer science. A high score will help eliminate any questions about whether you have what it takes to succeed. If you've already worked in the field and can get letters of recommendation from your employer or supervisor raving about your skill with computers and technical fields, all the better.

I just don't love math. Will this hold me back?

It really shouldn't. Logic, not math, is key to understanding computing, and when you get to the managerial level, other skills are even more important. William A. Schaffer, author of *High-Tech Careers for Low-Tech People*, notes that over 60 percent of the techies he interviewed about what skills they consider to be vital to high-tech success mentioned, to his surprise, communication. He quotes one software-engineering VP as saying, "Excellence in communication. That means listening, writing, speaking...After all, that is what 95 percent of your people really do all day long."

This doesn't mean you won't have to use a lot of math skills in your school career. But if it's any consolation, you'll likely not be using them nearly as much once you graduate, especially if you choose to take on a job that's more targeted to management of people or information systems. A surprising number of people working in the field say that while they can do math, they never really enjoyed it in school. This may come as a surprise—after all, we tend to divide the world into liberal arts types and math and science types—but in reality, there's a lot of crossover. You'll need to use math while you're in school, and the better you understand the mathematical underpinning of the things you're working on, the more sophisticated your solutions can be. On a day-to-day basis, you can be a math-hating IT person—and you won't be alone!

Will a bachelor's degree be enough, or do I need a master's?

There's no one answer for every situation, but, in general, a bachelor's degree will get your foot in the door for many, many jobs. If you want a higher-level managerial job, an appropriate master's degree (or even a—gasp!—MBA) may be what you need to progress to the next level. It makes sense to get the focused bachelor's degree, spend a few years in the workforce, and figure out exactly what aspect of the IT world is most attractive to you. Remember that undergraduate programs can be fairly broad, letting you learn a little bit about a lot of things. A graduate program will be much more specific in focus, so it makes sense to get a good feel for what it is you want to do before spending the time and money. Also, if you end up with the right employer, they may agree to help finance your graduate or continuing education. So there are a lot of good reasons to wait.

Is a master's degree enough, or do I need to go on and get a doctorate?

There is almost no job outside of academia or very intense research fields in which you'll need a doctoral degree. Yes, if you want to teach at the university level or head up a NASA lab, you may need a Ph.D. or other doctorate, but for most positions, a master's is the highest you'll need to go. Indeed, in the job world (again, outside of research laboratories and academia), a doctoral degree may even brand you as someone who is too theoretical in his approach and doesn't have enough real-world experience. The impression can be that while you were studying all that high-level theoretical math, your competitor for the job was learning people management, troubleshooting, and other non-academic essentials.

I don't have an undergraduate degree, but I'd rather enroll in a master's program. Is that possible?

There are at least three ways that this might work out:

▶ Ask about combined B.S./M.S. programs. Many schools in this book offer this option (see Chapter 12). While you may not save a lot of time over the more traditional method (which is to say, enrolling in an undergraduate program and then transitioning into a master's program after you graduate), there are some economies to be gained in terms of prerequisites and transfer credits. You'll also have the guarantee that your undergraduate and graduate programs will be complementary.

▶ If you've taken some undergraduate courses at some point in your career, and/or have broad-based experience and some certifications, you may be able to parlay these into the equivalent of an accredited undergraduate degree, which would be accepted by any school in this book. See Chapter 11 for more details on alternative and unusual ways of earning college credit.

▶ If you have sufficient experience in the field, some schools will admit you to a graduate program based on your entrance exam scores and proof of your hands-on training and experience. Generally speaking, you'll need to have been operating at a fairly high level for three to five years to get this dispensation. We list these schools in Chapter 12 and give details in the school-by-school listings.

I'm interested in the business of IT. Would an MBA be better for me than a tech-focused master's degree?

Five years ago, this would have been a more difficult question to answer, as MBAs tended to be very traditional—you learned about human resources, strategic planning, accounting, and the like, with optional concentrations in fields such as international business or business law. These days, however, many business schools have caught up with the times and are offering tech-focused MBAs. You'll still need to decide if you're more of a techie or more of a businessperson. If the thought of five-year cash-flow projections and currency-exchange fluctuations make your eyes roll back in your head, you might want to avoid the MBA. No matter how tech-focused the program is, it will still be for businesspeople who are interested in technology, not technologists who are interested in business.

Right now, you may not be sure in which direction you want to go. Take the time to think about how you'd answer that most cliché of job-interview questions: Where do you see yourself in five years? If the answer involves hands-on technology development, or even management of teams doing hands-on development, support, or implementation, the MBA might not be the right direction. If the business administration side of it really interests you, though, you might want to look into a tech-focused MBA. If you're envisioning starting your own company and already have a fair amount of hands-on tech knowledge, the real-world business case studies and problem-solving you'll get in a good MBA program might be a big key to your success.

Can I do my degree online? Will employers accept an online degree?

More and more schools are taking their degree programs online, and computer fields are, not surprisingly, at the head of the pack. If you have a computer and an e-mail account, you can probably find a degree program that will allow you to study with little or no in-person attendance. When you combine this with credit for existing credentials and other real-life learning, you may be able to get your degree more quickly and easily than you ever suspected was possible. But even if you're starting from ground zero, you will almost certainly be able to find an online program that suits your needs.

Appendix C indexes schools that offer distance-learning programs, and those programs are described in detail in Chapter 12 (which gives the skinny on 199 schools and their degree programs, ranging from the traditional to the Internet and encompassing everything in between).

As to whether your employer will accept an online degree, the answer is almost certainly yes, for a couple of reasons. First of all, diplomas don't state how you got your degree—an M.S.E.E. from Stanford is the same prestigious degree whether you sat in classrooms for two years or studied over the Internet. If you plan to study while employed, you may need to explain to your employer how you're doing your coursework, but it's highly unlikely that he or she will have any objections. Especially in technology-focused jobs, computer-based delivery of information is a daily reality. Your employer may have read about phony universities operating over the Internet, but as long as you're doing your program with a fully accredited school, you should be able to provide every assurance of the degree's legitimacy.

Is there any downside to online study?

In general, online programs are a great way for busy professionals to get the education they need. Programs vary—in some, you move at your own pace, downloading coursework as you need it; in others, you study along with a non-virtual classroom, so the instruction and the degree are virtually indistinguishable from those gained in a traditional classroom. However, we have heard from some Internet students that they miss the human interaction—kicking around ideas, collaborating on projects, grabbing a cup of coffee between classes with like-minded fellow-students. All of this but the coffee (no jokes here about Java-enabled sites!) can be duplicated via chat rooms, discussion forums, and e-mail, but still, it's not the same as rubbing shoulders the old-fashioned way. Whether you miss this or find it an insurmountable obstacle is something only you can answer. Some students are thrilled to get their coursework done online, participate in some online chat, and then get "face time" at work, with the family, or in any of a number of other ways. Others will never feel totally satisfied unless they're crammed into an uncomfortable plastic chair, desperately taking notes while watching a real flesh-and-blood professor pace back and forth, jingling keys in his or her pocket. If you're intrigued by the idea of online study, give some careful thought to which of these scenarios is most appealing.

Will my skills go out of date? How can I guard against this?

To somewhat oversimplify, an IT education consists of two sorts of skill sets, one that goes out of date and another that doesn't. Let's begin with that second set. Corny as it may sound, learning how to learn is an important skill. Employers often require a college degree less for the actual learning that took place in the classroom than for the sign that you're a person who's capable of the sort of mental discipline required to get a college degree. Jason Zien, About.com's Internet industry expert, points out that some of the best things you'll get out of college are learning to work well with others, leadership, and independent problem-solving. These aren't the kind of skills that go out of date, and their importance in the workplace can't be over-estimated.

That said, some of your line-by-line skills are going to go out of date, and you need to stay on top of the industry. What exact areas you need to focus on depend on your area of specialization. Network people may not need to know about e-commerce innovations, and if you're working in Visual Basic, you may not need to stay up on all the debates around Linux. Read industry magazines, find the best Web sites (your professors will be able to point you in good directions here), and keep an active network—of humans, not cables. If you find that most of your Visual Basic–using contacts are learning Java, pay attention. Your company may pay to send you to training courses and, if it doesn't, you'll need to keep an eye on what training and certifications will help you keep current. The companion book to this one, *Get Certified and Get Ahead* (Osborne/McGraw-Hill) by Anne Martinez, can help you determine which certifications might be useful and what you can expect to pay for them.

Remember, the most important thing you can do for yourself and your career is to stay plugged in. Find an online chat group you like and drop in regularly. Go out for coffee or drinks with people in your industry every so often, and ask them what's new. (One friend of ours just made the jump to a big IT job and doubled his salary as a result of having a beer every so often with one of his company's competitors. The fact that he's smart and talented helped too, but he would never have come to their attention if he hadn't made the effort to know folks socially.) Never stop learning and you'll never end up out of date.

CHAPTER 3

Researching and Applying to an Undergraduate Program

Whether you're a high school junior looking at where you'll be heading off to in a year or so or a midcareer professional going back for the degree you never thought you'd need after ten years in the workforce, certain questions apply. This chapter is targeted more to the first-time college-goer—adult students might wish to skim this chapter, and then turn to Chapter 7, which addresses concerns and questions common to the older student. Here, we'll go over the steps you should take on your way to enrolling in the undergraduate IT program of your dreams (grad students, skip ahead to the next chapter), highlight some common problems people run into and mistakes they make, and offer solutions.

Reality Check: Is This the Right Field for You?

You've read about the amazing market for trained technology workers. You've seen the statistics on starting salaries (significantly higher than you're likely to find in most other fields). You've bought this book. You want to get in on this exciting field. Most likely, the next step is figuring out precisely which field you'd like to pursue (computer science versus MIS versus information technology, and so forth), choosing the right school, and getting your application process underway. That's what the bulk of this chapter covers. However, it's worth taking a moment to consider whether this really is your field.

One more thing to remember is that "this field" covers a wide range of options. Popular computer and IT specializations are described in detail in Chapter 5, but the following is a quick look at areas you might choose to major in.

The Six Most Popular Tech Majors

While you will find dozens and dozens of degree titles available to you, the vast majority of undergraduate IT students get their degrees in one of the six areas described below.

COMPUTER SCIENCE

While CS is a catchall major that can encompass many aspects of the tech world, it is generally more science-oriented than focused on engineering, applications, programming, or even mathematics. Computer science involves more research and theoretical study than other disciplines, yet it still happens to be the most marketable computer major out there, mostly due to name recognition (although computer engineering is rapidly catching up).

ELECTRICAL ENGINEERING

At the opposite end of the spectrum is a major that deals with the most physical aspect of IT: gadgets and electronics, silicon boards and copper wire, transformers and circuits. This major has often been seen as a bit downmarket or "voc-tech," but many hardware visionaries got their start here. Electrical engineering is the field for you if you're interested in the basic principles behind motherboards, networking, power distribution, and circuit design.

COMPUTER ENGINEERING

Some CE programs are just electrical engineering dressed up in a new title for the new millennium. However, a real specialized CE track is developing at the better schools, featuring a multilevel approach to computers. This approach looks at how computers are built and how to fix them, as well as everything from networking and digital storage to software design and hardware/software integration.

SOFTWARE ENGINEERING

This field has become more and more popular in recent years, and for good reason. Though it's impossible for any one person to design new hardware without a lot of financial help, almost anyone with a basic background in programming can design new software, and entrepreneurs and visionaries are drawn to the possibilities.

COMPUTER INFORMATION SYSTEMS

Usually, CIS is a traditional computer science curriculum with less in the way of theory, programming, and higher mathematics—leaving more room for study in other fields and/or other hands-on information technology issues. Sometimes, however, there's a strong business-operations focus.

INFORMATION SCIENCE

This major focuses on information storage and retrieval, including how to design search engines, compare and sort data automatically, and make it all useful in a real-world setting.

OTHER POPULAR IT FIELDS

Other fields you may wish to look into include:

▶ Artificial intelligence and cognitive neural systems, on the more theoretical end of things

▶ Applied computer science and client-server technology, on the more service-oriented end

▶ New interdisciplinary fields such as telecommunications, computer-aided graphic design, computational mathematics, and management information systems

All of these are described in greater depth in Chapter 5.

Deciding on an IT Degree

A recent study from George Mason University reported that 43 percent of non-IT workers wish they had majored in a technical field. What that means is that the word is out—this is a hot field of study. But is it right for you? At the most basic level, ask yourself whether you like (or at least, are good at) math, or if you just like computers (or would like to make a lot of money). Reality check! If you don't like math, you're not going to enjoy a field of study in computer science, where your first year of specialization is likely to include such courses as calculus and linear algebra. If you expect to specialize in theoretical computer science, especially at the graduate level, it gets more intense, with courses in probability, combinatorics, graph theory, and topology.

Even a seemingly "artistic" concentration such as computer graphics involves a fair amount of math when you get into point plotting, surface algorithms, and the like. Still, if the thought of other aspects of the program, such as intensive C programming, animation, and 2-D to 3-D conversion are exciting, maybe the math will feel like a reasonable price to pay. After all, this isn't a theoretical math field—you're learning math as a tool to help you do the real work of programming. In many programming and systems design projects, logic is more important than math, which you may find heartening.

Just be sure you're picking a concentration you're interested in, or a few years down the line, when you're in the computer lab late at night running simulations and pounding extra-dark roast to keep your eyes open, you're going to wish you'd listened to that guidance counselor who tried to steer you toward commercial arts, business administration, or other computer-related but less math-intensive fields.

By the same token, some students do the opposite—even if they might be interested, they turn away from IT because they think that all IT gives them is the chance to sit in front of a computer running some kind of program—when actually IT has a myriad of exciting tasks that do not involve any terminal at all. Don't let this image of day-in/day-out keyboarding faze you. Follow your interest and give yourself a chance to check out IT degrees and the professions they lead you to.

If you're having questions about whether this is, indeed, what you want to be doing, spend a little time talking to high school guidance counselors or college admissions people. There may well be a computer-focused program out there that's not exactly IT-driven, but that suits your needs and interests. For instance, you might be interested in sales and marketing, in which case, you might want to look at a business major with an MIS minor. Or maybe you like Web design, in which case, a graphic design major with a concentration in digital projects is the way to go. There are many, many possible career paths in the technology world, and the right degree for you does exist.

To get a good feel for what you're going to be studying in various fields, take a look at Chapter 5, which breaks down the various fields of study mentioned above in much greater detail, and explains what you'll be focusing on in each. Then you can look at Appendix B, "Subject Index," and check out the listings for schools that offer a field you find intriguing. So, for example, if you're intrigued by MIS, you'd first check out Chapter 5, and find that, in general, MIS is less math and technology-driven, and more focused on business solutions. That intrigues you, so you go to the Subject Index and find 35 undergraduate degrees listed in the field. Reading the listings, you find that some programs are more people-oriented (training you to help out the end users), while others focus more on network solutions. This will help you apply to only those programs that will really suit your needs.

⊙ **COMMON PROBLEM**
Choosing an IT degree field because it seems like it'll lead to a good job, then finding out you're not suited to this field of study.

✔ **SOLUTION**
Do your research! If you like computers and have a flair for math and/or logic, the right program is out there. Read the listings in this book thoroughly, and you'll probably find something that will work for you. If not, you really do need to evaluate whether you'd be happier doing something computer-related, such as a more business-focused MIS program (we only list those with a strong technology component), an art-targeted computer animation degree, and so on.

Imagine yourself working on a computer-related task—that is, a system, a program or an activity designed to help other people be more productive through computing—then ask yourself if this is what you will enjoy doing. Write down your immediate reaction, because usually your first thought is your truest one. Still not sure? Try working in computer-related part-time jobs that will give you experience in what IT jobs are like. A big plus—you'll have real-life experience to bring to your school applications and to part-time jobs or internships once in school.

Picking a School

You've decided that there is, indeed, an IT degree out there for you, whether it's a philosophy and neurolinguistic-programming-tinged artificial intelligence program or a number-crunching B.S. in computer science. There are thousands of colleges and universities to choose from—which one is right for you? Buying this book was a good first step—in the 199 schools listed in Part II, you will almost certainly find the one that will suit your needs and help you get the degree you want. But there's more to picking a school than just making sure it offers the degree you want (or think you want!). Other factors to consider are discussed in the sections that follow.

Academics

If you're a C student, it may not be realistic to apply to the most prestigious schools. There may be a state school that can meet your needs—and then, once you've gotten some great grades in your freshman and sophomore years, you can always look at transferring to that top-rated school. A more extreme version of this is to look at community colleges. Often overlooked, these schools can be a low-cost way of building credits, and some have quite an impressive track record for sending their students on to good, even Ivy League, destinations. If you have shaky grades or not much money, look into your local community colleges, and ask them about transfer rates for computer science students. You might be pleasantly surprised—and save some money, too!

Location, Location, Location

It's easy to fall in love with a school's program without thinking about where you'll be spending the next four years or so of your life. If you hate the snow, maybe that New England–based school isn't for you, no matter how great their computer lab looks. If your finances aren't great and you live near a good state school, maybe it wouldn't be so terrible to live at home and save money during your first couple of years. If you want or need to work while attending school, what are the job opportunities in the area? An isolated school might not offer the same career flexibility as one in a central city area. On the other hand, if you're easily distracted, maybe that isolated school will help to keep you focused.

Look at the Program

IT is enough of an evolving field that there are some significant differences between programs from school to school, even if the program is called exactly the same thing. A B.S. in informational systems might be a highly technical IT-solutions-focused program, or it might be what in days gone by was known as library science. An MIS degree might involve high-level theoretical study of computer systems and how they work, or it might be a business-oriented program of interest mainly to future office managers. If the school is prestigious and has a great location, but it just doesn't offer exactly what you want, stop right there. The wrong degree from the right school isn't going to make you happy or fulfilled in your career.

As you read through the programs in this book, keep these factors in mind. Look at them with an eye to what you want out of a program, what the school can offer you, whether it's in a place you'd like to be, and whether, realistically, you're the kind of student they're looking for.

Remember, too, that you can get creative with your degree program. You may be able to put together a package that includes credit for prior experience, distance-learning courses over the Internet, and traditional classroom learning at the school of your choice. These options will be discussed in greater depth in Chapters 8 and 11.

High School Students: An Action Timeline

Picking the right school is only part of the preparation and application process. This section will map out the path to take to get you where you want to be.

First, let's assume a fairly ideal situation. The reality is that most students don't start thinking seriously about college until senior year of high school. That said, if you're sure you know what you want as early as junior year, there's a lot you can do to improve your chances of getting into the school of your dreams— if you have the time, resources, and motivation to pursue it. We know this isn't the case for every student, so the timeline below may not work for everyone. Still, it's useful to know what you should do in an ideal world, even if your situation is not quite so ideal. We'll look at some helpful workarounds in the "Common Problems" section of this topic.

Junior Year of High School

In their junior year, many students are only just starting to think about college. After all, it's more than two years away. Understandable as this is, the earlier you start your planning, the easier the process will be. The following hints will get you well on your way to those precious acceptance letters—which, in turn, will make senior year a lot less stressful.

✔ Begin collecting information about colleges. This book is a great start—it should help you choose the top schools for your field of interest. Check out Web sites, write for information, and attend college nights if they're offered at your school.

✔ In the fall, sign up and study for the Preliminary SAT/National Merit Scholarship Qualifying Test. Good scores on this important (though nonessential) test will increase your attractiveness to schools and widen your financial aid possibilities.

✔ Think about visiting local colleges if there are any around, just to get a feel for what campus life is like.

✔ In February, sign up and start studying for the SAT.

✔ If at all possible, plan to visit some campuses you're interested in come spring or summer.

✔ Look at the classes you're planning to take in your senior year. Make sure they'll be appropriate for your chosen field of study—the more math and computer science you can get in, the better, especially advanced placement courses. But colleges also look for well-rounded students, so don't neglect extracurricular activities, volunteer work, and all those other great résumé-builders.

The Summer Before Senior Year

You may have to work, you may have family vacation plans, but hey, you've got three months. Try to spend some portion of that time getting ready for the big college applications blitz.

✔ If at all possible, visit some of the colleges you're interested in, and meet with admissions staff, financial aid people, and members of the computer science faculty. Have a look at the computer lab facilities and see how good they look to you. Drop by the career center, and see if they seem technologically savvy and well staffed. Do they have relationships with any major tech employers? Do they know what the hot fields in technology are right now?

✔ Look for an appropriate summer job. If you can afford to, it's better to work for free in your field than to take a decent-paying job that's totally unrelated. Volunteering in your school's computer lab is better than waiting tables. Admissions committees look for evidence that you're committed to a field, and a summer job can make a big difference. It can also give you good material for entrance essays, if any of the schools you're interested in require them, and a boss or supervisor is a great source for a letter of recommendation.

✔ If any of the schools you're interested in require an essay or personal statement, start working on it. You'd be surprised how hard these can be to get right—and how valuable they can be in getting you noticed. See "Entrance Essays" later in this chapter for specific tips.

◎ **COMMON PROBLEM**
You can't afford to do campus visits.

✔ **SOLUTION**
Campus visits are very highly recommended, but not absolutely essential. While it is true that there is nothing like sitting in a school cafeteria or on a campus green to check out the atmosphere, sitting in a couple of classes and listening to a popular professor, meeting your student advisor in person, and so on, for some this just won't be financially doable. Try all the options at hand—maybe you have a high school graduation check that could be used for airfare? Still and all, if worst comes to worst, you can still make an informed decision. Many school Web sites give a good feel for the school, and catalogs can be useful, too. Think of specific questions you may have—what's the racial mix at the school (if that's important to you), are there many women in computer sciences, how much does it rain in the winter. These are all valid questions to ask of an admissions person, whether by e-mail or on the phone. If your funds are limited (and whose aren't!), you might want to see if you can squeeze out a visit to just your top three schools.

Senior Year

This is a very busy and stressful—as well as exciting—time for most students, and you may have a hard item staying focused. Make those calendars and time-lines, and post them where you can't miss being reminded of what you need to do. You're almost there!

✔ Check out the admissions, financial aid, and housing deadlines for all the schools you're interested in. Create a calendar or checklist listing all-important documents and their deadlines so you don't miss any important dates. There are a lot of them—financial aid and housing deadlines are often quite different from application deadlines. Different schools require different documentation, from you or from your parents, depending on your age and tax status. This can feel like a full-time job while you're also trying to finish out your last year of high school with good grades (and yes, colleges do look at your senior year grades), but the preparation pays off.

✔ Take the SAT and have your scores sent to your top schools.

✔ Narrow your choices and apply to the schools that best fit your needs. See "Picking a School" earlier for suggestions on how to choose schools. The following sections provide tips on how to make yourself more appealing to school admissions boards.

⊙ **COMMON PROBLEM**
You are most of the way through senior year before being able to focus on a school or maybe even choose a major.

✔ **SOLUTION**
There's no law that says you have to go to college right out of high school. Even if you miss every application deadline, you should just see how much you can get accomplished right away (maybe one school you're interested in has a late admissions deadline). But if you have to work for six months or a year before enrolling, it won't make that much difference in the long run. In fact, you'll make a little extra money and have some real-world experience to bring to the classroom. Once you get to college, you'll find students ranging from the whiz kids who skipped two grades and enrolled at age 15 to the returning professionals in their forties. You won't stand out.

✔ Receive those all-important fat acceptance envelopes, pick the school of your choice, and get ready for a great experience. Don't throw away a thin envelope thinking it's just a rejection. This sounds like a dumb piece of advice, but it happened to one student we know of—and it turned out that thin envelope was a request for just one more piece of information before acceptance could be completed. This story had a happy ending—she eventually opened the envelope and got them what they needed in time, but it could have been a disaster. Open your mail and read it the instant you get it!

Entrance Exams

Nobody likes exams. Well, okay, somebody out there probably does, but not anyone we want to meet any time soon. The good news is that entrance exam scores are becoming less and less important to admissions committees. After years of evidence that scores are a useful, but not a vital, predictor of college success, schools are shifting their emphasis. Many now look more closely at applicants' overall grades, the number of AP (advanced placement) courses they took in high school, their essays, their extracurricular activities, and all those things that say more about a person than a numerical score.

Indeed, some schools have dispensed with entrance exams altogether (Bowdoin College in Maine led the pack, way back in 1969). Still, even if a school doesn't require exams, it just makes sense to take them. High scores will still be impressive and may overweigh some other weaknesses in your application. And the top schools do still, in general, use test scores as a way of weeding through stacks and stacks of highly qualified applicants.

The tests you're likely to encounter are described in the following sections.

PSAT

Offered during the junior year of high school, this test is not required anywhere, but it is a good idea to take it. Co-sponsored by the College Board and National Merit Scholarship Corporation, this test's goal is to assess critical reading, math problem-solving, and writing skills. It is very similar to the SAT I and SAT II and is a great way to practice for these key tests. In addition, a high score puts you in line for scholarships and other perks. The PSAT is administered by high schools; talk to your guidance counselor about how to sign up. You can take the test before your junior year, but until then it won't qualify you for scholarships.

SAT I

The SAT I is the basic SAT, which measures verbal and math ability. Most schools still require this test for admission, and there are a wealth of software packages, books, and courses available to help you prepare. Studies have found that preparation is important, but that you can get as much out of a $17.95 book as you could from a $900 test-prep course (and yes, the courses can be that expensive!). What it really comes down to is discipline—force yourself to spend a few hours a week with the book or the online program, and you'll likely do fine. One article, in the prestigious *U.S. News and World Report* education section, even suggested that superhigh scores can have a downside—students with perfect SAT scores and no extracurricular activities were seen as not being well-rounded, and were often rejected by admissions committees. Take that with a grain of salt, of course. If you have perfect scores and a great transcript, plus some extracurriculars, the odds that anyone will hold a perfect score against you are low.

SAT II

These focused subject tests are offered in a range of fields. You may want or need to take them in either of the math concentrations available. There is no computer- or technology-specific concentration, though we guess that will change over time.

ACT

Virtually all schools accept the ACT in place of the SAT I, though some express a preference for the SAT. The test is broken into sections focusing on English, reading, mathematics, and science reasoning. This last section is useful for future technology majors, and you may wish to take the ACT if only to convince the school of your choice of your aptitude for computer sciences, if your transcript isn't as strong as it could be in that area.

AP

Advanced Placement exams are an opportunity for high school students who've taken AP classes to demonstrate their abilities—and sometimes even get college credits, advanced college standing, or both with high scores. Different high schools offer different AP programs, but if you're lucky, you'll be able to take computer science and calculus.

TOEFL

The Test of English as a Foreign Language is given to international students looking to study in the United States. Many programs specify a required score on this test as an admissions prerequisite for people whose first language is other than English.

Entrance Essays

You might feel that in a technically focused program, verbal skills are less important than they would be in, say, English literature—and, to some degree, that's true. Still, to reiterate, schools are interested in well-rounded students, and a math genius who can't string two sentences together isn't likely to do well in the university environment (or in the workplace, despite all the folklore about reclusive techie types). So, while your essay may not be a make or break factor in the application process, it is important to put some thought and effort into it.

As one admissions counselor puts it, "It may be the hardest and most anxiety-producing question you've ever had to answer: Who are you and why do you deserve to get into college (in 500 words or less)?" You want to avoid what another admissions dean calls "McEssay"—those that begin with something like, "As captain of

⊙ **COMMON PROBLEM**
You just don't have much relevant experience with which to impress admissions people.

✔ **SOLUTION**
Don't worry too much. At the undergraduate level, your potential is more important than your accomplishments. Yes, it's nice if you helped redesign your high school's database system—but most of the people you're up against never did that either. Enthusiasm and aptitude mean a lot more. In many programs, you don't have to declare your major until junior year, so you have two years to get those great math and computer science grades on your college record. At some schools, it may even be better to just enter as "undeclared." Often, the computer science department is highly competitive, and you may have a better chance coming in undeclared even if you could have had the option to declare as computer science (or whatever your desired field may be). Once you're admitted to the school, it's much easier to get into the specific program you want, and then you'll no longer be undeclared.

the debate team, I learned the value of hard work, cooperation, and a positive atti- tude." Generalizations and feel-good statements just won't cut it. Give them clear, interesting details. If you can tie your topic to your choice of major, all the better. The goal is to be engaging and real. There are many wonderful resources out there to help you ace the essay; we recommend some in Appendix D, "Resources." Don't leave this until last, and don't send your first or even your second draft. Have some- one you trust read it—a parent, an English teacher, or a guidance counselor—and really think about their responses. For good and bad essays, see Chapter 4 on per- sonal statements. While it is targeted to graduate students, the hints are essentially the same: be personal, interesting, relevant, and specific. Don't be boring, generic, or have a "what you can do for me" attitude. A good essay shows why you will be an asset to the school. A bad one can do all sorts of things—make you look sloppy, self- ish, unprepared, or boring. Don't fall into any of these traps.

 NOTE *Don't forget, even if you don't have to declare your major until later, to make yourself known to the department! Stop by the office, let them know that you intend to declare, and ask for advice. A good program advisor will steer you toward the better classes even outside their department. ("Don't take Linear Algebra 103 with Smith, he's cranky and grades everyone down. Lewis's class is much better." That sort of thing.) Also, if the major has a limited number of openings, the better known you are, the more likely you are to get in. (Within reason, of course...you don't want to be known as that kid who just won't stop bugging us about his chances of getting in.)*

Returning to School As an Adult

How much of the above applies to adult students? Some, but not all. Many schools waive much of the admissions process for people who are termed "adult" or "re- entry" students—usually anyone over the age of 25 or so (the exact definition varies from school to school). You will almost certainly not have to take exams, and you may not need to do the essay or other parts of the normal admissions packet.

Of course, you should consider the programs offered, the schools, and your qualifications as carefully as any prospective applicant—and indeed, you'll prob- ably have a better handle on the exact career path you'd like to take and what you'll need to get there.

Chapter 7 focuses on strategies for the adult student, whether you're taking your first college class ever or going to grad school after a bachelor's degree fol- lowed by 26 years in the workforce.

Special Focus: International Students

Every year, thousands and thousands of people come from overseas to study at American universities. With the U.S.'s role as a leader in many high-tech fields, an IT degree from a U.S. school is a hot ticket in many economies. In addition, the government is looking at easing restrictions on visas for foreign workers, in part to help meet the need for qualified IT professionals. It is likely that foreign nationals with an IT degree from a U.S. school will have certain visa and work-permit advantages. So the time is right to investigate this option. This is a topic big enough for an entire book, but we offer just a few pointers to get you started.

Research

While campus visits may be out, and local guidance counselors are unlikely to know much about American schools, the Internet makes it relatively easy to research what you need, and the United States Information Agency's advising centers (there are more than 400, in places from Albania to Zimbabwe) provide information on schools and immigration. Check them out at http://exchanges.state.gov/.

In addition, every school listed in this book has a Web site, and many of them are extremely helpful. While the site itself may not answer every question about attending from your home country, it will almost certainly guide you to the e-mail address of someone who can answer your questions. If an office of international students or other such facility isn't listed, write to the admissions office, with a subject line to your e-mail saying something like "Seeking Information for International Students." It will almost certainly get to the right place. If you haven't heard anything in a week or so, try again. Within reason, it never hurts to be persistent.

Cost

It won't be cheap. There is little or no financial aid available for international students. You will need to look into local grants and assistance programs, which do exist in many places. The restrictions on international students working while studying in America have been loosening up in recent years, and often even greater exceptions can be made in cases of extreme financial hardship.

In general, international students are allowed to work up to 20 hours a week. You will be required to show your college grades to the INS (the Immigration and Naturalization Service, which monitors foreign nationals in the U.S.), and your school will get in trouble if you are found to be working more than you are allowed. Be sure you discuss any employment with your school, to make sure there are no surprises.

However, there's more to consider than just whether or not you are allowed to work. Remember, you will be studying full time. Combining this with professional employment, even at "only" 20 hours a week, can lead to burnout and academic problems. Adjusting to a new country and unfamiliar workplace traditions are additional stresses, and it's important to remember that your studies come first.

In an actual case, several students who were lured into working for other international business owners with the prospects of getting visas were overworked with less pay than U.S. citizens, given unrealistic deadlines, and were not allowed to take off days when they had exams or papers to finish. Check everything out carefully, and go to your academic advisor if you have any questions or concerns about a work offer.

Language

In every school listed in this book, English skills are required, and virtually every one requires a satisfactory grade on the TOEFL. This test can be taken online.

Loneliness and Alienation

Studying in the U.S. can be expensive, and it can be alienating—you're a long way from home, in a new and different culture. It's helpful to ask the schools you're considering applying to how many international students are enrolled and what countries are best represented. Also, ask whether there's an international-student office available to help you with immigration and visa issues, and to provide networking and other support. Many schools have special orientation programs for international students, including special help negotiating the school bureaucracy and sometimes even programs on American culture to help you adapt. Many international students have found that visiting a local embassy is a great way to meet new friends (or even just to have a familiar meal!).

Loneliness is a real problem, and you should neither brush it off nor be embarrassed about it. The embassy may offer programs where you can volunteer and work, which is a good way of getting to know good people from your home country. Embassies may also have lists of associations and youth groups in the community that are resources for students and offer scholarships and stipend help. Getting invited to homes that serve the food you are familiar with will help you find a "home away from home," which in turn can help you become more relaxed and happy, and thus more successful in school. Embassies and consulates are listed in the local phone book, or ask at the international students' office at school for assistance.

CHAPTER 4

Researching and Applying to a Graduate School

Whether you're a dedicated computing whiz just finishing up your undergraduate degree and looking to keep on learning in your chosen field, an adult professional eager for a career shift, or anyone in between, the decision to go to graduate school is an exciting and significant one. You'll be dedicating some serious time, money, and effort to this endeavor, and getting a lot out of it. This chapter will show you how to choose the right program and get accepted. We'll also discuss some options that may not have occurred to you, and look at common problems and practical solutions.

Reality Check: Why Go to Grad School?

If you're already working in (or toward) an IT field, you probably know the answer to this question. While it's not that difficult or unusual for a recent college graduate to be snapped up into a good job with a nice salary in today's hot job market, it's also true that those hires tend to top out. People with equal (or even lesser) skills who also have an advanced degree in the field are seen as better value for the money and are chosen for advancement. Of course, it's not always true—even college dropouts can make it big, as a certain Mr. Bill Gates can tell you. Still, survey after survey shows graduate-degree-holders earning 10 to 100 percent more than employees with bachelor's degrees.

⊙ **COMMON PROBLEM**
Wanting or needing an advanced degree to move up in your career (or enter an IT-focused career), but not being sure exactly what to study.

✔ **SOLUTION**
Read the listings in Chapter 12 carefully, and narrow down which programs seem best for you, based on the criteria outlined below. Then get on the phone or on your e-mail and contact people at those schools. Put some effort into determining which schools will best meet your needs.

If you're looking to make a career shift, an advanced degree is a great entrée. In many graduate programs, your background is less important than your interest and aptitude, so don't worry that a lack of experience or a nontechnical undergraduate degree will be seen as a big negative. In reading through the detailed school listings in Chapter 12, you'll get a good sense of which schools are best for returning adult students. While in school, you'll gain skills and make networking contacts that will virtually assure a job in your field when you graduate.

Money and career advancement are both good reasons to go back and get a master's degree in your field. But they're not the only reasons. Especially at the doctoral level, graduate degrees can be all about research. If you're fascinated by computer systems and want to be on the cutting edge, helping develop the systems of tomorrow, there are programs that can help get you there. While pure research and academic jobs tend to follow from a Ph.D., there are master's-level programs that can get you started down this track. Again, the detailed listings in Chapter 12 can help you determine which programs are more nuts-and-bolts career-oriented and which will lead into research and theory.

Choosing the Right Graduate Program

A national news magazine recently reported that the average student spends more time shopping for a new car than choosing a graduate program. Don't be one of those students—you should take a lot of programs for a test drive before you choose one. After all, you may end up spending much more money on a graduate education than on a used Honda, and you can always trade in the car.

If you're planning to go straight from an undergraduate program into graduate school, you have a wonderful resource available to you—your professors. Granted, they may show a bit of chauvinism and initially insist that the school you're currently attending is the best and your only logical choice for your next degree. But if you've done your research and know that, actually, it's not, only the least helpful of people would refuse to assist you in your decision. Don't go into an advisor's office with little or no preplanning done and say something like, "Where should I go to grad school?" Instead, do your research, following the hints in this book, and come up with five to ten best options. Lay these out for the advisor (or your favorite professor in your field, or both), explain your reasoning, and ask for advice. Academics often have friends and colleagues at other schools, and may be able to give you the inside scoop on one of your chosen programs. In addition, once they see your interests and reasoning, they may be able to suggest another school that hadn't made your first cut, but would be perfect.

If you're currently in school, but not in an IT program, don't let that stop you. Find out when the dean of the school of computer sciences has office hours and make an appointment. Explain that you're not currently in the IT field, but are planning to attend graduate school in the field and you'd like some assistance in narrowing down your school choices. Be prepared for questions about why you're switching emphasis and about your dedication. The answers you come up with will be a great foundation for the personal statements you'll be writing later when it comes time to fill out those grad school applications.

If you've been out of school for more than a few years, you may no longer have access to your undergraduate alma mater and professors. You might still want to drop an e-mail or give a call to professors you remember fondly, as most will be flattered and happy to advise a former student. If this just doesn't feel like an option, it's not that big a deal. Using the hints below, you can still find the right program for you.

So, of the thousands of programs out there, which is the right one for you? Unless you're absolutely sure of the field you want to focus on, you should begin by reading Chapter 5, which details the differences between programs—information science versus information technology, computer science versus computer systems, and so forth. However, you will find there's a lot of overlap, and similar programs are called different things at different schools. Close reading of their listings in this book and communication with the schools you choose will help you decide. Here are some other, non-program-specific things to keep in mind while doing your research.

Reputation

Especially at the graduate level, a program's reputation, even a specific faculty member's, is more important than the school's itself. Do some research to find out who the hot people and departments are in your field. A few insider hints:

▶ Talk to professors at your college or, if you're out of school, make an appointment to visit a nearby college and talk to people there. Talk to junior as well as senior faculty—younger professors often are more clued in to where the hot and happening research is going on.

▶ Read professional journals and see who's publishing in fields you find interesting. Find out where they teach.

▶ Network with students who are already studying in your chosen field, preferably at schools you're considering. Go to the home page for a school you're interested in, and click on the relevant faculty members' Web pages. These often list research assistants, who will be studying almost exactly what you want to study. Write a brief, polite e-mail asking whether they'd be willing to answer some questions about the program. Most will be happy to once they realize you're not asking for a lot of their time. Ideally, it would be great to meet these folks for a cup of coffee, but realistically, you'll probably communicate via phone or e-mail. Ask a few well-chosen questions: What do they like best about the program? What do they like least? If they had it to do over, would they have chosen this school? Are faculty as good in the classroom as in the lab or is the school a "research mill"? What advice would they have for someone planning to apply? Find out about program culture as well—if it's intense and research-focused, and you do better in a collaborative, team-based environment, this is important to know.

Location

Don't be so taken with the quality of a program or the credentials of its faculty that you neglect where you'll be spending the next two years of your life. Sure, you can live anywhere and stand anything for two years, but do you want to? If you are miserable in the heat, a school in steamy Florida might meet your academic needs, but leave you moping around the air-conditioned library all weekend. It's easy to think this sort of thing doesn't matter because you'll be working so hard for those two years. In fact, the happier and more engaged you are, the better you'll do in school and the more of a positive impression you'll make on the professors who will be recommending you for jobs in the field (or not!).

Perhaps more important at the graduate level, many experts recommend that you go to school where you want to work. You will meet faculty, staff, and even fellow students who have leads on internships, jobs, and networking opportunities in the local area, and it would be career suicide *not* to take advantage of these opportunities. So think about whether a school in a rural area will suit your needs and personality or if you'd be better off in a bustling urban center. If the top school for what you want to do is in Georgia, but you know you'll be moving to California after you graduate, think about whether this is the smartest course of action.

On the other hand (this is why these decisions are never easy!), not all experts agree. Some would say, go to the absolute best school in your field and deal with relocation later. You'll want to weigh all of these factors and come up with what works best for you. If the Georgia and California programs are equally strong, and faculty seem equally good, location is a good tiebreaker. If, on the other hand, the school in the less desirable location really offers you the best program for your needs, look long and hard before making the decision. Don't be dazzled by the venerable name of an institution or a nice location, but also take a look at what exactly you will learn and how.

Cost

It's a fact of life—graduate school is expensive. You'll probably spend $10,000 to $30,000 on your advanced degree, so you want to be sure you get the best bang for your buck. Don't let the sticker shock scare you off. There are good schools in the lower price range and, conversely, the pricier schools often have good financial aid, including fellowships and assistantships offering tuition aid that doesn't need to be paid back. We go into this in greater detail in Chapter 6, but do be aware that you should start researching how you're going to pay around the same time you start looking at where you want to go.

 NOTE *Be an informed consumer. Some programs, particularly at the doctoral level, won't commit to funding you until you've successfully completed the first year. Make sure you understand what constitutes success, so there are no unpleasant surprises.*

To get a quick idea of the options, turn to the Subject Index (Appendix B) and look at a few schools that offer the degree you're interested in. Then turn to the schools' listings in Chapter 12 to look up the tuition costs. Remembering that these prices are only approximations (different students have different mitigating circumstances and tuition prices change all the time), do some spot comparing. Here are a couple of examples:

► If you're looking for a master's degree in computer science, you could pay a little over $4,000 at New Mexico State University or almost $40,000 at Dartmouth.

► A doctorate in electrical engineering can range from $5,500 for a resident at Texas Tech to $75,000 at MIT.

A couple of other things to look at are whether there's any penalty for withdrawing. If you don't like the program, what happens? Some schools will refund your tuition, others will do so only with a substantial penalty.

Finally, it's useful to do a "cost per credit" analysis. The number of hours required for a program can vary rather widely—while the standard is 30, it may be lower if a thesis is required, and may be as high as 39 or more. This makes a big difference when you're looking at value for the money. While the bottom-line figure is still important, it can be instructive to figure out what you're paying by the credit hour as well.

Other Considerations

Location, cost, and reputation are the three most relevant factors for many students. However, there's a lot more to consider when winnowing down your top choices. Basically, you're acting as a detective, trying to figure out how good a school's IT program *really* is. Of course no school is going to confess that they're still working the kinks out of their offerings. But you can ask a few pointed questions that help you determine whether they can offer you everything you need. Every program listed in this book has been checked out and found to be good, but that doesn't mean it will necessarily fit your needs. You may also run across interesting programs that aren't listed here, as schools are continually upgrading their IT offerings to keep pace with demand. Some things to consider include:

Is the program new?   That might seem like a plus, as it would imply fresh and up to date. On the other hand, it might also mean that this program is not as well funded as it could be and that the bugs haven't been worked out of it. In general, go for the established program with seasoned faculty and a real track record.

How about that faculty?   Who teaches in this program? What are their credentials? Is there a good mix of academia and real-world experience? Are their adjunct faculty from top IT employers?

What's the equipment like? (And who gets to use the good stuff?)   Find out whether they have state-of-the-art servers, remote access, and mainframe connectivity. Do they teach you a diversity of platforms—Unix, Mac, and PC? If it's important to you, are they Linux-friendly? How's their Internet connection speed? What sort of equipment is available in the labs? What will you get to work on?

How's student access?   Will you be able to log on from home (or dorms), laptop wireless, library, and classroom labs?

What about internships? Job placement? Career counseling?   Have career advisors recently worked in the real world? Are there specific IT-focused career people or will you be talking to a generic "one size fits all" counselor? Does the department have agreements with major local companies to get internships and student jobs for enrollees?

What else does this school or program have to offer you?   Are there special scholarships, great support groups, or other intangibles that might make a difference?

As you read through the programs in this book, keep these factors in mind. Look at them with an eye to what you want out of a program, what the school can offer you, whether it's in a place you'd like to be, and whether, realistically, you're the kind of student they're looking for.

Remember, too, that you can get creative with your graduate-degree program. You may be able to put together a package that includes credit for prior experience, distance-learning courses over the Internet, and traditional classroom learning at the school of your choice. These options will be discussed in greater depth in Chapters 8 and 11.

Preadmissions Timetable

Ideally, you should start the process of choosing and applying to a graduate school a year and a half before you plan to actually begin studying. Yes, you can do everything more quickly, but it's not wise. You're about to dedicate a lot of time and money to a course of study that can dramatically change your life for the better, and it just makes sense to take the time to do it right. If you absolutely know which school and program is right for you, and have already taken your GRE exams, the process can be a lot faster. Keep in mind that at many institutions, applying early is to your advantage. If the school has what's called "rolling admissions," you may be admitted ahead of the deadline. At the very least, your early application shows your enthusiasm and gives the admissions committee more time to evaluate you.

The following timetable assumes you'll take six months to prepare, and then apply a year before you want to attend graduate school. Again, it can be done more quickly, but this is the ideal.

Six Months Before You Apply

As with any important and expensive decision, the more time you can dedicate to this process, the better. If you can take a year to research schools, check out faculty, and refine your goals, that's great. If not, you can do what you need to do given a six-month head start. The following checklist shows you how:

✔ Go through this book, select the schools that seem to be of greatest interest to you. Remember—it's not free to apply to graduate schools. It takes time and effort, and there's usually an application fee from $25 to $100. Depending on how competitive the programs are that you're looking at, pick ten or so to focus on, with the intention of narrowing it down to the three to five you'll actually apply to.

✔ Check out the schools' Web sites, talk to faculty members and students, get a real picture of whether this is a place you'd like to spend a couple of years.

✔ Register for the GRE and look into taking a test-prep class. In particular, if you've been out of school for a while, you're also out of practice taking standardized tests. A good test-prep book can help, but many community colleges and university extension programs offer reasonably priced test-prep courses that are well worth the investment. Shop around—you may pay as much as $900 or as little as $150 for essentially the same information. Take as many sample tests as you can to get back in the swing. See Appendix D, "Resources," for test-prep books and services that offer courses.

✔ Start looking into financial aid options. If appropriate, approach your employer about corporate educational assistance. See Chapter 10 for more advice on this.

✔ Start thinking about who you'll have write your letters of recommendation. See below for more advice on whom to approach and how to approach them.

Three Months Before You Apply

Once the groundwork is done, you need to get serious! You'll want to take exams as early as possible, if only to get the anxiety of preparation behind you. Other tasks will flow naturally from this timeline.

✔ Take the GRE and, if required, the TOEFL (see below for details on these tests).

✔ Request application materials from your chosen schools. Standard wisdom is to apply to your top two or three schools, and then one or two "safety valves"— less competitive schools that you wouldn't mind attending if your top schools don't admit you. It's up to you how many schools you apply to—but remember, you'll need letters of recommendation for each. If you ask for too many letters, even in these days of easy copy-and-paste, you'll wear out your writers and, perhaps worse, come off to them as indecisive, which may affect the quality of the letters they end up writing.

✔ If the school requires a written personal statement, start on a draft of it. While this statement is less vital in the computer sciences than it would be in, say, law or medicine, it's still important. This is your chance to highlight why you'll be a great candidate, and is especially vital if you're coming from a nontechnical background or had less than stellar grades as an undergraduate. See below for more advice.

✔ Check on admissions deadlines and ask whether the schools you're applying to have rolling admissions.

✔ Ask for your letters of recommendation.

A Year Before You Plan to Enroll

Most schools require that everything be sent in a year before enrollment. If you're having trouble getting everything together, check on deadlines and see if there's any flexibility. The best strategy is to plan well in advance so you don't have to ask for special exceptions to be made.

✔ Confirm that your letter-writers sent in the letters of recommendation you requested or, depending on the school's requirements, collect the sealed letters to send in with your application.

✔ Send in your completed applications.

✔ Check to see whether there are separate deadlines and forms for financial aid, and be sure you meet those deadlines as well.

Six Months Before You Plan to Enroll

Six months before your enrollment date, everything should be falling into place. Now's the time to make a final decision on a school and do your wrap-up with references and other resources.

✔ Check with the schools to make sure they've received everything.

✔ If you're accepted by more than one school, do a close comparison to make sure you pick the right one. Revisit all the criteria discussed above—not just academic reputation, but location, facilities, and financial aid. The second-choice school that's willing to give you a full scholarship may be better in your circumstances than the top-notch one that expects you to pay your own way. Be realistic, but not defeatist. Sometimes the best school simply is the best school, and you should go for it, even if it means student loans for years to come.

✔ Let the schools you didn't choose know you won't be attending, so they can offer your spot to another candidate.

✔ Write to the people who wrote your letters of recommendation, thanking them and letting them know where you'll be attending graduate school. This isn't just a nice courtesy, it may be vital later on if you need them for other networking purposes!

TIP *Your letters don't have to be long. In fact, most professionals prefer a one- or two-paragraph letter to a two- or three-page missive. Avoid the temptation to include too much personal information (the professor doesn't care how your cat is doing or whether you'll be living on campus). Simply remind them who you are, let them know the good news, and thank them sincerely.*

⊙ **COMMON PROBLEM**

Missing financial aid deadlines. Often, in the excitement of applying for admission, students miss financial aid deadlines, which can be a real problem if you're admitted but don't have the funds to attend!

✔ **SOLUTION**

The first thing to do is to make sure you *don't* miss those deadlines! Read everything from the admissions office and, if the financial aid information isn't clear, call or e-mail to confirm. If you do miss a deadline, however, the school may be lenient if you've already been accepted. Call up, make your case, and ask if there are any options available to accepted students who've missed the deadline. Generally speaking, a school that has accepted you will try to make it possible for you to attend, but this is a less than ideal position to find yourself in. Try to avoid it in the first place by looking for *every* key date mentioned in your admissions packet.

Entrance Exams

Just about every school listed in this book requires the general Graduate Record Examination (GRE) for admission to graduate programs; some require an advanced GRE as well. Good scores will help make you more attractive to an admissions committee, especially if your background isn't as strong in technical fields as you might wish. If English is not your first language, most schools also require the Test of English as a Foreign Language (TOEFL).

Graduate Record Exam

The computer-based general GRE is administered year round at testing centers around the world. Check out the Web site at http://www.gre.org/ to find the center nearest you. The subject tests are given three times a year, using the paper-based test rather than a computer-based model. The general test is divided into three parts: English, math, and logic. Even though the latter two categories may be more relevant for your career in computer science, you'll want to do well on all three parts, as many schools take your aggregate score into account.

Some programs require that you take the subject exam in computer science and/or math; some even suggest that engineering and physics might be useful. It's up to you how much unrequired testing you want to subject yourself to, but we recommend that you at least take the computer science test. It consists of about 70 questions specifically tailored to students who plan to seek a graduate degree in computer science, and it assumes that you've taken courses at least to the level of an undergraduate major in the field. If you've worked or studied extensively in IT-related areas, you should do fine even if your undergraduate degree was in something totally unrelated. The questions are classified approximately as follows: software systems and methodology (35 percent), computer organization and architecture (20 percent), theory (25 percent), mathematical background (15 percent), and advanced topics such as artificial intelligence, modeling, and simulation (5 percent).

The math subject test (as differentiated from the general math GRE, which doesn't go beyond basic algebra) is about 66 questions. It focuses on abstract algebra, linear algebra, and the ability to prove theorems and create counter-examples. About a quarter of the questions require knowledge in other areas, such as complex analysis, topology, combinatorics, probability, statistics, number theory, and algorithmic processes. Many of these are skills you'll need in certain advanced computer fields, so you would be well advised to take the test if your chosen programs are math-heavy. This is another reason to do good research before choosing the programs to focus on.

TOEFL

The Test of English as a Foreign Language is given to international students looking to study in the U.S. Many programs specify a required score on this test as an admissions prerequisite for people whose first language is other than English. The test is available at centers around the world; see http://www.toefl.org/ for the location closest to you. Some school also require the Test of Written English (TWE), which is given at the same centers, although sometimes only on some of the test dates. If you're an international student and the TWE is required of you, be sure that you check with your testing center to make sure this test will be administered.

The Personal Statement

Many schools require a brief personal statement, detailing why you feel you would do well in the program, what experience you bring, and sometimes also a narrative breakdown of your transcript. For instance, you might be asked to explain classes with generic titles such as Math 101. This is a great opportunity to show why you are the right person for this program. Treat the statement like a job interview—remembering that old saying about showing what you will do for them, rather than what they can do for you. A statement such as "I want to attend your school because it is the best in its field" is much less attractive than one along the lines of, "I feel that my strong background in computer science and my dedication to research will be an asset to your top-rated program." An example of a good personal statement is shown in Figure 4-1 and a bad one is shown in Figure 4-2.

The following numbered list of points corresponds to the numbers in Figure 4-1, indicating the qualities found in a good personal statement:

❶   It's great to start with a personal anecdote—this grabs the reader's attention and draws them into your story. This woman immediately becomes "the girl who got spanked for taking a blender apart," much more memorable than "I've always wanted to go to Yale #324." Just be sure the anecdote ties into why you're interested in IT study, even if humorously as here, and be sure it doesn't make you look stupid or irresponsible—the fact that this story happened when she was five, clearly stated up front, removes that concern.

❷   Heeding the old maxim, "show, don't tell," this applicant demonstrates that she's interested in IT because she's well suited and has a strong background, rather than because it's "the flavor of the moment." An admissions committee wants to know that students will stick with the program, and she's making it clear that she has both the ability and the interest to do just that.

❸   She's showing that she understands the degree, and why she's a good candidate. This is not a "one size fits all" essay, and it shows.

❹   She does several things here: shows initiative, lets them know she's interested in women and minorities (always under-represented in tech programs), and makes it clear that she's not just a techie geek, she's also a people person.

❺   Good closing, shows personality and sense of humor, but in proportion—most of the statement is serious and professional, so it's all right to open and close on a lighter note.

1 I was only five when it happened, but I'll never forget the look on my mother's face. She had only left me alone for a few minutes, but in that time, I'd managed to get the blender partially disassembled and was moments from sticking a screwdriver straight into the motor. While the spanking I got that day dissuaded me from such home demolition projects for many years, I never lost my curiosity about how things work and how I might make them work better.

2 As I progressed through high school and my undergraduate studies, my interest in how things work kept developing. While I've never lost the thrill of taking something apart to see how it works (these days I put it back together myself, usually making some improvements on the way), I've also learned that "how it works" is a very big and exciting field. Far beyond nuts, bolts, and soldering irons, I have developed a passion for mathematic solutions, for writing code, and for helping others understand and love technology as much as I do.

3 That joy in both working with computers and helping others has made me think that I would be a good network administrator, and that your M.S. in Computer Engineering and Systems is a perfect match for my strengths.

4 In addition to my strong mathematic and computer skills, as shown in my grades from my undergraduate B.S. in Computer Science (see attached transcript), I bring some additional "pluses" to your program. As an undergraduate, I established Montoya University's first-ever networking group for women of color in technology. In organizing this group, I did recruitment, set up a Web site and an e-mail system, and got private funding from a number of local corporations to purchase training equipment. In our second year, I convinced those corporations to sponsor IT internships for women of color, and I am proud to say that the little coffee klatch I started four years ago is now a thriving independent training and development organization with almost 100 members.

5 In sum, I'm an able technician, a good organizer, an eager student, and a dedicated problem-solver, and I feel that I would be an asset to your impressive program. And if you have a blender that needs some work, I still have that screwdriver!

FIGURE 4-1 A good personal statement

> ❶   I would like to go to graduate school because at this point in my career, it is the logical next step and I am told it is essential for getting ahead in the field of technology. I have selected Yale for your good reputation, and feel that a degree from your school will be a great asset to me as a technician and a manager.
>
> ❷   While my grades aren't as good as they could be, I know that I will do better in grad school, as I am a very hard worker and it is important to me to succeed. I did not, for instance, do well in english as an undergrad because it wasn't important or interesting to me, but I will do well in my graduate studies, because sucess here is a matter of great importance.
>
> ❸   So, in closing, I would like to say that attending Harvard would mean a lot to me, and that it would fulfill my lifelong dream of attending an Ivy League school. Thank you for your attention to this application, and I hope to hear form you with good news soon.

Figure 4-2 A bad personal statement

The following numbered list of points corresponds to the numbers in Figure 4-2, indicating the places where the letter-writer failed to compose a compelling personal statement:

❶ First mistake: a "what you can do for me" attitude—and the most common and boring opener. Never start an essay "I would like to go to graduate school because…" Admissions officers are sick of seeing it, and you don't want to make them yawn. In addition, Yale knows it has not just a good but a great reputation. It's fine to talk about why you want to go to a particular school— essential, even—but this is bland to the point of offensiveness, which then raises a question as to whether this is a copy-and-paste essay being sent to several schools. Committees see a lot of this, and they can spot those essays. Instead, speak very specifically about the program, the professors, and the resources. Show that you've done your homework.

❷ Bad all over. Why call attention to bad grades if there's nothing you can say besides dissing undergrad English? If your grades are just average, best not to mention them at all, but instead focus on your strengths. If the marks are truly poor, mention them but put a positive spin on it. Did you improve in your last semester and go on to work in the field? Do you have accolades from bosses or professors explaining that you do, indeed, work hard and well? Is there anything else you can highlight about yourself or your achievements to take away the sting of a roster of Cs? Finally, spell check, spell check, spell check. An essay with typos makes you look stupid, or at the very least sloppy, neither of which is a good impression to make.

❸ Um...weren't we applying to Yale? You may think this is an unlikely error, but it happens more than you might think. Students adapt one essay to several schools, copy and paste, and forget to change the name. A great way to get yourself tossed in the "reject" pile. Finally, the school is not here to fulfill your dreams, it's here to turn out IT professionals who will be an asset to the community and reflect well on their alma mater. This student doesn't seem to get that or to have any clear idea of why he wants the degree, or even what degree he's going for.

Note how long a statement they require (usually no more than 1,500 words, which is about two pages), and don't go over. Read over their requirements and review the list of classes you'll be taking once accepted, then tailor your essay to this picture. For example, if you didn't take a lot of software-engineering classes in school, but you had a summer internship at a software company, be sure to mention this. Remember that schools are looking for reasons not to admit you as well as reasons to let you in, so don't focus on the negative.

A bad personal statement probably won't land you in the reject pile so long as your undergraduate grades, letters of recommendation, and GRE scores are good, but a great statement can really help your application. Remember that graduate students often end up as teaching or research assistants, and a good written presentation is a big plus for those areas. Don't send a school your first or even your second or third draft. If you're still in college, have a trusted professor or an academic counselor look your statement over and make suggestions. If you've been out of school for a while, show it to a significant other, a colleague, or someone else whose opinion you trust. Really listen to their critiques, and rework it to fit.

You might even consider hiring a professional editor to look over your most important applications. Look in the Yellow Pages or on the Net under "Editorial Services." Most editors charge an hourly rate of no more than $20 to $40, and looking over your application shouldn't take more than a couple of hours. Typos, grammatical errors, misspellings, and other mistakes can make you look sloppy and will detract from your image as a careful professional who seeks admission into a top-notch program.

Letters of Recommendation

In general, letters from professors carry more weight than those from employers or other professional colleagues. If you've been out of school for a while, contact your undergraduate alma mater and see if key professors are still there. Even if it's been years since you took classes with them, they may remember you. If not, they may be willing to dig into old course registers, remind themselves of who you are, and write a letter anyway. Most professors want to see their students succeed and are happy to help. If you still live near your alma mater, make an appointment and go meet with them. It's much harder to say no face to face—especially if you can remind them of something you did in the class, or even just talk about how they inspired you.

If you've been out of school and in the workforce for many years, you may need to rely on letters from employers or colleagues instead. First, though, contact the schools you're interested in, and see if they have any guidelines for people in your situation. Some will waive the requirement for letters of recommendation if you've been working in your field for some years. Others may ask for only one letter, usually from your employer, instead of the usual two or three. If they do require more than one, think of outside contractors or clients you may have worked with, or others who can speak on behalf of your talents, dedication, and intelligence.

As with any situation where you're asking for a favor, make it as easy as possible for your letter-writers to deliver. Provide them with the proper forms from the school and with addressed, stamped envelopes. Ask if they'd like anything else to refer to—your academic transcripts, your résumé, or your personal statement for the application. Some schools ask to have the letters sent directly to them, others want them sent to you sealed, with the writers' signatures over the seal, to ensure confidentiality and authenticity. Be sure the letter-writers know that they can have complete confidentiality, although if they offer to let you see a first draft, take them up on it. It can be a great ego boost and also allow you to correct any minor errors. A month or so after you've asked people to write your letters, drop them an e-mail to ask how it's going. You don't want to hassle them, but you also don't want them to miss the deadline.

Returning to School As an Adult

It is increasingly common for people to take a few (or many) years in the workplace before going on to a graduate degree. In fact, a recent study showed that more than half of all students working toward a master's degree or doctorate were over 30. So, if you're one of these students, you're far from alone.

Chapter 7 focuses in detail on strategies for the older student, but here we'd like to just briefly note that age and experience are quite often advantages rather than disadvantages in graduate school. At the admissions level, you may have real-world experience and skills that make you particularly attractive to admissions committees. Once in the classroom, you're likely to be more confident and career-focused, and less likely to be afraid of professors or of speaking up in class. Interpersonal skills learned in the workplace often transfer well to the classroom, allowing you to take a leadership role and get what you need out of your classes.

Special Focus: International Students

Every year, thousands and thousands of people come from overseas to study at American universities. With the U.S.'s role as a leader in many high-tech fields, an IT degree from a U.S. school is a hot ticket in many economies. In addition, the government is looking at easing restrictions on visas for foreign workers, in part to help meet the need for qualified IT professionals. It is likely that foreign nationals with an IT degree from a U.S. school will have certain visa and work-permit advantages. So the time is right to investigate this option. This is a topic big enough for an entire book, but here we offer just a few pointers to get you started.

Research

While campus visits may be out, and local guidance counselors are unlikely to know much about U.S. schools, the Internet makes it relatively easy to research what you need, and the United States Information Agency's advising centers (there are more than 400, in places from Albania to Zimbabwe) provide information on schools and immigration. Check them out at http://exchanges.state.gov/.

In addition, every school listed in this book has a Web site, and many of them are extremely helpful. While the site itself may not answer every question about attending from your home country, it will almost certainly guide you to the e-mail address of someone who can answer your questions. If an office of international students or other such facility isn't listed, write to the admissions office, with a subject line to your e-mail saying something like "Seeking Information for International Students." It will almost certainly get to the right place. If you haven't heard anything in a week or so, try again. Within reason, it never hurts to be persistent.

Cost

It won't be cheap. There is little or no financial aid available for international students. You will need to look into local grants and assistance programs, which do exist in many places. The restrictions on international students working while studying in the U.S. have been loosening up in recent years, and often even greater exceptions can be made in cases of extreme financial hardship.

In general, international students are allowed to work up to 20 hours a week. You will be required to show your college grades to the INS (the Immigration and Naturalization Service, which monitors foreign nationals in the U.S.), and your school will get in trouble if you are found to be working more than you are allowed. Be sure you discuss any employment with your school to make sure there are no surprises.

However, there's more to consider than just whether or not you are allowed to work. Remember, you will be studying full time. Combining this with professional employment, even at *only* 20 hours a week, can lead to burnout and academic problems. Adjusting to a new country and unfamiliar workplace traditions are additional stresses. It's also important to remember that your studies come first.

In an actual case, several students who were lured into working for other international business owners with the prospects of getting visas were overworked with less pay than U.S. citizens, given unrealistic deadlines, and were not allowed to take off days when they had exams or papers to finish. Check everything out carefully, and go to your academic advisor if you have any questions or concerns about a work offer.

Language

In every school listed in this book, English skills are required, and virtually every one requires a satisfactory grade on the TOEFL. This test can be taken online.

Loneliness and Alienation

Studying in the U.S. can be expensive, and it can be alienating—you're a long way from home, in a new and different culture. It's helpful to ask the schools you're considering applying to how many international students are enrolled and what countries are best represented. Also ask whether there's an international-student office available to help you with immigration and visa issues, and to provide networking and other support. Many schools have special orientation programs for international students, including special help negotiating the school bureaucracy and sometimes even programs on American culture to help you adapt.

CHAPTER 5

Understanding Degrees and Specializations

If you've decided that you definitely want an IT degree, the next question will almost certainly be, which one? There are so many degrees out there—indeed, it's possible to say without much exaggeration that there's a degree for everyone— that choosing can be bewildering. It doesn't help that different degrees are called different things depending on which school you're looking into. Do you want an Sc.B. in computer systems or a B.S. in management information systems? An M.S. in software engineering or an M.S. in computer science? How does the study of cognitive systems differ from that of artificial intelligence? Even the experts can get lost in a sea of degrees, titles, and specializations, so it's no wonder the novice feels a little overwhelmed.

All the degrees and fields of study you're likely to encounter are discussed in this chapter. Where a field can vary widely (mainly the generic fields such as computer science), this is noted, so that at least when you make initial inquiries to a school, you'll be aware of the sorts of questions you need to ask. (For example, programs vary in whether they are more hardware- or software-oriented. If one emphasis is important to you, it's vital you get that cleared up early, before you waste any time or money.) Keep in mind that some ambiguity is inherent in this field given how new it is. After all, universities have had 800 years to decide what a philosophy degree should entail, and they still can't agree. IT degrees are less than a decade old at many universities, and the ground rules are still being worked out. If anything seems unclear, ask a lot of questions.

Particularly, keep in mind what your end goal is for any degree. It's harder if you don't know what you want to do career-wise, but spend some time talking to guidance counselors and try to get a basic idea. If the business side of things fascinates you, for instance, you'll want to steer more toward MIS. If you'd like to focus on hard-core engineering and design, you'll want to find the programs that are more hardware-focused. Most program advisors will be plugged in to the jobs graduates are most suited for and will be happy to share that information. Don't forget to ask!

Undergraduate Degrees

There are two standard undergraduate degree titles: the associate's degree (also known as a two-year degree) and the bachelor's (a four-year degree). This book doesn't really deal with associate's degrees, but the most common associate's degree titles are Associate of Arts (A.A.), Associate of Science (A.S.), and Associate of Applied Science (A.A.S.). As far as IT degrees go, the A.A. degrees are usually the least specialized, the A.A.S. degrees the most specialized, and the A.S. degrees somewhere in between. The associate's degree is a perfectly valid option if you want a general educational credential that's a step up from a high school diploma, but don't necessarily need to be a college graduate.

If you think you'd like an associate's degree, your best bargain is probably your local community college. An associate's degree from one regionally accredited community college is pretty much as good as an associate's degree from any other regionally accredited community college.

However, when people talk about degrees in general, they almost always mean a bachelor's or higher. The bachelor's is the piece of paper that makes you a college graduate—and, as such, it gives you an edge. The bachelor's degree comes in a variety of shapes and sizes. Following are descriptions of the titles you're most likely to see as you start your research into the world of IT degrees. This is not an exhaustive list, but it's comprehensive and covers everything you'll find in Chapter 12.

Bachelor of Science (B.S.; also B.Sc., S.B., Sc.B.)

If you're going for a four-year IT degree, this is the standard credential you're likely to encounter, as most four-year undergraduate programs in engineering and the applied sciences are B.S. degrees. The B.S. tends to focus on mathematics and the natural sciences, leaving the fine arts and social sciences more or less on the back burner. If you want a focused old-school curriculum in your field of interest, this is probably your best bet.

Bachelor of Arts (B.A.; also A.B.)

The Bachelor of Arts (or, as they say at some fancier schools, "Artium Bachelor") tends to give students a broad liberal arts background. This isn't to say that the natural sciences and mathematics go completely ignored, but they're not usually given the sort of focus they might receive in a B.S. program. Think twice before enrolling in a B.A. in a technical field; to many, the degree still connotes "non-science," and suffers from a less technical image.

On the other hand, if you want to look like an outside-the-box thinker, this is not a bad credential to have. The B.A. in computer science has become a fairly common choice for students who prefer an IT-centered curriculum geared toward non-IT application areas, and thus the B.A. degree is now available with majors in such fields as computer engineering and computational mathematics.

In any case, getting a B.A. instead of a B.S. is not likely to hurt—unless vocational accreditation is important to you, that is. Very few B.A. programs hold ABET or CSAB accreditation. A few do, so check with your college anyway—you might get lucky!

Bachelor of Engineering (B.Eng.; also B.E.)

The Bachelor of Engineering makes the B.S. look like a generalist degree. Usually featuring an engineering-centered major of at least 54 credit hours, this degree is probably your best bet if you want a hard-core, highly focused curriculum with minimal abstract or theoretical coursework.

Bachelor of Electrical Engineering (B.E.E.)

Sometimes this is more focused than the B.Eng., sometimes actually less—but it almost always involves at least 54 semester hours of electrical engineering. If you're looking to build IT skills in networks, systems, programming, and software design, you won't find it in this degree program, generally a minus for most job seekers.

Bachelor of Software Engineering (B.Sw.E.)

This relatively new degree is essentially a B.Eng. designed specifically with software engineers in mind. In addition to programming, project management, and quality control, this program tends to also address computer science theory to some extent. Programming and project management are hot management-track fields, making this a good degree for people interested in quickly climbing the corporate ladder.

Bachelor of Business Administration (B.B.A.)

This is the white-collar answer to the B.Eng. Generally featuring a business-oriented core of 54 hours, this degree is the perfect ground-level management credential.

NOTE *To state the obvious, this is a non-techie degree. Even though you can specialize in computer fields, this degree is largely a business-based one. If you're not absolutely sure that you want to go for a management post upon graduation, you'll probably be better off with a less management-focused degree. If, however, you already have technical skills, this could be a great way to round out your education with an understanding of the business side of things.*

Bachelor of Applied Science (B.A.S.)

Generally speaking, this is an accelerated program designed for students who already hold a two-year associate's degree and would like to convert it to a four-year bachelor's degree. Arizona State University East, Bellevue University, the University of Houston at Clear Lake, and the University of Pennsylvania all offer programs along these lines. The B.A.S. can generally be completed in about two years, provided you have the right educational background. Be sure to thoroughly examine the IT offerings and make sure you'll be getting what you need in the time allotted in terms of technical training and project management experience.

Bachelor of Fine Arts (B.F.A.)

The Bachelor of Fine Arts traditionally focuses on a field of creative study, although it can also be tailored to other humanities-related fields. In recent years, IT-oriented B.F.A. programs in graphic design, multimedia, and so forth have started to crop up. If you're sure you want to do Web design or computer music rather than traditional IT design and maintenance, this may very well be the perfect degree for you. Be sure that the degree program you undertake is really tech-focused, not an arts program with some techie stuff thrown in to seem modern.

Bachelor of General Studies (B.G.S.; many similar programs of various titles)

This is a generalist adult learning bachelor's, also called a Bachelor of Liberal Studies or the like; nomenclatures vary from school to school. Although some scoff at this sort of degree as being too general, not tightly focused on any one field, it does have its advantages. It can usually be completed more quickly than its competitors, it's usually geared specifically toward reentry students, and it's usually a lot of fun. You're given a great deal more flexibility in this sort of program than you're ever likely to encounter in any of the more formal programs described above, and it accomplishes the same basic purpose: it gives you a formal four-year college degree, breaking the glass ceiling and even giving you the opportunity to pursue graduate work down the road. That said, you're taking a risk by getting a degree that's often seen as less rigorous. Be sure you're going to get good technical training, and be prepared to defend your education in job interviews.

Graduate Degrees

In the U.S., graduate degrees come in three broad varieties: the master's degree, the specialist (or engineer) degree, and the doctorate. These are discussed below, including distinctions between the sorts of degree titles you will see in each field. Master's programs generally involve one or two years of full-time work beyond the bachelor's degree. It's worth noting that many, but not all, master's programs involve a culminating experience of some kind—a thesis, a final project, or a comprehensive examination. Almost every doctorate requires a final project as well. You'll see different sorts of projects mentioned in the school listings in Chapter 12. Descriptions of these projects follow the title-by-title descriptions below, in the section that follows, "The Project, the Thesis, and the Comprehensive Examination."

Master of Arts (M.A.; also A.M.)

Typically, a Master of Arts in an information technology field will involve between 24 and 30 semester of hours of coursework and a culminating thesis.

Master of Science (M.S.; also S.M., Sc.M.)

The Master of Science can be either a research-oriented program like the M.A. or a professional program like the M.Eng.; most schools permit students to choose which approach they would prefer. The M.S. is pretty much the standard IT master's degree for research-oriented and professional graduate students alike, and its generally flexible nature makes it a fairly safe choice for any student.

Master of Engineering (M.Eng.; also M.E.)

Generally speaking, the Master of Engineering represents the opposite extreme from the M.A.: it is an engineering degree for engineers. Although some M.Eng. programs involve a thesis, it's far more likely to see a coursework-only M.Eng. or an M.Eng. that culminates in a capstone project (discussed in "The Project, the Thesis, and the Comprehensive Examination").

The drawback of this is that less research-oriented master's programs tend to make for a weaker doctoral application. If you think you might want to go for a Ph.D. down the road, you might be better off with an M.S.—although if the M.Eng. is particularly research-oriented, it may work just as effectively. As always, check specific master's program requirements versus specific doctoral entrance requirements and see if they line up.

Master of Software Engineering (M.Sw.E.; also M.S.E.)

Essentially an M.Eng. for programmers, this degree involves (necessarily) more theory than the average M.Eng. program, but is nevertheless usually considered a professional, rather than research-oriented, credential. Most M.Sw.E. programs culminate in a final programming project. Programming and project management are hot management-track fields, making this a good degree for people interested in quickly climbing the corporate ladder.

Master of Computer Science (M.C.S.; also M.C.I.S.)

The Master of Computer Science (or Master of Computer and Information Science) is generally a coursework-only degree designed for IT professionals. It is almost never research-oriented, so students who plan on applying to a strict Ph.D. program might be better off with an M.S. degree instead; the latter has original work and research requirements, which are more in line with original research work needed to complete the Ph.D. thesis.

Master of Electrical Engineering (M.E.E.)

The Master of Electrical Engineering is the electrical engineer's answer to the M.C.S. Although not generally geared toward doctoral work, the M.E.E. can be a perfect starting point for students who want to pursue the degree of Electrical Engineer (E.E.). Be sure that you'll get the broad-based IT training you need—some senior engineering students have been shocked and dismayed to find out that they learn nothing about networks, software, or programming, and need to get this information on their own while taking on an already rigorous engineering program. Don't let this happen to you.

Master of Computer Engineering (M.C.E.; also M.C.S.E.)

The Master of Computer Engineering (or Master of Computer Science and Engineering) is the computer engineer's answer to the M.C.S. and M.E.E. Please note that the abbreviation M.C.S.E. usually refers to Microsoft Certified Systems Engineer, so if this is your degree, you might want to spell it out on your résumé to avoid confusion.

Master of Business Administration (M.B.A.)

If you're eyeing a management job, this is the gold standard. The M.B.A. generally consists of 33 to 36 hours of coursework (although larger or smaller programs are not unheard of); a thesis, management project, or internship is sometimes involved. The M.B.A. can be tailored to the interests of IT-focused managers, but make no mistake about it: this is a manager's degree. If you're looking for a hard-core technical credential, this is probably not your best bet. Even a tech-focused M.B.A. may not give you the knowledge or training you need to lead technical projects. Be sure that you have the IT skills necessary (or that the program will give them to you) so you don't end up trying to manage projects or programs you don't understand (and end up seeing yourself in a Dilbert cartoon!).

Master of Fine Arts (M.F.A.)

The Master of Fine Arts has traditionally dealt with painting, music, or creative writing; now its repertoire has been expanded to include such fields as graphic design and technical communications.

The M.F.A. generally involves more coursework than the standard master's program and culminates in a creative project of some kind. If you're fairly certain that you'll want to do Web design, computer music, and so forth rather than management or traditional IT design and maintenance, this may be the perfect degree for you.

Master of Education (M.Ed.)

The Master of Education might be a wonderful choice if you're planning on doing IT work in a school setting (such as educational technology, computer science education, or instructional technology).

Electrical Engineer (E.E.), Computer Engineer (C.E.), and Computer Systems Engineer (C.S.E.)

If you already hold a master's degree in an IT field, would like a stronger credential, and don't necessarily think you'll ever want a doctorate, then the degree of Engineer might be perfect for you.

This degree normally involves 30 to 36 hours of post-master's graduate-level coursework. Students may also be required to undertake a comprehensive examination and/or a final project. Although it doesn't fall into the standard bachelor's-master's-doctorate framework, it is a widely recognized credential and might fit your needs perfectly.

Educational Specialist (Ed.S.)

The Ed.S. is the educator's answer to the degree of Engineer and involves essentially the same requirements (30 or more hours post-master's credit, possible final project, and comprehensive written exams). Ed.S. degrees in educational technology are quite common, and it may be possible to undertake one of these programs based even on a master's in another field provided you're willing to undertake the necessary prerequisite work (generally at least 12 to 15 hours of graduate-level coursework).

Doctor of Philosophy (Ph.D.; also D.Phil.)

In the U.S. educational system, the Ph.D. is generally considered to be the highest academic degree available. It involves a variable amount of coursework beyond the master's and a culminating dissertation (original contribution to the field of study). Sometimes examinations, teaching requirements, foreign language requirements, and/or internships make up part of the curriculum. While it is the usual method to obtain a master's degree first and then to apply for a doctorate, some doctorates are available to people who hold only a bachelor's. Usually, the time of study is a bit longer, and a master's is awarded partway through.

Doctor of Science (Sc.D.; also D.Sc. or D.S.)

Some students consider the Ph.D. to be a little too broad, theory-oriented, and academic. The Sc.D. aims to remedy this by focusing slightly more on applied aspects of the field of study. Some Sc.D. programs may permit students to undertake a project rather than a dissertation.

Doctor of Engineering (D.Eng.; also D.E.)

If even the Sc.D. is too dry and academic for you, there's still the Doctor of Engineering. This degree focuses very heavily on practical, hands-on study in the field. The curriculum generally involves several internships, a series of projects, and examinations. Students are generally given the option of undertaking a capstone project (sometimes called an "engineer's report") rather than the more traditional dissertation.

Doctor of Business Administration (D.B.A.)

This is the doctoral counterpart to the B.B.A. and M.B.A. It generally tends to be less research-oriented than a Ph.D. in Business Administration—and it always, of course, focuses on management issues.

The Project, the Thesis, and the Comprehensive Examination

Most (but certainly not all) master's programs conclude with a capstone project, a thesis, and/or a comprehensive written examination, as do many doctoral degrees. To understand the distinction, what follows is an examination of how your project might go if you were studying for an M.S. in Sandwich Engineering.

The *capstone project* would require that you build a certain kind of sandwich and write a short research paper explaining how you did it. You would then present the sandwich to the faculty committee with copies of your research paper. If they found the sandwich tasty and the research paper satisfactory, you would pass.

The *thesis* would require that you write a long, publishable work addressing, say, the effects of mustard on a turkey club sandwich. You might say that mustard removes the turkey's natural sweetness and gives the sandwich an aggressive, spicy taste, meaning that it would probably be better complemented with pumpernickel or rye than white bread. You would then bring your thesis to the faculty committee, and they would remind you that you didn't address the effects of mustard on a turkey club sandwich made on toasted wheat. You then modify your thesis to accommodate this new area of research, and they would probably be initially satisfied. You might then be asked to present an oral defense of your thesis before the committee. If you performed well and they liked your thesis, you would pass.

The *comprehensive written examination* might require that you take one-hour examinations on any four of the following nine topics: bread, turkey, ham, bologna, mayonnaise, ketchup, mustard, lettuce and tomato (approached as an interdisciplinary topic), and cheese. You would spend months preparing for this battery of examinations, sit down to take the test, and find yourself confronted with four hours worth of tough essay questions. If you presented satisfactory answers, you would pass.

As part of the M.S. program in Sandwich Engineering, you might or might not be expected to undertake a six-month internship wherein you make sandwiches part-time for a local deli. And after finishing, you might have trouble deciding whether you want to proceed to the research-oriented Ph.D. in Sandwich Engineering or the professional degree of Sandwich Engineer (Swch.E.). But as far as the M.S. in Sandwich Engineering goes, the coursework and culminating demonstration of knowledge (the capstone project, thesis, and/or comprehensive written examination) pretty much constitute the degree requirements for a master's program.

This metaphor applies to doctoral final projects as well. For example, the dissertation would simply be a longer and more rigorous version of the thesis. Because the dissertation is usually supposed to represent a truly original contribution to your field, you would strive to write something nobody's written about before—for example, a historical study of peanut butter sandwiches on pumpernickel.

Qualifying examinations for a doctoral program tend to be more or less similar to final master's examinations. In fact, some schools (with single M.S./Ph.D. tracks) allow the master's comprehensive examination to double as a doctoral qualifying examination.

Areas of Study and Specialization

Once you've decided on the degree you're going for, you need to figure out the area of study and perhaps the specialization. The *area of study* is what follows the "in" when you say, for instance, "I have an M.S. in computer science." An *area of specialization*, as you would guess from the name, represents a further emphasis in your study. Not every degree has an area of specialization. You may simply have an M.S. in computer science, or you may have an M.S. in computer science with a specialization in artificial intelligence. Usually, specialization is achieved by concentrating your electives in one area, but it may require extra work, perhaps in the form of an internship or a special project.

Describing the various areas in which you can earn a degree would seem simple enough, but the problem is that there's not much of a standard when it comes to just how schools name their programs—and there's even less of a standard when it comes to what constitutes a specialization. Some schools, for instance, might fire up a program in computer information systems that deals, in a systematic and thorough fashion, with computer information systems. Another program by the same name might be mostly management-oriented with only an 18-hour software applications component.

As for specializations, some computer science programs might be set up to accept 6 extra hours of programming (Introduction to C and Business COBOL) as a "software engineering track." Of course, you can go the other way too; we know of one liberal studies program that involves a 39-hour "concentration" in computer information systems. Usually one would think of a 39-hour concentration as a major, but not at this school (for whatever reason).

Furthermore, the line between a major and specialization may be even more confusingly blurred. The B.S.E. (Bachelor of Science in Engineering) and M.S.E. (Master of Science in Engineering) programs are good examples. Now, we know perfectly well that a B.S.E. in electrical engineering is a B.S.E. in electrical engineering and not a B.S. in engineering with a specialization in electrical engineering, but the degree itself is usually a "Bachelor of Science in Engineering in Electrical Engineering."

When it comes to applying for a job, the difference between a major and a specialization can be a big deal. While most businesses or graduate schools will accept a B.S. in electrical engineering with an emphasis in computer engineering as though it were a B.S. in computer engineering, these same businesses or graduate schools are not likely to be quite as charitable about a B.B.A. with a computer information systems emphasis. For this reason, it's usually safer (but not always essential, especially in uncommon fields) to go with a major rather than a specialization, provided you have that option. Majors come with specializations all their own—so rather than having a B.S. in electrical engineering with a computer engineering emphasis, you might go for a B.S. in computer engineering with a software engineering emphasis (or a B.S. in software engineering with a quality control emphasis).

Aren't sure what you want to specialize in just yet? Don't worry! It's not at all uncommon for a student to pick an emphasis after a semester, or even after the first or second year. If it's not clear whether special emphases are even offered at a school, or what exactly is involved in these special emphases, ask! Far too many people enroll in a program with only a vague idea of what will be involved and later find out it doesn't offer exactly what they need. This book is a great starting place for information, but you'll need to gather more.

If you're not sure of just what's out there, read on—but if you know exactly what you need to study, you can find it in Appendix B. You might still skim the subjects described below just to brush up on all the new fields that have cropped up over the last few years.

The Six Most Popular Information Technology Fields

Some bold trailblazers, gutsy leaders, and Einsteinian innovators want degrees as offbeat as they are. If you're one of those people, skip this section. Here we'll cover the best known and most popular information technology fields: computer science, electrical engineering, computer engineering, software engineering, computer information systems, and information science.

Computer Science

This is the granddaddy of them all: computer science, the stereotypical major of the stereotypical 1985 computer nerd. Well, that's not quite fair; there was a time when all "computer degrees" essentially were computer science degrees, so naturally computer science programs became a sort of catch-all for everything computer-related. Armed with a few courses in electrical engineering and soon-forgotten courses in COBOL and maybe Fortran, students could study computer science until they were (almost literally) blue in the face and come out of the program with a solid idea of how computers worked.

But the heart of computer science is, after all, science—not engineering, not applications, not programming, and not (quite) mathematics. This was once the field of Alan Turing, then it became the field of Bill Gates, and now—thanks to the fact that more specialized programs have taken the heat off of computer science as a discipline—it's becoming the field of Alan Turing once again.

Computer science still happens to be the most marketable computer major out there, mostly due to name recognition—but computer engineering is rapidly catching up. Don't be surprised to see computer science gradually become recognized as the very bleeding edge interdisciplinary field that it is, even as it takes a back seat per capita to computer engineering and computer information systems.

After all, the computer scientists of the previous generation have given us a lot of answers—but the beautiful thing about science is that more answers always seem to lead to even more questions.

Electrical Engineering

Here's the opposite end of the spectrum: you're dealing with circuits, gadgets, and electronics. You're fooling around with silicon boards and copper wire, transformers, circuits—things that dreams (and television sets) are made of.

What does this have to do with information technology? The physical aspects of information technology—how to design the machines, how to build them, how to maintain them, and even how to break them—are essentially electrical engineering issues. Computers are, after all, electrical beasts. We can't forget that.

But electrical engineering's immediate pertinence to information technology is beginning to diminish with the rise of computer engineering (see below). Most electrical engineering programs do still focus on computer design issues in their core requirements, and this isn't likely to change. And there's no doubt about it: electrical engineering will still tell you more about the most basic principles behind motherboards, networking, power distribution, and circuit design than any other single field likely ever will.

Computer Engineering

There was a time not very long ago when most computer engineering programs seemed to be modified electrical engineering tracks, and you'll still see a lot of that today. Still, computer engineering is starting to take on a mind of its own—and it's about time.

When you look at computer engineering programs, no matter how good they are, you're basically going to find two types: the old-school program (an electrical engineering curriculum with a few token computer science courses) and the new-school program. The new-school program essentially deals with computers on several levels. First, it addresses the basic electrical engineering principles behind computer hardware—and let's face it, electrical engineering will always be the backbone of computer hardware. Second, it addresses the unique theoretical and practical aspects of computer hardware—everything from design and maintenance to networking and digital storage. Finally, it deals with software engineering: what is computer logic, how do we give it instructions, and how do we create holistic hardware-software structures that seamlessly perform their tasks.

Now, this may sound a little familiar. Ten years ago, people might have told you that a computer science program was all about learning to work with computers—and they were right, in a way, because to a great extent that's all there was. But computer science now has other more abstract issues to consider. It's only natural that as science grows and engineering grows, we find that no single program can completely address them both as well as two separate programs can.

Software Engineering

Computer engineering is all well and good, but what if you want to focus your study on the engineering of software and software systems? This field has become more and more popular in recent years, and for good reason: while it's impossible for any one person to design new hardware without a lot of financial help, almost anyone with a basic background in programming can design new software—and it happens every day. This field is ripe for innovation.

Computer Information Systems

There are two kinds of majors in this field. The first, and most popular, basically looks like a traditional computer science curriculum with less in the way of theory, programming, and higher mathematics—leaving more room for study in other fields and/or other hands-on information technology issues.

The second version of this major is essentially a program in computer software applications plus management information systems. The idea is to approach computing from a business-oriented perspective and business from a computing-oriented perspective.

Information Science

You're probably thinking: isn't this a fancy new name for library science? Well, yes and no. Information science basically does deal with information storage and retrieval, but there's an awful lot more to information storage and retrieval these days than just plain library science. Information science teaches you how to design search engines (such as AltaVista or Lycos), compare and sort data automatically, and make it all useful to us humans. At least, that's the theory—sometimes this field wanders closer to computer information systems, and sometimes it wanders closer to library science.

Other Popular Information Technology Fields

There's something to be said for the road less traveled by, and sometimes it's even complimentary. Here you'll find a list of popular IT majors that fall outside of the "big six."

Applied Computer Science

Generally speaking, programs in this field focus on software applications and interdisciplinary uses of computers (such as informatics, computational biology, management information systems, and so forth).

Artificial Intelligence

Although computers-as-rational-agents is certainly a valid and relevant issue, most students in this field are busy designing neural nets and writing new algorithms in Lisp and Fortran. Make no mistake about it: artificial intelligence is as scientific as it is philosophical.

Client-Server Technology

This specialization deals basically with network technology, operating from the hierarchy of client-hub. Most modern programs in this field will involve operating systems study in both Unix and Windows NT.

Cognitive Neural Systems

How do networked computer "brains" operate, and how can we improve their function? This field wrestles with the question of how artificial intelligence relates to networking and vice versa.

Computer Systems Engineering

This field is very similar to computer engineering, but generally places more emphasis on hardware-software interaction, networking, and related fields.

End-User Support

This specialization focuses on technical support, a vitally important information technology field. Generally, students who specialize in this field can expect to study interpersonal communication, computer maintenance, and project management in addition to the more technical aspects of their major.

Microelectronics

This field usually focuses fairly exclusively on computer architecture and circuitry.

Networking

Programs in this field generally involve intensive study of both small-scale (LAN) and large-scale (WAN) intranets. The overall objective is to help computers work together in an efficient manner.

A Few Popular Interdisciplinary Fields

"Interdisciplinary" means combining two or more fields of study. Not every school offers interdisciplinary programs, but at those that do there are often interesting options for combining several of your interests or career directions. Some of these majors may seem impractical, and some of them may actually be impractical, but remember: you can't make a chord out of one note.

Accounting Information Systems
Over the years, information technology has begun to play a bigger role in the lives of accountants. This degree deals with information technology as it relates to accounting.

Algorithms, Optimization, and Combinatorics
This exciting new field of computational mathematics deals with the absolute latest mathematical theories that pertain, in a direct and meaningful fashion, to a variety of information technology fields.

Business Information Systems
This major tends to give about equal weight to computer information systems and business skills. Emphasis is generally placed on business-related computer skills and applications.

Cognitive Science
This cutting-edge interdisciplinary field addresses perception, memory, and logic from a variety of perspectives—including artificial intelligence and cognitive neural systems.

Computational Biology
This field deals largely with computational models of biological concept, such as computerized representations of DNA and the like. The approach of this program is largely theoretical, distinguishing it from health-related fields such as medical imaging technology.

Computational Mathematics
The mathematical questions that form the basis of computer science provide the heart of this field, while logic provides its soul.

Computer Graphic Design

This interdisciplinary field incorporates a lot of subdisciplines: digital publishing, Web design, word processing, image manipulation, rendered art, and more. This field deals with the broad question of just how you can use computers to generate graphical images.

Educational Technology

This field addresses the use of technology to educate students at all levels.

Electronic(s) Engineering Technology

Although one would normally see this as a subcategory of electrical engineering, programs in this field generally involve a good bit of study in computer software applications, management information systems, and the like.

Entertainment Technology

Focusing on exciting entertainment careers in movie special effects and video games, this field deals with the broad question of how one uses technology to entertain.

Human-Computer Interaction

This is information technology's answer to human factors engineering. Dedicated largely to the question of how we can make computers and people work together in a more pleasant and efficient manner, this field also addresses important philosophical concepts regarding the relationship between us and the technology we use.

Knowledge Discovery and Data Mining

This specialization deals with the specific question of automated data harvesting, sorting, and cataloging. It also addresses issues related to language technologies and software reliability.

Language Technologies

This field deals largely with the problem of how exactly one teaches a computer to read, write, speak, and listen.

Management Information Systems

There are essentially three aspects to this very popular field. First, it involves detailed study in management and business administration. Second, it involves a variable amount of study in computer information systems. And finally, it addresses decision sciences, logic, and related fields—fields that represent, to a great extent, the meeting place of management science and computer science.

Robotics

This field deals with electrical-mechanical interaction (this field is, in fact, sometimes called "electromechanical engineering"). As many complex electromechanical devices are operated by computer "brains," this field is highly relevant to information technology.

Telecommunications

This seems to be very much a buzzword field at the moment, so programs in this area tend to be highly diverse. Some are dedicated almost entirely to computer networking technology, others focus on radio and television, and still others are dedicated primarily to wireless communication. Some comprehensive programs in this field involve elements of all three disciplines.

How to Use This Information

You've just waded through a lot of facts, description, and details, many of which you'll probably never need. (How many folks really want or need to know about combinatorics, a sort of computing math too esoteric for all but the geekiest? Not many, but you will see it mentioned, which is why we gave it an entry.) It would be wonderful if we could end with a simple chart showing which degrees lead to which jobs. Unfortunately, it's just not that simple. While the listings give some guidance, and common sense can help you out quite a bit, many degrees lead people to a wide range of job possibilities. If you're not sure what you want to specialize in, the best advice is to do a lot of research (see the Chapter 1 resources in Appendix D, which will guide you to job descriptions and job-hunting resources), and then if you're still not sure, sign up for a very general field, such as plain old vanilla computer science. You can always narrow your field or transfer later if you discover that, in fact, your true passion is for combinatorics after all.

CHAPTER 6

Financial Aid Demystified

Paying for college. Those three simple words are enough to cause parents extreme anxiety, keep potential students awake at night—and, more seriously, keep those very same potential students from seriously pursuing an education. This is almost always the wrong way to go—the cliché is generally right, that the only thing more expensive than going to school is not going to school. In this chapter, we'll look at some of the basics of financial aid, step through your options, and discuss how to find out who has the money you need and how to get them to loan or (best case scenario) give it to you with a smile.

Will You Definitely Need Financial Aid?

These days, the answer to that question is almost certainly yes. The total cost of attending many private, independent schools is already somewhere around $100,000 for four years and climbing. And the very top graduate programs, though they require less dedicated time from you, may cost almost as much. Many people assume that financial aid is only for the academically brilliant, the truly needy, the young, or the full-time student. None of this is necessarily true. There's a lot of money available in the form of loans, grants, employer assistance, and more. Many experts go so far as to say that there's financial aid available for every single student who wants it. If you can afford to pay for your entire education out of your pocket without taking on any loans, that's great, but few people can realistically expect to do this. And even if you could, why not look for some merit-based grants? They're definitely out there.

What Kind of Financial Aid Is Available?

This chapter delineates the sorts of financial aid you're likely to encounter and offers hints and tips for securing the funding you need. There's a lot of turf to cover, and it may sometimes feel a bit overwhelming. One way to attack this is to start with the following list, which delineates the types of aid you're likely to encounter. Then skip to the back of the chapter for a handy Dos and Don'ts list. This provides a basic framework, and then you can dip into the rest of the chapter, reading the sections that interest you.

▶ Federal financial aid programs:

  ▶ Free money: Pell Grants and FSEOG

  ▶ Loans: Perkins loan, Stafford loan, and FPLUS

▶ State financial aid (free money and loans)

▶ Private loans

▶ Private foundation grants

▶ Employee assistance programs

Financial Aid Timelines

Whether you're a high school student planning your initial foray into college or someone who's worked in the IT field for a decade and now wants a master's degree in order to get ahead, you'll need to do some planning. These timelines lay out ideal planning structures. For the undergraduate, if you're not in high school, you'll need to adapt a bit, so just work backwards from the date you'd ideally like to enroll.

Undergraduate

Chapter 3 talked about setting up an ideal timeline for applying to schools. Here we look at a similar timeline for financial aid. If you can start researching scholarships, lining up work in your field, and so forth as early as your sophomore year, that's fabulous. However, the average student probably won't start focusing on college until at least junior year, so that's where we pick up this timeline.

JUNIOR YEAR OF HIGH SCHOOL

The more you can do at an early date, the better prepared you'll be when deadlines, exams, and requirements start piling up. Be prepared!

✔ As you start researching the schools you'll want to apply to, ask about financial aid opportunities and scholarships you might be eligible for.

✔ If your high school or a local college offers any sort of financial aid workshops, attend them. You'll get useful information and a psychological boost to start getting serious about your school-funding effort.

✔ Talk to your high school's guidance counselor about financial aid. He or she may be able to point you in interesting directions and help you set up an ideal timeline. If you set goals with the counselor and promise to check back with progress reports, this can serve as another motivator.

✔ Contact the appropriate state agency (see the listings later in this chapter) to find out what sort of state funding might be available to you.

Senior Year of High School

Here's where it all starts to get intense. There's a lot you need to do while taking your finals, saying goodbye to friends, and all the rest. Being well organized and aware of what's required is a great first step.

✔ Make a master plan for the year. What applications and forms are due when? You may want to make a big calendar and post it on your wall, to keep those deadlines always in the forefront of your mind.

✔ Apply for private scholarships.

✔ In November, get a Free Application for Federal Student Aid (FAFSA) form from your school guidance counselor or at http://www.fafsa.ed.gov/. Fill it out as soon as possible, but don't mail it until January 2, so as not to violate their procedure.

✔ In January, mail your FAFSA. You're penalized for sending it early, but as soon as it's okay to send (after January 1), timing counts. The earlier they receive your form, the more aid you're eligible for. Don't blow this one.

✔ In April, you should receive your financial aid notification awards. If you haven't received one by the date the school promises, call and ask whether it's been sent. Once you choose which school you'll be attending, write to the others to let them know you'll be declining the award. This frees up money for other applicants. Your award will come with some paperwork that needs to be filled out. Be sure you fill it out and return it in a timely fashion.

✔ By May you should have found out about private scholarships you've applied for. Again, if you haven't received anything, contact the foundations and ask about the status of your application. Never assume that no news is bad news—foundations are staffed by human beings, and mistakes are made. Your application may have been lost or misfiled, or the award notification sent to the wrong address.

The Summer Before School Starts

If at all possible, you should start trying to line up a college job even before high school graduation—maybe six months before you start college. However, if that's just not feasible, summer's the time to do it.

✔ Begin applying for a job at your school or in the surrounding area if at all possible. Visit (or if you haven't relocated yet, call or e-mail) the career center, send out résumés, meet with people who can give you letters of recommendation in your home town, and so forth.

✔ Even if you can't find anything in your field, work during the summer. Once you start school, every penny will count.

Once You're Enrolled

The timeline's the same every year that you're in college. Don't get lazy and forget. That's happened to all too many students who were well prepared for freshman year, but then got overwhelmed with final exams, the social whirl, and off-campus jobs, and forgot to file their paperwork. Don't let this happen to you.

✔ If you don't already have a campus job by September, now's the time to get one. Meet with the student career office and see what you can line up.

✔ During October through December, apply for private scholarships.

✔ In January, complete and send in your new FAFSA. Remember that this has to be done every year—renewal is not automatic.

✔ If you don't already have a summer job by March, start looking.

Graduate School

You'll note that this timeline's not too different from the undergraduate one, above. That's because the process, options, and forms are largely the same for graduate students. One additional factor, if you're working in the field already, is the notion of getting your employer to pay for your education. While the requirements in these situations vary from case to case, you'll find some basic heads-up reminders below. Be sure to investigate your personal situation carefully, using the hints in Chapter 10.

One Year Before Enrollment

As ever, the more research you can do, the better off you'll be.

✔ As you start researching the schools you'll want to apply to, ask about financial aid opportunities and scholarships you might be eligible for.

✔ Make a master plan for the year. What applications and forms are due when? You may want to make a big calendar and post it on your wall, to keep those deadlines always in the forefront of your mind.

✔ If your company offers any sort of employee assistance program, start researching it, and find out whether you'll be eligible and, if not, what you need to do to make yourself eligible.

✔ Contact the appropriate state agency (see the listings later in this chapter) to find out what sort of state funding might be available to you.

✔ Apply for private scholarships as early as possible.

✔ In November, get a FAFSA from the federal Web site (http://www.fafsa.ed.gov/). Fill it out as soon as possible, but don't mail it until January 2, so as not to violate their procedure.

✔ In January, mail your FAFSA. You're penalized for sending it early, but as soon as it's okay to send (after January 1), timing counts. The earlier they receive your form, the more aid you're eligible for. Don't blow this one.

Six Months Before Enrollment

You'll need to finalize things with your employer, figure out your financial realities, and get ready to switch gears from the work world back into academia (or, if you're going straight from undergrad to grad, into a different realm of academia). Being well organized and well informed gives you a great head start.

✔ If you're eligible for employee assistance, be sure all of your paperwork is done and that your employer understands your new schedule. Check with the human resources department to make sure everything's in place.

✔ In April, you should receive your financial aid notification awards. If you haven't received one by the date the school promises, call and ask whether it's been sent. Once you choose which school you'll be attending, write to the others to let them know you'll be declining the award. This frees up money for other applicants. Your award will come with some paperwork that needs to be filled out. Be sure you fill it out and return it in a timely fashion.

✔ By May you should have found out about private scholarships you've applied for. Again, if you haven't received anything, contact the foundations and ask about the status of your application. Never assume that no news is bad news—foundations are staffed by human beings, and mistakes are made. Your application may have been lost or misfiled, or the award notification sent to the wrong address.

ONCE YOU'RE ENROLLED

The timeline's the same every year that you're in college. Don't get lazy and forget. That's happened to all too many students who were well prepared at first, but then got overwhelmed with final projects, the social whirl, and off-campus jobs, and forgot to file their paperwork. Don't let this happen to you.

✔ During October through December, apply for private scholarships.

✔ In January, complete and send in your new FAFSA. Remember that this has to be done every year—renewal is not automatic.

Is There Financial Aid Available for Older Students?

In a word, yes. The nuts and bolts of obtaining financial aid are basically the same whether you're 18 or 48. While it is true that some scholarships from private foundations specify an age, these are almost equally divided between those for older and younger students. In addition, older students are more likely to be employed in a field that will pay for training.

One caveat is that it's still a little harder to find funding if you're a part-time student, which is true of many adults who are also working. Part-time students are technically eligible for most financial aid programs so long as they attend college at least half time, but in reality the available aid often goes to the full-time, more traditional candidates. In these cases, you just need to dig a little deeper—look for appropriate scholarships or foundation grants, or convince your employer to help fund your education. Things may be getting better—according to the *Chronicle of Higher Education*, more than a dozen states are looking at expanding financial aid for part-time students. Speak to your school's financial aid office to see whether your state is one. You might be pleasantly surprised.

A Note on Timing

The importance of good financial aid planning cannot be overstated. With major federal loan and grant programs, deadlines are absolutely inflexible. Miss one, and you've blown your chance for the money. Smaller foundations and school-based lending programs may be more flexible, but why risk it? Of course, nobody sets out to miss a deadline, but in the hurly-burly of deciding on a degree program, applying to schools, and all the rest, it's easy to forget about financial aid entirely, or to assume that the school will let you know when it's time to apply. Make inquiries about financial aid part of your initial approach to a school, and be meticulous about meeting and understanding the requirements and deadlines.

Some students wait until they're admitted to a school to start looking for financial aid, and by then it's usually too late. You can (and should) apply for financial aid before you're admitted to any school. The federal aid forms allow you to designate a number of schools to which you're applying, and to whom they'll send your information. Keep in mind that schools may not send out acceptance letters until June of any given year, but the deadline for federal aid forms is in February. Similarly, many private foundations have only one annual application date, and they can set it whenever they want.

In addition, be aware that some programs have limited amounts of money to give or lend. Employer-funded programs may send a limited number of employees to school, and often it's on a first-come, first-served basis. Similarly, private foundations may have rolling acceptance for their grants, and once they've given the money for the academic year, there's nothing left in the bank. Make financial aid research a part of your basic fact-finding mission. We give you some resources for getting started in this chapter and more in Appendix D, "Resources." Use them.

NOTE *Financial aid planning doesn't end after you get that first grant or loan. You'll need to reapply each year and revisit your needs, qualifications, and options. Once you're enrolled, you have the school's financial aid office available to help you. Make use of this resource.*

TIP *Financial aid offices are often crammed with students around big deadlines. Plan to get your paperwork in early. That way, when you have questions, someone will be able to take more time to help you, and the pressure will be off.*

What If You Do Blow a Deadline?

All is probably not lost. Call your financial aid office immediately, and ask what options are available for students in your situation. The school may be able to help you get your FAFSA in, or may be willing to give you preliminary approval without an official FAFSA, provided you give them the same information. Some schools offer short-term bridge loans to students awaiting delayed financial aid—ask if this is a possibility. In worst-case scenarios, consider borrowing from a bank or even against credit cards to bridge the gap between now and when you get some loan or grant money. Just be sure that you budget wisely and use the low-interest loan to pay back the other, higher-interest option. Robbing Peter to pay Paul may be a dumb but acceptable last-resort strategy for some, but once you're also robbing Bob, Fred, and Louie, you're setting yourself up for financial disaster.

What About Scholarship Search Services and Financial Aid Consultants?

The old-fashioned scholarship service may be fast becoming a thing of the past, as an increasing number of Web sites now offer free searches as part of a package of academic services. Thus, for a relatively small time investment, you can probably research what's available online. Only if you're really strapped for time should you think about paying any sort of fee to an individual to do just that research for you. However, there does seem to be a growth industry in professional college financial aid planners, and you may want to avail yourself of one of these experts.

The financial aid planners don't just help you find scholarships, although they will do that as part of their services. They'll also, for instance, help you find the right school (perhaps a more economical one that you'd overlooked, or one more likely to offer financial aid to someone of your gender, ethnicity, or economic background). They'll help you fill out your forms if you have a complex financial history, and show you legal, insider ways to maximize your perceived financial need. They'll be up on current tax law and employer assistance possibilities in your state, and give you advice for negotiating these waters.

Financial aid planners can be expensive, charging up to $150 an hour for their expertise. Be sure you find a good one, as there are sharks and phonies out there charging big bucks and delivering little. Start by asking the financial aid offices at some of your schools of choice—they can almost certainly recommend someone with expertise in the IT field. When you call to discuss the possibility of engaging a planner, ask them about their knowledge of computer science and IT programs, and ask for references from satisfied clients. A good planner will be happy to provide references—and happy to refer you on to someone else if IT is not his or her strong suit. This option may not be for everyone, but if you're serious about your education and have the money to invest, the right expert can literally save you tens of thousands of dollars.

Financial Aid Forms

Get used to filling out forms—you'll be doing a lot of it. There are three basic types of forms you're likely to see: the FAFSA, the CSS, and individual schools' forms. Here's what they are, why you need to know about them, and when you need to think about them.

The FAFSA: An Essential Form

The basic federal form you'll need to file is the Free Application for Federal Student Aid, known universally as the FAFSA. This form goes to a central processing facility, and that facility then sends your information back out to schools. Your institution of choice can provide you with the FAFSA, or you can get it online at http://www.fafsa.ed.gov/ (this site also has FAQs, though they're mainly targeted to high school students). Different schools have different deadlines for when you'll need to get the FAFSA in, but for maximum aid, hit the federal government's deadline of February 15. You'll also need to renew your application every year—more than one student has been rudely kicked off the educational gravy train for forgetting to send in that annual update. Don't let it happen to you.

The CSS Profile

Some schools also use something called a College Scholarship Service (CSS) profile to help them assess need for non-federal grants and loans at both the graduate and undergraduate levels. Read carefully through the financial aid materials from schools you're planning to apply to, as they may require both the CSS and the FAFSA. The CSS can also be filled out online, at http://www.collegeboard.org. (This site reorganizes frequently; go to the home page and follow the links to its financial aid section. This area will both explain the CSS and then let you fill it out.) If you don't have to fill out a CSS, don't. Not all schools require it and, more importantly, it has a tendency to make you look less needy, just by dint of the way it assesses income and assets.

School-Based Financial Aid Forms

Finally, most (if not all) schools will have their own financial aid applications for you to fill out, in addition to the FAFSA and possibly the CSS. The reason for this is that many schools have special scholarships—for instance, for minority students of computer engineering—and need to know whether you qualify. If you apply for any foundation grants to individuals or other private aid, there will be even more forms and deadlines. Make a calendar of what you're applying for, when you need to get forms in, and when you expect to hear back, and do your follow-up. Yes, this may feel like a part-time job, but it's one that can pay tens of thousands of dollars, so it's worthwhile. Try to remember that when you're up to your neck in triplicate forms and requests for tax data.

Federal Financial Aid Programs

Some 75 percent of all financial aid awarded in the U.S. comes from good ol' Uncle Sam. This includes both grants and loans, and by filing your FAFSA, you automatically put yourself in the running for both. Here are the basic federal programs, and what they have to offer. Throughout this section and those to follow, we'll be discussing undergraduate and graduate aid programs together, and many financial aid providers offer aid at all levels. If there are restrictions, we'll note them.

Pell Grants

Let's all hear it for Rhode Island senator Claiborne Pell, who came up with the fabulous idea of outright government grants (meaning you don't have to pay the money back) for deserving students. The grant that bears his name is only available to undergraduates working on their first bachelor's degree. It is need-based (as demonstrated by your FAFSA), and the amount awarded varies depending on a number of factors, including whether Congress has cut or increased the endowment, how many students apply, how much tuition costs at your school of choice, and various other criteria. Part-time students qualify, though for less money. The U.S. Department of Education guarantees that each participating school will receive enough money to pay the federal Pell Grants of its eligible students. This is the first place you should look for funding, as these grants are free money pure and simple.

FSEOG

The Federal Supplemental Educational Opportunity Grant Program (FSEOG) was established to help truly needy students bridge the gap between their available funds and their financial needs. Like the Pell Grant, it is for undergraduates only, but unlike the Pell, there's no guarantee every eligible student will be able to receive an FSEOG; students at each school are paid based on the availability of funds at that school. While the amount awarded can go as high as $4,000, most schools actually only have enough to shell out in the region of $1,000 to $2,000. Schools have their own definitions of extreme need; talk to your financial aid office if you think you might qualify. This is far preferable to overextending your personal credit, so if you're in a bind, look here before you look to private lenders.

Federal Perkins Loan

Available to both undergraduates and graduate students, this loan is interest-free while you're enrolled, and can be paid back over up to ten years once you graduate. Undergraduates can borrow up to $4,000 a year to a total of $20,000, while graduate students can borrow $6,000 a year up to a total of $40,000. Payments and interest start nine months after you graduate, although there are a number of options offered should you have dire financial need after graduation. If you drop to less than a half-time load of classes, it's handled the same as graduation, and you'll receive your first repayment notices nine months after the beginning of that semester.

One word of advice: a lot of people are nervous about borrowing up to $40,000, especially younger students who don't have much experience with consumer debt. Debt is a scary thing, and if you can avoid it, all the better. Still, it's worth considering that no one is ever likely to offer to loan you so much money on such favorable terms again in your adult life. Of course, you will have to pay this money back, and while it's likely that an IT degree will land you in a job that pays well enough to let you pay your loans off with a minimum of pain, they're still loans and in a worst-case scenario, job hunting while carrying a heavy load of debt can be stressful.

 TIP Be sure you have considered all funding alternatives before applying for loans. How about a savings set aside program where you save and then go to school when you have salted away enough tuition? Or save outside consulting fees just for your schooling. There are a lot of creative ways to fund an education that may not involve signing away your soul, even at an attractive rate of interest.

Federal Direct Student Loan Program

This relatively recent program lends money to both undergraduates and graduate students. The money comes from the federal government, but is distributed by a school's financial aid department. If you have demonstrated need, as assessed from your FAFSA, the loan is subsidized, which means the government pays the interest on it while you're enrolled in an approved program. However, even non-needy students qualify for an unsubsidized loan. In this case, interest accrues from day one, although the actual payment of that interest can be deferred until you graduate.

For undergraduates, the Federal Direct program lends up to $2,625 for the first year, $3,500 for the second, and $5,500 for the third, fourth, and fifth, after which point they assume you'll have earned your degree. Graduate students can borrow up to $18,500 per year.

Federal Stafford Loan Program

The particulars of the Stafford loan are almost exactly the same as those of the Federal Direct program—the only significant difference is that the money comes from private organizations (mainly banks, although also some educational foundations) rather than our tax dollars. Otherwise the dollar amounts and subsidized/unsubsidized details are the same: a loan of up to $2,625 for the first year, $3,500 for the second, and $5,500 for the third, fourth, and fifth. Graduate students can borrow up to $18,500 per year.

For both of these programs, there's a complicated formula for figuring out interest, based on current treasury-bill interest rates at the time you begin repayment. Ask financial aid officers to explain it to you if you want to know what your financial hit will be. The bottom line, as far as we're concerned, is that while not as great a deal as the Perkins loan, these are still decent bargains for students needing to borrow to fund their education.

Federal Parent Loans for Undergraduate Students

The FPLUS is only for undergrads who are still financially dependent on their parents. The amount parents can borrow is based on how expensive the school is, with financial need factored in. If your parents apply for an FPLUS and are turned down, you are automatically eligible for additional Stafford or Direct funds, so dependent students should always apply—it can't hurt, and it's just a check-box on the FAFSA application.

State Financial Aid

Each of the 50 states offers a variety of scholarships and grants in addition to participating in the federal programs listed above. Most of these programs are based on financial need, which each state assesses according to its own criteria, sometimes more generously than the federal government. So even if Uncle Sam doesn't think you're needy enough to qualify for supplemental aid, your state may have some extra cash for you. Some of the grants may be merit-based as well, which means that even if you're not financially needy according to the state's standards, your grades or talents may qualify you for extra money.

The criteria vary widely enough from state to state that there's no point in trying to list them all. Instead, contact the relevant state agency, listed below, to find out details that apply to you. In general, you need to have applied for federal aid and be a resident in the state where you're studying. Residency requirements vary not only from state to state, but even from school to school within a state. Usually they include a year's residency in the state, a state driver's license or ID card, a mailing address, and sometimes vehicle registration and/or insurance, state tax returns, or other documents. If you're attending a school away from your home state and aren't eligible for state aid your first year, don't forget that you probably will be in your second year of study—by which time you may be so intent on your studies that you forget all about this funding option. Don't—it can really help. Your school financial aid office should remind you of your new resident status when you go to talk about aid options for the coming year, but they're usually pretty busy and stressed out, so the more research you can do on your own the better.

As an example of what you might see, the state of Arkansas offers a range of grants, including:

The Academic Challenge Scholarship   This scholarship offers up to $2,500 annually for graduating high school seniors who complete the precollegiate core curriculum, have a 2.50 grade point average or better in those courses, achieve a 19 or better on the ACT, and demonstrate financial need. To apply for this scholarship, the student must be graduating from an Arkansas high school. He or she must submit a completed application to the state agency along with a seven-semester high school transcript and family federal income tax forms for the two years preceding high school graduation.

The Governor's Scholars Program   Offering up to $4,000 annually for graduating Arkansas high school seniors based on academic achievement, test scores, and leadership, this award pays tuition, mandatory fees, and room and board at an approved Arkansas college or university. This award is renewable annually for up to four years, including the initial award year, provided the recipient maintains a minimum cumulative college grade point average of 3.0 and completes a minimum of 24 semester credit hours or the equivalent per academic year. In order to be eligible for an Arkansas Governor's Scholar award, students must submit a program application by March 1, demonstrate leadership activity, and meet certain academic requirements.

The Missing in Action/Killed in Action (MIA/KIA) Dependents' Scholarship This scholarship pays for tuition and fees as well as room and board at any state-supported college or university for the dependents of an Arkansas citizen who was a prisoner of war or was missing or killed in action during the course of active military duty after January 1, 1960. This covers a bachelor's degree or a graduate or professional degree. To be eligible for an MIA/KIA Dependent's Scholarship, the student's parent or spouse must have been a resident of the state of Arkansas at the time he or she entered the military.

These are just three of a number of programs offered by the state of Arkansas, and each of the 50 states has its own programs. Look into the programs offered by your state of residence—there might be something perfect for you.

 TIP *Sometimes it will make sense to establish residency in a state in order to get a better deal on tuition or programs. This isn't something to undertake lightly—you'll need to uproot yourself and live somewhere for at least a year or more. Still, if it's an area you're interested in living in anyway, and the job prospects are good, you could do worse than moving somewhere for a couple of years, getting a job, becoming a resident, and then applying to the school of your dreams. If you don't get in, you'd better be happy with your new home state!*

Financial Aid Offices

The following is a list of financial aid offices, ordered by state. Each of these offices can help you find the right programs for you and determine whether you meet the eligibility criteria. The Web sites are often quite comprehensive and helpful, and should provide the jumping-off point for your search. It is worth noting that even though these sites belong to stable government entities, they seem to change quite frequently. Over a recent four-month period, at least five of the Web sites below changed their names, moved to other servers, or shifted to a different state agency's home page. There is almost always a "forwarding order" at the old URL, but these stay active for only so long. If you try one of these sites and get an "URL not found" message, don't despair. Enter the agency's name as a whole into your search engine of choice, and you'll almost certainly be directed to the new site.

Alabama

Alabama Commission on Higher
   Education
100 N. Union Street, P.O. Box 30200
Montgomery, AL 36130-2000
(334) 242-1998
http://www.ache/state.al.us/

Alaska

Alaska Commission on Postsecondary
   Education and Student Loan Corp.
3030 Vintage Boulevard
Juneau, AK 99801-7109
(907) 465-2962
http://www.state.ak.us/acpe/

Arizona

Arizona Commission for Postsecondary
   Education
2020 N. Central Avenue, #275
Phoenix, AZ 85004-4503
(602) 229-2591
http://www.acpe.asu.edu/

Arkansas

Arkansas Department of Higher
   Education
114 East Capitol
Little Rock, AR 72201-3818
(501) 371-2000
http://www.adhe.arknet.edu/

California

California Student Aid Commission
P.O. Box 419027
Rancho Cordova, CA 95741-9027
(916) 526-7590
http://www.csac.ca.gov/

Colorado

Colorado Commission on Higher
   Education
Colorado Heritage Center
1300 Broadway, 2nd Floor
Denver, CO 80203
(303) 866-2723
http://www.state.co.us/cche_dir/
   hecche.html

Connecticut

Connecticut Department of Higher
   Education
61 Woodland Street
Hartford, CT 06105-1855
(860) 947-1855
http://www.ctdhe.commnet.edu/

Delaware

Delaware Higher Education Commission
Carvel State Office Building
820 North French Street
Wilmington, DE 19801
(302) 577-3240
http://www.doe.state.de.us/high-ed/

District of Columbia

Office of Postsecondary Education,
    Research and Assistance
2100 Martin Luther King Jr. Avenue #401
Washington, DC 20020
(202) 727-3685
 http://www.washingtondc.gov/

Florida

Florida Department of Education
Office of Student Financial Assistance
325 W. Gaines Street
Tallahassee, FL 32399-0400
(850) 487-0049
http://www.bor.state.fl.us/

Georgia

Georgia Student Finance Commission
State Loans and Grants Division
2082 East Exchange Place, #200
Tucker, GA 30084
(800) 776-6878
http://www.gsfc.org/

Hawaii

Hawaii State Postsecondary Education
    Commission
University of Hawaii
2444 Dole Street, #202
Honolulu, HI 96822-2394
(808) 956-6624
http://www.k12.hi.us

Idaho

Idaho State Board of Education
650 West State Street
Boise, ID 83720
(208) 334-2270
http://www.sde.state.id.us/obse/htm

Illinois

Illinois Student Assistance Commission
1755 Lake Cook Road
Deerfield, IL 60015-5209
(847) 948-8550
http://www.isacl.org/

Indiana

State Student Assistance Commission of
    Indiana
150 W. Market Street, # 500
Indianapolis, IN 46204-2811
(317) 232-2350
http://www.ai.org/ssaci/

Iowa

Iowa College Student Aid Commission
200 10th Street, 4th Floor
Des Moines, IA 50309-3609
(515) 281-3501
http://www.state.ia.us/government/
    icsac/

Kansas

Kansas Board of Regents
700 SW Harrison, #1410
Topeka, KS 66603-3760
(785) 296-3517
http://www.kansasregents.org/

Kentucky

Kentucky Higher Education Assistance
  Authority
1050 US 127 S, #102
Frankfort, KY 40601-4323
(800) 928-8926
http://www.kheaa.state.ky.us/

Louisiana

Louisiana Student Financial
  Assistance Commission
P.O. Box 91202
Baton Rouge, LA 70821-9202
(800) 259-5626
http://www.doe.state.la.us/

Maine

Finance Authority of Maine
119 State House Station
Augusta, ME 04333-0949
(800) 228-3734
http://www.famemaine.com/

Maryland

Maryland Higher Education Commission
Jeffrey Building, 16 Frances Street
Annapolis, MD 21401-1781
(410) 974-5370
http://www.mhec.state.md.us/

Massachusetts

Massachusetts Education Financing
  Authority
330 Stuart Street, #304
Boston, MA 02116
(617) 727-9420
http://www.mefa.org/

Michigan

Michigan Higher Education Assistance
  Authority
Office of Scholarships and Grants
P.O. Box 30462
Lansing, MI 48909-7962
(888) 447-2687
http://www.mde.state.mi.us/

Minnesota

Minnesota Higher Education Services
  Office
1450 Energy Park Drive, #350
(800) 657-3866
http://www.mheso.state.mn.us

Mississippi

Mississippi State Institutions of
  Higher Learning
Financial Assistance Board
Office of Student Financial Aid
3825 Ridgewood Road
Jackson, MS 39211-6453
(601) 982-6663
http://www.ihl.state.ms.us/

Missouri

Missouri Coordinating Board for
  Higher Education
3515 Amazonas Drive
Jefferson City, MO 65109-5717
(573) 751-2361
http://www.mocbhe.gov/

Montana

Montana University System
2500 Broadway
Helena, MT 59620-3103
(406) 444-0078
http://www.montana.edu/

Nebraska

Nebraska Coordinating Commission
   for Postsecondary Education
140 N. 8th Street, #300
P.O. Box 95005
Lincoln, NE 68509-5005
(402) 471-2847
http://www.ccpe.state.ne.us

Nevada

University of Nevada-Reno
Office of Admissions Administration
   Records, MS 120
Reno, NV 89557
(775) 784-6181
http://www.unr.edu/

New Hampshire

New Hampshire Postsecondary
   Education Commission
2 Industrial Park Drive
Concord, NH 03301-8512
(603) 271-2555
http://www.state.nh.us/postsecondary/

New Jersey

New Jersey Higher Education Student
   Assistance Authority
4 Quakerbridge Plaza, Box 540
Trenton, NJ 08625
(800) 792-8670
http://www.hesaa.org/

New Mexico

New Mexico Commission on Higher
   Education
1068 Cerrillos Road
Santa Fe, NM 87501-4925
(800) 279-9777
http://www.nmche.org/

New York

New York State Higher Education
   Services Corporation
One Commerce Plaza
Albany, NY 12255
(518) 473-7087
http://www.hesc.state.ny.us/

North Carolina

North Carolina State Education
   Assistance Authority
P.O. Box 13663
Research Triangle Park, NC 27709-3663
(800) 700-1775
http://www.ncseaa.edu/

North Dakota

North Dakota Student Financial
   Assistance Program
600 E. Boulevard Avenue
Bismarck, ND 58505-0230
(701) 328-2960
http://www.nodak.edu/

Ohio

Ohio State Grants and Scholarships
309 S. 4th Street, Box 182452
Columbus, OH 43218-2452
(888) 833-1133
www.regents.state.oh.us/sgs/

Oklahoma
Oklahoma Tuition Aid Grant Program
500 Education Building, State Capitol
    Complex
Oklahoma City, OK 73105-4503
(405) 858-4356
http://www.okhighered.org/

Oregon
Oregon State Scholarship Commission
1500 Valley River Drive, #100
Eugene, OR 97401
(541) 687-7400
http://www.ous.edu/

Pennsylvania
Pennsylvania Higher Education
    Assistance Agency
200 N. 7th Street
Harrisburg, PA 17102-1444
(717) 720-2800
http://www.pheaa.org/

Rhode Island
Rhode Island Board of Governors for
    Higher Education
560 Jefferson Boulevard
Warwick, RI 02886
(800) 922-9855
http://www.uri.edu/ribog/

South Carolina
South Carolina Higher Education
    Tuition Grants Commission
1310 Lady Street, #811
Columbia, SC 29201
(803) 734-1200
http://www.state.sc.us/tuitiongrants/

South Dakota
South Dakota Department of Education
700 Governors Drive
Pierre, SD 57501-2291
(605) 773-3134
http://www.ris.sdbor.edu/

Tennessee
Tennessee Higher Education
    Commission
404 James Robertson Parkway, #1950
Nashville, TN 37243-0820
(800) 257-6526
http://www.state.tn.us/thec/

Texas
Texas Higher Education Coordinating
    Board
P.O. Box 12788, Capitol Station
Austin, TX 78711-2788
(800) 242-3062
http://www.thecb.state.tx.us/

Utah
Utah Education Assistance Authority
355 W. North Temple, #3 Triad, Suite 550
Salt Lake City, UT 84180-1205
(800) 418-8757
http://www.utahsbr.edu/

Vermont
Vermont Student Assistance
    Corporation
Champlain Mill, Box 2000
Winooski, VT 05404-9602
(802) 655-9602
http://www.vsac.org/

Virginia

State Council of Higher Education for
    Virginia
101 N. 14th Street, 9th Floor
Richmond, VA 23219
(804) 225-2628
http://www.schev.edu/

Washington

Washington State Higher Education
    Coordinating Board
917 Lakeridge Way SW, Box 43430
Olympia, WA 98504-3430
(360) 753-7850
http://www.hecb.wa.gov/

West Virginia

West Virginia State College and
    University Systems
1018 Kanawha Boulevard East, #700
Charleston, WV 25301
(304) 558-4614
http://wvde.state.wv.us/

Wisconsin

Higher Education Aids Board
P.O. Box 7885
Madison, WI 53707-7885
(608) 267-2206
http://www.heab.state.wi.us/

Wyoming

Wyoming College Commission
2020 Carey Avenue, 8th Floor
Cheyenne, WY 82002-0110
(307) 777-7763
http://www.k12.wy.us/higher_ed.html

Getting Money from Private Sources

Non-government money comes in two flavors, just like government money: loans
and grants. Ideally, you'll want to apply for as many grants as possible, as they
don't need to be paid back. However, in case the grants don't come through, it
makes sense to be looking at alternate sources of funding, including private loans.
Many banks and financial institutions are willing to loan you the money you need
for school, and they may have fewer restrictions on how you spend it. For instance,
you are not allowed to use federal education loan money to buy a car—which does
make sense, but if you live far from campus and work late in the computer lab, a
cheap reliable car may actually be a sensible educational purchase. Private loans
let you make that sort of decision.

We'll talk about private loan sources first, and then get into how to track down the best grant-providers. The only reason not to pursue every possible avenue is your own assessment of the time and money needed. After all, even if a bank offers to loan you money, you don't have to take the loan—and you'd be foolish not to take any grant offered you, unless it has stringent strings attached.

Private Loans

If federal and state loans don't cover all of your needs, or if you've missed deadlines or failed eligibility tests, private lenders can often help out. While most large banks have student loan divisions, the following have been rated as the best by a number of industry experts. If you have a good relationship with your bank, however, it doesn't hurt to ask them about loans for education. Rates do vary, so it makes sense to shop around for the best deal. Ask a lot of questions, including:

▶ How much can I borrow each school year?

▶ What is the total I can borrow over the course of my degree?

▶ What is the interest rate?

▶ Can payments be deferred while I'm in school?

▶ Is there any grace period after graduation or must I begin repaying the loan immediately? The answer to this question can range from no grace period up to about six months. Although you're likely to get a good job soon after graduation, this can provide a little cushion while you get settled.

▶ What is the repayment plan? Ask to see what your monthly payment will be, and how much you'll end up paying if you pay the minimum each month.

▶ Is there any penalty for early repayment? Some banks charge the same amount of total interest whether you take five or twenty years to pay back the loan—a great deal for the bank, not for you.

PROVIDERS OF PRIVATE EDUCATIONAL LOANS

While this may not be an exhaustive list, the following institutions are either the biggest or the most generous in the field, and are definitely of high repute. This doesn't mean you won't find other sources, but be sure to check them out carefully to make sure you're not being ripped off.

Bank of America

Student Banking Services

275 S. Valencia Avenue, 3rd Floor

Brea, CA 92823

(800) 442-0567

http://www.bankofamerica.com/
studentbanking/

Offers loans for both undergraduate
and graduate study.

Achiever Loan

KeyBank Education Finance

745 Atlantic Avenue

Boston, MA 02111

(800) KEY-LEND

http://www.key.com/educate/

Loans for both undergraduate and
graduate study.

TERI Loan

The Education Resources Institute

P.O. Box 312

330 Stuart Street, Suite 500

Boston, MA 02117-9123

(800) 255-8374

http://www.teri.org/

Loans for both undergraduate and
graduate study.

Citibank Student Loans

Undergraduate loans:

Citibank

P.O. Box 22945

Rochester, NY 14692-6805

(800) 692-8200

http://www.studentloan.com/

Graduate loans:

Citibank

99 Garnsey Road

Pittsford, NY 14534

(800) 946-4019

http://studentloan.citibank.com/

Graduate Access Loans

Access Group

P.O. Box 7430

Wilmington, DE 19803-0430

(800) 282-1550

http://www.accessgroup.org/

Loans for graduate study only.

Private Foundation Grants

There are more than 100,000 foundations in America, established to dispense
money to individuals who meet the foundation's criteria. A significant number of
these foundations are empowered to grant money for educational purposes. Your
school's financial aid office can often tell you where to look for grant money

that's been earmarked for computer science and IT studies. If you want to get creative, take a look at a book titled *Foundation Grants to Individuals*, available in any good reference library. This tome lists thousands of grants that individuals can apply for. Many are quite small and/or too specific ("$50 to graduates of Cedar Hills High School planning to study dentistry"), but there are interesting sources of free money out there for many people. Below, we list a sampling of private foundation grants. For more information on researching foundation grants, check out the Foundation Center, at http://fdcenter.org/.

When applying for grants, remember that private foundations can, within certain broad guidelines, set up their processes and requirements however they see fit. Application deadlines, application fees, eligibility requirements, and the like may vary widely from institution to institution. In addition, your school's financial aid office may not be able to help you out as much when you have questions—financial aid officers know the federal and state programs cold, but may not be as conversant with the ins and outs of private funding sources. If you're lucky, your school will have an office of grants, and/or someone in your department will be grant-savvy. If not, you'll have to do more of the work on your own. Be sure to fill out all of your paperwork, submit it on time, and supply whatever they want in the way of transcripts, letters of recommendation, and so forth. This can be a time-consuming process, so do some research up front and see which grants you're most likely to be a strong candidate for, based on their Web sites and inside tips from your department advisor.

Most experts recommend that you identify five or six grants that seem like good targets and focus your attention on them. You'll need to give each one real attention, writing a proposal that's targeted to the foundation, rather than a rote "give me money" form letter. If it's obvious you're applying to dozens of foundations using the same copy-and-paste application, those dozens of letters are all likely to end up in the recycle box. See Appendix D for leads on how to find more scholarships and how to write a winning proposal.

SOME FOUNDATIONS MAKING GRANTS TO IT STUDENTS

What follows is just a sampling of some of the more generous grants specifically designed for IT or computer science students. Remember, many grants are merely for "educational pursuits," and can be applied to any field of study.

American Association of University Women

2201 N. Dodge Street

P.O. Box 4030

Iowa City, IA 52243-4030

(319) 337-1716

http://www.aauw.org/3000/fdnfelgra.html

Generous grants to women studying at the graduate level in computer and information sciences.

AT&T Labs Fellowship for Women and Minorities

180 Park Avenue, Room C103

P.O. Box 971

Florsham Park, NJ 07932-0971

(908) 949-2943

http://www.research.att.com/academic/

Generous grants to women and minorities studying computer science, computer engineering, and information science at the graduate level. Also offers interesting summer internship programs for undergraduates in these fields.

Council on Library and Information Resources

A.R. Zipf Fellowship in Information Management

1755 Massachusetts Avenue NW, #500

Washington, DC 20036

(202) 939-4750

http://www.clir.org/activities/zipf/zipf.html

Awarded to a graduate student who shows leadership potential in the field of information management.

Fannie and John Hertz Foundation

P.O. Box 5032

Livermore, CA 94551-5032

(510) 373-1642

http://www.hertzfndn.org/awards.html

Generous and competitive merit-based awards for students working toward a Ph.D. in applied computer science, among other fields.

Foundation for Science and Disability

West Virginia University

Morgantown, WV 26506-6057

http://www.as.wvu.edu/~scidis/organize/fsd.html

Grants to graduate students in computer science fields who have a disability of some kind.

Institute of Electrical and Electronic Engineers Computer Society

Richard Merwin Student Scholarship

1730 Massachusetts Avenue NW

Washington, DC 20036-1992

(202) 371-1013

http://computer.org/students/schlrshp.htm

Applicants need to be a member of the Computer Society and be studying in computer science or computer engineering fields. Scholarships available at the undergraduate and graduate levels.

Society of Women Engineers

120 Wall Street, 11th Floor

New York, NY 10005-3902

(212) 509-9577

http://www.swe.org/ SWE/StudentServices/Scholarship/brochure.htm

A number of scholarships at the undergraduate and graduate levels for women studying in computer science fields. A number of the scholarships are awarded in conjunction with major employers in the field, such as Microsoft and 3M.

Xerox Corporation

Technical Minority Scholarship Program

907 Culver Road

Rochester, NY 14609

http://www.xerox.com/go/xrx/about_xerox/employment.jsp (from there, click on "College Recruiting")

Scholarships for undergraduate and graduate students in the fields of computer and software engineering and information management. Applicants need to be an ethnic minority, defined by Xerox as African American, Asian, Pacific Islander, American Indian, Native Alaskan, or Hispanic.

EMPLOYEE ASSISTANCE PROGRAMS

As noted above, many employers will fully or partially fund an employee's education, provided it's in some way related to the job. If you're already working in the IT field, it is absolutely worth approaching your employer about this. For more information on how to do so, see Chapter 10.

Summary: Dos and Don'ts

Here's a quick refresher on things to do and mistakes to avoid. Finding funding for your education is a complicated and exacting process, but the rewards are so potentially enormous that it really makes sense to spend the extra time and do it right.

Do

▶ Start your research as early as possible.

▶ Make up a calendar and be sure to chart (and hit) every deadline.

▶ Fill out your FAFSA as early as possible.

▶ Get creative! There are state and private grants that many folks don't investigate.

▶ Check out whether your employer has programs to help you.

▶ Consider delaying enrollment until you've saved up some money. It can make a big difference.

Don't

▶ Miss any deadlines.

▶ Accept a loan you don't truly need.

▶ Use your credit cards unless it's an emergency.

▶ Forget that you need to reapply for financial aid every year.

▶ Neglect to repay your student loans.

▶ Give up! There is money out there for every student. Some may just need to work a little harder or look a little longer.

CHAPTER 7

Going Back to School As an Adult

It's a common scenario: you found yourself in an interesting IT job as soon as you got out of high school, or maybe after a few years at a community college. You worked your way up and did quite well for yourself. Now, however, you're hitting a wall—younger people are being promoted over you because they have college degrees and you don't. Maybe you got your bachelor's degree, but realize after a few years (or decades!) in the workforce that a master's degree would help catapult you to the higher-level management position you want and deserve. Or maybe you're in the middle of a non-IT-focused career and want to go back, get an IT degree, and start afresh in a new, better, more rewarding field. But you're nervous. You don't want to go to school with a bunch of kids, you don't want to quit your job just yet, and you're not even sure you remember how to take tests. You're worried that you'll stand out on campus or that you won't be able to find the resources you need.

You Are Not Alone

Don't worry! While all of the concerns outlined above are perfectly normal, they are also easily overcome. Perhaps the most important thing for a prospective student in this position to realize is that you are not alone. According to the U.S. Department of Education, nearly half of all college students enrolled right now in schools in the U.S. are over the age of 24, and over one-third are older than 35. In other words, of the 10 million people studying for a degree right now, some 4 million are older than traditional "college age." (Throughout this chapter, we'll use "adult" to mean a student who's over 24. This is not to imply that 18-to-23-year-olds aren't adults, but this is the standard usage in the education field. Just so you know.)

Remember, too, that the increased earnings and prestige that go along with a college degree kick in at any age. You don't need to list the year your degree was awarded on your résumé—after all, an M.B.A. in e-commerce, for instance, speaks for itself, and is a great entrée to the upper echelons of business. As long as your degree is from a recognized school, employers don't care whether you earned it online while taking care of your family, through night classes, or by taking a couple of years out of the workforce. What matters is the knowledge you've gained and the value you bring to their company. Indeed, you can use job-interview spin control to make a persuasive case that your more recent study makes you a stronger candidate in the fast-changing world of IT and related fields. After all, a 36-year-old with a brand-new master's degree in a tech field has far more up-to-date knowledge than a 26-year-old with a two-year-old degree. Of course, it's not only wrong but also illegal for employers to consider age in hiring, but (a) some do anyway, and (b) more subtly, they consider how fresh your training and outlook are. So while any degree is good and any qualified candidate should be considered, a brand-new degree in an area of technical specialty such as e-commerce or data warehousing is certainly a great plus to bring to the table.

So why does the prospect of going back to school cause so much consternation for so many? There are several factors at work here. One is the fear of being older than everyone else in the classroom. Below, we talk about how your age may actually be an advantage—you've been out in the world, you're not afraid of adults (because you are one!), you know how to work hard. Indeed, adult students are generally seen as being more serious, more dedicated, and more goal-focused than their younger counterparts. One recent study at Pennsylvania State University showed that older students tend to get better grades than their younger classmates—probably due to a more established work ethic.

Yes, sitting in a classroom full of kids may seem disconcerting at first, but once the real work begins, age is fairly irrelevant. Evening and weekend classes tailored to working professionals or "reentry students" will have a much higher percentage of older students, and age becomes totally irrelevant when studying via distance learning. Unless you choose to tell your online professor and student support group your age, they never need to know.

Many schools offer special admissions seminars or open houses for adult students. Ask whether your top-choice colleges have such events, and decide if it would be worth attending. Look into programs at local schools, whether you plan to apply to them or not. You may well make some good networking contacts, get useful information on special financial aid options, or otherwise find it to be a rewarding way to spend an evening.

A Special Note for the Older Adult Student

If you're older than the 30s or 40s generally assumed when talking about adult students, you may be worried that you're just "too old for computers." Don't be. While it's true that people who grew up playing Nintendo may initially be more at home with programming languages and the like, our files are full of tales about grandmothers who take to programming like a fish to water. Senior-citizen advocacy groups such as the AARP and SeniorNet tell us that there are millions of people over 55 on the Internet, with more logging on every day. As long as you have a genuine interest in learning and an aptitude for logic and systematic thinking, you are not too old for IT, and never will be.

Advantages of Returning to School As an Adult

Most of the steps you'll need to take when going back to school after a gap in your education are the same as those outlined in Chapters 3 through 6—you'll need to pick the right school, go through their admissions process, decide on a field of specialization, and line up funding. However, as an adult student, you have some interesting additional options, benefits, and intangible pluses.

Different Admissions Requirements

While you can't count on all schools having different requirements for older students, some certainly do. For instance, it's quite likely that you won't have to take undergraduate entrance exams if you've been out of high school for more than five years. Similarly, many schools have special exemptions for veterans of the U.S. military. If you don't see any information on this in your top schools' literature, ask! All too often, catalogs and Web sites are written for the typical student, and may not note or highlight services for nontraditional applicants.

If you choose to do your first year or two at a community college, whether for reasons of finances or convenience, you'll almost certainly be able to transfer over to a four-year college or university without any entrance exams. Given that most community colleges offer classes geared to the needs of working adults, have open admissions policies, and are extremely affordable, this may be an option worth investigating, whatever your situation. Remember, your diploma and résumé only list where you graduated from, not how long it took you or how many schools you attended on the way!

 NOTE *Students planning to transfer credits should be aware that some schools may have quite stringent transfer policies—a B or better average, for example. So even if you are able to take courses at a community college, a low average won't get you into a top university. That said, a surprising number of community college students do take their high grades and low-cost learning and transfer it to Ivy League and other prestigious programs.*

At the graduate level, requirements surrounding entrance exams may be less flexible, but it's still worth inquiring. For instance, if you've worked in management for a few years and are looking to go back and get a tech-focused M.B.A., your managerial experience may excuse you from taking business entrance exams such as the Graduate Management Aptitude Test (GMAT).

Special Financial Options

Adult students are eligible for almost every financial aid option discussed in Chapter 6. The only likely restriction is that many of these sources are only available to full-time students or students maintaining at least half-time status, and if you're working and/or have a family, this may be a challenge to maintain. However, there are some additional options available to adult students.

Employer Assistance and Tax Benefits

We'll talk about this more in Chapter 10, but in brief, it's likely that your employer may have some money set aside for employee education, especially if you work for a big company and/or if you're already working in the IT field. Normally, this sort of assistance would be considered income and be taxable, but Uncle Sam has a lovely little loophole for undergraduate students. Up to $5,250 of employer-provided funding for undergraduate courses can be excluded from your taxes. There's no similar relief for graduate students yet, unfortunately.

Union Benefits

If you or a family member belong to a union, there may be even more money available. See Chapter 10 for more details.

More Tax Benefits

In 1997, Congress established several new benefits for adult college students. The Lifetime Learning tax credit is designed for working adults who are going back to school, and allows you to get tax credits for tuition and fees at the undergraduate or graduate level. There are some limits and restrictions (mainly on the amount of money you earn), but they're reasonable—basically, if you make over a certain amount, the benefit is phased out. One of the other new programs is the Hope Scholarship, designed for students in their first two years of college.

Penalty-Free IRA Withdrawals

If you've been working for a while and have money in an individual retirement account (IRA), you can probably withdraw those funds without the usual crippling penalties, provided you use the funds for educational expenses. While many financial advisors would caution against this option, warning that especially for the older student, retirement funds should be held sacrosanct, the possibility does exist, for better or worse.

Veterans' Benefits

If you're a veteran of U.S. military service, there is almost certainly money available for your education. The U.S. Department of Veterans Affairs has a comprehensive and helpful Web site, http://www.va.gov/, that can answer most or all of your questions. Even if your service was quite some time ago, there may be funding you can draw on under the old GI Bill.

PRIVATE LOANS

Chapter 6 discusses loan companies that offer reasonable-rate loans to students. As an adult with an established credit history, you're an attractive candidate for this sort of funding. However, ending up with education loans may narrow your options if you have to settle for a higher paying job even if one at a lesser salary might be the better fit, just to get rid of a heavy financial burden. Look at saving up first, even if it means delaying going to school for a bit, rather than getting heavily into debt.

FOUNDATION GRANTS

Foundation grants are discussed in greater depth in Chapter 6, but one thing to keep in mind is that there are a number of foundations set up specifically to aid older adults returning to college. There may be even more money available if you are female or a member of an ethnic minority. Ask the financial aid office at your schools of choice where you can find these foundations, or look through the latest edition of *Foundation Grants to Individuals* an extremely useful resource available at most libraries. This book, published by the nonprofit Foundation Center, lists almost 4,000 grants that individuals can apply for. While some are extremely specific and not worth one's time ($25 to graduates of a particular high school for use in studying gemology, for instance), many are widely applicable to students in a number of different fields.

STATE PROGRAMS

Finally, some states offer special programs for adults returning to college. To see whether your state does, contact the appropriate office, listed in Chapter 6.

Additional Support

While not every college has a full array of support services for adult students, it's the rare school that doesn't offer something. Often, there is a special office called something along the lines of an Adult Reentry Center, offering counseling and guidance for older students. (Key words to look for in an office name are *adult reentry, lifelong learning, returning adult, nontraditional student,* or *continuing studies.*) Services may include help in finding childcare or elder care, advice on special financial aid options, and counseling and/or support groups that allow older students to connect with others in the same boat, do some networking, and just talk about what it's like going back to school after a few (or many) years away.

If you've just been out of school for a couple of years, you may not feel that such a center has a lot to offer you, but it can't hurt to drop by and see what services they provide. After all, there may be scholarships you were unaware of or job-hunting seminars that could be of use. Finally, don't be afraid to ask for help. If you're feeling lost and overwhelmed by going back to school, the adult student center (or whatever it's called at your school) can help. Let them do so.

The Importance of Maturity and Professionalism

One intangible factor that older students often forget about is the fact that they've been out in the world and have a wider range of experiences than those who go straight from high school to college to graduate school. Of course, this varies from person to person—we've all known incredibly mature 19-year-olds and 50-year-old party animals, but in general, age and maturity are great assets in the classroom, for a number of reasons:

Focus   As someone who's been out of high school for a number of years, you're much better suited than the average recent grad to the task of figuring out what you know, what you don't know, and what you need to learn. Many younger students change majors several times, drift between programs, or realize near graduation that they've chosen the wrong field. The skills you've used to date in your career will also help you focus on the program you want and stick with it.

Maturity   In addition to this sort of career-focused direction, you also bring that focus and discipline to everyday studies. While you may be distracted by work and family life, you'll probably not be out all night drinking at parties! You understand the importance of deadlines and of doing a good job—after all, you've been faced with these realities in exchange for a paycheck rather than the somewhat more nebulous reward of a good grade. Experienced workers are more patient, able to focus, not easily stressed or distracted by the need to socialize or date, more disciplined, and hopefully more emotionally stable. As an older student, you have developed over time—and from your jobs—a clearer idea of what area of study you want to specialize in and as a result are more able to keep that focus.

Professionalism   Many students are intimidated by their professors, and thus lose valuable networking opportunities. As someone who's spent some time in the work world, you have interacted with people of all ages, perhaps in both a supervisory and supervised position. You know that just because someone is your supervisor (whether a boss or a professor) doesn't mean you can't be friends and exchange information to mutual benefit. Professors tell us that older students are much more comfortable asking questions, coming to office hours to check in, and following up potential job leads.

Some Important Questions Adult Students Are Asking

Okay, you've made the commitment. You've decided to go back to school and to get your IT degree, whether it's after taking a couple of years off between high school and college or returning after 20 years in the workforce to get the graduate degree that will help you advance to a higher level of management. You've read up on financial aid options, how to get academic support, and all the advantages adult students face, and you're ready to take the plunge. Still, a few questions remain. Below, we address a few of the most common concerns.

What About Work?

In an ideal world, you'll be able to choose whether to work while you go to school or to take the necessary two to four years off to concentrate on your degree full-time. There are advantages to both approaches. If you keep working, you may be able to get your employer to help pay for your degree, you'll avoid gaps on your résumé, and you'll end up owing less if you do need to borrow. However, you may also feel that the discipline of dedicating yourself 100 percent to study is the way for you. In this case, you'll finish school more quickly and have more time to devote to your studies. If you do have the opportunity to choose, put some real thought into which avenue will be best for you. Look at your finances, weigh where you are in your career, and make the choice that best suits your individual needs. If you choose the work route, it may be the toughest yet. You will need to juggle priorities—work, family, studying, and social life—all at once. So you really are taking on more of a load than if you studied full time.

Many people won't have the luxury of getting to choose. If you can't leave your job due to financial considerations, or simply because you don't want to give up a good position with room for growth once you've finished that degree, remember that it is possible to work and go to school. It may not be easy or relaxing, but it is rewarding, and millions of people do it. According to the U.S. Department of Education some 90 million adults participate in some sort of continuing education every year. The following sections describe some things to consider.

EMPLOYER ASSISTANCE

In Chapter 10, we talk about working with your employer to get the funding and the time you need to pursue your degree. Not every workplace offers money or other forms of support, but it can't hurt to ask. If you're a valued employee, your employer may allow you to work a flextime week or make other accommodations even if he or she can't provide you with any educational funding. Do be aware that many employer assistance programs are results-based—you only get your tuition (and sometimes compensation for books and fees) refunded after you've achieved a goal, such as a B in the coursework. There may be other restrictions, such as number of courses and credits taken per term.

NONTRADITIONAL CLASSES

As more and more adults return to school, colleges and universities are increasingly tailoring their programs to suit the needs of those adults. Typical options include night or weekend classes, extended programs wherein you take one or two classes a semester over a longer period of time, online or televised courses, and accelerated programs that jam more learning into a shorter period of time, a period which could perhaps be taken as leave from work. In Chapter 12, we list schools that offer distance learning, and also break out which other programs are best for working adults for other reasons (most weekend classes, best support for working professionals, and so on). For some, distance learning is a perfect solution. For others, the lack of flesh-and-blood interaction with a mentor and instructor and the face-to-face dynamics of group and class work make study at a distance unsatisfying.

MAKING A TIME AND A PLACE TO STUDY

It's easy to get overwhelmed by work and coursework, and you'll need to be firm with yourself. At the beginning of each course, ask each professor (whether it's in person or online) how many hours per week they expect you to spend on home-work, reading, computer labs, and so forth. Get a personal planner (use your PDA or a plain old-fashioned calendar) and schedule in your study time. Then stick to it! You may find that it's easiest for you to do your homework in your workplace after hours or on weekends—if your employer agrees to this and if you have a more powerful workstation at work than at home. If you do your coursework at home, set up a "homework station" and keep it dedicated to your studies.

Time-challenged professionals may benefit from these insider hints:

▶ Study in short, intense periods without taking frequent breaks (you can learn more when you're concentrating and focusing).

▶ Study in small chunks and at every opportunity—waiting in line, riding the bus or train, driving (by listening to tapes).

▶ Make studying part of your daily routine. It will soon become a habit.

▶ Look for projects and case studies you can do in class to help yourself see how the principles and theories you're learning can be made more relevant to your job or to other real-world scenarios.

▶ Explain things out loud to yourself in your own words. Yes, it sounds goofy, but this is a time-honored method of making sure you thoroughly understand the concepts. Otherwise, it's easy to read over something without truly com-prehending it.

What About My Family?

Just like the challenge of juggling work and school, juggling school and a family (and possibly work as well) is never going to be easy. However, it *is* possible, and the rewards far outweigh the challenges. The following sections describe some things to keep in mind.

GET YOUR FAMILY INVOLVED

Naturally, your strategies will be different depending on your situation—it's eas-ier to be sure your spouse understands the importance of your studies than to explain it to a four-year-old who wants a bedtime story when you have to review the Microsoft case one more time before the quiz. However, it's important that you do make your educational goals and ambitions clear to your family.

One single mother tells us that she has explained to her grammar-school-aged kids that mommy's going to school, too, and needs to do her homework. She helps her kids with their homework each night, and then they help her by playing quietly while she does her coursework. She tells them when she does well on tests, and their pride in her accomplishment helps them not feel abandoned when she needs to leave them with a sitter so she can go to computer lab.

With older children, or with a spouse who's feeling neglected, just be sure to make it very clear what your educational and career goals are, and how greatly this will benefit the family. Be sure to make time (schedule it in your planner if you have to!) for the occasional night out or family celebration, so you don't lose track of why you're doing this. You'll be surprised at the support you get.

CHILDCARE OPTIONS

With millions of adults returning to school each year, low-cost daycare is more common on campus. Ask admissions counselors about daycare options and/or visit the adult student services office. They may have information on informal non-school-sponsored daycare options, or let you post a notice on a real or electronic bulletin board looking for other parents with whom you can share the cost of a sitter.

NONTRADITIONAL CLASSES

More and more schools are offering alternatives to the traditional "sit in a classroom all day for four years" method of earning a degree. Many of these options work well for parents, including online or televised courses and accelerated programs that compress more learning into a shorter period of time. For instance, a class might meet all day Saturday for four Saturdays, and then switch to another class on the same schedule, allowing you to complete four classes in a four-month semester, but only go to campus once a week. See Chapter 12 for choices of nontraditional programs.

MAKING A TIME AND A PLACE TO STUDY

The demands of school and family can be overwhelming, and you need to set yourself up to succeed. Get a personal planner or calendar and schedule in your study time. If home is just too distracting due to active kids or the lure of the TV and the refrigerator, schedule your study time on campus or, if you're working and your employer agrees, at your office.

The following are some insider study hints:

▶ Figure out when your brain is at its sharpest and try to schedule your regular study period for that time. For some folks, that's first thing in the morning after exercise and coffee, for others it's in the early evening when the day's other work is done. Figure this out for yourself and take advantage of your circadian rhythms.

▶ Take good notes and then organize them later, creating a sort of personalized textbook or study plan. Order them from the more basic concepts to the most complex, and highlight the main concept.

▶ Rewrite key concepts in your own words to be sure you understand them. Rewriting things also helps get them into your brain much more firmly than simply reading them on paper or screen.

▶ Quiz yourself. Many students find that making up flashcards helps, and can be a good way to schedule in little study breaks when there's not much time for heavier work.

▶ Keep all your study materials in one place, but carry an emergency supply with you, whether that's a notebook, a special briefcase, or a set of flashcards. When the train breaks down and you're stuck in a tunnel for two hours, you'll be able to study rather than longing for those books back in your study nook at home.

▶ Review frequently to keep material fresh in your mind.

If you need to study at home, you can set yourself up for success here as well. Make yourself a study area in your computer room or den, and place yourself off limits to the world (including your family, the phone, and visitors) for a set period. It will seem hard at first, but if you stick to it, you'll soon develop a rhythm. If you find yourself wandering out to get coffee or snacks, start bringing them in to your work area when you start to work, so you'll have no excuse for breaking your concentration.

What If I Don't Remember How to Study?

This is a very common fear. Adult students often worry that they've forgotten how to study, or that younger students have mental skills and habits they can't possibly equal. Nothing could be further from the truth. While it is true that you may need to relearn some basics (whether or not cramming works for you, how to write a basic essay, and so forth), in fact the skills you've developed in the workplace more than transfer over into the academic environment. You'll need to process large amounts of incoming information, review it, and remember it under pressure. Sound like a day at work? The only real difference is that the information you need to absorb is more structured in school, and the tests are scheduled—unlike those awful moments when your boss calls on you at a meeting and you can't remember the figures you were supposed to have memorized.

There are a lot of great resources out there for adults who need to remember basic study skills, and we list them in Appendix D. Here's a lightning-quick summary of winning techniques, though, just to get you started.

Go to Class

Sounds obvious doesn't it? But when you're stressed by work and/or family requirements, it's easy to miss "just one class." Don't do it. Especially in an accelerated program, one class may contain truly vast amounts of useful information and, while you *can* make it up, it won't be easy. And don't just go—be fully engaged. Get there early, ask questions, make friends. You'll get more out of the material, and possibly make valuable networking contacts who may help you further your career (or share notes if you do miss a class, trade childcare, or other resources).

Take Notes

Studies show that students who take notes retain more knowledge than those who don't, even if they never look at those notes again. Something about the physical act of writing down material helps get it into your head. Taking *good* notes is even better, as they'll stand you in good stead when preparing for exams.

Be an Active Reader

When reading your textbook, don't just read the words. Highlight key concepts, take notes, and even consider making up flashcards and quizzing yourself. This may feel a little childish at first, but you're cramming a lot of technical information into your brain, and the more engaged you can be with the material, the more likely it is to stick.

ASK QUESTIONS

If something isn't clear in class, speak up. If you're still not getting it, and you don't want to take up more class time, see the professor in his or her office hours, or visit your on-campus learning center. If, for instance, you're having trouble mastering advanced calculus, working through some additional problems with a learning center tutor can be just the ticket. There's no shame in asking for help—remember, you're paying the school to deliver you an education, and to some degree, they owe you the support you need to make sure you get that education. Even if you aren't having trouble, keep asking questions! Ask your teacher to clarify the day's lessons, test content, or what he or she feels is truly important for you to take away from this course. Ask how he or she got started in IT.

MAKE TIME FOR REVIEW

Just attending class and labs and doing the homework probably isn't enough. You need to go back over key concepts to make sure they stick, and to develop a good base from which to learn more. Schedule a few hours a week for coursework review. This is a good time to give yourself flashcard quizzes, do additional review problems, or just read back over your notes and summarize important pieces of data.

JOIN A STUDY GROUP

A great way of reviewing is to get together with fellow students and go over materials once a week or so. This can be done in person or online. Many Internet-based programs offer a chat group as an automatic part of each class. If you're lucky, the professor will join the discussion group and offer additional support. Note that this is the case only with distance learning—in a face-to-face environment, it's unheard of for a professor to get involved in this sort of student chat. Sometimes concepts that are eluding you will become clear when discussed in a group, and if nothing else, the need to be prepared for your weekly sessions will force you to stay up on homework. If there's not already a study group for a given class, organize one yourself. This can also be a good résumé item if you need to demonstrate leadership skills later on. One caveat is that some students have found that their particular study group actually wastes time chatting away, arguing, gossiping about IT companies, latest and greatest products, and so forth. Watch out for this!

These are just a few of the many helpful suggestions available to adult learners. See Appendix D for books and Web sites that offer more advice.

CHAPTER 8

Using the Internet to Your Advantage

Five years ago, this would have been a very different chapter, and five years from now, it will no doubt be very different again. Even a few years ago, the data available on the Net was less than comprehensive. While there was a lot of information, it was not necessarily all that helpful, and a lot of the older, stodgier (but also more respected) schools were slow in getting useful material online. By contrast, five years from now, a chapter like this may be a very different animal as more and more information goes up on the Web. Already, studies tell us that more college research takes place on the Net than on paper, and this will only keep increasing. In a truly utopian future, information on the Web will one day be easy to find and to decipher. In a slightly more realistic scenario, books like this will still be a great help in sorting through the masses of information and using it more efficiently.

Things are already moving in that direction—most people start their college search on the Net and do research there. However, there is still a lot of bad information to be had and some downright sleazy operators looking to separate you from your money. This chapter will help you learn how to tell the good from the bad and the ugly, and find the right directions in which to look for more information.

This chapter is divided into two basic sections. The first tells how to do your pre-research on the Net—finding out about schools, getting insider information, and even applying to institutions online. The second section looks at the possibility of doing your entire degree online, and offers some basic guidelines for determining whether this is the right option for you.

Using the Internet for Research

As you no doubt know all too well, the Internet is both a fabulous tool for research and an incredible time-waster. Even when you're not sidetracked by other sites ("I'll research colleges in a minute, but first let's see if there's anything fun on eBay…"), getting quality information can be difficult. Sometimes you need to do several key-word searches before you hit on exactly what you want, which can be annoying. In this chapter and in Appendix D, "Resources," you'll find guidance to some good places to look first. Here's a bit of inspiration on the kinds of things you can do with some online research:

► Seek out and apply for scholarships, loans, and grants.

► Ask undergraduates in your field whether they're happy with the program, lab facilities, and so on. (How do you find them? It's entirely possible that there's a computer science association at the school, with membership posted online. If not, e-mail the department secretary and ask whether such a thing exists. Once you've got the contact info, you can fire away with questions.)

► Read back issues of the campus newspaper to get a sense of the social milieu, political climate, and research and job opportunities.

► Check out the syllabi for similar courses at different schools, to see which are best suited to your needs or interests.

► Find student teachers who can give you the lowdown on which professors have the best reputations and which ones you should avoid.

► Check out unofficial school sites and chat groups to see what the big gripes are—maybe you won't agree with them, but they can be illuminating.

Researching School-Specific Information

This book is a good starting place for finding out about IT programs online. If you want to check out other schools, or even get different evaluation criteria for these institutions, there are a number of Web sites that list schools and give various search criteria—cost, location, majors, and so on. Appendix D lists the most useful of these sites. Many of these sites have official relationships with colleges, allowing you to ask for more information, be added to mailing lists, or even complete your applications online.

Generally, these catchall sites are handy jumping-off places, but you'll want to go to individual school sites as well. Each listing in this book gives Web addresses, and the sites are rated as to usefulness, from one to four stars.

THINGS YOU'RE LIKELY TO FIND ON A SCHOOL'S WEB SITE

Just about every reputable college or university's Web site should give you at least these basics:

▶ Information about the college as a whole, and about the computer science (or other relevant) department in particular.

▶ Admission requirements.

▶ Exact degrees offered, and requirements, including course descriptions, for those degrees. This book lists such information, too, but it does change, and the school's Web site will detail any new requirements or programs.

▶ Application deadlines for admissions and financial aid.

▶ Tuition and fees.

SPECIAL FEATURES YOU MAY FIND ON SOME SITES

Here are some things that may or may not be available online at any given college or university. If you don't see them on a school's site, e-mail to ask. Maybe the links are non-intuitive or hard to find. If the information is not online, the admissions person or other official who reads your e-mail may be able to get it for you or direct you to a place where you can find it. If they get enough of this sort of e-mail, the school may consider improving its site!

Faculty and Staff Information

You're going to be spending months if not years of your life with these people, it makes sense to learn a little bit about them. While not every school site has faculty information, those institutions that are most proud of star performers often do. Sometimes you'll even get the e-mail addresses of key people whom you can query personally with further questions.

- ▶ Faculty biographies and research publications (great for finding out if the people in your possible future department are specialists in the areas that most interest you).

- ▶ Who's teaching the intro classes? You'll almost certainly be happier at a school where it's tenured faculty rather than grad students or adjunct professors.

- ▶ Chance to sign up for specialized information via an e-mail newsletter ("For more information on our developing IT programs...")

- ▶ Names of student teachers and graduate students who can provide insider information.

Useful Facts and Figures

Every semester, school Web sites are getting better, and as institutions compete for top students, admissions people are realizing that the Web site is often the first point of entry for serious candidates. Thus, they're putting more and better information online to help sell students on why this particular school is such a great choice.

- ▶ Student-to-teacher ratio. Will you get lost in the crowd, or is there a chance to really get to know your professors?

- ▶ Estimates of non-tuition and fees-related expenses you can expect, including books, software, housing, and food.

- ▶ Policies on transfer credits, life-experience learning, and credit by exams.

Information on Financial Aid and Job Placement

Career-minded students can often discover how much support they'll receive, and students interested in targeted scholarships and grants may also find useful information. If you don't see what you're looking for, send an e-mail! Maybe the "merit-based grants for minority students" page is about to go up.

▶ Non-school grants and fellowships of interest to IT students.

▶ Information on job-placement statistics. What percentage of graduates find jobs in IT right out of school? Does the school have an IT-savvy job-placement office? Does the computer science department have a special job-placement service, or are all students served by a one-size-fits-all office? If the latter, what's the success rate in IT?

▶ Does the department have programs to offer internships with top IT companies? What percentage of students participates in such programs?

Other Useful Links

Some school Web sites are really nothing more than "brochure-ware," but many can give you a really solid sense of the institution and its offerings. Poke around as much as possible, check out student pages, read the school newspaper, and otherwise get what you can out of every site.

▶ Links to the school library and research facilities.

▶ Links to unofficial student home pages.

▶ Links to the campus newspaper.

▶ Links to a CS or IT club or networking group for students.

▶ Information on student life. What resources are available? What's the male/female ratio? What's life like for minorities, gay and lesbian students, and others?

Networking Online

Many Web sites provide links to faculty members' Web pages, and these pages often list research assistants. These folks are a great and usually untapped resource for inside information. Write a brief, polite e-mail asking whether they'd be willing to answer some questions about the program. Most will be happy to once they realize you're not asking for a lot of their time. Ideally, it would be great to meet for a cup of coffee, but realistically, you'll probably communicate by phone or e-mail. Ask a few well-chosen questions: What do they like best about the program? What do they like least? If they had it to do over, would they choose this school? Are faculty as hot in the classroom as in the lab, or is the school a research mill? What advice would they have for someone planning to apply? Find out about program culture as well—if it's intense and research-focused, and you do better in a collaborative, team-based environment, this is important to know.

You can also network like this with faculty members. Find out who's likely to be teaching the classes you're interested in, and drop those professors an e-mail explaining that you're considering attending their institution, and asking similar questions to those delineated above. Many professors are pressed enough for time that they may not be able to get back to you, but many are very interested in student recruitment and outreach, so you might be surprised. Also, these professors might be too busy to write to you, but could forward your e-mail to a student assistant, which gives you another interesting networking contact. (Looking at faculty home pages is a great way to get a feel for whether they seem to be friendly, helpful, and engaged with students, as well as interested in your field. If you're a Java junkie and the faculty member's site looks like your grandma designed it, this may not be the institution for you.)

Finally, a school's site may give you information on networking connections if you have special considerations—if, for instance, you're a gay or minority student wondering whether you'll be happy in the town surrounding the campus, if you're female and wondering how well women are represented in the computer science department, or if you're an older student returning to college and wondering if there are resources for people like you. Look for club listings and links—Gay and Lesbian Student Council, African-American Student Office, Women in Science Club, Adult Reentry Office, and so on. Drop the club chairperson an e-mail detailing your concerns ("As an African-American student, I have some questions about attending college in small-town Mississippi, although I am quite attracted to your school's computer science program. Would anyone there have the time to answer some e-mail questions about life and culture in the region?"). The club chair, or whomever they refer you to, may end up being a wonderful source of information on all sorts of things, whether or not they're studying in the IT field.

Researching Financial Aid

Financial aid resources have been discussed in depth in Chapter 6, and a number of great Internet resources are listed in Appendix D under "Chapter 6." Here, then, let us just note that there is a lot of very helpful financial aid information on the Internet, and it's surprisingly accessible and well organized.

A number of sites allow you to search grant and loan options, customize to your personal needs, and apply online (see Appendix D for details). As these sites are easy to navigate, there's every reason to see what they have to offer. Many also give useful financial tools, such as college cost estimators, forms for determining your real financial needs, schedules showing how much student loans will cost you over the years at various rates of repayment, and even links to services that help with financial planning. If anyone asks for money for this information, be very suspicious. There's so much good stuff available for free that you should be sure of getting a very personalized and high-level service before you shell over any money.

Help with Exams

There's a great deal of helpful information on the Net about exams, both from the organizations that administer those exams (the College Board and the GRE) and from student assistance sites. One starting place is Scholar Stuff (http://www .scholarstuff.com/), an omnibus site that offers chat, financial aid information, and more. Their test preparation links take you to official sites that answer FAQs and give sample tests, as well as to mainstream test-prep companies that provide guidance, free test practice sites, and so forth.

This is definitely a case where what you get may not be what you pay for. Some great sites give away test-prep information for free, while others sell similar information for quite a lot of money. Do your research, check out the resources provided in this book, and shop sensibly. While you may decide that paying several hundred dollars for a test-prep course is the right move for you, you may also find that working through a few free online sample tests gives you the confidence you need to succeed.

Applying to Schools on the Internet

Hundreds and hundreds of schools accept online applications, whether through their own Web site or through a third-party site, such as the College Board (http://www.collegeboard.org/). Sometimes there is only an intermediary online step—you can, for instance, download application forms as PDFs, but need to fill them in by hand (or typewriter, if you can find one!) and snail-mail them in.

Unless you're nervous about privacy, there's really no reason not to apply online if your school of choice offers this option. While it probably won't get you to the top of the stack, there are some advantages—you can copy-and-paste similar information into several applications, and often you can apply for financial aid electronically at the same time. If you do worry about giving your credit card number over the Net, or if you have a slow or cranky connection, there's certainly no reason you can't apply the old-fashioned way.

 NOTE *Even if you do apply online, some schools may also require a paper printout of your electronic application. Don't forget this step, as it could delay or compromise your acceptance.*

Studying Online

Distance learning is nothing new, though you wouldn't know it by the fuss being made in some quarters. Back in the 1800s, a number of schools began providing coursework by post to people in various rural areas or outposts of empire (this latter being why the University of London had one of the first, and still one of the most comprehensive, distance programs). The Internet has made distance learning much, much simpler, with classes held in online forums, e-mail discussion groups, professors holding virtual "office hours," and access to libraries offered electronically.

A nice ancillary benefit of this Internet explosion is that employers and graduate schools are much more accepting of distance degrees than some might once have been. Twenty years ago, to say "I got my degree through correspondence" had the air of something vaguely downmarket or quaint, even though many respectable schools did (and do), in fact, offer correspondence degrees. Today, to say "I got my degree online" makes you sound like a hip, plugged-in techie. What a difference a delivery system makes!

Most distance-learning programs are specially targeted to working professionals. The average distance-learning student is over 25 years of age, employed, and with some existing college experience. More than half are female. Distance students have the reputation for being highly motivated—their rate of course completion is significantly higher than that of traditional on-campus students. Essentially, distance-learning students are adult, committed, and career-focused, and schools know it.

Beware of Slick Phonies

Just as distance learning has been around for almost 200 years, so have diploma mills. These phonies who sell you a worthless degree for anywhere from $100 to $20,000 are getting more clever and hard to tell from the real thing. A random Internet search for "distance learning" turns up a wealth of useful resources, and some truly dreadful fakes. You might wonder how a sensible person could be fooled by a fake school. Well, some of these fakes are remarkably clever—they require you to do coursework, they have official-sounding credentials, and some even ask you to fly to the "campus" (usually a rented facility) for graduation ceremonies.

The simplest way to determine whether a school is legitimate is to check out its accreditation. Chapter 9 tells you how to do this—and it's important to do so, as many phonies lie about accreditation or create false accrediting bodies to sign off on their programs. If you only deal with the schools listed in this book, you won't go wrong.

Components of an Online Program

To find out whether a school you're interested in offers what you want, first go to Appendix C and see whether it's listed as one that offers distance-learning programs. Then read the listing in Chapter 12. If you're still not sure (say, for instance, that you're interested in compressed video courses sent to your work-place, and the listing doesn't make it clear whether this is an option), e-mail the school and ask. Of the hundreds and hundreds of schools that offer online programs, each probably has a slightly different methodology. Here are some terms you may hear and some things to consider in deciding between programs:

Delivery methods   By definition, an online program is delivered over your computer. However, some programs also offer the option of getting videotaped lectures by mail, of watching courses broadcast on cable TV, and/or of receiving video feeds. In some cases, paper homework is also mailed to students; in others, all work is done electronically.

Synchronous versus asynchronous conferencing   Most online programs use asynchronous conferencing. As in any discussion group, you log on and read the latest posts, add your own, download any attachment that interests you, and so forth. In structured, for-credit forums, instructors generally give a date and time by which all posts must be received. Some programs also use synchronous conferences, more commonly known as live chat. Under this model, everyone must log on at a set time to participate. This is obviously difficult when students span time zones, and for that reason it isn't frequently utilized.

Structured versus unstructured learning   The majority of programs in this book expect students to progress through classes more or less on a normal semester (or quarter) plan. Some, however, are totally self-paced, allowing you to register whenever you want and progress through courses as you see fit (within some broad guidelines, but with great flexibility). While the latter may sound appealing in its freedom, many students find the lack of structure is isolating and hard to handle.

Level of support   Most online programs offer some official support in the form of chat or newsgroups. Many also have unofficial support, such as student forums and electronic study groups. If networking and support are important to you, be sure to ask what's available. As noted elsewhere in this book, it is important to keep up networking connections, and if you're not meeting those all-important connections face to face, you should be sure you can develop e-mail friendships with them. Present and former classmates and professors are great sources of job leads and other useful information, and you should cultivate these contacts.

Nontraditional credits   Chapter 11 details nontraditional credits in greater detail, but if you've been working in an IT field for some time, you very likely have some credit-worthy experience. Some schools are much more flexible than others in accepting credit from exams, prior schools, work-based training, and other life-experience learning. If it's not clear from the school's listing in Chapter 12 how much of this sort of credit will apply to the degree you're interested in, ask! You may be pleasantly surprised to discover that you've completed more of your degree than you ever expected.

Campus visits   These days, most distance programs can be done without ever visiting the school's campus. However, some programs do require a visit, either at the beginning of the degree for an orientation or at the end for final seminars and/or exams. The listings in Chapter 12 will make this clear.

Is Online Learning for You?

Only you can answer this question, but the odds are that it might be. If you're of traditional college age and looking forward to the complete campus experience, or if there's a great school near where you work and your employer can be flexible about your hours, perhaps there's no need to think about distance options. Similarly, if you know yourself and know that you simply can't learn unless you're in a structured classroom environment, you shouldn't disregard that knowledge. If you're a working professional, have a family, or don't want to relocate to go to school for some other reason, it's worth looking into online learning.

To determine if online learning is right for you, consider the following:

▶ If you're not a self-starter, you may not do well without the discipline of daily or weekly classes.

▶ In some online programs, you're pretty much working on your own, without a lot of direct feedback. As this form of learning becomes more popular, however, schools are working on ways to help students build a virtual community.

▶ If you're not sure whether you'll do well in this sort of environment, try it out first by taking one class online. See how it feels. Do you meet your deadlines? Do you feel supported? Do you feel isolated and alone? These are important markers.

▶ One of the most important factors to consider is whether the learning will be applicable in your current or chosen field. A degree is all very nice, but you need the learning that goes with it. Talk to your colleagues. These days, many IT professionals have taken online courses, and you can almost certainly find a colleague who can share his or her experiences and whether they have proved valuable. If you aren't in the IT fields, or don't have a colleague you can ask, contact the admissions officers at schools you're interested in. They may be able to hook you up with students who have completed or are working on online degrees, and you can ask questions at the source.

The opportunities for online research, application, and study are great now, and they'll only get better as more schools tailor their programs to the needs of working adults and to the strengths of the Internet as a delivery method. For more information on distance learning, see Appendix D for books and Web sites that can help you gain greater knowledge of this exciting and growing field.

CHAPTER 9

The Importance of Accreditation

When you start researching schools, you'll run into the truism that it's important to be sure a school is accredited before you do business with it. This is a useful piece of advice, as far as it goes, but few sources go on to note that there are many different types of accreditation, at least one of which is even worse than no accreditation at all. As noted elsewhere in this book, a random Internet search for any sort of degree program will turn up lots of good schools, and a few totally fake degree mills. It's important to know how to assess and evaluate a school, especially in these days of increased distance-learning options. After all, when totally legitimate and respected universities offer degree programs wholly online, it's easy for scam operators to disguise the fact that their "schools" have no campus, no faculty, and no legitimacy. As professional-looking color brochures, toll-free numbers, and snazzy Web sites have gotten easier and cheaper to maintain, phony schools are on the rise.

Why Are Fake Schools Allowed to Operate?

While various state agencies (as well as the FBI) have an interest in closing down fraudulent schools, the laws are not always clearly written or enforceable. Surely any school that will send you a Ph.D. in computer science by return mail for $100 is a fraud. But what if they require you to have two certifications and write a 10-page thesis for a bachelor's degree? Five certifications and a 100-page thesis for a master's? One man's degree mill is another's alternative university, and the ground rules keep changing.

That said, there are some fairly simple ways to tell whether a school is legitimate:

Physical location   It must have a physical location. Sorry, no physical location, no school as far as we're concerned. Virtual or no, in this day of virtual fakes, visiting the campus personally is a must. But recognize that many excellent schools operate from suites of offices in office buildings—no spacious lawns, football stadiums, and babbling brooks.

Resources   Libraries, campuses, buildings, cafeterias, and such—great universities have well-maintained physical plants. But an online program needs none of these things. Of course, it will have an excellent library service, but usually a library you can access, including full text of books and journals, from your home or office.

Faculty   The staff must be qualified with credentials. There is no substitute for a qualified faculty, but "qualified" often means demonstrated skills in the field and not necessarily letters after the name. Arguably, the three most successful computer entrepreneurs of the last decade—Gates, Dell, and Ellison— have no degrees whatsoever, but many students would feel it a privilege to study with them.

Established reputation   Traditions, alumni associations, professional ratings— the first two are nice to have, and even the online programs can have them. Ratings have become such a political thing, more than a few excellent schools opt out of cooperating with the raters. No one will deny that CalTech is a fine school, for example, but there are many people who feel the distance computer degrees of the never-rated New Jersey Tech are of comparable caliber.

Verifiable record of success and operation   Any legitimate school will be glad to give you the names and contact numbers of alumni who have agreed to be called or e-mailed by prospective students. This can be a valuable source of information.

The simplest thing is, of course, to limit your selection to the schools listed in this book; all of them have regional accreditation and many of them hold additional professional accreditation (the difference between and significance of these two types is defined below). If you are even tempted to look into buying a fake degree or certification, or to lie on your résumé, here is one word of warning: don't. As a result of increased publicity about fake Internet schools, credentials are being checked out today like never before. And anyway, you want all of the advantages that go with the piece of paper—the networking, the professional associations, the knowledge, the ability to go on and get further education in your field. None of these is available to holders of phony credentials.

What Is Accreditation?

Simply put, accreditation is a statement that a group of impartial experts have evaluated a school and found it to be beyond reproach. This situation is peculiar to the U.S., in that accreditation in this country is not an official government seal of approval. Most international schools are either operated directly by their nation's governments or given their degree-granting authority by those governments. In the U.S., accreditation is a purely voluntary, non-governmental process done by private organizations. Those organizations are, in turn, recognized and given authority by the U.S. Department of Education, but its authority is a bit confusing and less than absolute, as it's not the most powerful of bureaus (a number of presidents have talked about shutting it down, although this has, thankfully, not come to pass).

A number of unrecognized accrediting agencies exist, often established by bad schools for the purpose of accrediting themselves. Sometimes, in fact, the "agency" is just another line on the school's phone, answered by the same secretarial service. It's not enough to ask, "Is this school accredited?" You must then also ask, "By whom?" Almost every school has a page on its Web site discussing accreditation, but if you're suspicious at all, it's better to work backwards—go to the relevant accrediting agency's Web site and see whether they list the school in question. Few bad or phony schools go so far as to lie outright and claim to be accredited by one of the recognized agencies. Usually, they just list their unauthorized accreditation and assume that most students won't know the difference. Unfortunately, they're usually right.

How Does a School Become Accredited?

Every U.S. school was unaccredited at some time in its existence, even the most staid and respectable of institutions, although for most of them it was hundreds of years ago. These days, the way it works is that a new school upon opening its doors applies for accreditation to the appropriate regional agency. After a substantial preliminary investigation to determine that the school is operating legally and run legitimately, the agency will likely grant it provisional status. Typically, this step takes anywhere from several months to a number of years and, when completed, does not imply any kind of endorsement or recommendation. Rather, it's an indication that the school has taken the first step on the long path to full accreditation. Note that anyone can apply, and in fact, bad schools often put a line in their catalogs to the effect that, "We are planning to apply for accreditation," or "We expect to be accredited by such-and-such a date." This is a major warning sign. After all, someone may tell you that she expects to win the Nobel Prize for Literature or to be asked out on a date by George Clooney. Not necessarily a lie—maybe she does expect it, but that doesn't make it a credible remark.

Next, teams from the accrediting agency, generally composed of faculty members from already accredited institutions, will visit the school to watch it in operation and audit its procedures and policies. The visitations are conducted at regular points throughout the year, and allow the school to demonstrate its operations "on the hoof," and also to present copious amounts of required documentation detailing its legal status, academics, educational philosophy, curriculum, financial status, planning for the future, and so forth.

After these investigations and usually following at least two years of successful operation (sometimes a great deal longer), the school may advance to the status of "candidate for accreditation." This means, in essence, that the agency feels the school is probably worthy of accreditation, but needs a bit longer to prove itself. Some agencies skip this step and simply wait until they feel a school is worthy of accreditation rather than having a candidate step. The candidate status usually endures for two to six years, sometimes longer, until the agency feels the school is definitely worthy of its stamp of approval. Very few schools get to candidate status without going on to become accredited, but it has happened.

Once accreditation is awarded, the agency's evaluation team visits the school every five to ten years to ensure that it is still worthy of its approval. The status is always subject to review at any time should the school develop new programs or take any dramatic new turns.

Regional Accreditation

Generally, when people talk about accreditation, this is what they mean: accreditation granted by one of the U.S. regional agencies recognized by the government. Every school in this book has regional accreditation. If you're drawn to a school that is not listed in this book, do make sure you check what sort of accreditation it has; check with the school or with the relevant agency. As noted above, there's one sort of accreditation that's worse than none, and that's accreditation from a bad or fraudulent agency. You really can't go wrong with a school that holds accreditation from any of the agencies listed below.

Middle States Association of Colleges and Schools

Commission on Higher Education
3624 Market Street
Philadelphia, PA 19104
Phone: (215) 662-5606
Fax: (215) 662-5950
E-mail: info@msache.org
Web site: http://www.msache.org/

Responsible for schools located in Delaware, the District of Columbia, Maryland, New Jersey, Pennsylvania, Puerto Rico, and the Virgin Islands.

New England Association of Schools and Colleges

209 Burlington Road
Bedford, MA 01730-1433
Phone: (617) 271-0022
Fax: (617) 271-9050
E-mail: info@neasc.org
Web site: http://www.neasc.org/

Responsible for schools located in Connecticut, Maine, Massachusetts, New Hampshire, Rhode Island, and Vermont.

North Central Association of Colleges and Schools

30 North La Salle Street, Suite 2400
Chicago, IL 60602
Phone: (800) 621-8440
Fax: (312) 263-7462
E-mail: info@ncacihe.org
Web site: http://www.ncacihe.org/

Responsible for schools located in Arizona, Arkansas, Colorado, Illinois, Indiana, Iowa, Kansas, Michigan, Minnesota, Missouri, Nebraska, New Mexico, North Dakota, Ohio, Oklahoma, South Dakota, West Virginia, Wisconsin, and Wyoming.

Northwest Association of Schools and Colleges

11300 NE 33rd Place, Suite 120
Bellevue, WA 98004
Phone: (206) 827-2005
Fax: (206) 827-3395
E-mail: info@cocnasc.org
Web site: http://www.cocnasc.org/

Responsible for schools located in Alaska, Idaho, Montana, Nevada, Oregon, Utah, and Washington.

Southern Association of Colleges and Schools

1866 Southern Lane
Decatur, GA 30033
Phone: (800) 248-7701
Fax: (404) 679-4558
E-mail: dkollar@sacscoc.org
Web site: http://www.sacs.org/

Responsible for schools located in Alabama, Florida, Georgia, Kentucky, Louisiana, Mississippi, North Carolina, South Carolina, Tennessee, Texas, and Virginia.

Western Association of Schools and Colleges

985 Atlantic Avenue, Suite 100
Alameda, CA 94501
Phone: (510) 748-9001
Fax: (510)-748-9797
E-mail: wascsr@wascsenior.org
Web site: http://www.wascweb.org/

Responsible for schools located in California, Hawaii, Guam, and the Trust Territory of the Pacific.

The Special Case of National Accreditation

One interesting agency is the Distance Education and Training Council, a legitimate, government-recognized agency that deals exclusively with schools that offer most or all of their programs through distance learning. While the DETC does have a legitimate purpose—many new distance schools are too innovative or unusual for the mainstream agencies—they have also granted accreditation to some schools whose programs are of questionable repute. This is a topic of hot debate in distance-learning circles, and the verdict is far from in, but generally speaking, DETC accreditation is viewed in the education world as less rigorous than traditional regional accreditation. (Many regionally accredited schools also have distance programs.) This is not merely an academic debate, in either sense of the term. Quite a few regionally accredited schools will not accept DETC degrees for further education, and there are job descriptions and, particularly, corporate reimbursement plans that require a regionally accredited degree. Still, if you find an experimental new program on the Net and want to give it a go, you should make sure that at the very least it has DETC approval.

Distance Education and Training Council

1601 18th Street NW
Washington, DC 20009
Phone: (202) 234-5100
Fax: (202) 332-1386
E-mail: detc@detc.org
Web site: http://www.detc.org/

Professional Accreditation

In addition to academic accreditation, some discussion must also be devoted to the issue of professional accreditation. To qualify for professional accreditation, a school must not only undergo the rigorous academic and operational evaluations described above, but also an evaluation by an approved professional agency. These agencies are operated privately, but must be recognized by either the U.S. Department of Education or the Council on Higher Education Accreditation (CHEA, an independent non-governmental agency in Washington, DC), or both.

How Important Is Professional Accreditation?

If a school has regional accreditation, you can be sure that it's a legitimate and worthwhile institution. Professional accreditation is one more factor that might tip the scales a bit if you're torn between two schools, but it's very rarely essential. In engineering fields, the engineering-focused ABET accreditation is viewed as more relevant and therefore more prestigious than the comparable computer science CSAB accreditation. A very few graduate schools require applicants to have earned an ABET-accredited undergraduate engineering degree, while no graduate programs in the computer sciences require CSAB accreditation.

Both CSAB and ABET have commissions under them who do the actual evaluating. For ABET, it's the Engineering Accreditation Commission (EAC), which accredits programs in engineering (electrical/computer engineering and so forth) and the Technology Accreditation Commission (TAC), which deals with programs in technology (electronics engineering technology, computer technology, and so on) CSAB has only one, the Computer Science Accreditation Commission, which accredits B.S. and B.A. programs in computer science.

Note that both of these accreditations are for programs, not entire departments. Even very legitimate schools often blur this distinction, claiming on their Web sites that a department is "ABET accredited," when in fact only one program has this award. For instance, Clark Kent University's B.S. in computer engineering offered at the school's Smallville campus could be ABET-accredited, while the same program at the Metropolis campus might not be. It's not the engineering department itself that's accredited, only that particular degree in that particular field at that particular campus.

Most of this is relevant only at the undergraduate level, as few if any graduate IT programs have professional accreditation from either CSAB or ABET. If, however, you are interested in a tech-focused M.B.A., you might run across professional business accreditation. Again, it's hardly required, but for whatever reason, corporate recruiters look with more favor on M.B.A. degrees from professionally accredited schools, and this could give you an extra edge. The preferred M.B.A. accreditation comes from an accreditor called the International Association for Management Education (confusingly known as the AACSB, as its former title was the American Assembly of Collegiate Schools of Business, and they've changed their name but not their acronym).

Bottom line: there are hundreds of great schools, including many of those listed in this book, that don't have professional accreditation. However, if you're torn between two programs and need a deciding factor, professional accreditation (in addition, of course, to regional accreditation) is as good a one to use as any. One thing worth noting is that CSAB, the organization that accredits computer sciences programs, is soon likely to be acquired by ABET, which accredits engineering and technology. Its criteria are not likely to change, but it's still not clear exactly how this will play out.

The Professional Agencies

To investigate a school's professional accreditation, or for a more in-depth exploration of what qualifies an institution for accreditation, you can check out the relevant organizations' Web sites. These organizations can offer lists of their approved schools and other information about the field.

COMPUTER SCIENCES

As noted above, CSAB is in the process of being integrated into ABET, described below. It is not expected that this will affect their accreditation activities and, indeed, they are planning to expand out in the long term, performing accreditation of further specializations, such as information science. CSAB's current accreditation process focuses on programs that offer a broad general education in addition to the technical aspects of computer science. A very good program that is also very technology-focused with little requirement for breadth may therefore not qualify. The board's accreditation criteria are well and clearly spelled out on its Web site, which also offers a searchable database of accredited institutions.

Computing Sciences Accreditation Board, Inc.

184 North Street
Stamford, CT 06901
Phone: (203) 975-1117
Fax: (203) 975-1222
E-mail: csab@csab.org
Web site: http://www.csab.org/

Institutions are evaluated on a long list of criteria, basically divided into the following categories:

Objectives and assessments   Essentially, what the board looks at is whether the school sets goals for itself and whether it achieves them, particularly in the realms of student achievement and professional placement.

Student support   These criteria specify ideal class sizes, and call for good program descriptions and student advising.

Faculty   There is a long list of faculty criteria, including credentials, ratio of full-time faculty to adjuncts, requirements for faculty availability to students, ration of in-classroom time to research time, and professor/student ratios.

Curriculum   There are standards for what students should study, including general breadth requirements (one can't require only math and science, for instance), requirements for an ethics of computer science component to the program, and so forth.

Laboratories and computer facilities   These criteria specify what sort of computer equipment should be available to students, call for administrative support for those facilities, and note the need for long-term facility planning.

Institutional facilities   This requirement calls for networked classrooms, adequate student/faculty meeting space, subscriptions to trade journals for student use, and so on.

ENGINEERING AND TECHNOLOGY

ABET accreditation is well regarded, and focuses more on the technological and less on the broad-based general education side of life, in contrast with CSAB. The accreditation criteria are too long and involved to cite here (they are available as PDF downloads on the agency's Web site), but follow a similar vein to those noted above. Essentially, the agency concerns itself with making sure the faculty meet their standards, the school offers the students enough support, and subjects they consider important are required in each program. It is worth stating again that many schools that don't have this accreditation could, but they just don't feel the time and money are well invested in going through the process.

Accreditation Board for Engineering and Technology, Inc.

111 Market Place, Suite 1050
Baltimore, MD 21202
Phone: (410) 347-7700
Fax: (410) 625-2238
E-mail: accreditation@abet.org
Web site: http://www.abet.org/

M.B.A. ACCREDITORS

The most prestigious accreditor is the International Association for Management Education, formerly the American Assembly of Collegiate Schools of Business (and still referred to AACSB). This organization is the U.S.'s oldest business-school accreditor, and the one that deals with such schools as Harvard, Yale, Stanford, and dozens of others. Smaller colleges and universities tend to be accredited by the Association of Collegiate Business Schools and Programs. The Accrediting Council for Independent Colleges and Schools works mainly with community colleges and vocational schools, but does accredit a small number of M.B.A.-granting institutions. Finally, the International Assembly for Collegiate Business Education focuses on outcome-based business education (as opposed to ivory-tower academics).

The International Association for Management Education

600 Emerson Road, Suite 300
St. Louis, MO 63141
Phone: (314) 872-8481
Fax: (314) 872-8495
E-mail: webmaster@aacsb.edu
Web site: http://www.aacsb.edu/

The Association of Collegiate Business Schools and Programs

7007 College Boulevard, Suite 420
Overland Park, KS 66211
Phone: (913) 339-9356
Fax: (913) 339-6226
E-mail: acbsp@aol.com
Web site: http://www.acbsp.org/

The Accrediting Council for Independent Colleges and Schools

750 First Street NE, Suite 980
Washington, DC 20002-4241
Phone: (202) 336-6780
Fax: (202) 482-2593
E-mail: acics@acics.org
Web site: http://www.acics.org/

International Assembly for Collegiate Business Education

P.O. Box 25217
Overland Park, KS 66225
Phone: (913) 631-3009
Fax: (913) 631-9154
Web site: http://www.iacbe.org/

How to Use This Information in Making Your Decision

Accreditation from a recognized regional agency is important for a number of reasons. It ensures that the school is operating legitimately and that its credits and degrees will be accepted by other institutions. Most American universities operate on a semester unit or credit system, typically two semesters a year for four years to earn a bachelor's degree. Since 120 to 136 semester units are required to earn the degree, this means an average of 15 units (three to five classes at three to five units each) per semester. Master's degrees typically require 30 to 40 semester units. One common model, for instance, is a program requiring either 30 units plus a thesis, or 36 units with no thesis.

While there are a few good unaccredited programs, they are rare beasts, and it's simply safer to go with an accredited school. Choose one of the programs in this book, and you can't go wrong, accreditation-wise. Professional accreditation is a nice value-added feature for a program, but almost never essential (and, indeed, most of the prestigious research institutes forego CSAB accreditation). The only accreditation worse than no accreditation is when it's issued by a fraudulent agency. If you have any questions about the validity of a program's accreditation, go to the relevant agency's Web site, and see if the school is listed. And if you have any concerns about the accreditor itself, make sure it is listed on the site of the Council on Higher Education Accreditation (http://www.chea.org/).

For example, let's say you've heard about Aurora University's master's degree in information science and you're interested. However, you've never heard of the school, and you wonder whether it's legit. A quick scan of their Web site doesn't show anything on accreditation, but a keyword search turns up the claim that they're accredited by the Commission on Institutions of Higher Education of the North Central Association of Colleges and Schools. Flipping back in this chapter, you discover that the North Central Association would indeed be the right accreditor for an Illinois-based school. But you're the suspicious type. So you go to the agency's site, at http://www.ncacihe.org/. A link on the site's front page takes you to the searchable Directory of Institutions. Type in "Aurora," and hey presto, there's your verification.

Now, what about a trickier case? Let's say you've seen some advertisements for Cambridge State University and think they might be the school for you. The school doesn't seem to have a Web site (always a bad sign), so you look at the Web site for what would be their regional accreditor. They're in Louisiana, so that would be the Southern Association of Schools and Colleges. Nope, not listed. The school's catalog claims that the programs are accredited by World Association of Universities and Colleges (WAUC). You go to WAUC's site and, indeed, there's Cambridge State. But WAUC isn't listed in this chapter, and you're not sure if they're recognized by the U.S. government. Your next step is the Council of Higher Education Accreditation (CHEA), at http://www.chea.org/, and, indeed, WAUC is missing. You should have some serious questions before proceeding further.

This may sound like a big hassle, and you may wonder how dumb you'd have to be to be tricked by a phony school. Sadly, thousands and thousands of people are tricked every year. If anything seems the slightest bit fishy, take the time to do a spot of research. You'll be happy you did the next time you see one of those newspaper stories headlined, "Executive lied on résumé, fired from top job."

CHAPTER 10

Working with Your Employer

You need a degree to get a better job, but you can't quit your job to get a degree. Catch-22? Maybe not. Now more than ever, employers are hard-pressed to hang onto good employees, so you've got a bargaining chip. It's entirely possible that your employer may be willing to let you take some time off (or work flextime) to get a degree through conventional daytime courses. (Or to allow you extra time for homework or recuperation if you're taking night or online courses.) He or she may even be willing to help you pay for that degree in return for a commitment to work on for some time after the degree is earned. And once you've earned the degree, there's a good chance you can parlay it into a better job with your company—or, if that doesn't work out, you can take it somewhere else and get more money and more respect.

Getting Time Off to Study

It may not be as hard as it sounds. These days, there are so many degree programs geared to the needs of working professionals, it's not like you need to walk into your boss's office and say, "Excuse me, Mr. Burns, can I have four years off to go to college?"

In fact, if you study online, or through evening or weekend classes, you may not need to mention it to your boss at all. Still, you'll probably need time off at some point, whether to study for finals, attend graduation, or just take a break (Daytona Beach, anyone?), so it does make sense to let your supervisor know you're working on your degree. He or she may be concerned at first that this will be a distraction, but as long as you're prepared to show that it isn't, and your work doesn't suffer, they will almost certainly come to see it as a sign of your worth to the company.

Be aware, too, that you're looking at taking on a fairly large amount of stress. First of all, there's the pressure to get your schoolwork done and still hold up your end at work. Secondly, many employees fear they may lose political ground by going to school—that a junior employee may push them out while they're taking some informal leave for classes or just distracted with coursework. These aren't reasons not to better yourself, but if you haven't fully thought through the downside, you should. After all, it's better to be prepared for a downside that never occurs than to be blindsided when you can least afford it.

If you think through the ups and downs and decide that working while going to school is a good option for you, this book offers a number of useful resources. The Subject Index in Appendix B lists the programs best-suited to the needs of working professionals, and Appendix C features a number of undergraduate and graduate degrees that can be done entirely online. The bottom line is that you may not need time off to study at all. Still, if your employer offers the option of flextime, you may want to look into it, to give yourself the time you need in and around exams and deadlines for your big final class projects.

Will Your Boss Pay for Your Degree?

Sound crazy? Maybe not. Most large companies, and many smaller ones, have some sort of education reimbursement plan. Often, it's not well publicized or well understood, which may account for why some studies show that as few as 10 percent of employees use money that could be available to them for their education.

Employers know how important it is for their workforce to stay on top of new developments, especially in the technological fields. While this is frequently interpreted to mean that the employer will cover the cost of certifications or continuing education in technical fields, many will also consider funding degree-based higher education. Here are some hints and tips to keep in mind.

Find Out What's Available

If you don't have a clearly written employee manual, talk to someone in human resources. Does your company pay for education? Is there a definite policy? If not, to whom should you speak about your situation? Some larger companies also have scholarships for staff, and these are often badly publicized. Ask, ask, ask, and don't take "I don't know" for an answer. It may well be that there's a rule based on how long you've been with the company—for instance, you may have to work there for six months or a year before you're eligible for financial aid.

Make sure you have all the facts—it's happened that students enroll in a program just assuming they'll be reimbursed, and then find out they haven't met some obscure corporate requirement and they're out of pocket thousands of dollars.

Know, too, that it's unusual for a company to bear the full cost of education. Generally you can expect something like 50 to 100 percent of tuition to be reimbursed, but you'll likely have to pay for your own books and the like. In the math and computer science fields, these are not small expenses—a calculus book can easily run you $200, and that's just for one book! Then you need the solutions manual, the support software, and so on. Some companies reimburse proportionately, depending on the grade a student receives. Even though the student may pass the course with a B grade, the company may require a B+ or A for reimbursement. Know all of this before you start, to avoid surprises when you can least afford them.

Is This Job-Related?

There are some enlightened companies that pay for any education regardless of whether it benefits the employer, but those are few and far between. Generally, the first question will be, "Is this course related to your job?" If you're working in IT and see a future for yourself with the company, make a big case for how your education will benefit them. That is, if you're currently doing network support but are interested in a managerial position, make it clear that you're getting this education to get ahead in the company. Be honest. If your real goal is to jump ship as soon as you have the credentials, don't lie and say you're in it for the long haul. Reputations do travel, and you don't want to be seen as someone who lies to get money out of your employers. Of course, you don't have to tell the whole horrible truth to your supervisor, just remain vague ("The skills I'll gain in this program will help me to do a better job no matter what my title ends up being.").

It's not at all unusual for an employer to ask for a commitment from you—say, that you'll stay on for two to five years after you graduate. While this is almost certainly not legally enforceable, as a "gentleman's agreement" it may seem fair to you, and honoring such an agreement may be a reasonable choice for you to make, unless you're truly trapped in a Dilbert hell. In that case, you might want to consider leaving your job entirely and dedicating yourself to school full time, using the funding ideas in Chapters 6 and 7. Know, too, that it's fair for you to counteroffer when asked for such a commitment. Say, for instance, that you'll be happy to stay on, but you'd like to be guaranteed a raise and/or managerial title once you successfully complete your degree. You may not get this as a promise, but it can't hurt to try. If such promises are made, get them in writing. Supervisors change, companies get bought out, and even a totally trustworthy person's verbal say-so may not be something you can count on four years from now.

Note that any sort of financial assistance from your employer would normally be considered income and be taxable, but undergraduate students get a tax break—up to $5,250 of employer-provided funding for undergraduate courses can be excluded from your taxes. There's no similar relief for graduate students yet, unfortunately.

Get Creative

What if your employer doesn't offer any sort of education assistance? Fire up your chutzpah, and see if you can change that. Make an appointment with your supervisor, and come in prepared. This is a sales job, and the product you're selling is you, so it makes sense to give it your all. Explain why and how your education will benefit the company, and what you're willing to do to make it worthwhile to the workplace (for example, agreeing to stay on for a set amount of time after you earn your degree, using the workplace for school projects to give them unpaid consultant work, and so forth).

If they can't or won't give you straight-up tuition assistance, ask about a loan. There may be a policy whereby qualified employees can borrow for major expenses such as college, and pay it back at little or no interest. Some companies offer a prorated system. Say, for instance, you borrow $5,000. Over two years, that $5,000 would turn from a loan into a gift. So if you quit after a year, you'd only owe them $2,500. If your company doesn't have such a policy, suggest it be implemented. Remember that companies are looking for ways to retain trained staff. This sort of a benefit doesn't cost a lot in the grand scheme of things, and guarantees them a happy, well-trained, motivated workforce.

If you meet with no cooperation at all, this unsupportive employer may be bad for your career in other ways. Maybe the right thing to do is to find a better job—one at which your supervisor acknowledges the importance of ongoing training for IT professionals and is willing to help you develop in your career.

SOME FACTS TO SHARE WITH YOUR EMPLOYER

Studies show that a majority of employers offer at least some tuition assistance to employees. The figures quoted range from 70 to 90 percent of employers offering at least some help.

About half of these employers reimburse a full 100 percent of approved tuition costs, 18 percent reimburse between 50 and 90 percent, and the final 30 percent pay less than half.

Even part-timers can get some assistance—a quarter of all employers offer tuition assistance or reimbursement to part-time as well as full-time employees.

Special Advantages for Union Members

If you or a family member belongs to one of the 38,000 local unions in the U.S., there may be tuition benefit programs, grants, or scholarships available for you.

The AFL-CIO formerly published a book on college funding; this information is now available entirely online, at http://www.aflcio.org/scholarships/index.htm. The site is easy to use and well designed, allowing visitors to search for scholarships sponsored by national and international unions. Check with your local union office or contact the AFL-CIO for more information. Just for example, there are grants available for the children and grandchildren of professional engineers, and for aerospace workers and their children. The Web site is searchable by industry/union or by state. While you may not be a union member, perhaps one of your parents or grandparents was. It's worth looking into!

Okay, You Have the Degree. Now What?

Once you've earned your degree, whether it's a first-time bachelor's, a tech-focused M.B.A., or an M.S. in e-commerce, you're automatically more valuable to your company. Perhaps you've signed an agreement to stay on for a certain amount of time in exchange for tuition aid. That's fine, but you can still talk to your supervisor about an increase in pay or a better title. Your supervisor knows how hard it is to find good, qualified IT employees and should be happy to talk about how to keep you satisfied.

Getting the Promotion You Deserve

Every workplace is different, and only you know how best to approach your supervisor. In some settings, you might simply catch the relevant decision-maker when he or she's not busy, sit down, and have a quick informal chat to test the waters. ("Sue, I know it's six months until my annual review, and I was wondering what the proper procedure would be for looking at reevaluating my title and salary sooner rather than later, in light of my having completed that graduate IT program.") In more formal corporate settings, you should treat the conversation like a job interview. Schedule an appointment, dress up, and come prepared with a revised résumé that's targeted to your new objective in the company. This may seem a little unnatural or overly aggressive, but it's a great way to show your boss that you're serious, and force him or her to look at you and your credentials anew.

There are some great resources out there to help you design a résumé, come up with answers to tough questions, figure out what a fair market salary would be for the new you, and ace that interview, whether it's with your current boss or at a new company. See Appendix D, "Resources," for more guidance. Briefly, though, think about how you would answer the following questions. Even if your boss doesn't ask them, having thought it through will make your presentation more assured and polished. Practice at home with your significant other or a friend, or in front of the mirror. Yes, it sounds goofy, but this sort of preparation can really pay off—and wouldn't you be willing to look goofy for an extra $10,000 a year?

How have your skills improved? How will they benefit the organization?
Come up with real-life situations where you will now be more useful to the company. Mention hands-on job skills that your company needs and that you now possess. For example, if the company has a lot of proprietary software that tends to be buggy, discuss how your software engineering training will allow you to save time and money for line staff. If they're struggling with an outdated e-commerce engine, detail how you can save thousands of dollars that would have been spent on e-commerce consultants. You're uniquely situated to know your company's needs and weaknesses, and to show how you can help solve them.

Why should I pay you more money? Remember never to say that you *need* a raise. Need is totally irrelevant—you're worth more money, and you can produce the statistics to prove it. Appendix D (listed under "Chapter 1") points you toward salary information for your area. Concentrate on your skills and training and what they're worth on the open market. It seems as though it should be obvious what not to do, but it's shocking how many employees begin their plea for a raise with, "My kids are going to college and I can't afford tuition," or "I work really really hard, and you should reward that." It's not about what you need or how many late nights you work, it's about your skills and your worth. If your employer is unprofessional enough to steer into these waters (saying, for instance, "But doesn't your wife have a good job? Do you really need the raise?") gently get the conversation back on track with a statement along the lines of, "I don't think that's relevant right now. As I was saying, the average network administrator in this city makes $70,000 and..." Or, if you prefer, answer with "Yes, I do!" Then add, "The raise puts me in the average network administrator's salary range of $70,000 in the metro area. This would be great because I am very proud of our above-average network and its services."

Are you looking for another job? Employers appreciate loyalty, but they also can get complacent about your value if they don't think you're likely to leave. The best answer to a question like this is something along the lines of, "I would prefer to stay at the company, as I really enjoy my work, but if there's not a position available that matches my skills, I'll be forced to start looking at other offers."

Or you can say something like, "It's always good to see what's out there, but I certainly want to stay with you and I do appreciate having you as my mentor. There are many challenges I can work on here, and I have learned so much. I want to continue. What did you have in mind for me?"

If you take this approach, be prepared for the question to be thrown back at you, as in "What do you have in mind?" Be prepared to create your own job and discuss at length all the new initiatives you could work on thanks to the new degree.

 TIP *Even if you love your job, it doesn't hurt to keep your eyes open. Things change, companies fail, great supervisors leave and are replaced with awful ones. You should always know your market worth and have an idea about where you'd like to go next.*

Never lie—if you're job-hunting, you don't have to say so in so many words, but you shouldn't deny it either. Similarly, if you're not, don't invent phony job offers to get a raise. These sorts of mistruths can come back to haunt you—after all, you never know who your boss might chat with at the gym one morning! (It's amazing how many deals are done over chance meetings by the Stairmasters.)

Moving On

Sometimes, there just won't be a suitable position at your current company, or you'll be chafing at the opportunity to move on. In that case, you're well situated, given today's job market. Appendix D (listed under "Chapter 1") lists good sites for job-hunting and for researching a company you might want to work at. Some basic job-hunting tips:

Don't move on just for more money.   It's tempting when big dollar signs and stock options are dangled in front of you, but make sure the company you're looking at will be satisfying for you in the long term. If you feel the need for job security, working for a high-risk dot-com startup may be too much for your blood pressure. Conversely, if you crave excitement, a tech support job at a big firm, while well paid, might cause you to curl up and wilt from boredom.

Job-hunt on your own time.   There's nothing tackier than sending out job-hunting letters from your company's fax or e-mail, and prospective employers will notice. If you absolutely must print out résumés or letters at work, do it after hours or on weekends, and be absolutely sure you don't leave anything incriminating in the printer or photocopier. Even if your company has relaxed attitudes about using business e-mail for personal purposes, your boss can legally read everything you send out, and it doesn't look good to the person on the other end. After all, why would they want to hire someone who seems to spend his or her work hours looking for a better job!

Network, network, network.   It's been said before, and it will be said again: the best jobs don't show up in the paper or on even the best Web sites. They come about because someone you went to school with knows someone who's looking for just the right person, and they think you could be that person. If there's an alumni group for your program, stay in touch. If there's a local networking organization for IT professionals, go to their events. If there isn't one, consider starting one. As the organizer, you'll be the first to hear about great new job opportunities!

Whether your employer pays for your degree, promotes you once you have it, or fails to realize your new worth and loses you to a competitor, there's no question that the degree will be your ticket to a new and better work world. Be sure to take advantage of every truly attractive opportunity that presents itself, and you can't go wrong.

CHAPTER 11

Credit for Prior Learning

When you skim through college catalogs, you might find yourself thinking "Why do I have to take this course?" If you've been raised in a bilingual Spanish-English home, you might wonder why you need to take Spanish 101. If you've served as treasurer of a nonprofit organization for five years, why should you have to take Business Mathematics? If you earned repeated honors marks and aced high school calculus, do you really need Intermediate Algebra?

These are all very logical, fair questions. This chapter deals with some techniques you might be able to use to turn your prior learning into cold, hard credit.

Life Experience (Portfolio) Credit

As a simple, easy-to-grasp example, let's begin with the first scenario given: you grew up in a bilingual Spanish-English household, and your degree requires six hours of foreign language credit. And it just so happens that the college you're attending will grant up to six hours of life experience (portfolio) credit.

The concept behind portfolio learning is that it's the knowledge that counts, not how you got it. Whether Spanish 101– and 102–level knowledge was gained by sitting in a classroom or by being yelled at by your grandma, you deserve the credit. Does this mean you can get credit for Spanish 101 and 102? At many schools, the answer is a resounding yes. The general procedure for documenting life experience varies from college to college, but, generally speaking, you're looking at an essay and audiocassette, plus maybe a few letters of recommendation.

And that's it. None of this business of sitting in a classroom for 30 weeks listening to a room full of non-native speakers stumble through "Good morning!" and "Where is the restroom?"

You don't have to stop with Spanish 101 and 102, either. If you're a CPA, the CPA certification alone should be equal to several accounting courses. Same story if you're a Microsoft Certified Systems Engineer, logged in three years as a systems analyst, moderated large e-mail lists, or helped out in the open source movement. (If you've written functional software, all the better. It's hard to imagine a more solid demonstration of prior learning.)

Hundreds of colleges grant undergraduate credit through this method. If you're enrolled in a school, talk to your advisor. If you're not enrolled, talk to the adult learning or continuing education office. The admissions office may or may not have information on this option, and we've seen e-mails from admissions officers that openly deny a given program or procedure exists—even when it's advertised on the university Web page!

Appendix D lists a number of books dedicated entirely to portfolio evaluation. For many students, this really is the best option out there—and it's hard to imagine any student who could not legitimately put together at least one or two undergraduate life-experience portfolios. For example: even a recent high school graduate who spent his summers hanging ten could conceivably pull together some letters of recommendation documenting the time he spent surfing, throw in a five-minute video clip, and claim an hour or two of credit for his trouble.

Credit by Examination

This is probably the most traditional method of awarding credit based on prior learning. Many, many colleges will allow students to challenge midterm and final examinations even if they miss a number of classes, so this segues naturally into the next logical step: letting the student try his or her luck with the exam and doing away with the class altogether.

Can you do this? Well, yes and no. You're not likely to find many colleges that will say, "Hey, sure, take 15 hours worth of final exams this semester without attending any classes." But a number of well-respected traditional colleges do allow students to challenge final examinations without attending classes. The person you want to talk to in this situation is the professor.

Challenging courses by final exam has its drawbacks: it's expensive (expect to pay full course tuition whether you attend or not), it's precarious (there's not much room for rescheduling), and it only works in very small doses. In addition, it's also stressful—any test is a stress, especially if you want top grades. On top of that, consider that you'll be preparing and reviewing for the test while trying to complete other coursework. This can be a recipe for serious anxiety, so plan accordingly.

If you're set on taking on part or all of a degree by examination, it can be done. Charter Oak State College, Regents College, and Thomas Edison State College (all profiled in Chapter 12) allow students to complete degrees entirely based on off-campus examinations. Thousands of schools will also grant lower-level credit for these off-campus examinations (usually 6 to 12 hours, but sometimes much more).

The three most common "brands" of off-campus examinations are CLEP, DANTES, and RCE. We'll discuss these below.

In calculating costs for these examinations, remember to take into account the test proctor's (supervisor's) fee, which is usually about $10.

College Level Examination Program (CLEP)

P.O. Box 6600
Princeton, NJ 08541-6600
Phone: (609) 771-7865
Fax: (609) 771-7088
Web: http://www.collegeboard.com/clep/
E-mail: clep@info.collegeboard.com
Cost: $46/exam

With almost 3,000 participating colleges, this is the largest and most widely accepted credit-by-examination program in the world. CLEP examinations come in two varieties. CLEP general examinations cover broad subjects (such as humanities and the natural sciences) and are generally accepted for 6 to 8 hours of lower-level credit. CLEP subject examinations are generally patterned after specific common freshman and sophomore courses (Western Civilization I and II, Freshman English I and II, Macroeconomics, and so on) and are generally accepted for 3 or 4 hours of lower-level credit.

In addition to the general lower-level CLEP examinations available, a specific examination in Information Systems and Computer Applications (roughly equivalent to a 3-hour Introduction to Computers course) is available.

The College Board maintains a list of testing centers and cooperating universities on the Web site given above—so if you want to know whether a college accepts CLEP examinations for credit, that's the first place to check. But you'll also want to find out which CLEP examinations are accepted for credit at your school. Very few schools accept all CLEP examinations, and even fewer schools accept unlimited CLEP credit (as far as we know, it's only Charter Oak State College, Regents College, and Thomas Edison State College).

Defense Activity for Non-Traditional Education Support (DANTES)

Educational Testing Service
Rosedale Road
Princeton, NJ 08541
Phone: (609) 720-6740
Web: http://www.chauncey.com/dantes.html
E-mail: dantes@chauncey.com
Cost: $35/exam for civilians; free for military personnel

DANTES examinations (technically known as DANTES Subject Standardized Tests or DSSTs) were originally designed to fit the needs of active military personnel, but are now also available to civilians. About 1,500 universities accept credit for DSSTs, and DSSTs are available in a wider range of fields than CLEP examinations. Instead of being limited to standard courses, DSSTs are available in such diverse fields as business law, world religions, astronomy, anthropology, and technical writing. Some exams are even based on entertaining PBS miniseries such as

"Ethics in America," "The Civil War," "Art in the Western World," and "War and Peace in the Nuclear Age"—which means, essentially, that the most effective way to cram for some tests is to sit in front of a television for eight straight hours the night before.

Two IT-related DSSTs are available: Introduction to Computing and Management Information Systems.

egents College Examinations (RCE)

Administration Office

Regents College

mbia Circle

y, NY 12203-5159

: (888) 723-9267

18) 464-8777

http://www.regents.edu/099.htm

E-mail: testadmn@regents.edu

Cost: Average $200/exam for civilians; free for military personnel

Regents College Examinations (RCEs) are offered electronically through Sylvan Learning Centers (http://www.sylvanlearning.com/) nationwide. Originally designed by Regents College as part of their own external degree program (described in Chapter 12), RCEs have become a widely accepted form of credit by examination.

Most RCEs are offered in fields related to nursing, management, and the humanities. While there are no IT-related RCE examinations available at the time of this writing, new examinations are being developed on an almost constant basis.

Other Ways of Earning Credit

If all that only whets your appetite for more credit, here are a few more possible avenues you might consider:

Other examination systems The Thomas Edison College Examination Program (TECEP) of Thomas Edison State College, the Ohio University examinations, and even subject GREs can be possible sources of credit, depending on the university you're dealing with.

Certifications and on-the-job training   Many universities will accept credit (sometimes lots of credit) for non-academic training—especially if it has been recommended for credit by the American Council on Education (ACE). For more information, see Appendix D.

Military training   The American Council on Education (ACE) also recommends credit for almost any conceivable form of formal military training. For more information, see Appendix D.

Another great resource to check out is the little-known, but top-notch programs run by our very own U.S. Department of Agriculture—yep, the same folks who tell you how many servings of vegetables to eat each day. In addition to this invaluable service, they also offer federal training programs that are open to the general public, almost entirely by distance learning and at very reasonable prices. These programs are offered through the USDA graduate school, and the credits are accepted by most colleges and universities. For more information, check out http://www.grad.usda.gov/. It's your tax dollars at work.

In sum, there are a lot of ways to get legitimate college credit besides sitting in a classroom. You may have accumulated credits for things you've already done and not even realize they can be applied to your college degree. Read through the available resources on portfolio credit, look into the USDA's programs, and see what sort of jumpstart you may be able to give your college career. While it's not likely that (as the matchbook ads might say) you've already earned your degree without knowing it, you may well be able to skip some classes, save some time and money, and dedicate your efforts to the areas that really interest you.

PART II

Where to Go for Your IT Degree: The Best Colleges and Universities

In This Part

CHAPTER 12

The Top 199 IT Schools
in the U.S.

What follows is a complete set of listings for the top 199
information technology schools in the U.S., from American University to Yale and everything in between.

If you're looking for prestigious schools, they're all covered: MIT,
UCLA, Harvard, Yale, Brown, Carnegie Mellon, Berkeley, Stanford,
Princeton, and so on. If you're looking for something a bit more
affordable, you'll also find programs such as those at Charter Oak
State College where, if you play your cards right and have sufficient
life-experience learning under your belt, you can get a bachelor's
for a little over $1,500. For working adults who can't take time off,
or those who can't travel for family or other reasons, many schools
offer fully accredited, highly rigorous programs entirely online.
Appendix B, "Subject Index," and Appendix C, "Top Picks," help
steer readers toward the listings that might be most appropriate for
a range of special needs.

What You See Under the School's Name

At the top of every listing, you'll see the school's name followed by its mailing address. It's sad but true: many colleges just won't let you just send them mail to a general address anymore. It might get thrown away on the spot or processed through mail-sorting hell. So, pay close attention to the addresses given in this chapter—they're the ones that will get your letter to the right person in the right department. Sure, it's snail mail, so it might take a while to get to the right place, but it'll get there.

Web Site Address

To the right of the school's name, you'll find the school's Web site address. This will be the main Web site for the university. (Other sites will be listed under "Contact Information" later in the listing.) Typing in this URL should get you anywhere you want to go. Most major colleges and universities have placed their catalogs (or equivalent information) online, so this is probably the first place to look for information.

The little star rating next to the URL will tell you how useful the Web site is. Our ratings reflect these basic opinions:

½☆   Positively dreadful. The information an average student needs simply doesn't seem to be here.

☆   Workable but very limited. You might find the information you need here, but you probably won't.

☆½   A bit more manageable, but still incomplete. It might tell you everything you need to know, but you'll probably still find yourself requesting a catalog.

☆☆   There's nothing wrong with this site, but you won't want to e-mail home about it.

☆☆½   A bit better. You'll probably find everything you need to know here, and you probably won't give yourself eyestrain finding it.

☆☆☆   A really good site. All the general information you're likely to need is here and relatively easy to access.

☆☆☆½   Almost perfect. You will actually enjoy navigating this site.

☆☆☆☆   Truly perfect. Other schools should surf these sites and learn from them.

NOTE *The Web is a constantly changing beast, and the day you purchase this book, a school may finally have wised up and made its site a work of art. Worse, it's not unheard of for a school to change its Web address. It's not that common, especially for an established school like the 199 listed here, but if you do have trouble finding a site, just call the school and ask if the URL has changed.*

Year Established and Ownership

Directly under the Web site address, you'll find the year the college (as it existed at the time) opened its gates—but this doesn't always mean that it opened under the same name or ownership it has today.

Following the year-established date, you'll see the ownership line that tells you whether a school is public (state-funded) or private (independent). Public universities are generally inexpensive, large, diverse, and friendly toward reentry students. Private universities are generally more expensive, smaller, less diverse, and more traditional.

Most private universities are also under some form of religious ownership, which may or may not have any effect on the student's lifestyle. Where this may be an issue, it's noted in the school description, but none of the church-owned schools described in this book discourage students of other faiths from attending.

An Introduction to Each School

After the school's vital statistics, you'll find a few lines of text; this is basically a sound-bite summary of the institution and its offerings. This summary lets you know at a glance whether you're looking at a research institute or a small liberal arts college, whether it offers alternative means of earning credit (distance learning, evening classes, extension courses, and so forth), and other immediately important things. For example, if you're male, it's probably helpful to know up front that Smith is a woman's college and not coeducational.

This little paragraph is by no means intended as the last word on any school. For example, Rensselaer Polytechnic Institute is described later as a research institution even though it also offers a number of excellent programs designed specifically for working adults. And though Mills is without question a women's college, its graduate programs are open to both men and women.

Degrees Offered

If you love acronyms, you're in the right place. This section is a quick snapshot of what each school has to offer you in the way of IT degrees. However, be warned that not everything is listed here, only the most IT-focused programs. If a degree program has an IT component, but its primary focus is business (as with some MIS programs) or research (artificial intelligence, cognitive sciences), it will be listed at the bottom, under "Other Programs."

Don't be intimidated by all these crazy degree titles and majors—and you'll see quite a few (anybody want a Ph.D. in Algorithms, Optimization, and Combinatorics?). Don't feel like there necessarily has to be a difference between computer engineering and computer systems engineering; sometimes there isn't. Whenever you find yourself wondering "What the heck does *that* mean?" take a peek at Chapter 5, which describes all of these fields of emphasis in some detail.

NOTE *Every program in this book has full regional accreditation, per the exacting standards described in Chapter 9. Some also have the relevant professional accreditation, either in computer sciences (CSAB) or engineering (ABET). Those programs will be indicated in the text like this 🔵 and this 🔵, noting that additional accreditation. For a discussion of professional accreditation and its relevance, see Chapter 9.*

Approximate Cost of Degrees

So, how much will the degree run you? Well, that depends. The numbers listed are, essentially, an educated minimum guess, taking into account average tuition, fees, book costs, and estimated general out-of-pocket expenses—but not room and board, meals, transportation, and so forth. Also, note that actual tuition might be higher or lower for your circumstances, or even go up or down during the time you attend the school. But if you live off-campus at a location fairly close to the college, buy your own meals, and take on at least a half-time courseload, this is probably about how much the degree will end up costing you in the long run.

Sometimes tuition for students who are not residents of the state the school is located in is dramatically higher—but there are ways you can cut it down to size. If you live in a neighboring state and want to take on a program not offered in your home state, many colleges will at least partially waive nonresident tuition for residents of nearby states under a good-neighbor clause. When this good-neighbor discount applies across the board (regardless of whether you're taking on a program offered in your home state), it is marked as such—for example "Nonresident (New England)." It's still possible to negotiate some kind of good-neighbor arrangement with most colleges, however (especially colleges in New England and the prairie states).

Admissions Guidelines

This section is, quite specifically, defined as "guidelines" rather than "require-ments." Some of the qualifications needed are not negotiable, but many are. This section tells you what a school's ideal candidate will bring to the table, but often these requirements are negotiable.

UNDERGRADUATE

At the undergraduate level, for example, even the most basic guidelines are often negotiable. When you see "high school diploma required," it pretty much always means high school diploma or *equivalent*. We have never seen a school that forbids home-schoolers from attending, for instance, and some don't even require these home-schoolers to hold a GED diploma. You can also work around the high school diploma requirement at many schools by (a) scoring well on standardized tests and/or (b) documenting a considerable amount of work experience in the field. One student on record achieved unconditional admission into a bachelor's program at the age of 15 based on an exceptionally high ACT score. It can be done.

For those who have been out of school for a while and are a bit test-phobic: standardized test requirements are often waived for adult students. Some of the schools in this book have made this a point of official policy, and many others are quite willing to negotiate some kind of arrangement along these lines.

Finally, you can generally forget about freshman admission requirements if you've already earned at least a year's worth (30 semester hours) of college-level credits and have a good GPA to show for it. Most schools place transfer students in a special category all their own.

GRADUATE

This is a bit less negotiable; you pretty much do need a regionally accredited bach-elor's to get in (although it doesn't have to be in the same field as the graduate program you're applying for).

Students with a certain amount of documented work experience may be able to have the GPA and/or test requirements waived, however. It's also not at all unusual for universities to waive the GRE requirement in cases where the under-graduate GPA is honors-level solid.

Undergraduate Programs

This is the meat of the listing, describing in brief every program listed under the heading, and giving the lowdown on its strengths, emphases, accreditation, and optional fields of specialization. Do be aware that this isn't necessarily everything a school has to offer—look under "Other Programs," and also remember that almost every school will allow you to design your own program provided you can get faculty support.

Graduate Programs

Again, you'll find a snapshot of each graduate program the school has to offer, along with its strengths, optional emphases, and what sort of final project is required to graduate. The first thing you'll notice is that master's programs are described as 30-hour, 33-hour, and so forth—and you're probably wondering: whose hours?

That's an excellent question. To simplify matters, all master's programs are described based on a semester hour system; this will make it easy to compare the requirements of various programs regardless of the calendar system used. Quarter hours are converted into semester hours using a standard conversion so that, for example, a 45 quarter hour M.S. is, for instance, described as a 30 (semester) hour M.S.

Other Programs

These are programs that may be of interest to the IT student, but that are not, strictly speaking, IT programs. These include fields such as digital media arts, management information systems, cognitive science, technology management, informatics, and more. If you're looking for something on the fringe, you might actually want to look here first (all of these programs are listed in the Subject Index in Appendix B, making them easy to zero in on).

More Information

This section, as you might imagine from the header, covers any additional information that might be of use to the student, but that doesn't easily fit in other areas. For instance, here's where you'll find out about schools that offer unusually generous financial aid programs, those with interesting nontraditional options for earning credits, where to find satellite campuses in suburban areas, and so forth.

Contact Information

PHONE

Note that many toll-free general information or admissions numbers can get you routed through to pretty much anywhere you might want to go. If you find that your college search is burning a telephone-shaped hole in your wallet, try calling a school's general information number and asking to be transferred to the relevant department. After all, that's what the switchboard is for.

FAX

This is pretty self-explanatory, but here's a handy tip: always be sure to tell the person (or department) you're faxing exactly how you want to be reached. We've heard stories of prospective students who faxed questions on company letterhead, expecting to get a letter back. Instead, a reply was faxed back to a shared machine, and their little secret was out earlier than planned. Similarly, if you fax from a Kinko's or other public machine, be sure to specify that you want an e-mail or snail-mail response. If you find that the fax line just plain doesn't work, try again in a few days. If it still doesn't work, find another way to contact the university. Telephone numbers change, and you might be sending your request for information to a grandmother in Tennessee.

E-MAIL

E-mail is the cheapest way to send a letter. If you have e-mail, use it to ask questions, chat with faculty, and request paper information.

Extra!

Every so often, there's just a neat "fun fact" about a school that's worth noting. Did someone famous graduate from here? Has the school received a major award? Every so often, we'll let you in on these quirky details.

Armed with this wealth of information, you're ready to start the process of researching schools, writing away for information, and deciding on an educational path. Congratulations, you're about to embark on an incredibly rewarding process. Good luck!

American University   www.american.edu ☆☆☆

4400 Massachusetts Avenue, NW
Washington, DC 20016

Year established: 1893
Ownership: Private

This large, prestigious university offers a number of nontraditional options for students pursuing a program in information technology, including distance learning, evening classes, and an M.S. in Information Technology, which can be completed entirely through weekend study.

Degrees Offered

UNDERGRADUATE
B.S., Computer Information Systems
B.S., Computer Science

GRADUATE
M.S., Computer Information Systems
M.S., Computer Science

Approximate Cost of Degrees

UNDERGRADUATE
$80,500

GRADUATE
$26,000

Admissions Guidelines

UNDERGRADUATE
High school diploma, ACT and/or SAT

GRADUATE
Accredited bachelor's with 3.0 GPA on upper 60 hours

Undergraduate Programs

The B.S. program in Computer Science is strongly oriented toward theoretical foundations of the discipline. In its applied components, it tends to focus far more emphatically on software than on hardware issues.

The B.S. in Computer Information Systems is an interdisciplinary program focusing on programming, software applications, and business skills.

Graduate Programs

The M.S. in Computer Science is a 36-hour program based around evening classes and culminating in a comprehensive examination. Students may choose a thesis or non-thesis track.

The M.S. in Computer Information Systems is similar to the M.S. program in Computer Science, but may be completed entirely through weekend study.

Other Programs

A B.S. program in Multimedia Design and Development is available through the Department of Computer Science and Information Systems.

An M.F.A. in Film and Electronic Media is available. For more information, contact the Visual Media Division at (202) 885-2045.

More Information

American University offers a variety of nontraditional credit options, including evening, weekend, accelerated, and online classes. Reentry students may also bypass traditional undergraduate admission requirements through the individualized B.A. program. For more information on these options, contact the Division of Adult and Continuing Education at (202) 885-2513.

Contact Information

PHONE
General information: (202) 885-1000
Admissions: (202) 885-6000
International student services: (202) 885-3350
Graduate school: (202) 885-6064
CS/IS department: (202) 885-1470

E-MAIL
General information: einfo@american.edu
Admissions: afa@american.edu
International student services: iss@american.edu
CS/IS department: Kerry Sheehan
(ksheehan@american.edu)

Arizona State University East   www.east.asu.edu ☆☆☆½

7001 E. Williams Field Road
Mesa, AZ 85212

Year established: 1996
Ownership: Public

This new, midsize state university offers IT-related programs that are, more often than not, designed with reentry students specifically in mind. Weekend study, evening classes, on-site corporate cohort study, and online distance-learning options are available.

Degrees Offered

UNDERGRADUATE
B.A.S., Computer Systems Administration
B.A.S., Microcomputer Systems
B.A.S., Software Technology Applications
B.S., Computer Engineering Technology
🄰🄱🄴🅃 B.S., Electronic(s) Engineering Technology

GRADUATE
M.S.T., emphasis Computer Systems
M.S.T., emphasis Electronic Systems
M.S.T., emphasis Information Technology
M.S.T., emphasis Microelectronics

Approximate Cost of Degrees

UNDERGRADUATE, RESIDENT
$8,800–$13,800

UNDERGRADUATE, NONRESIDENT
$37,400–$46,700

GRADUATE, RESIDENT
$2,200–$3,800

GRADUATE, NONRESIDENT
$9,400–$12,800

Admissions Guidelines

UNDERGRADUATE (B.S.)
High school diploma, SAT and/or ACT

UNDERGRADUATE (B.A.S.)
Associate of Applied Science (A.A.S.) degree with 2.0 GPA

GRADUATE
Accredited bachelor's with 3.0 GPA on upper 60 hours

Undergraduate Programs

The B.S. program in Computer Engineering Technology is available in three tracks: general, software engineering technology, and software technology. Although the program is designed for future ABET accreditation, it does not seem to be ABET-accredited at the present time.

The ABET-accredited B.S. program in Electronic(s) Engineering Technology is available in three tracks: electronic systems, microelectronics, and telecommunications.

The B.A.S. programs in Computer Systems Administration, Microcomputer Systems, and Software Technology Applications are described as "capstone programs"; the faculty evaluates the student's A.A.S. degree to determine which prerequisites must be fulfilled. The B.A.S. curriculum plan is designed for adult students and can be completed in two years or less.

Graduate Programs

The Master of Science in Technology (M.S.T.) is a 30-hour program designed for reentry students; concentrations are available in Computer Systems, Electronic Systems, Information Technology, and Microelectronics. A minimum of 16 to 18 hours of credit in the major field is required. This is supplemented by 9 to 11 hours of credit in a closely related supporting field, a 3-hour research course, and an individualized final project.

Other Programs

Additional B.A.S. programs are offered in Digital Media Management, Digital Publishing, Instrumentation, Semiconductor Technology, and Technical Graphics through the Department of Technology and Applied Science.

An information technology concentration is available within the B.S. program in Industrial Technology. For more information, contact the

Department of Information and Management Technology at (480) 727-1005.

An M.S.T. in Management of Technology is offered through the Department of Technology and Applied Science.

Contact Information

Phone

General information: (480) 727-3278
Distance learning (online classes): (480) 965-6922
Electronic(s) and computer engineering technology: (480) 727-1137
Technology and applied sciences: (480) 727-1874

Fax

Electronics and computer engineering technology: (480) 727-1723
Technology and applied sciences: (480) 727-1089

E-mail

General information: asueast@asu.edu
Technology and applied sciences: ctas@asu.edu
Distance learning (online classes): dlt-tech@asu.edu
Distance learning (corporate, on-site): distance@asu.edu

Auburn University

www.auburn.edu ☆☆☆½

Undergraduate Admissions Office
202 Mary Martin Hall
Auburn, AL 36849

Graduate Admissions Office
106 Hargis Hall
Auburn, AL 36849-5122

Year established: 1856
Ownership: Public

This large public university is highly respected in the field of computer engineering, offering programs ranging from the extremely traditional Ph.D. program in Electrical Engineering to the innovative Bachelor of Software Engineering. Auburn has a clear and well-marked curricular flexibility that sets it apart from most institutions of its kind. Now offering evening classes and weekend study to supplement traditional programs—and entire degree programs that can be completed via distance learning—this school now has something to offer to the adult reentry student as well as the undistracted freshman.

Degrees Offered

Undergraduate
B.Sw.E.
(CSAB) B.S., Computer Science
(ABET) B.S., Computer Engineering
(ABET) B.S., Electrical Engineering

Graduate
M.E.E.
M.Sw.E.
M.S., Computer Science and Engineering
M.S., Electrical Engineering
Ph.D., Computer Science and Engineering

Ph.D., Electrical Engineering

Approximate Cost of Degrees

Undergraduate, Resident
$16,500

Undergraduate, Nonresident
$42,800

Master's, Resident
$3,800

Master's, Nonresident
$9,900

DOCTORATE, RESIDENT
$6,300

DOCTORATE, NONRESIDENT
$16,400

Admissions Guidelines

UNDERGRADUATE
High school diploma, SAT and/or ACT

GRADUATE
Accredited bachelor's, GRE (or GMAT)

Undergraduate Programs

The ABET-accredited B.S. program in Computer Engineering is an extremely hardware-focused curriculum that will prepare students for graduate work in the field.

The Bachelor of Software Engineering (B.Sw.E.) has replaced the software track of the B.S. in Computer Engineering degree. Although students are given an extremely solid background in programming and application development, the chief focus seems to be on complex, interacting software systems.

The CSAB-accredited B.S. in Computer Science is a general degree that provides a broad, largely software-centered background especially well-suited to students who want to pursue graduate studies in the field.

The ABET-accredited B.S. program in Electrical Engineering is more flexible and theory-focused than most undergraduate programs in the field.

Graduate Programs

The Master of Electrical Engineering (M.E.E.) is a 30-hour applied program in electrical engineering. No final project is required.

The Master of Software Engineering (M.Sw.E.) is a 32-hour program emphasizing high-level programming, hardware-software interaction, and inter-software compatibility. A capstone project is required. This program can be completed entirely via distance learning through the Graduate Outreach Program.

The M.S. in Computer Science and Engineering is a 30-hour program addressing hardware, software, and theoretical computer science. A final project or thesis is required. This program can be completed

entirely via distance learning through the Graduate Outreach Program.

The M.S. in Electrical Engineering is a 30-hour research-oriented program that culminates in a final project or thesis. All students in this program must spend at least one semester in full-time residence. Students are encouraged to build an individualized concentration within the field.

The Ph.D. in Computer Science and Engineering addresses hardware, software, and theoretical computer science. The program involves supervised research and culminates in a dissertation. This program can be completed partially via distance learning through the Graduate Outreach Office; one academic year of full-time residency is required.

The Ph.D. in Electrical Engineering emphasizes theoretical and research-related issues. Students must pass an entry examination shortly after enrolling in this program. A minimum of 15 quarter hours (10 hours) must be taken in a closely related field. Supervised research and a dissertation are required.

Other Programs

Auburn University offers a variety of Executive M.B.A. programs via distance learning, including an Executive Tech M.B.A. A Master of Management Information Systems (M.M.I.S.) is also available by distance learning or weekend study. For more information, contact the College of Business at (334) 844-4060.

M.S., M.Ed., and Ed.S. programs in Educational Technology are available through the College of Education. For more information, contact the Department of Educational Foundations, Leadership, and Technology at (334) 844-4460.

Contact Information

PHONE
General information: (334) 844-4000
Admissions (undergraduate): (334) 844-4080
Admissions (graduate): (334) 844-4700
Graduate Outreach Office: (888) 844-5300

E-MAIL
Admissions (undergraduate):
admissions@mail.auburn.edu
Admissions (graduate): gradadm@mail.auburn.edu

Azusa Pacific University

www.apu.edu ☆☆☆

901 E. Alosta Avenue
P.O. Box 7000
Azusa, CA 91702-7000

Year established: 1965
Ownership: Private

This midsize nondenominational Christian university offers traditional and nontraditional programs in a variety of fields. The availability of online classes, accelerated programs, life experience evaluation, and extension site make this university a convenient option for reentry students.

Degrees Offered

UNDERGRADUATE
B.S., Computer Information Systems (accelerated)
B.S., Computer Science

GRADUATE
M.S., Applied Computer Science and Technology

Approximate Cost of Degrees

UNDERGRADUATE
$53,200–$75,000

GRADUATE
$14,400

Admissions Guidelines

UNDERGRADUATE
High school diploma with 2.5 GPA

UNDERGRADUATE (ACCELERATED)
25+ years old, 60 hours transfer credit with 2.0 GPA, two years work experience

GRADUATE
Accredited bachelor's with 3.0 GPA

Undergraduate Programs

The accelerated B.S. in Computer Information Systems is an extremely nontraditional program designed for working adults. Sixty hours of prior coursework may be transferred into the program, and further credit can be earned immediately based on life experience. Remaining credit requirements are fulfilled through weekly classes and a required capstone project. Most students complete the program in about 15 months.

The traditional B.S. in Computer Science focuses on computer science theory and computer programming. Students in the program are required to undertake serious study in higher-level mathematics.

Graduate Programs

The M.S. in Applied Computer Science and Technology is designed for working professionals; classes usually meet weekly. Optional emphases are available in client/server technology, computer information systems, end-user support, software engineering, technical programming, and telecommunications. Students may choose to undertake a capstone project.

Other Programs

A Master of Education in Educational Technology degree is available; for more information, contact the program director at (626) 815-5480.

A B.S. in Management Information Systems is available through the accelerated model described above.

More Information

In addition to its main campus, Azusa Pacific University operates six satellite campuses in California (Menifee, Orange, San Bernardino, San Diego, Ventura, and Victorville).

Some distance-learning courses are offered through the Online APU program. For more information, contact the admissions office.

Contact Information

PHONE
(626) 969-3434 or (800) 825-5278

E-MAIL
Undergraduate admissions: krystal@apu.edu
Graduate school: Lisa Granillo (lgranill@apu.edu)
Accelerated programs: Krista Tice (ktice@apu.edu)
International students: Anita Gunadi (agunadi@apu.edu)

Ball State University   www.bsu.edu ☆☆

Muncie, IN 47306

Year established: 1965
Ownership: Public

This midsize state university offers nontraditional programs in computer, including a B.S. in Computer Science organized around work study and an M.S. in Computer Science that can be completed largely by distance learning.

Degrees Offered

UNDERGRADUATE
B.S., Computer Science

GRADUATE
M.S., Computer Science

Approximate Cost of Degrees

UNDERGRADUATE, RESIDENT
$31,800

UNDERGRADUATE, NONRESIDENT
$81,100

GRADUATE, RESIDENT
$8,000

GRADUATE, NONRESIDENT
$21,100

Admissions Guidelines

UNDERGRADUATE
High school diploma or equivalent

GRADUATE
Accredited bachelor's with 2.75 GPA (or 3.0 GPA on upper 60 hours)

Undergraduate Programs

The B.S. in Computer Science is available through four tracks: management information systems, physics and electronics, theory, and work-study. Students in the work-study program are paid for their internship.

Graduate Programs

The M.S. program in Computer Science can be completed almost entirely via distance learning; both thesis and non-thesis tracks are available.

Other Programs

A B.S. in Telecommunications is available; although the program is oriented toward radio and television, it does seem to have a significant information technology component. For more information, contact the College of Communication, Information and Media (CCIM) at (765) 285-6000.

An M.A. in Technology Education is available through the College of Applied Sciences and Technology. For more information, contact the Department of Industry and Technology at (765) 285-5642.

An M.B.A. with emphasis in information systems is available through the College of Business. The program can be completed on-site or through one of 65 off-campus locations.

More Information

Ball State University offers a variety of courses through off-campus extension, intensive courses, and distance learning. For more information, contact the School of Continuing Education and Public Service at (800) 872-0369.

Contact Information

PHONE
General information: (765) 289-1241
Admissions: (800) 482-4278
Computer science: (765) 289-1609

E-MAIL
General information: askbsu@bsu.edu
Admissions: askus@bsu.edu
Computer science: Bonita McVey (bmcvey@cs.bsu.edu)

Bellevue University

www.bellevue.edu ☆☆☆½

1000 Galvin Road South
Bellevue, NE 68005-3098

Year established: 1966
Ownership: Private

This midsize private university offers highly innovative programs in a range of fields related to information technology. The focus is predominantly business-oriented rather than technology-oriented. Several degrees may be completed online with no campus residency whatsoever.

Degrees Offered

UNDERGRADUATE
B.S., Business Information Systems
B.S., Computer Information Systems
B.S., E-Commerce

GRADUATE
M.S., Computer Information Systems

Approximate Cost of Degrees

UNDERGRADUATE
$22,500–$32,000

UNDERGRADUATE (ACCELERATED)
$9,300

GRADUATE
$9,400

Admissions Guidelines

UNDERGRADUATE
High school diploma or equivalent, SAT and/or ACT

UNDERGRADUATE (ACCELERATED)
60 hours college-level credit with 2.0 GPA

GRADUATE
Accredited bachelor's with 2.5 GPA on upper 60 hours. GRE required.

Undergraduate Programs

The B.S. in Business Information Systems is an accelerated program for students who have already completed 60 hours of college-level credit. It can be earned in as little as one year through coursework, credit by examination, and credit by life experience. Coursework requirements may be completed through online classes; no residency is required. Students may also choose to take evening and weekend residential courses offered at a variety of convenient locations throughout Nebraska and Iowa.

The B.S. in Computer Information Systems is available through a traditional four-year plan of study. Tracks are available in networking, software programming, and Web-based networking. Although this is an essentially traditional program, many courses may be completed online or through evening and weekend study.

Bellevue University also offers a 100 percent online B.S. in E-Commerce. An on-campus accelerated version of this program is currently under development.

Graduate Programs

The M.S. program in Computer Information Systems represents a sort of synthesis between computer science and management information systems; graduates of the program will have demonstrated competency in both fields. The program is designed for working adults and can be completed entirely through evening and weekend study.

Other Programs

B.A. and B.F.A. programs in Computer Graphic Design are available through a traditional four-year model. A concentration in Web-based graphic design is available.

A B.S. in Management Information Systems is offered under an accelerated arrangement similar to that of the B.S. program in Business Information Systems. They differ in that the Management Information Systems program involves business-related coursework and does not require any computer-related coursework beyond the 60 hours transferred into the program. As one might suspect, this means that the 60 hours transferred in must fulfill specific course prerequisites and satisfy the computer information systems component of the program. Like the B.S. in Business Information Systems, the B.S. in

Management Information Systems may be completed entirely through online classes.

The M.B.A. offered through the College of Business is available with two IT-related tracks: cyber law and management information systems.

More Information

Bellevue University offers a wide range of special programs and services to international students. For more information, e-mail intern@scholars.bellevue.edu.

Contact Information

Phone

General information: (402) 291-8100 or (800) 756-7920
Admissions office: (402) 293-3716 or (800) 756-7920, extension 3716

Accelerated programs: (402) 293-3711 or (800) 756-7920, extension 3711
Online programs: (402) 682-5069 or (800) 756-7920, extension 5069

Fax

General information: (402) 293-2020
Admissions office: (402) 293-3730
Online programs: (402) 682-5091

E-mail

Admissions office (IT programs): Glenda Masteller (grm@scholars.bellevue.edu)
Accelerated programs: Nancy King (npk@scholars.bellevue.edu)
Online programs: Kathy Consbruck (kathy@scholars.bellevue.edu)

Boise State University

www.boisestate.edu ☆☆☆

1910 University Drive
Boise, ID 83725

Year established: 1932
Ownership: Public

This midsize state university provides inexpensive programs in a variety of information technology fields. Evening classes, weekend study, and distance-learning options are available for reentry students.

Degrees Offered

Undergraduate

B.A.S., Computer Network Support Technology
B.A.S., Electronics Technology
(CSAB) B.S., Computer Science
(ABET) B.S., Electrical Engineering
B.S., Networking and Telecommunications

Graduate

M.S., Computer Science

Approximate Cost of Degrees

Undergraduate, Resident

$2,800–$18,000

Undergraduate, Nonresident

$4,800–$14,900

Graduate, Resident

$3,100–$5,000

Graduate, Nonresident

$5,000–$6,400

Admissions Guidelines

Undergraduate

High school diploma, ACT and/or SAT (unless over 21 and/or pursuing B.A.S.)

Graduate

Accredited bachelor's with 3.0 GPA, GRE usually required.

Undergraduate Programs

The B.A.S. is a most unusual program in that students are required to complete their major through an A.A.S. program in the field, then deal with broad distribution requirements at the upper level. This extremely vocational program seems to be designed primarily for reentry students and can be completed by evening classes.

The CSAB-accredited B.S. in Computer Science is a rather broad program that will provide students with a background in theory, software applications, and hardware suitable for graduate study.

The ABET-accredited B.S. in Electrical Engineering focuses largely on engineering science and on issues relevant to computer engineering.

The B.S. in Networking and Telecommunications is an interdisciplinary program focusing on issues in media technology and computer networking.

Graduate Programs

The 30-hour M.S. in Computer Science does not have established specializations, but students are encouraged to design their own plan of study based on generous free elective requirements. Students may choose a formal thesis or capstone project. A comprehensive examination is required.

Other Programs

The Division of Applied Technology offers additional B.A.S. programs in the following fields: accounting technology, administrative office technology, broadcast technology, business systems and computer technology, legal office technology, and marketing/management technology.

The College of Business offers a B.B.A. with optional concentrations in networking/telecommunications and computer information systems. For more information, contact the Department of

Computer Information Systems and Production Management at (208) 426-1181.

An M.Ed. with emphasis in educational technology is available. For more information, contact the Graduate College of Education at (208) 426-1731.

An M.S. in Instructional and Performance Technology is offered through the College of Engineering. The program can be completed on campus; a 100 percent online track is also available. For more information, contact the Department of Instructional and Performance Technology at (208) 426-1312.

Contact Information

PHONE
General information: (208) 426-1011
Admissions office: (208) 426-1820 or (800) 824-7017
Applied technology (B.A.S.): (208) 426-1431
Computer information systems: (208) 426-1181
Computer science: (208) 426-1172
Electrical engineering: (208) 426-4078

FAX
Applied technology (B.A.S.): (208) 426-3155
Computer information systems: (208) 426-1135
Computer science: (208) 426-1356
Electrical engineering: (208) 426-4800

E-MAIL
Admissions office: BSUinfo@boisestate.edu
Applied technology (B.A.S.): snarache@boisestate.edu
Computer information systems: cispomgen@boisestate.edu
Computer science: office@math-cs.boisestate.edu
Electrical engineering: cthrone@boisestate.edu

Boston University   www.bu.edu ☆☆☆

Office of Admissions
121 Bay State Road
Boston, MA 02215

Year established: 1869
Ownership: Private

This large private college addresses the needs of traditional students who desire an intensive, research-oriented background in computer engineering fields. It also effectively addresses the needs of nontraditional students who desire a convenient, management-oriented approach to information technology. Evening classes are available for all programs, and broader distance-learning options are currently being explored.

Degrees Offered

UNDERGRADUATE
B.S., Computer Science
🔲 B.S., Computer Systems Engineering
🔲 B.S., Electrical Engineering

GRADUATE
M.S., Computer Information Systems
M.S., Computer Science
M.S., Computer Systems Engineering
M.S., Electrical Engineering
M.S., Telecommunication
Ph.D., Computer Engineering
Ph.D., Electrical Engineering
Ph.D., Systems Engineering

Approximate Cost of Degrees

UNDERGRADUATE (ENGINEERING)
$95,100

UNDERGRADUATE (COMPUTER SCIENCE)
$28,800

MASTER'S (COMPUTER SCIENCE AND INFORMATION SYSTEMS, TELECOMMUNICATIONS)
$18,300

MASTER'S (ENGINEERING)
$35,700

DOCTORATE
$80,200

Admissions Guidelines

UNDERGRADUATE
High school diploma, SAT and/or ACT

GRADUATE
Accredited bachelor's

Undergraduate Programs

The B.S. program in Computer Science is offered through the Metropolitan College of Boston University, a vocationally oriented college established for reentry students. Coursework requirements are fulfilled by evening and weekend classes, and a few can even be completed via distance learning.

The ABET-accredited B.S. program in Computer Systems Engineering is an interdisciplinary program incorporating elements of computer engineering and systems engineering. The theoretical foundation for the program seems exceptionally strong, and the applied components of the program are broad and far-reaching.

The ABET-accredited B.S. program in Electrical Engineering uses the same basic pool of courses as the B.S. in Computer Systems Engineering, but differs in its major requirements. Like the B.S. in Computer Systems Engineering, the Electrical Engineering program seems to be designed primarily with full-time students in mind.

Graduate Programs

The M.S. programs in Computer Information Systems, Computer Science, and Telecommunications are offered through the Metropolitan College of Boston University. Evening classes, weekend study, and online courses are available, and a capstone project is required in each program. The M.S. in Computer Science is a largely software-oriented graduate-level computer science degree, while the M.S. in Computer Information Systems blends computer science with management information systems. The largely Internet-oriented M.S. in Telecommunication is very much a computer science degree that incorporates the disciplines of law, management, and technology.

The M.S. programs in Computer Systems Engineering and Electrical Engineering draw from a common pool of coursework, but differ in their distribution requirements. Both involve a research component, a student-defined specialization, and a capstone project.

Ph.D. programs in Computer Engineering, Electrical Engineering, and Systems Engineering are also available. The Ph.D. program in Computer Engineering is a broad degree that incorporates a significant amount of study in software engineering. The Ph.D. in Electrical Engineering is an extremely broad program incorporating a vast number of areas within the field. Although students are expected to specialize, breadth seems to be emphasized over depth. The Ph.D. program in Systems Engineering is an interdisciplinary program involving computer engineering, electrical engineering, and mechanical engineering. It is mainly oriented toward large, intelligent networks, robotics, control systems, and similarly integrative fields of study. All three programs require a considerable amount of supervised research and a dissertation or equivalent project.

Other Programs

B.F.A. and M.F.A. programs in Graphic Design are available. For more information, contact the School of the Arts at (617) 353-3350.

Contact Information

Phone

Admissions: (617) 353-2300
Metropolitan College: (617) 353-6000

Computer science: (617) 353-2566
Engineering: (617) 353-9760

Fax

Admissions: (617) 353-9695
Computer science: (617) 353-2367

E-mail

Admissions: admissions@bu.edu
Metropolitan College: met@bu.edu
Computer science: csinfo@bu.edu
Distance education: disted@bu.edu
Financial aid: finaid@bu.edu

Brigham Young University   www.byu.edu ★☆☆

Provo, UT 84602

Year established: 1875
Ownership: Private

This well-regarded private university offers an array of programs related to computer science and engineering. The undergraduate programs tend to have a strong theoretical bent, while the graduate programs allow vast room for student-specified focus. Evening classes, weekend study, extension sites, and distance learning are available.

Degrees Offered

Undergraduate

B.S., Computer Engineering
(CSAB) B.S., Computer Science
(ABET) B.S., Electrical Engineering
(ABET) B.S., Electronic(s) Engineering Technology

Graduate

M.S., Computer Science
M.S., Electrical Engineering
Ph.D., Computer Science
Ph.D., Electrical Engineering

Approximate Cost of Degrees

Undergraduate (LDS Church Members)

$11,800–$17,700

Undergraduate (Non-Members)

$17,700–$26,800

Master's (LDS Church Members)

$4,300–$6,200

Master's (Non-Members)

$6,500–$9,300

Doctorate (LDS Church Members)

$8,700–$12,700

Doctorate (Non-Members)

$15,600–$19,100

Admissions Guidelines

Undergraduate

High school diploma or equivalent. SAT and/or ACT recommended.

Graduate

Accredited bachelor's with 3.0 GPA, GRE (or GMAT) required

Undergraduate Programs

The hardware-oriented B.S. in Computer Engineering provides an extensive framework for further work and research in the field.

The CSAB-accredited B.S. in Computer Science is a broad, comprehensive program that emphasizes the theoretical foundations of the field.

The ABET-accredited B.S. in Electrical Engineering is primarily theory-based in its required courses. It provides students with generous opportunities for individualized specialization through its considerable base of upper-level free elective credit requirements. This program seems to be designed for dedicated students who have a solid idea in advance of which field they would like to study.

The ABET-accredited B.S. in Electronic(s) Engineering Technology includes an unusually strong computer information systems component.

Graduate Programs

The M.S. in Computer Science is a 30-hour program emphasizing the theoretical background and ramifications of the field. A thesis is required.

The M.S. in Electrical Engineering is a 30-hour program that requires students to design and submit an individualized plan of study. Any such plan of study must include a 9-hour specialization in computer engineering, electromagnetics, microelectronics and VLSI, or signals and systems. Students may undertake a thesis or non-thesis track.

The Ph.D. in Computer Science permits student-defined specialization through fairly generous free elective options. The program culminates in a dissertation. All students must also fulfill a teaching requirement.

The Ph.D. in Electrical Engineering is an individualized program structured in much the same manner as the M.S. in Electrical Engineering above. A dissertation is required. Students are also required to pass two examinations (an oral qualifying examination before submission of the dissertation prospectus, and a written comprehensive examination before advancement to candidacy).

More Information

The adjusted tuition for LDS church members should not be regarded as a exclusionary practice; the rationale for this discount is based on the practice of tithing. Brigham Young University welcomes qualified students of any creed provided that they are willing to abide by its nonsectarian campus code.

Contact Information

Phone

General information: (801) 378-4636
Admissions office: (801) 378-2507
Evening classes: (801) 378-2872
Distance learning: (801) 378-2868
Computer science: (801) 378-3027
Electrical and computer engineering: (801) 378-4012
Engineering and technology: (801) 378-4326

E-mail

Admissions office: admissions@byu.edu
Computer science: Jennifer Shadel (shadel@cs.byu.edu)
Electrical and computer engineering: Michelle Beus (mbeus@ee.byu.edu)
Electronic(s) engineering technology: Richard Helps (helpsr@byu.edu)

Brooklyn College

www.brooklyn.cuny.edu ☆☆

Office of Admissions
1201 Plaza Building
Brooklyn, NY 11210

Year established: 1930
Ownership: Public

As one of ten four-year colleges comprising the City University of New York, this large public university offers broad, interdisciplinary programs in several information technology fields. Some classes offered through the Computer and Information Science department may apply toward the CUNY Ph.D. in Computer Science. Evening classes, weekend study, and distance-learning courses are available.

Degrees Offered

UNDERGRADUATE
B.S., Computational Mathematics
B.S., Computer and Information Science

GRADUATE
M.A., Computer and Information Science
M.S., Information Systems

Approximate Cost of Degrees

UNDERGRADUATE, RESIDENT
$12,800–$16,200

UNDERGRADUATE, NONRESIDENT
$27,200–$36,500

MASTER'S, RESIDENT
$5,400–$7,000

MASTER'S, NONRESIDENT
$9,500–$12,200

DOCTORATE, RESIDENT
$6,500–$13,000

DOCTORATE, NONRESIDENT
$11,400–$22,400

Admissions Guidelines

UNDERGRADUATE
High school diploma required; SAT recommended

GRADUATE
Accredited bachelor's with 3.0 GPA;
GRE recommended

Undergraduate Programs
The interdisciplinary B.S. program in Computational Mathematics includes an exceptionally broad background in the natural and social sciences. Students may choose a computational or theoretical track.

Students in the B.S. program in Computer and Information Science may choose a track focusing on software issues or on computer engineering.

Graduate Programs
A 30-hour M.A. in Computer and Information Science is available; this seems to be a software-oriented rather than business-oriented program. Students may choose a thesis or non-thesis track; non-thesis track students must pass a comprehensive examination. A special preliminary "Group I" curriculum (consisting of intensive substitutes for undergraduate prerequisites) is available for students who do not possess an undergraduate degree in the field. Courses taken in this curriculum appear on the graduate transcript and are considered part of the earned degree, but do not apply toward the 30-hour core curriculum.

A computer-oriented 30-hour M.S. in Information Systems is available. As in the case of the M.A. in Computer and Information Science (see above), a "Group I" curriculum is available for those who lack the necessary undergraduate prerequisites. Students may choose a thesis or non-thesis track; non-thesis track students must pass a comprehensive examination.

Other Programs
Brooklyn College also offers a concurrent B.S. and M.P.S. in CIS/Economics designed for reentry students. No "direct track" to the M.P.S. seems to be available; students apply as undergraduates and complete both degree programs.

An interdisciplinary M.S. program in Computer Science and Health Science is available.

Some graduate-level courses offered through Brooklyn College's Department of Computer and Information Science may apply toward the City University of New York Ph.D. in Computer Science. For more information, contact the CUNY Graduate School and University Center at (212) 817-7000.

Contact Information

PHONE
General information: (718) 951-5000
Admissions office: (718) 951-5001
Computer and information science: (718) 951-5657

E-MAIL
adminqry@brooklyn.cuny.edu

Brown University

The College Admission Office
Box 1876
Providence, RI 02912

www.brown.edu ☆☆☆½

Year established: 1764
Ownership: Private

This large Ivy League university now offers a variety of nontraditional options for students, including evening classes and intensive summer sessions. Degrees are available at all levels.

Degrees Offered

Undergraduate
A.B., Computer Science
Sc.B., Computer Engineering
Sc.B., Computer Science
🔵 Sc.B., Electrical Engineering

Graduate
Sc.M., Computer Science
Sc.M., Electrical and Computer Engineering
Ph.D., Computer Science
Ph.D., Electrical and Computer Engineering

Approximate Cost of Degrees

Undergraduate
$97,300

Master's
$47,200

Doctorate
$103,900

Admissions Guidelines

Undergraduate
High school diploma, SAT and/or ACT

Graduate
Accredited bachelor's, GRE

Undergraduate Programs
The A.B. program in Computer Science is a broad program with a generous number of available free electives. Students must choose a two-course sequence (mild specialization) in artificial intelligence, software systems, systems, or theoretical computer science.

The Sc.B. in Computer Engineering is available with two concentrations: computers and multimedia signal processing.

The curriculum of the Sc.B. program in Computer Science has a slightly less theoretical focus than that of the A.B. program.

The ABET-accredited Sc.B. program in Electrical Engineering is one of the oldest of its kind in the country and, like most of Brown's programs, allows ample opportunity for student-directed specialization.

Graduate Programs
The Sc.M. in Computer Science focuses on applied computer science rather than theory. A project or thesis is required.

The Ph.D. in Computer Science focuses more or less equally in its course requirements on applied and theoretical computer science; students are encouraged to develop their own specializations using free electives. Qualifying examinations in programming and research method are required.

The highly flexible Sc.M. and Ph.D. programs in Electrical and Computer Engineering may be focused on one of the following two research tracks: computers, information, and systems (focusing on computer engineering, control systems, and multimedia signal processing) or solid-state and quantum electronics.

Other Programs
An Sc.B. in Computational Biology is also available through the Computer Science Department.

Contact Information

Phone
General information: (401) 863-1000
Admissions office: (401) 863-2378
Computer science: (401) 863-7600

Fax
Admissions office: (401) 863-9300
Computer science: (401) 863-7657
Engineering: (401) 863-2679

E-mail
Admissions: admissionundergraduate@brown.edu
Computer science: Kathy Kirman (kpk@cs.brown.edu)

Bucknell University   www.bucknell.edu ☆☆½

Lewisburg, PA 17837

Year established: 1846
Ownership: Private

This small, well-known liberal arts school offers programs in computer science and electrical engineering. Evening and distance-learning classes are available.

Degrees Offered

UNDERGRADUATE
B.A., Computer Science
CSAB B.S., Computer Science
B.S., Computer Science and Engineering
ABET B.S., Electrical Engineering

GRADUATE
M.S., Electrical Engineering

Approximate Cost of Degrees

UNDERGRADUATE
$95,900

GRADUATE
$47,900–$59,200

Admissions Guidelines

UNDERGRADUATE
High school diploma. GPA and test scores a factor.

GRADUATE
Accredited bachelor's with 2.8 GPA, GRE required

Undergraduate Programs

The CSAB-accredited B.S. in Computer Science is a straightforward undergraduate program with broad-based distribution requirements. The requirements for the B.A. are similar, but, as one might expect, involve a considerably larger liberal arts component.

The B.S. in Computer Science and Engineering blends applied course requirements from the computer science curriculum with hardware-relevant electrical engineering courses to present an inter-disciplinary curriculum resembling, in many respects, that of a computer engineering program.

Many of the required courses in computer science may be taken online, considerably reducing the time spent on campus.

The ABET-accredited B.S. in Electrical Engineering is a broad program; students are given virtually unlimited options for individualized specialization through broad free-elective requirements.

Graduate Programs

The M.S. program in Electrical Engineering is largely a research-oriented degree focusing on a capstone project (which may be an electrical engineering project or a formal thesis). Students generally form their coursework around the proposed topic, often integrating coursework and research from other departments (computer science, for instance) to augment the proposed plan of study.

More Information

Bucknell University offers need-based scholarships to a considerably large number of its students. For more information, contact the Office of Financial Aid at (570) 577-1331.

Contact Information

PHONE
General information: (570) 577-2000
Computer science and engineering: (570) 577-1394
Electrical engineering: (570) 577-1234

FAX
(570) 577-3760

E-MAIL
admissions@bucknell.edu

> ✴ **EXTRA!**
>
> Bucknell boasts one of the highest percentage of female engineering students in the country (24 percent of engineering majors at the university are female, compared to some 17 percent nationwide).

California Institute of Technology   www.caltech.edu ☆

1200 East California Boulevard
Pasadena, CA 91125

Year established: 1921
Ownership: Private

This major research institution offers considerable options to the traditionally minded graduate student and is beginning to branch out to better serve the needs of reentry students as well. Evening classes are available.

Degrees Offered

UNDERGRADUATE
B.S., Computer Science
 B.S., Electrical Engineering

GRADUATE
M.S., Electrical Engineering
Ph.D., Computation and Neural Systems
Ph.D., Computer Science
Ph.D., Electrical Engineering

Approximate Cost of Degrees

UNDERGRADUATE
$74,400

MASTER'S
$27,900

DOCTORATE
$65,100

Admissions Guidelines

UNDERGRADUATE
High school diploma, SAT required

GRADUATE
Accredited bachelor's, GRE required

Undergraduate Programs

The B.S. in Computer Science is, as you might expect, heavily research-oriented. Students are given a number of opportunities to participate in hands-on, active work in the field.

The ABET-accredited B.S. in Electrical Engineering is strongly theory-oriented. Students are given a rigorous education in the fundamentals of electrical engineering as a scientific discipline. Student-designed specializations may, with faculty approval, be an option.

Graduate Programs

The M.S. in Electrical Engineering is an intensive program well-anchored in the theoretical bases of the discipline. A thesis is required. Concentrations are available in communications and signal processing, computer engineering, control systems, electronic circuits, microwave and radio engineering, optoelectronics, and solid-state electronics. Students may also design their own concentrations with faculty approval.

The Ph.D. in Computation and Neural Systems represents an interdisciplinary study of computer networking, artificial intelligence, and cognitive science. Three 12-week laboratory rotations are required during the first year of the program. Students are required to define a specific, faculty-approved concentration related to the required dissertation.

Students who want to undertake the Ph.D. in Computer Science, but who have not already earned an acceptable M.S. in the field, may apply to the M.S. program and upgrade to the Ph.D. program upon completing all requirements (including a thesis). The Ph.D. program requires an oral comprehensive examination in addition to the dissertation. A minor in applied computation is available. It is extremely likely that Ph.D. students will be expected to participate in Cal Tech's innovative research projects.

The Ph.D. in Electrical Engineering involves 18 hours of graduate-level mathematics courses in addition to the required courses in electrical engineering. An oral comprehensive examination is required in addition to the standard dissertation. Concentrations are available in communications and signal processing, computer engineering, control systems, electronic circuits, microwave and radio engineering, optoelectronics, and solid-state electronics. Students may also design their own concentrations with faculty approval.

Contact Information

PHONE
General information: (626) 395-6811
Computer science: (626) 395-6244
Engineering: (626) 395-4104

FAX
Computer science: (626) 792-4257
Engineering: (626) 585-1729

★ EXTRA!

U.S. News and World Report voted Cal Tech the top national university in America for 2000.

California Polytechnic State University   www.calpoly.edu ☆☆☆½

Admissions Office
San Luis Obispo, CA 93407

Year established: 1942
Ownership: Public

This large, reputable state university offers undergraduate and graduate programs in computer engineering, computer science, and electrical engineering. The academic philosophy at this fine institution is "learn by doing," so all programs are extremely hands-on and focus more on application than theory. Evening classes and extension programs are available.

Degrees Offered

UNDERGRADUATE
B.S., Computer Engineering
 B.S., Computer Science
B.S., Electrical Engineering

GRADUATE
M.S., Computer Science
M.S., Electrical Engineering

Approximate Cost of Degrees

UNDERGRADUATE, RESIDENT (U.S. CITIZEN)
$6,400–$21,300

Undergraduate, Nonresident (U.S. Citizen)
$35,900–$100,100

Undergraduate, International
$29,000–$88,600

Graduate, Resident (U.S. Citizen)
$2,100–$11,700

Graduate, Nonresident (U.S. Citizen)
$11,000–$26,500

Graduate, International
$9,700–$22,200

Admissions Guidelines

Undergraduate
High school diploma recommended, ACT and/or SAT required

Graduate
Accredited bachelor's with 2.5 GPA on upper 60 hours, GRE required

Undergraduate Programs

The B.S. in Computer Engineering supports a broad, general background in the field. It seems that no specializations are offered as such, but that all aspects of computer engineering (computer architecture, digital system design, and so forth) are covered to some extent.

The B.S. program in Computer Science (accredited by both the CSAB and CSAC) is very oriented toward applied computer science. Hardware is emphasized slightly more than one would expect in a general computer science curriculum, the remainder of the major requirements focusing on programming and networking issues. This is not to say that the theoretical background is missing completely, of course, but it clearly takes a back seat in this rigorous, hands-on program.

The ABET-accredited B.S. in Electrical Engineering does allow some room for specialization in that students are given a large number of options with regard to upper-level electives. Students are also

required to choose one of two formal specializations: electronics or power systems.

Graduate Programs

The M.S. in Computer Science is a 45-quarter-hour (30-hour) program with required hands-on work in a variety of fields, most of them related to programming, database work, networking, and artificial intelligence. A thesis is required.

The M.S. in Electrical Engineering is a broad, hands-on program with generous opportunities for student specialization through broad elective credit requirements. Students must complete a capstone project and examination.

Other Programs

A Web-oriented B.S. in Graphic Communication is available. For more information, contact the Graphic Communications Department at (805) 756-1108.

More Information

Although Cal Poly welcomes international students, non–U.S. citizens are not eligible for financial aid.

Cal Poly offers diverse nontraditional options for adult students. For more information, contact the Extended Education Division at (805) 756-2053.

Contact Information

Phone
General information: (805) 756-1111
Financial aid: (805) 756-2927
Computer engineering: (805) 756-1229
Computer science: (805) 756-2824
Electrical engineering: (805) 756-2781

E-mail
Admissions office: admissions@calpoly.edu
Financial aid: financialaid@calpoly.edu
Computer engineering: cpeprogram@calpoly.edu
Computer science: computer-science@calpoly.edu
Electrical engineering: eedept@calpoly.edu

California State University—Chico   www.csuchico.edu ☆☆½

400 West First Street
Chico, CA 95929

Year established: 1887
Ownership: Public

This midsize state university offers residential programs at the undergraduate and graduate level in computer science, computer information systems, computer engineering, and electrical engineering. Online and evening classes are available.

Degrees Offered

UNDERGRADUATE
🅐 B.S., Computer Engineering
B.S., Computer Information Systems
🅒 B.S., Computer Science
🅐 B.S., Electrical/Electronic Engineering

GRADUATE
M.S., Computer Science
M.S., Electrical Engineering

Approximate Cost of Degrees

UNDERGRADUATE, RESIDENT
$7,000–$27,900

UNDERGRADUATE, NONRESIDENT
$36,500–$57,400

GRADUATE, RESIDENT
$2,100–$8,700

GRADUATE, NONRESIDENT
$9,500–$17,000

Admissions Guidelines

UNDERGRADUATE
High school diploma or equivalent, ACT and/or SAT

GRADUATE
Regionally accredited bachelor's, 2.75 on upper 60 hours (3.00 on upper 30)

Undergraduate Programs

The ABET-accredited B.S. in Computer Engineering is offered with three optional specializations: computer systems design, robotics and controls, and systems engineering.

The B.S. in Computer Information Systems seems to be largely oriented toward networking, artificial intelligence, and database management. It appears to be far less OS-specific than most CIS programs.

A CSAB-accredited B.S. in Computer Science is offered. Students must choose one of three tracks: general, math/science, or systems. The math/science track is the most theoretical by far, while the systems track is the most practical; the general track can safely be described as a sort of middle ground. Students who intend to pursue a graduate-level program in the field would probably be best served by the general track. Employees of participating corporations may complete this program entirely by distance learning.

The ABET-accredited B.S. in Electrical/Electronic Engineering is available with five optional patterns of specialization: communications, control systems, digital signal processing, digital systems, and electro-optics. Students who elect to pursue a pattern of specialization must undertake two to four courses and a senior project in the appropriate field.

Graduate Programs

The M.S. program in Computer Science is a 30-hour program. Students may choose to undertake either a thesis or a project as a capstone work. Students are required to fulfill a depth requirement by focusing on one of nine fields: artificial intelligence and expert systems, computer architecture, computer theory, data and file structures, graphics and image processing, operating systems/networks, programming languages and theory, simulation and mathematical computation, or software engineering/systems analysis. Employees of participating corporations may complete this program entirely by distance learning.

The M.S. in Electrical Engineering is a 30-hour program with thesis and non-thesis tracks. Students who undertake the non-thesis track must pass a comprehensive examination at the end of the program. Optional patterns of specialization are available in communication systems, control systems, digital signal processing, and digital systems.

Other Programs

A B.S. in Business Administration (emphasis management information systems) and an M.B.A. (emphasis management information systems) are available. For more information, contact the Department of Accounting and Management Information Systems at (530) 898-6463.

B.S. and M.S. programs in Instructional Technology are available. Students may pursue a B.A. in Communication Design with an emphasis in information and communication systems. For more information on these programs, contact the Department of Communication Design at (530) 898-4048.

An M.A. in Information and Communication Studies is also offered. For more information, contact the Department of Communication Arts and Sciences at (530) 898-5751.

Contact Information

PHONE
General information: (530) 898-4636
Admissions: (530) 898-4428 or (800) 542-4426
Financial aid: (530) 898-6451
Computer science: (530) 898-6442
Electrical and computer engineering: (530) 898-5343

FAX
Admissions: (530) 898-6456
Financial aid: (530) 898-6883
Electrical and computer engineering: (530) 898-4956

E-MAIL
Admissions: info@csuchico.edu
Financial aid: finaid@csuchico.edu
Engineering, computer science, and technology: help@ecst.csuchico.edu

---

California State University—Sacramento   www.csus.edu ☆☆☆

6000 J Street
Sacramento, CA 95819

Year established: 1948
Ownership: Public

Dubbed "the capital university," this midsize public university offers undergraduate programs in computer engineering, computer science, and electrical/electronic engineering. Graduate programs are offered in computer science, electrical/electronic engineering, and software engineering. Night classes are offered, a large extension program has been established, and special benefits are available for mature students.

Degrees Offered

UNDERGRADUATE
B.S., Computer Engineering
CSAB B.S., Computer Science
ABET B.S., Electrical and Electronic Engineering

GRADUATE
M.S., Computer Science
M.S., Electrical and Electronic Engineering
M.S., Software Engineering

Approximate Cost of Degrees

UNDERGRADUATE, RESIDENT
$5,700–$16,600

UNDERGRADUATE, NONRESIDENT
$34,700–$48,100

GRADUATE, RESIDENT
$2,000–$7,900

GRADUATE, NONRESIDENT
$9,300–$16,800

Admissions Guidelines

UNDERGRADUATE
High school diploma with 2.0 GPA

GRADUATE
Accredited bachelor's with 2.5 GPA on upper 60 hours, GRE required

Undergraduate Programs
The B.S. program in Computer Engineering is a broad, hands-on program with no formal specializations. The program seems to be largely oriented toward RISC systems; courses in VLSI and UNIX C play an integral role in the curriculum.

The CSAB-accredited B.S. program in Computer Science is broad, giving a great deal of background in the general sciences. The computer science requirements themselves seem to be slightly less hardware-oriented than one might expect, although there is a strong focus on programming and operating systems.

The ABET-accredited B.S. in Electrical and Electronic Engineering is offered with four possible areas of emphasis: analog and digital electronics, communication engineering, control systems, and power engineering.

Graduate Programs
The M.S. program in Computer Science emphasizes breadth rather than depth, covering a wide variety of specific areas within the field. A culminating thesis or capstone project is required. In some cases, students who have completed their bachelor's less than seven years prior to enrollment may be able to use some of their undergraduate credit in lieu of specific core graduate courses.

The M.S. program in Electrical and Electronic Engineering is offered with four possible areas of specialization: computer engineering, intelligent machines/robotics and controls, power engineering, and a broad specialization encompassing microwaves, circuits, devices, communications, and signals. As the required final project, students may choose to undertake a traditional thesis, a capstone project, or a comprehensive examination.

The M.S. program in Software Engineering seems to focus on hardware-software interaction and to have a stronger theory component than most programs in the field. A culminating thesis or capstone project is required. As in the case of the M.S. in Computer Science, students who have completed their bachelor's less than seven years prior to enrollment may be able to use some of their undergraduate credit in lieu of specific core graduate courses.

Other Programs
An M.B.A., with optional concentrations in management computer applications and management information systems, is available. For more information, contact the Office of Graduate Programs for the College of Business at (916) 278-6772.

More Information
Credit is available through a variety of residential, but nontraditional, means. For more information, contact the Office of Regional and Continuing Education at (916) 278-4433.

California State University at Sacramento offers a variety of benefits to its adult students: students age 25 and older fall under the Mature Admission Policy and need not have a 2.0 high school GPA, students 60 and older are eligible for a reduced rate, and specific scholarships are set aside for reentry students. For more information, contact the Office of Reentry Services at (916) 278-6750.

Contact Information

PHONE
General information: (916) 278-6011
Computer engineering: (916) 278-6834
Computer science: (916) 278-6834
Electrical and electronic engineering: (916) 278-6873

FAX
Computer science: (916) 278-6774
Engineering: (916) 278-5949

E-MAIL
Admissions: admissions@csus.edu
Financial aid: finaid@csus.edu
Graduate studies: gradctr@csus.edu
Computer engineering: Ronald Becker (rbecker@csus.edu)
Computer science: cscadv@gaia.ecs.csus.edu
Electrical and electronic engineering: Shelley Hedberg (hedbergs@ecs.csus.edu)

Carnegie Mellon University   www.cmu.edu ☆☆☆

5000 Forbes Avenue
Pittsburgh, PA 15213

Year established: 1967
Ownership: Private

This large, prestigious private university is particularly well known for its programs in computer science. With its stunning assortment of research-oriented on-campus options in innovative, cutting-edge technology fields, and an impressive foray into the world of distance learning, this research-oriented institution is far from stagnant.

Degrees Offered

UNDERGRADUATE
B.S., Computer Science
🅰 B.S., Electrical and Computer Engineering
B.S., Human-Computer Interaction

GRADUATE
M.H.C.I.
M.S.E.
M.S.I.T.
M.S., E-Commerce
M.S., Electrical and Computer Engineering
M.S., Knowledge Discovery and Data Mining
M.S., Language Technologies
Ph.D., Algorithms, Combinatorics, and Optimization
Ph.D., Computer Science
Ph.D., Electrical and Computer Engineering
Ph.D., Human-Computer Interaction
Ph.D., Language Technologies
Ph.D., Pure and Applied Logic

Approximate Cost of Degrees

UNDERGRADUATE
$170,200

MASTER'S
$42,600–$75,400

DOCTORATE
$127,700–$226,200

Admissions Guidelines

UNDERGRADUATE
High school diploma, SAT and/or ACT. SAT II subject tests are often required.

GRADUATE
Accredited bachelor's. Work experience and/or prerequisite knowledge usually expected.

Undergraduate Programs
The B.S. program in Computer Science is not itself specialized, but offers so many possible courses for elective credit that a number of very detailed, faculty-led individualized concentrations can be developed. Suggested concentrations range from graphics and virtual reality to scientific computing.

Students in the ABET-accredited B.S. program in Electrical and Computer Engineering choose one of five specializations: applied physics, signals and systems, circuits, computer hardware, or computer software. A capstone project is required.

The B.S. in Human-Computer Interaction can probably be described as an interdisciplinary program focusing on the overlap between computer science and human factors psychology. Two questions seem to dominate the field: the first is "How can we improve, as users, to make full use of computer technology?", and the second is "How can we modify computer technology to better serve us?" Subjects addressed in this program range from aesthetics to high-level programming. Students are required to undertake a capstone project.

Graduate Programs
The Master of Human-Computer Interaction (M.H.C.I.) degree is a largely professional, ten-course program that culminates in an original team project.

The Master of Software Engineering (M.S.E.) offers optional tracks in the economic and organizational environment of software systems, human-computer interaction, management of the software process, and real-time systems; students may also choose to undertake an individualized specialization. Participation in a team software system is offered as a capstone project. This program may be completed entirely through corporate-sponsored extension classes, and most of its core courses may be taken by distance learning as part of the online Certificate of Software Engineering (CSE) program.

The Master of Software Information Technology (M.S.I.T.) is a new program designed by the Software Engineering Institute with reentry students specifically in mind; both software engineering and applications are addressed. This program can be completed entirely by distance learning.

The M.S. in Electrical and Computer Engineering is a broad program offering a great deal of opportunity for faculty-led student specialization through broad elective credit requirements. A final project is required.

The M.S. in E-Commerce is a one-year program administered jointly by the School of Computer Science and the Graduate School of Industrial Administration.

The M.S. in Knowledge Discovery and Data Mining, offered by the Center for Automated Learning and Discovery (CALD), deals with computational linguistics, statistical modeling, and related fields. The field itself can probably be described as a theoretical approach to databases and their use. Students generally undertake a capstone project.

The M.S. in Language Technologies is an exciting, innovative program focusing on issues of computational linguistics. Research may culminate in a thesis if the student wants, but the general orientation of the M.S. is professional.

The Ph.D. in Algorithms, Combinatorics, and Optimization is administered jointly by the Computer Science Department, the Department of Mathematical Sciences, and the Graduate School of Industrial Administration. The field itself seems to represent a scholarly overlap between discrete mathematics and certain theoretical, highly abstract fundamentals of computer science.

Students undertaking the Ph.D. program in Computer Science generally focus their studies on the proposed doctoral thesis topic. Much of the program involves intensive full-time research rather than coursework.

The Ph.D. in Electrical and Computer Engineering deals, through its considerable breadth requirements, with the field as a whole. A doctoral thesis (dissertation) and comprehensive examination are required. Under certain circumstances, a promising student

with a B.S. in Electrical and Computer Engineering may proceed directly to the Ph.D. program.

The Ph.D. in Human-Computer Interaction is available in three tracks: computer science, design, and human sciences. The program involves a great deal of supervised research and a teaching requirement.

The Ph.D. program in Language Technologies is a research-oriented program focusing on computational linguistics and related fields. Students are required to undertake supervised research and to submit a doctoral thesis.

The Ph.D. in Pure and Applied Logic is administered jointly by the School of Computer Science, the Department of Mathematical Sciences, and the Department of Philosophy. In its pure logic component, it seems to deal primarily with issues involving symbolic/mathematical logic (geometry applied to philosophy or vice versa). In computer programming, an enviable opportunity presents itself in that symbolic logic can finally be, to some extent, applied; its implications can finally be studied in a semi-concrete fashion.

Other Programs

A partially Web-focused Master of Design (M.Des.) in Communication Planning and Design is available. For more information, contact the School of Design at (412) 268-2828.

A Master of Entertainment Technology, which can be tailored to a great extent to meet the needs of computer game designers, is available through the Information Technology Center. For more information, call (412) 268-8741.

A Master of Information Science Management (M.I.S.M.) is available. Although oriented toward business leadership, it seems to be far, far more CIS-oriented than the average program in management information systems. For more information, call (412) 268-4720 or (888) 634-9604.

A 16-month M.S. in Information Networking, integrating issues of computer science, electrical engineering, business, and telecommunications, is available. For more information, contact the Information Networking Institute at (412) 268-7195.

M.S. and Ph.D. programs in Robotics are also available. For more information, contact the Robotics Institute at (412) 268-3818.

More Information

Carnegie Mellon offers a wide variety of nontraditional class arrangements. For example, a graduate certificate in Software Engineering—comprising the core curriculum of the M.S.E. program—can be completed 100 percent nonresidentially. For more information, contact the Admissions Office.

Contact Information

PHONE

General information: (412) 268-2000
Computer science: (412) 268-2565

Electrical and computer engineering: (412) 268-2454
Human-computer interaction: (412) 268-6943
Knowledge discovery and data mining: (412) 268-1299
Language technologies: (412) 268-2623

E-MAIL

Computer science: scs@cs.cmu.edu
Human-computer interaction: HCII-masters@cs.cmu.edu
Knowledge discovery and data mining: cald@cs.cmu.edu
Language technologies: ltp@cs.cmu.edu

✴ **EXTRA!**

CMU was voted "Most Wired University" by Yahoo! Internet Life.

Case Western Reserve University　　www.cwru.edu ☆☆☆½

10900 Euclid Avenue
Cleveland, OH 44106

Year established: 1967
Ownership: Private

This private, research-oriented university offers a number of engineering-oriented programs in information technology fields. Evening classes, summer intensives, and on-site corporate classes are available. Still, the vast majority of CWRU's graduate programs seem to be oriented toward full-time study and research.

Degrees Offered

UNDERGRADUATE

B.A., Computer Science
B.S., Computer Science
 B.S.E., Computer Engineering
 B.S.E., Electrical Engineering
 B.S.E., Systems and Control Engineering

GRADUATE

M.S., Computer Engineering
M.S., Computing and Information Science
M.S., Electrical Engineering
M.S., Systems and Control Engineering
Ph.D., Computer Engineering
Ph.D., Computing and Information Science
Ph.D., Electrical Engineering
Ph.D., Systems and Control Engineering

Approximate Cost of Degrees

UNDERGRADUATE
$83,300

MASTER'S
$31,300

DOCTORATE
$62,500

Admissions Guidelines

UNDERGRADUATE
High school diploma, SAT and/or ACT

GRADUATE
Accredited bachelor's

Undergraduate Programs

While the B.A. in Computer Science has a fairly light major and gives the student a broad background in the liberal arts, the B.S. in Computer Science has a slightly more stringent major and less broad non-major distribution requirements.

The ABET-accredited B.S.E. in Computer Engineering is an interdisciplinary engineering program that places a great deal of emphasis on those principles of electrical and systems engineering most applicable toward computer engineering.

The ABET-accredited B.S.E. in Electrical Engineering provides options for interdisciplinary, student-defined specializations such as robotics and VLSI.

The ABET-accredited B.S.E. in Systems and Control Engineering provides options for interdisciplinary, student-defined specializations as well.

Graduate Programs

The M.S. in Computer and Information Science is theory-oriented, although students are also given a strong background in operating systems, programming, and application development. A capstone project is required.

The M.S. programs in Computer Engineering, Electrical Engineering, and Systems and Control Engineering are broad in their coursework requirements, but student specialization is encouraged through the use of free electives. A capstone project is required in all three programs.

The Ph.D. programs in Computer and Information Science, Computer Engineering, Electrical Engineering, and Systems and Control Engineering are all strongly research-oriented degrees patterned around the required dissertation.

Other Programs

A general Master of Engineering is available via on-site distance learning (offered through workplaces and other decentralized non-campus locations). For more information, contact the Executive Director of Professional Programs and Distance Learning at (216) 368-0598.

A Ph.D. in Management Information and Decision Sciences is also available; for more information, contact the Weatherhead School of Management at (216) 368-2030.

Contact Information

PHONE
General information: (216) 368-2000
Electrical/computer engineering and CIS:
(216) 368-2800

E-MAIL
Admissions (undergraduate):
admission@po.cwru.edu
Admissions (graduate): gradadmit@po.cwru.edu
Electrical/computer engineering and CIS: Robert V. Edwards (rve2@po.cwru.edu)

Central Michigan University   www.cmich.edu ☆☆☆☆

Admissions Office
Warriner Hall 102
Mount Pleasant, MI 48859

Year established: 1892
Ownership: Public

This midsize state university offers a variety of options to both traditional and nontraditional students in computer science and related fields. We are particularly impressed with the wide range of undergraduate options related directly and peripherally to information technology. Evening classes and distance-learning courses are available.

Degrees Offered

UNDERGRADUATE
B.S., Cognitive Science
B.S., Computer-Aided Manufacturing
B.S., Computer Science
B.S., Computer Technology
B.S., Electronic(s) Engineering Technology

GRADUATE
M.S., Computer Science

Approximate Cost of Degrees

UNDERGRADUATE, RESIDENT
$12,600

UNDERGRADUATE, NONRESIDENT
$37,200

GRADUATE, RESIDENT
$5,200

GRADUATE, NONRESIDENT
$10,300

Admissions Guidelines

UNDERGRADUATE
High school diploma required, ACT and/or SAT recommended

GRADUATE
Accredited bachelor's with 2.5 GPA on upper 60 hours

Undergraduate Programs
The B.S. in Computer Science is a broad program with a primary focus on software and theory. A special track is available for those who want to teach computer science in secondary schools.

The B.S. in Cognitive Science is an interdisciplinary program dealing, in its core, with issues of artificial intelligence and cognitive neural systems.

The B.S. in Computer-Aided Manufacturing is available with a computer-aided design (CAD) track.

The B.S. in Computer Technology is essentially a computer engineering program, but contains a unique component dealing with the long-term environmental effects of computer technology.

The B.S. program in Electronic(s) Engineering Technology involves study of programming, hardware design, computer-aided design (CAD), and manufacturing. Emphases are available in manufacturing engineering technology and mechanical engineering technology.

Graduate Programs
The M.S. in Computer Science is a broad program giving a comprehensive background in the field and opportunity for student specialization through free electives. Thesis and non-thesis tracks are available.

Other Programs
B.S. programs are also offered in Accounting Information Systems, Hospitality Information Systems, Management Information Systems, and Office Systems Administration. For more information, contact the Department of Business Information Systems at (517) 774-3554.

An M.A. in Educational Technology is also available. For more information, contact the Department of Teacher Education and Professional Development at (517) 774-3975.

A management-oriented M.S. in Information Systems, which involves a significant information technology component, is available. For more information, contact the Information Systems office at (517) 774-1910.

Contact Information

PHONE
General information: (517) 774-4000
Admissions: (517) 774-3076
Computer science: (517) 774-4418

FAX
Computer science: (517) 774-3728

E-MAIL
Admissions: cmuadmit@cmich.edu
Computer science: Gongzhu Hu (hu@cps.cmich.edu)

Charter Oak State College   www.cosc.edu ☆½

66 Cedar Street
Newington, CT 06111-2646

Year established: 1973
Ownership: Public

This college, the external degree program of the state of Connecticut, offers perhaps the quickest and least expensive way to earn an accredited bachelor's in an information technology field. All programs through this institution are completed 100 percent off-campus. Students may incorporate credit earned through traditional learning, undertake Charter Oak State's own distance-learning courses, or take advantage of a variety of other options (see below).

Degrees Offered

UNDERGRADUATE
B.A.G.S., emphasis Computer Science
B.S.G.S., emphasis Computer Science

Approximate Cost of Degrees

UNDERGRADUATE, RESIDENT
$1,300 and up

UNDERGRADUATE, NONRESIDENT
$1,500 and up

Admissions Guidelines

UNDERGRADUATE
Age 16 or older, 9 hours of college-level credit already earned

Undergraduate Programs

The B.A. in General Studies (B.A.G.S.) and B.S. in General Studies (B.S.G.S.) are earned 100 percent via distance learning. Students may take advantage of distance-learning courses offered by Charter Oak State, undertake contract learning with a Charter Oak State instructor, transfer in an unlimited number of courses (earned residentially or via distance learning) from any regionally accredited institu-

tions of higher learning, incorporate professional or military training, earn credit via examinations (CLEP, DANTES, and subject GREs), and evaluate prior life experience for credit.

The Computer Science emphasis *does not appear on the diploma*. It is, however, a fairly rigorous 30-hour template of required credit distribution that is functionally equivalent to a major. The emphasis of a B.A.G.S. or B.S.G.S. is stated on the transcript.

Other Programs

A General Studies concentration in Technology and Management is also available. Furthermore, students may (with faculty approval) design an individualized concentration in virtually any information technology field.

Contact Information

PHONE
(860) 666-4595

FAX
(860) 666-4852

E-MAIL
info@cosc.edu

Christopher Newport University   www.cnu.edu ☆☆☆½

1 University Place
Newport News, VA 23606

Year established: 1976
Ownership: Public

Formerly a campus of the College of William and Mary, this midsize public university offers several unique information technology programs. Evening classes, distance learning, and extension classes are available.

Degrees Offered

UNDERGRADUATE
🔲 B.S., Computer Engineering
B.S., Computer Science

GRADUATE
M.S., Applied Physics and Computer Science

Approximate Cost of Degrees

UNDERGRADUATE, RESIDENT
$12,000–$15,100

UNDERGRADUATE, NONRESIDENT
$35,100–$43,900

GRADUATE, RESIDENT
$4,500

GRADUATE, NONRESIDENT
$13,200

Admissions Guidelines

UNDERGRADUATE
High school diploma, SAT and/or ACT

GRADUATE
Accredited bachelor's with 3.0 GPA in major, GRE required

Undergraduate Programs

The ABET-accredited B.S. program in Computer Engineering gives a broad, formal background, which would provide suitable preparation for graduate study in the field.

The B.S. in Computer Science is available with an optional teacher certification track.

Graduate Programs

The M.S. in Applied Physics and Computer Science is a powerful, interdisciplinary 30-hour program emphasizing overlapping aspects of both fields. Students must specialize in computer science, instrumentation and advanced computer systems, modeling and simulation, and solid-state systems. The curriculum involves a final thesis/project and oral comprehensive examination.

Other Programs

A B.S. in Information Science is also available through the Department of Computer Science and Technology.

Contact Information

PHONE
General information: (757) 594-7000
Admissions: (757) 594-7015 or (800) 333-4268
Computer science/technology: (757) 594-7065

FAX
Admissions: (757) 594-7333

E-MAIL
admit@cnu.edu

Clemson University   www.clemson.edu ☆☆½

School of Engineering and Science
Clemson, SC 29634-5124

Year established: 1889
Ownership: Public

This highly respected, research-oriented institution offers an array of highly structured programs in information technology fields. Evening classes and distance-learning courses are available.

Degrees Offered

UNDERGRADUATE
B.A., Computer Science
CSAB B.S., Computer Science
ABET B.S., Computer Engineering
B.S., Computer Information Systems
ABET B.S., Electrical Engineering

GRADUATE
M.Eng., Electrical Engineering
M.S., Computer Engineering
M.S., Computer Science
M.S., Electrical Engineering
Ph.D., Computer Engineering
Ph.D., Computer Science
Ph.D., Electrical Engineering

Approximate Cost of Degrees

UNDERGRADUATE, RESIDENT
$13,900

UNDERGRADUATE, NONRESIDENT
$37,800

MASTER'S, RESIDENT
$5,200

MASTER'S, NONRESIDENT
$14,200

DOCTORATE, RESIDENT
$12,200

DOCTORATE, NONRESIDENT
$33,100

Admissions Guidelines

UNDERGRADUATE
High school diploma, SAT and/or ACT

GRADUATE
Accredited bachelor's, GRE required

Undergraduate Programs
The B.A. program in Computer Science seems to essentially be a liberal arts degree with a significant computer science concentration.

The ABET-accredited B.S. program in Computer Engineering gives students a broad background in the field.

The B.S. in Computer Information Systems is a business-oriented degree, although it still gives students a fairly strong information technology background.

The CSAB-accredited B.S. in Computer Science gives a broad, strong background in computer science. It is rather unique in that students are also required to choose a 12-hour application emphasis in a non-technical field (such as accounting or decision science).

The ABET-accredited B.S. program in Electrical Engineering is a structured, focused curriculum.

Graduate Programs
The M.S. programs in Computer Engineering, Computer Science, and Electrical Engineering are broad, 36-hour programs. Each student may choose one of three tracks: thesis, research paper, or non-thesis. Students in all tracks must pass an exit examination of some kind. Students in the Computer Engineering and Electrical Engineering programs must also choose a specialization from among the following: communications/digital signal processing, computer communications, computer systems architecture, control/robotics, electromagnetics, electronics, or power.

The Master of Engineering (M.Eng.) in Electrical Engineering is a professional program designed primarily for reentry students. No thesis is required.

The Ph.D. programs in Computer Engineering, Computer Science, and Electrical Engineering each incorporate a qualifying examination, teaching requirement, and final comprehensive examination in addition to the standard required dissertation.

Other Programs
An interdisciplinary M.F.A. in Fine Arts in Computing is also available. For more information, contact the Department of Computer Science at (864) 656-5868.

Contact Information

PHONE
Admissions: (864) 656-2287
Computer science: (864) 656-5868
Electrical and computer engineering: (864) 656-5900

E-MAIL
Admissions: cuadmissions@clemson.edu
Graduate school: graduateschool@clemson.edu

Cleveland State University   www.csuohio.edu ☆☆☆

1983 East 24th Street
Cleveland, OH 44115

Year established: 1964
Ownership: Public

This large state university offers residential programs in CIS and electrical/computer engineering at the undergraduate and graduate levels. Evening classes are available.

Degrees Offered

UNDERGRADUATE
🅰🅱🅴🆃 B.E.E.
B.S., Computer and Information Science
🅰🅱🅴🆃 B.S., Electronic(s) Engineering Technology
("2+2" program)

GRADUATE
M.C.I.S.
M.S., Electrical Engineering
D.E. (emphasis Electrical and Computer Engineering)

Approximate Cost of Degrees

UNDERGRADUATE, RESIDENT
$19,300

UNDERGRADUATE, NONRESIDENT
$38,000

MASTER'S, RESIDENT
$7,700

MASTER'S, NONRESIDENT
$15,300

DOCTORATE, RESIDENT
$12,900

DOCTORATE, NONRESIDENT
$25,500

Admissions Guidelines

UNDERGRADUATE
High school diploma or equivalent, ACT and/or SAT

GRADUATE
Accredited bachelor's and GRE (or GMAT, as appropriate)

Undergraduate Programs

The ABET-accredited Bachelor of Electrical Engineering is offered with two possible tracks: general and computer engineering. The general track is essentially a traditional, hands-on program in electrical engineering. In sharp contrast to many emphasis tracks in computer engineering, which sometimes merely require the student to replace several electrical engineering courses with upper-level hardware-oriented computer science courses, the computer engineering track of the B.E.E. focuses on both hardware and software issues with great intensity beginning in the first year of the program.

The B.S. in Computer and Information Science is offered with two possible tracks: computer information systems and computer science. The CIS track focuses heavily on software and is intended for students who plan to hit the proverbial ground running. The CS track emphasizes a broad theoretical background in computer science and would better fit a student who intends to undertake a graduate-level program in the field.

The ABET-accredited B.S. in Electronic(s) Engineering Technology is intended for students who already possess an associate's degree in a comparable field, but may, under certain circumstances, be an option for other students as well.

Graduate Programs

The Master of Computer and Information Science (M.C.I.S.) has three possible tracks: computer science, information systems, and systems programming. The computer science track focuses on CIS theory, the information systems track focuses on software applications, and the systems programming track seems to represent a middle ground of sorts between computer information systems and software engineering.

The 36-hour M.S. in Electrical Engineering offers concentrations in communication systems, computer systems, control systems, power systems, and semi-conductor devices. Students may choose a thesis or non-thesis track.

The Doctor of Engineering offers an emphasis in electrical and computer engineering, although this is an interdisciplinary program and no major, as such, is offered. For more information, contact the College of Engineering at (216) 687-2555.

Other Programs

Cleveland State University also offers a B.B.A. with emphasis in Information Systems. For more information, contact the College of Business at (216) 687-6952.

More Information

Cleveland State University's institutional roots can be traced back to the Cleveland YMCA that, in the 1880s, offered college courses to underprivileged students. Incorporated as the Association Institute (1906) and, later, Fenn College (1929), this program gradually grew in size; in 1964, it became a public university of the State of Ohio.

Over 50 percent of Cleveland State University's student body take advantage of the many available financial aid options. For more information, contact the admissions office.

Cleveland State University welcomes international students. For more information, contact the Center for International Services and Programs (CISP) at (216) 687-3910.

Contact Information

PHONE
General information: (216) 687-2000 or (888) 278-6446
Registrar: (216) 687-3700 or (888) 278-6446, extension 3700
Graduate admissions: (216) 687-3592 or (888) 278-6446, extension 3592
CIS: (216) 687-4760 or (888) 278-6446, extension 4760
Electrical engineering: (216) 687-2589 or (888) 278-6446, extension 2589
Technology: (216) 687-2559 or (888) 278-6446, extension 2559

FAX
Registrar: (216) 687-5501
Graduate admissions: (216) 687-9210

E-MAIL
admissions@csuohio.edu

College of William and Mary   www.wm.edu ☆☆☆

Department of Computer Science
P.O. Box 8795
Williamsburg, VA 23187-8795

Year established: 1693
Ownership: Public

This small, prestigious public university offers degrees in computer science at all levels. Evening classes are available.

Degrees Offered

UNDERGRADUATE
B.A., Computer Science
B.S., Computer Science

GRADUATE
M.S., Computer Science
Ph.D., Computer Science

Approximate Cost of Degrees

UNDERGRADUATE, RESIDENT
$9,200–$15,600

UNDERGRADUATE, NONRESIDENT
$56,400–$65,300

MASTER'S, RESIDENT
$4,500–$6,000

MASTER'S, NONRESIDENT
$18,400–$20,700

DOCTORATE, RESIDENT
$8,900–$10,900

DOCTORATE, NONRESIDENT
$27,600–$33,400

Admissions Guidelines

UNDERGRADUATE
High school diploma

GRADUATE
Accredited bachelor's, GRE required

Undergraduate Programs
The B.A. and B.S. programs in Computer Science involve a Concentration Writing Requirement wherein students are expected to undertake a philosophically significant written project in the field.

Graduate Programs
The 32-hour M.S. program in Computer Science is available with both thesis and non-thesis tracks. Non-thesis students are required to take a project course as part of the substituted coursework, while thesis students may do so or not as they choose. Optional tracks are available in computational operations research and computational science.

The Ph.D. in Computer Science is very dissertation-centered and does not involve a teaching requirement. A computational science track is available.

Other Programs
M.A., M.S., and Ph.D. programs in Applied Science with emphasis in computational science are available. For more information, contact the School of Applied Science at (757) 221-2563.

The computational science track is also available through the M.A., M.S., and Ph.D. programs in Physics. For more information, contact the Department of Physics at (727) 221-3500.

Contact Information

PHONE
General information: (757) 221-4000
Admissions: (757) 221-4223
Computer science: (757) 221-3455

FAX
Computer science: (757) 221-1717

E-MAIL
Computer science: info@cs.wm.edu

 EXTRA!

Former British Prime Minister Margaret Thatcher serves as chancellor of the College of William and Mary.

Colorado State University   www.colostate.edu ☆☆

Office of Admissions
Fort Collins, CO 80523-0015

Year established: 1870
Ownership: Public

This large state university offers a number of programs in information technology fields, which meet the needs of both traditional and nontraditional students. Evening classes, intensive courses, and distance learning are available. Most graduate degree programs described below may be completed mostly, or even entirely, via distance learning.

Degrees Offered

UNDERGRADUATE
B.S., Computer Science
ABET B.S., Electrical Engineering

GRADUATE
M.E.E.
M.S., Computer Science
M.S., Electrical Engineering
Ph.D., Computer Science
Ph.D., Electrical Engineering

Approximate Cost of Degrees

UNDERGRADUATE, RESIDENT
$12,900

UNDERGRADUATE, NONRESIDENT
$43,600

MASTER'S, RESIDENT
$6,800

MASTER'S, NONRESIDENT
$22,400

DOCTORATE, RESIDENT
$13,700

DOCTORATE, NONRESIDENT
$44,700

Admissions Guidelines

UNDERGRADUATE
High school diploma with 2.8 GPA, SAT and/or ACT recommended

GRADUATE
Accredited bachelor's required, GRE recommended

Undergraduate Programs
The B.S. program in Computer Science represents a fairly standard, well-rounded curriculum in the field. Students are given considerable opportunity to choose individualized concentrations through the generous 19 to 22 hours of free elective credit.

The ABET-accredited B.S. program in Electrical Engineering is available with specializations in computer engineering and optoelectronics.

Graduate Programs
The 30-hour Master of Electrical Engineering (M.E.E.) is based only on coursework and is designed primarily for reentry students. This program may be completed 100 percent online.

The 39-hour M.S. in Computer Science is a research-oriented program with a vast number of available informal focus areas to choose from. Thesis and non-thesis tracks are available. The coursework requirements for this program may be completed online.

The 30-hour M.S. in Electrical Engineering culminates in a thesis. Dozens of faculty-approved research focus areas are available, including (but not limited to) computer architecture, computer networks, neural networks, optical computing, parallel architectures, and VLSI design/testing. Students are encouraged to design a specialization around one or more of these research areas. The coursework requirements for this program may be completed online.

The Ph.D. in Computer Science requires two examinations in addition to the standard dissertation.

The Ph.D. in Electrical Engineering requires two batteries of examinations in addition to the standard dissertation. As is true in the case of the Electrical Engineering M.S. program, students are encouraged to design specializations around faculty-supported research interests. The coursework requirements for this program may be completed online.

Contact Information

PHONE
General information: (970) 491-1101
Admissions: (970) 491-6909
Computer science: (970) 491-5792
Electrical and Computer Engineering: (970) 491-6706

E-MAIL
Admissions: admissions@colostate.edu
Computer science: Sharon van Gorder (vangord@cs.colostate.edu)
Electrical and computer engineering: Karen Bross (kbross@engr.colostate.edu)

Columbia University

www.columbia.edu ☆☆☆

The Fu Foundation School of Engineering
and Applied Science
2960 Broadway
New York, NY 10027-6902

Year established: 1754
Ownership: Private

This massive private Ivy League university offers a vast array of programs in several information technology fields. Evening classes and distance-learning video courses are available.

Degrees Offered

UNDERGRADUATE
B.S., Computer Engineering
B.S., Computer Science
🅰 B.S., Electrical Engineering

GRADUATE
M.S., Computer Engineering
M.S., Computer Science
M.S., Electrical Engineering
C.S.E.
E.E.
Eng.Sc.D., Electrical Engineering
Ph.D., Computer Science
Ph.D., Electrical Engineering

Approximate Cost of Degrees

UNDERGRADUATE
$48,300

MASTER'S
$29,000

DOCTORATE
$53,100

Admissions Guidelines

UNDERGRADUATE
High school diploma, SAT and/or ACT

GRADUATE
Accredited bachelor's, GRE required

Undergraduate Programs
The B.S. program in Computer Engineering is one of very few in the country to use Java, rather than C, as its core programming language.

The B.S. in Computer Science is available with optional tracks in intelligent systems, systems, and theory.

The ABET-accredited B.S. program in Electrical Engineering represents a solid, standard curriculum in the field.

Graduate Programs
At this writing, an M.S. program in Computer Engineering is currently in the final stages of approval and should be ready very soon.

The M.S. in Electrical Engineering is available with heavily structured concentrations in lightwave (photonics) engineering, microelectronic circuits, microelectronic devices, multimedia networking, new media engineering, telecommunications, and wireless/mobile communications.

The M.S. and Ph.D. programs in Computer Science are designed primarily for research-minded students who would be interested in developing their own specializations with faculty assistance.

The Eng.Sc.D. and Ph.D. programs in Electrical Engineering are both research-oriented degrees, which require a qualifying examination and dissertation. The Eng.Sc.D. involves more hands-on work in the form of ongoing projects, while the Ph.D. is more research-oriented.

The degrees of Computer Systems Engineer (C.S.E.) and Electrical Engineer (E.E.) are post-Master's, non-thesis professional degrees designed primarily for reentry students.

Other Programs
An M.B.A. with emphasis in management of information, communications, and media is also available. For more information, call the Columbia Business School at (212) 854-5553.

Contact Information

PHONE
General information: (212) 854-1754
Admissions: (212) 854-1754
Computer science and engineering: (212) 939-7000
Electrical engineering: (212) 854-3105

FAX
Admissions: (212) 854-1754
Computer science and engineering: (212) 666-0140
Electrical engineering: (212) 932-9421

Columbus State University   www.colstate.edu ☆☆½

4225 University Avenue
Columbus, GA 31907-5645

Year established: 1958
Ownership: Public

This midsize state university "without boundaries" offers undergraduate and graduate programs in computer science, including a 100 percent online master's degree. A number of options are available for reentry students, including online, evening, and extension classes.

Degrees Offered

UNDERGRADUATE
B.S., Applied Computer Science
B.S., Computer Science

GRADUATE
M.S., Applied Computer Science (available online)

Approximate Cost of Degrees

UNDERGRADUATE, RESIDENT
$6,300–$9,700

UNDERGRADUATE, NONRESIDENT
$25,300–$38,700

GRADUATE, RESIDENT
$2,200–$3,300

GRADUATE, NONRESIDENT
$8,700–$13,100

Admissions Guidelines

UNDERGRADUATE
High school diploma, ACT and/or SAT

GRADUATE
Accredited bachelor's, GRE

Undergraduate Programs
The B.S. program in Computer Science is fairly standard. The B.S. program in Applied Computer Science builds on the basic Computer Science curriculum, waiving broader requirements and focusing on programming and software applications.

Graduate Programs
The M.S. in Applied Computer Science is described as having two "tracks," one being the residential program and one being the 100 percent online program. While the residential program is very similar to a traditional M.S. program in Computer Science, it is understood that the online track also addresses issues related to information technology management and business information systems.

Other Programs
A B.B.A. in Computer Information Systems is also available through the Abbott Turner College of Business. For more information, contact Dr. Bob Fleck at (706) 562-1657.

More Information
The University College program of Columbus State University is designed for reentry students; even students who don't meet the undergraduate admission requirements described above are encouraged to apply. For more information, contact the Division of Basic Studies at (706) 565-4016.

Contact Information

PHONE
General information: (706) 568-2001
Admissions: (706) 568-2035

FAX
(706) 568-2462

OTHER WEB SITES
Online programs: http://www.csuonline.edu/
Computer science: http://www.cs.colstate.edu/

E-MAIL
admissions@colstate.edu

Cornell University

Information and Referral Center
Day Hall Lobby
Ithaca, NY 14853-2801

www.cornell.edu ☆☆½

Year established: 1865
Ownership: Private

This large private university, one of the leading research institutions in the country, offers a variety of unique programs in computer science and electrical engineering. Evening classes are available.

Degrees Offered

UNDERGRADUATE
B.A., Computer Science
B.S., Computer Science
ABET B.S., Electrical Engineering

GRADUATE
M.Eng., Computer Science
M.Eng., Electrical Engineering
M.S., Electrical Engineering
Ph.D., Computer Science
Ph.D., Electrical Engineering

Approximate Cost of Degrees

UNDERGRADUATE, RESIDENT
$43,300

UNDERGRADUATE, NONRESIDENT
$83,600

MASTER'S
$25,400

DOCTORATE
$44,500

Admissions Guidelines

UNDERGRADUATE
High school diploma, SAT and/or ACT

GRADUATE
Accredited bachelor's, GRE required

Undergraduate Programs

The B.A. and B.S. programs in Computer Science are designed to permit students to use the generous free elective options available to create an individualized program suitable for work in other fields as well as computer science. Alternately, of course, students may choose to focus more completely on computer science.

The ABET-accredited B.S. program in Electrical Engineering allows for considerable individualized specialization through field electives.

Graduate Programs

The one-year, non-thesis M.Eng. programs in Computer Science and Electrical Engineering are designed for reentry students.

The Ph.D. in Computer Science requires a battery of examinations in addition to coursework and the standard dissertation.

The M.S. and Ph.D. programs in Electrical Engineering do not have any required courses. Students design a curriculum in electrical engineering with faculty assistance.

Contact Information

PHONE

General information: (607) 254-4636
Admissions: (607) 255-5241
Graduate school: (607) 255-4884

E-MAIL

Admissions (undergraduate): admissions@cornell.edu
Admissions (graduate): gradadmissions@cornell.edu
Computer science (undergraduate): ugrad@cs.cornell.edu
Computer science (graduate): grad@cs.cornell.edu
Electrical engineering (undergraduate): Paul Kintner (paul@ee.cornell.edu)
Electrical engineering (graduate): eemsphd@cornell.edu
Master of Engineering: meng@cornell.edu

Creighton University   www.creighton.edu ☆☆½

2500 California Plaza
Omaha, NE 68178

Year established: 1878
Ownership: Private

This small, prestigious Jesuit university offers a variety of special undergraduate and graduate programs for reentry students who seek a background in computer science and related management issues. Innovative programs in e-commerce and information technology management are now available for evening and weekend study.

Degrees Offered

UNDERGRADUATE
B.S., Applied Computer Science
B.S., Computer Science

GRADUATE
M.S., Computer Science
M.S., E-Commerce

Approximate Cost of Degrees

UNDERGRADUATE (TRADITIONAL)
$113,100

UNDERGRADUATE (UNIVERSITY COLLEGE)
$34,000–$68,000

GRADUATE
$14,800–$16,100

Admissions Guidelines

UNDERGRADUATE (TRADITIONAL)
High school diploma or equivalent with 2.75 GPA, ACT and/or SAT

UNDERGRADUATE (UNIVERSITY COLLEGE)
High school diploma with 2.0 GPA

GRADUATE
Accredited bachelor's required

Undergraduate Programs

The B.S. program in Computer Science represents a fairly standard four-year computer science curriculum, which should satisfy the prerequisite requirements of most graduate programs in the field. The B.S. program in Applied Computer Science is similar, but involves some business-related coursework. Both programs are available through evening and weekend classes to students in the University College program.

Graduate Programs

The 36-hour M.S. in Computer Science is available with a thesis track (requiring 10 courses and a thesis) or non-thesis track (requiring 11 courses and a major report). Students may, if they choose, use up to 6 hours of graduate courses in a business-related field to satisfy elective requirements. A comprehensive examination is required.

The M.S. in E-Commerce seems to be more business-oriented than technology-oriented, and can be completed entirely through evening and weekend study. A capstone project is required. A joint M.S./J.D. program in E-Commerce is also available.

Other Programs

Creighton University offers an M.S. in Information Technology Management. A management information systems emphasis is also available within the B.S. program in Business Administration.

More Information

Some distance-learning classes are currently under development; contact the University College for details.

Contact Information

PHONE

General information: (402) 280-2700 or (800) 282-5835
University College: (402) 280-2424 or (800) 637-4279
Graduate school: (402) 280-2870
Business administration/e-commerce: (402) 280-2850

E-MAIL

Admissions: admissions@creighton.edu
University College: univcol@creighton.edu
Graduate school: gradsch@creighton.edu

Dartmouth College

Department of Computer Science
6211 Sudikoff Laboratory
Hanover, NH 03755-3510

www.dartmouth.edu ☆☆

Year established: 1769
Ownership: Private

This small, prestigious Ivy League university has a long and impressive history as an innovative institution in the field of computer science. While its programs are fairly standard in their structure, they serve their function exceptionally well. Most of these programs function as though they were designed with traditional students in mind, but some evening classes are available.

Degrees Offered

UNDERGRADUATE

B.S., Computer Science

GRADUATE

M.S., Computer Science
Ph.D., Computer Science

Approximate Cost of Degrees

UNDERGRADUATE

$98,500

MASTER'S

$40,000

DOCTORATE

$86,200

Admissions Guidelines

UNDERGRADUATE

High school diploma

GRADUATE

Accredited bachelor's, GRE required

Undergraduate Programs

The B.S. program in Computer Science represents a fairly standard curriculum in the field in and of itself, but an interesting dual major program in computer science and engineering is available.

Graduate Programs

The M.S. and Ph.D. programs in Computer Science are extremely structured, but offer room for mild specialization through free electives.

Contact Information

PHONE
General information: (603) 646-1110
Undergraduate admissions: (603) 646-2875
Computer science: (603) 646-2206

FAX
Computer science: (603) 646-1672

E-MAIL
Computer science:
Computer.Science.Department@dartmouth.edu

 EXTRA!

The programming language BASIC was invented by two Dartmouth faculty members, Drs. John G. Kemeny and Thomas Kurtz.

DePaul University   www.depaul.edu ☆☆½

1 East Jackson Boulevard
Chicago, IL 60604

Year established: 1898
Ownership: Private

This prestigious university offers a wealth of undergraduate and graduate programs in a variety of information technology fields, and makes them available through almost all imaginable means: evening classes, weekend classes, conferencing, satellite campuses, and distance learning.

Degrees Offered

UNDERGRADUATE
B.A., Computing
B.S., Computer Science
B.S., Human-Computer Interaction
B.S., Information Systems

GRADUATE
M.A., Applied Technology
M.S., Computer Science
M.S., Distributed Systems
M.S., E-Commerce Technology
M.S., Human-Computer Interaction
M.S., Information Systems
M.S., Software Engineering
M.S., Telecommunications Systems
Ph.D., Computer Science

Approximate Cost of Degrees

UNDERGRADUATE
$52,900

GRADUATE, MASTER'S (M.A.A.T.)
$18,600

GRADUATE, MASTER'S (M.S.)
$22,700

DOCTORATE
$37,800

Admissions Guidelines

UNDERGRADUATE
High school diploma required

GRADUATE
Accredited bachelor's required, GRE recommended

Undergraduate Programs

The interdisciplinary B.A. in Computing offered through the School of New Learning is designed with reentry students specifically in mind. Offering an integrated curriculum that incorporates aspects of computing, philosophy, and the social sciences, this program can be completed in three years or less.

The B.S. program in Computer Science is well-secured in the theory-related aspects of the field. Tracks are available in traditional computer science and data analysis.

The B.S. program in Human-Computer Interaction incorporates aspects of the social sciences and computer science into a single, integrated curriculum.

The B.S. program in Information Systems is IT-focused and involves a strong base curriculum in programming theory.

Graduate Programs

The very IT-focused M.A. in Applied Technology is offered through the School of New Learning and designed specifically for reentry students. In addition to the above requirement, three years of work experience is required for admission. The program culminates with an individualized final review class. Specializations are available in applied information systems and applied telecommunications.

The M.S. in Computer Science is available with a thesis or non-thesis track; all students must pass a comprehensive examination. Specializations are available in artificial intelligence, computer graphics, computer vision, data analysis, database systems, data communications, and system foundations.

The M.S. in Distributed Systems primarily addresses the computer science of networks rather than of individual computers. No thesis is required, but all students must pass a comprehensive examination on the three required "core knowledge" courses, which are generally taken early in the program.

The M.S. in E-Commerce Technology addresses issues surrounding the booming dot.com marketplace. A thesis or project may be undertaken for credit, but neither are required. All students must pass a comprehensive examination on the three required "core knowledge" courses, which are generally taken early in the program.

The M.S. in Human-Computer Interaction draws on courses from a variety of computer science disciplines. All students must pass a comprehensive examination on the three required "core knowledge" courses, which are generally taken early in the program. Although no formal thesis or project is required, all students are required to take a capstone course.

The M.S. in Information Systems is a broad, but decisively IT-oriented program. A thesis or project may be undertaken for credit, but neither are required. All students must pass a comprehensive examination on the three required "core knowledge" courses, which are generally taken early in the program. Students may choose a general track or specialize in computer-supported collaborative work, data warehousing, e-commerce, IT project management, networking, or systems development.

The M.S. in Software Engineering is a structured program with minimal free electives. A thesis or project is required; students may specialize in project management, software development, or software systems.

The M.S. in Telecommunications Systems addresses the science of telecommunications-based networks and associated technology. All students must pass a comprehensive examination on three required "core knowledge" courses, which are generally taken early in the program. A special track in computer science is available. No thesis is required.

The Ph.D. in Computer Science requires students to take several subject-based examinations before proceeding to candidacy.

Other Programs

An M.S. in Management Information Systems is also available.

Contact Information

PHONE

General information: (312) 362-8000
Admissions: (312) 362-8300
Computer science/information science/telecommunications: (312) 362-8381
School of New Learning: (312) 362-8001

E-MAIL

admitdpu@wppost.depaul.edu

DeVry Institutes
www.devry.edu ☆☆☆

Administrative Offices
One Tower Lane
Oakbrook Terrace, IL 60181

Year established: 1931
Ownership: Private

This classic, almost stereotypical option for reentry students broke new ground in offering night school programs (which could, and still can, be completed entirely via evening classes) and weekend study programs. Still an object of ridicule to some because of its aggressive television marketing, this school is nevertheless a trailblazer that continues to offer rigorous, vocationally oriented information technology degrees to a vast number of reentry students all over the country. Distance-learning options are also under development.

Degrees Offered

UNDERGRADUATE
B.S., Computer Engineering Technology
B.S., Computer Information Systems
B.S., Electronic(s) Engineering Technology
B.S., Information Technology

Approximate Cost of Degrees

UNDERGRADUATE
$35,000

Admissions Guidelines

UNDERGRADUATE
High school diploma, SAT and/or ACT required.
Must be 17 or older.

Undergraduate Programs

The new B.S. in Computer Engineering Technology is slated for ABET evaluation within the next three years.

The B.S. program in Computer Information Systems is grounded in contemporary technology, emphasizing issues of applied computing over theory. Some courses in business-related information systems are required.

The B.S. in Electronic(s) Engineering Technology is designed with unusual interdisciplinarity; a 12-hour computer programming concentration is required as part of the program, for instance. Most extension sites offer this program as an ABET-accredited major.

The B.S. in Information Technology is an accelerated program designed for students who already possess a bachelor's degree in a non-IT field. Students who progress through the program quickly can complete it in a year.

Other Programs

The DeVry Institutes also offer B.S. programs in Technical Management and Telecommunications Management.

Master of Information Systems Management (M.I.S.M.) and Master of Telecommunications Management (M.T.M.) programs are also available. For more information, contact the Keller School of Management at (630) 574-1960 or (888) 535-5378.

More Information

DeVry Institutes are available in Arizona (Phoenix), California (Fremont, Long Beach, and Pomona), Georgia (Alpharetta and Decatur), Illinois (Addison and Chicago), Missouri (Kansas City), New Jersey (North Brunswick), New York (Long Island City), Ohio (Columbus), and Texas (Irving).

Contact Information

PHONE
(630) 571-7700 or (800) 733-3879

E-MAIL
obtWeb@dpg.devry.edu

Drexel University   www.drexel.edu ☆☆☆

3141 Chestnut Street
Philadelphia, PA 19104

Year established: 1891
Ownership: Private

This respected private university offers an array of information technology degrees through a variety of means. Several can be completed online, and all others can be at least partially completed through evening and weekend classes.

Degrees Offered

UNDERGRADUATE

B.S., Computer Engineering
CSAB B.S., Computer Science
ABET B.S., Electrical Engineering
B.S., Information Systems

GRADUATE

M.S., Electrical Engineering
M.S., Information Systems
Ph.D., Electrical Engineering

Approximate Cost of Degrees

UNDERGRADUATE

$73,600

MASTER'S

$18,000

DOCTORATE

$33,100

Admissions Guidelines

UNDERGRADUATE

High school diploma, SAT and/or ACT

GRADUATE

Accredited bachelor's, 3.0 GPA on upper 60 hours

Undergraduate Programs

The hands-on B.S. program in Computer Engineering is offered through the School of Evening and Professional Studies and is designed with reentry students in mind.

The CSAB-accredited B.S. program in Computer Science is offered through the School of Evening and Professional Studies and is designed with reentry students in mind. Students are encouraged to design their own specializations, but specializations are offered in artificial intelligence, data structures and algorithms, numerical and scientific computing, operating systems, and programming languages.

The ABET-accredited B.S. program in Electrical Engineering is offered through the Department of Electrical and Computer Engineering. Concentrations are available in computer engineering, computers, controls and robotics, electronics, power and energy, and telecommunications.

The B.S. in Information Systems is offered through the School of Information Science and Technology as well as the School of Evening and Professional Studies. The field of information systems as it is represented at Drexel is a heavily software-oriented IT field presented with a strong theory-focused base. It could be described as the backbone of Drexel's IT programs and is not, as is the case at many universities, a library or decision science program. Concentrations in the B.S. program are available in analysis and design, distributed systems, information resource management, and knowledge-based systems.

Graduate Programs

The M.S. program in Electrical Engineering is offered through the Department of Electrical and Computer Engineering. Full-time students are required to either complete a thesis or author a peer-reviewed, published article; part-time students are encouraged to do so, but not required. Specializations are available in computers and digital circuits, electrophysics, power systems, and systems.

The M.S. program in Information Systems may be completed online. Work experience may be evaluated for up to 9 hours of credit.

The Ph.D. program in Electrical Engineering requires that students become an active part of Drexel University's research environment. A written examination is also required, as well as the standard dissertation.

Other Programs

B.B.A. and M.B.A. programs with emphasis in technology management are available; the latter may be completed online. For more information, contact the Management Department of the Bennett S. LeBow College of Business at (215) 895-2143.

An M.S. in Library and Information Science with emphasis in management of digital information is available and may be completed online. For more information, contact the Department of Information Science and Technology.

Contact Information

PHONE

Admissions: (800) 237-3935
Engineering: (215) 895-2210
Evening classes/professional studies: (215) 895-2167
Information science/technology: (215) 895-2474

E-MAIL

Admissions: admissions@drexel.edu
Engineering: coess@drexel.edu
Evening classes/professional studies: coeps@drexel.edu
Information science/technology: IST.INFO@cis.drexel.edu

Duke University

www.duke.edu ☆½

Durham, NC 27708

Year established: 1924
Ownership: Private

This well-known university, particularly renowned for its business administration programs, also offers a number of rigorous programs in computer science and electrical engineering. Evening classes are available.

Degrees Offered

UNDERGRADUATE

B.A., Computer Science
B.S., Computer Science
(ABET) B.S., Electrical Engineering

GRADUATE

M.S., Computer Science
M.S., Electrical and Computer Engineering
Ph.D., Computer Science
Ph.D., Electrical and Computer Engineering

Approximate Cost of Degrees

UNDERGRADUATE

$93,300

MASTER'S

$21,600

DOCTORATE

$36,000

Admissions Guidelines

UNDERGRADUATE

High school diploma, SAT and/or ACT

GRADUATE

Accredited bachelor's, GRE required

Undergraduate Programs

The B.A. in Computer Science is designed to support double majors with non-technical fields, while the B.S. in Computer Science is designed to support double majors with technical fields. Both programs, on their own, represent a standard curriculum in the field.

The ABET-accredited B.S. in Electrical Engineering requires that students choose two concentrations from among the following: computer engineering, control systems, electromagnetic fields and optics, and solid-state electronics/circuits.

Graduate Programs

The 36-hour M.S. in Computer Science involves both a required thesis and a required concentration. Concentrations are available in algorithms, artificial intelligence, scientific computing, and systems.

The 30-hour M.S. in Electrical and Computer Engineering is available with thesis, project, and coursework-only tracks.

The Ph.D. in Computer Science involves two consecutive semester-long projects culminating in publication-quality reports. Upon completing this requirement, the student undertakes a qualifying examination, then proceeds to the standard dissertation and broad coursework requirements. Concentrations are available in algorithms, artificial intelligence, scientific computing, and systems.

The 60-hour Ph.D. in Electrical and Computer Engineering involves a qualifying examination in addition to the standard dissertation. Students who apply using an M.S.E.E. from another institution may apply a maximum of 15 hours toward Ph.D. requirements.

Contact Information

PHONE
General information: (919) 684-8111
Admissions (undergraduate): (919) 684-3214
Admissions (graduate): (919) 684-3913
Continuing education: (919) 684-2621
Computer science: (919) 660-6500

E-MAIL
askduke@admiss.duke.edu

Embry-Riddle Aeronautical University   www.erau.edu ☆☆☆

Embry-Riddle Aeronautical University (Florida)
600 S. Clyde Morris Boulevard
Daytona Beach, FL 32114-3900

Year established: 1927
Ownership: Private

Embry-Riddle Aeronautical University (Arizona)
3200 Willow Creek Road
Prescott, AZ 86301-3720

This midsize private university is possessed by the spirit of an old, by-the-book engineering school. The programs resonate with the basic idea of character-building hard work rather than formal academic study. This approach gives Embry-Riddle's programs a unique, Spartan character that distinguishes them from the pack. If Embry-Riddle's curricula remain rugged and old-fashioned, however, its delivery methods have certainly not. With evening and weekend classes at both campuses, and more than 100 extension sites, this is an institution that suits freshmen and reentry students equally well.

Degrees Offered

UNDERGRADUATE
B.S., Computer Engineering
B.S., Computer Science
ABET B.S., Electrical Engineering

GRADUATE
M.S.E.

Approximate Cost of Degrees

UNDERGRADUATE
$16,900

GRADUATE
$8,600

Admissions Guidelines

UNDERGRADUATE
High school diploma, SAT and/or ACT

GRADUATE
Accredited bachelor's

Undergraduate Programs
The hardware-oriented B.S. in Computer Engineering is available through both the Daytona Beach and Prescott campuses. Much of the program may be completed via distance learning.

The B.S. in Computer Science is offered through the Daytona Beach and Prescott campuses. This is a highly structured program that emphasizes applied computer science through individual and team projects.

The hands-on, ABET-accredited B.S. in Electrical Engineering is offered only through the Prescott campus.

Graduate Programs
The Master of Software Engineering (M.S.E.) program addresses the field from a variety of practical approaches; emphasis is placed on problem-solving. A thesis or equivalent research project is required.

Other Programs
A B.S. in Management of Technical Operations is available through all sites; an M.S. in Technical Management is available through the Daytona Beach campus and various extension sites.

Contact Information

PHONE
General information (Florida): (904) 226-6000 or (800) 222-3728
Admissions (Florida): (904) 226-6100 or (800) 862-2416
General information (Arizona): (520) 708-3728 or (800) 888-3728
Admissions (Arizona): (520) 708-3728 or (800) 888-3728
Extension programs: (904) 226-6910 or (800) 522-6787

E-MAIL
General information (Florida): admit@db.erau.edu
General information (Arizona): admit@pr.erau.edu
Extension programs: ecinfo@db.erau.edu
Distance learning: Indstudy@cts.db.erau.edu

Emporia State University   www.emporia.edu ☆☆☆

1200 Commercial Street
Emporia, KS 66801-5087

Year established: 1863
Ownership: Public

This former teacher's college offers solid, inexpensive undergraduate programs in computer science. Evening classes and distance learning are available.

Degrees Offered

UNDERGRADUATE
B.S.B., Computer Information Systems
B.S., Computer Science

Approximate Cost of Degrees

UNDERGRADUATE, RESIDENT
$8,400

UNDERGRADUATE, NONRESIDENT
$26,200

Admissions Guidelines

UNDERGRADUATE
High school diploma or equivalent

Undergraduate Programs
The B.S. in Business (B.S.B) with a major in Computer Information Systems is a surprisingly IT-oriented program, which focuses intensely on software and networking issues.

The B.S. in Computer Science is grounded in the mathematical foundations of the field. In its applied component, it seems most focused on software engineering and programming issues.

Other Programs

An M.S. in Instructional Design and Technology is also available. For more information, contact the Teacher's College at (316) 341-5367.

Contact Information

PHONE

General information: (316) 341-1200 or (877) 468-6378
Computer information systems: (316) 341-5346
Computer science: (316) 341-5281

FAX

Computer information systems: (316) 341-6346

E-MAIL

Computer information systems: acis@emporia.edu
Computer science: Chuck Pheatt
(pheattch@esumail.emporia.edu)

Florida Institute of Technology

www.fit.edu ☆☆☆

150 West University Boulevard
Melbourne, FL 32901-6975

Year established: 1958
Ownership: Private

This research-oriented institution, most well known for its programs in aviation, aeronautics, and space studies, also offers a variety of programs in information technology at all levels. Evening classes, extension courses, and distance learning are available.

Degrees Offered

UNDERGRADUATE

- B.S., Computer Engineering
- B.S., Computer Science
- B.S., Electrical Engineering

GRADUATE

M.S., Computer Engineering
M.S., Computer Information Systems
M.S., Computer Science
M.S., Electrical Engineering
Ph.D., Computer Engineering
Ph.D., Computer Science
Ph.D., Electrical Engineering

Approximate Cost of Degrees

UNDERGRADUATE

$73,800

MASTER'S

$27,700

DOCTORATE

$46,100

Admissions Guidelines

UNDERGRADUATE

High school diploma with 2.8 GPA, SAT and/or ACT recommended

GRADUATE

Accredited bachelor's with 3.0 GPA, GRE recommended

Undergraduate Programs

The ABET-accredited B.S. in Computer Engineering begins with a broad base in theory, then narrows its focus and emphasizes a thoroughly lab-oriented, practical curriculum during the junior and senior years.

The CSAB-accredited B.S. in Computer Science is available with optional specializations in information systems and software development.

The ABET-accredited B.S. in Electrical Engineering focuses on a systems-oriented approach during the senior year.

Graduate Programs

The 30-hour M.S. in Computer Engineering is available with both thesis and non-thesis tracks. Students in the latter track must pass a capstone written examination.

The 30-hour M.S. in Computer Information Systems emphasizes software and database issues, although hardware issues are (somewhat surprisingly) also addressed. No thesis is required, but all students must pass a final examination. This program is available via extension.

The 32-hour M.S. in Computer Science focuses intensely on software engineering issues; beyond this, students are given a great deal of flexibility in choosing an area of emphasis. A thesis is required. This program is available via extension.

The 30-hour M.S. in Electrical Engineering is designed to effectively accommodate the needs of both part-time and full-time students; both thesis and non-thesis tracks are available. Students in the latter track must pass a capstone written examination. Specializations are available in electromagnetics, physical electronics, and systems and information processing.

The Ph.D. in Computer Engineering requires two examinations in addition to the standard dissertation. Students are encouraged to focus on areas of interest to them.

The Ph.D. in Computer Science requires a comprehensive examination in addition to the standard dissertation. Students are given a great deal of flexibility in choosing an area of emphasis.

The Ph.D. in Electrical Engineering requires two examinations in addition to the standard dissertation. Concentrations are available in control, electromagnetics, physical electronics, signal processing, systems and information processing, and telecommunications.

Other Programs

An M.S. program in Aviation Computer Science is also available through the Computer Science department.

M.S. programs in Management (emphasis Computer Information Systems) and Systems Engineering (emphasis Information Systems) are available through the School of Extended Studies. Both programs may be completed via extension or distance learning.

More Information

In addition to its sites in Florida (Orlando, Patrick AFB/Kennedy Space Center, and Tampa Bay), the School of Extended Graduate Studies has established extension programs in Alabama (Redstone Arsenal), Maryland (Aberdeen Proving Ground and Patuxent River), New Jersey (Northeast), and Virginia (Fort Lee, National Capital, and Hampton Roads).

Contact Information

Phone
General information: (321) 674-8000
Admissions: (321) 674-8030 or (800) 888-4348
Extended graduate studies (extensions/distance learning): (321) 674-8880
Computer science: (321) 674-8763
Electrical and computer engineering: (321) 674-8060
Software engineering: (321) 674-8874

E-mail
Admissions (undergraduate): admissions@fit.edu
Admissions (graduate): grad-admissions@fit.edu
Computer engineering: compeng@ee.fit.edu
Computer science: www@cs.fit.edu
Electrical engineering: Webmaster@ee.fit.edu

Fordham University   www.fordham.edu ☆☆½

Office of Undergraduate Admission
Thebaud Hall
441 East Fordham Road
New York, NY 10458-5191

Year established: 1841
Ownership: Private

This midsize-to-large Jesuit college offers programs through primarily traditional delivery methods in a strong academic environment. Although the institution seems to be tradition-oriented, a variety of special programs for adult students are being developed. Evening classes and intensive weekend classes are available. Branch campuses are available throughout the New York City area.

Degrees Offered

UNDERGRADUATE
B.A., Computer Science
B.S., Computer Science
B.A., Information Science

GRADUATE
M.S., Computer Science

Approximate Cost of Degrees

UNDERGRADUATE
$78,700

GRADUATE
$17,300

Admissions Guidelines

UNDERGRADUATE
High school diploma with 3.0 GPA, SAT and/or ACT

GRADUATE
Accredited bachelor's, GRE required

Undergraduate Programs
The B.A. and B.S. programs in Computer Science represent a fairly standard curriculum in the field; the B.A. program requires six fewer major electives than the B.S. program.

The B.A. in Information Science is an application-oriented degree that addresses software engineering and database management.

Graduate Programs
The M.S. program in Computer Science is available through three tracks: thesis-centered, course-based (general), and course-based (specialized). The thesis-centered track involves a 6-hour thesis and 24 hours of coursework; no specialization is required. The general course-based track involves 33 hours of coursework, while the specialized track involves 21 hours of broad coursework and 9 hours of coursework in an individualized, faculty-approved research area.

More Information
Fordham University is currently developing a program called "College at Sixty" (so named because of its location on 60th Street). This program, which centers on intensive daytime and evening courses, is designed specifically for adults age 50 and older.

Contact Information

PHONE
Admissions: (718) 817-4000, (212) 636-6710, or (800) 367-3426
Computer science: (718) 817-4480

FAX
Admissions: (718) 367-9404
Computer science: (718) 817-4488

E-MAIL
Admissions: enroll@fordham.edu
Computer science: cis@murray.fordham.edu

George Mason University

www.gmu.edu ☆☆☆☆

4400 University Drive
Fairfax, VA 22030-4444

Year established: 1957
Ownership: Public

With its innovative programs in interdisciplinary information technology fields, this school looks to be a marvelous research institute cleverly disguised as a midsize state university. Evening classes, intensive courses, credit by examination, and distance learning are available.

Degrees Offered

UNDERGRADUATE
B.S., Computer Engineering
B.S., Computer Science
⒜ B.S., Electrical Engineering

GRADUATE
M.A., Telecommunications
M.S., Computer Engineering
M.S., Computer Science
M.S., Electrical Engineering

M.S., Information Systems
M.S., Software Systems Engineering
M.S., Telecommunications
Ph.D., Computational Sciences and Informatics
Ph.D., Computer Science
Ph.D., Electrical and Computer Engineering
Ph.D., Information Technology and Engineering

Approximate Cost of Degrees

UNDERGRADUATE, RESIDENT
$16,900

UNDERGRADUATE, NONRESIDENT
$56,300

MASTER'S, RESIDENT
$7,700

MASTER'S, NONRESIDENT
$21,900

DOCTORATE, RESIDENT
$14,100

DOCTORATE, NONRESIDENT
$39,900

Admissions Guidelines

UNDERGRADUATE
High school diploma, SAT and/or ACT

GRADUATE
Accredited bachelor's with 3.0 GPA on upper 60 hours, GRE recommended

Undergraduate Programs

The B.S. program in Computer Science represents a standard curriculum in the field, well-suited as a base for graduate-level study.

The B.S. program in Computer Engineering allows for considerable specialization through the use of free electives. Pre-approved specializations are available in digital networks, high performance computers/VHDL, signal processing, and VLSI/VHDL.

The ABET-accredited B.S. program in Electrical Engineering involves a considerable amount of study in the theoretical background of electrical engineering. As is typical of George Mason University's programs, the B.S.E.E. allows for specializa-

tion through the use of free electives. Pre-approved specializations are available in communications/signal processing, computer engineering, control systems, and electronics.

Graduate Programs

The M.A. in Telecommunications is a highly innovative, interdisciplinary program focusing on telecommunications technology and its impact on business and society as a whole. Concentrations are available in educational technology, information systems, international telecommunications, management and policy, production theories and practice, and telecommunications systems. The program concludes with a semester-long, team-oriented research seminar.

The M.S. program in Electrical Engineering is available with thesis and non-thesis tracks, the non-thesis track involving a shorter capstone research paper. Concentrations are available in communications, computer engineering, control and robotics, electronics/electromagnetics/optoelectronics, and signal processing.

The M.S. program in Computer Engineering is also available with thesis and non-thesis tracks, the non-thesis track involving a shorter capstone research paper. Concentrations are available in digital systems design, computer networks, distributed computing systems, and microprocessor/embedded systems.

The M.S. program in Computer Science is available with thesis, non-thesis, and project tracks. Concentrations are available in artificial intelligence, computer systems, image processing/graphics, parallel/distributed computing, and software engineering.

The M.S. program in Information Systems is extremely IT-oriented, focusing on issues of data analysis and software engineering. Project and non-project tracks are available.

The M.S. in Software Systems Engineering is available with thesis and non-thesis tracks. Students may design their own concentrations with faculty approval.

The M.S. program in Telecommunications differs from the M.A. program (see above) in that it is essentially a pure IT/engineering program. Although some interdisciplinarity is involved, the M.S. is essentially a hands-on degree for individuals who would like to undertake intensive study in the specific discipline of telecommunications design, analysis, and implementation. No thesis is required.

Concentrations are available in modeling of telecommunications systems, network applications, network technologies, systems engineering of telecommunications, and wireless communications.

The Ph.D. in Computational Sciences and Informatics is a broad, interdisciplinary program incorporating computer science and information systems as it relates to other scientific disciplines. Research specializations are available in bioinformatics, computer design of materials, computational fluid dynamics, global change, and space sciences.

The Ph.D. in Computer Science involves a qualifying examination (taken near the beginning of the program) and a comprehensive examination (taken near the end). The standard dissertation is, of course, also required. Students may design their own concentrations with faculty approval, but pre-approved concentrations are available in artificial intelligence, computer systems, databases, imaging, information and information security, parallel and distributed systems, and software engineering.

The Ph.D. in Electrical and Computer Engineering involves a qualifying examination and a teaching requirement in addition to the standard dissertation. Specializations are available in communications and networking, computer engineering, control and robotics, electronics/photonics/electromagnetics, and signal processing.

The Ph.D. in Information Technology and Engineering requires a student-defined 18-hour specialization and a comprehensive examination in addition to the standard dissertation.

Contact Information

PHONE
General information: (703) 993-1000
Admissions: (703) 993-2400
Computational sciences and informatics: (703) 993-1990
Computer science: (703) 993-1530
Electrical and computer engineering: (703) 993-1569
Information technology and engineering: (703) 993-1505
Software systems engineering: (703) 993-1640
Telecommunications (M.A.): (703) 993-3699

FAX
Admissions: (703) 993-2392
Computational sciences and informatics: (703) 993-1993
Computer science: (703) 993-1710
Electrical and computer engineering: (703) 993-1601
Information technology and engineering: (703) 993-1734
Software systems engineering: (703) 993-1638
Telecommunications (M.A.): (703) 993-8714

E-MAIL
Admissions: admissions@gmu.edu
Computational sciences and informatics: pbecker@gmu.edu
Computer science: csinfo@cs.gmu.edu
Electrical and computer engineering: ece@gmu.edu
Information technology and engineering: sitegrad@gmu.edu
Telecommunications (M.A.): casgrad@gmu.edu

Georgia Institute of Technology   www.gatech.edu ☆☆½

Atlanta, GA 30332

Year established: 1885
Ownership: Public

This old-school engineering school has gone new-school, offering programs in a variety of innovative interdisciplinary information technology fields through a variety of delivery methods. Evening classes, intensive classes, and distance learning are available.

Degrees Offered

UNDERGRADUATE
- (ABET) B.S., Computer Engineering
- (CSAB) B.S., Computer Science
- (ABET) B.S., Electrical Engineering

GRADUATE
- M.S., Computer Science
- M.S., Electrical and Computer Engineering
- M.S., Human-Computer Interaction
- M.S., Information Design and Technology
- Ph.D., Algorithms, Combinatorics, and Optimization
- Ph.D., Computer Science
- Ph.D., Electrical and Computer Engineering

Approximate Cost of Degrees

UNDERGRADUATE, RESIDENT
$13,000

UNDERGRADUATE, NONRESIDENT
$45,600

MASTER'S, RESIDENT
$5,100

MASTER'S, NONRESIDENT
$18,100

DOCTORATE, RESIDENT
$7,500

DOCTORATE, NONRESIDENT
$27,100

Admissions Guidelines

UNDERGRADUATE
High school diploma, SAT and/or ACT required

GRADUATE
Accredited bachelor's with 3.0 GPA, GRE recommended

Undergraduate Programs

The ABET-accredited B.S. program in Computer Engineering shares its core requirements with the Electrical Engineering program, and the B.S.C.E. seems to indeed resemble the E.E. program in its emphases. Very little attention is paid to software engineering, the bulk of the program being dedicated to hardware issues.

The CSAB-accredited B.S. program in Computer Science is available with specializations in computer systems, data management systems, educational technology, graphics and visualization, intelligent systems, networking and telecommunications, software engineering, theory, and usability.

The ABET-accredited B.S. program in Electrical Engineering is very much oriented toward microelectronics, so much so that it resembles the Computer Engineering program (see above) in many respects.

Graduate Programs

The 36-hour M.S. program in Computer Science is available with thesis, non-thesis, and project tracks.

The 36-hour M.S. in Electrical and Computer Engineering is available with thesis and non-thesis tracks. Students specialize in individualized, faculty-approved research areas.

The M.S. program in Human-Computer Interaction represents an interdisciplinary collaboration of the College of Computing, the Graphics, Visualization, and Usability (GVU) Center, the School of Literature, Communications, and Culture, and the School of Psychology.

The 36-hour M.S. program in Information Design and Technology requires a project or thesis and an individualized, faculty-approved specialization.

The Ph.D. program in Algorithms, Combinatorics, and Optimization represents an interdisciplinary collaboration of the College of Computing, the School of Industrial and Systems Engineering, and the School of Mathematics. It represents in many respects the application of computer science to mathematics, and has a significant information technology component.

The Ph.D. programs in Computer Science and Electrical and Computer Engineering require a comprehensive examination in addition to the standard dissertation. As is true in the case of the M.S. offered through the same department (see above), students specialize in individualized, faculty-approved research areas.

Other Programs

M.A. and Ph.D. programs in the History of Technology are also available. For more information, contact the Division of History, Technology, and Society at (404) 894-6828.

An Executive M.B.A. program in Management of Technology is available. For more information, contact the Dupree College of Management at (404) 894-5606.

Contact Information

PHONE
General information: (404) 894-2000
Algorithms, combinatorics, and optimization: (404) 894-2593
Computer science: (404) 894-3152

Electrical and computer engineering: (404) 894-2900
Human-computer interaction: (404) 894-4672
Information design and technology: (404) 894-2730

E-MAIL
Computer science: communications@cc.gatech.edu
Electrical and computer engineering: info@ece.gatech.edu
Human-computer interaction: hci-ms@gvu.gatech.edu
Information design and technology: idt-info@lcc.gatech.edu

Harvard University   www.harvard.edu ★☆

Academic Office
Division of Engineering and Applied Sciences
Pierce Hall 110A
Cambridge, MA 02138

Year established: 1636
Ownership: Private

This unparalleled university offers a variety of interdisciplinary, research-oriented programs in computer science at every level. Evening classes are available.

Degrees Offered

UNDERGRADUATE
A.B., Computer Science

GRADUATE
S.M., Computer Science
Ph.D., Computer Science

Approximate Cost of Degrees

UNDERGRADUATE
$90,800

MASTER'S
$33,100

DOCTORATE
$52,800

Admissions Guidelines

UNDERGRADUATE
High school diploma, SAT and/or ACT required

GRADUATE
Accredited bachelor's, GRE required

Undergraduate Programs
The A.B. in Computer Science is a highly abstract, interdisciplinary program that emphasizes the theoretical fundamentals of computer science and its applications in diverse fields. Formal interdisciplinary concentrations are available in cognitive science, computer science and mathematics, economics, electrical engineering, and linguistics.

Graduate Programs
The S.M. and Ph.D. programs in Computer Science are offered through the School of Engineering and Applied Sciences as a whole rather than by a formal department of computer science. As such, they are defined to a great extent by the student's predilections and research interests. Both programs are organized around the final project (the thesis in the case of the S.M., the dissertation in the case of the Ph.D.), and virtually any series of courses may be

feasible provided it meets with faculty approval. Students are not only permitted to undertake inter-disciplinary research projects, they are encouraged to do so.

Other Programs

A Ph.D. in Information Technology and Management is offered jointly by the School of Engineering and Applied Sciences and Harvard Business School.

Contact Information

PHONE
Engineering and applied sciences: (617) 495-2833

E-MAIL
Engineering and applied sciences: info@deas.harvard.edu
Admissions (E&AS): admissions@deas.harvard.edu

✳ **EXTRA!**

Microsoft CEO Steve Ballmer is a Harvard graduate (his degree is in mathematics).

Howard University

www.howard.edu ☆☆☆

Office of Admission
2400 Sixth Street NW
Washington, DC 20059

Graduate School of Arts and Sciences
Fourth and College Streets NW
Washington, DC 20059

Year established: 1867
Ownership: Private

This highly respected university offers extremely intensive programs at all levels in several information technology fields. Evening classes are available.

Degrees Offered

UNDERGRADUATE
 B.S., Electrical Engineering
B.S., Systems and Computer Science

GRADUATE
M.C.S.
M.Eng., Electrical Engineering
Ph.D., Electrical Engineering

Approximate Cost of Degrees

UNDERGRADUATE
$66,600

MASTER'S
$14,400

DOCTORATE
$33,600

Admissions Guidelines

UNDERGRADUATE
High school diploma, SAT and/or ACT

GRADUATE
Accredited bachelor's, GRE recommended

Undergraduate Programs

The ABET-accredited B.S. program in Electrical Engineering offers concentrations in communications theory/signal processing, computer engineering, microwave and antennas, and solid-state electronics.

The CSAB-accredited B.S. in Systems and Computer Science is oriented toward software engineering and data structures.

Graduate Programs

The 30-hour Master of Computer Science (M.C.S.) is an extremely focused program grounded primarily in issues of programming and software engineering. No thesis is required.

The Master of Engineering (M.Eng.) in Electrical Engineering may be undertaken as a traditional 30-hour research master's (with 24 credit hours of coursework and a 6-hour thesis) or as a 33-hour professional master's (with 33 hours of coursework and two comprehensive subject examinations). Concentrations are available in antennas/microwaves and communications, control engineering, power systems, signal processing, and solid-state electronics.

The 72-hour Ph.D. in Electrical Engineering requires two comprehensive examinations as well as the standard dissertation.

Other Programs

Howard University also offers an M.B.A. with an e-commerce specialization. This program may be completed entirely by distance learning. For more information, visit Howard University Online (http//www.howarduniversityonline.com).

Contact Information

PHONE

Admissions: (202) 806-2900 or (800) 822-6363
Computer science: (202) 806-6595
Electrical engineering: (202) 806-6585

E-MAIL

Admissions: admission@howard.edu
Engineering and computer science:
ceacs@howard.edu

Illinois Institute of Technology   www.iit.edu ★★★½

3300 South Federal Street
Chicago, IL 60616-3793

Year established: 1890
Ownership: Private

This private, professionally oriented institution offers a variety of unique information technology programs at all levels. Evening classes, intensive courses, and extension programs are available. Almost all programs (even through the doctoral level) may be completed part-time.

Degrees Offered

UNDERGRADUATE

ABET B.S., Computer Engineering
B.S., Computer Information Systems
B.S., Computer Science
ABET B.S., Electrical Engineering
B.S., Internet Communication

GRADUATE

M.E.C.E.
M.S., Computer Science
M.S., Computer Systems Engineering
M.S., E-Commerce

M.S., Electrical Engineering
M.T.S.E.
Ph.D., Computer Science
Ph.D., Electrical Engineering

Approximate Cost of Degrees

UNDERGRADUATE

$70,000

MASTER'S

$21,300

DOCTORATE

$39,000

Admissions Guidelines

UNDERGRADUATE
High school diploma, SAT and/or ACT recommended

GRADUATE
Accredited bachelor's, GRE recommended

Undergraduate Programs
The ABET-accredited B.S. programs in Computer Engineering and Electrical Engineering permit students to essentially spend the bulk of their senior year pursuing student-designed, faculty-approved specializations.

The B.S. in Computer Information Systems is an interdisciplinary, software-oriented degree that emphasizes the use of computer applications in a faculty-approved field of the student's choice.

The B.S. in Computer Science is a structured program that places a great deal of weight on the theoretical background of the field.

The B.S. in Internet Communication addresses the Internet from the dual perspective of information technology and the social sciences.

Graduate Programs
The Master of Electrical and Computer Engineering (M.E.C.E.) is a professional degree designed primarily for reentry students. No thesis is required. Concentrations are available in communication systems, computer communication, computer engineering, control systems, electromagnetics, electronics, networks, photonics and optics, power systems, and signal processing. Students are also encouraged to design their own concentration tracks.

The M.S. in Computer Science is available in four tracks: general, computer networking and telecommunications, intelligent information systems, and software engineering. No thesis is required.

The M.S. in Computer Systems Engineering integrates aspects of computer engineering, software engineering, and systems engineering. A thesis may be undertaken for credit, but is not required. Concentrations are available in computer hardware design, computer systems software, and networks/telecommunications.

The M.S. in E-Commerce is essentially a professional degree for budding dot-com entrepreneurs.

The M.S. program in Electrical Engineering presents an option for students to define a highly specialized professional or research-oriented curriculum through the use of free electives. A thesis may be undertaken for credit, but is not required.

Concentrations are available in communication theory and signal processing, computer engineering, networks/electronics/electromagnetics, and power/control systems.

The Master of Telecommunications and Software Engineering (M.T.S.E.) is a professional degree designed primarily for reentry students. No thesis is required.

The Ph.D. in Computer Science involves a broad qualifying examination and a comprehensive examination in addition to the standard dissertation.

The Ph.D. in Electrical Engineering involves a broad qualifying examination, a comprehensive examination in the field of specialization, and a publication requirement in addition to the standard dissertation.

Other Programs
An M.S. for Teachers (M.S.T.) in Computer Science is also available.

Contact Information

PHONE
General information: (312) 567-3000
Admissions: (312) 567-3025 or (800) 448-2329
Computer science: (312) 567-5150
E-commerce: (312) 906-6522
Electrical and computer engineering: (312) 567-3400

FAX
Computer science: (312) 567-5067
Electrical and computer engineering: (312) 567-8976

E-MAIL
Admissions: admission@iit.edu
Computer science: info@cs.iit.edu
E-commerce: Martin Bariff (bariff@iit.edu)

Indiana University—Bloomington   www.iub.edu ☆☆☆

107 S. Indiana Avenue
Bloomington, IN 47405-7000

Year established: 1838
Ownership: Public

As the capital campus of Indiana's public university system, this institution is well-grounded in tradition. At the same time, it shows no signs of slowing down; with new programs in informatics and human-computer interaction, IUB has managed to stay on the cutting edge of the information technology field. Reentry students are also given a number of options, ranging from evening classes and summer intensives to (at the undergraduate level) distance learning. Most programs can likely be completed part-time.

Degrees Offered

UNDERGRADUATE
B.A., Computer Science
B.S., Computer Science
B.S., Informatics

GRADUATE
M.S., Computer Science
M.S., Human-Computer Interaction
Ph.D., Computer Science

Approximate Cost of Degrees

UNDERGRADUATE, RESIDENT
$15,000

UNDERGRADUATE, NONRESIDENT
$49,800

MASTER'S, RESIDENT
$5,800

MASTER'S, NONRESIDENT
$16,800

DOCTORATE, RESIDENT
$10,600

DOCTORATE, NONRESIDENT
$30,900

Admissions Guidelines

UNDERGRADUATE
High school diploma, SAT and/or ACT required

GRADUATE
Accredited bachelor's, GRE required; subject GRE also recommended

Undergraduate Programs

The B.A. and B.S. programs in Computer Science represent solid, broad-based curricula in the field. The two degrees differ significantly only in their respective concentration requirements.

The B.S. in Informatics is essentially a computer information systems program designed with a versatile applied, broad-based interdisciplinary focus. Informatics can be applied to the health sciences, for instance, or perhaps to accounting. The emphasis is somewhat less business-oriented than most programs of its kind, though of course students may always choose to apply informatics to business administration or related fields.

Graduate Programs

The 30-hour M.S. in Computer Science places significant weight on programming and software engineering. A thesis, project, or examination may be undertaken (in lieu of an additional 9 hours of coursework), but these are not required.

The Ph.D. in Computer Science involves a qualifying examination in addition to the standard dissertation.

The 36-hour M.S. in Human-Computer Interaction is offered through the School of Informatics. Like most curricula in the field, this program places a decidedly heavy emphasis on software engineering and graphics as they pertain to computer interfaces. A thesis or project is required.

Other Programs

A Ph.D. in Cognitive Science may be undertaken in conjunction with the Department of Computer Science to create a beast that resembles, to a great extent, a Ph.D. in Cognitive Neural Systems. It's worth noting that the program itself doesn't look IT-oriented, but the opportunity for IT specialization is certainly there. For more information, contact the Cognitive Science program at (812) 855-2722.

Contact Information

PHONE
General information: (812) 855-4848
Admissions: (812) 855-0661
Computer science: (812) 855-1502

Informatics/HCI: (812) 856-5754

E-MAIL
Admissions: iuadmit@indiana.edu
Computer science (undergraduate):
ug-info@cs.indiana.edu
Computer science (graduate):
gradvise@cs.indiana.edu
Informatics/HCI: emmerson@indiana.edu

Indiana University/ Purdue University—Indianapolis

www.iupui.edu ☆☆½

425 University Boulevard
Indianapolis, IN 46202-5143

Year established: 1969
Ownership: Public

When the two largest public university systems in Indiana converge on a single campus, this is the result one might expect: a scrambling, hectic metropolitan innovation factory that can never afford the luxury of stagnation. Through its budding School of New Media and cooperative projects with other campuses, this is clearly one of the top schools to watch. Most graduate programs can be completed entirely via evening classes. Short intensive courses and distance learning are also available.

Degrees Offered

UNDERGRADUATE
B.S., Computer Science
B.S., Computer Technology
(ABET) B.S., Electrical Engineering
(ABET) B.S., Electrical Engineering Technology

GRADUATE
M.S., Computer and Information Science
M.S., Electrical Engineering
Ph.D., Electrical Engineering

Approximate Cost of Degrees

UNDERGRADUATE, RESIDENT
$14,700

UNDERGRADUATE, NONRESIDENT
$45,600

MASTER'S, RESIDENT
$6,000

MASTER'S, NONRESIDENT
$17,000

DOCTORATE, RESIDENT
$10,900

DOCTORATE, NONRESIDENT
$31,200

Admissions Guidelines

UNDERGRADUATE
High school diploma required, SAT and/or ACT recommended

GRADUATE
Accredited bachelor's with 3.0 GPA, GRE recommended

Undergraduate Programs
The B.S. in Computer Science is available with tracks in computing science (applied computer science) and scientific computing (informatics and computational science).

The B.S. in Computer Technology is available in three tracks: business, standard, and technical.

The ABET-accredited B.S. curriculum in Electrical Engineering represents a structured, hands-on program in the field.

Graduate Programs

The 30-hour M.S. in Computer and Information Science is available with a thesis track and a project track. Specializations are available in bioinformatics, databases and data mining, networks and distributed systems, software engineering, and visualization.

The 30-hour M.S. in Electrical Engineering is available with thesis and non-thesis tracks. Considerable research opportunities are available, particularly in computer engineering and related fields.

The Ph.D. in Electrical Engineering is likely reserved for students who have completed their M.S.E.E. at IUPUI, but other qualified students may be accepted with faculty approval.

Other Programs

B.S. and M.S. programs in Media Arts and Science are also available; these programs include a strong computer graphics component. For more information, contact the School of New Media at (317) 278-7666.

Contact Information

PHONE
General information: (317) 274-4591
Computer science: (317) 274-9727
Engineering and Technology: (317) 274-9726

E-MAIL
Computer science: admissions@cs.iupui.edu
Engineering and Technology: etinfo@engr.iupui.edu

Iowa State University

www.iastate.edu ☆☆½

Ames, IA 50011

Year established: 1858
Ownership: Public

This prominent state university, boasts a computing museum and a well-known faculty in computer science. With evening classes, intensive courses, and distance learning as options, this institution can be as useful to the seasoned reentry student as it is to many promising young freshmen.

Degrees Offered

UNDERGRADUATE
ABET B.S., Computer Engineering
CSAB B.S., Computer Science
ABET B.S., Electrical Engineering

GRADUATE
M.S., Computer Engineering
M.S., Computer Science
M.S., Electrical Engineering
Ph.D., Computer Science
Ph.D., Electrical Engineering

Approximate Cost of Degrees

UNDERGRADUATE, RESIDENT
$11,600–$15,600

UNDERGRADUATE, NONRESIDENT
$38,900–$52,100

MASTER'S, RESIDENT
$6,900

MASTER'S, NONRESIDENT
$20,300

DOCTORATE, RESIDENT
$13,400

DOCTORATE, NONRESIDENT
$39,400

Admissions Guidelines

UNDERGRADUATE
High school diploma required, SAT and/or ACT recommended

GRADUATE
Accredited bachelor's required, GRE recommended

Undergraduate Programs

The ABET-accredited B.S. in Computer Engineering is free from the electrical engineering emphasis that defines so many programs in the field, and is instead a program clearly oriented toward computer engineering as a specific, integral discipline.

The CSAB-accredited B.S. in Computer Science is a largely software-oriented program with unusually strong options in artificial intelligence and neural networks.

The ABET-accredited B.S. in Electrical Engineering is fairly standard and does not stray too far from what one would describe as the established regular program in the field. The program looks quite solid, but there is not much in it that stands out. Certainly a student who completes this program will be well prepared for graduate work in the field, as it includes significant applied and theoretical components.

Graduate Programs

The M.S. programs in Computer Engineering and Electrical Engineering may culminate in a thesis if the student wants, but a non-thesis track (culminating in a faculty-approved independent study project of some kind) is also available in both programs. Both programs may be completed almost entirely by distance learning.

The M.S. in Computer Science culminates with a required thesis project that may, at the student's discretion, be a formal thesis or research paper. Students who choose the latter option must take one additional course.

The Ph.D. in Computer Science requires a comprehensive examination, a standard thesis, and a research skills requirement. Students may satisfy the research skills component by earning a B grade on a sequence of two upper-level English courses, by publishing a paper in a peer-reviewed journal, or by demonstrating competency in a foreign language.

The Ph.D. in Electrical Engineering requires a comprehensive examination in addition to the standard dissertation. Students are also expected to pursue one of four faculty-approved specializations: communications and signal processing, control systems, electromagnetics, electromagnetics, and power.

Other Programs

The Department of Computer Science can collaborate with the Department of Psychology to create a Ph.D. in Computer Science oriented toward cognitive science or a Ph.D. in Neuroscience oriented toward cognitive neural systems. Contact the Department of Computer Science for more information.

Contact Information

PHONE
General information: (515) 294-4111 or (800) 262-3810
Distance Learning: (515) 294-7470 or (800) 854-1675
Computer science: (515) 294-4377
Electrical and Computer Engineering: (515) 294-5933

FAX
Computer science: (515) 294-0258
Electrical and Computer Engineering: (515) 294-9273

E-MAIL
General information: online@iastate.edu
Computer science: Janey Nicholas
(jnichol@iastate.edu)
Electrical and Computer Engineering:
ece@ee.iastate.edu

 EXTRA!

Iowa State is home to the Atanasoff-Berry Computer (ABC), the world's first digital computer.

Jackson State University

www.jsums.edu ☆☆½

1400 John R. Lynch Street
Jackson, MS 39217

Year established: 1877
Ownership: Public

This midsize urban university offers undergraduate and graduate programs in computer science, and has recently begun to offer programs in computer engineering as well. Reentry students may want to take advantage of JSU's evening classes and extension courses.

Degrees Offered

UNDERGRADUATE
B.S., Computer Engineering
(CSAB) B.S., Computer Science

GRADUATE
M.S., Computer Science

Approximate Cost of Degrees

UNDERGRADUATE, RESIDENT
$13,200

UNDERGRADUATE, NONRESIDENT
$24,600

GRADUATE, RESIDENT
$4,000

GRADUATE, NONRESIDENT
$9,200

Admissions Guidelines

UNDERGRADUATE
High school diploma, SAT and/or ACT required

GRADUATE
Accredited bachelor's with 3.0 GPA required, GRE recommended

Undergraduate Programs

The B.S. in Computer Engineering is available with tracks in hardware engineering, software engineering, and telecommunications.

The CSAB-accredited B.S. in Computer Science is a theory-oriented degree. Students work from a broad, comprehensive background in mathematics toward programming, data analysis, and software engineering.

Graduate Programs

The 36-hour M.S. in Computer Science focuses on programming and software engineering. Students may choose a thesis or project track; all students in the program must pass a comprehensive examination.

Other Programs

An M.S.Ed. in Technology Education is also available. For more information, contact the Department of Technology at (601) 968-2466.

Contact Information

PHONE
General information: (601) 968-2121 or (800) 848-6817
Admissions: (601) 968-2100
Computer engineering: (601) 313-9044
Computer science: (601) 968-2105

FAX
(601) 968-2237

E-MAIL
admappl@ccaix.jsums.edu

Johns Hopkins University   www.jhu.edu ☆☆½

Office of Admissions
140 Garland Hall
3400 North Charles Street
Baltimore, MD 21218

Year established: 1876
Ownership: Private

This respected, research-oriented institution offers a variety of programs geared toward both traditional and reentry students. Evening classes and intensive short courses are available.

Degrees Offered

UNDERGRADUATE

B.A., Computer Science
B.S., Computer Science
B.A., Electrical and Computer Engineering
B.S., Computer Engineering
(ABET) B.S., Electrical Engineering

GRADUATE

M.S.E., Computer Science
M.S.E., Electrical and Computer Engineering
M.S., Information and Telecommunications Systems
Ph.D., Computer Science
Ph.D., Electrical Engineering

Approximate Cost of Degrees

UNDERGRADUATE

$94,700

MASTER'S

$35,500

DOCTORATE

$59,200

Admissions Guidelines

UNDERGRADUATE

High school diploma, SAT and/or ACT required

GRADUATE

Accredited bachelor's required, GRE often required

Undergraduate Programs

The B.A. in Computer Science is oriented toward software engineering and databases. A 6-hour foreign-language concentration is required.

The B.A. in Electrical and Computer Engineering allows for a great deal of flexibility. A 6-hour foreign language concentration is required.

The B.S. in Computer Engineering is a highly structured program that emphasizes hardware issues slightly more than it emphasizes software issues.

The B.S. in Computer Science is very similar to the B.A. in its orientation; software engineering and databases are emphasized heavily. The B.S. major is larger than the B.A. major (by 12 credit hours), and does not require a foreign language concentration.

The ABET-accredited B.S. in Electrical Engineering is also described as a B.S.E.E. in Electrical and Computer Engineering, and does indeed allow for a great deal of study in computer hardware.

Graduate Programs

The Master of Science in Engineering (M.S.E.) in Computer Science is offered through the Department of Computer Science. The base of the program is a 24-hour coursework requirement; students may then choose to undertake a thesis, a suitable project, or 6 hours of additional coursework to fulfill the remaining requirements.

The Master of Science in Engineering (M.S.E.) in Electrical and Computer Engineering is, like the Computer Science M.S.E., based around a mandatory 24-hour coursework requirement and a floating 6-hour requirement that may be fulfilled by a thesis, project, or coursework.

Although it is most certainly an IT-oriented program, the M.S. in Information and Telecommunications Systems does involve a business component. The program concludes with a faculty-approved capstone project. Concentrations are available in advanced technology and electronic commerce, information systems, and telecommunications systems.

Students in the Computer Science Ph.D. program must fulfill an 8-course breadth requirement;

students are then required to undertake two projects and report on them before proceeding to the comprehensive examination.

Following the comprehensive examination, students may proceed to the standard dissertation.

The Ph.D. in Electrical Engineering is a research-oriented program wherein the student picks a faculty advisor early on and proceeds with this advisor through the conclusion of the dissertation. A qualifying examination is required.

Other Programs

A business-oriented B.S. in Information Systems is available through the School of Professional Studies and Business Education. For more information, contact the Division of Business/Information Systems at (410) 516-0775.

A Master of Music (M.Mus.) in Computer Music is available. For more information, contact the Peabody Conservatory's Computer Music Department at (410) 659-8107.

Contact Information

PHONE
Admissions (undergraduate): (410) 516-8171
Admissions (graduate): (410) 516-8174
Computer science: (410) 516-8775
Electrical and computer engineering: (410) 516-7033
Information and telecommunications systems: (410) 516-0777

FAX
Computer science: (410) 516-6134
Electrical and computer engineering: (410) 516-5566

E-MAIL
Admissions (undergraduate): gotojhu@jhu.edu
Admissions (graduate): gradadm@jhu.edu
Computer science: Nancy Scheeler (nancy@cs.jhu.edu)
Electrical and computer engineering: ece@jhu.edu
Information and telecommunications systems: itsinfo@jhu.edu

Kansas State University   www.ksu.edu ☆☆☆☆

Admissions Office
119 Anderson Hall
Manhattan, KS 66506

Year established: 1863
Ownership: Public

This large state university offers highly rigorous programs in information technology fields at all levels. Evening classes, intensive courses, and distance learning are available; in fact, all required courses for the master's degrees in electrical engineering and software engineering may be completed via distance learning.

Degrees Offered

UNDERGRADUATE
(CSAB) B.A., Computer Science
(CSAB) B.S., Computer Science
B.A., Information Systems
B.S., Information Systems
(ABET) B.S., Computer Engineering
(ABET) B.S., Electrical Engineering

GRADUATE
M.S., Computing and Information Sciences
M.S., Electrical Engineering

M.S.E.
Ph.D., Computer Science

Approximate Cost of Degrees

UNDERGRADUATE, RESIDENT
$8,400

UNDERGRADUATE, NONRESIDENT
$34,800

MASTER'S, RESIDENT
$9,000

Master's, Nonresident
$24,300

Doctorate, Resident
$13,700

Doctorate, Nonresident
$47,400

Admissions Guidelines

Undergraduate
High school diploma, ACT required

Graduate
Accredited bachelor's with 3.0 GPA

Undergraduate Programs

The ABET-accredited B.S. in Computer Engineering gives roughly equal weight to hardware and software engineering issues.

The CSAB-accredited B.A. and B.S. programs in Computer Science represent fairly standard, well-rounded programs in the field. The major requirements of both programs are essentially the same.

The ABET-accredited B.S. in Electrical Engineering is designed to give students a stronger-than-average background in the theoretical framework supporting electrical engineering as a field. Students are required to choose a specialization in bioengineering, communication systems and signal processing, digital systems, electronic systems and devices, or power systems.

The B.A. and B.S. programs in Information Systems are heavily oriented toward programming and software engineering. Strong, intensive, and focused almost completely on information technology itself, the Information Systems curriculum of Kansas State University bears little resemblance to the business-oriented programs in information systems offered at many universities.

Graduate Programs

The 33-hour M.S. in Computer and Information Sciences allows for a 12-hour student-defined specialization. Students may undertake a thesis or project for credit, but are not required to do so.

The 30-hour M.S. in Electrical Engineering is available with thesis, report, and coursework-only tracks. The coursework-only track of this program may be completed entirely via distance learning.

The 33-hour Master of Software Engineering (M.S.E.) focuses on a student-defined application area; the capstone project is a software portfolio consisting of various creative projects undertaken as part of the program. This degree may be completed almost entirely via distance learning; only one short visit to the actual campus is required.

The Ph.D. in Computer Science involves three qualifying examinations in addition to course requirements and the standard dissertation.

Other Programs

A Ph.D. in Engineering, with emphasis in electrical and computer engineering, is also available. For more information, contact the College of Engineering at (785) 532-5590.

Contact Information

Phone
Admissions: (785) 532-6250
Continuing education and distance learning: (800) 432-8222
Computer and information science: (785) 532-6350
Electrical and computer engineering: (785) 532-5600

Fax
Admissions: (785) 532-6393
Computer and information science: (785) 532-7353
Electrical and computer engineering: (785) 532-1188

E-mail
General information: kstate@ksu.edu
Computer and information science: office@cis.ksu.edu
Online programs: Ellen Stauffer (estauff@dce.ksu.edu)
Electrical and computer engineering (undergraduate): undergrad@eece.ksu.edu
Electrical and computer engineering (graduate): grad@eece.ksu.edu

Lamar University

www.lamar.edu ☆☆☆

4400 Martin Luther King Boulevard
P.O. Box 10009
Beaumont, TX 77710

Year established: 1923
Ownership: Public

This midsize state university offers enticing information technology options at all levels for traditional and reentry students alike. Evening classes and distance learning are available.

Degrees Offered

UNDERGRADUATE
B.S., Computer Science
ⒶⒷⒺⓉ B.S., Electrical Engineering

GRADUATE
M.E., Electrical Engineering
M.E.S., Electrical Engineering
M.S., Computer Science
D.Eng., Electrical Engineering

Approximate Cost of Degrees

UNDERGRADUATE, RESIDENT
$6,700

UNDERGRADUATE, NONRESIDENT
$27,700

MASTER'S, RESIDENT
$5,700

MASTER'S, NONRESIDENT
$21,100

DOCTORATE, RESIDENT
$11,500

DOCTORATE, NONRESIDENT
$42,300

Admissions Guidelines

UNDERGRADUATE
High school diploma, SAT and/or ACT required

GRADUATE
Accredited bachelor's, GRE required

Undergraduate Programs
The B.S. program in Computer Science is oriented toward software and theory.

The ABET-accredited B.S. in Electrical Engineering permits students to choose an optional computer engineering track.

Graduate Programs
The Master of Engineering (M.E.) and Master of Engineering Science (M.E.S.) are both 36-hour programs. The primary difference seems to be that the former is a professional degree with no required thesis, while the latter is a research-oriented degree with a required thesis.

The 37-hour M.S. in Computer Science is available with thesis and project tracks. Students must choose a specialization in artificial intelligence, computer architecture, databases, graphics and multimedia, simulation, or software engineering.

The Doctor of Engineering (D.Eng.) is a highly research-focused degree, which culminates in completion of a "field of study." The field of study requirement essentially involves concentrated coursework in a given field, completion of supervised research, and a formal report.

Other Programs
A B.B.A. in Management Information Systems is also available through the College of Business. For more information, contact the Department of Management Information Systems at (409) 880-8635.

Contact Information

PHONE
General information: (409) 880-7011
Computer science: (409) 880-8775
Electrical engineering: (409) 880-8746

E-MAIL
Computer science: csdept@hal.lamar.edu
Electrical engineering: eece@hal.lamar.edu

Lehigh University

www.lehigh.edu ☆☆½

27 Memorial Drive West
Bethlehem, PA 18015

Year established: 1865
Ownership: Private

This highly respected university offers information technology degrees at all levels. Evening classes and distance learning are available.

Degrees Offered

UNDERGRADUATE
B.A., Computer Science
CSAB B.S., Computer Science
ABET B.S., Computer Engineering
ABET B.S., Electrical Engineering

GRADUATE
M.Eng., Electrical Engineering
M.S., Computer Engineering
M.S., Computer Science
M.S., Electrical Engineering
Ph.D., Computer Science
Ph.D., Electrical Engineering

Approximate Cost of Degrees

UNDERGRADUATE
$96,000

MASTER'S
$32,000

DOCTORATE
$58,800

Admissions Guidelines

UNDERGRADUATE
Accredited bachelor's, SAT and/or ACT required

GRADUATE
Accredited bachelor's with 2.75 overall GPA and 3.0 GPA on upper 60 hours, GRE required

Undergraduate Programs

The B.A. and B.S. programs in Computer Science are identical in their major courses. They differ only in accreditation (the B.S. is CSAB-accredited, while the B.A. is not) and general distribution requirements (the B.S. requires 12 hours of additional credit in the natural sciences). Both represent a broad, largely theory-oriented study of the field.

The ABET-accredited B.S. in Computer Engineering provides a strong background in the theoretical foundations of the field. Specializations are available in communications, computer architecture, digital signal processing, digital systems, image processing, software engineering, system software, and VLSI circuit design.

The ABET-accredited B.S. in Electrical Engineering represents a broad, highly structured curriculum in the field, stressing the theoretical fundamentals of electrical engineering as a scientific discipline.

Graduate Programs

The 30-hour M.Eng. in Electrical Engineering is a professional, hands-on program representing a series of practical, design-oriented courses. A final project is required.

The 36-hour M.S. in Computer Engineering is a highly structured program involving hands-on research as well as intensive study in the abstract, theoretical fundamentals of the field. A thesis is required.

The 33-hour M.S. in Computer Science is a largely theory-focused, research-oriented program. A thesis is required.

The 36-hour M.S. in Electrical Engineering is research-oriented; students may design mild specializations to fit their interests. A thesis is required.

The Ph.D. programs in Computer Science and Electrical Engineering involve two written examinations (one comprehensive, one specialized) in addition to the standard dissertation.

Other Programs

B.S. and M.B.A. programs in Business Information Systems are also available. For more information, contact the Department of Management and Marketing at (610) 758-4743.

An M.S. in Management of Technology is offered via distance learning. For more information, contact the Office of Distance Education at (610) 758-5794.

Contact Information

PHONE
General information: (610) 758-3000
Admissions (undergraduate): (610) 758-3100
Admissions (graduate/engineering and applied science): (610) 758-6310
Computer science and electrical/computer engineering: (610) 758-3065

FAX
Admissions (undergraduate): (610) 758-4361
Admissions (graduate/engineering and applied science): (610) 758-5623
Computer science and electrical/computer engineering: (610) 758-6279

Louisiana State University   www.lsu.edu ☆☆½

Office of Undergraduate Admissions
110 Thomas Boyd Hall
Baton Rouge, LA 70803

LSU Graduate School
114 David Boyd Hall
Baton Rouge, LA 70803

Year established: 1853
Ownership: Public

This large state-funded university offers research-oriented and vocational programs in information technology at all levels. Evening classes and distance learning are available.

Degrees Offered

UNDERGRADUATE
🎓 B.S., Computer Engineering
B.S., Computer Science
🎓 B.S., Electrical Engineering

GRADUATE
M.S., Computer Science
M.S., Electrical and Computer Engineering
Ph.D., Computer Science
Ph.D., Electrical and Computer Engineering

Approximate Cost of Degrees

UNDERGRADUATE, RESIDENT
$10,900

UNDERGRADUATE, NONRESIDENT
$27,200

MASTER'S, RESIDENT
$4,100

MASTER'S, NONRESIDENT
$10,300

DOCTORATE, RESIDENT
$11,000

DOCTORATE, NONRESIDENT
$27,500

Admissions Guidelines

UNDERGRADUATE
High school diploma, SAT and/or ACT required

GRADUATE
Accredited bachelor's, GRE required

Undergraduate Programs
The B.S. in Computer Science is oriented toward software engineering and programming issues.

The ABET-accredited B.S. in Computer Engineering is a well-rounded program, incorporating courses in VLSI design, computer architecture, digital systems, and related fields into a broad theoretical framework.

The ABET-accredited B.S. in Electrical Engineering is oriented toward design of complex electronic systems.

Graduate Programs

The 36-hour M.S. in Computer Science centers on a student-defined, faculty-approved specialization that may be interdisciplinary in its scope. A comprehensive examination is required. The program culminates in a thesis or systems design project; this thesis or project must fall within the chosen field of specialization.

The 36-hour M.S. program in Electrical and Computer Engineering is available with concentrations in computer engineering, electronics, power, and systems engineering. Students may choose a thesis or non-thesis track.

The Ph.D. in Computer Science requires a comprehensive examination in addition to the standard dissertation. Students are encouraged to participate in some of the many ongoing research projects taking place at Louisiana State.

The Ph.D. program in Electrical and Computer Engineering is highly individualized; students design a course plan in the field with faculty approval. A comprehensive examination is required in addition to the standard dissertation.

Other Programs

The Louisiana State University M.B.A. program is available with concentrations in enterprise information systems, human resource information systems, and marketing information technology. For more information, contact the Ourso College of Business at (225) 388-8867.

Contact Information

PHONE

Admissions (undergraduate): (225) 388-1175
Admissions (graduate): (225) 388-2311
Computer science: (225) 388-1495
Electrical and computer engineering: (504) 388-5241

FAX

Computer science: (225) 388-1465
Electrical and computer engineering: (504) 388-5200

E-MAIL

Admissions (undergraduate): mmoore2@lsumvs.sncc.lsu.edu
Admissions (graduate): gradadm@lsu.edu
Computer science: Lynette Jackson (lynette@bit.csc.lsu.edu)
Electrical and computer engineering: Alan H. Marshak (marshak@gate.ee.lsu.edu)

Loyola University—Chicago   www.luc.edu ☆☆☆

6525 N. Sheridan Road
Chicago, IL 60626

Year established: 1870
Ownership: Private

This prestigious Jesuit university offers software-oriented undergraduate and graduate programs in computer science. Evening classes and extension courses are available.

Degrees Offered

UNDERGRADUATE
B.S., Computer Science

GRADUATE
M.S., Computer Science

Approximate Cost of Degrees

UNDERGRADUATE
$71,000

GRADUATE
$15,400

Admissions Guidelines

UNDERGRADUATE
Accredited bachelor's, SAT and/or ACT required

GRADUATE
Accredited bachelor's with 3.0 GPA, GRE required

Undergraduate Programs

The B.S. program in Computer Science focuses on programming and software engineering through the lens of theoretical computer science.

Graduate Programs

The 30-hour M.S. program in Computer Science gives a broad-based summary through five ground-level courses (advanced computer architecture, algorithms and complexity, object-oriented programming, operating systems, and software engineering). The remaining 15 hours are all comprised of free electives, giving students a great deal of flexibility in designing a tailored curriculum. An internship is strongly encouraged. No thesis is required.

Other Programs

B.B.A. and M.B.A. programs with emphases in information systems management and e-commerce are available through the Graduate School of Business. For more information, contact the Information Systems and Operations Management Department at (312) 915-7050.

More Information

In addition to the two primary campuses in Chicago, LUC operates campuses in Maywood and Willmette, Illinois.

Contact Information

PHONE
General information: (773) 274-3000
Computer science: (773) 508-3558

FAX
Computer science: (773) 508-2123

E-MAIL
Computer science: info@math.luc.edu

Marquette University

www.marquette.edu ☆☆☆

P.O. Box 1881
Milwaukee, WI 53201-1881

Year established: 1881
Ownership: Private

This midsize private university offers programs at all levels in information technology fields; rigorous, applied programs based on sound theoretical foundations abound. Evening classes are available.

Degrees Offered

UNDERGRADUATE
B.S., Computer Engineering
B.S., Computer Science
🅰️ B.S., Electrical Engineering

GRADUATE
M.S., Computing
M.S., Electrical and Computer Engineering
Ph.D., Electrical and Computer Engineering

Approximate Cost of Degrees

UNDERGRADUATE
$66,900

GRADUATE
$18,400

Admissions Guidelines

UNDERGRADUATE
High school diploma, SAT and/or ACT required

GRADUATE
Accredited bachelor's required, 3.0 GPA and GRE recommended

Undergraduate Programs

The B.S. program in Computer Engineering is available with specializations in computer system design, knowledge-based systems, and software engineering. Students can also, with faculty approval, design an individualized specialization.

The B.S. in Computer Science is largely programming-focused, although theory is also stressed.

The ABET-accredited B.S. in Electrical Engineering can be completed via one of two specialized tracks: electronic engineering or computer engineering.

Graduate Programs

The 36-hour M.S. program in Computing is available in three tracks: standard coursework with thesis, standard coursework only, and bioinformatics. The first two represent a standard tech-oriented M.S. program in Computer Information Systems. The bioinformatics track, offered in conjunction with the Medical College of Wisconsin, involves a 6-hour research project in lieu of a thesis.

The M.S. program in Electrical and Computer Engineering is available in three tracks: coursework with thesis, coursework with essay, and coursework only. The first two are 30-hour curricula, while the latter represents 36 hours of coursework.

The Ph.D. in Electrical and Computer Engineering requires two qualifying examinations (one oral, one written) in addition to coursework requirements and the standard dissertation. Coursework emphases are available in antennas and propagation, artificial intelligence and expert systems, computer science and engineering, control systems, digital signal and speech processing, electric drives and power electronics, materials science, microwaves, power systems and devices, and solid-state devices. While Marquette's Web page makes the very clear statement that these do not constitute formal specializations, many would in fact regard these concentrations as being roughly equivalent in depth to a mild formal specialization.

Other Programs

A B.S. in Computational Mathematics is available through the computer science department, as are M.S. and Ph.D. programs in the interdisciplinary field of Mathematics, Statistics, and Computer Science.

Contact Information

Phone
Admissions: (414) 288-7302 or (800) 222-6544
Computer science: (414) 288-7573

Fax
Computer science: (414) 288-5472

E-mail
General information: go2marquette@marquette.edu
Admissions: admissions@marquette.edu
Computer science: Douglas Harris
(doug@marque.mscs.mu.edu)
Electrical and computer engineering:
 eece@marquette.edu

Marshall University

www.marshall.edu ☆☆½

400 Hal Greer Boulevard
Huntington, WV 25755

Marshall University Graduate College
100 Angus E. Peyton Drive
South Charleston, WV 25303-1600

Year established: 1837
Ownership: Public

This large public university offers highly innovative undergraduate and master's-level programs in information technology. Evening classes, extension courses, and distance learning are available.

Degrees Offered

Undergraduate
B.S.I.S.T., Computer and Information Technology

Graduate
M.S., Information Systems

Approximate Cost of Degrees

Undergraduate, Resident
$9,800

Undergraduate, Nonresident
$26,000

Graduate, Resident
$4,400

Graduate, Nonresident
$14,200

Admissions Guidelines

UNDERGRADUATE
High school diploma, ACT required

GRADUATE
Accredited bachelor's with 2.75 GPA, GRE required

Undergraduate Programs

The B.S. in Integrated Science and Technology (B.S.I.S.T.) in Computer and Information Technology approaches the field from the broad perspective of mathematics and computational science. The Computer and Information Technology major consists of a 24-hour theoretical base and an 18-hour applied focus.

Graduate Programs

The 33-hour M.S. in Information Systems is strongly oriented toward software systems engineering. No thesis is required.

Other Programs

An M.S. in Technology Management is also available. For more information, contact the department at (304) 696-6007.

Contact Information

PHONE
Admissions (undergraduate): (304) 696-3160
Admissions (graduate): (304) 746-1901

E-MAIL
General information: webmaster@marshall.edu
Information systems: cite@marshall.edu

Massachusetts Institute of Technology   www.mit.edu ★★★½

Admissions Office
MIT, Room 3-108
77 Massachusetts Avenue
Cambridge, MA 02139-4307

Graduate and Special Student Admissions
MIT, Room 3-103
77 Massachusetts Avenue
Cambridge, MA 02139

Year established: 1861
Ownership: Private

Regarded by many as the top information technology school in the country, this prestigious research-oriented institution offers programs at all levels in a variety of information technology fields. Pay special attention to "Other Programs" (below), as MIT offers a vast number of interdisciplinary programs to fit the needs of almost any student. Evening classes are available. This school has also made a promising first step into the world of distance learning.

Degrees Offered

UNDERGRADUATE
CSAB ABET S.B., Computer Science and Engineering
CSAB ABET S.B., Electrical Engineering and Computer Science
ABET S.B., Electrical Science and Engineering

GRADUATE
M.Eng., Electrical Engineering and Computer Science
M.S., Electrical Engineering and Computer Science
C.S.E.
E.E.
Sc.D., Electrical Engineering and Computer Science
Ph.D., Electrical Engineering and Computer Science

Approximate Cost of Degrees

UNDERGRADUATE
$100,000

MASTER'S
$41,700

DOCTORATE
$75,000

Admissions Guidelines

UNDERGRADUATE
High school diploma, SAT and/or ACT required

GRADUATE
Accredited bachelor's required, GRE required for non-engineering programs

Undergraduate Programs
The ABET-accredited and CSAB-accredited S.B. program in Computer Science and Engineering, the ABET-accredited and CSAB-accredited S.B. program in Electrical Engineering and Computer Science, and the ABET-accredited S.B. program in Electrical Science and Engineering follow the same basic structural credit distributions, but differ in specific core course requirements. All three programs are available with concentrations in artificial intelligence and applications, bioelectrical engineering, communication/control/signal processing, computer systems and architecture, devices/circuits/systems, electrodynamics and energy systems, and theoretical computer science.

Graduate Programs
The Master of Engineering (M.Eng.) in Electrical Engineering and Computer Science is available with concentrations in artificial intelligence and applications, bioelectrical engineering, communication/control/signal processing, computer systems and architecture, devices/circuits/systems, electrodynamics and energy systems, and theoretical computer science. A thesis is required.

The M.S. in Electrical Engineering and Computer Science focuses on a student-defined, faculty-approved area of specialization; it is somewhat less intensive and rigid than the M.Eng. program in this field. A thesis is required.

The Engineer degrees in Computer Science (C.S.E.) and Electrical Engineering (E.E.) are founded on the basic M.Eng./M.S. model. Students must be accepted for an M.Eng. or M.S. program in Electrical Engineering and Computer Science, then specialize in Computer Science or Electrical Engineering by undertaking additional coursework in the field. A thesis is required.

The Sc.D. and Ph.D. programs in Electrical Engineering and Computer Science differ only in specific course distribution requirements. A qualifying examination is required in addition to the standard dissertation. Students who have not earned an accredited master's degree will be expected to complete the M.Eng. program before enrolling in an Sc.D. or Ph.D. program. Students who have completed a master's in the field at another university may be required to undertake the S.M. program before going on to the Sc.D. or Ph.D. program. In any case, students are generally expected to complete an MIT master's degree of some kind before pursuing an MIT doctorate.

Other Programs
The Ph.D. in Applied Mathematics offers opportunities for world-class research in theoretical computer science. For more information, contact the Graduate Department of Mathematics at (617) 253-2689.

S.B. and Ph.D. programs in Brain and Cognitive Sciences are available; these programs can be tailored to meet the interests of a student who intends to pursue research in artificial intelligence and cognitive neural systems. For more information, contact the Department of Brain and Cognitive Sciences at (617) 253-0482.

S.B. and S.M. programs in Comparative Media Studies are available through the School of Humanities and Social Science. For more information, contact the program office at (617) 253-3599.

An S.M. in Medical Informatics (intended primarily for physicians who want to expand their skills) is available. For more information, contact the Graduate Department of Health Sciences and Technology at (617) 258-7084.

The Sloan School of Management offers a Ph.D. in Management with optional emphases in information technologies and management of technological innovation. For more information, contact the Sloan doctoral program office at (617) 253-7188.

An executive S.M. in Management of Technology is available. For more information, contact the technology management office of the Sloan School of Management at (617) 253-7166.

An S.B. in Management Science is also available with an optional emphasis in information technologies. For more information, contact the undergraduate programs office of the Sloan School of Management at (617) 253-8614.

The S.B., S.M., and Ph.D. programs in Media Arts and Sciences can be tailored to fit the needs of a student who wants to specialize in computer-related art forms. For more information, contact the MIT Media Laboratory at (617) 253-0300.

The S.M. and Ph.D. programs in Operations Research are available with optional concentrations in computer science and management information systems. For more information, contact the MIT Operations Research Center at (617) 253-3601.

Highly innovative S.B. and Ph.D. programs in the field of Science, Technology, and Society are available. For more information, contact the office of the program coordinator at (617) 253-3452.

An S.M. in System Design and Management is available both residentially and via distance learning. For more information, contact Leaders for Manufacturing and System Design and Management at (617) 253-1055.

S.M. and Ph.D. programs in Technology and Policy are also available. For more information, contact the Technology and Policy Academic Office at (617) 253-7693.

Contact Information

PHONE
General information: (617) 253-1000
Admissions (undergraduate): (617) 253-4791
Admissions (graduate): (617) 253-2917
Electrical engineering and computer science (undergraduate): (617) 253-7329
Electrical engineering and computer science (graduate): (617) 253-4603

FAX
Electrical engineering and computer science: (617) 258-7354

E-MAIL
Admissions (undergraduate, freshmen): mitfrosh@mit.edu
Admissions (undergraduate, international): mitintl@mit.edu
Admissions (undergraduate, transfer): mittransfer@mit.edu
Admissions (graduate): mitgrad@mit.edu
Electrical engineering and computer science (undergraduate): ug@eecs.mit.edu
Electrical engineering and computer science (graduate): grad-ap@eecs.mit.edu

Mills College

www.mills.edu ☆☆☆☆

5000 MacArthur Boulevard
Oakland, CA 94613-1301

Year established: 1852
Ownership: Private

This small private college offers unique interdisciplinary options in computer science at the undergraduate and graduate levels. Evening classes are available.

Degrees Offered

UNDERGRADUATE
B.S., Computer Science

GRADUATE
M.A., Interdisciplinary Computer Science

Approximate Cost of Degrees

UNDERGRADUATE
$72,000–$112,400

GRADUATE
$16,700–$32,300

Admissions Guidelines

UNDERGRADUATE
High school diploma, ACT and/or SAT required

GRADUATE
Accredited bachelor's required, GRE recommended

Undergraduate Programs
The B.S. in Computer Science is a highly structured program oriented toward theory (particularly computational mathematics) and software engineering.

Graduate Programs

The 36-hour M.A. in Interdisciplinary Computer Science is based around a core battery of courses in software engineering and theoretical computer science. From this basic framework, students work within an individualized, faculty-approved track. A thesis is required.

More Information

Although Mills is a women's college at the undergraduate level, all graduate programs are available to students of either gender.

Contact Information

PHONE

Admissions (undergraduate): (800) 876-4557
Admissions (graduate): (510) 430-3309
Computer science: (510) 430-2201

FAX

Admissions (undergraduate): (510) 430-3314
Admissions (graduate): (510) 430-2159

E-MAIL

Admissions (undergraduate): admission@mills.edu
Admissions (graduate): grad-studies@mills.edu

☀ **EXTRA!**

Mills was the first women's college to offer a major in computer science.

Minnesota State University—Mankato   mankato.msus.edu ☆☆½

Undergraduate Admissions Office
209 Wigley Administration Center
Mankato, MN 56001

College of Graduate Studies and Research
125 Wigley Administration Center
Mankato, MN 56001

Year established: 1868
Ownership: Public

This midsize public university offers an array of unique programs in information technology. Evening classes and extension courses are available.

Degrees Offered

UNDERGRADUATE

B.S., Computer Engineering
B.S., Computer Engineering Technology
B.S., Computer Information Science
B.S., Computer Science
 B.S., Electrical Engineering
 B.S., Electronic(s) Engineering Technology

GRADUATE

M.S., Computer Science

M.S.E., Electrical Engineering
M.S.E., Mechatronics

Approximate Cost of Degrees

UNDERGRADUATE, RESIDENT

$12,000

UNDERGRADUATE, NONRESIDENT (KANSAS, MICHIGAN, MISSOURI, OR NEBRASKA)

$17,000

UNDERGRADUATE, NONRESIDENT (NORTH DAKOTA)
$12,000

UNDERGRADUATE, NONRESIDENT (SOUTH DAKOTA)
$12,800

UNDERGRADUATE, NONRESIDENT (WISCONSIN)
$12,500

UNDERGRADUATE, NONRESIDENT (OTHER)
$23,200

GRADUATE, RESIDENT
$5,500

GRADUATE, NONRESIDENT (NORTH OR SOUTH DAKOTA)
$4,800

GRADUATE, NONRESIDENT (WISCONSIN)
$5,300

GRADUATE, NONRESIDENT (OTHER)
$8,200

Admissions Guidelines

UNDERGRADUATE
High school diploma, ACT required

GRADUATE
Accredited bachelor's with 2.75 overall GPA (or 3.0 GPA on upper 60 hours), GRE required

Undergraduate Programs

The new B.S. program in Computer Engineering is available with optional faculty-approved concentrations in advanced digital systems, communications, digital signal processing, networking, and system design.

The new B.S. program in Computer Engineering Technology deals with computer hardware and, to a lesser extent, with general principles of electronics.

The B.S. program in Computer Information Science is primarily oriented toward data analysis and software engineering.

The B.S. program in Computer Science is highly theory-oriented and includes a complete minor in mathematics among its distribution requirements.

The ABET-accredited B.S. program in Electrical Engineering is available with optional faculty-approved concentrations in communications, controls, digital systems, and microelectronics design.

The ABET-accredited B.S. program in Electronic(s) Engineering Technology represents a highly structured standard curriculum in the field.

Graduate Programs

The 34-hour M.S. in Computer Science requires a thesis and comprehensive examination in addition to the standard coursework. This is a highly structured program that focuses primarily on applied computer science.

The 32-hour M.S.E. in Electrical Engineering requires a thesis or capstone engineering project. Faculty-approved concentrations are available in communications systems, control/biomedical systems, digital systems, and materials/microelectronics.

The 32-hour M.S.E. in Mechatronics requires a thesis or capstone engineering project. Faculty-approved concentrations are available in robotics and smart systems.

Other Programs

A B.S. in Management Information Systems is available through the Department of Computer Science.

More Information

Until last year, Minnesota State University at Mankato was known as Mankato State University.

Contact Information

PHONE
General information: (800) 722-0544
Admissions (undergraduate): (507) 389-1822
Admissions (graduate): (507) 389-2321
Computer and information science: (507) 389-2968

FAX
Admissions (graduate): (507) 389-5974

E-MAIL
Admissions (undergraduate):
admissions@mankato.msus.edu
Admissions (graduate): grad@mankato.msus.edu
Computer and information science:
cisdept@mankato.msus.edu

Mississippi State University   www.msstate.edu ☆☆☆½

Office of Admissions
P.O. Box 6305
Mississippi State, MS 39762

Graduate School
P.O. Box G
Mississippi State, MS 39762-5507

Year established: 1878
Ownership: Public

This major state-funded institution offers a wide variety of information technology programs at all levels. Several innovative interdisciplinary programs have also been developed (see "Other Programs"). Evening classes, extension courses, and distance learning are available.

Degrees Offered

UNDERGRADUATE
(ABET) B.S., Computer Engineering
(CSAB) B.S., Computer Science
(ABET) B.S., Electrical Engineering

GRADUATE
M.S., Computer Engineering
M.S., Computer Science
M.S., Electrical Engineering
Ph.D., Computational Engineering
Ph.D., Computer Engineering
Ph.D., Computer Science
Ph.D., Electrical Engineering

Approximate Cost of Degrees

UNDERGRADUATE, RESIDENT
$7,200

UNDERGRADUATE, NONRESIDENT
$15,100

MASTER'S, RESIDENT
$6,000

MASTER'S, NONRESIDENT
$12,200

DOCTORATE, RESIDENT
$11,400

DOCTORATE, NONRESIDENT
$23,100

Admissions Guidelines

UNDERGRADUATE
High school diploma, SAT and/or ACT required

GRADUATE
Accredited bachelor's with 2.75 GPA on upper 60 hours required, GRE recommended

Undergraduate Programs
The ABET-accredited B.S. in Computer Engineering blends a solid background in theoretical computer science with hands-on research in applied electrical and software engineering.

The CSAB-accredited B.S. in Computer Science is a theory-oriented program that allows generous room for student specialization through its 18 hours of major electives.

The ABET-accredited B.S. program in Electrical Engineering offers informal senior year specializations in computer systems, electromagnetics, feedback control systems, high voltage, microelectronics, power systems, signal processing, and telecommunications.

Graduate Programs
The M.S. programs in Computer Engineering and Electrical Engineering are identical in their basic structural elements, differing only in specific course requirements. Both require an oral examination. Thesis (30-hour) and non-thesis (33-hour) tracks are available.

The 32-hour M.S. in Computer Science is available with faculty-approved specializations in advanced scientific computing, artificial intelligence, computer architecture, database systems, graphics and visualization, high performance computing, programming languages and systems, and software engineering. Students can choose a thesis or cap-stone project. The coursework requirements for this program can be completed via distance learning.

The Ph.D. in Computer Science requires two examinations in addition to the standard disserta-tion. Students must specialize in artificial intelli-gence, graphics and visualization, high performance computing, or software engineering. Much of this program can be completed via distance learning; contact the department for details.

The Ph.D. programs in Computer Engineering and in Electrical Engineering require a qualifying exam-ination in addition to the standard dissertation. Students must design a plan of study that satisfies the faculty and program committee.

Other Programs

The School of Business offers a B.S. in Business Information Systems; a business information sys-tems concentration is also available in the M.S.B.A. and D.B.A. programs. Contact the Department of Management and Information Systems at (662) 325-3928 for more information.

A new, computer-graphics-oriented M.F.A. in Elec-tronic Visualization is available. For more informa-tion, contact the Department of Art at (662) 325-2970.

M.S. and Ph.D. programs in Computational Engi-neering are also available. For more information, contact the Engineering Research Center for Compu-tational Field Simulators at (662) 325-8278.

M.S., Ed.S., and Ed.D. programs in Instructional Technology are available. For more information, contact the Department of Technology and Educa-tion at (662) 325-2281.

A B.S. in Office Systems and Technologies is avail-able through the Department of Technology and Education. For more information, contact the pro-gram office at (662) 325-2280.

Contact Information

Phone
Admissions (undergraduate): (662) 325-2224
Admissions (graduate): (662) 325-7400
Computer science: (662) 325-2756
Electrical and computer engineering: (662) 325-3912

Fax
Admissions (undergraduate): (662) 325-7360
Admissions (graduate): (662) 325-1967
Computer science: (662) 325-8997
Electrical and computer engineering: (662) 325-2298

E-mail
General information: msuinfo@ur.msstate.edu
Admissions (undergraduate):
admit@admissions.msstate.edu
Admissions (graduate): grad@grad.msstate.edu
Computer science: office@cs.msstate.edu
Electrical and computer engineering:
office@ece.msstate.edu

Montana State University—Bozeman   www.montana.edu ★★★

Office of Admissions
P.O. Box 172180
Bozeman, MT 59717-2180

College of Graduate Studies
108 Montana Hall
P.O. Box 172580
Bozeman, MT 59717-2580

Year established: 1893
Ownership: Public

This highly regarded public university offers undergraduate and graduate programs in information technology fields. The overall emphasis of these programs is very much "old school"; the computer science bachelor's degree program is, for example, very much a traditional computer science bachelor's. Still, these very traditional programs are becoming available through some very nontraditional means. Reentry students may wish to take advantage of the evening class, extension course, weekend study, and distance-learning options available.

Degrees Offered

UNDERGRADUATE

B.S., Computer Engineering
(CSAB) B.S., Computer Science
(ABET) B.S., Electrical Engineering

GRADUATE

M.S., Computer Science
M.S., Electrical Engineering

Approximate Cost of Degrees

UNDERGRADUATE, RESIDENT

$11,900

UNDERGRADUATE, NONRESIDENT

$34,900

GRADUATE, RESIDENT

$6,700

GRADUATE, NONRESIDENT

$15,300

Admissions Guidelines

UNDERGRADUATE

High school diploma, SAT and/or ACT required

GRADUATE

Accredited bachelor's, GRE required

Undergraduate Programs

The B.S. program in Computer Engineering represents a solid, well-rounded curriculum in the field.

The CSAB-accredited B.S. program in Computer Science is oriented toward software engineering and theoretical computer science.

The ABET-accredited B.S. in Electrical Engineering culminates in a semester-long team capstone project.

Graduate Programs

The 30-hour M.S. program in Computer Science represents a standard, theory-based curriculum in the field. Students can choose to complete the program with a thesis or with a capstone project. Montana residents can fulfill all degree requirements through distance learning and extension classes.

Other Programs

A B.S. in Technology Education is also available. For more information, contact the College of Education, Health, and Human Development at (406) 994-5950.

The Ph.D. in Engineering has an optional electrical and computer engineering concentration. For more information, contact the College of Engineering at (406) 994-2272.

Montana State—Bozeman and Montana Tech offer a joint, 100 percent online Master of Project Engineering and Management (M.P.E.M.). For more information, contact the Department of Chemical Engineering at (406) 994-2221.

Contact Information

PHONE

Admissions (undergraduate): (406) 994-6617
Admissions (graduate): (406) 994-4145
Electrical and computer engineering: (406) 994-2505

FAX

Electrical and computer engineering: (406) 994-5958

E-MAIL

Admissions (undergraduate):
registrar@montana.edu
Admissions (graduate): gradstudy@montana.edu
Computer science: csinfo@cs.montana.edu
Electrical and computer engineering:
eedept@ee.montana.edu

Montana Tech of the University of Montana

www.mtech.edu ☆☆☆½

1300 West Park Street
Butte, MT 59701

Year established: 1893
Ownership: Public

This public, vocational technical institute offers a wide variety of options for reentry students, including extension courses, evening classes, and distance learning. Although its programs have a definitive emphasis in applied computer science, they can be tailored to fit the needs of research-minded students as well.

Degrees Offered

UNDERGRADUATE
B.S., Business and Information Technology
B.S., Computer Science

Approximate Cost of Degrees

UNDERGRADUATE, RESIDENT
$5,600–$13,900

UNDERGRADUATE, NONRESIDENT
$16,300–$40,700

Admissions Guidelines

UNDERGRADUATE
High school diploma required, SAT and/or ACT generally required (may be waived)

Undergraduate Programs
The B.S. program in Business and Information Technology is strongly oriented toward business software, data analysis, and information science; it is much more of an IT program than a business program.

The B.S. program in Computer Science is unusually research-friendly and allows opportunity for student specialization through free electives.

Other Programs
An online Master of Project Engineering and Management (M.P.E.M.) is offered jointly with Montana State University—Bozeman. For more information, contact the Department of Environmental Engineering at (406) 496-4239.

Contact Information

PHONE
Admissions: (406) 496-4178 or (800) 445-8324
Business and information technology: (406) 496-4401
Computer science: (406) 496-4366

FAX
Business and information technology: (406) 496-4704
Computer science: (406) 496-4133

E-MAIL
admissions@po1.mtech.edu

National Technological University   www.ntu.edu ☆☆☆

700 Centre Avenue
Fort Collins, CO 80526

Year established: 1984
Ownership: Private

This massive educational consortium of 45 universities offers unparalleled opportunities for students who want to undertake a degree nonresidentially. NTU does not offer on-campus degrees as such. Students complete their degrees via corporate extension site courses, video courses and satellite television courses, and distance learning.

Degrees Offered

GRADUATE
M.S., Computer Engineering
M.S., Computer Science
M.S., Electrical Engineering
M.S., Software Engineering

Approximate Cost of Degrees

GRADUATE
$22,500

Admissions Guidelines

GRADUATE
Accredited bachelor's with 2.9 GPA required

Graduate Programs
The 30-hour M.S. in Computer Engineering gives roughly equal weight to hardware and software issues in its core requirements. Students choose two of the following fields for specialization: algorithms and data structures, computer architecture, computational methods and theory, computer software, digital systems, intelligent systems, software engineering, and software techniques. No thesis is required.

Although the 30-hour M.S. in Computer Science primarily emphasizes theory in its core requirements, hardware and software issues are addressed in survey form. Students choose two of the following fields for specialization: algorithms and data structures, computer architecture, computational methods and theory, computer software, intelligent systems, software engineering, and software techniques. No thesis is required. This program can be completed online.

The 33-hour M.S. in Electrical Engineering addresses a broad array of topics related both directly and peripherally to the field. In its core requirements, it seems to be primarily geared toward digital systems. Concentrations are available in electromagnetics, microelectronics, and circuits. No thesis is required.

The 33-hour M.S. in Software Engineering includes courses on software reliability among its core requirements, and seems to place much more emphasis on the fundamental philosophy of software engineering than it does on specific methodologies and applications. Students choose two of the following fields for specialization: computer software, intelligent systems, software engineering, and software techniques. No thesis is required.

Other Programs

M.S. programs in Management of Technology, Systems Engineering, and Telecommunications are available. Students can also choose to undertake an individualized "special topics" M.S. with faculty approval.

More Information

The following institutions offer courses through NTU: Arizona State University, Auburn University, Boston University, Clemson University, Colorado State University, Columbia University, Florida Gulf Coast University, George Washington University, Georgia Institute of Technology, Illinois Institute of Technology, Iowa State University, Kansas State University, Kettering University, Lehigh University, Massachusetts Institute of Technology, Michigan State University, Michigan Technological University, New Jersey Institute of Technology, New Mexico State University, North Carolina State University, Northeastern University, Oklahoma State University, Old Dominion University, Purdue University, Rensselaer Polytechnic Institute, Southern Methodist University, University of Alabama (Huntsville and Tuscaloosa), University of Alaska (Fairbanks), University of Arizona, University of Arkansas, University of California (Berkeley and Davis), University of Colorado (Boulder), University of Delaware, University of Florida, University of Idaho, University of Illinois (Urbana-Champaign), University of Kentucky, University of Maryland (College Park), University of Massachusetts (Amherst), University of Michigan, University of Minnesota, University of Missouri (Rolla), University of Nebraska (Lincoln), University of New Mexico, University of Notre Dame, University of South Carolina, University of Southern California, University of Tennessee (Knoxville), University of Washington, University of Wisconsin (Madison), and Vanderbilt University.

Contact Information

PHONE
(970) 495-6400 or (800) 582-9976

FAX
(970) 484-0668

E-MAIL
admissions@mail.ntu.edu

New Jersey Institute of Technology　　www.njit.edu ☆☆☆½

University Heights, NJ 07102

Year established: 1881
Ownership: Public

This major state-funded research institution offers top-tier programs at all levels in a variety of information technology fields through an almost unparalleled variety of delivery methods. Evening classes, extension courses, and distance learning are all available. Several of the programs described below can be completed entirely by distance learning.

Degrees Offered

UNDERGRADUATE

CSAB B.A., Computer Science
CSAB B.S., Computer Science
B.A., Information Systems
ABET B.S., Computer Engineering
ABET B.S., Electrical Engineering
B.S.E.T., Computer Technology
ABET B.S.E.T., Electrical and Computer Engineering

GRADUATE

M.S., Computer Engineering
M.S., Computer Science
M.S., Electrical Engineering
M.S., Information Systems
M.S., Telecommunications
Ph.D., Computer and Information Science
Ph.D., Computer Engineering
Ph.D., Electrical Engineering

Approximate Cost of Degrees

UNDERGRADUATE, RESIDENT

$13,000–$31,200

UNDERGRADUATE, NONRESIDENT

$21,700–$57,300

MASTER'S, RESIDENT

$6,100–$15,900

MASTER'S, NONRESIDENT

$8,300–$21,200

DOCTORATE, RESIDENT

$10,200–$31,800

DOCTORATE, NONRESIDENT

$13,900–$42,300

Admissions Guidelines

UNDERGRADUATE

High school diploma, SAT and/or ACT required

GRADUATE

Accredited bachelor's with 2.8 GPA required, GRE recommended

Undergraduate Programs

The ABET-accredited B.S. program in Computer Engineering gives roughly equal weight to hardware and software issues. Specializations are available in advanced computer architecture, computer networking, and parallel processing.

The CSAB-accredited B.A. in Computer Science leans slightly more toward applied computing issues than the B.S., which is very much the standard computer science degree. The standard curriculum of computer science as represented by the B.S. consists of a solid background in the natural sciences that then "zooms in" on computation, algorithms, and related theoretical aspects of computer science. This standard curriculum does approach applied issues in hardware and software engineering, but generally relegates them to the junior and senior years. This program can be completed by distance learning.

The ABET-accredited B.S. in Electrical Engineering is a very broad program that represents all major areas of the field; computer hardware is addressed in a particularly emphatic manner in the core requirements. Specializations are available in biomedical instrumentation, communications, controls, power systems, and radio/microwave/fiber optics.

The B.A. in Information Systems tackles the basic issues of applied computer science head-on without straying too far in the direction of management information systems. This program can be completed via distance learning.

The B.S.E.T. in Computer Technology focuses more or less evenly on software engineering, computer hardware, and management.

The ABET-accredited B.S.E.T. in Electrical and Computer Engineering offers optional tracks in biomedical electronics, computer systems, and telecommunications.

Graduate Programs

The 30-hour M.S. in Computer Engineering is available with optional concentrations in computer networking, machine vision systems, microprocessor-based systems, parallel computing systems, and VLSI design. Students can choose a thesis or capstone project track. The thesis is generally a publishable work of 40 to 60 pages that presents a solution to a research problem, while the capstone project is a faculty-approved demonstration of learned practical skill in the field.

The 30-hour M.S. in Computer Science is available with optional concentrations in artificial intelligence, computer algorithms and theory of computing, computer communications and networking, computer systems and parallel/distributed processing, database and knowledge-based engineering, image processing and computer graphics, information systems applications and management, numerical computation, software engineering, and systems analysis/simulation/modeling. Students can choose a thesis or capstone project track. The thesis is generally a publishable work of 40 to 60 pages that presents a solution to a research problem, while the capstone project is a faculty-approved demonstration of learned practical skill in the field. This program can be completed by distance learning.

The 30-hour M.S. in Electrical Engineering is available with optional concentrations in communications, computer systems, control systems, digital signal processing, energy conversion and power, microwave and lightwave engineering, and solid-state materials/devices/circuits. No thesis is required.

The 36-hour M.S. in Information Systems is a primarily software-focused program with optional concentrations in biomedical informatics, data analysis and modeling tools, electronic enterprise design, evaluation methods and tools, interdisciplinary information systems, management information systems, and multimedia communication. No thesis is required. This program can be completed by distance learning.

The 30-hour M.S. in Telecommunications is available with optional concentrations in communication systems, information technologies, management and administration, and networking. No thesis is required.

The Ph.D. in Computer Engineering requires one year of full-time residency and a qualifying examination in addition to the standard dissertation.

The Ph.D. in Computer and Information Science requires that students specialize in computer science or information systems. A teaching requirement and one year of full-time residency comprise essential parts of the program. The standard dissertation is required.

The Ph.D. in Electrical Engineering requires that students specialize in biomedical engineering, communications, computer systems, control systems, digital signal processing, energy conversion and power, microwave and lightwave engineering, or solid-state materials/devices/circuits. A qualifying

examination and one year of full-time residency are required in addition to the standard dissertation.

Other Programs

NJIT's Department of Computer and Information Science and the University of Medicine and Dentistry of New Jersey (UMDNJ) jointly offer M.S. and Ph.D. degrees in Biomedical Informatics. For more information, contact the NJIT biomedical informatics program office at (973) 596-3383.

The B.S. and M.S. programs in Management are available with an electronic commerce specialization. A specialization in management of technology is also available in the M.B.A. program, which may soon be completed by distance learning. For more information, contact the School of Management at (973) 596-3248.

A B.S.E.T. in Telecommunications Management Technology is also available. For more information, contact the program coordinator at (973) 596-6078.

Contact Information

PHONE
Admissions: (973) 596-3300 or (800) 925-6548
Computer science and information systems: (973) 596-3366
Computer technology: (973) 596-2878
Electrical and computer engineering: (973) 596-3512
Electrical and computer technology: (973) 596-8190
Telecommunications: (973) 596-3534

FAX
Computer science and information systems: (973) 596-5777
Electrical and computer engineering: (973) 596-5680
Electrical and computer technology: (973) 642-4184

E-MAIL
Computer engineering: Jacob Savir (savir@oak.njit.edu)
Computer science and information systems: Joseph Leung (leung@cis.njit.edu)
Computer technology: Marie-Therese Daulard (daulard@adm.njit.edu)
Electrical and computer technology: William Barnes (barnesw@adm.njit.edu)
Telecommunications: Alexander Haimovich (haimovic@megahertz.njit.edu)

New Mexico Highlands University   www.nmhu.edu ☆☆☆½

Box 9000
Las Vegas, NM 87701

Year established: 1893
Ownership: Public

This midsize state-funded university offers solid, theory-oriented computer science degrees at the undergraduate level and unique, mind-blowing interdisciplinary programs at the graduate level. Evening classes are available.

Degrees Offered

UNDERGRADUATE
B.A., Computer Science
B.S., Computer Science

GRADUATE
M.A., Media Arts and Computer Science
M.S., Media Arts and Computer Science

Approximate Cost of Degrees

UNDERGRADUATE, RESIDENT
$7,500–$9,300

UNDERGRADUATE, NONRESIDENT
$9,300–$30,300

GRADUATE, RESIDENT
$2,300–$2,800

GRADUATE, NONRESIDENT
$2,800–$8,000

Admissions Guidelines

UNDERGRADUATE
High school diploma, SAT and/or ACT required

GRADUATE
Accredited bachelor's required, GRE recommended

Undergraduate Programs
The B.A. program in Computer Science represents a curriculum focused almost entirely on theory and software issues. An information systems specialization is available.

The B.S. program in Computer Science is identical in its core major requirements to the B.A., but offers an optional concentration in software and hardware systems rather than information systems. The software and hardware systems concentration essentially constitutes a computer engineering minor and gives the program more of an applied focus.

Graduate Programs
The 36-hour M.A. in Media Arts and Computer Science integrates an interdisciplinary humanities curriculum with graduate-level study in computer science. The specialization forms the point of consilience between computer science and media arts. Students must choose a specialization from among the following faculty-approved options: cognitive science, computer graphics, design studies, digital audio and video production, multimedia systems, or networking technology. A thesis is required; the thesis must relate in some way to the area of specialization.

The 36-hour M.S. in Media Arts and Computer Science is similar in its core requirements to the M.S., but allows for greater flexibility in choosing an area of specialization and final capstone work. Students must choose a specialization from among the following faculty-approved options: cognitive science, computer graphics, multimedia systems, or networking technology. A thesis or other capstone project is required. Because of the highly interdisciplinary nature of this program, the capstone project can take on a variety of forms provided that it meets faculty approval and is related in some manner to the area of specialization.

Other Programs
The Department of Mathematics and Computer Science also offers individualized B.A. and B.S. programs. With faculty approval, these programs can be tailored to fit the needs of students who want to focus on an extremely specific area in computer science and mathematics (such as artificial intelligence, computer networking, or software engineering).

A B.B.A. with emphasis in Information Systems is available. For more information, contact the School of Business at (505) 454-3230.

A B.A. in Technology Education is also available. For more information, contact the School of Education at (505) 454-3357.

Contact Information

PHONE
General information: (505) 425-7511
Admissions (undergraduate): (505) 454-3593
Admissions (graduate): (505) 454-3266

Computer science: (505) 454-3302
Media arts and computer science: (505) 454-3230

FAX
Admissions: (505) 454-3552

E-MAIL
Admissions (undergraduate):
Admissions@nmhu.edu
Admissions (graduate): graduate@venus.nmhu.edu
Computer science: Curtis Sollohub
(csollohub@venus.nmhu.edu)
Media arts and computer science: Wayne Summers
(wsummers@cs.nmhu.edu)

New Mexico State University   www.nmsu.edu ☆☆☆

Office of Admissions
P.O. Box 30001
Las Cruces, NM 88003-8001

Year established: 1888
Ownership: Public

This major state-funded institution offers programs at all levels in information technology fields. Although NMSU has an extremely strong faculty research base to work from and would have every right to be research-oriented, it seems to be equally focused on serving the needs of reentry students through its weekend study, extension site, and distance-learning options. NMSU also accepts up to 30 hours of undergraduate credit (25 percent of a bachelor's degree) in credit-by-examination earned through DANTES and CLEP examinations.

Degrees Offered

UNDERGRADUATE
B.S., Computer Science
(ABET) B.S., Electrical Engineering
(ABET) B.S.E.T., Electronic(s) and Computer Engineering Technology

GRADUATE
M.S., Computer Science
M.S., Electrical Engineering
Ph.D., Computer Science

Approximate Cost of Degrees

UNDERGRADUATE, RESIDENT
$10,000

UNDERGRADUATE, NONRESIDENT
$32,700

MASTER'S, RESIDENT
$3,700

MASTER'S, NONRESIDENT
$4,000–$9,000

DOCTORATE, RESIDENT
$6,700

DOCTORATE, NONRESIDENT
$8,000–$20,900

Admissions Guidelines

UNDERGRADUATE
High school diploma, SAT and/or ACT required

GRADUATE
Accredited bachelor's required, GRE recommended

Undergraduate Programs

The B.S. in Computer Science represents a ground-level introduction to the field as a scientific discipline; this gradually expands to algorithms and computation, eventually reaching out to encompass software engineering and related applied disciplines. Even in this, the program never strays far from its scientific roots; structures of programming and structures of databases are studied, patterns are examined, and the end result is a relentlessly scientific, relentlessly fundamental curriculum in the field.

The ABET-accredited B.S. in Electrical Engineering places a heavy, decisive focus on computer hardware and complex digital systems in its core requirements. Specializations are available in communications/telemetry/signal processing, computer engineering, control systems, electric energy systems, electromagnetics, electronic circuit design, microelectronics, and photonics. Students can also design an original specialization with faculty approval.

The ABET-accredited B.S. in Engineering Technology (B.S.E.T.) in Electronic(s) and Computer Engineering Technology emphasizes microelectronics and digital systems while integrating business and management issues into the curriculum.

Graduate Programs

The 33-hour M.S. in Computer Science is based in the mathematical and foundations of the field, emphasizing software engineering in its applied components. A thesis is ordinarily required, but students can elect to undertake a special computer science project with faculty approval.

The M.S. in Electrical Engineering is available through a 30-hour coursework and thesis track (culminating in a publishable work addressing a research problem), a 33-hour coursework and project track (culminating in a creative electrical engineering project), or a 36-hour coursework-only track. Students work within faculty-approved parameters to define a primary area of specialized study.

The Ph.D. program in Computer Science is designed around a student-defined specialization that should match a faculty research interest. A qualifying examination is required in addition to the standard dissertation.

Other Programs

A B.S. in Business Computer Systems is also available. For more information, contact the Department of Accounting and Business Computer Systems at (505) 646-2944.

A Ph.D. program in Engineering (with optional emphasis in electrical and computer engineering) is also available. For more information, contact the main office of the College of Engineering at (505) 646-2911.

Contact Information

PHONE
General information: (505) 646-0111
Admissions (undergraduate): (505) 646-3121 or (800) 662-6678
Admissions (graduate): (505) 646-2736
Computer science: (505) 646-3723
Electrical and computer engineering: (505) 646-3115
Electronics and computer engineering technology: (505) 646-3452

FAX
Computer science: (505) 646-1002
Electrical and computer engineering: (505) 646-1435
Electronics and computer engineering technology: (505) 646-8107

E-MAIL
Admissions (undergraduate): admissions@nmsu.edu
Admissions (graduate): gradinfo@nmsu.edu
Computer science: csoffice@cs.nmsu.edu
Electrical and computer engineering: Steven Castillo (scastill@nmsu.edu)
Electronic(s) and computer engineering technology: Jeff Beasley (jbeasley@gauss.nmsu.edu)

New York Institute of Technology   www.nyit.edu ☆☆½

Central Islip Campus
P.O. Box 9029
Central Islip, NY 11722-9029

Manhattan Campus
1855 Broadway
New York, NY 10023-7692

The Dorothy and Alexander Schure Old Westbury Campus
P.O. Box 8000
Old Westbury, NY 11568-8000

Year established: 1955
Ownership: Private

This private, vocationally oriented institution offers a variety of programs in information technology disciplines and related interdisciplinary fields through three campuses in the metropolitan New York area and one satellite campus in Fort Lauderdale, Florida. Evening classes, weekend study, and distance learning are available; many of NYIT's programs can be completed entirely through these nontraditional means.

Degrees Offered

UNDERGRADUATE
B.S., Computer Science
ABET B.S., Electrical Engineering
ABET B.Tech., Electrical Engineering Technology

GRADUATE
M.S., Computer Science
M.S., Electrical Engineering

Approximate Cost of Degrees

UNDERGRADUATE
$54,400

GRADUATE
$16,200

Admissions Guidelines

UNDERGRADUATE
High school diploma, SAT required

GRADUATE
Accredited bachelor's, GRE required

Undergraduate Programs
The B.S. program in Computer Science is based on its most fundamental level on the disciplines that form the scientific core of the field. From this framework, students specialize in an area of applied computer science during the senior year. Pre-approved specializations are available in computer graphics and distributed systems, but each student is encouraged to design an individualized plan of study. This program is offered through all three campuses and can be completed via evening and weekend study.

The ABET-accredited B.S. program in Electrical Engineering is available with an optional computer engineering minor. The program itself focuses on digital systems and microelectronics, so even those who don't want to undertake the computer engineering track per se will likely gain an understanding of the basic principles behind computer hardware. This program is offered through the Manhattan and Old Westbury campuses and can be completed via evening and weekend study.

The ABET-accredited Bachelor of Technology (B.Tech.) in Electrical Engineering Technology is available with an optional computer technology minor. The core requirements focus on issues of design, reliability, and quality control. This program is offered through the Manhattan and Old Westbury campuses and can be completed via evening and weekend study.

Graduate Programs

The 36-hour M.S. in Computer Science offers a broad-based curriculum in the field with core components in theory, computation, software applications, and software design. A thesis or capstone project is required. This program is offered through all three campuses and can be completed via evening and weekend study.

The 36-hour M.S. in Electrical Engineering is based around a faculty-approved, student-designed specialization. Students have an opportunity to specialize in virtually all popular areas of electrical and computer engineering. The program as a whole is oriented more toward digital systems and hardware than toward software engineering, although software engineering is addressed and it is quite likely that a student will be able to negotiate a specialization in this field. No thesis is required. This program is offered through the Manhattan and Old Westbury campuses and can be completed via evening and weekend study.

Other Programs

Programs in Computer Graphics (B.F.A.), Technology Education (B.S.), and Instructional Technology (M.S.) are available through the Manhattan and Old Westbury campuses.

A B.S. program in Telecommunications Management is available through all three campuses. The program can also be completed online or via evening and weekend study.

An M.B.A. program with emphasis in management of information systems is available through all three campuses and can be completed via evening and weekend study.

More Information

NYIT also operates a campus in Ft. Lauderdale, Florida. Interested parties should contact the Central Islip campus for details.

Contact Information

PHONE

Admissions (Central Islip campus): (631) 348-3047 or (800) 873-6948
Admissions (Manhattan campus): (212) 261-1640
Admissions (Old Westbury campus): (516) 686-7931 or (800) 345-6948

FAX

Admissions (Central Islip campus): (631) 348-0912
Admissions (Manhattan campus): (212) 977-3460
Admissions (Old Westbury campus): (516) 686-7613

E-MAIL

admissio@nyit.edu

New York University

www.nyu.edu ☆☆☆

Office of Admissions
22 Washington Square North
New York, NY 10011-9191

Year established: 1831
Ownership: Private

With more than 36,000 students, this is the largest private university and research institution in the U.S. and a natural top-tier choice for traditional students. This doesn't mean that nontraditional students are left out in the cold entirely, however; NYU has recently been particularly aggressive in recruiting nontraditional students. Evening classes and weekend study are available.

Degrees Offered

UNDERGRADUATE

B.A., Computer Science

GRADUATE

M.S., Computer Science
M.S., Information Systems
M.S., Scientific Computing
Ph.D., Computer Science

Approximate Cost of Degrees

UNDERGRADUATE
$97,300

MASTER'S
$23,800

DOCTORATE
$49,200

Admissions Guidelines

UNDERGRADUATE
Accredited bachelor's, SAT required

GRADUATE
Accredited bachelor's, GRE required

Undergraduate Programs
The general track of the B.A. program in Computer Science is definitively oriented toward theory and study of the discipline's structural foundations. A computer applications track is available for students who want to apply computing to other fields.

Graduate Programs
The 36-hour M.S. in Computer Science requires a core examination, but does not require a thesis. Specializations are available in applications programming, artificial intelligence, computer architecture, databases and distributed computing, graphics, multimedia and telecommunications, numerical analysis, and software engineering.

The 39-hour M.S. in Information Systems is an interdisciplinary program that addresses the application of computer science principles to the broader fields of information and decision science. No thesis is required.

The 36-hour M.S. in Scientific Computing, offered through the Courant Institute of Mathematical Sciences, focuses on algorithms, combinatorics, and related mathematical foundations of computing. A computational thesis is required.

The Ph.D. in Computer Science requires that students pass three subject examinations in addition to the standard dissertation.

Other Programs
M.A. and Ph.D. programs in the interdisciplinary field of Education, Communications, and Technology are also available. For more information, contact the department at (212) 998-5176.

Students may simultaneously complete a NYU bachelor's in biology, computer science, mathematics, or physics and a Stevens Institute Bachelor of Engineering in electrical, computer, or mechanical engineering. For more information, contact the program advisor at (212) 998-8130.

A Master of Professional Studies (M.P.S.) in Interactive Telecommunications is also available. For more information, contact the ITP Department of Tisch School of the Arts at (212) 998-1880.

The Ph.D. program in Neural Science may be of interest to students interested in cognitive neural systems and artificial intelligence. For more information, contact the Center for Neural Science at (212) 998-7780.

Contact Information

PHONE
General information: (212) 998-1212
Admissions (undergraduate): (212) 998-4500
Admissions (graduate): (212) 998-8050
Computer science/information systems:
(212) 998-3011
Scientific computing: (212) 998-3256

FAX
Admissions (undergraduate): (212) 995-4902
Admissions (graduate): (212) 995-4557
Scientific computing: (212) 995-4121

E-MAIL
Admissions (undergraduate): admissions@nyu.edu
Admissions (graduate): gsas.admissions@nyu.edu
Computer science/information systems:
admissions@cs.nyu.edu
Scientific computing: huntington@cims.nyu.edu

North Carolina State University   www.ncsu.edu ☆☆

Director of Admissions
Box 7103
Raleigh, NC 27695-7103

Graduate School
Box 7102
Raleigh, NC 27695-7102

Year established: 1889
Ownership: Public

This major public university offers strong research opportunities in information technology fields at the graduate level and sound, well-rounded programs at the undergraduate level. Evening classes, weekend study, and distance learning are available.

Degrees Offered

UNDERGRADUATE
🔲 B.S., Computer Engineering
🔲 B.S., Computer Science
🔲 B.S., Electrical Engineering

GRADUATE
M.C.S.
M.S., Computer Engineering
M.S., Computer Networking
M.S., Computer Science
M.S., Electrical Engineering
Ph.D., Computer Engineering
Ph.D., Computer Science
Ph.D., Electrical Engineering

Approximate Cost of Degrees

UNDERGRADUATE, RESIDENT
$8,800

UNDERGRADUATE, NONRESIDENT
$42,900

MASTER'S, RESIDENT
$2,400

MASTER'S, NONRESIDENT
$16,100

DOCTORATE, RESIDENT
$3,900

DOCTORATE, NONRESIDENT
$26,900

Admissions Guidelines

UNDERGRADUATE
High school diploma, SAT and/or ACT required

GRADUATE
Accredited bachelor's with 3.0 GPA required, GRE recommended

Undergraduate Programs

The ABET-accredited B.S. program in Computer Engineering gives a broad background in computer hardware and software engineering, then zeroes in on a student-defined, faculty-approved concentration and interdisciplinary electives during the senior year.

The CSAB-accredited B.S. program in Computer Science requires that students specialize in computer architecture, databases, graphics, management information systems, operating systems, or software engineering. A minor in computer programming is also available.

The ABET-accredited B.S. program in Electrical Engineering gives a broad background in linear systems and computer engineering during the first three years, then focuses on a student-defined, faculty-approved concentration and interdisciplinary electives during the senior year.

Graduate Programs

The 30-hour Master of Computer Science (M.C.S.) is designed for reentry students and is perfect for students who want to take on a graduate program in computer science on a convenient part-time basis.

This is a professional degree focusing on applied issues in hardware, software engineering, and applications. No thesis or final project is required.

The 36-hour M.S. in Computer Engineering gives roughly equal weight to hardware and software engineering. No thesis is required.

The 30-hour M.S. in Computer Science is intended primarily for students who want to proceed to doctoral work. A thesis and comprehensive examination are required. Students can design a 9-hour specialization (minor) in a non-CS field and thereby, with faculty approval, create an interdisciplinary M.S. program.

The 36-hour M.S. in Computer Networking deals with both small- and large-scale computer networking; telecommunications and hardware-software interaction are also addressed. No thesis is required.

The 36-hour M.S. in Electrical Engineering addresses a broad range of electrical engineering issues, but can be tailored to focus on computer engineering. No thesis is required.

The Ph.D. in Computer Engineering is designed to encourage student-initiated informal specialization in the primary area of dissertation research.

The Ph.D. in Computer Science requires preliminary oral and written examinations in addition to the standard dissertation.

The Ph.D. in Electrical Engineering is designed to encourage student-initiated informal specialization in the primary area of dissertation research.

Other Programs

Programs in Technology Education are available at all levels. For more information, contact the department of Math, Science, and Technology Education at (919) 515-2238.

Contact Information

PHONE

General information: (919) 515-2011
Admissions (undergraduate): (919) 515-2434
Admissions (graduate): (919) 515-2872
Computer science: (919) 515-2858
Electrical and computer engineering (undergraduate): (919) 515-5087
Electrical and computer engineering (graduate): (919) 515-5090

FAX

Computer science: (919) 515-7896
Electrical and computer engineering: (919) 515-5523

E-MAIL

Admissions (undergraduate): undergradadmissions@ncsu.edu
Computer science (undergraduate): undergrad@csc.ncsu.edu
Computer science (graduate): graduate@csc.ncsu.edu
Electrical and computer engineering (undergraduate): jjb@eos.ncsu.edu
Electrical and computer engineering (graduate): ECEDirGradProg@ncsu.edu

North Dakota State University — www.ndsu.nodak.edu ☆☆

1301 North University
Fargo, ND 58105

Year established: 1890
Ownership: Public

This midsize public university offers rigorous, well-rounded programs at all levels in information technology fields. Evening classes, weekend study, and distance learning are available.

Degrees Offered

UNDERGRADUATE

B.A., Computer Science
CSAB B.S., Computer Science
ABET B.S., Electrical Engineering

GRADUATE

M.S., Computer Science
M.S., Electrical Engineering
Ph.D., Computer Science

Approximate Cost of Degrees

UNDERGRADUATE, RESIDENT
$11,100

**UNDERGRADUATE, NONRESIDENT
(MINNESOTA)**
$11,600

UNDERGRADUATE, NONRESIDENT (OTHER)
$16,100–$27,700

MASTER'S, RESIDENT
$3,900

MASTER'S, NONRESIDENT
$10,300

DOCTORATE, RESIDENT
$6,400

DOCTORATE, NONRESIDENT
$17,200

Admissions Guidelines

UNDERGRADUATE
High school diploma, ACT required

GRADUATE
Accredited bachelor's with 3.0 GPA required, GRE recommended

Undergraduate Programs

The CSAB-accredited B.S. program in Computer Science represents a broad program of study based on coursework in the structural and theoretical foundations of the discipline. The B.A. program places less of an emphasis on theory and relies primarily on an applied component, stressing interdisciplinary computing.

The ABET-accredited B.S. in Electrical Engineering includes a particularly strong curricular base in digital systems and computer engineering.

Graduate Programs

The 29-hour M.S. in Computer Science is a highly research-oriented program that focuses on abstract, structural issues in computer science. This is not to say that it lacks an applied component—it would also function reasonably well as a professional master's—but the overall approach of the program seems to be highly organic. A thesis is optional.

The M.S. in Electrical Engineering is available with concentrations in biomedical engineering, communication and signal processing, computers, controls, electromagnetics, electronics, and power systems. A thesis is optional.

The Ph.D. in Computer Science requires a qualifying examination in addition to the standard dissertation.

Other Programs

NDSU offers a B.B.A. with emphasis in management information systems. For more information, contact the College of Business Administration at (701) 231-8651.

The Ph.D. in Engineering is available with an electrical engineering focus. For more information, contact the Department of Electrical and Computer Engineering at (701) 231-7019.

Contact Information

PHONE
Admissions (undergraduate): (701) 231-8643
Admissions (graduate): (701) 231-7033
Computer science: (701) 231-8562
Electrical engineering: (701) 231-7019

FAX
Admissions (graduate): (701) 231-8098

E-MAIL
Admissions (undergraduate):
nuadmiss@plains.nodak.edu
Admissions (graduate): ndsu-grad@plains.nodak.edu

Northeastern University   www.northeastern.edu ☆☆☆

Office of Undergraduate Admissions
150 Richards Hall
360 Huntington Avenue
Boston, MA 02115

Graduate School of Computer Science
161 Cullinane Hall
360 Huntington Avenue
Boston, MA 02115

Graduate School of Engineering
130 Snell Engineering Center
360 Huntington Avenue
Boston, MA 02115

Year established: 1898
Ownership: Private

This major private research institution offers intensive programs at all levels. Of particular interest to reentry students, however, is Northeastern's "cooperative education" agreement whereby a student can complete some degree requirements as on-the-job learning. Evening classes, weekend study, extension courses, and distance learning are also available.

Degrees Offered

UNDERGRADUATE
CSAB B.S., Computer Science
ABET B.S., Electrical Engineering
B.S.E.T., Computer Technology
ABET B.S.E.T., Electrical Engineering Technology

GRADUATE
M.S., Computer Science
M.S., Computer Systems Engineering
M.S., Electrical and Computer Engineering
Ph.D., Computer Science
Ph.D., Electrical and Computer Engineering

Approximate Cost of Degrees

UNDERGRADUATE
$77,600

GRADUATE
$23,400

Admissions Guidelines

UNDERGRADUATE
High school diploma, SAT and/or ACT required

GRADUATE
Accredited bachelor's, GRE required

Undergraduate Programs

The CSAB-accredited B.S. in Computer Science addresses abstract structural elements of computer science at great depth, based on a foundation of scientific inquiry. During the junior and senior years, applied issues in computer science proceed from these structural elements.

The B.S. in Engineering Technology (B.S.E.T.) in Computer Technology emphasizes hardware slightly more than software and focuses on hardware-software interface issues (such as low-level programming and operating systems theory).

The ABET-accredited B.S. in Electrical Engineering involves a rigorous curriculum focusing on complex digital systems, microelectronics, and computer engineering.

The ABET-accredited B.S. in Engineering Technology (B.S.E.T.) in Electrical Engineering Technology involves a solid curriculum in digital systems, analog and digital electronics, circuit analysis, and distributed systems.

Graduate Programs

The 32-hour M.S. in Computer Science is available with concentrations in artificial intelligence, communication and networks, databases, graphics and image processing, operating systems and computer architecture, programming languages and compilers, software engineering, and theory. No thesis is required.

The 32-hour M.S. in Computer Systems Engineering is available with concentrations in computer-aided design/manufacturing and engineering software design. Computer systems engineering represents an interdisciplinary program involving computer science and engineering and industrial engineering. Emphasis is placed on applied engineering of computer systems in the context of other engineering fields. No thesis is required.

The 29-hour M.S. in Electrical and Computer Engineering is hardware-oriented in its core requirements, although students are welcome to incorporate software engineering into the program through elective credit. A thesis or capstone project is required for full-time students, but part-time students are exempt from this requirement.

The Ph.D. in Computer Science requires two examinations in addition to the standard dissertation. Coursework requirements are based around a faculty-approved, student-defined plan of study, which should be related to the field of the dissertation.

The Ph.D. in Electrical and Computer Engineering requires two examinations in addition to the standard dissertation. Residency requirements can be satisfied by one year of full-time study or two consecutive years of part-time study.

Other Programs

Northeastern University also offers a High Technology M.B.A. program addressing management of technology (especially information technology). Contact the College of Business Administration at (617) 373-3232 for more information.

Contact Information

PHONE

Admissions (undergraduate): (617) 373-2200
Computer science: (617) 373-2462
Electrical and computer engineering: (617) 373-4159
Engineering technology: (617) 373-2500

FAX

Admissions (undergraduate): (617) 373-8780
Computer science: (617) 373-5121
Electrical and computer engineering: (617) 373-8970
Engineering technology: (617) 373-2501

E-MAIL

Admissions (undergraduate):
 undergrad-admissions@neu.edu
Computer science (undergraduate):
undergradschool@ccs.neu.edu
Computer science (graduate):
gradschool@ccs.neu.edu
Engineering technology: info@lis.coe.neu.edu

✶ EXTRA!

Northeastern's IT-focused M.B.A. was voted the top "Techno-MBA" in America by *Computerworld* (http://www.computerworld.com/).

Northwestern University www.northwestern.edu ☆☆½

633 Clark Street
Evanston, IL 60208

Year established: 1851
Ownership: Private

Offering programs in information technology at all levels, this major private research institution is also well-suited for the reentry student. Evening classes are available.

Degrees Offered

UNDERGRADUATE
B.A., Computing and Information Systems
[ABET] B.S., Computer Engineering
[ABET] B.S., Electrical Engineering

GRADUATE
M.S., Electrical and Computer Engineering
Ph.D., Computer Science
Ph.D., Electrical and Computer Engineering

Approximate Cost of Degrees

UNDERGRADUATE
$98,600

MASTER'S
$37,000

DOCTORATE
$61,600

Admissions Guidelines

UNDERGRADUATE
High school diploma, SAT and/or ACT required

GRADUATE
Accredited bachelor's, GRE required

Undergraduate Programs
The B.A. in Computing and Information Systems approaches software issues from an extremely solid, structural base of abstract theory. This program leads to an unusually strong philosophical foundation and would be a natural choice for a student who plans on graduate work in the field.

The ABET-accredited B.S. in Computer Engineering is available with pre-approved faculty specializations in computer architecture and systems design, embedded systems design, parallel and distributed computing, robotics, and VLSI/CAD.

The ABET-accredited B.S. in Electrical Engineering is available with pre-approved faculty specializations in biomedical engineering, communication systems and networks, computer systems design, control systems, digital signal processing, electromagnetic waves and devices, electronic circuits, photonics, and solid-state electronics.

Graduate Programs
The 24-credit-hour M.S. in Electrical and Computer Engineering is focused fairly strongly on digital system theory and design. A thesis or project is required.

Faculty research interests for the Ph.D. in Computer Science include artificial intelligence, distributed interactive systems, human-computer interaction, software engineering, and theoretical computer science. One year of full-time residency and a qualifying examination are required in addition to the standard dissertation.

The Ph.D. in Electrical and Computer Engineering requires that students focus on computer engineering, photonics, solid-state engineering, or systems. A qualifying examination is required in addition to the standard dissertation.

Other Programs
A Ph.D. in Accounting and Information Systems is also available. For more information, contact the J.L. Kellogg Graduate School of Management at (847) 491-3427.

A B.A. in Cognitive Science is available. For more information, contact the department at (847) 491-5190.

The Ph.D. in Neuroscience can be focused on artificial intelligence. For more information, contact the Neuroscience Institute at (847) 491-2862.

Contact Information

PHONE
General information: (847) 491-3741
Admissions (graduate): (847) 491-7264
Computer science: (847) 467-1174
Electrical and computer engineering: (847) 491-3338

FAX
Admissions (graduate): (847) 491-5070
Computer science: (847) 491-5258
Electrical and computer engineering: (847) 491-4455

E-MAIL
Admissions (undergraduate): ug-admission@nwu.edu
Computer engineering (undergraduate): Majid Sarrafzadeh (majid@ece.nwu.edu)
Computer science: compsci@cs.nwu.edu
Electrical engineering (undergraduate): Prem Kumar (kumarp@ece.nwu.edu)
Electrical and computer engineering (graduate): grad@ece.nwu.edu

Nova Southeastern University   www.nova.edu ☆☆☆

3301 College Avenue
Fort Lauderdale, FL 33314

Year established: 1964
Ownership: Private

This pioneer in nontraditional education offers programs at all levels for reentry adults. All of NSU's programs can be completed through its many cohort groups and extension sites. Online courses are also available (and some programs can be completed entirely online).

Degrees Offered

UNDERGRADUATE
B.S., Computer Information Systems
B.S., Computer Science

GRADUATE
M.S., Computer Information Systems
M.S., Computer Science
Ph.D., Computer Information Systems
Ph.D., Computer Science

Approximate Cost of Degrees

UNDERGRADUATE
$43,900

MASTER'S
$14,200

DOCTORATE
$20,700

Admissions Guidelines

UNDERGRADUATE
High school diploma required, SAT and/or ACT recommended

GRADUATE
Accredited bachelor's, GRE required

Undergraduate Programs

The B.S. program in Computer Information Systems is a highly focused, applied program in programming, data analysis, and software engineering.

The B.S. program in Computer Science approaches the field from the dual perspectives of mathematics and structural computer science theory. The program would serve as an excellent introduction to a standard graduate program in the field.

Graduate Programs

The 36-hour M.S. in Computer Information Systems addresses basic issues of computer theory and software engineering in an organic, comprehensive fashion. No thesis is required. This program can be completed online.

The 36-hour M.S. in Computer Science focuses on highly abstract, structural elements of the field. Almost every imaginable component of computer science is addressed, including software engineering, networking, and human-computer interaction. No thesis is required. This program can be completed online.

The Ph.D. programs in Computer Science and Computer Information Systems give students a wide variety of available courses to choose from. The standard dissertation is required. There is no residency requirement.

Other Programs

Ph.D. programs in Information Science and Information Systems are also available through the Department of Computer Science.

Graduate programs in instructional technology are also available. For more information, contact the Fischler Graduate School of Education and Human Services at (954) 262-8500.

A M.S. in Management Information Systems is also available. For more information, contact the Wayne Huizenga Graduate School of Business at (954) 262-5000.

Contact Information

PHONE
General information: (954) 262-7300 or (800) 541-6682
Computer science/information systems:
(954) 262-2002 or (800) 986-2247, extension 2002

E-MAIL
Admissions (undergraduate): dodder@nova.edu
Computer science/information systems: Bonnie Bowers (bowersb@scis.nova.edu)

Ohio State University   www.ohio-state.edu ☆☆½

Columbus, OH 43210

Year established: 1870
Ownership: Public

This major state university offers programs at all levels in information technology fields in an environment well-suited for both traditional and nontraditional students. Evening classes, distance learning, and life experience credit are available.

Degrees Offered

UNDERGRADUATE
B.A., Computer and Information Science
B.S., Computer and Information Science
B.S., Computer Science and Engineering
🅰🅱️🅴🆃 B.S., Electrical Engineering

GRADUATE
M.S., Computer and Information Science
M.S., Electrical Engineering
Ph.D., Computer and Information Science
Ph.D., Electrical Engineering

Approximate Cost of Degrees

UNDERGRADUATE, RESIDENT
$16,500

UNDERGRADUATE, NONRESIDENT
$48,300

MASTER'S, RESIDENT
$24,900

MASTER'S, NONRESIDENT
$38,900

DOCTORATE, RESIDENT
$41,400

DOCTORATE, NONRESIDENT
$64,800

Admissions Guidelines

UNDERGRADUATE
High school diploma, SAT and/or ACT required

GRADUATE
Accredited bachelor's with 3.0 GPA required; GRE and GRE subject test recommended

Undergraduate Programs
The B.S. program in Computer Science and Engineering is available with tracks in hardware-software systems, information systems, and software systems.

The B.A. and B.S. programs in Computer and Information Science are focused primarily on software and computer science theory.

The ABET-accredited B.S. in Electrical Engineering is available with computer engineering and electrical engineering tracks. The computer engineering track includes courses in both hardware and software engineering (emphasizing the former), while the electrical engineering track surveys virtually the entire discipline.

Graduate Programs
The 33-hour M.S. in Computer and Information Science can culminate in a thesis or in a battery of five written examinations. The former track is generally chosen by students who plan on proceeding to doctoral work or research.

The 30-hour M.S. in Electrical Engineering can culminate in a thesis or a comprehensive examination in a specific subject area (biomedical engineering, communications, computer engineering, control, electrical power systems, or electromagnetics/optics).

The Ph.D. in Computer and Information Science requires two examinations in addition to the standard dissertation.

The Ph.D. in Electrical Engineering requires two examinations and one year of full-time residency in addition to the standard dissertation.

Other Programs
The B.S. in Business Administration is available with an information systems specialization. This specialization is administered jointly by the

Department of Computer and Information Science and the Max M. Fisher College of Business.

A B.S. in Health Information Management is available. For more information, contact the HIMS Division of the School of Allied Medical Professions at (614) 292-0567.

Contact Information

PHONE
General information: (614) 292-6446
Admissions (undergraduate): (614) 292-3980
Admissions (graduate): (614) 292-9444
Computer and information science: (614) 292-5813
Electrical engineering: (614) 292-2572

FAX
Admissions (undergraduate): (614) 292-4818
Admissions (graduate): (614) 292-3895
Computer and information science: (614) 292-2911
Electrical engineering: (614) 292-7596

E-MAIL
Admissions (undergraduate):
telecounseling@fa.adm.ohio-state.edu
Admissions (graduate): gradadmiss@osu.edu
Computer science (undergraduate):
undergrad@cis.ohio-state.edu
Computer science (graduate): Elizabeth O'Neill
(oneill@cis.ohio-state.edu)
Electrical engineering (graduate):
eegrad@ee.eng.ohio-state.edu

Ohio University

Athens, OH 45701

www.ohiou.edu ☆☆☆

Year established: 1804
Ownership: Public

This major public university offers intensive, highly structured programs at all levels. Evening classes and distance learning are available.

Degrees Offered

UNDERGRADUATE
B.S., Computer Science
ABET B.S., Electrical Engineering

GRADUATE
M.S., Electrical Engineering
Ph.D., Electrical Engineering

Approximate Cost of Degrees

UNDERGRADUATE, RESIDENT
$19,200

UNDERGRADUATE, NONRESIDENT
$40,400

MASTER'S, RESIDENT
$11,900

MASTER'S, NONRESIDENT
$22,800

DOCTORATE, RESIDENT
$28,600

DOCTORATE, NONRESIDENT
$54,800

Admissions Guidelines

UNDERGRADUATE
High school diploma, SAT and/or ACT required

GRADUATE
Accredited bachelor's with 2.7 GPA required, GRE recommended

Undergraduate Programs
The B.S. in Computer Science represents a well-rounded program solidly grounded in mathematics and theoretical computer science. As part of the program, students must pass a foreign language requirement.

The ABET-accredited B.S. in Electrical Engineering is available with tracks in electrical engineering and computer engineering. The computer engineering track is largely hardware-oriented, although software engineering is addressed to some extent.

Graduate Programs

The 40-hour M.S. in Electrical Engineering is available with an optional computer science track. A thesis is required.

The Ph.D. in Electrical Engineering is available with an optional computer science. A comprehensive examination (which includes both oral and written components) is required in addition to the standard dissertation.

Other Programs

A B.B.A. with emphasis in management information systems is also available. For more information, contact the Department of Management Information Systems at (740) 593-0646.

A 43-hour M.A. in Telecommunications is available with an optional interactive communication emphasis. For more information, contact the School of Telecommunications at tcomschool@ohiou.edu.

Contact Information

PHONE

General information: (740) 593-1000
Admissions (undergraduate): (740) 593-4100

E-MAIL

Admissions (undergraduate): FRSHINFO@ohiou.edu
Admissions (graduate): gradstu@www.ohiou.edu
Engineering/computer science: Valerie Pettit
(pettit@homer.ece.ohiou.edu)

Oklahoma State University   osu.okstate.edu ★★★

Center for Academic Services
324 Student Union
Stillwater, OK 74078-1012

Year established: 1890
Ownership: Public

This major research-oriented state university offers programs at all levels in information technology disciplines and related interdisciplinary fields (see "Other Programs"). Evening classes, weekend study, and distance learning are available.

Degrees Offered

UNDERGRADUATE

B.S., Computer Science
ABET B.S., Electrical Engineering
ABET B.S., Electronics Technology

GRADUATE

M.Eng., Electrical Engineering
M.S., Computer Science
M.S., Electrical Engineering
Ph.D., Computer Science
Ph.D., Electrical Engineering

Approximate Cost of Degrees

UNDERGRADUATE, RESIDENT
$10,200

UNDERGRADUATE, NONRESIDENT
$28,700

MASTER'S, RESIDENT
$3,700

MASTER'S, NONRESIDENT
$10,500

DOCTORATE, RESIDENT
$7,300

DOCTORATE, NONRESIDENT
$20,900

Admissions Guidelines

UNDERGRADUATE
High school diploma, SAT and/or ACT required

GRADUATE
Accredited bachelor's with 3.0 GPA on upper 60 hours required, GRE recommended

Undergraduate Programs

The B.S. program in Computer Science is oriented primarily toward mathematics, theoretical computer science, and structural issues of computing. The program provides an excellent introduction to graduate work in the field.

The ABET-accredited B.S. program in Electrical Engineering focuses on issues in circuit design, digital systems, computer engineering, and control theory.

The ABET-accredited B.S. program in Electronics Technology gives students a rigorous background in digital systems, microelectronics, and related fields.

Graduate Programs

The 33-hour M.Eng. (Master of Engineering) in Electrical Engineering is a professional degree culminating in a capstone project. Although no formal specializations are available, students are given the opportunity to explore the field through electives.

The 30-hour M.S. in Computer Science requires two examinations in addition to the coursework requirements and thesis.

The 30-hour M.S. in Electrical Engineering is available with concentrations in most of the Electrical Engineering Ph.D. research areas (see below). A thesis is required.

The Ph.D. program in Computer Science is available with concentrations in computer organization and operating systems, information systems, numerical analysis and optimization, programming languages, and theoretical computer science. Three examinations (two written, one oral) are required in addition to the standard dissertation.

The Ph.D. program in Electrical Engineering is available with coursework and research concentrations in communications, computer system design, control theory, digital and analog VLSI design, electronics, expert system development, intelligent control, microwave remote sensing, laser applications, optoelectronics, parallel processing, power economics, renewable energy systems, and speech/

image signal processing. Two examinations are required in addition to the standard dissertation.

Other Programs

M.S. programs in Accounting Information Systems and Management Information Systems are also available. For more information, contact the program director at (405) 744-5111.

M.S. and Ed.D. programs in Educational Technology are also available. For more information, contact the College of Educational Studies at osu-coe@okstate.edu.

An M.S. in Telecommunications Management is offered through the Department of Computer Science. For more information, contact the program office at (405) 744-9000.

Contact Information

PHONE
Admissions (undergraduate): (405) 744-6858
Admissions (graduate): (405) 744-6368
Computer science: (405) 744-5668
Electrical and computer engineering: (405) 744-5157
Electronics technology: (405) 744-5716

FAX
Computer science: (405) 744-9097
Electrical engineering: (405) 744-9198

E-MAIL
Admissions (undergraduate): admit@okstate.edu
Admissions (graduate): grad-i@okstate.edu
Electrical engineering: R. Ramakumar (ramakum@master.ceat.okstate.edu)

Old Dominion University   web.odu.edu ★★★½

Office of Admissions
108 Alfred B. Rollins Jr. Hall
Norfolk, VA 23529

Year established: 1930
Ownership: Public

This major public research-oriented university offers programs at all levels in a variety of cutting-edge information technology fields. Evening classes are available, as is distance learning. Several programs can, in fact, be completed entirely via distance learning.

Degrees Offered

UNDERGRADUATE
🅰 B.S., Computer Engineering
B.S., Computer Engineering Technology
B.S., Computer Science
B.S., E-Commerce
🅰 B.S., Electrical Engineering
🅰 B.S., Electrical Engineering Technology

GRADUATE
M.E., Computer Engineering
M.E., Electrical Engineering
M.S., Computer Engineering
M.S., Computer Science
M.S., E-Commerce Systems
M.S., Electrical Engineering
Ph.D., Computer Science
Ph.D., Electrical Engineering

Approximate Cost of Degrees

UNDERGRADUATE, RESIDENT
$15,600

UNDERGRADUATE, NONRESIDENT
$48,000

MASTER'S, RESIDENT
$6,700

MASTER'S, NONRESIDENT
$17,700

DOCTORATE, RESIDENT
$13,300

DOCTORATE, NONRESIDENT
$35,400

Admissions Guidelines

UNDERGRADUATE
High school diploma, SAT and/or ACT

GRADUATE
Accredited bachelor's, GRE required

Undergraduate Programs
The ABET-accredited B.S. program in Computer Engineering heavily emphasizes digital systems and circuit design.

The B.S. program in Computer Engineering Technology addresses both hardware and software issues, but emphasizes the former. The lower-level curriculum of this program is virtually identical to that of the ABET-accredited B.S. in Electrical Engineering Technology.

The B.S. program in Computer Science emphasizes the basic structural and philosophical dimensions of the field; in its applied component, this program emphasizes software far more than it does hardware. This program can be completed by distance learning.

The new B.S. in E-Commerce addresses Internet marketing, technology management, data analysis, computer applications, security, and other issues affecting Internet commerce. This program is offered through the College of Business and Public Administration.

The ABET-accredited B.S. program in Electrical Engineering emphasizes systems design, microelectronics, and circuit design. Students can design an upper-level specialization using elective course options.

The ABET-accredited B.S. program in Electrical Engineering Technology primarily emphasizes power and control systems; computer engineering also comprises a significant portion of the major. This program can be completed by distance learning.

Graduate Programs
The 30-hour Master of Engineering (M.E.) in Computer Engineering is a professional degree intended primarily for reentry students. No thesis is required. The curriculum strongly favors a systems-oriented approach.

The 30-hour Master of Engineering (M.E.) in Electrical Engineering is a professional degree intended primarily for reentry students. No thesis is required.

The 30-hour M.S. in Computer Engineering is a highly research-oriented program designed primarily, but not exclusively, for students who want to continue on to a Ph.D. program. A thesis is required. The curriculum strongly favors a systems-oriented approach.

The 34-hour M.S. in Computer Science is available with an optional computer information sciences track. The program culminates in a comprehensive examination, followed by either a thesis or a capstone project.

Beginning in Fall 2001, an M.S. in E-Commerce Systems will be available. This highly innovative program, the first we've seen of its kind, adapts virtually all aspects of management science to Internet commerce in a concise, integral fashion. The program culminates in an e-commerce project demonstrating learned knowledge in the field. This program will be offered through the College of Business and Public Administration.

The 30-hour M.S. in Electrical Engineering is a highly research-oriented program designed primarily, but not exclusively, for students who want to continue on to a Ph.D. program. A thesis is required. Primary research interests are classified into the three broad areas of computer engineering, physical science, and systems science.

The Ph.D. program in Computer Science includes a teaching requirement. In addition to the standard dissertation, two examinations and two consecutive semesters of full-time residency are required.

The Ph.D. program in Electrical Engineering requires two semesters of full-time residency. Two examinations are required in addition to the standard dissertation.

Other Programs

An e-commerce specialization is also available in the M.B.A. program of the College of Business and Public Administration.

Contact Information

Phone
Admissions: (757) 683-4845 or (800) 348-7926
Electrical and computer engineering technology: (757) 683-3775
Computer science/electrical and computer engineering: (757) 683-5874

Fax
Electrical and computer engineering technology: (757) 683-5655

E-mail
Admissions: admit@odu.edu
Computer engineering technology: F.M. Williams (fwilliam@odu.edu)
E-commerce: John Barker (jbarker@odu.edu)
Electrical and computer engineering: Heather Jones (jones@ece.odu.edu)
Electrical engineering technology: John Hackworth (jhackwor@odu.edu)

Oregon Graduate Institute of Science and Technology

www.ogi.edu ☆☆☆½

Office of Academic and Student Services
20000 N.W. Walker Road
Beaverton, OR 97006-8921

Year established: 1963
Ownership: Private

This major private research institute offers an array of unique graduate programs in information technology. Most programs can be completed at least largely by part-time study; in addition, evening classes and distance learning are available.

Degrees Offered

Graduate
M.S., Computer Science and Engineering
M.S., Electrical and Computer Engineering
M.Sw.E.
Ph.D., Computer Science and Engineering
Ph.D., Electrical and Computer Engineering

Approximate Cost of Degrees

Master's
$23,600

Doctorate
$47,300

Admissions Guidelines

GRADUATE

Accredited bachelor's, GRE required

Graduate Programs

The 30-hour M.S. in Computer Science and Engineering is available in two tracks: research and professional. The research track requires a thesis. The professional track is available with heavy concentrations in adaptive systems, computational finance, computer security, data-intensive systems, human-computer interfaces, software engineering, software engineering for industry professionals, spoken language systems, and systems software. The student can also design an individualized specialization with faculty approval.

The 30-hour M.S. in Electrical and Computer Engineering is available in two tracks: research and professional. The research track requires a thesis. The professional track is available with heavy concentrations in communication and signal processing, computational finance, computer engineering, electronic circuit design, electronic packaging, information processing, multimedia systems, semiconductor processing and device physics, and VLSI design. The student can also design an individualized specialization with faculty approval.

The 28-hour Oregon Master of Software Engineering (M.Sw.E.) is offered jointly with Oregon State University, Portland State University, and the University of Oregon. The program culminates in a 6-hour software engineering practicum (supervised work).

The Ph.D. in Computer Science and Engineering is available with concentrations in adaptive systems and applications, human-computer interactive systems,

programming languages and software engineering, systems software, and theory.

The Ph.D. in Electrical and Computer Engineering is a highly research-oriented program that differs in its course requirements depending on the research focus of the dissertation. No curricula are set in stone; each student designs an individualized plan of study with faculty approval. A comprehensive examination is required.

Other Programs

An M.S. in Computational Finance is also available through the Department of Computer Science and Engineering.

An M.S. in Management in Science and Technology is available both residentially and by distance learning. For more information, contact the department at (877) 468-6644.

Contact Information

PHONE

Admissions: (503) 748-1027 or (800) 685-2423
Computer science and engineering: (503) 748-1151
Electrical and computer engineering: (503) 748-1418
Software engineering: (503) 725-2900

FAX

Admissions: (503) 748-1285
Computer science and engineering: (503) 748-1553
Software engineering: (503) 725-2910

E-MAIL

Admissions: admissions@admin.ogi.edu
Computer science and engineering: csedept@cse.ogi.edu
Electrical and computer engineering: johansen@ece.ogi.edu

Pace University   www.pace.edu ☆☆½

1 Pace Plaza   Year established: 1906
New York, NY 10038   Ownership: Private

This private metropolitan university offers programs at all levels. Most of these degrees geared quite specifically toward the professional goal of getting one's IT degree and getting ahead. Evening classes, weekend study, and distance learning are available.

Degrees Offered

UNDERGRADUATE
B.A., Computer Science
🅒 B.S., Computer Science
B.S., Information Systems
B.S., Professional Computer Studies

GRADUATE
M.S., Computer Science
M.S., Information Systems
M.S., Telecommunications
D.P.S., Computing

Approximate Cost of Degrees

UNDERGRADUATE
$60,500

MASTER'S
$20,700

DOCTORATE
$41,400

Admissions Guidelines

UNDERGRADUATE
High school diploma, SAT and/or ACT required

GRADUATE
Accredited bachelor's required, GRE recommended

Undergraduate Programs

The B.A. program in Computer Science approaches the field from a broad background in the humanities, social sciences, and natural sciences. The concentration focuses on theoretical issues in computer science pertinent to other fields and, in its applied component, on interdisciplinary uses of computing.

The CSAB-accredited B.S. in Computer Science approaches the discipline from a broad natural science background, proceeding gradually into structural field issues and gradually moving toward a study of new computing methodologies. The program is highly software-focused in its applied components.

The heavily software-oriented B.S. in Information Systems focuses on the use of computer information systems in the workplace. Programming, software engineering, and structural computer science issues are addressed in some depth.

The B.S. in Professional Computer Studies focuses heavily on software applications and computer programming. The program is strongly office-focused and does not address issues of theoretical computer science or structural computing in very much depth.

Graduate Programs

The 36-hour M.S. in Computer Science gives students exceptional flexibility in choosing specific areas of study. No thesis is required, although students may undertake one if they want.

The 36-hour M.S. in Information Systems addresses software engineering in some depth while touching on issues of management and policy. No thesis is required.

The M.S. in Telecommunications is a highly structured program focusing on computer telecommunications, but addressing other telecommunications fields in reasonable depth. No thesis is required.

The Doctor of Professional Studies (D.P.S.) in Computing involves a team software development project during the first year of coursework, a student-defined faculty-approved specialization during a second, and the standard dissertation during the third. The program focuses heavily on computer applications and engineering. The program can be completed entirely through evening and weekend study and is intended for students who work full-time.

Other Programs

B.B.A., M.B.A., and D.P.S. programs with emphasis in business information systems are offered through the Lubin School of Business. For more information, contact the Lubin administrative office at (212) 346-1487.

A B.S. program in Office Information Systems is also offered through the Department of Computer and Information Science.

More Information

Pace University operates seven campuses in the general New York City area: three in New York City, two in White Plains, one in Pleasantville, and another in Briarcliff Manor.

Contact Information

PHONE
General information: (800) 784-7223
Admissions (undergraduate): (212) 346-1323
Admissions (graduate): (212) 346-1531
Computer and information science: (212) 346-1687

E-MAIL
Computer science: Kenneth Norz
(knorz@fsmail.pace.edu)

Pennsylvania State University— University Park

www.psu.edu ☆☆½

Undergraduate Admissions Office
201 Shields Building, Box 3000
University Park, PA 16804-3000

Year established: 1855
Ownership: Public

This institution, the flagship college of a major state university, offers solid programs at all levels in an array of information technology fields. Evening classes, weekend study, extension sites, and distance learning are available.

Degrees Offered

UNDERGRADUATE
(ABET) B.S., Computer Engineering
B.S., Computer Science
(ABET) B.S., Electrical Engineering
B.S., Information Sciences and Technology

GRADUATE
M.Eng., Computer Science and Engineering
M.S., Computer Science and Engineering
M.S., Electrical Engineering
Ph.D., Computer Science and Engineering
Ph.D., Electrical Engineering

Approximate Cost of Degrees

UNDERGRADUATE, RESIDENT
$25,300

UNDERGRADUATE, NONRESIDENT
$53,800

MASTER'S, RESIDENT
$10,300

MASTER'S, NONRESIDENT
$21,200

DOCTORATE, RESIDENT
$17,200

DOCTORATE, NONRESIDENT
$35,300

Admissions Guidelines

UNDERGRADUATE
High school diploma, SAT and/or ACT required

GRADUATE
Accredited bachelor's, GRE required

Undergraduate Programs

The ABET-accredited B.S. program in Computer Engineering emphasizes software slightly more than it does hardware. Mathematical and theoretical foundations of the field are emphasized more than one would generally expect.

The B.S. program in Computer Science seamlessly integrates the study of theoretical computer science with applied computing. Students begin study in both areas at the very beginning of the program and continue studying both until the very end.

Because the coursework is distributed in such a fashion, there is little of the "theoretical foundation" dynamic that one generally sees in a computer science curriculum.

The ABET-accredited B.S. in Electrical Engineering allows for senior-level specialization in virtually every common electrical engineering field (such as analog and digital electronics, control systems, and digital signal processing) and some very uncommon ones (such as image processing and space science). A senior project is required.

The B.S. program in Information Sciences and Technology is available with tracks in information/society/public policy, information systems development, and information technology integration.

Graduate Programs

The 30-hour Master of Engineering (M.Eng.) in Computer Science and Engineering emphasizes theory and software systems. No thesis is required, but the student must either submit or publish a suitable research paper while enrolled in the program.

The 30-hour M.S. in Computer Science and Engineering emphasizes theory and software systems. A thesis is required.

The 32-hour M.S. in Electrical Engineering is available with specializations in computer engineering, electromagnetic fields and propagation, electronic materials/devices/circuits, lasers/electro-optics, and signals/systems. Students can opt for a thesis or publishable research paper as their final project. Students who undertake the former need only take 24 hours of formal coursework, while students who undertake the latter will need to take 32 hours.

The Ph.D. program in Computer Science and Engineering requires two examinations in addition to the standard dissertation.

The Ph.D. program in Electrical Engineering requires two examinations in addition to the standard dissertation. Students must also fulfill two consecutive semesters of full-time residency.

Contact Information

Phone
Admissions (undergraduate): (814) 865-5471
Computer science and engineering: (814) 865-9505
Electrical engineering: (814) 863-2788
Information sciences and technology: (877) 690-1266 or (814) 865-3528

Fax
Computer science and engineering: (814) 865-3176
Electrical engineering: (814) 865-7065
Information sciences and technology: (814) 865-5604

E-mail
Admissions (undergraduate): admissions@psu.edu
Admissions (graduate): gadm@oas.psu.edu
Computer science and engineering: corl@cse.psu.edu
Electrical engineering: Glenna Young (gryece@engr.psu.edu)
Information sciences and technology: ISTinfo@psu.edu

Portland State University   www.pdx.edu ☆☆☆

P.O. Box 751
Portland, OR 97207

Year established: 1946
Ownership: Public

Considered by many to be a pioneer in the field of nontraditional education, this respected metropolitan university offers programs at all levels in information technology fields. Evening classes, weekend study, credit by examination, and distance learning are available.

Degrees Offered

Undergraduate
(ABET) B.S., Computer Engineering
(CSAB) B.S., Computer Science
(ABET) B.S., Electrical Engineering

Graduate
M.S., Computer Science
M.S., Electrical and Computer Engineering
M.Sw.E.
Ph.D., Electrical and Computer Engineering

Approximate Cost of Degrees

UNDERGRADUATE, RESIDENT
$18,000

UNDERGRADUATE, NONRESIDENT
$51,000

MASTER'S, RESIDENT
$3,100

MASTER'S, NONRESIDENT
$5,400

DOCTORATE, RESIDENT
$5,200

DOCTORATE, NONRESIDENT
$9,000

Admissions Guidelines

UNDERGRADUATE
High school diploma, SAT and/or ACT required

GRADUATE
Accredited bachelor's, GRE required

Undergraduate Programs

The ABET-accredited B.S. in Computer Engineering is a hardware-oriented program, although students may focus more on software through major electives. A senior project is required.

The CSAB-accredited B.S. in Computer Science focuses on theoretical computer science, computer systems engineering, and software engineering. Students must complete a two-semester capstone software engineering project.

The ABET-accredited B.S. in Electrical Engineering incorporates intensive study in electromagnetics, thermodynamics, and circuit design. A senior project is required.

Graduate Programs

The 28-hour Oregon Master of Software Engineering (M.Sw.E.) is offered jointly with the Oregon Graduate Institute of Science and Technology, Oregon State University, and the University of Oregon. The program culminates in a 6-hour software engineering practicum (supervised work).

The 30-hour M.S. in Computer Science is available with specializations in databases, languages, systems, and theory. A thesis or project paper (a research paper on a project undertaken by the student or team of students as part of the program) is required.

The 30-hour M.S. in Electrical and Computer Engineering is available with specializations in analog and digital circuit design, application-specific integrated circuit design, automatic control theory, communications, computer architecture and systems, computer vision, design automation, electromagnetics, image processing, integrative circuit device modeling and processing, neural networks, optics and laser systems, parallel processing, power electronics, power and energy, robotics, signal processing, solid-state devices, and VLSI design. The program generally culminates in a thesis, but students can (with faculty approval) undertake a project instead.

The Ph.D. in Electrical and Computer Engineering requires two examinations in addition to the standard dissertation.

Other Programs

An M.B.A. with emphasis in management of information technology is available. For more information, contact the Student Services Office of the School of Business Administration at (503) 725-3712.

Contact Information

PHONE
General information: (503) 725-3000
Admissions: (503) 725-3511 or (800) 547-8887
Computer science: (503) 725-4036
Electrical and computer engineering: (503) 725-3806

FAX
Computer science: (503) 725-3211
Electrical and computer engineering: (503) 725-3807

E-MAIL
Admissions: admissions@pdx.edu
Computer science: cmps@cs.pdx.edu
Electrical and computer engineering: eed@ee.pdx.edu

Princeton University

www.princeton.edu ☆☆☆

Princeton, NJ 08544

Year established: 1746
Ownership: Private

This prestigious research-oriented institution offers programs at all levels in information technology fields. Although its doctoral programs are intensive, full-time research endeavors and not for the squeamish, its professional master's programs are designed to accommodate reentry students and can be completed on a part-time basis. Evening classes are available.

Degrees Offered

UNDERGRADUATE
A.B., Computer Science
🅐 B.S., Electrical Engineering
B.S.E., Computer Science

GRADUATE
M.Eng., Computer Science
M.Eng., Electrical Engineering
Ph.D., Applied and Computational Mathematics
Ph.D., Computer Science
Ph.D., Electrical Engineering

Approximate Cost of Degrees

UNDERGRADUATE
$98,500

MASTER'S
$36,900

DOCTORATE
$61,600

Admissions Guidelines

UNDERGRADUATE
High school diploma, SAT and/or ACT, SAT II required

GRADUATE
Accredited bachelor's, GRE required

Undergraduate Programs
The A.B. in Computer Science gives students a generous 18 hours of major electives. The required background of the program focuses primarily on structural computing theory and hardware.

The ABET-accredited B.S. in Electrical Engineering is available with informal specializations in communications/signal processing/control, computer engineering, optical engineering, and solid-state electronics.

The B.S. in Engineering (B.S.E.) in Computer Science is oriented toward computer systems and hardware engineering.

Graduate Programs
The 24-hour M.Eng. in Computer Science is a highly profession-oriented program that is particularly well-suited for reentry students. No thesis or final project is required.

The 24-hour M.Eng. in Electrical Engineering is a highly profession-oriented program that seems particularly well-suited for reentry students. No thesis or final project is required.

The Ph.D. in Applied and Computational Mathematics is available to a limited number of exceptionally promising students each year. A general examination is required in addition to the standard dissertation.

The Ph.D. in Computer Science requires two examinations in addition to the standard dissertation. The entire program must be completed full-time. Princeton undertakes a vast amount of research in a diverse array of fields, so students will be able to undertake a dissertation study in virtually any field of interest. Interdisciplinary topics are encouraged.

The Ph.D. in Electrical Engineering requires two examinations in addition to the standard dissertation. Research specializations are available in computer engineering, electronic materials and devices, information sciences and systems, and optics/optoelectronic engineering.

Contact Information

PHONE
Admissions (undergraduate): (609) 258-3060
Admissions (graduate): (609) 258-3034

Applied and computational mathematics:
(609) 258-3008
Computer science: (609) 258-5030
Electrical engineering (undergraduate):
(609) 258-4625
Electrical engineering (graduate): (609) 258-6728

FAX
Admissions (undergraduate): (609) 258-6743
Admissions (graduate): (609) 258-6180
Computer science: (609) 258-1771

E-MAIL
Computer science (undergraduate): Doug Clark
(doug@cs.princeton.edu)
Computer science (graduate):
gradinfo@cs.princeton.edu
Electrical engineering (undergraduate): Sharad
Malik (sharad@ee.princeton.edu)
Electrical engineering (graduate): Karen Williams
(ski@ee.princeton.edu)

✷ EXTRA!

Jeff Bezos, Amazon.com CEO and *Time* magazine's "Man of the Year 1999," is a
Princeton graduate. Alan Turing, the father of artificial intelligence, earned his
Ph.D. from Princeton.

Purdue University—West Lafayette   www.purdue.edu ☆☆½

West Lafayette, IN 47907

Year established: 1869
Ownership: Public

This highly respected Big Ten state university offers programs at all levels in a variety of information technology fields. Evening classes, weekend courses, and distance learning are available.

Degrees Offered

UNDERGRADUATE
B.S., Computer Science
B.S., Computer Engineering
B.S., Computer Technology
 B.S., Electrical Engineering
 B.S., Electrical Engineering Technology

GRADUATE
M.S., Computer Science
M.S., Electrical Engineering
M.S.E., Electrical and Computer Engineering
M.S.T., Computer Technology
M.S.T., Electrical Engineering Technology
Ph.D., Electrical and Computer Engineering
Ph.D., Computer Science

Approximate Cost of Degrees

UNDERGRADUATE, RESIDENT
$17,900

UNDERGRADUATE, NONRESIDENT
$52,400

MASTER'S, RESIDENT
$6,700

MASTER'S, NONRESIDENT
$19,600

DOCTORATE, RESIDENT
$11,200

DOCTORATE, NONRESIDENT
$32,800

Admissions Guidelines

UNDERGRADUATE
High school diploma, SAT and/or ACT required

GRADUATE
Accredited bachelor's required, 3.0 GPA and GRE recommended

Undergraduate Programs

The B.S. in Computer Engineering takes a definite systems approach, incorporating elements of both hardware and software engineering. In its prerequisites, the program seems to be slightly more hardware-focused than software-focused. The opportunity for software specialization is nevertheless there, thanks for a generous helping of available courses in the field and free elective credit options.

The B.S. in Computer Science focuses primarily on structural issues and software development.

The B.S. in Computer Technology is available with specializations in applications development and programming, business and manufacturing knowledge, interpersonal skills, systems and database development, and telecommunications and networking.

The ABET-accredited B.S. in Electrical Engineering focuses on electronic circuit design, computer engineering, and related topics. Students are given generous opportunity for specialization through elective credit options.

The ABET-accredited B.S. in Electrical Engineering Technology gives roughly equal weight to electrical engineering issues and project management issues.

Graduate Programs

The 30-hour M.S. in Computer Science focuses intensively on structural, theoretical, and software-oriented issues in the field. No thesis is required. An optional specialization in computational science and engineering is available in conjunction with the Department of Electrical and Computer Engineering.

The M.S. in Electrical Engineering is available with specializations in automatic control, biomedical engineering, communications and signal processing, computer engineering, energy sources and systems, fields and optics, solid-state devices and materials, and VLSI/circuit design. No thesis is required.

The M.S. in Engineering (M.S.E.) in Electrical and Computer Engineering approaches electrical and computer engineering from within the broader theoretical background of engineering science. No thesis is required.

The M.S. in Technology (M.S.T.) programs in Computer Technology and Electrical Engineering Technology represent interdisciplinary, non-thesis curricula designed for reentry students.

The Ph.D. program in Computer Science requires two examinations in addition to the standard dissertation. An optional computational science and engineering track is available, which incorporates elements of electrical and computer engineering into the broader computer and computational science major.

The Ph.D. program in Electrical and Computer Engineering requires three examinations in addition to the standard dissertation. Students are given opportunity to specialize in a customized research area. An optional computational science and engineering track is available, which incorporates elements of mathematics and computer science into the broader electrical and computer engineering major.

Other Programs

B.S. and M.S.T. programs in Computer Graphics are also available through the School of Technology. For more information, contact the Department of Computer Graphics at (765) 494-4585.

B.S. and M.S.T. programs in Computer-Integrated Manufacturing Technology are available; the B.S. program is ABET-accredited. For more information, contact the CIMT Department at (765) 494-7515.

Students can elect to undertake an interdisciplinary M.S. in Statistics and Computer Science. For more information, contact the Computer Science Department.

Purdue University offers an M.S. in Technology (M.S.T.) that can be completed entirely through distance learning and weekend residencies. The program uses a cohort model whereby students complete the program as a team, progressing at roughly the same pace. For more information, contact the program office at gradprog@tech.purdue.edu.

Contact Information

PHONE
General information: (765) 494-4600
Admissions (undergraduate): (765) 494-1776
Admissions (graduate): (765) 494-2600

Computer science (undergraduate): (765) 494-6595 or (800) 320-6132

Computer science (graduate): (765) 494-6004

Computer technology: (765) 494-4545

Electrical and computer engineering: (765) 494-3536

Electrical engineering technology: (765) 494-7484

Fax

Admissions (undergraduate): (765) 494-0544

Computer technology: (765) 496-1212

Electrical and computer engineering: (765) 494-3544

E-mail

Admissions (undergraduate): admissions@purdue.edu

Admissions (graduate): gradinfo@purdue.edu

Computer science (undergraduate): undergrad-info@cs.purdue.edu

Computer science (graduate): grad-info@cs.purdue.edu

Electrical and computer engineering (undergraduate): eceugo@ecn.purdue.edu

Electrical and computer engineering (graduate): ecegrad@ecn.purdue.edu

---

Regents College — www.regents.edu ☆☆☆

7 Columbia Circle
Albany, NY 12203-5159

Year established: 1971
Ownership: Private

This highly innovative and completely unique school awards undergraduate degrees to students based on prior coursework, credit by examination, or new coursework from any regionally accredited institution (regardless of the delivery method). Military and professional programs that have been evaluated by ACE/PONSI can also be applied toward a degree. Regents College was formerly the external degree program of the University of the State of New York, but became proprietary in 1998.

Degrees Offered

Undergraduate

B.S., Computer Information Systems

B.S., Computer Technology

(ABET) B.S., Electronic(s) Engineering Technology

Approximate Cost of Degrees

Undergraduate

$1,600 and up

Admissions Guidelines

Undergraduate

A high school diploma or equivalent is usually required, but exemptions are possible.

Undergraduate Programs

Regents does not offer undergraduate courses as such, but will accept unlimited nonduplicating transfer credit from courses taken at any regionally accredited (or equivalent) institution. Professional courses recognized by the American Council on Education (ACE) can also be used, in some cases, to satisfy degree requirements. Regents College will also grant credit for some military training. All degrees offered by Regents College can be completed 100 percent nonresidentially.

Regents accepts most recognized forms of credit by examination, including CLEP, DANTES, AP, and subject GRE examinations. Regents also offers proprietary Regents College Examinations (RCEs) in a variety of fields.

In January 2000, Regents College announced that it would accept the Microsoft Certified Software Engineering (MCSE), Microsoft Computer Professional (MCP), and Comp TIA certifications for credit toward its B.S. in Computer Information Systems. This innovative degree seems to be the most popular of Regents' technology offerings.

The B.S. in Computer Technology is extremely hardware-oriented and could easily be classified as a computer engineering program. Eight laboratory courses are required (one physics laboratory and seven computer hardware laboratories). These courses can be taken at any regionally accredited university (or non-U.S. equivalent).

The ABET-accredited B.S. in Electronic(s) Engineering Technology requires (in addition to credit requirements) an Integrated Technology Assessment (ITA), a comprehensive examination that seems to be similar to a portfolio evaluation.

Graduate Programs

It seems extremely likely that Regents College will offer a master's of some kind in an information technology field beginning in 2002. No further information is currently available.

Other Programs

Regents College also offers a general B.S. in Technology with a number of possible concentrations, including computer technology and electronics/instrumentation.

Students in Regents College's M.S.N. program can choose an informatics concentration.

More Information

Non-U.S. students are encouraged to apply and can, in most cases, complete a Regents College degree without leaving their home country.

Students who actively serve in a branch of the military are eligible to receive discounts and other benefits.

Contact Information

Phone
(518) 464-8500 or (888) 647-2388

Fax
(518) 464-8777

Other Web Sites
CIS: http://www.itdegree.com/

E-mail
rcinfo@regents.edu

 EXTRA!

Shareware gaming top dog Steve Moraff, of MoraffWare (http://www.moraff.com/), is a Regents College graduate.

Rensselaer Polytechnic Institute   www.rpi.edu ☆☆½

110 8th Street
Troy, NY 12180

Year established: 1824
Ownership: Private

This highly respected private research institution offers programs at all levels in a vast array of standard and interdisciplinary information technology fields. Interdisciplinarity is indeed the focus of Rensselaer; dual majors are encouraged at the undergraduate level, and an individualized M.S. program (see "Other Programs") permits students to undertake graduate-level study in any reasonable field of their choice. Several programs can be completed entirely via distance learning. Evening classes, weekend study, and extension classes are also available.

Degrees Offered

UNDERGRADUATE

🔵 B.S., Computer and Systems Engineering
B.S., Computer Science
🔵 B.S., Electrical Engineering
B.S., Information Technology

GRADUATE

M.Eng., Computer and Systems Engineering
M.Eng., Electrical Engineering
M.S., Cognitive Systems Engineering
M.S., Computer and Systems Engineering
M.S., Computer Science
M.S., Electrical Engineering
M.S., Information Technology
D.Eng., Computer and Systems Engineering
D.Eng., Electrical Engineering
Ph.D., Computer and Systems Engineering
Ph.D., Computer Science
Ph.D., Electrical Engineering
Ph.D., Information Technology

Approximate Cost of Degrees

UNDERGRADUATE
$89,200

MASTER'S
$23,900

DOCTORATE
$43,900

Admissions Guidelines

UNDERGRADUATE
High school diploma, SAT and/or ACT required

GRADUATE
Accredited bachelor's, GRE required

Undergraduate Programs

The ABET-accredited B.S. in Computer and Systems Engineering incorporates elements of hardware and software design, VLSI design and maintenance, and computer systems theory into an integrated curriculum representing a broad, intensive, and fundamentally rigorous base in the field.

The B.S. program in Computer Science is directed primarily toward a study of theoretical computer science. The approach is decisively applied, interdisciplinary, and systems-oriented.

The ABET-accredited B.S. in Electrical Engineering is available with concentrations in automatic control and robotics, communications and signal processing, computer hardware/VLSI design, computer systems and applications, electromagnetics and plasma engineering, electronics and circuits, manufacturing, and solid-state electronics/ microelectronics.

The B.S. in Information Technology is designed for students who want to apply computer information systems to a second field. Students can choose from dozens of pre-approved secondary fields or design their own.

Graduate Programs

The 30-hour M.Eng. programs in Computer and Systems Engineering and in Electrical Engineering represent a broad curriculum in the field designed specifically for reentry students. Emphasis is placed on applied, rather than theoretical, issues. No thesis is required. The M.Eng. in Electrical Engineering can be completed via distance learning.

The 30-hour M.S. in Cognitive Systems Engineering is a highly innovative, interdisciplinary program entailing advanced study in computer and systems engineering, artificial intelligence, and psychology. A final project is required.

The 30-hour M.S. program in Computer Science is a highly student-defined program that rests primarily on issues of theoretical computer science and software engineering. A capstone software engineering project (with an attached written report) is required.

The 30-hour M.S. programs in Computer and Systems Engineering and in Electrical Engineering are highly structured programs that represent well-rounded, practical curricula. A thesis or project is generally required, but may be waived in cases where the student has already demonstrated equivalent skill or experience. These programs can be completed via distance learning.

The 30-hour M.S. in Information Technology is a highly interdisciplinary program focusing primarily on information technology and secondarily on an applied, non-IT related field for information technology application. No thesis is required.

The Ph.D. in Computer Science requires three examinations in addition to the standard dissertation.

The D.Eng. and Ph.D. programs in Computer and Systems Engineering represent strikingly similar curricular requirements; they differ primarily in the nature of their respective final projects. The D.Eng. thesis is essentially a project report that solves an applied engineering problem (which may be software-oriented, hardware-oriented, or both), while the Ph.D. thesis is a standard, research-oriented dissertation.

The D.Eng. and Ph.D. programs in Electrical Engineering are both highly intensive, focusing on digital circuit design, solid-state electronics, and related fields in their coursework requirements. They differ primarily in the nature of their respective final projects. The D.Eng. thesis is essentially a project report (that solves an applied engineering problem), while the Ph.D. thesis is a standard, research-oriented dissertation.

The Ph.D. in Information Technology is available with concentrations in artificial intelligence and cognitive science, computational sciences and engineering, computer communications and networks, computer-mediated communication, data mining and knowledge discovery, discrete event simulation, educational technologies, electronic arts, electronic commerce, and human-computer interaction. Two examinations are required in addition to the standard dissertation.

Other Programs

M.B.A. and M.S. programs in Computer Science Management are available by distance learning. For more information, contact the Department of Professional and Distance Education at (518) 276-7787.

An M.F.A. in Electronic Arts is available. For more information, contact the Department of Electronic Arts at (518) 276-4778.

An individualized professional M.S. can be designed in virtually any field. This 30-hour program requires no thesis and can be completed by distance learning. For more information, contact Kim Scalzo at (518) 276-8351.

The M.S. in Applied Science is available with optional specializations in microelectronics manufacturing and parallel/scientific computation. For more information, contact the Department of Applied Science at (518) 276-6305.

The M.S. and Ph.D. programs in Communication and Rhetoric can be tailored to the interests of a student who wants to undertake graduate-level research in computer-mediated communication. For more information, contact the Department of Communication and Rhetoric at (518) 276-6469.

M.B.A. and M.S. programs in Management of Technology are available with a unique optional track in Sino-U.S. technological business management. For more information, contact the Lally School of Management and Technology at (518) 276-6845.

The M.S. in Philosophy emphasizes artificial intelligence in its course requirements and primary research areas. For more information, contact the Department of Philosophy, Psychology, and Cognitive Science at (518) 276-6472.

An M.S. in Post-Professional Informatics and Architecture is available. This highly innovative program examines the impact of spatial modeling and simulation on architecture and related fields. For more information, contact the School of Architecture at (518) 276-6478.

The M.S. and Ph.D. programs in Science and Technology Studies can be undertaken as humanities-oriented study programs in information technology. For more information, contact the Department of Science and Technology Studies at (518) 276-6413.

B.S., M.B.A., and M.S. programs in Technological Entrepreneurship are also available. For more information, contact the Severino Center for Technological Entrepreneurship at (518) 276-8398.

Contact Information

PHONE

General information: (518) 276-6000
Admissions (undergraduate): (518) 276-6216
Admissions (graduate): (518) 276-6789
Cognitive systems engineering: (518) 276-8266
Computer science: (518) 276-8326
Electrical and computer/systems engineering: (518) 276-2554
Information technology: (518) 276-2660

FAX

Information technology: (518) 276-6687

E-MAIL

Admissions (undergraduate): admissions@rpi.edu
Admissions (graduate): grad-services@rpi.edu
Cognitive systems engineering: Ron Noel (noelr@rpi.edu)
Computer science: info@cs.rpi.edu
Electrical and computer/systems engineering: gradinfo@ecse.rpi.edu

Rice University

6100 Main Street
Houston, TX 77005

www.rice.edu ☆☆

Year established: 1912
Ownership: Private

This large, research-oriented private university offers programs at all levels in standard and nonstandard information technology fields. Several of the graduate programs are geared specifically toward the needs of reentry students. Evening classes are available.

Degrees Offered

UNDERGRADUATE

B.A., Computational and Applied Mathematics
B.A., Computer Science
B.S., Computer Science
B.A., Electrical and Computer Engineering
ABET B.S., Electrical Engineering

GRADUATE

M.A., Computational and Applied Mathematics
M.C.A.M.
M.C.S.
M.C.S.E.
M.E.E.
M.S., Electrical and Computer Engineering
Ph.D., Computational and Applied Mathematics
Ph.D., Computer Science
Ph.D., Electrical and Computer Engineering

Approximate Cost of Degrees

UNDERGRADUATE
$63,200

MASTER'S
$23,700

DOCTORATE
$39,500

Admissions Guidelines

UNDERGRADUATE
High school diploma, SAT and/or ACT required

GRADUATE
Accredited bachelor's with 3.0 GPA, GRE required

Undergraduate Programs

The B.A. in Computational and Applied Mathematics is available with informal concentrations in dif-ferential equations, operations research, optimization, and numerical analysis.

The B.A. and B.S. programs in Computer Science are effectively identical in their major requirements, differing only in broad distribution requirements. Specializations are available in architecture, computational science, foundations, human-computer interaction, and software systems.

The B.A. in Electrical and Computer Engineering is a largely individualized program that allows students to undertake specialized study in the area(s) of their choice, including (but not limited to) digital systems design, software engineering, and electromagnetics.

The ABET-accredited B.S. in Electrical Engineering is available with specializations in bioengineering, computer engineering, electronic circuits and devices, quantum electronics, and systems.

Graduate Programs

The 36-hour M.A. in Computational and Applied Mathematics addresses issues at the most complex, fundamental levels of computer science theory and applied mathematics. A thesis is required.

The 30-hour Master of Computational and Applied Mathematics (M.C.A.M.) is a professional program designed primarily for reentry students. Students are given great opportunity to construct an individualized specialization through major electives. No thesis is required.

The 30-hour Master of Computational Science and Engineering (M.C.S.E.) is a highly interdisciplinary professional program designed primarily for reentry students. Students are given great opportunity to construct an individualized specialization through major electives. No thesis is required.

The 30-hour Master of Computer Science (M.C.S.) is a highly flexible professional program designed primarily for reentry students. Students are given a great opportunity to construct an individualized specialization through major electives. No thesis is required.

The 30-hour Master of Electrical Engineering (M.E.E.) is a professional program designed for reentry students. Students are given a great deal of flexibility in designing a primary specialization track. No thesis is required.

The 30-hour M.S. in Electrical and Computer Engineering is available with optional specializations in bioengineering, computer engineering, physical electronics, and systems. A thesis is required.

The Ph.D. in Computational and Applied Mathematics requires two examinations in addition to the standard dissertation.

The Ph.D. in Computer Science can be tailored to fit the needs of individual students. Two examinations are required in addition to the standard dissertation.

The Ph.D. in Electrical and Computer Engineering is available with optional specializations in bioengineering, computer engineering, physical electronics, and systems. Two examinations are required in addition to the standard dissertation.

Other Programs

A Ph.D. in Computational Biology is offered jointly with Baylor School of Medicine and the University of Houston. For more information, contact the program office at (713) 527-4752.

Contact Information

PHONE
General information: (713) 348-8101
Admissions (undergraduate): (713) 348-4036 or (800) 527-6957
Admissions (graduate): (713) 348-4002
Computational and applied mathematics: (713) 348-4805
Computer science: (713) 348-4834
Electrical and computer engineering: (713) 348-4020

FAX
Admissions (undergraduate): (713) 348-5952
Admissions (graduate): (713) 348-4806
Computational and applied mathematics: (713) 348-5318
Computer science: (713) 348-5930
Electrical and computer engineering: (713) 348-5686

E-MAIL
Admissions (undergraduate): admission@rice.edu
Admissions (graduate): graduate@rice.edu
Computational and applied mathematics: caam@caam.rice.edu
Computer science: Iva Jean Jorgensen (ivajean@cs.rice.edu)
Electrical and computer engineering: elec@rice.edu

Rivier College
www.rivier.edu ☆☆☆

420 Main Street
Nashua, NH 03060-5086

Year established: 1933
Ownership: Private

This small private liberal arts college offers undergraduate and graduate programs in computer science that seem particularly well-suited for reentry students. Evening classes and credit by life experience are available.

Degrees Offered

UNDERGRADUATE
B.S., Computer Science

GRADUATE
M.S., Computer Science

Approximate Cost of Degrees

UNDERGRADUATE
$42,600

MASTER'S
$16,700

Admissions Guidelines

UNDERGRADUATE
High school diploma required. SAT and/or ACT required unless age 24 or older.

GRADUATE
Accredited bachelor's, GRE required

Undergraduate Programs
The B.S. in Computer Science is strongly oriented toward software engineering and applications. Students undertake a solid, but not excruciating, curriculum in computational mathematics as part of the program requirements.

Graduate Programs
The 33-hour M.S. in Computer Science focuses primarily on issues in programming, applications, and software systems engineering. No thesis is required.

Other Programs
A B.S. in Information Management is also available. For more information, contact the Department of Business Administration at (603) 888-1311, extension 8237.

Contact Information

PHONE
Admissions (undergraduate): (603) 888-1311 or (800) 447-4843
Admissions (graduate): (603) 897-8219
Computer science: (603) 897-8571

FAX
Admissions (graduate): (603) 897-8810

E-MAIL
General information: info@rivier.edu
Admissions (undergraduate): rivadmit@rivier.edu
Admissions (graduate): giadmissions@rivier.edu
Computer science: Teresa Magnus (tmagnus@rivier.edu)

Rochester Institute of Technology   www.rit.edu ☆☆

Rochester, NY 14623

Year established: 1829
Ownership: Private

This prestigious research-oriented institution offers a variety of highly innovative interdisciplinary programs at the undergraduate and graduate levels in a vast array of possible fields. Evening classes, weekend study, extension courses, and distance learning are available. A number of the programs described below can be completed entirely through distance learning.

Degrees Offered

UNDERGRADUATE
B.S., Computational Mathematics
(ABET) B.S., Computer Engineering
(ABET) B.S., Computer Engineering Technology
(CSAB) B.S., Computer Science
(ABET) B.S., Electrical Engineering
(ABET) B.S., Electrical Engineering Technology
B.S., Information Technology
(ABET) B.S., Microelectronics Engineering
B.S., Software Engineering
(ABET) B.S., Telecommunications Engineering Technology

GRADUATE
M.Eng., Microelectronics Manufacturing Engineering
M.S., Computer Engineering
M.S., Computer Science
M.S., Electrical Engineering
M.S., Information Technology
M.S., Software Development and Management

Approximate Cost of Degrees

UNDERGRADUATE
$69,300

GRADUATE
$19,500

Admissions Guidelines

UNDERGRADUATE
High school diploma, SAT and/or ACT required

GRADUATE
Accredited bachelor's, GRE required

Undergraduate Programs

The B.S. in Computational Mathematics focuses on solving modeling, simulation, and design problems through the use of computational mathematics principles.

The ABET-accredited B.S. in Computer Engineering focuses primarily on hardware issues, although software issues are also given significant attention.

The ABET-accredited B.S. in Computer Engineering Technology focuses more on software than hardware issues, but permits students to informally specialize in virtually any aspect of the field.

The CSAB-accredited B.S. in Computer Science is available with optional concentrations in artificial intelligence, computer graphics, computer science theory, digital systems design, networking and distributed systems, parallel computing, software engineering, and systems software.

The ABET-accredited B.S. in Electrical Engineering focuses on digital systems, electronic circuits, and theoretical issues in electrical and computer engineering.

The ABET-accredited B.S. in Electrical Engineering Technology allows room for, and encourages, individualized specialization within the field.

The B.S. in Information Technology is a highly interdisciplinary program addressing issues in programming, networking, and human-computer interaction.

The ABET-accredited M.S. in Microelectronics Engineering deals with the fundamentals of computer architecture, focusing on practical issues in microcomputer design and manufacturing.

The B.S. in Software Engineering focuses heavily on scientific software and software systems. The program will in all likelihood be submitted for ABET review within the next three years.

The ABET-accredited B.S. in Telecommunications Engineering Technology focuses on issues of computer networking and computer telecommunications. Some management issues are also addressed.

Graduate Programs

The 32-hour M.Eng. in Microelectronics Manufacturing Engineering focuses on complex design issues in microelectronics manufacturing. No thesis is required. This program can be completed via distance learning.

The 30-hour M.S. in Computer Engineering permits the student to specialize in a field of his or her choice. A thesis is required.

The 30-hour M.S. in Computer Science allows a great deal of room for student specialization through the generous 13 hours of elective credit options. A thesis or project is required.

The 30-hour M.S. in Electrical Engineering deals primarily with issues of digital systems design, VLSI design, and electronics/circuits. A thesis or project is required.

The 36-hour M.S. in Information Technology integrates study of interdisciplinary computing, networking, programming, and human-computer interaction into a single curriculum. A thesis or project is required. Concentrations are available in electronic commerce, interactive multimedia development, learning and performance technology, project management, software development, and telecommunications technology. This program can be completed via distance learning.

The 32-hour M.S. in Software Development and Management incorporates study of software engineering, systems engineering, and supervision into an integrated curriculum suitable for students who want to actively supervise and participate in software development. No thesis is required. This program can be completed via distance learning.

Other Programs

An ABET-accredited B.S. in Computer-Integrated Manufacturing Engineering Technology (available residentially or through distance learning), an ABET-accredited B.S. in Electrical/Mechanical Engineering Technology, and an M.S. in Computer Integrated Manufacturing are available. For more information, contact the department at (716) 475-7070.

More Information

Rochester Institute of Technology offers a vast number of information technology programs at the associate's level through the National Technical

Institute for the Deaf (NTID). These programs not only give under-served students opportunity to obtain credentials from a top-notch university, they also provide them with degrees that can be easily segued into one of the four-year bachelor's programs described above. For more information on this highly innovative and (we hope) trend-setting program, send an e-mail to NTIDMC@rit.edu.

Contact Information

PHONE
General information: (716) 475-2411
Distance learning: (716) 475-5089 or (800) 225-5748
Computational mathematics: (716) 475-6529
Computer engineering: (716) 475-2399
Computer science: (716) 475-2995
Electrical and computer engineering: (716) 475-2379
Electrical and computer engineering technology: (716) 475-2179
Information technology (undergraduate): (716) 247-7453
Information technology (graduate): (716) 475-2202
Microelectronics manufacturing engineering: (716) 475-2035
Software engineering: (716) 475-5461

FAX
Distance learning: (716) 475-5077
Computer engineering: (716) 475-5041
Computer science: (716) 475-7100
Software engineering: (716) 475-7909

E-MAIL
Distance learning: DISTED@rit.edu
Computational mathematics: Patricia Clark (pacsma@rit.edu)
Computer engineering: Marilyn Simpatico (maseec@ritvax.isc.rit.edu)
Computer science: csdept@cs.rit.edu
Information technology (undergraduate): Al Biles (jab@it.rit.edu)
Information technology (graduate): Rayno Niemi (rdn@it.rit.edu)
Microelectronics manufacturing engineering: Lynn Fuller (lffeee@rit.edu)
Software engineering: Lana Verschage (lana@cs.rit.edu)

Rutgers—The State University of New Jersey
www.rutgers.edu ☆½

New Brunswick Campus
New Brunswick, NJ 08901

Year established: 1927
Ownership: Public

This major state university offers rigorous, highly structured programs at all levels. Evening classes and weekend study are available. Rutgers operates campuses and extension sites throughout the state of New Jersey.

Degrees Offered

UNDERGRADUATE
B.A., Computer Science
B.S., Computer Science
🔵 B.S., Electrical and Computer Engineering

GRADUATE
M.S., Computer Science
M.S., Electrical Engineering
Ph.D., Computer Science
Ph.D., Electrical Engineering

Approximate Cost of Degrees

UNDERGRADUATE, RESIDENT
$22,600

UNDERGRADUATE, NONRESIDENT
$45,700

MASTER'S, RESIDENT
$20,300

MASTER'S, NONRESIDENT
$29,800

DOCTORATE, RESIDENT
$33,900

DOCTORATE, NONRESIDENT
$49,700

Admissions Guidelines

UNDERGRADUATE
High school diploma, SAT and/or ACT required

GRADUATE
Accredited bachelor's with 3.0 GPA, GRE required

Undergraduate Programs

The B.A and B.S. programs in Computer Science integrate issues in applied computing into a curriculum consisting of computational mathematics and structural computer science. An optional specialization in numerical analysis is available.

The ABET-accredited B.S. in Electrical and Computer Engineering is available with computer engineering and electrical engineering tracks.

Graduate Programs

The 30-hour M.S. in Computer Science allows for informal student specialization through the use of generous free elective options. A thesis is generally required, but students can opt for a final essay (supplemented by additional coursework) instead.

The M.S. in Electrical Engineering is available with concentrations in communications engineering, computer engineering, digital signal processing, solid-state electronics, and systems/control. No thesis is required.

The Ph.D. in Computer Science requires a qualifying examination in addition to the standard dissertation.

The Ph.D. in Electrical Engineering requires two examinations in addition to the standard dissertation.

Other Programs

A B.S. in Information Systems is available through the Newark campus.

Contact Information

PHONE
General information: (732) 932-4636
Admissions (graduate): (732) 932-7711
Computer science: (732) 445-3546
Electrical and computer engineering: (732) 445-3262

FAX
Admissions (graduate): (732) 932-8231
Computer science: (732) 445-0537
Electrical and computer engineering: (732) 445-2820

E-MAIL
Computer science (undergraduate): Barbara Carroll (bcarroll@cs.rutgers.edu)
Computer science (graduate): Valentine Rolfe (rolfe@cs.rutgers.edu)
Electrical engineering (undergraduate): UndergraduateAdmission@ece.rutgers.edu
Electrical engineering (graduate): GraduateAdmission@ece.rutgers.edu

Sacred Heart University   www.sacredheart.edu ☆☆☆

5151 Park Avenue
Fairfield, CT 06432

Year established: 1953
Ownership: Private

This small Catholic liberal arts school offers undergraduate and graduate programs in computer science with a very strong, very focused information technology bent. What really makes Sacred Heart stand out, though, is its emphasis on serving the needs of nontraditional students. With extension sites and branch campuses throughout Connecticut, night classes, weekend study options, and distance learning, this school is one of the best-kept secrets in Connecticut.

Degrees Offered

UNDERGRADUATE
B.S., Computer Science

GRADUATE
M.S., Computer and Information Science

Approximate Cost of Degrees

UNDERGRADUATE
$58,900

GRADUATE
$22,100

Admissions Guidelines

UNDERGRADUATE
High school diploma, SAT required

GRADUATE
Accredited bachelor's, GRE required

Undergraduate Programs
The B.S. in Computer Science is available with specializations in computer science and information technology. This broad-based and flexible program can be tailored to meet the needs of almost any student.

Graduate Programs
The 39-hour M.S. in Computer and Information Science is an unusually flexible program that can be tailored to the needs of full-time researchers and reentry professionals alike. Fifteen-hour concentrations are available in computer science and information technology. No thesis is required, but can be undertaken for credit at the student's discretion.

Contact Information

PHONE
General information: (203) 371-7999
Admissions (undergraduate): (203) 371-7880
Admissions (graduate): (203) 371-7830 or
(800) 288-2498
Computer and information science (graduate):
(203) 371-7792

FAX
Admissions (graduate): (203) 365-7500

E-MAIL
Admissions (undergraduate): Karen Guastelle
(Guastelk@sacredheart.edu)
Distance learning: Nancy Sidoti (sidotin
@sacredheart.edu)
Computer and information science: Venu Dasigi
(dasigi@shu.sacredheart.edu)

San Jose State University   www.sjsu.edu ★★★

1 Washington Square
San Jose, CA 95192

Year established: 1857
Ownership: Public

This midsize state university offers programs at the undergraduate and graduate levels in a range of information technology fields. Evening classes and distance learning are available.

Degrees Offered

UNDERGRADUATE
B.S., Applied and Computational Mathematics
(ABET) B.S., Computer Engineering
(CSAB) B.S., Computer Science
(ABET) B.S., Electrical Engineering

GRADUATE
M.S., Computer Engineering
M.S., Computer Science
M.S., Electrical Engineering

Approximate Cost of Degrees

UNDERGRADUATE, RESIDENT
$5,700

UNDERGRADUATE, NONRESIDENT
$37,200

GRADUATE, RESIDENT
$3,400

GRADUATE, NONRESIDENT
$12,200

Admissions Guidelines

UNDERGRADUATE
High school diploma, SAT and/or ACT required

GRADUATE
Accredited bachelor's with 2.5 GPA on upper 60 hours required, GRE recommended. For graduate engineering programs, an ABET-accredited bachelor's is required.

Undergraduate Programs
The B.S. in Applied and Computational Mathematics is available with emphases in applied mathematics and statistics.

The ABET-accredited B.S. in Computer Engineering gives roughly equal weight to hardware and software engineering.

The CSAB-accredited B.S. in Computer Science is available with informal emphases in artificial intelligence, computation theory, database management, graphics, networking, programming languages, scientific computing, and software engineering.

The ABET-accredited B.S. in Electrical Engineering is a highly structured program that addresses all major areas of the field.

Graduate Programs
The 30-hour M.S. in Computer Engineering is available with specializations in computer design, computer networks, computer vision, microcomputers and embedded systems, multimedia applications, and software engineering. A thesis or project is required.

The 30-hour M.S. in Computer Science is a broad-based program that addresses all major aspects of the field in a survey fashion, though student specialization is both permitted and encouraged. The program can culminate in a thesis or final paper. The latter option requires that students take an additional elective course to round out the curriculum.

The 30-hour M.S. in Electrical Engineering is available with specializations in communications and signal processing, control and power electronics, digital system design, and electronics/electronic devices. A thesis or project is required.

Other Programs
The B.S. in Business Administration is available with emphases in management information systems and accounting information systems. For more information, contact the department at (408) 924-3506.

An instructional technology concentration is available within the M.A. program in Education. For more information, contact the Division of Educational Leadership and Development at (408) 924-3620.

An M.F.A. in Art with emphasis in digital media is available. For more information, contact the Art and Design Graduate Office at (408) 924-4346.

Contact Information

PHONE
General information: (408) 924-1000
Computer engineering: (408) 924-4150
Computer science: (408) 924-5100
Electrical engineering: (408) 924-3950

FAX
Computer engineering: (408) 924-4153

E-MAIL
General information: sjsupao@sjsu.edu
Computer engineering: cise@email.sjsu.edu

Santa Clara University

www.scu.edu ☆☆½

500 El Camino Real
Santa Clara, CA 95053

Year established: 1851
Ownership: Private

This venerable private university offers engineering-oriented information technology programs at the undergraduate and graduate levels. Evening classes are available.

Degrees Offered

UNDERGRADUATE
🔳 B.S., Computer Engineering
B.S., Computer Science
🔳 B.S., Electrical Engineering

GRADUATE
M.S., Computer Engineering
M.S., Electrical Engineering
M.S., Software Engineering
Ph.D., Computer Engineering
Ph.D., Electrical Engineering

Approximate Cost of Degrees

UNDERGRADUATE
$83,200

MASTER'S
$31,200

DOCTORATE
$52,000

Admissions Guidelines

UNDERGRADUATE
High school diploma, SAT and/or ACT required

GRADUATE
Accredited bachelor's, GRE required

Undergraduate Programs

The B.S. program in Computer Science is available with informal specializations in foundations (theoretical computer science), graduate-level preparation (which essentially covers the upper-level basics of an average CSAB-accredited program), numerical computation (computational mathematics, algorithms, and combinatorics), and software (programming and software engineering).

The ABET-accredited B.S. in Computer Engineering places more weight on hardware than it does on software. Students are given a considerable number of courses to choose from in constructing upper-level study plans.

The ABET-accredited B.S. in Electrical Engineering focuses on student and faculty research. Students are given the opportunity to essentially tailor the program to fit personal research interests.

Graduate Programs

The 30-hour M.S. in Computer Engineering addresses graduate-level concerns in computational science and theoretical computer engineering, focusing at times on such areas as compiler design and networking principles. No thesis is required.

The 30-hour M.S. in Electrical Engineering focuses on digital systems by default, but can be tailored to the research interests of individual students. No thesis is required.

The 30-hour M.S. in Software Engineering focuses intensively on computer software issues, giving scant attention to project management and other non-IT issues. A final project is required.

The degrees of Computer Engineer (C.E.) and Electrical Engineer (E.E.) are individualized programs designed by the student in consultation with a faculty member. Requirements for these programs vary depending on the student's academic and professional background.

The Ph.D. in Computer Engineering requires a qualifying examination in addition to the standard dissertation. A one-year full-time residency requirement must also be fulfilled.

The Ph.D. in Electrical Engineering requires two examinations in addition to the standard dissertation. A one-year full-time residency requirement must also be fulfilled.

Contact Information

PHONE
General information: (408) 554-4000
Admissions (undergraduate): (408) 554-4700
Computer engineering: (408) 554-4483
Electrical engineering: (408) 554-4482

FAX
Admissions (undergraduate): (408) 554-5255
Computer engineering: (408) 554-5474

Seattle University   www.seattleu.edu ☆☆☆

900 Broadway
Seattle, WA 98122-4340

Year established: 1891
Ownership: Private

This respected private university offers undergraduate and graduate programs in several key areas of information technology, all in the very heart of the West Coast IT industry. Evening classes are available.

Degrees Offered

UNDERGRADUATE
B.A., Computer Science
CSAB B.S., Computer Science
ABET B.S., Electrical Engineering

GRADUATE
M.Sw.E.

Approximate Cost of Degrees

UNDERGRADUATE
$64,400

GRADUATE
$24,200

Admissions Guidelines

UNDERGRADUATE
High school diploma, SAT and/or ACT required

GRADUATE
Accredited bachelor's, GRE required

Undergraduate Programs

The B.A. in Computer Science is a rather flexible program. Students can effectively design a major based on a rigorous background in the liberal arts and natural sciences. Interdisciplinary study is valued at the upper level, though it is of course also possible to undertake a simple computer science major.

The CSAB-accredited B.S. in Computer Science is available with three tracks: general (a traditional computer science program), business (computer science with business information), and mathematics (computer science with a stronger emphasis on computational mathematics).

The ABET-accredited B.S. in Electrical Engineering culminates in a three-quarter team electrical engineering project.

Graduate Programs

The 30-hour Master of Software Engineering (M.Sw.E.) addresses specific issues in applied software engineering, broader structural issues in software systems, and other relevant issues such as quality control and project management. A final software engineering project is required.

Contact Information

PHONE
General information: (206) 296-6000
Computer science and software engineering:
(206) 296-5510
Electrical engineering: (206) 296-5970

FAX
Computer science and software engineering:
(206) 296-5518

E-MAIL
Computer science and software engineering:
Everald Mills (mills@seattleu.edu)
Electrical engineering: eedept@seattleu.edu

Smith College   www.smith.edu ☆☆☆½

Office of Admission
Northampton, MA 01063

Year established: 1871
Ownership: Private

This small private liberal arts college has recently established itself as the first women's college in the country to offer programs through a Department of Engineering; we're delighted to learn of this and hope that it represents a trend. Individualized options in information technology may also be available at the graduate level (see "Other Programs"). Evening classes are available.

Degrees Offered

UNDERGRADUATE
B.S., Computer Science
S.B.E.S., Computer Engineering
S.B.E.S., Electrical Engineering

Approximate Cost of Degrees

UNDERGRADUATE
$93,600

Admissions Guidelines

UNDERGRADUATE
High school diploma, SAT and/or ACT required

Undergraduate Programs

The B.S. program in Computer Science is available with formal concentrations in computer science and language, mathematical foundations of computer science, and systems. Students are also permitted—even encouraged—to design individualized concentrations.

The new Bachelor of Science in Engineering Science (S.B.E.S.) programs in Computer Engineering

and Electrical Engineering look to be designed according to ABET specifications and will likely be submitted to ABET within the next five years.

Other Programs

It may be possible to design an individualized program of study in an information technology field. For more information, contact the Office of Graduate Studies at (413) 585-3050.

Contact Information

PHONE
General information: (413) 585-4900
Admissions: (413) 585-2500
Computer science: (413) 585-3804
Engineering: (413) 585-7000

FAX
Admissions: (413) 585-2527

E-MAIL
Admissions: admission@smith.edu
Computer science: orourke@cs.smith.edu
Engineering: principia@science.smith.edu

South Dakota State University   web.sdstate.edu ☆☆½

SDSU Admissions Office
Box 2201
Brookings, SD 57007

Year established: 1881
Ownership: Public

This midsize state university offers extremely inexpensive engineering-oriented information technology programs at the undergraduate and graduate levels. Evening classes, credit by examination, and distance learning are available.

Degrees Offered

UNDERGRADUATE
B.S., Computer Science
(ABET) B.S., Electrical Engineering
B.S.T., Electronic(s) Engineering Technology

GRADUATE
M.S.E., Computer Science
M.S.E., Electrical Engineering

Approximate Cost of Degrees

UNDERGRADUATE, RESIDENT
$7,700

UNDERGRADUATE, NONRESIDENT (MINNESOTA)
$8,700

UNDERGRADUATE, NONRESIDENT (IOWA AND NEBRASKA)
$23,800

UNDERGRADUATE, NONRESIDENT (OTHER)
$24,600

GRADUATE, RESIDENT
$2,200

GRADUATE, NONRESIDENT (MINNESOTA)
$2,400

GRADUATE, NONRESIDENT (IOWA AND NEBRASKA)
$6,600

GRADUATE, NONRESIDENT (OTHER)
$6,900

Admissions Guidelines

UNDERGRADUATE
High school diploma, ACT required

GRADUATE
Accredited bachelor's, GRE required

Undergraduate Programs

The B.S. in Computer Science emphasizes a strong scientific and theoretical base. In its applied components, the program tends to favor software engineering.

The ABET-accredited B.S. in Electrical Engineering is available with emphases in biomedical engineering, communications and advanced electronics, computers and digital hardware, electronic materials and devices, image processing, and power systems.

The B.S. in Technology (B.S.T.) in Electronic(s) Engineering Technology incorporates elements of management and quality control into a professional, hands-on curriculum.

Graduate Programs

The 36-hour M.S. in Engineering (M.S.E.) programs in Computer Science and in Electrical Engineering feature a 15-hour core (7 hours of engineering science and 8 hours of electives), a 14-hour specialization, and a 6-hour thesis or 6-hour project in the area of specialization.

Contact Information

PHONE
Admissions (undergraduate): (800) 952-3541
Admissions (graduate): (605) 688-4181
Computer science: (605) 688-5719
Electrical engineering: (605) 688-4526
Electronic(s) engineering technology: (605) 688-6417

FAX
Admissions (graduate): (605) 688-6167
Computer science: (605) 688-5878
Electrical engineering: (605) 688-5880
Electronic(s) engineering technology: (605) 688-5041

E-MAIL
Admissions (graduate): davisd@adm.sdstate.edu
Computer science: bergumg@mg.sdstate.edu
Electrical engineering: finchr@mg.sdstate.edu
Electronic(s) engineering technology: Jerry Sorensen (sorensej@mg.sdstate.edu)

Southern Methodist University   www.smu.edu ☆☆½

School of Engineering and Applied Science
3145 Dyer Street
Dallas, TX 75205-0338

Year established: 1911
Ownership: Private

This private university offers structured information technology programs at all levels. Evening classes, credit by examination, and distance learning are available. Several of the programs described below can be completed almost entirely by distance learning.

Degrees Offered

UNDERGRADUATE
B.A., Computer Science
B.S., Computer Science
(ABET) B.S., Computer Engineering
(ABET) B.S., Electrical Engineering

GRADUATE
M.S., Computer Engineering
M.S., Computer Science
M.S., Electrical Engineering
M.S., Software Engineering
M.S., Telecommunications
Ph.D., Computer Engineering
Ph.D., Computer Science

Approximate Cost of Degrees

UNDERGRADUATE
$65,700

MASTER'S
$21,600

DOCTORATE
$39,600

Admissions Guidelines

UNDERGRADUATE
High school diploma, SAT and/or ACT required

GRADUATE
Accredited bachelor's with 3.0 GPA, GRE required in some programs (Computer Engineering, Computer Science, and Electrical Engineering)

Undergraduate Programs
The B.A. in Computer Science incorporates a 40-hour computer science major into a broad curriculum based soundly in the natural sciences and humanities. The program is slightly less flexible in its major requirements than the B.S. in Computer Science (see below).

The ABET-accredited B.S. in Computer Engineering balances software engineering and computer hardware to create a sturdy, well-rounded curriculum.

The B.S. in Computer Science is available with an optional pre-medical specialization. The program itself is primarily theory-oriented, but integrates software engineering into the structured curriculum.

The ABET-accredited B.S. in Electrical Engineering is available with specializations in biomedical engineering, computer engineering, and telecommunications engineering.

Graduate Programs
The 30-hour M.S. in Computer Engineering integrates aspects of the standard graduate-level computer science curriculum (such as algorithms, combinatorics, artificial intelligence, and data systems) into an applied, rigorously directed computer engineering program. No thesis is required. This program can be completed almost entirely by distance learning.

The 30-hour M.S. in Computer Science is available with optional concentrations in algorithms, architecture, artificial intelligence, and software. No thesis is required. This program can be completed almost entirely by distance learning.

The 30-hour M.S. in Electrical Engineering represents a traditional curriculum in the field well-grounded in theory. No thesis is required. This program can be completed almost entirely by distance learning.

The 30-hour M.S. in Software Engineering integrates elements of software reliability, quality control, and project management into a stringent, focused programming-focused curriculum. No thesis is required. This program can be completed almost entirely by distance learning.

The 30-hour M.S. in Telecommunications addresses virtually all major areas of the field, including ATM transactions, telephones, and fiber optic communications. The primary emphasis, however, seems to be on IT-relevant telecommunications in fields such as Internet communications, intelligent systems, video compression, and data communication. No thesis is required. This program can be completed almost entirely by distance learning.

The Ph.D. in Computer Engineering addresses computer science theory more closely than most doctoral programs of its kind. Two examinations are required in addition to the standard dissertation.

The Ph.D. in Computer Science is available with concentrations in algorithms engineering, artificial intelligence, computer architecture, computer arithmetic, computer networks, data and knowledge engineering, mathematical programming, natural language processing, parallel and distributed processing, and software engineering/systems. Two examinations are required in addition to the standard dissertation.

Other Programs

The Department of Electrical Engineering also offers a B.S. in Telecommunications Systems.

Contact Information

Phone
Computer science and engineering: (214) 768-3083
Electrical engineering and telecommunications: (214) 768-3113

Fax
Computer science and engineering: (214) 768-3085
Electrical engineering and telecommunications: (214) 768-3573

E-mail
Admissions (undergraduate): enrolserv@mail.smu.edu
Computer science and engineering: Beth Minton (beth@seas.smu.edu)
Electrical engineering and telecommunications: eehelp@seas.smu.edu

Southern Polytechnic State University   www.spsu.edu ☆☆☆

1100 South Marietta Parkway
Marietta, Georgia 30060

Year established: 1948
Ownership: Public

This midsize vocational state university offers innovative information technology programs at the undergraduate and graduate levels. Evening classes and distance learning are available.

Degrees Offered

Undergraduate
B.S., Computer Engineering Technology
B.S., Computer Science
B.S., Electrical Engineering Technology
B.S., Telecommunications Engineering Technology

Graduate
M.S., Computer Science
M.S., Electrical Engineering Technology
M.S., Software Engineering

Approximate Cost of Degrees

Undergraduate, Resident
$8,500

Undergraduate, Nonresident
$30,200

Graduate, Resident
$3,700

Graduate, Nonresident
$13,500

Admissions Guidelines

Undergraduate
High school diploma with 2.0 GPA, SAT and/or ACT required

Graduate
Accredited bachelor's, GRE required

Undergraduate Programs

The B.S. in Computer Engineering Technology is available with specializations in embedded systems and networks. Students are also encouraged to design individualized specializations to fit their interests.

The B.S. in Computer Science gives roughly equal weight to theory and applied computer science. Students are given the opportunity to specialize during their junior and senior years.

The B.S. in Electrical Engineering Technology is available with specializations in communications engineering technology, digital engineering technology, power engineering technology, and telecommunications engineering technology.

The B.S. in Telecommunications Engineering Technology is focused almost entirely on computer networking of all kinds. The general thrust of the program deals (as one might expect) with Internet and intranet systems engineering.

Graduate Programs

The 32-hour M.S. in Computer Science is a structured, rigorous program in which students focus on specific target areas of computer science in a survey fashion. A thesis or project is required.

The 32-hour M.S. in Electrical Engineering Technology seems to focus on digital engineering technology, although students are given the opportunity to design specializations to fit their needs. A thesis or project is required.

The new 32-hour M.S. in Software Engineering does not delve into project management or quality control in great depth. Instead, it focuses almost entirely on practical, hands-on issues in software engineering and the structural concepts they rely upon. A project is required.

Contact Information

PHONE
Admissions: (770) 528-7281
Computer science: (770) 528-7406
Electrical and computer engineering technology: (770) 528-7246

E-MAIL
General information: web@spsu.edu
Computer science: compsci@spsu.edu

St. Cloud State University   www.stcloudstate.edu ☆☆☆½

720 4th Avenue South
St. Cloud, MN 56301-4498

Year established: 1869
Ownership: Public

This midsize state university offers affordable programs in information technology fields through a variety of delivery methods, including evening classes, weekend study, life experience credit, and distance learning.

Degrees Offered

UNDERGRADUATE
B.S., Applied Computer Science
CSAB B.S., Computer Science
ABET B.S., Electrical Engineering

GRADUATE
M.S., Computer Science

Approximate Cost of Degrees

UNDERGRADUATE, RESIDENT
$14,200

UNDERGRADUATE, NONRESIDENT (NORTH AND SOUTH DAKOTA, WISCONSIN)
$14,200

UNDERGRADUATE, NONRESIDENT (OTHER)
$26,100

GRADUATE, RESIDENT
$4,800

GRADUATE, NONRESIDENT (NORTH AND SOUTH DAKOTA, WISCONSIN)
$4,800

GRADUATE, NONRESIDENT (OTHER)
$7,100

Admissions Guidelines

UNDERGRADUATE
High school diploma, ACT required

GRADUATE
Accredited bachelor's with 2.75 GPA, GRE required

Undergraduate Programs

The B.S. in Applied Computer Science focuses on computer applications and programming.

The CSAB-accredited B.S. in Computer Science approaches issues in software engineering and applications from a broad framework in computer science theory.

The ABET-accredited B.S. in Electrical Engineering provides students with an unusually flexible curriculum in the field.

Graduate Programs

The 32-hour M.S. in Computer Science addresses artificial intelligence and computer systems engineering as part of its core curriculum, permitting further student specialization through the use of elective courses. No thesis is required.

Other Programs

A B.S. in Business Computer Information Systems is also available. For more information, contact the program center at (320) 255-2174.

A B.S. in Computer Science Education is also available through the Department of Computer Science.

B.A., B.S., and M.S. programs in Information Media are also available. For more information, contact the Center for Information Media at (320) 255-2062.

Contact Information

PHONE
General information: (320) 255-0121
Admissions (undergraduate): (320) 255-2244 or (800) 369-4260
Admissions (graduate): (320) 255-2113
Computer science: (320) 255-4966
Continuing studies: (320) 255-3081

FAX
Admissions (graduate): (320) 654-5371

E-MAIL
Admissions (undergraduate):
SCSU4U@stcloudstate.edu
Admissions (graduate):
grads@condor.stcloudstate.edu
Continuing studies: ccs@condor.stcloudstate.edu

St. Mary's University

www.stmarytx.edu ☆☆☆

One Camino Santa Maria
San Antonio, TX 78228

Year established: 1852
Ownership: Private

This unique and highly respected institution carries with it an emphasis on rigorous, focused study in specific fields. Although students are given a great amount of flexibility in designing their programs, it will become rapidly obvious that these programs are designed with no "spare credits" in mind. Still, if its curriculum is traditional in tone, St. Mary's programs are designed to accommodate the needs of nontraditional students. Evening classes, extension courses, and weekend study are available.

Degrees Offered

UNDERGRADUATE

B.A., Computer Information Systems
B.A., Computer Science and Application Systems
B.S., Computer Engineering
B.S., Computer Science
🄰🄱🄴🄳 B.S., Electrical Engineering
B.S., Software Engineering and Computer Applications

GRADUATE

M.S., Computer Information Systems
M.S., Computer Science
M.S., Electrical Engineering
M.S., Software Engineering

Approximate Cost of Degrees

UNDERGRADUATE

$53,200

GRADUATE

$20,000

Admissions Guidelines

UNDERGRADUATE

High school diploma, SAT and/or ACT required

GRADUATE

Accredited bachelor's, GRE required

Undergraduate Programs

The B.A. in Computer Information Systems is strongly oriented toward programming, software engineering, and computer applications.

The B.A. in Computer Science and Application Systems primarily addresses issues in software engineering and database issues, although students are given a strong base in theoretical computer science.

The B.S. in Computer Engineering emphasizes hardware engineering, although software engineering is also given considerable weight. This program has all the earmarks of having been designed around established ABET standards.

The B.S. in Computer Science approaches issues of applied computing through the lens of a broad, rigorous background in computational mathematics and theoretical computer science.

The ABET-accredited B.S. in Electrical Engineering integrates issues of quality control and economics into a solid, well-rounded, and structured electrical engineering curriculum.

The innovative B.S. program in Software Engineering and Computer Applications incorporates computer-aided design, programming, quality control, and interdisciplinary applied computing into a single, unified curriculum.

Graduate Programs

The 36-hour M.S. in Computer Information Systems is largely oriented toward information technology, but also includes a significant management component. No thesis is required. Students who do not work in an information technology field can be required to undertake an internship as part of the program.

The 36-hour M.S. in Computer Science integrates study in a vast number of computer science disciplines; particularly innovative offerings are available in artificial intelligence and computer networking. A comprehensive examination is required; a thesis is not.

The 36-hour M.S. in Electrical Engineering is available with concentrations in computer engineering and electrical engineering. No thesis is required.

The 36-hour M.S. in Software Engineering incorporates elements of quality control, computer programming, and computer science into a solid, integrated curriculum. No thesis is required.

Contact Information

PHONE

Admissions: (210) 436-3126 or (800) 367-7868

FAX

Admissions: (210) 431-6742

E-MAIL

General information: info@www.stmarytx.edu
Admissions (undergraduate): admissions@www.stmarytx.edu
Admissions (graduate): gradschool@www.stmarytx.edu
Computer science (undergraduate): Arthur Hanna (csart@stmarytx.edu)
Computer science (graduate): Douglas Lee Hall (cshall@stmarytx.edu)

Stanford University

www.stanford.edu ☆☆☆½

Office of Undergraduate Admission
520 Lasuen Mall, Old Union 232
Stanford CA 94305-3005

Graduate Admissions Office
Room 132, Old Union
Stanford, CA 94305-3005

Year established: 1891
Ownership: Private

This top-notch private university offers programs at all levels in the standard information technology fields and allows for a wide variety of very nonstandard specializations within these fields. Evening classes, extension courses, and distance learning are available. Stanford's M.S. in Electrical Engineering can be completed online.

Degrees Offered

UNDERGRADUATE
B.S., Computer Science
B.S., Computer Systems Engineering
🅐 B.S., Electrical Engineering

GRADUATE
M.S., Computer Science
M.S., Electrical Engineering
E.E. (professional degree)
Ph.D., Computer Science
Ph.D., Electrical Engineering

Approximate Cost of Degrees

UNDERGRADUATE
$92,200

MASTER'S
$35,400

DOCTORATE
$59,000

Admissions Guidelines

UNDERGRADUATE
SAT required

GRADUATE
Accredited bachelor's, GRE required

Undergraduate Programs

The B.S. in Computer Science is firmly grounded in the theoretical and structural elements of computer science, but allows an extraordinary amount of flexibility in its applied components.

The B.S. in Computer Systems Engineering approaches computer engineering from a theoretical and structural perspective, placing emphasis on the foundational aspects of the field.

The ABET-accredited B.S. in Electrical Engineering is available with specializations in computer hardware, computer software, controls, electronics, fields and waves, and signal processing/telecommunications.

Graduate Programs

The 30-hour M.S. in Computer Science is available with specializations in artificial intelligence, databases, human-computer interaction, numerical analysis and scientific computation, real-world computing, software theory, systems, and theoretical computer science. No thesis is required. Although students can undertake a thesis to earn a distinction in research, this particular M.S. in Computer Science is designed to serve as a terminal degree and should not be regarded as a stepping-stone for doctoral work.

The 30-hour M.S. in Electrical Engineering is available with specializations in computer hardware, computer software systems, control and systems engineering, communication systems, electronic circuits, electronic devices/sensors/technology, fields/waves/radio science, image systems, lasers/optoelectronics/quantum electronics, network systems, signal processing, solid-state materials and devices, telecommunications, and VLSI design. No thesis is required. This program can be completed entirely via distance learning.

The professional degree of Electrical Engineer (E.E.) requires 30 hours of credit beyond the master's degree and a thesis.

The Ph.D. in Computer Science requires two examinations (a computer systems examination and a computer theory examination) in addition to the standard dissertation.

The Ph.D. in Electrical Engineering requires an examination in addition to the standard dissertation.

Contact Information

PHONE
General information: (650) 723-2300
Admissions (undergraduate): (650) 723-2091
Admissions (graduate): (650) 723-4291
Computer science: (650) 723-2273
Electrical engineering: (650) 725-3706

FAX
Admissions (undergraduate): (650) 723-6050
Computer science: (650) 725-7411

E-MAIL
Admissions (undergraduate):
undergrad.admissions@forsythe.stanford.edu
Admissions (graduate):
ck.gaa@forsythe.stanford.edu

★ **EXTRA!**

Intel president and CEO Craig Barrett earned all of his degrees (B.S., M.S., and Ph.D.) from Stanford.

Stevens Institute of Technology   www.stevens.edu ☆☆½

Castle Point on Hudson
Hoboken, NJ 07030

Year established: 1870
Ownership: Private

This major private university offers programs at all levels in a variety of traditional and not-so-traditional information technology fields. From e-business to electrical engineering and everything in between, Stevens has demonstrated itself to be one of very few clear leaders in the world of academic information technology. Evening classes, weekend study, extension courses, and distance learning are available.

Degrees Offered

UNDERGRADUATE
 B.S., Computer Engineering
ⓒˢᵃᵇ B.S., Computer Science
ᴬᵇᵉᵗ B.S., Electrical Engineering
B.S., E-Business

GRADUATE
M.Eng., Computer Engineering
M.Eng., Electrical Engineering
M.S., Computer Science
M.S., Information Systems
C.E.
E.E.
Ph.D., Computer Engineering
Ph.D., Computer Science
Ph.D., Electrical Engineering

Approximate Cost of Degrees

UNDERGRADUATE
$84,700

MASTER'S
$26,100

DOCTORATE
$43,600

Admissions Guidelines

UNDERGRADUATE
High school diploma, SAT and/or ACT required

GRADUATE
Accredited bachelor's with 3.0 GPA, GRE required

Undergraduate Programs

The ABET-accredited B.S. in Computer Engineering is a versatile program, which can be tailored equally well to the interests of a microelectronics engineer or a Unix system administrator.

The CSAB-accredited B.S. in Computer Science is available with concentrations in financial systems, intelligent design and manufacturing, and mathematics. Like all CSAB-accredited programs, Stevens's program proceeds from a broad, intensive background in mathematics and the natural sciences.

The new B.S. in E-Business incorporates elements of information systems and traditional business administration into a unified curriculum designed specifically for the budding dot-com entrepreneur.

The ABET-accredited B.S. in Electrical Engineering focuses on microelectronics and digital systems in its core requirements.

Graduate Programs

The 30-hour Master of Engineering (M.Eng.) in Computer Engineering is available with formal concentrations in computer systems, data communications and networks, digital systems design, image processing and visual environments, information systems, and software engineering. No thesis is required.

The 30-hour M.Eng. in Electrical Engineering is available with formal concentrations in computer architecture and digital systems, electronics and materials, microelectronic devices and circuits, photonic devices and systems, signal processing for communications, telecommunications engineering, and wireless communications. No thesis is required.

The 30-hour M.S. in Computer Science is available with formal concentrations in computer communications, database systems, programming languages and compilers, software design, and theoretical computer science. No thesis is required.

The 33-hour M.S. in Information Systems is available with formal concentrations in computer science, e-commerce, information management, project management, and telecommunications management. No thesis is required.

The degrees of Computer Engineer (C.E.) and Electrical Engineer (E.E.) are individualized professional programs designed for students who already hold a master's degree, but who do not want to undertake a doctoral research program. A final project is required.

The Ph.D. in Computer Engineering is available with formal concentrations in computer architecture and digital systems design, computer and information engineering, image and signal processing, intelligent systems, and software engineering. A qualifying examination is required in addition to the standard dissertation.

The Ph.D. in Computer Science is available with formal concentrations in computer communications, database systems, programming languages and compilers, software design, and theoretical computer science. A qualifying examination is required in addition to the standard dissertation.

The Ph.D. in Electrical Engineering is available with formal concentrations in computer architecture and digital systems design, intelligent systems, signal and image processing, and telecommunications engineering. A qualifying examination is required in addition to the standard dissertation.

Other Programs

A Master of Technology Management (M.T.M.) program is also available. For more information, contact the program office at (201) 216-8903.

M.S. and Ph.D. programs in Information Management, Technology Management, and Telecommunications Management are offered through the Wesley J. Howe School of Technology Management. For more information, contact the school at (201) 216-8255.

Contact Information

PHONE
General information: (201) 216-5000
Admissions (undergraduate): (201) 216-5228
Admissions (graduate): (201) 216-5234
Computer science: (201) 216-5328
E-business: (201) 216-5550
Electrical and computer engineering: (201) 216-5623
Information systems: (201) 216-8255

FAX
Admissions (undergraduate): (201) 216-8326
Admissions (graduate): (201) 216-8044
Computer science: (201) 216-8249

E-business and information systems: (201) 216-5385
Electrical and computer engineering: (201) 216-8246

E-MAIL
Admissions (undergraduate):
admissions@stevens-tech.edu
Admissions (graduate):
thegradschool@stevens-tech.edu
Computer science: Dr. Adriana Compagnoni
(abc@cs.stevens-tech.edu)
Electrical and computer engineering: Fran Flanigan
(fflaniga@stevens-tech.edu)
Information systems and e-business: Michael Poli
(mpoli@stevens-tech.edu)

State University of New York—Albany   www.albany.edu ★★★½

University at Albany
1400 Washington Avenue
Albany, NY 12222

Year established: 1844
Ownership: Public

This major branch of the New York state university system offers innovative programs at all levels in computer science. Evening classes and distance learning are available.

Degrees Offered

UNDERGRADUATE
B.A., Computer Science
B.S., Computer Science

GRADUATE
M.S., Computer Science
Ph.D., Computer Science

Approximate Cost of Degrees

UNDERGRADUATE, RESIDENT
$21,400

UNDERGRADUATE, NONRESIDENT
$35,300

MASTER'S, RESIDENT
$8,000

MASTER'S, NONRESIDENT
$13,300

DOCTORATE, RESIDENT
$13,400

DOCTORATE, NONRESIDENT
$22,100

Admissions Guidelines

UNDERGRADUATE
High school diploma, SAT and/or ACT required

GRADUATE
Accredited bachelor's, GRE required

Undergraduate Programs
The B.A. and B.S. programs in Computer Science are largely identical in their major requirements, focusing on applied software issues from the perspective of theoretical computer science. Optional specializations in business information systems and computational/applied mathematics are available.

Graduate Programs

The 32-hour M.S. in Computer Science draws from a broad base in theoretical computer science, focusing on programming and software engineering in its applied components. A comprehensive written examination and a thesis are required.

The Ph.D. in Computer Science requires two examinations and an ongoing project in addition to the standard dissertation. The ongoing project is generally completed prior to the candidacy stage.

Other Programs

Emphases in human resource information systems and management information systems are available through the School of Business. For more information, contact the school at (518) 442-4981.

Contact Information

PHONE
Admissions (undergraduate): (800) 293-7869
Admissions (graduate): (800) 440-4723
Computer science: (518) 442-4270

FAX
Computer science: (518) 442-5638

E-MAIL
Admissions: ugadmissions@albany.edu
Computer science: info@cs.albany.edu

State University of New York—Buffalo   www.buffalo.edu ★★★

Undergraduate Admissions
17 Capen Hall
Box 601660
Buffalo, NY 14260-1660

Graduate School
410 Capen Hall
Buffalo, NY 14260-1608

Year established: 1846
Ownership: Public

This large state university offers programs at all levels in several major information technology fields. Of particular interest are the most uncommon interdisciplinary graduate programs, which encompass both computer science and computer engineering. Evening classes are available.

Degrees Offered

UNDERGRADUATE
B.S., Computer Engineering
B.A., Computer Science
B.S., Computer Science
🔵 B.S., Electrical Engineering

GRADUATE
M.Eng., Electrical Engineering
M.S., Computer Science and Engineering
M.S., Electrical Engineering
Ph.D., Computer Science and Engineering
Ph.D., Electrical Engineering

Approximate Cost of Degrees

UNDERGRADUATE, RESIDENT
$21,100

UNDERGRADUATE, NONRESIDENT
$40,700

MASTER'S, RESIDENT
$20,900

MASTER'S, NONRESIDENT
$30,900

DOCTORATE, RESIDENT
$34,900

DOCTORATE, NONRESIDENT
$51,400

Admissions Guidelines

UNDERGRADUATE
High school diploma, SAT and/or ACT required

GRADUATE
Accredited bachelor's, GRE required

Undergraduate Programs
The B.S. in Computer Engineering gives roughly equal weight to hardware and software engineering. Students are given an opportunity to specialize through the use of free electives.

The B.A. and B.S. programs in Computer Science are virtually identical in their major requirements; both emphasize software engineering and applications from a strong theoretical base.

The ABET-accredited B.S. in Electrical Engineering places great emphasis on computer engineering and electronics.

Graduate Programs
The 30-hour Master of Engineering (M.Eng.) in Electrical Engineering is a professional degree designed primarily for reentry students. The program caps off with a final, two-semester project.

The 30-hour M.S. in Computer Science and Engineering requires that students specialize in computer engineering or computer science. A thesis or project is required. Students in the computer engineering track must specialize further in hardware or software systems, while students in the computer science track must specialize further in artificial intelligence, algorithms and theory, or systems.

The 30-hour M.S. in Electrical Engineering requires that students choose from among the following concentrations: communications and signals, controls and energy systems, digital electronics, or microelectronics/photonics. Students can choose to undertake a thesis or project.

The Ph.D. in Computer Science and Engineering requires that students specialize in computer engineering or computer science. Two examinations are required in addition to the standard dissertation. Students in the computer engineering track must specialize further in hardware or software systems, while students in the computer science track must specialize further in artificial intelligence, algorithms and theory, or systems.

The Ph.D. in Electrical Engineering requires that students choose from among the following concentrations: communications and signals, controls and energy systems, digital electronics, or microelectronics/photonics. Two examinations are required in addition to the standard dissertation.

Other Programs
A management information systems concentration is available within the B.S. program in Business Administration. For more information, contact the Department of Business Administration at (716) 645-3204.

Contact Information

PHONE
Admissions (undergraduate): (888) 822-3648
Admissions (graduate): (716) 645-2939
Computer science and engineering: (716) 645-3180
Electrical engineering: (716) 645-2422

FAX
Computer science and engineering: (716) 645-3464
Electrical engineering: (716) 645-3656

E-MAIL
Admissions (undergraduate):
ubadmitweb@admissions.buffalo.edu
Computer science and engineering (undergraduate):
cse-uginfo@cse.buffalo.edu
Computer science and engineering (graduate):
csdgs@cs.buffalo.edu
Electrical engineering: Betty Brown
(blbrown@acsu.buffalo.edu)

State University of New York— Empire State College

www.esc.edu ☆☆

One Union Avenue
Saratoga Springs, NY 12866-4391

Year established: 1971
Ownership: Public

As the official adult education and external degree program of SUNY, this institution offers entire individualized degrees through credit by examination, life experience credit, transfer credit, distance learning, and/or on-campus evening and weekend classes. Although all programs can be completed completely nonresidentially, Empire State College also operates extension sites throughout the state of New York through which students can, if they so choose, take face-to-face courses.

Degrees Offered

UNDERGRADUATE
B.A., emphasis in almost any field
B.P.S., emphasis in almost any field
B.S., emphasis in almost any field

Approximate Cost of Degrees

UNDERGRADUATE, RESIDENT
$2,250 and up

UNDERGRADUATE, NONRESIDENT
$4,900 and up

Admissions Guidelines

UNDERGRADUATE
High school diploma and/or acceptable SAT/ACT score required

Undergraduate Programs

The Empire State College program of the State University of New York offers totally individual programs to students throughout the world, and can accommodate a program of study in virtually any information technology field. All degrees can be completed entirely off-campus, either through distance learning or through one of Empire State's many extension sites.

More Information

SUNY Empire State College has recently begun to expand its graduate offerings, and it would not surprise us if a master's in an information technology field were to become an option fairly soon.

Contact Information

PHONE
(518) 587-2100 or (800) 847-3000

FAX
(518) 587-3033

E-MAIL
Kirk Starczewski, Director of College Relations
(kstarcze@esc.edu)

State University of New York— Stony Brook

www.sunysb.edu ☆☆½

Admissions Office
118 Administrative Building
SUNY Stony Brook
Stony Brook, NY 11794-1901

Year established: 1957
Ownership: Public

Regarded by many as the most prestigious of SUNY's campuses, this major research-oriented university offers programs at all levels in the standard information technology fields. Evening classes and extension courses are available.

Degrees Offered

UNDERGRADUATE
ⒶⒷⒺ⒯ B.S., Computer Engineering
B.S., Computer Science
ⒶⒷⒺ⒯ B.S., Electrical Engineering
B.S., Information Systems

GRADUATE
M.S., Computer Science
M.S., Electrical Engineering
Ph.D., Computer Science
Ph.D., Electrical Engineering

Approximate Cost of Degrees

UNDERGRADUATE, RESIDENT
$19,900

UNDERGRADUATE, NONRESIDENT
$38,400

MASTER'S, RESIDENT
$9,500

MASTER'S, NONRESIDENT
$14,600

Admissions Guidelines

UNDERGRADUATE
High school diploma, SAT and/or ACT required

GRADUATE
Accredited bachelor's, GRE required

Undergraduate Programs
The ABET-accredited B.S. in Computer Engineering generally emphasizes hardware more than it does software, although students can tip the balance a bit through clever use of electives.

The B.S. in Computer Science is available with optional specializations in artificial intelligence, computer networks and communications, database systems, graphics, hardware, multimedia, operating systems, programming languages and software engineering, and theory.

The ABET-accredited B.S. in Electrical Engineering is available with specializations in bioengineering, communications and signal processing, control and systems, electromagnetic fields/fiber-optic systems, electronic circuits and devices, power and energy systems, and solid-state electronics.

The decisively IT-oriented B.S. in Information Systems deals with design and management of computer databases, computer media, and the like.

Graduate Programs
The 36-hour M.S. in Computer Science approaches virtually every element of the field in a systematic fashion. A thesis or project is required.

The 30-hour M.S. in Electrical Engineering is available with specializations in communications, computer engineering, electromagnetics and optics, signal processing, and solid-state electronics/circuits. No thesis is required.

The Ph.D. in Computer Science permits a student to undertake some coursework specialization in his or her field of dissertation research. Two examinations are required in addition to the standard dissertation.

The Ph.D. in Electrical Engineering hinges on the student's individualized, faculty-approved plan of study. Two examinations are required in addition to the standard dissertation.

Contact Information

PHONE
Admissions (undergraduate): (631) 632-6868
Computer science: (631) 632-8470
Electrical and computer engineering: (631) 632-8420

FAX
Computer science: (631) 632-8334
Electrical and computer engineering: (631) 632-8494

E-MAIL
Admissions (undergraduate):
ugadmissions@notes.cc.sunysb.edu
Computer Science (undergraduate):
grace@cs.sunysb.edu
Computer Science (graduate):
graduate@cs.sunysb.edu
Electrical and computer engineering:
postmaster@sbee.sunysb.edu

Syracuse University

www.syracuse.edu ☆☆½

Syracuse, NY 13244

Year established: 1870
Ownership: Private

This major private university offers programs at all levels in a number of information technology fields. Evening classes, weekend study, and distance learning are available.

Degrees Offered

UNDERGRADUATE
B.S., Computer and Information Science
🅰 B.S., Computer Engineering
🅰 B.S., Electrical Engineering

GRADUATE
M.S., Computational Science
M.S., Computer Engineering
M.S., Computer and Information Science
M.S., Electrical Engineering
M.S., Systems and Information Science
Ph.D., Computer and Electrical Engineering
Ph.D., Computer and Information Science

Approximate Cost of Degrees

UNDERGRADUATE
$81,500

MASTER'S
$30,600

DOCTORATE
$51,000

Admissions Guidelines

UNDERGRADUATE
High school diploma, SAT and/or ACT required

GRADUATE
Accredited bachelor's, GRE required

Undergraduate Programs
The ABET-accredited B.S. in Computer Engineering is available with hardware-oriented and software-oriented tracks; both emphasize structural aspects of their respective disciplines.

The B.S. in Computer and Information Science gives a great deal of weight to computer networking and software engineering. Minors in computational mathematics and neuroscience are available, permitting students to undertake a genuinely interdisciplinary program in computational science or cognitive neural systems.

The ABET-accredited B.S. in Electrical Engineering is available with specializations in communications, control, electromagnetics, and VLSI design/maintenance.

Graduate Programs
The 33-hour M.S. in Computational Science is a marvelous interdisciplinary program in mathematics, computer science, and computational engineering. Although highly theoretical in its orientation, this program is particularly well suited to the needs of reentry students. No thesis is required.

The 33-hour M.S. in Computer and Information Science is a rigorous, professional program that emphasizes structural, software-oriented, and interdisciplinary aspects of the discipline. No thesis is required.

The 30-hour M.S. in Computer Engineering emphasizes hardware much more than it does software. A thesis or project is required.

The 30-hour M.S. in Electrical Engineering emphasizes digital systems and electronics. A thesis or project is required.

The 33-hour M.S. in Systems and Information Science emphasizes combinatorics, software systems, software applications, and the more structural elements of theoretical computer science. No thesis is required.

The Ph.D. in Computer and Electrical Engineering requires an examination in addition to the standard dissertation.

The Ph.D. in Computer and Information Science requires two comprehensive written examinations in addition to the standard dissertation.

Other Programs

An M.S. in Telecommunications and Network Management is available and can be completed almost entirely via distance learning. For more information, contact the School of Information Studies at (315) 443-2911.

Contact Information

PHONE

General information: (315) 443-1870
Engineering and computer science: (315) 443-2545

E-MAIL

Admissions (undergraduate): orange@syr.edu
Admissions (graduate): gradsch@summail.syr.edu
Continuing education: parttime@uc.syr.edu
Distance learning: suisdp@uc.syr.edu
Engineering and computer science: inquire@ecs.syr.edu

Temple University   www.temple.edu ☆☆☆

1801 North Broad Street
Philadelphia, PA 19122

Year established: 1884
Ownership: Public

This major, research-oriented public university offers a number of traditional and nontraditional programs at every level. While the bachelor's programs in computer science seem to be modeled after the highly theoretical offerings of the 1980s, the graduate programs in e-commerce are cutting-edge and innovative (even considered against other programs in this cutting-edge, innovative field!). Evening classes and distance learning are available.

Degrees Offered

UNDERGRADUATE

B.A., Computer Science
B.S., Computer Science
🅰 B.S., Electrical Engineering Technology
🅰 B.S.E., Electrical Engineering

GRADUATE

M.S., Computer Science
M.S., E-commerce
M.S.E., Electrical Engineering
Ph.D., Computer and Information Science

Approximate Cost of Degrees

UNDERGRADUATE, RESIDENT

$26,300

UNDERGRADUATE, NONRESIDENT

$47,100

MASTER'S, RESIDENT

$10,400

MASTER'S, NONRESIDENT

$14,300

DOCTORATE, RESIDENT

$23,400

DOCTORATE, NONRESIDENT

$32,300

Admissions Guidelines

UNDERGRADUATE

High school diploma with 2.0 GPA, SAT and/or ACT required

GRADUATE

Accredited bachelor's, GRE required

Undergraduate Programs

The B.A. in Computer Science is a fairly traditional program that approaches applied computing—largely programming and software applications—from a broad background in theoretical computer science and computational mathematics.

The B.S. is similar to the B.A. in major requirements, but differs in overall credit distribution.

The ABET-accredited B.S. in Electrical Engineering Technology focuses on digital systems and electronics.

The ABET-accredited B.S.E. in Electrical Engineering is a fairly broad program addressing the theoretical base of electrical engineering from a rigorous mathematical background.

Graduate Programs

The 30-hour M.S. in Computer Science deals primarily with abstract, theoretical issues in the field; zooming in on software engineering in its applied component, it culminates in a final project. No thesis is required.

The 30-hour M.S. in E-commerce is designed for professionals who already hold an M.B.A. and want to improve their skills in the information technology sector. No thesis is required. This program is designed to be completed through evening classes.

The 30-hour M.S. in Engineering (M.S.E.) in Electrical Engineering permits students to pursue research interests in such diverse fields as intelligent instrumentation systems and speech processing. A thesis is required.

The Ph.D. in Computer and Information Science is available with intensive research concentrations in artificial intelligence and applications, information systems, and software systems. In addition to the standard dissertation, a teaching internship and two examinations are required.

Other Programs

The Fox School of Business and Management offers a B.B.A.(with emphasis in information systems), an M.B.A. (with emphases in e-commerce, information systems, and management information systems), and an M.S. in Business Administration (emphasis information systems), which can be completed by distance learning. For more information, contact the Fox School at (215) 204-7676.

The Ph.D. program in Engineering is available with optional concentrations in computer-aided manufacturing and computer engineering. For more information, contact the College of Engineering at (215) 204-7800.

Contact Information

PHONE
General information: (215) 204-7000
Admissions (undergraduate): (215) 204-7200
Admissions (graduate): (215) 204-1380
Computer science: (215) 204-8450
Electrical engineering: (215) 204-8089

FAX
Computer science: (215) 204-5082

E-MAIL
Admissions (undergraduate):
tuadm@vm.temple.edu
Admissions (graduate): tugrad@blue.temple.edu
Computer science: admissions@cis.temple.edu
Electrical engineering: John Helferty
(jhelfert@nimbus.temple.edu)

Texas A&M University   www.tamu.edu ☆☆☆

Admissions and Records
College Station, TX 77842-1265

Year established: 1876
Ownership: Public

This large public research university offers both research-oriented and professional programs at all levels in information technology fields. Evening classes, weekend study, extension courses, and distance learning are available.

Degrees Offered

Undergraduate

ABET B.S., Computer Engineering
CSAB B.S., Computer Science
ABET B.S., Electrical Engineering
ABET B.S., Electronics Engineering Technology
ABET B.S., Telecommunications Engineering Technology

Graduate

M.C.E.
M.C.S.
M.Eng., Electrical Engineering
M.S., Computer Engineering
M.S., Computer Science
M.S., Electrical Engineering
Ph.D., Computer Engineering
Ph.D., Computer Science

Approximate Cost of Degrees

Undergraduate, Resident
$5,400

Undergraduate, Nonresident
$33,000

Master's, Resident
$3,200

Master's, Nonresident
$11,000

Doctorate, Resident
$6,200

Doctorate, Nonresident
$21,400

Admissions Guidelines

Undergraduate
High school diploma, SAT and/or ACT required

Graduate
Accredited bachelor's, GRE required

Undergraduate Programs

The ABET-accredited B.S. in Computer Engineering is a largely hardware-focused program that emphasizes a strong practical background in electrical engineering.

The CSAB-accredited B.S. in Computer Science is available with informal specializations in algorithms, artificial intelligence and cognitive modeling, computational science, computer systems and architecture, computer vision, graphics, languages and computability, networking, robotics, and software systems. Students who perform exceptionally well may be permitted to incorporate graduate-level courses into their junior and senior year plan.

The ABET-accredited B.S. in Electrical Engineering is available with an optional computer engineering track. Informal specializations are available in computer engineering, controls and communications, microelectronic circuit design, and power systems/electromagnetics/electro-optics.

The ABET-accredited B.S. in Electronics Engineering Technology emphasizes circuit design and digital systems. The program is very to-the-point, offering a professional major that requires refreshingly few management courses.

The ABET-accredited B.S. in Telecommunications Engineering Technology is a comprehensive, structured program that deals with wireless communication as well as computer networking issues (although the information technology aspects of the program are the most prominent).

Graduate Programs

The 36-hour Master of Computer Engineering (M.C.E.) is a professional degree designed primarily for reentry students. No thesis is required.

The 36-hour Master of Computer Science (M.C.S.) is a professional degree designed primarily for reentry students. No thesis is required.

The 36-hour Master of Engineering (M.Eng.) in Electrical Engineering is available with specializations in analog/mixed signals, biomedical imaging, computer engineering, control systems, electric power systems/power electronics, electromagnetics/microwaves, electronic materials, solid-state electronics/electro-optics, and telecommunications/signal processing. An internship is required.

The 36-hour M.S. in Computer Engineering could probably be described as a professional program approached from a research-oriented perspective. A thesis is required.

The 36-hour M.S. in Computer Science is a research-oriented program well suited for students who want to undertake a laboratory post or progress to a doctoral program. A thesis is required.

The 32-hour M.S. in Electrical Engineering is available with specializations in analog/mixed signals, biomedical imaging, computer engineering, control systems, electric power systems/power electronics, electromagnetics/microwaves, electronic materials, solid-state electronics/electro-optics, and telecommunications/signal processing. A thesis is required.

The Ph.D. program in Computer Engineering allows immense flexibility in its credit distribution requirements; students can specialize in virtually any computer engineering research area. Two examinations are required in addition to the standard dissertation. Students are expected to publish at least one article in a refereed journal prior to graduation.

The Ph.D. program in Computer Science emphasizes theoretical and computational aspects of the field, though this flexible curriculum allows students to address or focus on other areas as they see fit. Two examinations are required in addition to the standard dissertation. Students are expected to publish at least one article in a refereed journal prior to graduation.

Other Programs

A Master of Education (M.Ed.) in Educational Technology is also available. This program can be completed by distance learning. For more information, contact the Department of Curriculum and Instruction at (409) 845-7276.

A D.Eng. (Doctor of Engineering) is also available and can be (to an extent) tailored toward an electrical engineering or computer engineering focus. For more information, contact the College of Engineering at (979) 845-1321.

Contact Information

PHONE

General information: (979) 845-3211
Admissions: (409) 845-1004
Computer science and engineering: (979) 845-5534
Electrical engineering: (409) 845-7441
Electronics engineering technology: (979) 845-5966
Telecommunications engineering technology: (409) 845-5966

FAX

Computer science and engineering: (979) 847-8578
Electrical engineering: (409) 845-6259
Electronics engineering technology: (979) 847-9396

E-MAIL

Admissions: admissions@tamu.edu
Computer science and engineering: Elena Catalena (elena@cs.tamu.edu)
Electrical engineering: Deana Totzke (deana@ee.tamu.edu)
Electronics engineering technology: J. Morgan (morganj@entc.tamu.edu)
Telecommunications engineering technology: catala@entc.tamu.edu

Texas Christian University   www.tcu.edu ☆☆½

2800 S. University Drive
Fort Worth, TX 76129

Year established: 1873
Ownership: Private

This midsize private university offers traditional undergraduate programs in computer science and electrical engineering. Evening classes are available.

Degrees Offered

UNDERGRADUATE

(CSAB) B.S., Computer Science
(ABET) B.S.E., emphasis Electrical Engineering

Approximate Cost of Degrees

UNDERGRADUATE

$47,500

Admissions Guidelines

UNDERGRADUATE
High school diploma, SAT and/or ACT required

Undergraduate Programs
The CSAB-accredited B.S. in Computer Science represents a basic, traditional curriculum in the field well grounded in theoretical computer science and computational mathematics. In its applied components, the program heavily emphasizes programming and databases.

The ABET-accredited B.S. in Engineering with emphasis in Electrical Engineering represents a traditional, broad, and scientific approach to the field grounded in mathematics and the natural sciences.

More Information
Until recently, Texas Christian University also offered a Master of Software Engineering (M.Sw.E.) program. Unfortunately, there was apparently not sufficient general interest in this program and it is now closed. It is quite likely that TCU will revive this program at a later date if there is a demand for it.

Contact Information

PHONE
General information: (817) 257-7000
Admissions: (817) 921-7490 or (800) 828-3764
Computer science: (817) 257-7166
Engineering: (817) 257-7677

FAX
Admissions: (817) 921-7268
Computer science: (817) 257-7110
Engineering: (817) 257-7704

E-MAIL
Admissions: frogmail@tcu.edu
Computer science: J. Richard Rinewalt (d.Rinewalt@tcu.edu)
Engineering: Cynthia Baker (c.a.baker@tcu.edu)

Texas Tech University   www.texastech.edu ☆☆

Office of Admissions and School Relations
McClellan Hall, Box 45005
Lubbock, TX 79409-5005

Graduate Admissions
Box 41030
Lubbock, Texas 79409-1030

Year established: 1923
Ownership: Public

This large state university offers engineering-focused programs at all levels in several popular information technology fields. Evening classes, weekend study, credit by examination, and distance learning are available.

Degrees Offered

UNDERGRADUATE
B.S., Computer Engineering
B.S., Computer Science
B.S., Electrical Engineering
🄰 B.S., Electronic(s) Engineering Technology

GRADUATE
M.S., Computer Science
M.S., Electrical Engineering
M.S., Software Engineering
Ph.D., Computer Science
Ph.D., Electrical Engineering

Approximate Cost of Degrees

UNDERGRADUATE, RESIDENT
$4,900

UNDERGRADUATE, NONRESIDENT
$32,500

MASTER'S, RESIDENT
$3,300

MASTER'S, NONRESIDENT
$11,000

DOCTORATE, RESIDENT
$5,500

DOCTORATE, NONRESIDENT
$18,400

Admissions Guidelines

UNDERGRADUATE
High school diploma, SAT and/or ACT required

GRADUATE
Accredited bachelor's, GRE required

Undergraduate Programs

The B.S. in Computer Engineering emphasizes software over hardware in its core requirements. Students are permitted to essentially design their curriculum during the junior and senior years through the use of major electives.

The B.S. program in Computer Science proceeds from a sturdy theoretical base in mathematics and the natural sciences to study in applied issues such as programming and software applications.

The B.S. program in Electrical Engineering offers informal specializations in communications, electromechanical engineering, electronics, optoelectronics, power, and signals/systems.

The ABET-accredited B.S. in Electronic(s) Engineering Technology addresses practical issues in design, function, and maintenance of electronics (primarily digital systems). A significant portion of this program can be completed by examination.

Graduate Programs

The 36-hour M.S. in Computer Science is available with optional tracks in artificial intelligence and robotics, computer-aided design systems, parallel and distributed systems, and software engineering. In lieu of a track, students can undertake a thesis; otherwise, no thesis is required. A final comprehensive examination is required.

The 36-hour M.S. in Electrical Engineering allows for a number of elective courses in communications, electronics, and power systems. A thesis and final examination are required.

The 36-hour M.S. in Software Engineering is a highly structured program emphasizing software systems and quality control principles. A final comprehensive examination is required, but a thesis is not. This program can be completed by distance learning.

The Ph.D. in Computer Science is available with optional tracks in artificial intelligence and robotics, computer-aided design systems, parallel and distributed systems, and software engineering. Two examinations are required in addition to the standard dissertation.

The Ph.D. in Electrical Engineering allows for a number of elective courses in communications, electronics, and power systems. Two examinations are required in addition to the standard dissertation.

Other Programs

Texas Tech University also offers a B.B.A. with emphasis in management information systems, an M.B.A. with emphasis in management information systems, M.S. programs in Management Information Systems and Telecom Technology/Network Management, and a Ph.D. in Management Information Systems. For more information, contact the Department of Management at (806) 742-3176.

An interdisciplinary M.Eng. is available with concentrated tracks in electrical engineering and software engineering. This program can be completed by distance learning. For more information, contact the College of Engineering at (806) 742-3451.

Contact Information

PHONE
General information: (806) 742-2011
Admissions (undergraduate): (806) 742-1480
Admissions (graduate): (806) 742-2787
Computer science: (806) 742-3527
Engineering technology: (806) 742-3538
Software engineering: (806) 742-1189

FAX
Admissions (undergraduate): (806) 742-0980
Computer science and software engineering: (806) 742-3519
Engineering technology: (806) 742-1699

E-MAIL
Admissions: nsr@ttu.edu
Computer science: Penny Ohlhaver
(penny.ohlhaver@coe.ttu.edu)
Electronic(s) engineering technology:
etsa@coe3.coe.ttu.edu
Software engineering: Gopal Lakhani
(lakhani@cs.ttu.edu)

Thomas Edison State College   www.tesc.edu ☆½

101 W. State Street
Trenton, NJ 08608-1176

Year established: 1972
Ownership: Public

As the external degree program of the state of New Jersey, this institution offers undergraduate information technology degrees through nontraditional delivery methods. Students can complete all degrees 100 percent off-campus through online courses, credit by examination, life experience credit, certification evaluations, on-the-job training, transfer credit, and military experience.

Degrees Offered

UNDERGRADUATE
B.A., Computer Science
B.S.A.S.T., Computer Science Technology
B.S.A.S.T., Electrical Technology
B.S.A.S.T., Electronic(s) Engineering Technology

Approximate Cost of Degrees

UNDERGRADUATE, RESIDENT
$1,400 and up

UNDERGRADUATE, NONRESIDENT (U.S.)
$1,800 and up

UNDERGRADUATE, NONRESIDENT (NON-U.S.)
$2,100 and up

Admissions Guidelines

UNDERGRADUATE
High school diploma required

Undergraduate Programs

The B.A. in Computer Science integrates study of the discipline into a curriculum focused on the liberal arts. Like all of TESC's degree programs, the B.A. in Computer Science is flexible.

The B.S.A.S.T. in Computer Science Technology involves a 21-hour AST core and an 18-hour science and mathematics core in addition to the 33-hour major. The program essentially represents a software-oriented computer engineering curriculum.

The B.S.A.S.T. in Electrical Technology emphasizes power systems and electronics.

The B.S.A.S.T. in Electronic(s) Engineering Technology emphasizes digital systems, communications, and signal processing.

Other Programs

A B.S.A.S.T. in Engineering Graphics (which includes a CAD concentration) is also available.

A B.S. in Business Administration can be customized with an 18-hour emphasis in computer information systems.

Contact Information

PHONE
(609) 292-6565 or (888) 442-8372

FAX
(609) 984-8447

E-MAIL
admissions@tesc.edu

Tufts University   www.tufts.edu ☆☆½

Medford, MA 02155

Year established: 1852
Ownership: Private

This major private university offers programs at all levels in traditional information technology fields. Graduate programs tend to be more research-oriented than professional, but are still practical enough to fit the needs of most reentry students. Evening classes are available.

Degrees Offered

UNDERGRADUATE
B.A., Computer Science
B.S., Computer Science
(ABET) B.S., Computer Engineering
(ABET) B.S., Electrical Engineering

GRADUATE
M.S., Computer Science
M.S., Electrical Engineering
Ph.D., Computer Science
Ph.D., Electrical Engineering

Approximate Cost of Degrees

UNDERGRADUATE
$100,500

MASTER'S
$37,700

DOCTORATE
$62,800

Admissions Guidelines

UNDERGRADUATE
High school diploma, SAT and/or ACT required

GRADUATE
Accredited bachelor's, GRE required

Undergraduate Programs

The B.A. in Computer Science offered through the College of Liberal Arts approaches computer science applications from a broad background in the humanities, social sciences, mathematics, and natural sciences. The B.S. in Computer Science offered through the College of Engineering is a bit more to the point, addressing computational mathematics, natural science, and the massive Computer Science major as a single, integrated field of study. A relevant minor in multimedia arts is available.

The ABET-accredited B.S. in Computer Engineering features a hardware-oriented curriculum. The program is flexible at the upper level and permits a considerable amount of student-directed informal specialization. Particularly appropriate minors are available in computer science, multimedia arts, and engineering management.

The ABET-accredited B.S. in Electrical Engineering permits extensive student specialization through the use of free electives. Particularly relevant minors are available in biomedical engineering and engineering management.

Graduate Programs

The 30-hour M.S. in Computer Science emphasizes theoretical computer science and applied software engineering. A thesis or final project is required.

The 30-hour M.S. in Electrical Engineering is available with an optional electro-optics specialization. A thesis or final project is required.

The Ph.D. in Computer Science requires a qualifying examination in addition to a dissertation. Data compression and scientific computation have been identified as particularly strong research areas.

The Ph.D. in Electrical Engineering requires a qualifying examination in addition to a dissertation. Electro-optics and Fourier optics have been identified as particularly strong research areas.

Contact Information

PHONE
General information: (617) 628-5000
Admissions (undergraduate): (617) 627-3170
Admissions (graduate): (617) 627-3395
Electrical engineering and computer science: (617) 627-3217

FAX
Admissions (undergraduate): (617) 627-3860
Admissions (graduate): (617) 627-3016
Electrical engineering and computer science: (617) 627-3220

E-MAIL
Admissions (undergraduate): UAdmissInquiry@Infonet.Tufts.Edu
Admissions (graduate): gsas@infonet.tufts.edu

Tulane University   www2.tulane.edu ☆☆☆

6823 St. Charles Avenue
New Orleans, LA 70118

Year established: 1834
Ownership: Private

This large private university offers standard information technology degrees at every level, but Tulane's graduate research possibilities are anything but standard. Evening classes are available.

Degrees Offered

UNDERGRADUATE
- (CSAB) B.S., Computer Science
- (ABET) B.S.E., Computer Engineering
- (ABET) B.S.E., Electrical Engineering

GRADUATE
M.S., Computer Science
M.S.E., Electrical Engineering
Sc.D., Computer Science
Sc.D., Electrical Engineering
Ph.D., Computer Science
Ph.D., Electrical Engineering

Approximate Cost of Degrees

UNDERGRADUATE
$96,900

MASTER'S
$36,300

DOCTORATE
$60,500

Admissions Guidelines

UNDERGRADUATE
High school diploma, SAT and/or ACT required

GRADUATE
Accredited bachelor's, GRE required

Undergraduate Programs

The ABET-accredited B.S.E. in Computer Engineering offers particularly strong elective courses in artificial intelligence, neural networks, robot reasoning, and related field. The program is also unusually strong in computational mathematics. Although hardware forms the core of the program, it is decisively more software- and theory-oriented in its elective options. Double majors are available in computer science and electrical engineering.

The CSAB-accredited B.S. in Computer Science approaches software issues from a background in computational mathematics and the natural sciences. The program is unusually strong in artificial intelligence (and related fields), databases, computational science, and software engineering. Double majors are available in electrical engineering and computer engineering.

The ABET-accredited B.S.E. in Electrical Engineering offers particularly strong elective courses in digital systems, electronics, and related fields. Double majors are available in computer engineering and computer science.

Graduate Programs

The 30-hour M.S. in Computer Science is unusually strong in its computational science offerings. A comprehensive examination is required; students can choose either a thesis or project as a culminating project.

The 30-hour M.S. in Engineering (M.S.E.) in Electrical Engineering requires a comprehensive examination in addition to the standard culminating project, which can be either a thesis or project.

The Ph.D. in Computer Science requires two examinations in addition to the standard dissertation. Particularly strong research areas are available in artificial intelligence, computer systems, computing theory, and programming languages.

The Ph.D. in Electrical Engineering requires two examinations in addition to the standard dissertation. Tulane University is extremely well known for its research in power systems and digital signal processing.

Contact Information

PHONE

General information: (504) 865-5000
Admissions (undergraduate): (504) 865-5731 or
(800) 873-9283
Admissions (graduate): (504) 865-5100
Electrical engineering and computer science:
(504) 865-5785

FAX

Electrical engineering and computer science: (504)
862-3293

E-MAIL

General information: pr@tulane.edu
Admissions (undergraduate):
undergrad.admission@tulane.edu
Electrical engineering and computer science:
admasst@eecs.tulane.edu

University of Alabama in Huntsville   www.uah.edu ☆☆

Huntsville, AL 35899

Year established: 1950
Ownership: Public

This major research-oriented state university offers innovative programs at every level in a variety of information technology fields. Considerable opportunity is provided for specialized research, and most of the bachelor's-
level and master's-level programs are quite accommodating to professional reentry students as well. Evening
classes are available.

Degrees Offered

UNDERGRADUATE

CSAB B.S., Computer Science
ABET B.S.E., Computer Engineering
ABET B.S.E., Electrical Engineering

GRADUATE

M.S., Computer Science
M.S.E., Computer Engineering
M.S.E., Electrical Engineering
Ph.D., Computer Science
Ph.D., Electrical and Computer Engineering

Approximate Cost of Degrees

UNDERGRADUATE, RESIDENT

$12,900

UNDERGRADUATE, NONRESIDENT

$26,400

MASTER'S, RESIDENT

$6,300

MASTER'S, NONRESIDENT

$12,400

DOCTORATE, RESIDENT

$10,500

DOCTORATE, NONRESIDENT

$20,600

Admissions Guidelines

UNDERGRADUATE

High school diploma required. SAT and/or ACT also
required if high school diploma is less than five
years old.

GRADUATE

Accredited bachelor's, GRE required

Undergraduate Programs

The CSAB-accredited B.S. in Computer Science
focuses on programming in its applied components
while drawing from a rigorous theoretical base in
computational mathematics.

The ABET-accredited B.S. in Engineering (B.S.E.) in Computer Engineering is a highly structured program that gives roughly equal weight to hardware and software issues. The program takes a strongly systems-oriented approach.

The ABET-accredited B.S. in Engineering (B.S.E.) in Electrical Engineering places considerable emphasis on circuits, digital signal processing, and VLSI design. Students are given a generous 18 hours of upper-level electives, allowing room for a substantially student-defined specialization.

Graduate Programs

The 33-hour M.S. in Computer Science is available with specializations in artificial intelligence, computer architecture, computer graphics, data and information technology, image processing, languages and systems, software engineering, and theoretical computer science. A thesis is optional, but a comprehensive examination is required.

The 36-hour M.S.E. in Computer Engineering is available with specializations in computer systems architectures, parallel and distributed processing, software engineering, and VLSI/electronics. A thesis is optional, but a comprehensive examination is required.

The 36-hour M.S.E. in Electrical Engineering is available with specializations in communications and radar, control theory, digital signal processing, electromagnetics and plasma, electronics and VLSI, and opto-electronics. Students can also specialize in a computer engineering field with faculty approval. A thesis is optional, but a comprehensive examination is required.

The Ph.D. in Computer Science is available with specializations in artificial intelligence, computer architecture, computer graphics, data and information technology, image processing, languages and systems, software engineering, and theoretical computer science. Two examinations are required in addition to the standard dissertation, and a six-

month full-time residency requirement must be fulfilled.

The Ph.D. in Electrical and Computer Engineering is available with specializations in artificial intelligence and neural networks, digital and neural computer architecture, digital signal processing, hardware design, network theory, parallel processing, software engineering, and VLSI/electronics. Two examinations are required in addition to the standard dissertation, and a six-month full-time residency requirement must be fulfilled.

Other Programs

A B.S. in Business Administration, with emphasis in management information systems, is available; also offered through the College of Administrative Science is an M.S. in Management Information Systems. For more information on these programs, contact the Office of Academic Assistance of the College of Administrative Science at (256) 890-6024.

The Department of Electrical Engineering participates in an innovative interdepartmental Ph.D. program in electro-optics.

Contact Information

PHONE

Admissions (undergraduate): (256) 890-6070 or (800) 824-2255
Admissions (graduate): (256) 890-6002
Computer science: (256) 890-6088
Electrical engineering: (256) 890-6316

E-MAIL

Admissions (undergraduate):
admitme@email.uah.edu
Admissions (graduate): deangrad@uah.edu
Computer science: info@cs.uah.edu
Electrical engineering (undergraduate):
eceinfo@eb.uah.edu
Electrical engineering (graduate): ecegrad@uah.edu

University of Alabama—Birmingham   www.uab.edu ☆☆☆

Office of Undergraduate Admissions
260 Hill University Center
1400 University Boulevard
Birmingham, AL 35294-1150

Graduate School, Main Office
511 Hill University Center
1400 University Boulevard
Birmingham, AL 35294-1150

Year established: 1966
Ownership: Public

This major state university offers programs at all levels in computer science in electrical engineering. Although the overall emphasis of these programs seems to be field-based, opportunities for research are certainly present. Interdisciplinary options in cognitive science and health informatics (see "Other Programs") are also offered. Evening classes and distance learning are available.

Degrees Offered

UNDERGRADUATE
B.S., Computer Science
🅰 B.S., Electrical Engineering

GRADUATE
M.S., Computer and Information Science
M.S., Electrical Engineering
Ph.D., Computer and Information Science
Ph.D., Electrical Engineering

Approximate Cost of Degrees

UNDERGRADUATE, RESIDENT
$12,900

UNDERGRADUATE, NONRESIDENT
$27,100

MASTER'S, RESIDENT
$4,400

MASTER'S, NONRESIDENT
$8,200

DOCTORATE, RESIDENT
$7,400

DOCTORATE, NONRESIDENT
$13,700

Admissions Guidelines

UNDERGRADUATE
High school diploma with 2.0 GPA, SAT and/or ACT required

GRADUATE
Accredited bachelor's with 3.0 GPA, GRE required

Undergraduate Programs

The B.S. in Computer Science approaches study of applied software applications and software engineering from a broad, rigorous background in mathematics and the natural sciences. An optional specialization in telecommunications and computer networking is available.

The ABET-accredited B.S. in Electrical Engineering focuses on circuit design, electronics, and electromechanical engineering.

Graduate Programs

The 36-hour M.S. in Computer and Information Science is a largely application-focused program that incorporates elements of theoretical computer science and software engineering. No thesis is required.

The 30-hour M.S. in Electrical Engineering is very emphatically a hands-on program that adequately serves the needs of research-minded students as well as reentry professionals. Specializations are available in communication systems, computer systems, control systems, and power systems. A final design-oriented thesis or project is required.

The Ph.D. in Computer and Information Science requires a qualifying examination in addition to the standard dissertation. Students must fulfill a residency requirement consisting of one year of full-time study.

The Ph.D. in Electrical Engineering is available with specializations in communication systems, computer systems, control systems, and power systems. A qualifying examination is required in addition to the standard dissertation.

Other Programs

An interdisciplinary Ph.D. in Cognitive Science is offered through the departments of biomedical engineering, computer and information science, physiology and biophysics, psychology, and vision science. This program can be tailored to the interests of a student who wants to undertake intensive study and research in cognitive neural systems. For more information, contact the program director at (205) 934-3850.

An M.S. in Health Informatics is also available. For more information, contact the program office at (205) 934-3509.

Contact Information

PHONE

Admissions (undergraduate): (205) 975-5433 or (800) 421-8743
Admissions (graduate): (205) 934-8227.
Computer and information science: (205) 934-2213
Electrical and computer engineering: (205) 934-8410

FAX

Admissions (graduate): (205) 934-8413
Computer and information science: (205) 934-5473

E-MAIL

Admissions (undergraduate):
UndergradAdmit@uab.edu
Admissions (graduate): gradschool@uab.edu
Electrical and computer engineering:
ecewebc@eng.uab.edu

University of Alabama—Tuscaloosa   www.ua.edu ☆☆☆

Office of Undergraduate Admissions
Box 870132
Tuscaloosa, AL 35487-0132

Graduate School
Box 870118
Tuscaloosa, AL 35487-0118

Year established: 1831
Ownership: Public

This major state university offers programs at all levels in traditional information technology fields. A variety of research options are present, but this institution seems to effectively serve the needs of professional students as well. Evening classes, weekend study, and distance learning are available.

Degrees Offered

UNDERGRADUATE

(CSAB) B.S., Computer Science
(ABET) B.S., Electrical Engineering

GRADUATE

M.S., Computer Science
M.S., Electrical Engineering
Ph.D., Computer Science
Ph.D., Electrical Engineering

Approximate Cost of Degrees

Undergraduate, Resident
$15,500

Undergraduate, Nonresident
$34,900

Master's, Resident
$5,500

Master's, Nonresident
$12,300

Doctorate, Resident
$9,200

Doctorate, Nonresident
$20,500

Admissions Guidelines

Undergraduate
High school diploma with 2.0 GPA, SAT and/or ACT required

Graduate
Accredited bachelor's with 3.0 GPA, GRE required

Undergraduate Programs

The CSAB-accredited B.S. in Computer Science approaches the primarily theoretical and software-oriented major curriculum based on a broad, rigorous background in mathematics and the natural sciences.

The ABET-accredited B.S. in Electrical Engineering focuses on digital systems and electronics in its core requirements, but can be tailored to individual student interests. A computer engineering track (recognized by ABET as an accredited major in computer engineering) is available.

Graduate Programs

The 33-hour M.S. in Computer Science focuses on software engineering issues in its core requirements, but allows for a great deal of student-directed specialization. A thesis, project, or comprehensive examination is required.

The 32-hour M.S. in Electrical Engineering is available with formal concentrations in communications and controls, electromagnetics and materials, electronics and computer engineering, and power systems. A thesis is generally required, but can be waived under special circumstances.

The Ph.D. in Computer Science requires a qualifying examination in addition to the standard dissertation.

The Ph.D. in Electrical Engineering is available with formal concentrations in communications and controls, electromagnetics and materials, electronics and computer engineering, and power systems. Two examinations are required in addition to the standard dissertation.

Other Programs

A highly regarded M.B.A. in management information systems is available, as are B.S. and M.S. programs in the field. For more information, contact the Culverhouse College of Commerce and Business Administration at (205) 348-7443.

Contact Information

Phone
Admissions (undergraduate): (205) 348-5666 or (800) 933-2262
Admissions (graduate): (205) 348-5921
Computer science: (205) 348-6363

Fax
Admissions (graduate): (205) 348-0400
Computer science: (205) 348-0219

E-mail
Admissions (undergraduate):
uaadmit@enroll.ua.edu
Admissions (graduate, international):
intergradapply@aalan.ua.edu
Admissions (graduate, U.S.):
usgradapply@aalan.ua.edu
Computer science: dept@cs.ua.edu
Electrical and computer engineering: Lloyd Morley
(lmorley@coe.eng.ua.edu)

University of Alaska—Anchorage   www.uaa.alaska.edu ☆☆

Enrollment Services
3211 Providence Drive
Anchorage, AK 99508-8046

Year established: 1954
Ownership: Public

This midsize public university offers strong, hands-on undergraduate programs in computer science with several intensive concentrations to choose from. Evening classes, extension courses, and weekend study options are available.

Degrees Offered

UNDERGRADUATE
B.A., Computer Science
B.S., Computer Science

Approximate Cost of Degrees

UNDERGRADUATE, RESIDENT
$9,800

UNDERGRADUATE, NONRESIDENT
$29,400

Admissions Guidelines

UNDERGRADUATE
High school diploma with 2.5+ GPA, SAT and/or ACT required

Undergraduate Programs

The University of Alaska at Anchorage offers both B.A and B.S. programs in Computer Science. The B.A. in Computer Science is designed for students who want to pursue a broad, interdisciplinary course of study focusing on software-oriented computing.

The B.S. in Computer Science is available via three different tracks: traditional, information science, and scientific computing. The traditional track provides a broad background in both applied and theoretical computer science and seems to be particularly geared toward students who will be pursuing a graduate degree in the field. The information science track focuses on applied computer science and software issues; its curriculum is very similar to that of the B.A. in Computer Science described above. The scientific computing track is largely theoretical in its orientation and is designed for students who seek a strong, extensive background in the principles behind computer science as a discipline.

Other Programs

The University of Alaska at Anchorage offers a Bachelor of Business Administration with emphasis in Management Information Systems.

A number of certificates and associate's degree programs are also available in a variety of IT-related fields, most notably office information systems and electronics. For more information, contact the Community and Technical College at (907) 786-6400.

Contact Information

PHONE
Enrollment services: (907) 786-1480
College of arts and sciences: (907) 786-1707

FAX
(907) 786-4888

E-MAIL
Enrollment services: Kris Keays
(ankmk1@uaa.alaska.edu)
Math and natural sciences: Carol Frentress
(ancjf@uaa.alaska.edu)

University of Alaska—Fairbanks   www.uaf.edu ☆☆☆

Office of Admissions
P.O. Box 757480
Fairbanks, Alaska 99775-7480

Year established: 1917
Ownership: Public

This major state university offers extremely traditional programs in computer science and electrical engineering at the undergraduate level, but shifts into innovative course and research offerings at the graduate level. Evening classes and extension courses are available.

Degrees Offered

UNDERGRADUATE
CSAB B.S., Computer Science
ABET B.S., Electrical Engineering

GRADUATE
M.E.E.
M.S., Computer Science
M.S., Electrical Engineering
Ph.D., Electrical Engineering

Approximate Cost of Degrees

UNDERGRADUATE, RESIDENT
$11,000

UNDERGRADUATE, NONRESIDENT
$32,000

MASTER'S, RESIDENT
$6,200

MASTER'S, NONRESIDENT
$12,100

DOCTORATE, RESIDENT
$10,300

DOCTORATE, NONRESIDENT
$20,200

Admissions Guidelines

UNDERGRADUATE
High school diploma with 2.0 GPA, SAT and/or ACT required

GRADUATE
Accredited bachelor's required, GRE required only if GPA is below 3.0

Undergraduate Programs

The CSAB-accredited B.S. in Computer Science is a traditional program that approaches computer science from a decisively theoretical perspective. In its applied components, it tends to emphasize databases and programming.

The ABET-accredited B.S. in Electrical Engineering is available with research specializations in communications engineering, computer engineering, power engineering, and space systems engineering.

Graduate Programs

The 32-hour Master of Electrical Engineering (M.E.E.) is a professional degree designed primarily for reentry students. No thesis is required, but students must pass a comprehensive examination at the end of the program.

The 30-hour M.S. in Computer Science permits students to choose one of two tracks: software engineering (which focuses on project management and systems-oriented programming) or technical computer science (which emphasizes programming and computational mathematics). A thesis and comprehensive examination are required.

The 30-hour M.S. in Electrical Engineering is a highly structured, strongly research-oriented program culminating in a required thesis and comprehensive examination.

The Ph.D. in Electrical Engineering is specifically described as an interdisciplinary program and can incorporate courses from a variety of secondary fields. Students design a faculty-approved plan of study that culminates in the standard dissertation.

Contact Information

PHONE
Admissions: (907) 474-7500 or (800) 478-1823
Computer science: (907) 474-7332
Electrical engineering: (907) 474-7137

FAX
Admissions: (907) 474-5379
Electrical engineering: (907) 474-5135

E-MAIL
Admissions: fyapply@uaf.edu
Computer science: fycs@uaf.edu
Electrical engineering: fyee@uaf.edu

University of Arizona   www.arizona.edu ☆☆

Tucson, AZ 85721

Year established: 1885
Ownership: Public

This major public university offers programs at all levels in traditional information technology fields. Evening classes, weekend study, and distance learning are available.

Degrees Offered

UNDERGRADUATE
🅰 B.S., Computer Engineering
B.S., Computer Science
🅰 B.S., Electrical Engineering

GRADUATE
M.S., Computer Science
M.S., Electrical and Computer Engineering
Ph.D., Computer Science
Ph.D., Electrical and Computer Engineering

Approximate Cost of Degrees

UNDERGRADUATE, RESIDENT
$12,800

UNDERGRADUATE, NONRESIDENT
$41,000

MASTER'S, RESIDENT
$4,800

MASTER'S, NONRESIDENT
$15,400

DOCTORATE, RESIDENT
$8,000

DOCTORATE, NONRESIDENT
$25,700

Admissions Guidelines

UNDERGRADUATE
High school diploma, SAT and/or ACT required

GRADUATE
Accredited bachelor's, GRE required

Undergraduate Programs

The ABET-accredited B.S. in Computer Engineering gives roughly equal weight to software engineering and hardware issues. Students are given an opportunity to specialize at the upper levels.

The B.S. in Computer Science focuses on issues in computational mathematics, operating systems, databases, and programming. This well-rounded curriculum seems well suited to a research-minded student.

The ABET-accredited B.S. in Electrical Engineering is a highly structured program designed with emphasis on digital systems, signal processing, and power systems.

Graduate Programs

The 30-hour M.S. in Computer Science works from a 12-hour core in computer science theory, then allows the rest for student electives. No thesis is required, but all students must pass a comprehensive examination.

The 30-hour M.S. in Electrical and Computer Engineering is a highly structured program allowing for 6 hours of graduate level field electives. No thesis is required, but all non-thesis students must pass a six-part comprehensive examination.

The Ph.D. in Computer Science requires two examinations in addition to the standard dissertation. The program itself focuses on advanced theoretical issues in computational mathematics and structural computer science.

The Ph.D. in Electrical and Computer Engineering requires two examinations in addition to the standard dissertation. The program places emphasis on digital systems, electronics, and computer engineering.

Other Programs

B.S.B.A., M.B.A., M.S., and Ph.D. programs in Management Information Systems are available. For more information, contact the MIS department of the Eller College of Business and Public Administration at (520) 621-2748.

Contact Information

PHONE
General information: (520) 621-2211
Admissions (graduate): (520) 621-7808
Computer science: (520) 621-6613

FAX
Computer science: (520) 621-4246

E-MAIL
Admissions (undergraduate): appinfo@arizona.edu
Computer science (graduate): gradadmissions@cs.arizona.edu
Electrical engineering (undergraduate): James Boyless (boyless@ece.arizona.edu)
Electrical engineering (graduate): Tami Whelan (whelan@ece.arizona.edu)

University of Arkansas—Fayetteville www.uark.edu ☆☆½

Fayetteville, AR 72701

Year established: 1871
Ownership: Public

This large state university offers programs at the undergraduate and graduate levels in several major information technology fields. Those considering a doctoral program may also want to investigate the interdisciplinary Ph.D. in Engineering (see "Other Programs"). Evening classes, weekend study, extension courses, and distance learning are available.

Degrees Offered

UNDERGRADUATE
B.A., Computer Science
B.S., Computer Science
🅐 B.S., Computer Systems Engineering
🅐 B.S., Electrical Engineering

GRADUATE
M.S., Computer Engineering
M.S., Computer Science
M.S., Electrical Engineering

Approximate Cost of Degrees

UNDERGRADUATE, RESIDENT
$17,400

UNDERGRADUATE, NONRESIDENT
$38,600

MASTER'S, RESIDENT
$9,200

MASTER'S, NONRESIDENT
$18,400

DOCTORATE, RESIDENT
$15,300

DOCTORATE, NONRESIDENT
$30,700

Admissions Guidelines

UNDERGRADUATE
High school diploma, SAT and/or ACT required

GRADUATE
Accredited bachelor's with 2.5 GPA, GRE required

Undergraduate Programs

The B.A. program in Computer Science involves a 29-hour major and emphasizes interdisciplinary computing, while the B.S. in Computer Science involves a 44-hour major and emphasizes a strong, traditional background in theoretical computer science. Both programs focus on programming and software applications in their applied component.

The ABET-accredited B.S. in Computer Systems Engineering is a strongly hardware-focused program that provides students with a solid background in low-level programming, software-hardware interfacing, and structural computer system theory.

The ABET-accredited B.S. in Electrical Engineering is available with informal specializations in computers and digital systems, electronic circuits, energy processing systems and control, and telecommunications.

Graduate Programs

The 36-hour M.S. in Computer Science focuses on advanced issues in theoretical computer science and software engineering. A thesis is encouraged, but not required.

The 30-hour M.S. in Computer Engineering focuses intensively on both hardware and software issues on a graduate-level survey basis. A thesis is generally required, and qualifying examinations can be required at the discretion of the faculty.

The 30-hour M.S. in Electrical Engineering is available with informal specializations in computers and digital systems, electronic circuits, energy processing systems and control, and telecommunications. A thesis is generally required, and qualifying examinations can be required at the discretion of the faculty.

The new Ph.D. in Computer Science requires a comprehensive examination in addition to the standard dissertation. Coursework focuses on theoretical issues in computer science such as artificial intelligence and human-computer interaction.

Other Programs

A Master of Education (M.Ed.) in Educational Technology is also available. For more information, contact the Department of Educational Leadership, Counseling, and Foundations at (501) 575-4207.

An interdisciplinary Ph.D. in Engineering is offered with concentrations in computer engineering and electrical engineering. For more information, contact the College of Engineering at (501) 575-3051.

Contact Information

PHONE

General information: (501) 575-2000
Admissions (undergraduate): (501) 575-5346
Admissions (graduate): (501) 575-4401
Computer science and engineering: (501) 575-6036
Electrical engineering: (501) 575-3005

FAX

Computer science and engineering: (501) 575-5339
Electrical engineering: (501) 575-7967

E-MAIL

Admissions (undergraduate):
uafadmis@comp.uark.edu
Admissions (graduate): gradinfo@cavern.uark.edu

University of Arkansas—Little Rock   www.uarl.edu ☆☆½

2801 South University Avenue
Little Rock, AR 72204-1099

Year established: 1927
Ownership: Public

This midsize state university offers field-oriented, professional undergraduate and graduate programs in hardware- and software-oriented information technology fields. Evening classes are available.

Degrees Offered

UNDERGRADUATE

CSAB B.S., Computer Science
ABET B.S., Electronics and Computer Engineering Technology

GRADUATE

M.S., Computer and Information Science

Approximate Cost of Degrees

UNDERGRADUATE, RESIDENT

$14,900

UNDERGRADUATE, NONRESIDENT

$32,100

GRADUATE, RESIDENT

$5,000

GRADUATE, NONRESIDENT

$10,700

Admissions Guidelines

UNDERGRADUATE

High school diploma, SAT and/or ACT required

GRADUATE

Accredited bachelor's with 3.0 GPA, GRE required

Undergraduate Programs

The CSAB-accredited B.S. in Computer Science approaches issues in databases and software engineering from a broad theoretical base in computational mathematics. This program actually involves a course in COBOL as its programming language component.

The ABET-accredited B.S. in Electronics and Computer Engineering Technology focuses on microprocessors, digital systems, and IT management issues. A minor in computer-aided manufacturing is available.

Graduate Programs

The 34-hour M.S. in Computer and Information Science focuses on systems-oriented software and database issues. A thesis or project is required.

Other Programs

A B.B.A. with emphasis in computer information systems is also available through the College of Business. For more information, contact the program chair at (501) 569-8851.

Contact Information

PHONE

General information: (501) 569-3000
Admissions (undergraduate): (501) 569-3127
Admissions (graduate): (501) 569-3206
Computer and information science: (501) 569-8130
Engineering technology: (501) 569-8200

E-MAIL

Admissions (undergraduate): adminfo@ualr.edu
Admissions (graduate): graddept@ualr.edu

University of California—Berkeley   www.berkeley.edu ☆☆

Berkeley, CA 94720

Year established: 1873
Ownership: Public

This top research-oriented public university offers programs at all levels in the most common information technology fields. Berkeley is unique in that it brings together curricular requirements that would seem mutually exclusive (ABET-accredited Electrical Engineering and CSAB-accredited Computer Science majors) while dividing methodological approaches on a hairline (for instance, students who complete an M.S. are not even considered eligible for the D.Eng. unless they first complete the M.Eng.). Evening classes and distance learning are available.

Degrees Offered

UNDERGRADUATE
B.A., Computer Science
CSAB ABET B.S., Electrical Engineering and Computer Science

GRADUATE
M.Eng., Electrical Engineering
M.S., Computer Science
M.S., Electrical Engineering
D.Eng., Electrical Engineering
Ph.D., Computer Science
Ph.D., Electrical Engineering

Approximate Cost of Degrees

UNDERGRADUATE, RESIDENT
$17,900

UNDERGRADUATE, NONRESIDENT
$58,600

MASTER'S, RESIDENT
$7,200

MASTER'S, NONRESIDENT
$22,500

DOCTORATE, RESIDENT
$12,000

DOCTORATE, NONRESIDENT
$37,500

Admissions Guidelines

UNDERGRADUATE
High school diploma with 2.8 GPA, SAT and/or ACT required

GRADUATE
Accredited bachelor's with 3.0 GPA, GRE required

Undergraduate Programs

The B.A. in Computer Science provides a unique opportunity for students who want to pursue a program in interdisciplinary computing from a top information technology school.

The ABET-accredited and CSAB-accredited B.S. in Electrical Engineering and Computer Science is a rigorous, structured, and intensive program that addresses issues in digital systems, theoretical computer science, software engineering, and various electrical engineering fields from a broad background in the natural sciences and computational mathematics. This program seamlessly integrates the traditional structure of a CSAB-accredited Computer Science program into an intense, hands-on engineering focus of an ABET-accredited Electrical Engineering program. Specializations are available in bioelectronics, circuits and systems, computer sciences, and electronics.

Graduate Programs

The 30-hour M.S. programs in Electrical Engineering and Computer Science are intensively research-oriented programs designed primarily for students who want to pursue research on a professional basis or proceed to doctoral study. A thesis is required.

The 36-hour Master of Engineering (M.Eng.) in Electrical Engineering is designed for working professionals who want to pursue a hands-on curriculum in the field. The program culminates in a final examination. A computer engineering specialization is available.

The Doctor of Engineering (D.Eng.) in Electrical Engineering is designed for working professionals who want to undertake advanced study in applied electrical engineering. A culminating project and dissertation are required. A computer engineering specialization is required.

The Ph.D. programs in Computer Science and Electrical Engineering require two written examinations and one year of full-time residency in addition to the standard dissertation.

Other Programs

Master's and Ph.D. programs in Information Management and Systems are available. For more information, contact the School of Information Management and Systems at (510) 642-1464.

Contact Information

PHONE
Admissions (undergraduate): (510) 642-3175
Computer science: (510) 642-1042
Electrical engineering: (510) 642-3214

FAX
Computer science: (510) 642-5775

E-MAIL
Admissions (undergraduate):
ouars@uclink4.berkeley.edu
Admissions (graduate): gradadm@uclink4.berkeley.edu
Electrical engineering/computer science (graduate):
gradadm@eecs.berkeley.edu

✴ **EXTRA!**

Apple co-founder Steve Wozniak is a Berkeley graduate. Sun Microsystems co-founder Bill Joy earned his M.S. in electrical engineering and computer science from Berkeley, but this was obviously not enough to keep him busy. While he was there, he also led the effort to design Berkeley Unix (better known as BSD).

University of California—Davis   www.ucdavis.edu ☆☆☆

One Shields Avenue
Davis, CA 95616

Year established: 1908
Ownership: Public

This major, research-oriented university offers programs at all levels in standard computer science and engineering fields. Evening classes are available.

Degrees Offered

UNDERGRADUATE
 B.S., Computer Engineering
B.S., Computer Science
ABET CSAB B.S., Computer Science and Engineering
ABET B.S., Electrical Engineering

GRADUATE
M.S., Computer Science
M.S., Electrical and Computer Engineering
Ph.D., Computer Science
Ph.D., Electrical and Computer Engineering

Approximate Cost of Degrees

UNDERGRADUATE, RESIDENT
$19,500

UNDERGRADUATE, NONRESIDENT
$58,700

MASTER'S, RESIDENT
$22,900

MASTER'S, NONRESIDENT
$37,600

DOCTORATE, RESIDENT
$38,100

DOCTORATE, NONRESIDENT
$62,600

Admissions Guidelines

UNDERGRADUATE
High school diploma, SAT and/or ACT required

GRADUATE
Accredited bachelor's, GRE required

Undergraduate Programs
The ABET-accredited B.S. in Computer Engineering gives roughly equal weight to hardware and software issues. Students can construct extensive, informal specialization tracks through the use of free electives.

The B.S. in Computer Science includes specific components in hardware, software, and theory. Students are given the option to emphasize one or more of these focal points, or to divide elective credit more or less evenly among them.

The ABET-accredited and CSAB-accredited B.S. in Computer Science and Engineering essentially consists of the standard CSAB-accredited B.S. in Computer Science with sufficient credit depth in electronics and computer engineering to justify ABET accreditation. Given the rigorous curricular structures demanded by each form of accreditation, this program is surprisingly flexible.

The ABET-accredited B.S. in Electrical Engineering is available with formal specializations in analog electronics, digital electronics, electromagnetics, physical electronics, and signal processing/communications.

Graduate Programs

The 36-hour M.S. in Computer Science focuses on issues in software engineering, computational mathematics, and fairly abstract theoretical issues in computer science (such as artificial intelligence, networking principles, and so forth). Students can elect to undertake a thesis or comprehensive written examination.

The 36-hour M.S. in Electrical and Computer Engineering focuses on digital systems, physical electronics, and signal processing. Students can elect to undertake a thesis or comprehensive written examination.

The Ph.D. in Computer Science requires two examinations in addition to the standard dissertation. Each student designs a plan of study based on personal research interests.

The Ph.D. in Electrical and Computer Engineering requires two examinations in addition to the standard dissertation. Students must also complete a residency requirement (consisting of two consecutive semesters of full-time study) and a teaching requirement.

Other Programs

An interdisciplinary, ABET-accredited B.S. program in Electrical Engineering and Materials Science is offered through the Department of Electrical and Computer Engineering.

Contact Information

PHONE
General information: (530) 752-1011
Admissions (undergraduate): (530) 752-2971
Admissions (graduate): (530) 752-0655
Computer science: (530) 752-7004
Electrical and computer engineering: (530) 752-0583

FAX
Admissions (graduate): (530) 752-6222
Computer science: (530) 752-4767
Electrical and computer engineering: (530) 752-8428

E-MAIL
Admissions (undergraduate):
undergradadmissions@ucdavis.edu
Admissions (graduate): gradadmit@ucdavis.edu
Electrical and computer engineering (undergraduate):
ugradinfo@ece.ucdavis.edu
Electrical and computer engineering (graduate):
gradinfo@ece.ucdavis.edu

University of California—Irvine   www.uci.edu ☆☆☆

Irvine, CA 92697

Year established: 1965
Ownership: Public

This major state university offers programs at all levels in a variety of information technology fields ranging from the traditional (electrical engineering) to the nontraditional (embedded systems). Evening classes are available.

Degrees Offered

UNDERGRADUATE
🅐 B.S., Computer Engineering
B.S., Computer Science
🅐 B.S., Electrical Engineering

GRADUATE
M.S., Electrical and Computer Engineering
M.S., Embedded Systems
M.S., Information and Computer Science

M.S., Knowledge Discovery
Ph.D., Electrical and Computer Engineering
Ph.D., Information and Computer Science

Approximate Cost of Degrees

UNDERGRADUATE, RESIDENT
$19,800

UNDERGRADUATE, NONRESIDENT
$61,100

MASTER'S, RESIDENT
$10,400

MASTER'S, NONRESIDENT
$25,900

DOCTORATE, RESIDENT
$17,400

DOCTORATE, NONRESIDENT
$43,200

Admissions Guidelines

UNDERGRADUATE
High school diploma with 2.8 GPA, SAT and/or ACT required

GRADUATE
Accredited bachelor's with 3.0 GPA, GRE required

Undergraduate Programs

The ABET-accredited B.S. in Computer Engineering focuses more on hardware than software, but permits a considerable amount of student specialization through the use of field electives.

The B.S. in Computer Science is a flexible program that surveys virtually the entire field in its core requirements, but its elective course offerings in cognitive neural systems really stand out.

The ABET-accredited B.S. in Electrical Engineering is available with formal specializations in electro-optics and solid-state devices, power systems, and systems/signal processing.

Graduate Programs

The 36-hour M.S. in Electrical and Computer Engineering is available with formal tracks in computer systems and software, electrical engineering, and networks/distributed computing. The program can culminate in a thesis or final examination.

The 30-hour M.S. in Embedded Systems focuses on multilevel hardware-software and software-software interaction. Formal concentrations are available in distributed and networked embedded systems, embedded software, embedded system architectures, microelectronic embedded systems, system reliability and fault tolerance, and theoretical foundations of embedded systems. No thesis is required.

The 36-hour M.S. in Information and Computer Science is available with formal concentrations in algorithms and data structures, artificial intelligence, computer systems and networks, computer systems design, computing and organizations/policy/society, and software. The program can culminate in a thesis or final examination.

The 30-hour M.S. in Knowledge Discovery is a highly innovative program focusing on data mining and automated knowledge sorting-and-retrieval systems (for example, databases created and accessed by artificial intelligence routines) from the general perspective of software engineering. No thesis is required.

The Ph.D. in Electrical and Computer Engineering is available with formal tracks in computer systems and software, electrical engineering, and networks/distributed computing. Two examinations are required in addition to the standard dissertation.

The Ph.D. in Information and Computer Science is available with formal concentrations in algorithms and data structures, artificial intelligence, computer systems and networks, computer systems design, computing and organizations/policy/society, and software. Two examinations are required in addition to the standard dissertation.

Contact Information

PHONE
General information: (949) 824-5011
Admissions (undergraduate): (949) 824-6703
Admissions (graduate): (949) 824-7296
Computer and information science: (949) 824-7403
Electrical and computer engineering: (949) 824-4821

FAX
Admissions (undergraduate): (949) 824-7708
Admissions (graduate): (949) 824-2095
Computer and information science: (949) 824-4056
Electrical and computer engineering: (949) 824-3779

E-MAIL
Admissions (graduate): ogs@uci.edu
Computer and information science:
foffice@ics.uci.edu
Electrical and computer engineering (graduate):
ecegrad@ece.uci.edu

University of California—Los Angeles   www.ucla.edu ☆☆☆½

Box 951361
Los Angeles, CA 90095-1361

Year established: 1919
Ownership: Public

This major public university indisputably represents the cutting edge of technological research. Programs at all levels are available in traditional information technology fields, but these standard-looking, cookie-cutter-sounding majors hide a sea of innovative research programs. Evening classes are available.

Degrees Offered

UNDERGRADUATE

CSAB B.S., Computer Science
ABET CSAB B.S., Computer Science and Engineering
ABET B.S., Electrical Engineering

GRADUATE

M.S., Computer Science
M.S., Electrical Engineering
Ph.D., Computer Science
Ph.D., Electrical Engineering

Approximate Cost of Degrees

UNDERGRADUATE, RESIDENT
$20,800

UNDERGRADUATE, NONRESIDENT
$61,500

MASTER'S, RESIDENT
$8,900

MASTER'S, NONRESIDENT
$23,900

DOCTORATE, RESIDENT
$14,800

DOCTORATE, NONRESIDENT
$39,800

Admissions Guidelines

UNDERGRADUATE
High school diploma, SAT and/or ACT required

GRADUATE
Accredited bachelor's, GRE required

Undergraduate Programs

The CSAB-accredited B.S. in Computer Science is a well-rounded program that addresses applied and theoretical computing based on a broad background in the natural sciences. This program is largely software-oriented in its applied components.

The CSAB-accredited and ABET-accredited B.S. in Computer Science and Engineering approaches the field from a primarily hardware-centered perspective. This highly structured program leaves relatively little room for student-defined specialization.

The ABET-accredited B.S. in Electrical Engineering is available with informal specializations in communications and telecommunications, control systems, electromagnetics, integrated circuits and systems, operations research, photonics and opto-electronics, plasma electronics, signal processing, and solid-state electronics.

Graduate Programs

The 36-hour M.S. in Computer Science is available with informal specializations in artificial intelligence, biological systems, computer programming languages and systems, computer science theory, computer systems architecture, database and knowledge-based systems, network modeling and analysis, physical systems, and scientific computing. Students can choose to finish off the program with a thesis or comprehensive examination.

The 36-hour M.S. in Electrical Engineering is available with formal concentrations in communications and telecommunications, control systems, electromagnetics, integrated circuits and systems, operations research, photonics and optoelectronics, plasma electronics, signal processing, and solid-state electronics. Students can choose to finish off the program with a thesis or comprehensive examination.

The Ph.D. in Computer Science is available with informal tracks in artificial intelligence, biological systems, computer programming languages and systems, computer science theory, computer systems architecture, database and knowledge-based systems, network modeling and analysis, physical systems, and scientific computing. Coursework requirements are defined solely based on student and faculty research interests and vary from individual to individual. Two examinations are required in addition to the standard dissertation.

The Ph.D. in Electrical Engineering is available with formal concentrations in communications and telecommunications, control systems, electromagnetics, integrated circuits and systems, operations research, photonics and optoelectronics, plasma electronics, signal processing, and solid-state electronics. Coursework requirements are defined almost entirely based on student and faculty research interests and vary from individual to individual. Two examinations are required in addition to the standard dissertation.

Other Programs

Master's and Ph.D. programs in Library Information Systems are also available. For more information, contact the Department of Information Studies at (310) 825-8799.

Contact Information

PHONE

General information: (310) 825-4321
Admissions (undergraduate): (310) 825-3101
Admissions (graduate): (310) 825-1711
Computer science: (310) 825-3886
Electrical engineering: (310) 825-2647

FAX

Admissions (undergraduate): (310) 206-1206
Computer science: (310) 825-2273
Electrical engineering: (310) 206-8495

E-MAIL

Admissions (undergraduate):
ugadm@saonet.ucla.edu

University of California—San Diego   www.ucsd.edu ☆☆½

9500 Gilman Drive
La Jolla, CA 92093

Year established: 1962
Ownership: Public

This large public university offers programs at all levels in the hottest information technology fields. With graduate programs well suited to research-minded students and reentry students alike, this university has pretty much any traditional program one could ask for. Evening classes are available.

Degrees Offered

UNDERGRADUATE

B.A., Computer Science
B.S., Computer Science
B.S., Computer Science and Engineering
(ABET) B.S., Electrical Engineering

GRADUATE

M.Eng., Electrical and Computer Engineering
M.S., Computer Science
M.S., Computer Science and Engineering
M.S., Electrical Engineering
Ph.D., Computer Science
Ph.D., Electrical and Computer Engineering

Approximate Cost of Degrees

UNDERGRADUATE, RESIDENT
$19,400

UNDERGRADUATE, NONRESIDENT
$60,100

MASTER'S, RESIDENT
$7,800

MASTER'S, NONRESIDENT
$23,100

DOCTORATE, RESIDENT
$13,100

DOCTORATE, NONRESIDENT
$38,500

Admissions Guidelines

UNDERGRADUATE
High school diploma with 2.8 GPA, SAT and/or ACT required

GRADUATE
Accredited bachelor's with 3.0 GPA, GRE required

Undergraduate Programs
The B.A. and B.S. programs in Computer Science draw on a background in the natural sciences and mathematics, focusing on theoretical computer science in their major requirements. The B.S. has a more focused major conforming largely to CSAB standards, while the B.A. has a smaller major and places more weight on broader degree requirements.

The largely hardware-oriented B.S. in Computer Science and Engineering is a flexible program designed for students who want to undertake a broad, well-rounded curriculum in the field—a curriculum grounded, but not entrenched, in basic principles of digital systems and signal processing.

The ABET-accredited B.S. in Electrical Engineering is available with informal concentrations in communication systems, computer design, controls and systems theory, electronic circuits and systems, electronic devices and materials, machine intelligence, networks, photonics, queuing systems, and software systems. Students can also design their own specializations with faculty approval.

Graduate Programs
The 32-hour Master of Engineering (M.Eng.) in Electrical and Computer Engineering is a professional degree designed for working adults. No culminating project or examination is required.

The 33-hour M.S. in Computer Science is available with formal concentrations in artificial intelligence, communication networks, computer architecture and compilers, cryptography and security, database and information retrieval, design automation for microelectronic designs, distributed and fault-tolerant computing, multimedia systems, parallel and scientific computing, software engineering, and storage systems. Students can also design their own specializations with faculty approval. The program can culminate in a thesis or comprehensive examination, depending solely on student preference.

The 33-hour M.S. in Computer Science and Engineering gives roughly equal weight to hardware and software issues. Roughly half of the curriculum is student-defined. The program as a whole culminates in a thesis or comprehensive examination, depending on student preference.

The 32-hour M.S. in Electrical Engineering centers on a student-defined, faculty-approved plan of focused study. A thesis or comprehensive examination is required.

The Ph.D. in Computer Science is available with formal concentrations in artificial intelligence, complexity theory and theory of algorithms, computer-aided design, data and knowledge base systems, network security and cryptography, parallel and high-performance computation, processor architecture and compilation, semantics, software engineering, and systems. Students can also design their own specializations with faculty approval. Two examinations are required in addition to the standard dissertation.

The Ph.D. in Electrical and Computer Engineering is available with formal concentrations in advanced manufacturing, applied ocean sciences, applied optics and photonics, communication theory and systems, computer engineering, electronic circuits and systems, electronic devices and materials, intelligent systems/robotics/control, magnetic recording, radio and space science, and signal/image processing. Two examinations are required in addition to the standard dissertation.

Contact Information

PHONE
General information: (858) 534-2230
Admissions: (858) 534-4831
Computer science and engineering (undergraduate): (858) 534-3621
Computer science and engineering (graduate): (858) 534-3622
Electrical and computer engineering (undergraduate): (858) 822-3590
Electrical and computer engineering (graduate): (858) 822-3580

FAX
Computer science and engineering: (858) 534-7029

E-MAIL
Admissions: admissionsinfo@ucsd.edu

University of Central Oklahoma   www.ucok.edu ☆☆

100 N. University Drive
Edmond, OK 73034

Year established: 1890
Ownership: Public

This midsize state university offers unique interdisciplinary options in applied computing. Evening classes are available.

Degrees Offered

UNDERGRADUATE
B.S., Computing Science

Approximate Cost of Degrees

UNDERGRADUATE, RESIDENT
$8,900

UNDERGRADUATE, NONRESIDENT
$20,300

Admissions Guidelines

UNDERGRADUATE
High school diploma, ACT required

Undergraduate Programs
The B.S. in Computing Science is an interdisciplinary program consisting of a standard computer science curriculum (focusing on theory and software applications) and an area of computing application. Areas of applications are available in accounting, biology, economics, general business, management, marketing, mathematics, and psychology. Students can design individualized areas of application with faculty approval.

Other Programs
The B.B.A. program of the College of Business Administration is available with an optional management information systems emphasis. For more information, contact the Office of Undergraduate Admissions (405) 974-3366.

The M.S. in Applied Mathematical Sciences is available with a computer science specialization. For more information, contact the College of Mathematics and Sciences at (405) 974-2461.

Contact Information

PHONE
General information: (405) 974-2000
Admissions (undergraduate): (405) 974-3366
Admissions (graduate): (405) 974-3341
Mathematics and sciences: (405) 974-2461

E-MAIL
Admissions (undergraduate): 4ucoinfo@ucok.edu
Admissions (graduate): gradcoll@aix1.ucok.edu
Mathematics and sciences: mathsci@aix1.ucok.edu

University of Chicago   www.uchicago.edu ☆☆½

5801 South Ellis Avenue
Chicago, IL 60637

Year established: 1891
Ownership: Private

This prestigious, private university offers what seems at first glance to be a standard curriculum. The approach of the University of Chicago is anything but standard, however; here computer science is more an art than a science, more a craft than a profession. A student who undertakes any of these programs is obviously in for a treat. Evening classes and weekend study are available.

Degrees Offered

UNDERGRADUATE
B.A., Computer Science
B.S., Computer Science

GRADUATE
S.M., Computer Science
Ph.D., Computer Science

Approximate Cost of Degrees

UNDERGRADUATE
$97,300

MASTER'S
$41,300

DOCTORATE
$68,900

Admissions Guidelines

UNDERGRADUATE
High school diploma, SAT and/or ACT required

GRADUATE
Accredited bachelor's required, GRE strongly recommended

Undergraduate Programs

The B.A. and B.S. programs in Computer Science are largely identical in their major requirements, differing primarily in general credit distribution. Both programs are available with specializations in advanced systems, artificial intelligence, and numerical analysis. The B.S. is available with a minor in computational neuroscience.

Graduate Programs

The 33-hour S.M. in Computer Science includes required components in artificial intelligence, computational science, systems, and theory. A thesis is required. A special "conversion" track is available for students who want to undertake the S.M. program, but who lack the requisite undergraduate and/or professional background.

The Ph.D. in Computer Science requires a comprehensive candidacy examination in addition to the standard dissertation. All students must satisfy a research-oriented foreign language requirement.

Contact Information

PHONE
General information: (773) 702-1234
Admissions (undergraduate): (773) 702-8650
Computer science: (773) 702-6011

FAX
Admissions (undergraduate): (773) 702-4199

E-MAIL
Computer science: admissions@cs.uchicago.edu

University of Cincinnati   www.uc.edu ☆☆☆

2624 Clifton Avenue
Cincinnati, OH 45221

Year established: 1819
Ownership: Public

This major public university has fired up a variety of innovative programs to augment its well-established traditional offerings. Evening classes, weekend study, extension courses, and distance learning are available. Most of the undergraduate programs described below, including all programs in engineering technology, can be partially completed (and funded) through co-op arrangements.

Degrees Offered

UNDERGRADUATE
B.A.G.S., emphasis Information Technology
🅰 B.S., Computer Engineering

B.S., Computer Engineering Technology
B.S., Computer Science
🅰 B.S., Electrical Engineering
🅰 B.S., Electrical Engineering Technology
B.S., Information Engineering Technology

GRADUATE
M.S., Computer Engineering
M.S., Computer Science
M.S., Electrical Engineering
Ph.D., Computer Science and Engineering
Ph.D., Electrical Engineering

Approximate Cost of Degrees

UNDERGRADUATE, RESIDENT
$24,000

UNDERGRADUATE, NONRESIDENT
$55,500

MASTER'S, RESIDENT
$10,300

MASTER'S, NONRESIDENT
$18,100

DOCTORATE, RESIDENT
$17,200

DOCTORATE, NONRESIDENT
$30,200

Admission Guidelines

UNDERGRADUATE
High school diploma, SAT and/or ACT required

GRADUATE
Accredited bachelor's with 3.0 GPA, GRE required

Undergraduate Programs

The Bachelor of Applied and General Studies (B.A.G.S.) in Information Technology is designed specifically for reentry students. This program is designed to be completed through traditional coursework, distance learning, individualized study, weekend study, extension courses, evening study, or any mix of the above.

The ABET-accredited B.S. in Computer Engineering integrates computer science theory, software engineering, and electronics into a single cohesive curriculum.

The new B.S. in Computer Engineering Technology primarily stresses electronics, signal processing, logic circuits, and other hardware aspects of computer engineering.

The B.S. in Computer Science focuses on theory, emphasizing broad theoretical aspects of software engineering in its applied components.

The ABET-accredited B.S. in Electrical Engineering emphasizes digital systems, microelectronics, and signal processing.

The ABET-accredited B.S. in Electrical Engineering Technology stresses electronics, logic circuits, signal processing and networking, and hardware-software interaction.

The B.S. in Information Engineering Technology is, in effect, a degree in software and database engineering technology. Emphasis is placed on programming, multimedia applications, hardware-software interaction, and software engineering.

Graduate Programs

The 30-hour M.S. in Computer Engineering approaches computer engineering from a broad systems-oriented perspective, drawing fields as diverse as computer science theory and electronics into a single, unified curriculum. A thesis is required.

The 30-hour M.S. in Computer Science focuses on software engineering and theoretical computer science. A thesis is required.

The 30-hour M.S. in Electrical Engineering is available with research tracks emphasizing electronic materials/devices or systems engineering. A thesis is required.

The Ph.D. in Computer Science and Engineering is available with research tracks emphasizing computer engineering or computer science. A qualifying examination is involved in addition to the standard coursework and dissertation requirements.

The Ph.D. in Electrical Engineering is available with research tracks emphasizing electronic materials/devices or systems engineering. A qualifying examination is involved in addition to the standard coursework and dissertation requirements.

Other Programs

An information systems emphasis is available within the B.B.A. program. The M.B.A. program offers emphases in information technology and in management of advanced technology and innovation. For more information, contact the College of Business Administration at (513) 556-7030.

Contact Information

PHONE
General information: (513) 556-6000
Admissions: (513) 556-1100
Applied and general studies (B.A.G.S.): (513) 556-6932
Computer engineering: (513) 556-2214
Computer science: (513) 556-1813
Electrical and computer engineering technology:
(513) 556-6558
Electrical engineering: (513) 556-4753

FAX
Admissions: (513) 556-1105
Applied and general studies (B.A.G.S.): (513) 556-3280
Electrical and computer engineering technology:
(513) 556-5328
Electrical engineering and computer science:
(513) 556-7326

E-MAIL
General information: uc.web.general@uc.edu
Admissions: admissions@uc.edu
Computer engineering: Dr. Karen Davis
(karen.davis@uc.edu)
Computer science: Dr. Chia-Yung Han
(chia.han@uc.edu)

University of Colorado—Boulder   www.colorado.edu ☆☆☆

Boulder, CO 80309

Year established: 1876
Ownership: Public

This major state university offers standard and nonstandard information technology programs at every level. Evening classes, distance learning, extension courses, and weekend study are available.

Degrees Offered

UNDERGRADUATE
B.S., Computer Science
🅰 B.S., Electrical and Computer Engineering
🅰 B.S., Electrical Engineering

GRADUATE
M.Eng., Computer Science
M.Eng., Electrical Engineering
M.S., Computer Science
M.S., Electrical Engineering
M.S., Telecommunications
Ph.D., Computer Science
Ph.D., Electrical Engineering

Approximate Cost of Degrees

UNDERGRADUATE, RESIDENT
$17,200

UNDERGRADUATE, NONRESIDENT
$68,200

MASTER'S, RESIDENT
$11,600

MASTER'S, NONRESIDENT
$42,400

DOCTORATE, RESIDENT
$19,400

DOCTORATE, NONRESIDENT
$70,600

Admissions Guidelines

UNDERGRADUATE
High school diploma, SAT and/or ACT required

GRADUATE
Accredited bachelor's required, GRE recommended

Undergraduate Programs
The B.S. in Computer Science represents a traditional curriculum in the field that approaches issues of software engineering, software applications, and theoretical computer science from a broad, interdisciplinary background in mathematics and the natural sciences. Opportunities for co-op work study and overseas study are available.

The ABET-accredited B.S. in Electrical and Computer Engineering focuses on digital systems, hardware-software interaction, and theoretical computer science.

The ABET-accredited B.S. in Electrical Engineering takes a primarily theory-oriented approach to the field. The program is extremely flexible in its applied components, allowing ample room for student-defined specialization.

Graduate Programs

The 33-hour M.Eng. programs in Computer Science and in Electrical Engineering are intended primarily for reentry students who work in the field and want to improve their academic credentials. No thesis is required. These programs can be completed entirely through coursework taken at approved corporate extension sites.

The 30-hour M.S. in Computer Science is a flexible program that can be structured and restructured to fit student research interests. A thesis or written comprehensive examination is required.

The 30-hour M.S. in Electrical Engineering is available with informal concentrations in biomedical engineering, communication engineering and signal processing, computer engineering, control systems, electromagnetics, optics, power engineering, propagation and remote sensing, solid-state materials, and VLSI/CAD. A thesis or written comprehensive examination is required. This program can be completed almost entirely through coursework taken at approved corporate extension sites.

The 40-hour M.S. in Telecommunications focuses on IT-relevant concerns. A thesis or project is required.

The Ph.D. in Computer Science involves no specific course requirements; the student works with key faculty members to design an individualized program of study. Components are available in artificial intelligence, database systems, numerical computation, operating systems, parallel processing, programming languages, software engineering, and theory.

The Ph.D. in Electrical Engineering is available with informal concentrations in biomedical engineering, communication engineering and signal processing, computer engineering, control systems, electromagnetics, optics, power engineering, propagation and remote sensing, solid-state materials, and VLSI/CAD.

A qualifying examination is required in addition to the standard dissertation. Students must fulfill a residency requirement consisting of two consecutive semesters of full-time study.

Contact Information

PHONE
General information: (303) 492-1411
Admissions (undergraduate): (303) 492-2456
Computer science: (303) 492-7514
Electrical and computer engineering: (303) 492-7327

FAX
Computer science: (303) 492-2844

E-MAIL
Admissions (undergraduate): apply@colorado.edu
Computer science (undergraduate): David Smith (David.Smith@Colorado.EDU)
Computer science (graduate): Vicki Kunz (Vicki.Kunz@Colorado.EDU)
Electrical and computer engineering: eceinfo@schof.colorado.edu

---

University of Connecticut   www.uconn.edu ★★☆

Storrs, CT 06269

Year established: 1881
Ownership: Public

This large public, research-oriented university offers programs at all levels in traditional information technology fields. Evening classes, weekend study, distance learning, and statewide extension courses are available.

Degrees Offered

UNDERGRADUATE

B.S., Computer Engineering
B.S., Computer Science
ABET CSAB B.S., Computer Science and Engineering
ABET B.S., Electrical Engineering

GRADUATE

M.S., Computer Science and Engineering
M.S., Electrical Engineering
Ph.D., Computer Science and Engineering
Ph.D., Electrical Engineering

Approximate Cost of Degrees

UNDERGRADUATE, RESIDENT

$25,300

UNDERGRADUATE, NONRESIDENT

$60,400

MASTER'S, RESIDENT

$9,400

MASTER'S, NONRESIDENT

$22,000

DOCTORATE, RESIDENT

$15,700

DOCTORATE, NONRESIDENT

$36,700

Admissions Guidelines

UNDERGRADUATE

High school diploma, SAT and/or ACT generally
required (but can be waived for adult students)

GRADUATE

Accredited bachelor's with 3.0 GPA, GRE required

Undergraduate Programs

The hardware-oriented B.S. in Computer Engineering is available with formal concentrations in communications and computer networks, real-time computing systems, and VLSI design/fabrication.

The B.S. in Computer Science approaches issues in computer science theory, programming, and software engineering from a broad background in mathematics and the natural sciences.

The ABET-accredited and CSAB-accredited B.S. in Computer Science and Engineering deals with both fields from a primarily systems-oriented perspective. Formal concentrations are available in computer architecture and networks, graphics and imaging, and software engineering.

The ABET-accredited B.S. in Electrical Engineering is available with optional formal concentrations in computer engineering, electronic circuits and instrumentation, microelectronics, systems, and telecommunications.

Graduate Programs

The 30-hour M.S. in Computer Science and Engineering focuses on hardware-software interaction, software engineering, and theory. No thesis is required, but all students must pass a comprehensive written examination.

The 33-hour M.S. in Electrical Engineering is available with tracks in control/communication systems and electromagnetics/physical electronics. A written comprehensive examination is required; a thesis is not.

The Ph.D. in Computer Science and Engineering involves a foreign language requirement, a full year of full-time residency, and two examinations in addition to the standard dissertation. Students design individualized, faculty-approved plans based on personal research interests.

The Ph.D. in Electrical Engineering involves a foreign language requirement and a qualifying examination in addition to the standard dissertation. Students largely design individualized plans of study, but can focus their core requirements in the general direction of control/communication systems or electromagnetics/physical electronics.

Contact Information

PHONE

General information: (860) 486-2000
Admissions: (860) 486-3137
Computer science and engineering: (860) 486-3719
Electrical and computer engineering: (860) 486-4816

FAX

Admissions: (860) 486-3137
Electrical and computer engineering: (860) 486-2447

E-MAIL

Admissions (undergraduate):
beahusky@uconnvm.uconn.edu
Admissions (graduate):
MBalinsk@gris.grad.uconn.edu
Computer science and engineering:
Dr. Reda Ammar (reda@engr.uconn.edu)

University of Delaware

www.udel.edu ☆☆½

Newark, DE 19716

Year established: 1833
Ownership: Public

This major public university offers programs at all levels in the standard information technology fields. Students are encouraged to pursue independent study and research. Evening classes, distance learning, extension courses, and weekend study are available.

Degrees Offered

UNDERGRADUATE
B.A., Computer Science
B.S., Computer Science
B.C.E.
ⒶⒷⒺⓉ B.E.E.

GRADUATE
M.E.E.
M.S., Computer Science
Ph.D., Computer Science
Ph.D., Electrical Engineering

Approximate Cost of Degrees

UNDERGRADUATE, RESIDENT
$21,800

UNDERGRADUATE, NONRESIDENT
$55,400

MASTER'S, RESIDENT
$8,200

MASTER'S, NONRESIDENT
$20,800

DOCTORATE, RESIDENT
$13,700

DOCTORATE, NONRESIDENT
$34,700

Admissions Guidelines

UNDERGRADUATE
High school diploma, SAT and/or ACT required

GRADUATE
Accredited bachelor's with 3.0 GPA, GRE required

Undergraduate Programs

The B.A. and B.S. programs in Computer Science are roughly identical in their major requirements, differing largely in their general credit distribution requirements. Both approach the field from a broad, well-rounded background in mathematics and the natural sciences. The computer science major focuses on issues in software applications, theory, and programming.

The Bachelor of Computer Engineering (B.C.E.) takes a decisively hardware-oriented approach in its emphasis on digital systems, signal processing, and VLSI design.

The ABET-accredited Bachelor of Electrical Engineering (B.E.E.) centers primarily on a student-defined concentration within the field. The core requirements of this program tend to emphasize the theoretical background of the field, allowing considerable room for independent research.

Graduate Programs

The 30-hour Master of Electrical Engineering (M.E.E.) is available with formal specializations in integrated circuit fabrication technology and electromagnetics/optics. No thesis is required.

The 30-hour M.S. in Computer Science focuses on theory and hardware-software interaction. No thesis is required.

The Ph.D. in Computer Science involves a foreign language requirement and two examinations in addition to the standard coursework and dissertation requirements.

The Ph.D. in Electrical Engineering involves two written comprehensive examinations in addition to the standard coursework and dissertation requirements.

Contact Information

PHONE
General information: (302) 831-2000
Admissions (undergraduate): (302) 831-8125
Computer and information science: (302) 831-2712
Electrical and computer engineering: (302) 831-2405

FAX
Electrical and computer engineering: (302) 831-4316

E-MAIL
Admissions: admissions@udel.edu

University of Denver www.du.edu ☆☆☆½

2199 South University Boulevard
Denver, CO 80208

Year established: 1864
Ownership: Private

This large private university offers sound, theory-focused programs at all levels in information technology fields. Evening classes, extension courses, and distance learning are available.

Degrees Offered

UNDERGRADUATE
B.A., Applied Computing
(ABET) B.S., Computer Engineering
B.S., Computer Science
(ABET) B.S., Electrical Engineering

GRADUATE
M.S., Computer Engineering
M.S., Computer Science
M.S., Computer Science and Engineering
M.S., Electrical Engineering
Ph.D., Mathematics and Computer Science

Approximate Cost of Degrees

UNDERGRADUATE
$80,300

MASTER'S
$30,100

DOCTORATE
$50,200

Admissions Guidelines

UNDERGRADUATE
High school diploma, SAT and/or ACT required

GRADUATE
Accredited bachelor's, GRE required

Undergraduate Programs

The B.A. in Applied Computing is an extremely flexible, interdisciplinary program designed for students who want to apply computers to a specific, non-IT field (graphic design, health informatics, physics, and so forth).

The ABET-accredited B.S. in Computer Engineering emphasizes software in its core requirements, but a number of elective courses are available in software engineering.

The B.S. in Computer Science focuses on computational mathematics and issues in theoretical computer science. This program is particularly well-suited for students who want to eventually pursue graduate-level research in computer science.

The ABET-accredited B.S. in Electrical Engineering emphasizes digital systems, electronics, and signal processing in its core requirements, but a number of elective courses are available in other fields.

Graduate Programs

The 30-hour M.S. in Computer Engineering is available with concentrations in artificial and machine intelligence, computer/data communications and networks, computer systems and architecture, and communication systems and digital signal processing. No thesis is required.

The 32-hour M.S. in Computer Science focuses on issues in software engineering, programming, and advanced theoretical computer science. No thesis is required.

The 32-hour M.S. in Computer Science and Engineering incorporates theoretical computer science and applied computer engineering into a single, integrated curriculum. No thesis is required.

The 30-hour M.S. in Electrical Engineering is available with concentrations in electromagnetics/ quantum optics/semiconductors, signal processing and communications, and systems/controls. No thesis is required.

The Ph.D. in Mathematics and Computer Science is an interdisciplinary program focusing on theoretical computer science and advanced principles of applied and theoretical mathematics. A student-defined specialization in computational mathematics would certainly be within the boundaries of this program. A qualifying examination is required in addition to the standard coursework and dissertation requirements.

Other Programs

Interdisciplinary B.A. and M.A. programs in Digital Media Studies are also available. For more information, drop an e-mail to Dr. Jeff Rutenbeck (jrutenbe@du.edu).

The M.B.A. program of the Daniels College of Business is available with an information technology track. For more information, contact the college at (303) 871-3416.

Contact Information

PHONE
General information: (303) 871-2000
Admissions (undergraduate): (303) 871-2036 or (800) 525-9495
Admissions (graduate): (303) 871-3119 or (877) 871-3119
Computer science: (303) 871-2453

FAX
Admissions (undergraduate): (303) 871-3301
Admissions (graduate): (303) 871-4566
Computer science: (303) 871-3010

E-MAIL
Admissions (undergraduate): admission@du.edu
Admissions (graduate): grad-adm@du.edu
Computer science: info@cs.du.edu

University of Florida

www.ufl.edu ☆☆☆

Gainesville, FL 32611

Year established: 1853
Ownership: Public

This large state university offers research-oriented and professional programs in information technology at all levels. Evening classes, distance learning, and weekend study are available.

Degrees Offered

UNDERGRADUATE
B.S., Computer Science
🆎 B.S., Computer Engineering
🆎 B.S., Electrical Engineering

GRADUATE
M.Eng., Electrical and Computer Engineering
M.S., Computer Science
M.S., Electrical and Computer Engineering
C.I.S.E.
E.C.E.
Ph.D., Computer Science
Ph.D., Electrical and Computer Engineering

Approximate Cost of Degrees

UNDERGRADUATE, RESIDENT
$11,800

UNDERGRADUATE, NONRESIDENT
$41,200

MASTER'S, RESIDENT
$6,800

MASTER'S, NONRESIDENT
$20,400

DOCTORATE, RESIDENT
$11,300

DOCTORATE, NONRESIDENT
$34,100

Admissions Guidelines

UNDERGRADUATE
High school diploma with 2.0 GPA, SAT and/or ACT required

GRADUATE
Accredited bachelor's with 3.0 GPA, GRE required

Undergraduate Programs

The B.S. in Computer Science focuses on programming and software engineering. While students are given a solid background in theoretical computer science, the program as a whole focuses on application, maintenance, and development.

The ABET-accredited B.S. in Computer Engineering is available with specializations in computer information systems/engineering software and electrical/computer engineering hardware.

The ABET-accredited B.S. in Electrical Engineering is available with specializations in computers/communications/systems and controls, electromagnetics/power and photonics, and electronic devices/circuits.

Graduate Programs

The 33-hour M.Eng. and M.S. degrees in Electrical and Computer Engineering are available with specializations in communications, computer systems and networks, devices and physical electronics, digital signal processing, electric energy systems, electromagnetics, electronic circuits, intelligent and information systems, phonics, and systems/control. Neither program requires a thesis.

The 33-hour M.S. in Computer Science focuses on theory and software engineering. Formal specializations are available in algorithms and high performance computing, computer systems and architecture, database systems, intelligent systems, and software engineering. All students must pass a written comprehensive examination. No thesis is required.

The degree of Computer and Information Science Engineer (C.I.S.E.) is a unique post-master's program focusing on professional issues in the field. Formal specializations are available in algorithms and high performance computing, computer systems

and architecture, database systems, intelligent systems, and software engineering. A thesis is required.

The degree of Electrical and Computer Engineer (E.C.E.) is a unique, post-master's program focusing on professional issues in the field. Formal specializations are available in communications, computer systems and networks, devices and physical electronics, digital signal processing, electric energy systems, electromagnetics, electronic circuits, intelligent and information systems, photonics, and systems/control. A thesis is required.

The Ph.D. in Computer and Information Science is available with specializations in algorithms and high performance computing, computer systems and architecture, database systems, intelligent systems, and software engineering. Two written examinations are required in addition to the standard coursework and dissertation requirements.

The Ph.D. in Electrical and Computer Engineering is available with research specializations in communications, computer systems and networks, devices and physical electronics, digital signal processing, electric energy systems, electromagnetics, electronic circuits, intelligent and information systems, photonics, and systems/control. Two written examinations are required in addition to the standard coursework and dissertation requirements.

Other Programs

The B.S. in Business Administration is available with an emphasis in computer and information science; an M.S. in Decision and Information Sciences is also available. For more information, contact the Warrington College of Business at (352) 392-2397, extension 1217.

The new B.S. and M.S. programs in Digital Arts and Sciences are designed for students who want to work in the fields of graphic design and multimedia development. For more information, contact the Department of Computer and Information Science.

Contact Information

PHONE
General information: (352) 392-3261
Admissions (undergraduate): (352) 392-1365
Admissions (graduate): (352) 392-1582
Computer and information science: (352) 392-1200
Electrical and computer engineering: (352) 392-0912

FAX
Computer and information science: (352) 392-1220
Electrical and computer engineering: (352) 392-8671

E-MAIL
Admissions (undergraduate): freshman@ufl.edu
Admissions (graduate): gradinfo@ufl.edu
Computer/information science (undergraduate):
Janet King (janet@cise.ufl.edu)

Computer/information science (graduate): Dr. D.D.
Dankel, II (ddd@cise.ufl.edu)
Computer engineering (undergraduate): Steve
Permann (steve@ece.ufl.edu)
Electrical engineering (undergraduate): Laurel
Edvardsson (laurie@eng.ufl.edu)
Electrical/computer engineering (graduate):
info@graduate.ece.ufl.edu

University of Georgia

Athens, GA 30602

www.uga.edu ☆☆☆

Year established: 1785
Ownership: Public

This large public university offers degrees at all levels in computer science and related interdisciplinary fields. Of particular interest is the M.S. in Artificial Intelligence, which addresses the issue from a variety of IT and non-IT perspectives. Evening classes, weekend study, extension courses, and distance learning are available.

Degrees Offered

UNDERGRADUATE
B.S., Computer Science

GRADUATE
M.S., Artificial Intelligence
M.S., Computer Science
Ph.D., Computer Science

Approximate Cost of Degrees

UNDERGRADUATE, RESIDENT
$14,800

UNDERGRADUATE, NONRESIDENT
$45,200

MASTER'S, RESIDENT
$6,300

MASTER'S, NONRESIDENT
$17,700

DOCTORATE, RESIDENT
$10,500

DOCTORATE, NONRESIDENT
$29,500

Admissions Guidelines

UNDERGRADUATE
High school diploma, SAT and/or ACT required

GRADUATE
Accredited bachelor's, GRE required

Undergraduate Programs
The B.S. in Computer Science focuses on programming and software engineering issues from a broad background in computational mathematics and theoretical computer science.

Graduate Programs
The 33-hour M.S. in Artificial Intelligence focuses on interdisciplinary issues in computer science, electromechanical engineering, semantics, psychology, and philosophy. A thesis is required.

The 32-hour M.S. in Computer Science heavily emphasizes theoretical computer science, computational mathematics, and software engineering. A thesis is required.

The Ph.D. in Computer Science offers formal research concentrations in artificial intelligence, computational science, computer architecture, distributed information systems, image processing and vision, modeling and simulation, parallel processing, and theory. Two comprehensive written examinations are involved in addition to the standard coursework and dissertation requirements.

Other Programs
M.Ed., Ed.S., and Ph.D. programs are available in Instructional Technology and Computer-Based

Education. For more information, contact the College of Education at (706) 542-3810.

The Terry College of Business B.B.A. is available with a management information systems concentration. For more information, call the college at (706) 542-8100.

A telecommunications emphasis is available within the Bachelor of Journalism (B.J.) program. For more information, contact the Department of Journalism at (706) 542-1704.

Contact Information

PHONE
General information: (706) 542-3000
Admissions (undergraduate): (706) 542-2112

Admissions (graduate): (706) 542-1739
Artificial intelligence: (706) 542-0358
Computer science: (706) 542-2911

FAX
Admissions (undergraduate): (706) 542-1466
Computer science: (706) 542-2966

E-MAIL
Admissions (undergraduate):
undergrad@admissions.uga.edu
Admissions (graduate): gradadm@uga.edu
Distance learning: usgis@uga.edu
Artificial intelligence: Angie Paul
(aspaul@ai.uga.edu)
Computer science: mjp@cs.uga.edu

University of Hawaii at Manoa www.uhm.hawaii.edu ☆☆☆

2444 Dole Street
Honolulu, HI 96822

Year established: 1907
Ownership: Public

This major state university offers an array of information technology programs, ranging from the highly traditional ABET-accredited B.S. in Electrical Engineering to the highly innovative Ph.D. in Communications and Information Sciences. Evening classes, weekend study, and distance learning are available.

Degrees Offered

UNDERGRADUATE
B.A., Information and Computer Science
B.S., Information and Computer Science
(ABET) B.S., Electrical Engineering

GRADUATE
M.S., Electrical Engineering
M.S., Information and Computer Science
Ph.D., Communications and Information Sciences
Ph.D., Electrical Engineering
Ph.D., Information and Computer Science

Approximate Cost of Degrees

UNDERGRADUATE, RESIDENT
$16,600

UNDERGRADUATE, NONRESIDENT
$42,500

MASTER'S, RESIDENT
$7,700

MASTER'S, NONRESIDENT
$16,600

DOCTORATE, RESIDENT
$12,900

DOCTORATE, NONRESIDENT
$27,700

Admissions Guidelines

UNDERGRADUATE
High school diploma, SAT and/or ACT required

GRADUATE
Accredited bachelor's required, GRE generally required (but may be waived for electrical engineering M.S. program)

Undergraduate Programs
The ABET-accredited B.S. in Electrical Engineering emphasizes electronics, signal processing, and computer engineering. A considerable portion of this program can be completed by distance learning.

The B.A. and B.S. programs in Information and Computer Science are roughly identical in their major requirements, differing largely in overall credit distribution requirements. Students are encouraged to design individualized tracks.

Graduate Programs

The 30-hour M.S. in Electrical Engineering is available with formal tracks in computers, electrophysics, and systems. No thesis is required.

The 30-hour M.S. in Information and Computer Science focuses on software engineering and theoretical computer science. A thesis or project is required.

The Ph.D. in Communications and Information Sciences is an interdisciplinary program offered through the Departments of Communication, Decision Sciences, Information and Computer Science, and Library and Information Systems. Specializations are available in communication and information theories, computer software systems, data communications, information storage/retrieval, management information systems, organizational communication, and policy/planning. Students must pass a written comprehensive examination in addition to satisfying the standard dissertation and coursework requirements.

The Ph.D. in Electrical Engineering involves three written comprehensive examinations in addition to the standard dissertation and coursework requirements.

The Ph.D. in Information and Computer Science emphasizes theoretical computer science. Students must pass a written comprehensive examination in addition to satisfying the standard dissertation and coursework requirements.

Other Programs

A management information systems emphasis is available within the B.B.A. program of the Department of Management and Industrial Relations. For more information, contact the College of Business Administration at (808) 956-8215.

An M.Ed. in Educational Technology is available through the College of Education. For more information, contact the Department of Educational Technology at (808) 956-7671.

Contact Information

Phone
General information: (808) 956-8111
Communications and information sciences: (808) 956-5815
Electrical engineering: (808) 956-7586
Information and computer science: (808) 956-7420

Fax
Communications and information sciences: (808) 956-5835
Electrical engineering: (808) 956-3427
Information and computer science: (808) 956-3548

E-mail
Communications and information sciences: Rebecca Knuth (knuth@hawaii.edu)
Electrical engineering: eeoffice@spectra.eng.hawaii.edu

University of Houston

www.uh.edu ☆☆☆½

4800 Calhoun Road
Houston, TX 77204

Year established: 1927
Ownership: Public

This major public university is definitely one to watch. With programs at every level in traditional and highly nontraditional fields of study and new programs being added to the mix on a regular basis, this world-class university will soon be acknowledged as the major contender that it so obviously is. Evening classes, extension courses, and distance learning are available.

Degrees Offered

Undergraduate
B.S., Computer Engineering
(CSAB) B.S., Computer Science
(ABET) B.S., Electrical Engineering

(ABET) B.S.T., Computer Engineering Technology
(ABET) B.S.T., Electrical Technology

Graduate
M.E.E.
M.S., Computer and Systems Engineering

M.S., Computer Science
M.S., Electrical and Computer Engineering
M.Tech., Microcomputer Systems
Ph.D., Computer and Systems Engineering
Ph.D., Computer Science
Ph.D., Electrical and Computer Engineering

Approximate Cost of Degrees

UNDERGRADUATE, RESIDENT
$13,300

UNDERGRADUATE, NONRESIDENT
$34,100

MASTER'S, RESIDENT
$5,000

MASTER'S, NONRESIDENT
$12,400

DOCTORATE, RESIDENT
$7,700

DOCTORATE, NONRESIDENT
$19,900

Admissions Guidelines

UNDERGRADUATE
High school diploma with 2.5 GPA, SAT and/or ACT required

GRADUATE
Accredited bachelor's, GRE required

Undergraduate Programs

The B.S. in Computer Engineering focuses on hardware-software interaction and software engineering. This highly flexible program allows a considerable amount of room for student-defined specialization.

The CSAB-accredited B.S. in Computer Science approaches issues in software engineering and theory from a broad background in computational mathematics and the natural sciences. Tracks are available in business information systems and computational science.

The ABET-accredited B.S. in Electrical Engineering is available with two possible tracks: electrical engineering (with optional specializations in electromagnetics and solid-state devices, electronics, power and controls, and signals/communications)

and computer engineering. The latter track focuses a great deal more on hardware issues than does the B.S. in Computer Engineering.

The ABET-accredited B.S. in Technology (B.S.T.) in Computer Engineering Technology deals primarily with issues related to programming and software engineering.

The ABET-accredited B.S.T. in Electrical Technology is available with tracks in control systems and electrical power.

Graduate Programs

The 36-hour Master of Electrical Engineering (M.E.E.) is available with three possible tracks: electrical engineering (with optional specializations in control systems, electromagnetics and microelectronics, electronics and computers, power systems, and signals/communications), industrial power systems, and telecommunications. No thesis is required.

The 30-hour M.S. in Computer and Systems Engineering focuses on hardware-software interaction and low-level programming. A thesis is required.

The 30-hour M.S. in Computer Science deals primarily with advanced issues in software engineering and applications. A thesis is strongly encouraged, but a 36-hour non-thesis track is available. This program can be completed almost entirely by extension.

The 30-hour M.S. in Electrical and Computer Engineering is available with research specializations in applied electromagnetics, biomedical engineering, computer engineering, control systems, electronics, intelligent systems, microelectronics, optoelectronics, power systems, signal and image processing, telecommunications, and well logging (yes, well logging). A thesis is required. This program can be completed almost entirely by extension.

The 34-hour Master of Technology (M.Tech.) in Microcomputer Systems emphasizes digital systems, neural nets, and hardware-hardware interaction. No thesis is required.

The Ph.D. in Computer and Systems Engineering focuses on advanced research issues in hardware-software interaction and low-level programming. A qualifying examination is required in addition to the standard dissertation and coursework requirements.

The Ph.D. in Computer Science focuses on advanced theoretical issues in computer science; in its applied components, the program tends to emphasize software engineering. A qualifying examination and one year of full-time residency are involved in addition to the standard dissertation and coursework requirements. Students may, at faculty discretion, be asked to fulfill a foreign language requirement.

The Ph.D. in Electrical Engineering is available with research specializations in applied electromagnetics, biomedical engineering, computer engineering, control systems, electronics, intelligent systems, microelectronics, optoelectronics, power systems, signal and image processing, telecommunications, and well logging. A qualifying examination is required in addition to the standard dissertation and coursework requirements.

Other Programs

M.Ed. and Ed.D. programs in Instructional Technology are available through the College of Education. For more information, contact the Department of Curriculum and Instruction at (713) 743-4977.

B.B.A., M.B.A., and Ph.D. programs are available with tracks in management information systems. For more information, contact the College of Business at (713) 743-1010.

The ABET-accredited B.S.T. in Mechanical Technology is available with a computer drafting design concentration. The upper-level requirements for this program can be completed by distance learning. For more information, contact the university.

Contact Information

PHONE
General information: (713) 743-2255
Admissions: (713) 743-1010
Computer science: (713) 743-3350
Electrical and computer engineering: (713) 743-4400

FAX
Computer science: (713) 743-3335
Electrical and computer engineering: (713) 743-4444

E-MAIL
Admissions: admissions@uh.edu
Computer science (undergraduate): undergra@cs.uh.edu
Computer science (graduate): gradinfo@cs.uh.edu
Electrical and computer engineering: Dr. Frank Claydon (fclaydon@pop.uh.edu)
Technology: Katherine Lambert (klambert@bayou.uh.edu)

University of Houston—Clear Lake   www.cl.uh.edu ☆☆☆

2700 Bay Area Boulevard
Houston, TX 77058

Year established: 1974
Ownership: Public

This unique state-funded university is dedicated solely to upper-level and graduate-level education. Evening classes, weekend study, extension courses, and distance learning are available.

Degrees Offered

UNDERGRADUATE
B.S., Computer Information Systems
B.S., Computer Sciences
B.S., Computer Systems Engineering

GRADUATE
M.S., Computer Engineering
M.S., Computer Information Systems
M.S., Computer Sciences
M.S., Software Engineering

Approximate Cost of Degrees

UNDERGRADUATE (UPPER 60 HOURS), RESIDENT
$7,100

UNDERGRADUATE (UPPER 60 HOURS), NONRESIDENT
$21,000

GRADUATE, RESIDENT
$5,000

GRADUATE, NONRESIDENT
$10,000

Admissions Guidelines

UNDERGRADUATE
Associate's degree or 54 hours college credit, 2.0 GPA, good standing with last institution attended, and TASP exam (or exemption from TASP exam) required. Students with fewer hours of college credit can be admitted provisionally.

GRADUATE
Accredited bachelor's with good standing, GRE required

Undergraduate Programs
The B.S. in Computer Information Systems is an intensive program focused on issues in programming, software engineering, and hardware-software interaction.

The B.S. in Computer Systems Engineering focuses on networking and hardware-software interaction.

The B.S. in Computer Sciences focuses on software engineering, programming, and theoretical computer science. This highly flexible program allows considerable room for student-defined specialization.

Graduate Programs
The 36-hour M.S. in Computer Engineering is available with formal specializations in computer systems networking and telecommunications. No thesis is required.

The 36-hour M.S. in Computer Information Systems is available with formal specializations in database systems and networking. The program focuses intensively on hardware-software interaction issues,

software engineering, and theory. No thesis is required.

The 36-hour M.S. in Computer Sciences is available with formal specializations in graphics and image processing, knowledge systems and databases, and computer systems. No thesis is required.

The 36-hour M.S. in Software Engineering is available with formal specializations in information management, mission- and safety-critical systems, and software management. No thesis is required. The entire program can be completed through extension courses offered at various locations throughout Texas.

Other Programs
An M.S. in Instructional Technology is also available. For more information, contact the School of Education at (281) 283-3615.

B.S., M.B.A., and M.S. programs are available in management information systems. For more information, contact the College of Business and Public Administration at (281) 283-3100.

Contact Information

PHONE
General information: (281) 283-7600
Admissions: (281) 283-2508
Computer information systems: (281) 283-3864
Computer sciences: (281) 283-3865

E-MAIL
Computer information systems: Dr. Kwok-Bun Yue (yue@cl.uh.edu)
Computer sciences: Dr. Sadegh Davari (davari@cl.uh.edu)
Software engineering: SE@cl.uh.edu

University of Idaho   www.uidaho.edu ☆☆½

Moscow, ID 83844

Year established: 1889
Ownership: Public

This large public university offers traditional information technology programs at all levels through a variety of delivery methods, both traditional and otherwise. Both M.Eng. programs described below can be completed nonresidentially. Evening classes, weekend study, extension courses, and distance learning are available.

Degrees Offered

UNDERGRADUATE
ABET B.S., Computer Engineering
CSAB B.S., Computer Science
ABET B.S., Electrical Engineering

GRADUATE
M.Eng., Computer Engineering
M.Eng., Electrical Engineering
M.S., Computer Engineering
M.S., Computer Science
M.S., Electrical Engineering
Ph.D., Computer Science
Ph.D., Electrical Engineering

Approximate Cost of Degrees

UNDERGRADUATE, RESIDENT
$14,600

UNDERGRADUATE, NONRESIDENT
$38,200

MASTER'S, RESIDENT
$5,800–$8,800

MASTER'S, NONRESIDENT
$14,800–$17,400

DOCTORATE, RESIDENT
$9,700–$14,600

DOCTORATE, NONRESIDENT
$24,700–$29,000

Admissions Guidelines

UNDERGRADUATE
High school diploma with 2.0 GPA, SAT and/or ACT required

GRADUATE
Accredited bachelor's, GRE required

Undergraduate Programs
The ABET-accredited B.S. in Computer Engineering focuses on digital systems, electronics, and other hardware-related issues.

The CSAB-accredited B.S. in Computer Science focuses heavily on theory and databases.

The ABET-accredited B.S. in Electrical Engineering is available with specializations in communication systems, control systems, digital signal processing, digital systems, electromagnetics, electronics, and power systems.

Graduate Programs
The 36-hour M.Eng. programs in Computer Engineering and Electrical Engineering are designed with reentry students in mind. No thesis is required, and either program can be completed entirely by distance learning and/or extension courses.

The 36-hour M.S. in Computer Engineering focuses on hardware-software interaction, software engineering, and networking. A thesis is encouraged, but not required.

The 36-hour M.S. in Computer Science focuses on theory within its core components. An optional 15-hour software engineering focus is available. A thesis is encouraged, but not required.

The 36-hour M.S. in Electrical Engineering focuses on digital systems, electronics, and control systems. A thesis is encouraged, but not required.

The Ph.D. in Computer Science can be tailored to meet the research interests of nearly any student. A preliminary examination is required of all students, and a qualifying examination is required of all students who do not possess an M.S. in Computer Science. Two semesters of full-time residency are required in addition to the standard coursework and dissertation requirements.

The Ph.D. in Electrical Engineering is available with research emphases in communication systems, computer engineering, control systems, digital signal processing, digital systems, electromagnetics, electronics, and power systems.

Two semesters of full-time residency are required in addition to the standard coursework and dissertation requirements.

Other Programs
An information systems emphasis is available within the B.S. in the Business program. For more information, contact the Department of Business at (208) 885-7341.

Contact Information

PHONE
General information: (208) 885-6111
Admissions (undergraduate): (208) 885-6326 or (888) 884-3246
Admissions (graduate): (208) 885-4001

Computer science: (208) 885-6589
Electrical engineering: (208) 885-6554

E-MAIL
General information: info@uidaho.edu
Admissions (undergraduate): admappl@uidaho.edu

Admissions (graduate): gadms@uidaho.edu
Computer engineering: James Frenzel
(jfrenzel@uidaho.edu)
Computer science: chair@cs.uidaho.edu
Electrical engineering: Becky Huffman
(becky@ee.uidaho.edu)

University of Iowa · www.uiowa.edu ☆☆☆

Iowa City, IA 52242

Year established: 1847
Ownership: Public

This major state university offers programs at all levels in the hottest information technology fields. Evening classes, weekend study, and distance learning are available.

Degrees Offered

UNDERGRADUATE
B.A., Computer Science
B.S., Computer Science
(ABET) B.S., Electrical Engineering

GRADUATE
M.C.S.
M.S., Computer Science
M.S., Electrical and Computer Engineering
Ph.D., Computer Science
Ph.D., Electrical and Computer Engineering

Approximate Cost of Degrees

UNDERGRADUATE, RESIDENT
$16,800

UNDERGRADUATE, NONRESIDENT
$66,200

MASTER'S, RESIDENT
$7,100

MASTER'S, NONRESIDENT
$18,600

DOCTORATE, RESIDENT
$11,900

DOCTORATE, NONRESIDENT
$31,000

Admissions Guidelines

UNDERGRADUATE
High school diploma, SAT and/or ACT required

GRADUATE
Accredited bachelor's with 2.5 GPA, GRE required

Undergraduate Programs

The B.A. and B.S. programs in Computer Science are roughly identical in their major requirements, differing primarily in general credit distribution. The former places more weight on a solid liberal arts education, while the latter involves more credit in mathematics and the natural sciences.

The ABET-accredited B.S. in Electrical Engineering focuses on electronics, signal processing, and computer engineering.

Graduate Programs

The 30-hour Master of Computer Science (M.C.S.) is available with formal specializations in artificial intelligence, computation science, programming languages, software engineering, and in systems and networks. A capstone project is required.

The 33-hour M.S. in Computer Science is available with formal specializations in artificial intelligence, computation science, programming languages, software engineering, and in systems and networks. A thesis is required.

The 30-hour M.S. in Electrical and Computer Engineering focuses on electronics, networking, signal processing, hardware-software interaction, and software engineering. No thesis is required.

The Ph.D. in Computer Science requires two written examinations in addition to the standard coursework and dissertation requirements.

The Ph.D. in Electrical and Computer Engineering focuses on digital systems, electronics, signal processing, and hardware-software interaction.

Other Programs

M.A. and Ph.D. programs in Instructional Design and Technology are also available. For more information, contact the College of Education at (319) 335-5995.

Contact Information

PHONE
General information: (319) 335-3500

Admissions: (319) 335-3847 or (800) 553-4692
Computer science: (319) 335-0713

FAX
Computer science: (319) 335-3624

E-MAIL
Computer science: csinfo@cs.uiowa.edu
Electrical and computer engineering:
ece@eng.uiowa.edu

University of Kansas

Lawrence, KS 66045

www.ukans.edu ☆☆½

Year established: 1864
Ownership: Public

This large public university offers programs at all levels in the most popular information technology fields. Evening classes, weekend study, and distance learning are available.

Degrees Offered

UNDERGRADUATE
(ABET) B.S., Computer Engineering
(CSAB) B.S., Computer Science
(ABET) B.S., Electrical Engineering

GRADUATE
M.S., Computer Engineering
M.S., Computer Science
M.S., Electrical Engineering
D.Eng., Electrical Engineering
Ph.D., Computer Science
Ph.D., Electrical Engineering

Approximate Cost of Degrees

UNDERGRADUATE, RESIDENT
$14,600

UNDERGRADUATE, NONRESIDENT
$42,300

MASTER'S, RESIDENT
$5,400

MASTER'S, NONRESIDENT
$14,300

DOCTORATE, RESIDENT
$9,000

DOCTORATE, NONRESIDENT
$23,800

Admissions Guidelines

UNDERGRADUATE
High school diploma, SAT and/or ACT required

GRADUATE
Accredited bachelor's, GRE required

Undergraduate Programs

The ABET-accredited B.S. in Computer Engineering gives roughly equal weight to electronics, programming, and hardware-software interaction.

The CSAB-accredited B.S. in Computer Science is a heavily programming-focused degree, although students are given a solid background in theory as well.

The ABET-accredited B.S. in Electrical Engineering focuses on circuits, control systems, and signal processing.

Graduate Programs

The 30-hour M.S. in Computer Engineering focuses on networking in its core requirements. No thesis is required.

The 30-hour M.S. in Computer Science focuses on theory and software engineering. No thesis is required.

The 30-hour M.S. in Electrical Engineering primarily deals with signal processing and telecommunications in its core requirements. No thesis is required.

The D.Eng. in Electrical Engineering requires a supervised industrial internship and qualifying examination in addition to the standard coursework and dissertation requirements.

The Ph.D. in Computer Science is available with tracks emphasizing applied computing or theoretical computer science. A qualifying examination is required in addition to the standard coursework and dissertation requirements.

The Ph.D. in Electrical Engineering is available with tracks emphasizing computer engineering or telecommunications. A qualifying examination is required in addition to the standard coursework and dissertation requirements.

Contact Information

PHONE
General information: (785) 864-2700
Admissions (undergraduate): (785) 864-3911
Admissions (graduate): (785) 864-4141
Electrical engineering and computer science:
(785) 864-4620

FAX
Electrical engineering and computer science:
(785) 864-3226

E-MAIL
Admissions (undergraduate): adm@ukans.edu
Admissions (graduate): graduate@raven.cc.ukans.edu

University of Louisville

www.louisville.edu ☆☆½

S. Third Street
Louisville, KY 40292

Year established: 1798
Ownership: Public

This major public university offers unique programs at all levels in several information technology fields. Evening classes, weekend study, and distance learning are available.

Degrees Offered

UNDERGRADUATE
B.S., Computer Information Systems
B.S., Electrical Engineering
CSAB B.S., Engineering Mathematics and Computer Science

GRADUATE
ABET M.Eng., Electrical Engineering
ABET M.Eng., Engineering Mathematics and Computer Science
M.S., Computer Science
Ph.D., Computer Science and Engineering
Ph.D., Electrical Engineering

Approximate Cost of Degrees

UNDERGRADUATE, RESIDENT
$17,000

UNDERGRADUATE, NONRESIDENT
$40,700

MASTER'S, RESIDENT
$6,800

MASTER'S, NONRESIDENT
$16,600

DOCTORATE, RESIDENT
$11,400

DOCTORATE, NONRESIDENT
$27,700

Admissions Guidelines

UNDERGRADUATE
High school diploma, SAT and/or ACT required

GRADUATE
Accredited bachelor's with 2.5 GPA, GRE required

Undergraduate Programs

The B.S. in Computer Information Systems focuses on software applications, programming, and management information systems. The program is offered through the College of Business and Public Administration.

The B.S. in Electrical Engineering focuses on signal processing and networking, digital systems, and computer engineering.

The CSAB-accredited B.S. in Engineering Mathematics and Computer Science focuses on programming and hardware-software interaction.

Graduate Programs

The 30-hour ABET-accredited Master of Engineering (M.Eng.) in Electrical Engineering focuses on digital systems, signal processing and networking/telecommunications, and computer engineering. A thesis is required, and all students must pass a final comprehensive examination.

The 30-hour ABET-accredited Master of Engineering (M.Eng.) in Engineering Mathematics and Computer Science focuses on programming, software engineering, theory, and hardware-software interaction. A thesis is required, and all students must pass a final comprehensive examination.

The 36-hour M.S. in Computer Science focuses on computer science theory and software engineering. No thesis is required.

The Ph.D. in Computer Science and Engineering involves a qualifying examination in addition to the standard coursework and dissertation requirements.

The Ph.D. in Electrical Engineering focuses on computer engineering, physical electronics, and signal processing. A qualifying examination is required in addition to the standard coursework and dissertation requirements.

Contact Information

PHONE
General information: (502) 852-5555 or (800) 334-8635
Computer engineering and computer science: (502) 852-6304
Computer information systems: (502) 852-6440
Electrical and computer engineering: (502) 852-6289

FAX
Computer information systems: (502) 852-7557

E-MAIL
Admissions (undergraduate):
admitme@louisville.edu
Admissions (graduate):
gradmit@gwise.louisville.edu

University of Maine

Orono, ME 04469

www.umaine.edu ☆☆☆

Year established: 1865
Ownership: Public

This major research-oriented public university offers programs at all levels in the hottest information technology fields. Evening classes, weekend study, extension courses, and distance learning are available.

Degrees Offered

UNDERGRADUATE
B.A., Computer Science
(CSAB) B.S., Computer Science
(ABET) B.S., Computer Engineering
(ABET) B.S., Electrical Engineering
(ABET) B.S., Electrical Engineering Technology

GRADUATE
M.S., Computer Engineering
M.S., Computer Science
M.S., Electrical Engineering
Ph.D., Computer Science
Ph.D., Electrical Engineering

Approximate Cost of Degrees

UNDERGRADUATE, RESIDENT
$22,600

UNDERGRADUATE, NONRESIDENT
$54,000

MASTER'S, RESIDENT
$8,800

MASTER'S, NONRESIDENT
$20,300

DOCTORATE, RESIDENT
$14,600

DOCTORATE, NONRESIDENT
$33,800

Admissions Guidelines

UNDERGRADUATE
High school diploma, SAT and/or ACT required

GRADUATE
Accredited bachelor's, GRE required

Undergraduate Programs

The B.A. in Computer Science and the CSAB-accredited B.S. in Computer Science are fairly similar in their major courses, differing largely in general distribution requirements. While the B.A. incorporates a broad liberal arts and social sciences background into the curriculum, the B.S. focuses more on IT-pertinent foundations such as mathematics and the natural sciences.

The ABET-accredited B.S. in Computer Engineering is available with formal concentrations in communications, computer graphics, digital control, integrated circuit design, machine vision, power systems, and robotics.

The ABET-accredited B.S. in Electrical Engineering is available with formal concentrations in analog electronics, communications and signal processing, computer hardware, digital electronics, fields/waves/devices, and in power and industrial control.

The ABET-accredited B.S. in Electrical Engineering Technology incorporates study of manufacturing, management, and quality control into a solid electrical engineering curriculum.

Graduate Programs

The 30-hour M.S. in Computer Engineering emphasizes computer hardware, hardware-software interaction, and software engineering. A thesis is required.

The 30-hour M.S. in Computer Science focuses on theory and software issues. A thesis or project is required.

The 30-hour M.S. in Electrical Engineering emphasizes systems engineering, electronics, and signal processing. A thesis is required.

The Ph.D. programs in Computer Science and Electrical Engineering each require a comprehensive examination in addition to the standard coursework and dissertation requirements.

Contact Information

PHONE
Admissions (undergraduate): (207) 581-1561 or (877) 486-2364
Admissions (graduate): (207) 581-3217
Computer science: (207) 581-3941
Electrical and computer engineering: (207) 581-2223

FAX
Admissions (undergraduate): (207) 581-1213
Admissions (graduate): (207) 581-3232

E-MAIL
Admissions (undergraduate): UM-ADMIT@MAINE.EDU
Admissions (graduate): graduate@maine.edu
Computer science: Ellen Johndro (EllenJohndro@umit.maine.edu)

University of Maryland University College

www.umuc.edu ☆☆☆

3501 University Boulevard East
Adelphi, MD 20783

Year established: 1950
Ownership: Public

As the adult learning campus for the University of Maryland system, the University College offers undergraduate and graduate degrees at all levels. All programs can be completed through weekend study, evening classes, life experience credit, transfer credit, and/or distance learning.

Degrees Offered

UNDERGRADUATE
B.A., Computer and Information Science
B.S., Computer and Information Science
B.A., Computer Information Technology

B.S., Computer Information Technology
B.A., Computer Science
B.S., Computer Science
B.A., Computer Studies
B.S., Computer Studies

GRADUATE

M.S., Computer Systems Management
M.S., Electronic Commerce
M.S., Information Technology
M.S., Telecommunications Management
M.Sw.E.

Approximate Cost of Degrees

UNDERGRADUATE, RESIDENT
$24,400

UNDERGRADUATE, NONRESIDENT
$32,300

UNDERGRADUATE, ACTIVE-DUTY MILITARY (RESIDENT OR NONRESIDENT)
$17,700

GRADUATE, RESIDENT
$10,500

GRADUATE, NONRESIDENT
$14,300

Admissions Guidelines

UNDERGRADUATE
High school diploma required, SAT and/or ACT recommended

GRADUATE
Accredited bachelor's, GRE required

Undergraduate Programs

The major in Computer and Information Science is available with informal concentrations in database systems, languages and systems, networking and distributed systems, and software engineering. This program can be completed by distance learning.

The new major in Computer Information Technology focuses on applied computing, quality control issues, and hardware-software interaction.

The major in Computer Science is really a very traditional one for its field, focusing primarily on theory and programming issues.

The interdisciplinary major in Computer Studies focuses on computing rather than computer science, computer engineering, or computer information systems. Emphasis is placed on study of computers, software applications, and their practical use. This program can be completed by distance learning.

Graduate Programs

The 36-hour M.S. in Computer Systems Management is available with formal concentrations in applied computer systems, database systems and security, information resources management, and software development management. A final project is required. This program can be completed by distance learning.

The new 33-hour M.S. in Electronic Commerce focuses on dot-com business strategies and technologies. A final project is required.

The new 36-hour M.S. in Information Technology is available with informal concentrations in computer systems, databases, information technology management, software systems, and telecommunications. A final project is required.

The 39-hour M.S. in Telecommunications Management focuses as much on formal telecommunications science and engineering as it does on management. No thesis is required. This program can be completed by distance learning.

The 36-hour Master of Software Engineering (M.Sw.E.) addresses programming, project management, and quality assurance from a systems-oriented perspective. A capstone project is required. This program can be completed by distance learning.

Other Programs

B.A. and B.S. programs in Information Systems Management are also available and can be completed by distance learning. For more information, contact the undergraduate admissions office.

M.S. programs in Management (with emphasis in management information systems) and Technology Management are also available and can be completed by distance learning. For more information, contact the graduate admissions office.

Contact Information

PHONE
Admissions (undergraduate): (301) 985-7000 or (800) 283-6832
Admissions (graduate): (301) 985-4617 or (800) 283-6832
Computer science and information technology: (301) 985-7787

E-MAIL
General information: info@umuc.edu
Computer and information science: Dr. S.K. Bhaskar (sbhaskar@nova.umuc.edu)
Computer science: Dr. Nicholas Duchon (duchon@nova.umuc.edu)
Computer studies: A.K. Huseonica (ahuseonica@umuc.edu)

Computer systems management: Dr. Paul F.G. Keller (pkeller@polaris.umuc.edu)
Electronic commerce: Bob Ouellette (rouellette@umuc.edu)
Information technology: John Richardson (jrichardson@umuc.edu)
Software engineering: mswe@umuc.edu
Telecommunications management: Dr. Bernard Carver (bcarver@umuc.edu)

University of Maryland   www.maryland.edu ☆☆☆

College Park, MD 20742

Year established: 1856
Ownership: Public

This cutting-edge public university offers programs at every level in all the hottest information technology fields. Evening classes, weekend study, corporate extension courses, and distance learning are available.

Degrees Offered

UNDERGRADUATE
B.S., Computer Engineering
B.S., Computer Science
ABET B.S., Electrical Engineering

GRADUATE
M.Eng., Electrical Engineering
M.S., Computer Science
M.S., Electrical Engineering
M.S., Telecommunications
Ph.D., Computer Science
Ph.D., Electrical Engineering

Approximate Cost of Degrees

UNDERGRADUATE, RESIDENT
$24,600

UNDERGRADUATE, NONRESIDENT
$53,500

MASTER'S, RESIDENT
$11,800

MASTER'S, NONRESIDENT
$17,200

DOCTORATE, RESIDENT
$19,700

DOCTORATE, NONRESIDENT
$32,800

Admissions Guidelines

UNDERGRADUATE
High school diploma, SAT and/or ACT required

GRADUATE
Accredited bachelor's, GRE required

Undergraduate Programs

The B.S. in Computer Engineering stresses computational mathematics, networking, and software engineering.

The B.S. in Computer Science is available with informal specializations in computer systems, information processing, numerical analysis, programming languages and software engineering, and theory of computing.

The ABET-accredited B.S. in Electrical Engineering is available with informal specializations in communications and signal processing, computer engineering, controls, electrophysics, microelectronics, and power systems.

Graduate Programs

The 33-hour Master of Engineering (M.Eng.) in Electrical Engineering is a professional degree designed specifically for reentry students. No thesis is required.

The 30-hour M.S. in Computer Science is available with informal specializations in artificial intelligence, computer systems, database systems, programming languages, scientific computing, software engineering, theory of computing, and visual/geometric computing. No thesis is required.

The 30-hour M.S. in Electrical Engineering focuses on digital systems, electronics, and communications/signal processing. No thesis is required.

The new 35-hour M.S. in Telecommunications incorporates study of relevant policy and management issues into a solid, rigorous telecommunications engineering curriculum. A final project is required.

The Ph.D. program in Computer Science involves two comprehensive written examinations in addition to the standard coursework and dissertation requirements.

The Ph.D. program in Electrical Engineering involves a qualifying examination in addition to the standard coursework and dissertation requirements.

Contact Information

PHONE
General information: (301) 405-1000
Admissions (graduate): (301) 405-4198
Computer science (undergraduate): (301) 405-2672
Computer science (graduate): (301) 405-2664
Electrical and computer engineering (undergraduate): (301) 405-3685
Electrical and computer engineering (graduate): (301) 405-3681
Telecommunications: (301) 405-8189

FAX
Admissions (graduate): (301) 314-9305
Computer science: (301) 405-6707

E-MAIL
Admissions (graduate): gradmit@deans.umd.edu
Computer science (undergraduate): ugrad@cs.umd.edu
Computer science (graduate): csgradof@cs.umd.edu
Electrical and computer engineering (undergraduate): eeadvise@deans.umd.edu
Electrical and computer engineering (graduate): eneegrad@deans.umd.edu
Telecommunications: Asante Shakuur (ashakuur@eng.umd.edu)

University of Massachusetts—Amherst   www.umass.edu ☆☆☆

Amherst, MA 01003

Year established: 1863
Ownership: Public

This major public university offers degrees at all levels in the most popular information technology fields. Evening classes, weekend study, extension courses, and distance learning are available.

Degrees Offered

UNDERGRADUATE
B.S., Computer Science
🄰🄱🄴 B.S., Computer Systems Engineering
🄰🄱🄴 B.S., Electrical Engineering

GRADUATE
M.S., Computer Science
M.S., Electrical and Computer Engineering
Ph.D., Computer Science
Ph.D., Electrical and Computer Engineering

Approximate Cost of Degrees

UNDERGRADUATE, RESIDENT
$19,300

UNDERGRADUATE, NONRESIDENT
$51,900

MASTER'S, RESIDENT
$5,500

MASTER'S, NONRESIDENT
$16,300

DOCTORATE, RESIDENT
$9,100

DOCTORATE, NONRESIDENT
$27,200

Admissions Guidelines

UNDERGRADUATE
High school diploma with 2.0 GPA, SAT and/or ACT required

GRADUATE
Accredited bachelor's, GRE required

Undergraduate Programs

The B.S. in Computer Science is an intensively software-focused and programming-focused curriculum in the field stemming from a broad, significant background in theory and computational mathematics.

The ABET-accredited B.S. in Computer Systems Engineering incorporates computer hardware and software engineering into a single, cohesive curriculum. Students are given generous opportunity to specialize through the use of field electives.

The ABET-accredited B.S. in Electrical Engineering focuses on electronics and signal processing.

Graduate Programs

The 30-hour M.S. in Computer Science focuses on theory, software engineering, and hardware-software interaction. A thesis or research paper is required.

The 30-hour M.S. in Electrical and Computer Engineering broadly addresses a variety of issues in the field in its core requirements; students are given the opportunity to specialize in specific research fields as they wish. A thesis or research paper is required. This program can be completed by distance learning.

The Ph.D. programs in Computer Science and in Electrical and Computer Engineering each involve a written comprehensive examination and two consecutive semesters of full-time residency in addition to the standard coursework and dissertation requirements.

Contact Information

PHONE

General information: (413) 545-0111
Admissions (undergraduate): (413) 545-0222
Admissions (graduate): (413) 545-0721
Computer science: (413) 545-2744
Electrical and computer engineering: (413) 545-0962

FAX

Admissions (undergraduate): (413) 545-4312
Admissions (graduate): (413) 577-0010
Computer science: (413) 545-1249
Electrical and computer engineering: (413) 545-4611

E-MAIL

Admissions (undergraduate):
mail@admissions.umass.edu
Admissions (graduate): gradadm@resgs.umass.edu
Computer science: Dr. Jim Kurose
(kurose@cs.umass.edu)

University of Massachusetts—Lowell   www.uml.edu ☆☆☆

1 University Avenue
Lowell, MA 01854

Year established: 1894
Ownership: Public

This major research-oriented public university offers cutting-edge programs at all levels in several major information technology fields. Evening classes, extension courses, and distance learning are available.

Degrees Offered

UNDERGRADUATE
(CSAB) B.S., Computer Science
(ABET) B.S., Electrical Engineering
(ABET) B.S., Electronic(s) Engineering Technology

GRADUATE
M.S., Communications Engineering
M.S., Computer Engineering
M.S., Computer Science
M.S., Information Processing
M.S., Telecommunications
M.S.Eng., Electrical Engineering
D.Eng., Electrical and Computer Engineering
Sc.D., Computer Science

Approximate Cost of Degrees

UNDERGRADUATE, RESIDENT
$21,900

UNDERGRADUATE, NONRESIDENT
$49,800

MASTER'S, RESIDENT
$4,900

MASTER'S, NONRESIDENT
$13,900

DOCTORATE, RESIDENT
$8,200

DOCTORATE, NONRESIDENT
$23,200

Admissions Guidelines

UNDERGRADUATE
High school diploma, SAT and/or ACT required

GRADUATE
Accredited bachelor's, GRE required

Undergraduate Programs
The CSAB-accredited B.S. in Computer Science primarily addresses theory and software engineering issues from a broad, comprehensive background in mathematics and the natural sciences.

The ABET-accredited B.S. in Electrical Engineering is available with the following tracks: traditional electrical engineering, computing foundations (permitting some study of computer science theory), and computing concentration (permitting extensive study of computer science and software engineering).

The ABET-accredited B.S. in Engineering Technology (B.S.E.T.) in Electronic(s) Engineering Technology focuses on electronics, networking, and computer programming.

Graduate Programs
The 33-hour M.S. in Communications Engineering focuses on an impressive array of networking and signal processing processes. No thesis is required.

The 33-hour M.S. in Computer Engineering can be tailored to fit personal research interests. No thesis is required.

The 30-hour M.S. in Computer Science deals primarily with issues in theory, software engineering, and software applications. No thesis is required.

The 33-hour Master of Science in Engineering (M.S.Eng.) in Electrical Engineering emphasizes electronics, signal processing, and neural systems. No thesis is required.

The 33-hour M.S. in Information Processing emphasizes software applications, human-computer interaction, and databases. No thesis is required.

The 33-hour M.S. in Telecommunications is strongly oriented toward computer networking, intranet, and Internet technologies. No thesis is required.

The Doctor of Engineering (D.Eng.) in Electrical and Computer Engineering can be tailored to suit the needs of virtually any student interested in the field. A qualifying examination is involved in addition to the standard coursework and dissertation requirements.

The Doctor of Science (Sc.D.) in Computer Science involves a qualifying examination in addition to the standard coursework and dissertation requirements.

Contact Information

PHONE
Admissions (undergraduate): (978) 934-3931 or (800) 410-4607
Admissions (graduate): (978) 934-2381 or (800) 656-4723
Computer science: (978) 934-3620
Electrical and computer engineering: (978) 934-3300

FAX
Admissions (undergraduate): (978) 934-3086
Admissions (graduate): (978) 934-3022

E-MAIL
Admissions (undergraduate): admissions@uml.edu
Admissions (graduate): graduateschool@uml.edu
Computer science: computer-science@uml.edu
Electrical and computer engineering: Dr. Michael Fiddy (MichaelFiddy@uml.edu)

University of Memphis   www.memphis.edu ★★½

Memphis, TN 38152

Year established: 1912
Ownership: Public

This cutting-edge public university offers undergraduate and graduate programs in engineering-focused information technology fields. Evening classes, weekend study, and distance learning are available.

Degrees Offered

UNDERGRADUATE
B.S., Computer Engineering
🄰 B.S., Electrical Engineering
🄰 B.S.E.T., Computer Engineering Technology
🄰 B.S.E.T., Electronic(s) Engineering Technology

GRADUATE
M.S., Electrical Engineering

Approximate Cost of Degrees

UNDERGRADUATE, RESIDENT
$15,800

UNDERGRADUATE, NONRESIDENT
$37,900

MASTER'S, RESIDENT
$6,700

MASTER'S, NONRESIDENT
$15,000

Admissions Guidelines

UNDERGRADUATE
High school diploma, SAT and/or ACT required

GRADUATE
Accredited bachelor's, GRE required

Undergraduate Programs

The B.S. in Computer Engineering focuses on software engineering, low-level programming, and hardware-software interaction.

The ABET-accredited B.S. in Electrical Engineering is available with optional specializations in computer engineering, electrophysics, and in systems and signals.

The ABET-accredited B.S. in Engineering Technology (B.S.E.T.) in Computer Engineering Technology focuses on applied computing in fields such as computer-aided design (CAD), programming, and databases.

The ABET-accredited B.S. in Engineering Technology (B.S.E.T.) in Electronic(s) Engineering Technology focuses chiefly on circuit design, signal processing, and related concerns.

Graduate Programs

The 30-hour M.S. in Electrical Engineering is available with formal specializations in automatic control systems, communications and propagation systems, electro-optical systems, and engineering computer systems. A thesis is required.

Other Programs

The M.S.E.T. (M.S. in Engineering Technology) is available with an electronics emphasis. For more information, contact the department at (901) 678-3300.

The M.S. and Ph.D. programs in Mathematical Sciences are available with a computer science track. For more information, contact the Department of Mathematical Sciences at (901) 678-2482.

B.B.A., M.B.A., and M.S.B.A. programs are available with a management information systems emphasis through the Fogelman College of Business and Economics. For more information, contact Dr. Lloyd Brooks at (901) 678-4651.

Contact Information

PHONE
Admissions (undergraduate): (901) 678-2111
Admissions (graduate): (901) 678-2911
Computer engineering technology: (901) 678-2227
Electrical engineering: (901) 678-2175
Electronic(s) engineering technology: (901) 678-3292

FAX
Admissions (graduate): (901) 678-5023
Computer engineering technology: (901) 678-5145
Electrical engineering: (901) 678-5469
Electronic(s) engineering technology: (901) 678-5145

E-MAIL
Admissions: admissions@memphis.edu

University of Michigan—Dearborn   www.umd.umich.edu ☆☆½

4901 Evergreen Road
Dearborn, MI 48128

Year established: 1959
Ownership: Public

This state university offers cutting-edge programs in engineering-focused information technology fields. Evening classes, weekend study, and extension courses are available.

Degrees Offered

UNDERGRADUATE
CSAB B.S., Computer and Information Science
B.S.E., Computer Engineering
ABET B.S.E., Electrical Engineering

GRADUATE
M.S., Computer and Information Science
M.S.E., Computer Engineering
M.S.E., Electrical Engineering
M.S., Software Engineering

Approximate Cost of Degrees

UNDERGRADUATE, RESIDENT
$20,900

UNDERGRADUATE, NONRESIDENT
$51,100

GRADUATE, RESIDENT
$12,100

GRADUATE, NONRESIDENT
$30,600

Admissions Guidelines

UNDERGRADUATE
High school diploma, SAT and/or ACT required

GRADUATE
Accredited bachelor's with 3.0 GPA required. GRE recommended.

Undergraduate Programs

The CSAB-accredited B.S. in Computer and Information Science is available with formal tracks in computer science (emphasizing theory, computational mathematics, and the traditional emphases of the major) and information systems (emphasizing software, applied computing, and business information systems).

The new B.S. in Engineering (B.S.E.) in Computer Engineering focuses on theory, software engineering, and digital systems design. Students can undertake a dual degree track whereby they can concurrently earn B.S.E. degrees in Electrical Engineering and Computer Engineering.

The ABET-accredited B.S.E. in Electrical Engineering is available with formal specializations in computers, digital systems, and electrical engineering.

Students may use one of these tracks or develop individualized specializations. Students can undertake a dual degree track whereby they can concurrently earn B.S.E. degrees in Electrical Engineering and Computer Engineering.

Graduate Programs

The 30-hour M.S. in Computer and Information Science is available with formal specializations in computer graphics and geometric modeling, computer networks, database management, information systems, software engineering, and system software. No thesis is required.

The 30-hour M.S. in Engineering (M.S.E.) in Computer Engineering allows a great deal of room for student-defined research tracks. The department seems to be particularly strong in the areas of intelligent systems and geometric modeling. No thesis is required.

The 30-hour M.S.E. in Electrical Engineering also allows a great deal of room for student-defined research tracks. The department seems to be particularly strong in the areas of computer engineering, digital systems design, and signal processing. No thesis is required.

The new 30-hour M.S. in Software Engineering is available with formal specializations in advanced software techniques, information engineering, intelligent systems, software design, software process management, software safety and security, and user interface design. A thesis or project is required.

Contact Information

PHONE
General information: (313) 593-5000
Admissions (undergraduate): (313) 593-5100
Admissions (graduate): (313) 593-1494
Computer and information science: (313) 436-9145
Electrical and computer engineering: (313) 593-5420

FAX
Electrical and computer engineering: (313) 593-9967

E-MAIL
Admissions: umdgoblu@umd.umich.edu
Computer and information science: Dr. Bruce Maxim (bmaxim@umich.edu)
Electrical and computer engineering: eceweb@umdsun2.umd.umich.edu

University of Minnesota—Twin Cities   www.umn.edu/tc ☆☆

Minneapolis, MN 55455

Year established: 1851
Ownership: Public

This Big Ten research university offers programs at all levels in the most popular information technology fields. Evening classes, extension courses, weekend study, and distance learning are available. The M.S. in Software Engineering may be completed entirely through weekend study.

Degrees Offered

UNDERGRADUATE
B.A., Computer Science
B.S., Computer Science
B.Comp.E.
B.E.E.

GRADUATE
M.C.I.S.
M.E.E.
M.S., Computer Engineering
M.S., Computer Science
M.S., Electrical Engineering
M.S., Software Engineering
Ph.D., Computer Science
Ph.D., Electrical Engineering

Approximate Cost of Degrees

UNDERGRADUATE, RESIDENT
$22,600

UNDERGRADUATE, NONRESIDENT
$55,200

MASTER'S, RESIDENT (COMPUTER SCIENCE)
$10,800

MASTER'S, NONRESIDENT (COMPUTER SCIENCE)
$19,700

MASTER'S, RESIDENT (SOFTWARE ENGINEERING)
$14,600

MASTER'S, NONRESIDENT (SOFTWARE ENGINEERING)
$27,500

DOCTORATE, RESIDENT
$17,900

DOCTORATE, NONRESIDENT
$32,800

Admissions Guidelines

UNDERGRADUATE
High school diploma, SAT and/or ACT required (ACT preferred)

GRADUATE
Accredited bachelor's, GRE required

Undergraduate Programs

The Bachelor of Computer Engineering (B.Comp.E.) is a primarily hardware-oriented program, although students are given the opportunity to specialize in software-focused fields if they so wish.

The Bachelor of Electrical Engineering (B.E.E.) is available with specializations in biomedical engineering, computer-aided design (CAD), computer architecture and software, computer engineering, computer networks, control systems, electrical engineering, electric energy systems, microelectronics and materials, optics and magnetics, and telecommunications/signal processing.

The B.A. and B.S. programs in Computer Science offer identical core requirements (emphasizing theoretical computer science, programming, and hardware-software interaction), but differ in their general credit distribution requirements.

Graduate Programs

The 31-hour Master of Computer and Information Science (M.C.I.S.) is designed with reentry students primarily in mind. The degree emphasizing software engineering, databases, and computer science theory. No thesis is required.

The 30-hour Master of Electrical Engineering (M.E.E.) is a professional program designed primarily for reentry students. No thesis is required.

The new 30-hour M.S. in Computer Engineering focuses on hardware issues. A thesis or project is required.

The 31-hour M.S. in Computer Science focuses on theory, software engineering, and hardware-software interaction. A thesis or research paper is required.

The 30-hour M.S. in Electrical Engineering focuses on digital systems, electronics, and signal processing. A thesis or project is required.

The 36-hour executive M.S. in Software Engineering focuses on quality assurance and project management issues in addition to structural software engineering issues, programming, and hardware-software interaction. A capstone project is required. This two-year program, designed specifically with reentry students in mind, can be completed entirely through weekend study.

The Ph.D. in Computer Science is available with research specializations in artificial intelligence, computer engineering, numerical analysis, software systems, and theory. A comprehensive examination is required in addition to the standard coursework and dissertation requirements.

The Ph.D. in Electrical Engineering requires a comprehensive written examination in addition to the standard coursework and dissertation requirements.

Contact Information

PHONE
Admissions (undergraduate): (612) 625-2008 or (800) 752-1000
Computer engineering (graduate): (612) 625-8041
Computer science: (612) 625-4002
Electrical and computer engineering (undergraduate): (612) 624-9803
Electrical engineering (graduate): (612) 626-7192

FAX
Admissions (undergraduate): (612) 626-1693
Computer science and engineering: (612) 625-0572
Electrical and computer engineering: (612) 625-4583

E-MAIL
Admissions (undergraduate): admissions@tc.umn.edu
Computer engineering (undergraduate): undergraduatestudies@ece.umn.edu
Computer engineering (graduate): gradinfo@compengr.umn.edu
Computer science (graduate): dgs@cs.umn.edu
Electrical engineering (undergraduate): undergraduatestudies@ece.umn.edu
Electrical engineering (graduate): graduatestudies@ece.umn.edu
Software engineering: degrees@cdtl.umn.edu

University of Missouri—Columbia www.missouri.edu ☆☆☆

Columbia, MO 65211

Year established: 1839
Ownership: Public

This major public research university offers programs at all levels in computer science and engineering. Evening classes, weekend study, and distance learning are available.

Degrees Offered

UNDERGRADUATE
B.A., Computer Science
B.S., Computer Science
ABET B.S., Computer Engineering
ABET B.S., Electrical Engineering

GRADUATE
M.S., Computer Engineering
M.S., Computer Science
Ph.D., Computer Science and Engineering

Approximate Cost of Degrees

UNDERGRADUATE, RESIDENT
$21,700

UNDERGRADUATE, NONRESIDENT
$34,500

MASTER'S, RESIDENT
$7,400

MASTER'S, NONRESIDENT
$11,900

DOCTORATE, RESIDENT
$12,400

DOCTORATE, NONRESIDENT
$19,900

Admissions Guidelines

UNDERGRADUATE
High school diploma, ACT required

GRADUATE
Accredited bachelor's, GRE required

Undergraduate Programs
The B.A. and B.S. programs in Computer Science are largely similar in formal major requirements, but differ in their general priorities. While the B.A. in Computer Science is effectively a liberal arts degree with a strong major in the field, the B.S. in Computer Science focuses on the computer science major and builds the general curriculum around this major.

The ABET-accredited B.S. in Computer Engineering focuses on digital systems, hardware-software interaction, and theory.

The ABET-accredited B.S. in Electrical Engineering focuses on digital systems, circuits, and signal processing.

Graduate Programs
The 30-hour M.S. in Computer Engineering focuses to a great extent on software engineering and the interplay between software engineering and hardware. The program can culminate in a thesis or project.

The 30-hour M.S. in Computer Science is a largely theory-oriented program, although a great deal of hands-on study is also required. A thesis or project is required.

The Ph.D. in Computer Science and Engineering involves a comprehensive examination in addition to the standard coursework and dissertation requirements.

Contact Information

PHONE
General information: (573) 882-2121
Admissions (undergraduate): (573) 882-7786
Admissions (graduate): (573) 882-6311
Electrical engineering: (573) 882-6387

FAX
Admissions (graduate): (573) 884-5454
Electrical engineering: (573) 882-0397

E-MAIL
Admissions (undergraduate): mu4u@missouri.edu
Admissions (graduate): info@grad.missouri.edu
Computer engineering and computer science: gradsec@cecs.missouri.edu

 EXTRA!
Missouri boasts the nation's oldest Department of Electrical Engineering (founded 1884).

University of Montana
www.umt.edu ☆☆☆

Missoula, MT 59812

Year established: 1893
Ownership: Public

This major public university offers undergraduate and graduate programs in computer science. Evening classes, weekend study, and distance learning are available.

Degrees Offered

UNDERGRADUATE
(CSAB) B.S., Computer Science

GRADUATE
M.S., Computer Science

Approximate Cost of Degrees

UNDERGRADUATE, RESIDENT
$14,200

UNDERGRADUATE, NONRESIDENT
$26,500

MASTER'S, RESIDENT
$7,900

MASTER'S, NONRESIDENT
$16,700

DOCTORATE, RESIDENT
$13,200

DOCTORATE, NONRESIDENT
$27,800

Admissions Guidelines

UNDERGRADUATE
High school diploma, SAT and/or ACT required

GRADUATE
Accredited bachelor's with 3.0 GPA, GRE required

Undergraduate Programs

The CSAB-accredited B.S. in Computer Science proceeds from a broad theoretical base to a well-rounded applied curriculum in programming and software engineering. Optional tracks in business systems and software systems are available.

Graduate Programs

The 36-hour M.S. in Computer Science focuses on hardware-software interaction, theoretical computer science, and databases. The program can be completed with a thesis or project.

Contact Information

PHONE
General information: (406) 243-0211
Admissions: (406) 243-6266 or (800) 462-8636

FAX
Computer science: (406) 243-5139

E-MAIL
Admissions: admiss@selway.umt.edu

University of Nebraska—Lincoln   www.unl.edu ☆☆☆

Lincoln, NE 68588

Year established: 1869
Ownership: Public

This Big Ten university offers undergraduate and graduate programs in the most essential information technology fields. Evening classes, weekend study, and distance learning are available.

Degrees Offered

UNDERGRADUATE
(ABET) B.S., Computer Engineering
B.S., Computer Science
(ABET) B.S., Electrical Engineering

GRADUATE
M.S., Computer Science
M.S., Electrical Engineering
Ph.D., Computer Science

Approximate Cost of Degrees

UNDERGRADUATE, RESIDENT
$18,000

UNDERGRADUATE, NONRESIDENT
$35,400

MASTER'S, RESIDENT
$5,600

MASTER'S, NONRESIDENT
$10,600

DOCTORATE, RESIDENT
$9,300

DOCTORATE, NONRESIDENT
$17,600

Admissions Guidelines

UNDERGRADUATE
High school diploma, SAT and/or ACT required

GRADUATE
Accredited bachelor's, GRE required

Undergraduate Programs

The ABET-accredited B.S. in Computer Engineering focuses on computer hardware, networking, and hardware-software interaction.

The B.S. in Computer Science is available with optional specializations in applications, computational mathematics, hardware, and software.

The ABET-accredited B.S. in Electrical Engineering is available with informal specializations in devices and waves, electronic circuits, and systems.

Graduate Programs

The 30-hour M.S. in Computer Science is available with a general track (a well-rounded, traditional curriculum in computer science) and a computer engineering track (with optional specializations in computer communications and networking, design implementation, system level architectures, and in vision, image processing, and graphics). A thesis or capstone project is required.

The 30-hour M.S. in Electrical Engineering focuses on electronics, digital circuits, and signal processing/telecommunications. No thesis is required, but all students must pass a qualifying examination.

The Ph.D. in Computer Science involves two written comprehensive examinations in addition to the standard coursework and dissertation requirements.

Contact Information

PHONE
General information: (800) 742-8800
Admissions (undergraduate): (402) 472-2023
Admissions (graduate): (402) 472-2878
Computer science and engineering: (402) 472-2401
Electrical engineering: (402) 472-3771

FAX
Computer science and engineering: (402) 472-7767
Electrical engineering: (402) 472-4732

E-MAIL
Admissions (undergraduate): nuhusker@unl.edu
Admissions (graduate): gradadmissions@unl.edu
Computer science and engineering: info@cse.unl.edu

University of Nebraska—Omaha   www.unomaha.edu ☆☆½

6001 Dodge Street
Omaha, NE 68182

Year established: 1908
Ownership: Public

This small public university offers highly innovative programs in several popular information technology fields. Of particular interest are the cutting-edge graduate offerings in telecommunications and the nontraditional Bachelor of General Studies, which can be completed entirely through off-campus study. Distance learning, credit by examination, evening classes, extension courses, and weekend study are available.

Degrees Offered

UNDERGRADUATE
B.G.S., concentration in Computer Science
B.S., Computer Engineering
B.S., Computer Science
B.S., Electronics Engineering
🅐🅑🅔🅣 B.S., Electronic(s) Engineering Technology

GRADUATE
M.Eng., Telecommunications Engineering
M.S., Computer Science
M.S., Electrical Engineering
M.S., Telecommunications Engineering

Approximate Cost of Degrees

UNDERGRADUATE, RESIDENT
$14,100

UNDERGRADUATE, NONRESIDENT
$31,100

GRADUATE, RESIDENT
$5,200

GRADUATE, NONRESIDENT
$10,500

Admissions Guidelines

UNDERGRADUATE
High school diploma, SAT and/or ACT required

GRADUATE
Accredited bachelor's, GRE required

Undergraduate Programs

The Bachelor of General Studies (B.G.S.) is available with a 30-hour concentration in Computer Science. This program can be completed through distance learning, evening classes, weekend study, transfer credit, and a variety of other means. The 9-hour residency requirement can now be fulfilled through online courses, meaning that the B.G.S. can be completed entirely by distance learning if the student so wishes.

The B.S. in Computer Engineering focuses on electronics, networking, and hardware-software interaction.

The B.S. in Computer Science focuses on theoretical issues, software applications, and programming. Students can largely customize the upper-level Computer Science curriculum to meet personal research interests, but must meet faculty approval before doing so.

The B.S. in Electronics Engineering focuses on communications, digital systems, and related issues. A telecommunications track is available.

The ABET-accredited B.S. in Electronic(s) Engineering Technology focuses on complex information technology hardware, networking technology, and technology management issues.

Graduate Programs

The 36-hour Master of Engineering (M.Eng.) in Telecommunications Engineering deals primarily with fiberoptics, wireless communication, and computer networking. No thesis is required. All students must choose a 9-hour secondary area of study in business administration, information systems, or math and statistics.

The M.S. in Computer Science focuses on software engineering and hardware-software interaction. Students can elect to undertake a 36-hour coursework track culminating in an examination or a 30-hour research track culminating in a thesis.

The 33-hour M.S. in Electrical Engineering focuses on digital systems and telecommunications issues in its core requirements, but can be tailored to fit the interests of virtually any student. All students must pass a qualifying examination. The program culminates with a thesis or project.

The proposed M.S. in Telecommunications Engineering primarily addresses issues in fiberoptics, wireless communication, and computer networking. This program will probably be available beginning in the fall of 2001.

Other Programs

B.S. and M.S. programs in Management Information Systems are also available. For more information, contact the College of Information Science and Technology at (402) 554-2380.

Contact Information

PHONE
General information: (402) 554-2800
Admissions (undergraduate): (402) 472-2023 or (800) 742-8800
Admissions (graduate): (402) 554-2341
Bachelor of General Studies (B.G.S.): (402) 554-2370
Computer and electronics engineering: (402) 554-4980
Computer science: (402) 554-2423
Telecommunications engineering: (402) 554-3628

FAX
Admissions: (402) 554-3472
Bachelor of General Studies (B.G.S.): (402) 554-2231
Computer and electronics engineering: (402) 554-2289
Computer science: (402) 554-3284

E-MAIL
Admissions (undergraduate): unoadm@unomaha.edu
Admissions (graduate): graduate@unomaha.edu

Computer and electronics engineering:
CEEN@unomaha.edu
Computer science (undergraduate):
ugprog@cs.unomaha.edu

Computer science (graduate):
gprog@cs.unomaha.edu
Telecommunications engineering: Dr. Hamid Sharif-Kashani (hsharif@unomha.edu)

University of Nevada—Las Vegas   www.unlv.edu ☆☆☆

4505 Maryland Parkway
Las Vegas, NV 89154

Year established: 1957
Ownership: Public

This midsize public university offers programs at all levels in traditional information technology fields. Evening classes and extension courses are available.

Degrees Offered

UNDERGRADUATE
B.A., Computer Science
CSAB B.S., Computer Science
B.S., Computer Engineering
ABET B.S., Electrical Engineering

GRADUATE
M.S., Computer Science
M.S., Electrical Engineering
Ph.D., Computer Science
Ph.D., Electrical Engineering

Approximate Cost of Degrees

UNDERGRADUATE, RESIDENT
$12,900

UNDERGRADUATE, NONRESIDENT (REGIONAL/"GOOD NEIGHBOR")
$22,000

UNDERGRADUATE, NONRESIDENT (OTHER)
$40,800

MASTER'S, RESIDENT
$9,400

MASTER'S, NONRESIDENT (REGIONAL/"GOOD NEIGHBOR")
$15,700

MASTER'S, NONRESIDENT (OTHER)
$30,300

DOCTORATE, RESIDENT
$15,600

DOCTORATE, NONRESIDENT (REGIONAL/"GOOD NEIGHBOR")
$26,100

DOCTORATE, NONRESIDENT (OTHER)
$50,500

Admissions Guidelines

UNDERGRADUATE
High school diploma with 2.5 GPA, SAT and/or ACT required. Must be 15 or older.

GRADUATE
Accredited bachelor's with 2.75 GPA, GRE required

Undergraduate Programs
The B.A. in Computer Science represents a flexible, interdisciplinary curriculum in the field. Applied computing issues tend to be emphasized, although theoretical computer science is also addressed.

The B.S. program in Computer Engineering focuses on digital systems, circuit design, and hardware-software interaction.

The CSAB-accredited B.S. in Computer Science focuses on issues in theoretical computer science, programming, and hardware-software interaction.

The ABET-accredited B.S. in Electrical Engineering is available with informal specializations in communications, computer engineering, controls, digital signal processing, electromagnetics, electronics, power, and solid-state electronics.

Graduate Programs
The 30-hour M.S. in Computer Science focuses on theory and software engineering. A thesis or project is required.

The 30-hour M.S. in Electrical Engineering is available with informal specializations in communications, computer engineering, control systems, electromagnetics and optics, electronics, power systems, signal processing, and solid-state electronics. A thesis or project is required.

The Ph.D. in Computer Science involves two comprehensive written examinations in addition to the standard coursework and dissertation requirements.

The Ph.D. in Electrical Engineering involves three comprehensive written examinations in addition to the standard coursework and dissertation requirements.

Contact Information

PHONE
General information: (702) 895-3011

Admissions (undergraduate): (702) 895-3443 or (800) 334-8658
Admissions (graduate): (702) 895-3320
Computer science: (702) 895-3681
Electrical and computer engineering: (702) 895-4183

FAX
General information: (702) 895-3850
Admissions (graduate): (702) 895-4180

E-MAIL
Admissions (undergraduate):
undrgradadmision@ccmail.nevada.edu
Admissions (graduate):
gradcollege@ccmail.nevada.edu
Computer science: syracuse@cs.unlv.edu
Electrical and computer engineering:
iyer@ee.unlv.edu

University of Nevada—Reno   www.unr.edu ☆☆½

Reno, NV 89557

Year established: 1874
Ownership: Public

This prominent state-funded university offers degrees at all levels in hands-on information technology fields. Evening classes and distance learning are available.

Degrees Offered

UNDERGRADUATE
B.S., Computer Science
🔵 B.S., Electrical Engineering

GRADUATE
M.S., Computer Engineering
M.S., Computer Science
M.S., Electrical Engineering
Ph.D., Computer Engineering
Ph.D., Electrical Engineering

Approximate Cost of Degrees

UNDERGRADUATE, RESIDENT
$13,400

UNDERGRADUATE, NONRESIDENT
$23,100

GRADUATE, RESIDENT
$5,200

GRADUATE, NONRESIDENT
$9,000

Admissions Guidelines

UNDERGRADUATE
High school diploma with 2.5 GPA, SAT and/or ACT required

GRADUATE
Accredited bachelor's with 2.75 GPA, GRE required

Undergraduate Programs
The B.S. in Computer Science focuses on theory and software engineering.

The ABET-accredited B.S. in Electrical Engineering focuses on digital systems and electronics. A computer engineering specialization is available.

Graduate Programs
The 32-hour M.S. in Computer Engineering involves minimal core requirements, focusing instead on faculty-approved student research interests. While

the program tends to favor hardware issues in its core requirements, elective research opportunities are so prominent that students can essentially create a software engineering curriculum. A thesis or research paper is required.

The 32-hour M.S. in Computer Science is available with specializations in artificial intelligence and machine learning, computability and theory of computing, computational science and engineering, computer engineering and architecture, computer systems and networks, graphics and image processing, object oriented technology, parallel and distributed systems, programming languages and design, and software engineering. A thesis or research paper is required.

The 32-hour M.S. in Electrical Engineering involves minimal core requirements, focusing instead on faculty-approved student research interests. A thesis or research paper is required. All students must pass a written comprehensive examination.

The Ph.D. programs in Computer Engineering and Electrical Engineering each involve two written examinations in addition to the standard coursework and dissertation requirements.

Contact Information

PHONE
General information: (775) 784-1110
Admissions: (775) 784-6865
Computer engineering: (775) 784-4313
Computer science: (775) 784-6974
Electrical engineering: (775) 784-6944

FAX
Computer science and engineering: (775) 784-1877
Electrical engineering: (775) 784-6627

E-MAIL
General information: webmaster@unr.edu
Computer engineering: Dr. Carl Looney (looney@cs.unr.edu)
Computer science: Dr. George Bebis (bebis@cs.unr.edu)
Electrical engineering: Dr. John Kleppe (kleppe@ee.unr.edu)

University of New Hampshire   www.unh.edu ★★☆

Durham, NH 03824

Year established: 1866
Ownership: Public

This major public university offers undergraduate and graduate programs in standard information technology fields. Evening classes are available.

Degrees Offered

UNDERGRADUATE
CSAB B.S., Computer Science
ABET B.S., Electrical Engineering

GRADUATE
M.S., Computer Science
M.S., Electrical Engineering
Ph.D., Computer Science
Ph.D., Computer Engineering

Approximate Cost of Degrees

UNDERGRADUATE, RESIDENT
$31,800

UNDERGRADUATE, NONRESIDENT
$67,300

MASTER'S, RESIDENT
$11,600

MASTER'S, NONRESIDENT (NEW ENGLAND)
$15,900

MASTER'S, NONRESIDENT (OTHER)
$25,000

DOCTORATE, RESIDENT
$19,400

DOCTORATE, NONRESIDENT (NEW ENGLAND)
$26,600

DOCTORATE, NONRESIDENT (OTHER)
$41,600

Admissions Guidelines

UNDERGRADUATE
High school diploma, SAT and/or ACT required

GRADUATE
Accredited bachelor's, GRE required. (GRE Computer Science Subject Test strongly recommended for relevant programs.)

Undergraduate Programs
The CSAB-accredited B.S. in Computer Science progresses from a strong theoretical base to a rigorous, hands-on curriculum in software engineering and programming. Minors in computer applications and computer technology are also available.

The ABET-accredited B.S. in Electrical Engineering is available with optional tracks in computer engineering and in signals and systems.

Graduate Programs
The 30-hour M.S. in Computer Science focuses on theoretical issues in the field, although a significant software engineering component is involved. Students are encouraged to design individualized specializations reflecting their research interests. A thesis is required in the default track, but students can also elect for a non-thesis track which involves 30 additional hours of coursework and a comprehensive examination.

The 30-hour M.S. in Electrical Engineering allows vast room for student-defined specialization through the use of electives. A thesis or project is generally required in the standard track, but students may also undertake a coursework track that culminates in a comprehensive examination.

The Ph.D. in Computer Science focuses on design-oriented theoretical issues. A written qualifying examination is required in addition to the standard coursework and dissertation requirements.

The Ph.D. in Electrical Engineering focuses on complex, hands-on design issues. Two written examinations are required in addition to the standard coursework and dissertation requirements.

Contact Information

PHONE
Admissions: (603) 862-1360
Computer science: (603) 862-3778
Electrical and computer engineering: (603) 862-1357

FAX
Computer science: (603) 862-3493

E-MAIL
Admissions (undergraduate): admissions@unh.edu
Admissions (graduate): grad.school@unh.edu
Computer science: Dr. Ted Sparr (tms@cs.unh.edu)
Electrical and computer engineering:
ece.dept@unh.edu

University of New Haven www.newhaven.edu ☆☆½

300 Orange Avenue
West Haven, CT 06516

Year established: 1920
Ownership: Private

This unique private university offers undergraduate and graduate programs in standard information technology fields. Evening classes are available.

Degrees Offered

UNDERGRADUATE
B.S., Computer Science
(ABET) B.S., Electrical Engineering

GRADUATE
M.S., Computer and Information Science
M.S., Electrical Engineering

Approximate Cost of Degrees

UNDERGRADUATE
$40,400

MASTER'S
$23,900

DOCTORATE
$39,900

Admissions Guidelines

UNDERGRADUATE
High school diploma, SAT and/or ACT required

GRADUATE
Accredited bachelor's required, GRE strongly recommended

Undergraduate Programs
The B.S. in Computer Science focuses on theory, computational mathematics, and programming.

The ABET-accredited B.S. in Electrical Engineering is available with specializations in communications, control, digital systems, and power.

Graduate Programs
The 48-hour M.S. in Computer and Information Science focuses on theory and software engineering. A thesis or project is required.

The 36-hour M.S. in Electrical Engineering is available with tracks in computer engineering and electrical engineering. No thesis is required.

Contact Information

PHONE
General information: (800) 342-5864
Admissions: (203) 932-7319
Computer science: (203) 932-7159
Electrical and computer engineering: (203) 932-7165

FAX
Computer science: (203) 932-7158
Electrical and computer engineering: (203) 931-6091

E-MAIL
Admissions (undergraduate):
adminfo@charger.newhaven.edu
Admissions (graduate):
gradinfo@charger.newhaven.edu
Electrical engineering: Dr. Ali Golbazi
(golbazi@charger.newhaven.edu)

University of New Mexico   www.unm.edu ★★☆

Albuquerque, NM 87131

Year established: 1889
Ownership: Public

This major public university offers degrees at all levels in established information technology fields. Evening classes, extension courses, and distance learning are available.

Degrees Offered

UNDERGRADUATE
(ABET) B.S., Computer Engineering
(CSAB) B.S., Computer Science
(ABET) B.S., Electrical Engineering

GRADUATE
M.S., Computer Science
M.S., Electrical Engineering
Ph.D., Computer Science
Ph.D., Electrical Engineering

Approximate Cost of Degrees

UNDERGRADUATE, RESIDENT
$13,900

UNDERGRADUATE, NONRESIDENT
$41,300

MASTER'S, RESIDENT
$5,500

MASTER'S, NONRESIDENT
$15,600

DOCTORATE, RESIDENT
$9,100

DOCTORATE, NONRESIDENT
$26,100

Admissions Guidelines

UNDERGRADUATE
High school diploma with 2.25 GPA, SAT and/or ACT required

GRADUATE
Accredited bachelor's with 3.0 GPA, GRE required

Undergraduate Programs

The ABET-accredited B.S. in Computer Engineering is a predominantly hardware-oriented program, although students are also given opportunity to study software engineering.

The CSAB-accredited B.S. in Computer Science integrates a study of theoretical and applied computing into a broad, comprehensive background in mathematics and the natural sciences.

The ABET-accredited B.S. in Electrical Engineering focuses on digital systems, signal processing and telecommunications, and computer engineering.

Graduate Programs

The 32-hour M.S. in Computer Science emphasizes theoretical computer science, although students are also exposed to study in databases and software engineering. No thesis is required.

The 32-hour M.S. in Electrical Engineering is available with optional specializations in computer engineering, physical electronics and photonics, and in signals and systems. No thesis is required.

The Ph.D. in Computer Science requires two batteries of comprehensive examinations in addition to the standard coursework and dissertation requirements.

The Ph.D. in Electrical Engineering involves a rigorous qualifying examination in addition to the standard coursework and dissertation requirements.

Contact Information

Phone
General information: (505) 277-0111
Admissions (undergraduate): (505) 277-2446
Admissions (graduate): (505) 277-2711
Computer science: (505) 277-3112
Electrical and computer engineering: (505) 277-2436

Fax
Computer science: (505) 277-6927
Electrical and computer engineering: (505) 277-1439

E-mail
Admissions (graduate): gradstud@unm.edu
Computer science: csinfo@cs.unm.edu
Electrical and computer engineering: info@eece.unm.edu

University of North Carolina—Chapel Hill   www.unc.edu ☆☆☆

Chapel Hill, NC 27599

Year established: 1793
Ownership: Public

This highly respected midsize public university offers strong, software-focused graduate programs in computer science. At the undergraduate level, a computer science concentration is available within the mathematics B.S. program. Evening classes are available.

Degrees Offered

Graduate
M.S., Computer Science
Ph.D., Computer Science

Approximate Cost of Degrees

Master's, Resident
$9,800

Master's, Nonresident
$37,300

Doctorate, Resident
$16,300

Doctorate, Nonresident
$62,100

Admissions Guidelines

Graduate
Accredited bachelor's with 3.0 GPA on upper 60 hours, GRE required

Graduate Programs

The 30-hour M.S. in Computer Science focuses heavily on programming and software engineering. As part of the program, each student must participate (preferably as part of a team) in the design of a software product. No thesis is required.

The Ph.D. in Computer Science involves two examinations in addition to the standard coursework and dissertation requirements.

Other Programs

A computer science specialization is available within the mathematics B.S. program. For more information, contact the Department of Mathematics at (919) 962-0198.

Contact Information

PHONE
General information: (919) 962-2211

Admissions (undergraduate): (919) 966-3621
Admissions (graduate): (919) 966-2611
Computer science: (919) 962-1700

FAX
Admissions (undergraduate): (919) 962-3045
Computer science: (919) 962-1799

E-MAIL
Admissions (undergraduate): uadm@email.unc.edu
Admissions (graduate): gradinfo@unc.edu
Computer science: geninfo@cs.unc.edu

University of North Carolina—Charlotte www.uncc.edu ☆☆½

9201 University City Boulevard
Charlotte, NC 28223-0001

Year established: 1946
Ownership: Public

This major public university offers programs at all levels in the most popular information technology fields. Evening classes, extension courses, and distance learning are available.

Degrees Offered

UNDERGRADUATE
B.A., Computer Science
B.S., Computer Science
B.A., Information Science
B.S., Computer Engineering
ABET B.S., Electrical Engineering
ABET B.S., Electrical Engineering Technology

GRADUATE
M.S., Computer Science
M.S., Electrical Engineering
M.S., Information Technology
Ph.D., Electrical Engineering
Ph.D., Information Technology

Approximate Cost of Degrees

UNDERGRADUATE, RESIDENT
$12,500

UNDERGRADUATE, NONRESIDENT
$41,600

MASTER'S, RESIDENT
$4,700

MASTER'S, NONRESIDENT
$15,600

DOCTORATE, RESIDENT
$7,800

DOCTORATE, NONRESIDENT
$26,000

Admissions Guidelines

UNDERGRADUATE
High school diploma, SAT and/or ACT required

GRADUATE
Accredited bachelor's with 3.0 GPA, GRE required

Undergraduate Programs

The major in Computer Science focuses on theory, hardware-software interaction, programming, and software applications. An optional computer engineering specialization is available.

The B.A. in Information Science incorporates management courses into a fairly solid, rigorous IT curriculum emphasizing theory and software applications.

The B.S. in Computer Engineering is available with specializations in communications, computer architecture, design and testing, and device electronics and technology.

The ABET-accredited B.S. in Electrical Engineering focuses on electronics, digital systems, and communications.

The ABET-accredited B.S. in Electrical Engineering Technology is available as a special "2+2" degree completion program or a traditional four-year, on-campus program. The "2+2" program is designed for students who have earned at least 54 hours of college credit and can be completed almost completely through extension courses, video courses, and online distance learning. Students can choose to specialize in computer engineering technology.

Graduate Programs

The 30-hour M.S. in Computer Science is available with research specializations in computer networks and communication, decision support systems, data visualization, enterprise integration, evolutionary computing, intelligent information systems, knowledge discovery and data mining, parallel programming, and robotics. A thesis or comprehensive written examination is required.

The 30-hour M.S. in Electrical Engineering is available with optional specializations in communications, computer engineering, controls, power systems, optoelectronics, and microelectronics. No thesis is required. This program can be completed entirely through night classes.

The 30-hour M.S. in Information Technology is available with specializations in advanced database and knowledge discovery, financial services, management, and marketing. A capstone project is required.

The Ph.D. in Electrical Engineering involves a written comprehensive examination in addition to the standard coursework and dissertation requirements.

The Ph.D. in Information Technology involves one year of full-time residency and a core comprehensive examination in addition to the standard coursework and dissertation requirements.

Contact Information

PHONE
General information: (704) 547-2000
Admissions (undergraduate): (704) 547-2213
Admissions (graduate): (704) 547-3366
Computer science: (704) 547-4880
Electrical and computer engineering: (704) 547-2302
Engineering technology: (704) 547-2305

FAX
Admissions (undergraduate): (704) 510-6483
Electrical and computer engineering: (704) 547-2352

E-MAIL
Admissions (undergraduate):
unccadm@email.uncc.edu
Admissions (graduate): gradadm@email.uncc.edu
Computer science: Dr. Richard Lejk (lejk@uncc.edu)
Electrical and computer engineering: Dr. Farid Tranjan (tranjan@uncc.edu)
Information technology: Dr. Bill Chu (billchu@uncc.edu)

University of North Dakota   www.und.edu ☆☆½

University Station
Grand Forks, ND 58202

Year established: 1883
Ownership: Public

This major public university offers undergraduate and graduate programs in the most popular information technology fields. Evening classes, corporate extension classes, and distance learning are available. This university, widely recognized for its excellent graduate programs in aeronautical and space sciences, offers an aeronautics specialization within the electrical engineering major.

Degrees Offered

UNDERGRADUATE
B.A., Computer Science
(CSAB) B.S., Computer Science
(ABET) B.S., Electrical Engineering

GRADUATE
M.Eng., Electrical Engineering
M.S., Computer Science
M.S., Electrical Engineering

Approximate Cost of Degrees

UNDERGRADUATE, RESIDENT
$15,800

UNDERGRADUATE, NONRESIDENT
$32,400

GRADUATE, RESIDENT
$6,400

GRADUATE, NONRESIDENT (MINNESOTA)
$7,300

GRADUATE, NONRESIDENT (SOUTH DAKOTA, MONTANA, MANITOBA, SASKATCHEWAN)
$8,600

GRADUATE, NONRESIDENT (OTHER)
$13,500

Admissions Guidelines

UNDERGRADUATE
High school diploma required, SAT and/or ACT required if under age 25

GRADUATE
Accredited bachelor's with 2.75 GPA, GRE required

Undergraduate Programs
The B.A. in Computer Science is intended for students who want to major in computer science, but would prefer that the bulk of their degree be otherwise devoted to the liberal arts.

The CSAB-accredited B.S. in Computer Science focuses on theory, programming, and hardware-software interaction.

The ABET-accredited B.S. in Electrical Engineering is available with an optional focus in aerospace engineering or computer science. Much of this program can be completed through corporate extension courses.

Graduate Programs
The 33-hour professional Master of Engineering (M.Eng.) in Electrical Engineering is available with optional specializations in energy systems, high frequency devices and fields, and systems engineering. No thesis is required.

The M.S. in Computer Science is available with two tracks, one emphasizing research and one emphasizing applied computing. The 30-hour research track focuses on theory and computational mathematics, and requires a thesis. The 32-hour applied computing track focuses on software engineering and programming and does not require a thesis. Both tracks require a comprehensive written examination.

The 30-hour M.S. in Electrical Engineering is available with optional specializations in energy systems, high frequency devices and fields, and systems. Students are encouraged, but not required, to undertake a thesis.

Contact Information

PHONE
General information: (701) 777-2011 or (800) 225-5863
Computer science: (701) 777-4107
Electrical engineering: (701) 777-4332

FAX
Computer science: (701) 777-3330

E-MAIL
Admissions: Heidi Kippenhan (heidikippenhan@mail.und.nodak.edu)
Undergraduate information: enrolser@sage.und.nodak.edu
Computer science: csdept@cs.und.edu
Electrical engineering: Arnold Johnson (ARNOLD_JOHNSON@mail.und.nodak.edu)

University of North Florida   www.unf.edu ☆☆☆½

4567 St. Johns Bluff Road, South
Jacksonville, FL 32224-2645

Year established: 1972
Ownership: Public

This small public university offers undergraduate and graduate programs dealing with hardware and software aspects of information technology. Evening classes, weekend study, and distance learning are available.

Degrees Offered

UNDERGRADUATE
(CSAB) B.S., Computer and Information Sciences
(ABET) B.S., Electrical Engineering

GRADUATE
M.S., Computer and Information Sciences

Approximate Cost of Degrees

UNDERGRADUATE, RESIDENT
$13,600

UNDERGRADUATE, NONRESIDENT
$42,900

GRADUATE, RESIDENT
$7,100

GRADUATE, NONRESIDENT
$20,800

Admissions Guidelines

UNDERGRADUATE
High school diploma, SAT and/or ACT required

GRADUATE
Accredited bachelor's with 3.0 GPA, GRE, and/or accredited graduate degree

Undergraduate Programs

The B.S. in Computer and Information Sciences is available with formal tracks in computer science, information science, and information systems. The computer science track is accredited by the Com-puter Science Accreditation Commission (CSAC) of the CSAB.

The ABET-accredited B.S. in Electrical Engineering is available with formal tracks emphasizing computer design or system design.

Graduate Programs

The 30-hour M.S. in Computer and Information Sciences emphasizes databases, software engineering, and hardware-software interaction. A thesis is generally required, but students can elect instead to undertake a 36-hour coursework track. Students who choose this option must pass a comprehensive examination.

Contact Information

PHONE
General information: (904) 620-1000
Admissions: (904) 620-2624
Computer and information sciences: (904) 620-2985
Electrical engineering: (904) 620-2970

FAX
Computer and information sciences: (904) 620-2988
Electrical engineering: (904) 620-2975

E-MAIL
Admissions: admissions@unf.edu
Computer and information sciences: Dr. Judith Solano (jsolano@unf.edu)
Electrical engineering: Dr. Joseph Campbell (jlcampbe@unf.edu)

University of North Texas

www.unt.edu ☆☆½

Denton, TX 76203

Year established: 1890
Ownership: Public

This major public university offers traditional programs at all levels in computer science and engineering technology. Evening classes, weekend study, and distance learning are available.

Degrees Offered

UNDERGRADUATE
B.A., Computer Science
(CSAB) B.S., Computer Science
(ABET) B.S., Electronic(s) Engineering Technology

GRADUATE
M.S., Computer Science
Ph.D., Computer Science

Approximate Cost of Degrees

UNDERGRADUATE, RESIDENT
$15,000

UNDERGRADUATE, NONRESIDENT
$41,000

MASTER'S, RESIDENT
$5,200

MASTER'S, NONRESIDENT
$12,900

DOCTORATE, RESIDENT
$8,600

DOCTORATE, NONRESIDENT
$21,500

Admissions Guidelines

UNDERGRADUATE
High school diploma, SAT and/or ACT required

GRADUATE
Accredited bachelor's, GRE required

Undergraduate Programs
The B.A. in Computer Science is a broad, interdisciplinary, hands-on program designed for students who seek a solid background in applied computing.

The CSAB-accredited B.S. in Computer Science focuses on theory, software engineering, and hardware-software interaction.

The ABET-accredited B.S. in Electronic(s) Engineering Technology focuses on applied electrical and computer engineering issues. Digital systems, signal processing, computer hardware, and computer software applications are addressed with reasonable depth.

Graduate Programs
The M.S. in Computer Science focuses on theory and software engineering. Students may elect to undertake the 33-hour thesis track, the 36-hour project track, or the 39-hour coursework-only track.

The Ph.D. in Computer Science requires two batteries of written examinations in addition to the standard dissertation and coursework requirements.

Other Programs
The general M.S. in Engineering Technology can be tailored to electronics engineering. For more information, contact the program director at (940) 565-2363.

Contact Information

PHONE
Admissions (undergraduate): (940) 565-2681 or (800) 868-8211
Admissions (graduate): (940) 565-2636 or (888) 868-4723
Computer science: (940) 565-2767
Engineering technology: (940) 565-2022

FAX
Computer science: (940) 565-2799
Engineering technology: (940) 565-2666

E-MAIL
Admissions (graduate): gradsch@unt.edu
Computer science (undergraduate): ugradinfo@cs.unt.edu
Computer science (graduate): gradinfo@cs.unt.edu
Engineering technology: etec@unt.edu

University of Notre Dame   www.nd.edu ☆☆☆

Notre Dame, IN 46556

Year established: 1842
Ownership: Private

This prestigious research university offers programs at all levels in electrical engineering and in computer science and engineering. Evening classes are available.

Degrees Offered

UNDERGRADUATE
(ABET) B.S., Computer Engineering
B.S., Computer Science
(ABET) B.S., Electrical Engineering

GRADUATE
M.S., Computer Science and Engineering
M.S., Electrical Engineering
Ph.D., Computer Science and Engineering
Ph.D., Electrical Engineering

Approximate Cost of Degrees

UNDERGRADUATE
$97,400

MASTER'S
$47,500

DOCTORATE
$79,200

Admissions Guidelines

UNDERGRADUATE
High school diploma, SAT and/or ACT required

GRADUATE
Accredited bachelor's, GRE required

Undergraduate Programs

The ABET-accredited B.S. in Computer Engineering is a clearly and unrepentantly hardware-focused program that nevertheless addresses issues in software engineering and computational mathematics.

The B.S. in Computer Science incorporates elements of theory, software applications, programming, and computer hardware. The curriculum for this program seems to be more engineering-focused than most in the field.

The ABET-accredited B.S. in Electrical Engineering focuses on electronics in its core requirements, but this highly flexible curriculum allows ample room for student-defined specialization.

Graduate Programs

The 30-hour M.S. programs in Computer Science and Engineering and in Electrical Engineering are highly focused, research-based programs designed primarily for students who want to pursue a doctorate in the field. A thesis and oral comprehensive examination are required for both degrees.

The Ph.D. in Computer Science and Engineering involves a qualifying examination in addition to the standard coursework and dissertation requirements. Research specializations are available in artificial intelligence, distributed computing, electronic design automation, operating systems, parallel computing algorithms, pipelined and parallel architectures, and VLSI algorithms and circuit design.

The Ph.D. in Electrical Engineering involves a qualifying examination in addition to the standard coursework and dissertation requirements. Research specializations are available in communication systems, control systems, high-speed circuits and devices, nanoelectronics, optoelectronics, semiconductor materials and devices, and signal and image processing.

Contact Information

PHONE
General information: (219) 631-5000
Admissions (undergraduate): (219) 631-7505
Admissions (graduate): (219) 631-7706
Computer science and engineering: (219) 631-8320
Electrical engineering: (219) 631-5480

FAX
Admissions (undergraduate): (219) 631-8865
Computer science and engineering: (219) 631-9260
Electrical engineering: (219) 631-4393

E-MAIL
Admissions (undergraduate): admissio.1@nd.edu
Admissions (graduate): GradAd.1@nd.edu

University of Oregon

Office of Admissions
240 Oregon Hall
1217 University of Oregon
Eugene, OR 97403-1217

www.uoregon.edu ☆☆☆

Year established: 1877
Ownership: Public

This major public university offers programs at all levels in the most prominent information technology fields. Evening classes, weekend study, extension courses, and distance learning are available.

Degrees Offered

UNDERGRADUATE
B.S., Computer and Information Science
B.S., Computer Information Technology

GRADUATE
M.S., Computer and Information Science
M.Sw.E.
Ph.D., Computer Science

Approximate Cost of Degrees

UNDERGRADUATE, RESIDENT
$19,200

UNDERGRADUATE, NONRESIDENT
$59,300

MASTER'S, RESIDENT
$12,000

MASTER'S, NONRESIDENT
$19,400

DOCTORATE, RESIDENT
$20,000

DOCTORATE, NONRESIDENT
$32,300

Admissions Guidelines

UNDERGRADUATE
High school diploma with 3.0 GPA, SAT and/or ACT required

GRADUATE
Accredited bachelor's, GRE required

Undergraduate Programs
The B.S. in Computer and Information Science addresses issues in theory, software engineering, and databases from a background in mathematics and the natural sciences.

The new B.S. in Computer Information Technology is designed specifically for students who want to apply computer information technology toward business, library science, neuroscience, and other fields not generally associated with a standard computer science curriculum.

Graduate Programs
The 37-hour M.S. in Computer and Information Science deals primarily with theory, software engineering, and hardware-software interaction. No thesis is required.

The 28-hour Oregon Master of Software Engineering (M.Sw.E.) is offered jointly with the Oregon Graduate Institute of Science and Technology, Oregon State University, and Portland State University. The program culminates in a 6-hour software engineering practicum (supervised work).

The Ph.D. in Computer Science involves components in algorithms and complexity, computer architecture, and programming languages. An oral comprehensive examination is required in addition to the standard coursework and dissertation requirements.

Contact Information

PHONE
General information: (541) 346-1000
Admissions: (541) 346-3201 or (800) 232-3825
Computer science: (541) 346-4408
Software engineering: (503) 725-2900

FAX
Admissions: (541) 346-5815
Computer science: (541) 346-5373
Software engineering: (503) 725-2910

E-MAIL
Admissions: Martha Pitts
(mpitts@oregon.uoregon.edu)
Computer and information science:
Dr. Sarah Douglas (douglas@cs.uoregon.edu)

University of Pennsylvania   www.upenn.edu ☆☆☆

3451 Walnut
Philadelphia, PA 1904

Year established: 1740
Ownership: Private

This major private research university offers traditional and highly nontraditional programs at all levels in an array of information technology fields. Evening classes, extension courses, co-op study, and distance learning are available.

Degrees Offered

UNDERGRADUATE
B.A.S., Computer Science
B.S.E., Computer and Telecommunications
Engineering
B.S.E., Computer Science and Engineering
(ABET) B.S.E., Electrical Engineering

GRADUATE
M.S.E., Computer Science
M.S.E., Electrical Engineering
Ph.D., Computer and Information Science
Ph.D., Electrical Engineering

Approximate Cost of Degrees

UNDERGRADUATE
$105,800

MASTER'S
$39,700

DOCTORATE
$66,100

Admissions Guidelines

UNDERGRADUATE
High school diploma, SAT and/or ACT required

GRADUATE
Accredited bachelor's, GRE required

Undergraduate Programs
The Bachelor of Applied Science (B.A.S.) in Computer Science is an interdisciplinary program focusing on mathematics, engineering, and computer science as a triune major, computer science being the most prominent of the three.

The Bachelor of Science and Engineering (B.S.E.) in Computer Science approaches the field from a strong engineering perspective. This program is, as one might expect, very hands-on; a great deal of laboratory work is involved.

The highly innovative B.S.E. program in Computer and Telecommunications Engineering emphasizes computer-telecommunications interaction issues—which is to say, modulation/demodulation, data transmission, and both small-scale (intranet) and large-scale (Internet) networking.

The ABET-accredited B.S.E. in Electrical Engineering is available with formal specializations in microelectronic circuit sand systems, photonics and electronic materials, and signals and communications.

Graduate Programs
The 30-hour Master of Science and Engineering (M.S.E.) in Computer Science focuses largely on computational mathematics and software engineering. No thesis is required.

The 30-hour M.S.E. in Electrical Engineering can be completed through a standard model similar to the computer science M.S.E. above, or students may elect to complete the program through an 11-month, paid industrial "externship." In such a scenario, on-the-job work forms the basis of the thesis.

The Ph.D. in Computer and Information Science involves a written comprehensive examination and teaching practicum in addition to the standard coursework and dissertation requirements.

The Ph.D. in Electrical Engineering involves a qualifying examination in addition to the standard coursework and dissertation requirements.

Other Programs
B.A.S. programs in Computational Biology, Computer and Cognitive Science, and Digital Media Design are also available. For more information, contact the Department of Computer and Information Science.

A Ph.D. in Operations and Information Management is available through the Wharton School. For more information, contact the program office at (215) 898-4877.

Contact Information

PHONE
General information: (215) 898-5000
Admissions (undergraduate): (215) 898-7507
Computer and information science: (215) 898-8560
Electrical engineering: (215) 898-9241

FAX
Computer and information science: (215) 898-0587
Electrical engineering: (215) 573-2068

E-MAIL
Computer and information science:
cis-info@cis.upenn.edu

University of Pittsburgh   www.pitt.edu ☆☆☆

Pittsburgh, PA 15260

Year established: 1787
Ownership: Public

This large public university offers programs at all levels in computer science, information science, and electrical engineering. Evening classes and distance learning are available.

Degrees Offered

UNDERGRADUATE
B.S., Computer Engineering
B.S., Computer Science
⒜ B.S., Electrical Engineering
B.S., Information Science

GRADUATE
M.S., Computer Science
M.S., Electrical Engineering
M.S., Information Science
M.S., Telecommunications
Ph.D., Computer Science
Ph.D., Electrical Engineering
Ph.D., Information Science

Approximate Cost of Degrees

UNDERGRADUATE, RESIDENT
$29,700

UNDERGRADUATE, NONRESIDENT
$60,400

MASTER'S, RESIDENT
$14,600

MASTER'S, NONRESIDENT
$28,500

DOCTORATE, RESIDENT
$24,400

DOCTORATE, NONRESIDENT
$47,600

Admissions Guidelines

UNDERGRADUATE
High school diploma, SAT and/or ACT required

GRADUATE
Accredited bachelor's, GRE required

Undergraduate Programs

The new B.S. in Computer Engineering gives roughly equal weight to hardware and software issues.

The B.S. in Computer Science focuses on theory, programming, and hardware-software interaction.

The ABET-accredited B.S. in Electrical Engineering is available with specializations in computers, electronics, and telecommunications/signal processing.

The B.S. in Information Science focuses on databases, software applications, software engineering, and human-computer interaction.

Graduate Programs

The 30-hour M.S. in Computer Science is available with optional concentrations in artificial intelligence and software engineering. A thesis or project is required.

The 30-hour M.S. in Electrical Engineering is available with specializations in bioengineering, computer engineering, control, electronics, image processing/computer vision, and signal processing/communications. No thesis is required.

The 36-hour M.S. in Information Science incorporates study of cognitive science and computational mathematics into a curriculum dedicated largely to software applications and software engineering. No thesis is required. An optional track emphasizing medical informatics is available.

The 48-hour M.S. in Telecommunications focuses on technical issues in computer networking and telecommunications, although policy and management issues are also addressed. A thesis or capstone project is required.

The Ph.D. in Computer Science involves two comprehensive examinations in addition to the standard coursework and dissertation requirements.

The Ph.D. in Electrical Engineering involves a qualifying examination in addition to the standard coursework and dissertation requirements. Concentrations are available in bioengineering, computer engineering, control, electronics, image processing/computer vision, and signal processing/communications.

The Ph.D. in Information Science involves a qualifying examination in addition to the standard coursework and dissertation requirements. An optional track emphasizing telecommunications is available.

Contact Information

Phone
General information: (412) 624-4141
Admissions (undergraduate): (412) 624-7488
Computer science: (412) 624-8490
Electrical engineering: (412) 624-8000

Information science and telecommunications: (412) 624-9400

Fax
Computer science: (412) 624-8854
Electrical engineering: (412) 624-8003
Information science and telecommunications: (412) 624-2788

E-mail
Admissions (undergraduate): oafa+@pitt.edu
Computer science: Dr. Siegfried Treu (treu@cs.pitt.edu)
Electrical engineering: eedept@ee.pitt.edu
Information science and telecommunications: isadmit@sis.pitt.edu

---

University of Rhode Island   www.uri.edu ☆☆☆

Kingston, RI 02881

Year established: 1892
Ownership: Public

This major public research university offers rigorous programs at all levels in the most preeminent information technology fields. Most of these programs emphasize hands-on work and research; students should expect to spend almost as much time in the laboratory as they spend in the classroom. Evening classes, weekend study, and extension courses are available.

Degrees Offered

Undergraduate
ABET B.S., Computer Engineering
B.S., Computer Science
ABET B.S., Electrical Engineering

Graduate
M.S., Computer Science
M.S., Electrical Engineering
Ph.D., Electrical Engineering

Approximate Cost of Degrees

Undergraduate, Resident
$17,500

Undergraduate, Nonresident (Regional)
$24,200

Undergraduate, Nonresident (Other)
$50,400

Graduate, Resident
$6,800

Graduate, Nonresident (Regional)
$9,500

Graduate, Nonresident (Other)
$16,700

Admissions Guidelines

Undergraduate
High school diploma, SAT and/or ACT required

Graduate
Accredited bachelor's, GRE required

Undergraduate Programs
The ABET-accredited B.S. in Computer Engineering focuses on hardware issues, networking, hardware-software interaction, and low-level programming.

The B.S. in Computer Science represents a traditional curriculum in the field focusing primarily on theory, software engineering, and databases.

The ABET-accredited B.S. in Electrical Engineering primarily addresses circuits, electronics, signal processing, and computer engineering.

Graduate Programs

The M.S. in Computer Science is available with formal research specializations in analysis of algorithms, artificial intelligence, computer-aided education, computer architecture, databases, distributed computing, expert systems, graphical user interfaces, numerical analysis, operating systems, programming languages, real time systems, simulation, software engineering, statistical computation, symbolic and algebraic computation, theory of computation, and VLSI systems. Students may elect to undertake a 32-hour thesis track, a 30-hour non-thesis track (culminating in a research paper), and 40-hour applied non-thesis track. All students must pass a written comprehensive examination.

The 30-hour M.S. in Electrical Engineering is available with formal research specializations in acoustics and underwater acoustics, biomedical engineering, computer engineering and VLSI, communication theory, digital signal processing, electrical

and optical properties of materials, electromagnetic fields and optical communication, and systems theory. A thesis or research paper is required.

The Ph.D. in Electrical Engineering involves a written qualifying examination in addition to the standard coursework and dissertation requirements.

Other Programs

The Ph.D. in Applied Mathematical Sciences is available with a computer science specialization. Contact the Department of Computer Science for more information.

Contact Information

PHONE
General information: (401) 874-1000
Admissions (undergraduate): (401) 874-7000
Admissions (graduate): (401) 874-2262
Computer science: (401) 874-2701
Electrical engineering: (401) 874-2506

E-MAIL
Admissions (undergraduate):
uriadmit@uriacc.uri.edu
Admissions (graduate): urigrad@uriacc.uri.edu
Computer science: department@cs.uri.edu

University of Rochester   www.rochester.edu ☆☆½

Office of Admissions
University of Rochester
Box 270251
Rochester, NY 14627-0251

Year established: 1850
Ownership: Private

This large private university offers research-oriented programs in computer science and electrical engineering. Evening classes are available.

Degrees Offered

UNDERGRADUATE
B.A., Computer Science
B.S., Computer Science
🅰🅱🅴🆃 B.S., Electrical Engineering

GRADUATE
M.S., Electrical Engineering
Ph.D., Computer Science
Ph.D., Electrical Engineering

Approximate Cost of Degrees

UNDERGRADUATE
$97,700

MASTER'S
$28,200

DOCTORATE
$50,000

Admissions Guidelines

UNDERGRADUATE
High school diploma, SAT and/or ACT required

GRADUATE
Accredited bachelor's, GRE required

Undergraduate Programs
The major in Computer Science is available with informal specializations in computer systems, natural language and knowledge representation, theory, and vision and robotics.

The ABET-accredited B.S. in Electrical Engineering is available with specializations in biomedical engineering, computers, signals/systems/communications, VLSI design, and waves/devices.

Graduate Programs
The 30-hour M.S. in Electrical Engineering can be tailored to fit the needs of virtually any student. No thesis is required.

The Ph.D. in Computer Science involves a comprehensive written examination and teaching internship in addition to the standard coursework and dissertation requirements.

The Ph.D. in Electrical Engineering is available with research concentrations in biomedical ultrasound and biomedical engineering, integrated electronics and computer engineering, microelectromechanics and electrostatics, optoelectronics, signal/image processing and communications, and superconductivity and solid-state electronics.

Contact Information

PHONE
General information: (716) 275-6111
Admissions: (716) 275-3221 or (888) 822-2256
Computer science: (716) 275-5671
Electrical and computer engineering: (716) 275-4054

FAX
Admissions: (716) 461-4595
Computer science: (716) 273-4556
Electrical and computer engineering: (716) 275-2073

E-MAIL
Admissions: Admit@admissions.rochester.edu
Electrical and computer engineering:
eceinfo@ece.rochester.edu

University of South Carolina www.sc.edu ★★★

Columbia, SC 29208

Year established: 1801
Ownership: Public

This major public, research-oriented university offers programs at all levels in computer engineering, computer science, and electrical engineering. Evening classes, weekend study, and distance learning are available.

Degrees Offered

UNDERGRADUATE
(ABET) B.S., Computer Engineering
B.S., Computer Information Systems
(CSAB) B.S., Computer Science
(ABET) B.S., Electrical Engineering

GRADUATE
M.E., Computer Engineering
M.E., Electrical Engineering
M.S., Computer Engineering
M.S., Computer Science
M.S., Electrical Engineering
Ph.D., Computer Engineering
Ph.D., Computer Science
Ph.D., Electrical Engineering

Approximate Cost of Degrees

UNDERGRADUATE, RESIDENT
$19,300

UNDERGRADUATE, NONRESIDENT
$44,800

MASTER'S, RESIDENT
$7,800

MASTER'S, NONRESIDENT
$14,900

DOCTORATE, RESIDENT
$13,000

DOCTORATE, NONRESIDENT
$24,900

Admissions Guidelines

UNDERGRADUATE

High school diploma, SAT and/or ACT required

GRADUATE

Accredited bachelor's, GRE required

Undergraduate Programs

The ABET-accredited B.S. in Computer Engineering focuses on hardware, theory, and hardware-software interaction in its core requirements.

The B.S. in Computer Information Systems focuses on databases, information systems, software applications, software engineering, and hardware-software interaction.

The CSAB-accredited B.S. in Computer Science focuses on theory and software applications.

The ABET-accredited B.S. in Electrical Engineering focuses on electronics and computer engineering.

Graduate Programs

The 30-hour Master of Engineering (M.E.) programs in Computer Engineering and Electrical Engineering are designed primarily for reentry students who want to increase their practical knowledge of the field. No thesis is required.

The 30-hour M.S. programs in Computer Engineering and Electrical Engineering are primarily research-oriented degrees well suited to students who want to pursue doctoral work later. A thesis is required.

The 33-hour M.S. in Computer Science is a well-rounded program that addresses both theory and software applications in a rigorous, comprehensive fashion. A thesis or project is required.

The Ph.D. programs in Computer Engineering and Electrical Engineering each involve a qualifying examination in addition to the standard coursework and dissertation requirements.

The Ph.D. in Computer Science requires two comprehensive examinations in addition to the standard coursework and dissertation requirements.

Contact Information

PHONE

General information: (803) 777-7000
Admissions (undergraduate): (803) 777-7700
Admissions (graduate): (803) 777-4243
Computer science and engineering: (803) 777-4195
Electrical engineering: (803) 777-4195

FAX

Admissions (undergraduate): (803) 777-0101
Admissions (graduate): (803) 777-2972
Computer science and engineering: (803) 777-8045
Electrical engineering: (803) 777-8045

E-MAIL

Admissions (undergraduate): admissions-ugrad@sc.edu
Admissions (graduate): gradapp@sc.edu
Electrical engineering (undergraduate): Leck Mason (mason@ece.sc.edu)
Electrical engineering (graduate): Theresa Masters (masters@ece.sc.edu)

University of Southern California www.usc.edu ☆☆½

Los Angeles, CA 90089-0911

Year established: 1879
Ownership: Private

This major private university offers programs at all levels in the hottest information technology fields. Evening classes, weekend study, extension courses, and distance learning are available.

Degrees Offered

UNDERGRADUATE

B.S., Computer Engineering and Computer Science
B.S., Computer Science
ABET B.S., Electrical Engineering

GRADUATE

M.S., Computer Engineering
M.S., Computer Science
M.S., Electrical Engineering
M.S., Systems Architecture and Engineering

E.E.
Ph.D., Computer Engineering
Ph.D., Computer Science
Ph.D., Electrical Engineering

Approximate Cost of Degrees

UNDERGRADUATE
$94,500

MASTER'S
$35,500

DOCTORATE
$59,100

Admissions Guidelines

UNDERGRADUATE
High school diploma, SAT and/or ACT required

GRADUATE
Accredited bachelor's, GRE required

Undergraduate Programs
The B.S. in Computer Engineering and Computer Science focuses on issues in software engineering, hardware systems, and hardware-software engineering. A minor in multimedia systems is available.

The B.S. in Computer Science focuses on theory, programming, and software systems. A minor in multimedia systems is available.

The ABET-accredited B.S. in Electrical Engineering focuses on computer engineering, electronics, and signal processing.

Graduate Programs
The 27-hour M.S. in Computer Engineering addresses both hardware and software issues from a holistic, systems-oriented perspective. No thesis is required. This program can be completed by distance learning.

The 27-hour M.S. in Computer Science is available with formal specializations in computer networks, multimedia and creative technologies, robotics and automation, and software engineering. No thesis is required. This program can be completed by distance learning.

The 27-hour M.S. in Electrical Engineering is available with formal specializations in aerospace controls, computer networks, multimedia and

creative technology, systems architecture and engineering, and VLSI design. No thesis is required. This program can be completed by distance learning.

The 30-hour M.S. in Systems Architecture and Engineering is available with formal specializations in artificial intelligence and neural networks, automation and control systems, communications and signal processing, computer and information systems, construction, engineering management systems, integrated media systems, manufacturing systems, software process architecture, and systems. No thesis is required. This program can be completed by distance learning.

The degree of Electrical Engineer (E.E.) is a 30-hour, post-master's program designed for professional engineers. A qualifying examination is required in addition to a final supervised project. All course requirements for this program can be completed by distance learning.

The Ph.D. programs in Computer Engineering and Electrical Engineering involve one year of full-time residency in addition to the standard coursework and dissertation requirements.

The Ph.D. program in Computer Science involves one year of full-time residency and a written qualifying examination in addition to the standard coursework and dissertation requirements.

Other Programs
An M.S. in Integrated Media Systems is also available. For more information, contact the Department of Computer Science.

Contact Information

PHONE
General information: (213) 740-1111
Admissions (undergraduate): (213) 740-8899
Admissions (graduate): (213) 740-5686
Computer science: (213) 740-4496
Electrical engineering: (213) 740-4700

FAX
Computer science: (213) 740-7285
Electrical engineering: (213) 740-8677

E-MAIL
Computer science: csdept@pollux.usc.edu
Electrical engineering: eepdept@mizar.usc.edu

University of Tennessee   www.utk.edu ☆☆

Knoxville, TN 37996

Year established: 1794
Ownership: Public

This major public university offers programs at all levels in every major information technology field. Evening classes, weekend study, extension courses, and distance learning are available.

Degrees Offered

UNDERGRADUATE
B.S., Computer Engineering
B.S., Computer Science
🄰 B.S., Electrical Engineering

GRADUATE
M.S., Computer Science
M.S., Electrical Engineering
M.S., Information Sciences
Ph.D., Computer Science
Ph.D., Electrical Engineering

Approximate Cost of Degrees

UNDERGRADUATE, RESIDENT
$17,000

UNDERGRADUATE, NONRESIDENT
$42,300

MASTER'S, RESIDENT
$6,700

MASTER'S, NONRESIDENT
$16,300

DOCTORATE, RESIDENT
$11,200

DOCTORATE, NONRESIDENT
$27,100

Admissions Guidelines

UNDERGRADUATE
High school diploma, SAT and/or ACT required

GRADUATE
Accredited bachelor's, GRE required

Undergraduate Programs

The B.S. in Computer Engineering focuses largely on hardware issues and hardware-software interaction.

The B.S. in Computer Science focuses on theory, programming, and software applications.

The ABET-accredited B.S. in Electrical Engineering is available with optional specializations in communications, controls, computers, electronics, and power systems.

Graduate Programs

The 30-hour M.S. in Computer Science culminates in a thesis or comprehensive examination.

The M.S. in Electrical Engineering is available with a 30-hour track culminating in a thesis or a 33-hour track culminating in a project.

The 42-hour M.S. in Information Sciences can be tailored to fit individual student needs. A thesis or comprehensive written examination is required. This program can be completed almost entirely through distance learning.

The Ph.D. in Computer Science involves a comprehensive examination in addition to the standard coursework and dissertation requirements.

The Ph.D. in Electrical Engineering involves two batteries of comprehensive examinations in addition to the standard coursework and dissertation requirements. Research specializations are available in circuit theory, communication theory, computers, control systems, electro-optics, electromagnetic theory, plasma engineering, power electronics, power systems, and solid-state engineering.

Contact Information

PHONE
General information: (865) 974-1000
Admissions (undergraduate): (865) 974-2184
Admissions (graduate): (865) 974-3251
Computer science: (865) 974-5067
Electrical engineering: (865) 974-3461
Information sciences: (865) 974-2148

FAX
Computer science: (865) 974-4404
Electrical engineering: (865) 974-5483
Information sciences: (865) 974-4967

E-MAIL
Admissions (undergraduate): admissions@utk.edu
Admissions (graduate): gsinfo@utk.edu
Computer science: info@cs.utk.edu

Electrical engineering: Courtney Smith (courtney-smith@mail.ee.utk.edu)
Information sciences: sis@utk.edu

University of Tennessee Space Institute   www.utsi.edu ☆☆½

B.H. Goethert Parkway
Tullahoma, TN 37388-9700

Year established: 1964
Ownership: Public

This technology-focused public university offers intensive, research-oriented graduate programs in computer science and electrical engineering. Evening classes and extension courses are available.

Degrees Offered

GRADUATE
M.S., Computer Science
M.S., Electrical Engineering
Ph.D., Electrical Engineering

Approximate Cost of Degrees

MASTER'S, RESIDENT
$6,700

MASTER'S, NONRESIDENT
$16,300

DOCTORATE, RESIDENT
$11,200

DOCTORATE, NONRESIDENT
$27,100

Admissions Guidelines

GRADUATE
Accredited bachelor's, GRE required

Graduate Programs
The 30-hour M.S. in Computer Science focuses largely on theory, although students are also given opportunity to study more applied aspects of the discipline. A thesis or project is required.

The 33-hour M.S. in Electrical Engineering focuses for the most part on electronics, digital systems, and communications. A thesis or project is required.

The Ph.D. in Electrical Engineering can be earned at UTSI only under special circumstances, and only after students pass a qualifying examination at the University of Tennessee, Knoxville.

Contact Information

PHONE
General information: (888) 822-8874
Admissions: (931) 393-7432
Computer science: (931) 393-7296
Electrical engineering: (931) 393-7457

FAX
Admissions: (931) 393-7346

E-MAIL
Admissions: admit@utsi.edu
Computer science: Dr. Bruce Whitehead (bwhitehe@utsi.edu)
Electrical engineering: Dr. Roy Joseph (rjoseph@utsi.edu)

University of Texas at Arlington   www.uta.edu ☆☆½

701 South Nedderman Drive
Arlington, TX 76019

Year established: 1895
Ownership: Public

This major public university offers degrees at all levels in a variety of information technology fields. Evening classes, weekend study, extension courses, and distance learning are available. Two of the programs described below (the M.S. programs in CSE and EE) can be completed entirely online, and another (the M.Sw.E.) can be completed almost entirely by extension.

Degrees Offered

UNDERGRADUATE

(ABET) (CSAB) B.S., Computer Science and Engineering
(ABET) B.S., Electrical Engineering
B.S., Information Systems

GRADUATE

M.C.S.
M.Eng., Computer Science and Engineering
M.Eng., Electrical Engineering
M.S., Computer Science
M.S., Computer Science and Engineering
M.S., Electrical Engineering
M.S., Information Systems
M.Sw.E.
Ph.D., Computer Science
Ph.D., Computer Science and Engineering
Ph.D., Electrical Engineering

Approximate Cost of Degrees

UNDERGRADUATE, RESIDENT
$18,900

UNDERGRADUATE, NONRESIDENT
$46,100

MASTER'S, RESIDENT
$6,200

MASTER'S, NONRESIDENT
$12,600

DOCTORATE, RESIDENT
$10,300

DOCTORATE, NONRESIDENT
$21,000

Admissions Guidelines

UNDERGRADUATE
High school diploma, SAT and/or ACT required

GRADUATE
Accredited bachelor's, GRE required

Undergraduate Programs

The ABET-accredited and CSAB-accredited B.S. in Computer Science and Engineering focuses largely on theory, software engineering, and hardware-software interaction.

The ABET-accredited B.S. in Electrical Engineering is available with optional tracks emphasizing computing or biomedical engineering.

Graduate Programs

The 38-hour Master of Computer Science (M.C.S.) is designed primarily for working professionals and is particularly well suited for reentry students. A project is generally required, but may be waived for students who can document equivalent work experience.

The 38-hour Master of Engineering (M.Eng.) programs in Computer Science and Engineering and in Electrical Engineering are designed primarily for working professionals and are particularly well suited for reentry students. Both programs generally require a project, but this requirement may be waived for students who can document equivalent work experience.

The 31-hour M.S. in Computer Science is a primarily research-oriented degree focusing on theory and software applications. A thesis is required.

The 31-hour M.S. in Computer Science and Engineering is a primarily research-oriented degree focusing on theory, software engineering, telecommunications, and hardware-software interaction. A thesis is required. This program can be completed by distance learning.

The 36-hour M.S. in Electrical Engineering is a highly flexible program and can be tailored to fit the needs of virtually any student. A thesis is required. This program can be completed by distance learning.

The 37-hour professional Master of Software Engineering (M.Sw.E.) is delivered by streaming video to various corporate extension sites throughout north Texas. A project is required.

The Ph.D. programs in Computer Science and in Computer Science and Engineering involve two written comprehensive examinations in addition to the standard coursework and dissertation requirements.

The Ph.D. in Electrical Engineering is available with research specializations in applied physical electronics, communications, electromagnetic fields/microwave systems/optics, energy systems, high frequency microelectronic devices and circuits, microprocessors and digital systems, signal processing, and systems and controls. Two comprehensive written examinations are involved in addition to the standard coursework and dissertation requirements.

Other Programs

Management-oriented B.S. and M.S. programs in Information Systems are also available. For more information, contact the department at (817) 272-3502.

Contact Information

PHONE

General information: (817) 272-2222
Admissions (undergraduate): (817) 272-6287
Admissions (graduate): (817) 272-3186
Distance learning: (817) 272-3021
Computer science and engineering: (817) 272-3785
Electrical engineering: (817) 272-2672

FAX

Computer science and engineering: (817) 272-3784
Electrical engineering: (817) 272-2253

E-MAIL

General information: mavmail@uta.edu
Computer science and engineering:
cseinfo@cse.uta.edu
Electrical engineering: eeinfo@engineering.uta.edu

University of Texas at Austin   www.utexas.edu ☆☆☆

Austin, TX 78712

Year established: 1883
Ownership: Public

This large public university offers programs at all levels in computer sciences and electrical engineering. Evening classes, weekend study, co-op study, extension courses, and distance learning are available.

Degrees Offered

UNDERGRADUATE

B.A., Computer Sciences
B.S., Computer Sciences
ABET B.S., Electrical Engineering

GRADUATE

M.A., Computer Sciences
M.S., Computer Sciences
M.S.E., Electrical and Computer Engineering
M.S.E., Software Engineering
Ph.D., Computer Sciences
Ph.D., Electrical and Computer Engineering

Approximate Cost of Degrees

UNDERGRADUATE, RESIDENT
$13,600

UNDERGRADUATE, NONRESIDENT
$39,400

MASTER'S, RESIDENT
$5,800

MASTER'S, NONRESIDENT
$13,600

DOCTORATE, RESIDENT
$9,700

DOCTORATE, NONRESIDENT
$22,600

Admissions Guidelines

UNDERGRADUATE

High school diploma, SAT and/or ACT required

GRADUATE

Accredited bachelor's, GRE required

Undergraduate Programs

The major in Computer Sciences focuses on theory, programming, and hardware-software interaction.

The ABET-accredited B.S. in Electrical Engineering focuses largely on electronics, communications, and digital systems in its core requirements. A computer engineering track (which holds separate ABET accreditation) is also available.

Graduate Programs

The 39-hour M.A. in Computer Sciences is available with specializations in analysis of algorithms and programs, artificial intelligence, automatic theorem proving, communication protocols, computer architecture, computer networks, database management, formal theory of programming languages, graphics, mathematical software, multimedia, natural language processing, neural networks, numerical analysis, operating systems, parallel programming, program verification, real-time systems, system modeling, theoretical computer sciences, and VLSI. A thesis is required.

The 36-hour M.S. in Computer Sciences is available with specializations in analysis of algorithms and programs, artificial intelligence, automatic theorem proving, communication protocols, computer architecture, computer networks, database management, formal theory of programming languages, graphics, mathematical software, multimedia, natural language processing, neural networks, numerical analysis, operating systems, parallel programming, program verification, real-time systems, system modeling, theoretical computer sciences, and VLSI. No thesis is required.

The 33-hour Master of Science in Engineering (M.S.E.) in Electrical and Computer Engineering is available with formal specializations in biomedical engineering, computer engineering, electromagnetics and acoustics, energy systems, manufacturing systems engineering, plasma/quantum electronics/optics, solid-state electronics, and telecommunications/information systems engineering. A thesis or project is required.

The 33-hour Master of Science in Engineering (M.S.E.) in Software Engineering is designed primarily for reentry students who already work in the field. A project is required.

Depending on student research interests, the Ph.D. in Computer Sciences may focus on application, systems, or theory in its course requirements. A qualifying examination is involved in addition to the standard coursework and dissertation requirements.

The Ph.D. in Electrical and Computer Engineering follows a student-defined, faculty-approved program of study, which may include research, internship, and other components in addition to the standard coursework and dissertation requirements.

Other Programs

Several programs are available in management information systems: the B.B.A. is available with a management information systems emphasis, an M.S. in Science and Technology Commercialization is available, and a Ph.D. in Management Science and Information Systems is also offered through the Department of Management and Information Science. For more information, contact the Red McCombs School of Business at (512) 471-5921.

Contact Information

PHONE
Admissions (undergraduate): (512) 475-7440
Admissions (graduate and international): (512) 475-7390
Computer sciences: (512) 471-7316
Electrical and computer engineering: (512) 471-6179

FAX
Admissions (undergraduate): (512) 475-7475
Admissions (graduate and international): (512) 475-7395
Computer sciences: (512) 471-8885
Electrical and computer engineering: (512) 471-5532

E-MAIL
Admissions (undergraduate): frmn@uts.cc.utexas.edu
Admissions (graduate): adgrd@utxdp.dp.utexas.edu
Admissions (international): adint@utxdp.dp.utexas.edu
Computer sciences (undergraduate): under-info@cs.utexas.edu
Computer sciences (graduate): csadmis@cs.utexas.edu

University of Texas at Dallas   www.utdallas.edu ☆☆☆½

P.O. Box 830688
Richardson, TX 75083-0688

Year established: 1969
Ownership: Public

This large public university offers degrees at all levels in a variety of information technology fields. Evening classes, weekend study, extension courses, co-op study, and distance learning are available. The master's degree programs in computer science and electrical engineering can be completed online.

Degrees Offered

UNDERGRADUATE
B.S., Computer Science
ABET B.S., Electrical Engineering

GRADUATE
M.S., Computer Engineering
M.S., Computer Science
M.S., Electrical Engineering
M.S., Telecommunications Engineering
Ph.D., Computer Science
Ph.D., Electrical Engineering

Approximate Cost of Degrees

UNDERGRADUATE, RESIDENT
$17,100

UNDERGRADUATE, NONRESIDENT
$45,900

MASTER'S, RESIDENT
$8,400

MASTER'S, NONRESIDENT
$19,000

DOCTORATE, RESIDENT
$14,100

DOCTORATE, NONRESIDENT
$31,700

Admissions Guidelines

UNDERGRADUATE
High school diploma, SAT and/or ACT required

GRADUATE
Accredited bachelor's with 3.0 GPA, GRE required

Undergraduate Programs

The B.S. in Computer Science focuses on computational mathematics, computer science theory, software applications, and programming.

The ABET-accredited B.S. in Electrical Engineering emphasizes communication systems, electronics, and digital circuits.

Graduate Programs

The 33-hour M.S. in Computer Engineering is available with formal specializations in computer architecture, computer systems, and VLSI systems. No thesis is required.

The 33-hour M.S. in Computer Science is available with optional tracks in software engineering and in networks and telecommunications. No thesis is required. This program can be completed by distance learning.

The 33-hour M.S. in Electrical Engineering is available with formal concentrations in communication and signal processing, digital microelectronics systems, digital systems, materials and systems, optical devices, solid-state devices and circuits, and wireless communications systems. No thesis is required. This program can be completed by distance learning.

The 33-hour M.S. in Telecommunications Engineering is available with formal concentrations in array processing, digital communications, high-speed networks, mobile communications, optical communications, and speech processing. No thesis is required.

The Ph.D. programs in Computer Science and Electrical Engineering each involve qualifying examinations in addition to the standard coursework and dissertation requirements.

Contact Information

PHONE
General information: (972) 883-2111
Admissions (undergraduate): (972) 883-2341 or (800) 889-2343
Computer science: (972) 883-2185
Electrical engineering: (972) 883-6755

FAX
General information: (972) 883-6803

E-MAIL
Admissions (undergraduate):
ugrad-admissions@utdallas.edu
Admissions (graduate):
grad-admissions@utdallas.edu
Electrical engineering: Dr. William Frensley
(frensley@utdallas.edu)
Computer science (graduate):
cs-grad-info@utdallas.edu

University of Texas at San Antonio   www.utsa.edu ☆☆½

6900 North Loop, 1604 West
San Antonio, TX 78249-0619

Year established: 1969
Ownership: Public

This major public university offers hands-on programs at the undergraduate and graduate levels in computer science and electrical engineering. Evening classes, weekend study, extension courses, and distance learning are available.

Degrees Offered

UNDERGRADUATE
B.S., Computer Science
(ABET) B.S., Electrical Engineering

GRADUATE
M.S., Computer Science
M.S., Electrical Engineering
Ph.D., Computer Science

Approximate Cost of Degrees

UNDERGRADUATE, RESIDENT
$13,100

UNDERGRADUATE, NONRESIDENT
$40,200

MASTER'S, RESIDENT
$5,700

MASTER'S, NONRESIDENT
$13,800

DOCTORATE, RESIDENT
$9,500

DOCTORATE, NONRESIDENT
$23,000

Admissions Guidelines

UNDERGRADUATE
High school diploma, SAT and/or ACT required

GRADUATE
Accredited bachelor's with 3.0 GPA, GRE required

Undergraduate Programs

The B.S. in Computer Science focuses on theory, computational mathematics, and software engineering.

The ABET-accredited B.S. in Electrical Engineering is available with particularly strong computer engineering options.

Graduate Programs

The 36-hour M.S. in Computer Science focuses on theory and computational mathematics in its core requirements, but can be tailored to fit a variety of interests. A thesis, project, or series of research papers is required.

The 36-hour M.S. in Electrical Engineering focuses on electronics, digital systems, communications, and computer engineering. A thesis or comprehensive examination is required.

The Ph.D. in Computer Science is available with optional specializations in high-performance computational techniques and high-performance programming environments. A qualifying examination is required in addition to the standard coursework and dissertation components.

Other Programs

An M.S. in Management of Technology is available and can be completed almost entirely by distance learning. For more information, contact the program office at (210) 458-5372.

Contact Information

PHONE
Admissions (undergraduate): (210) 458-4599 or (800) 669-0919
Admissions (graduate): (210) 458-4330
Computer science: (210) 458-4453
Engineering: (210) 458-4490

FAX
Engineering: (210) 458-5589

E-MAIL
Admissions (graduate): graduatestudies@utsa.edu
Computer science: Dr. Richard Sincovec (sincovec@cs.utsa.edu)
Engineering: info@voyager1.utsa.edu

University of Toledo

www.utoledo.edu ☆☆½

Department of Electrical Engineering and Computer Science
The College of Engineering
2801 West Bancroft
Toledo, OH 43606-3390

Year established: 1872
Ownership: Public

This midsize public university offers degrees at all levels in electrical engineering and a top-notch, double-accredited undergraduate program in computer science and engineering. Evening classes, weekend study, co-op study, extension courses, and distance learning are available.

Degrees Offered

UNDERGRADUATE
[ABET] [CSAB] B.S., Computer Science and Engineering
[ABET] B.S., Electrical Engineering
[ABET] B.S.E.T., Electronic(s) Engineering Technology

GRADUATE
M.S., Electrical Engineering
Ph.D., Electrical Engineering

Approximate Cost of Degrees

UNDERGRADUATE, RESIDENT
$18,400

UNDERGRADUATE, NONRESIDENT
$43,900

GRADUATE, RESIDENT
$9,700

GRADUATE, NONRESIDENT
$19,300

DOCTORATE, RESIDENT
$16,200

DOCTORATE, NONRESIDENT
$32,100

Admissions Guidelines

UNDERGRADUATE
High school diploma, SAT and/or ACT required

GRADUATE
Accredited bachelor's, GRE required

Undergraduate Programs

The ABET-accredited and CSAB-accredited B.S. in Computer Science and Engineering is organized around co-op work. The program gives roughly equal weight to theory and hands-on work, but deals with both in a rigorous and comprehensive manner.

The ABET-accredited B.S. in Electrical Engineering is organized around co-op work study plans whereby students gain hands-on knowledge in the field.

The ABET-accredited B.S. in Engineering Technology (B.S.E.T.) in Electronic(s) Engineering Technology stresses computer engineering, quality control, software reliability, hardware-software interaction, and communications.

Graduate Programs

The 36-hour M.S. in Electrical Engineering is available with concentrations in applied computational systems, applied electrosciences and control systems, communications and signal processing, and software and intelligent systems. No thesis is required.

The Ph.D. in Electrical Engineering is available with concentrations in applied computational systems, applied electrosciences and control systems, communications and signal processing, and software and intelligent systems. A qualifying examination is involved in addition to the standard coursework and dissertation requirements.

Other Programs

An information systems concentration is available within the M.B.A. program. Før more information, contact the program division at (419) 530-2420.

An M.S. in Engineering with emphasis in computer science is also available. For more information, contact the Department of Electrical Engineering and Computer Science.

Contact Information

PHONE
General information: (419) 530-4242
Admissions (undergraduate): (419) 530-8888
Admissions (graduate): (419) 530-4723
Admissions (international): (419) 530-1200
Electrical engineering and computer science:
(419) 530-8150

FAX
Electrical engineering and computer science:
(419) 530-8146

E-MAIL
Admissions (undergraduate):
enroll@utnet.utoledo.edu

University of Tulsa   www.utulsa.edu ☆☆☆

600 South College
Tulsa, OK 74104

Year established: 1894
Ownership: Private

This major private university offers programs at all levels in computer science and electrical engineering.
Evening classes are available.

Degrees Offered

UNDERGRADUATE
⬤ B.S., Computer Science
⬤ B.S., Electrical Engineering

GRADUATE
M.E., Electrical Engineering
M.S., Computer Science
M.S., Electrical Engineering
Ph.D., Computer Science

Approximate Cost of Degrees

UNDERGRADUATE
$58,900

MASTER'S
$20,600

DOCTORATE
$34,300

Admissions Guidelines

UNDERGRADUATE
High school diploma, SAT and/or ACT required

GRADUATE
Accredited bachelor's with 3.0 GPA, GRE required

Undergraduate Programs
The CSAB-accredited B.S. in Computer Science
focuses on theory and software applications. An
optional computer information systems specialization is available.

The ABET-accredited B.S. in Electrical Engineering focuses on electronics, digital circuits, and communication systems.

Graduate Programs
The 30-hour Master of Engineering (M.E.) in Electrical Engineering is designed primarily for professionals who want to increase their knowledge in the field. No thesis is required.

The 33-hour M.S. in Computer Science focuses on theory and software applications. A thesis or project is required.

The 30-hour M.S. in Electrical Engineering is a flexible, research-oriented program suitable for students who want to pursue doctoral work. A thesis or project is required.

The Ph.D. in Computer Science involves a two-semester internship, one year of full-time residency, and a battery of written comprehensive examinations in addition to the standard coursework and dissertation requirements.

Other Programs
The B.S. program in Applied Mathematics is available with an optional computer science specialization. For more information, contact the computer science department.

A Master of Engineering and Technology Management (M.E.T.M.) is also available. For more information, contact Rebecca Holland (rebecca-holland@utulsa.edu).

Contact Information

PHONE
General information: (918) 631-2000
Admissions (undergraduate): (918) 631-2307 or (800) 331-3050
Admissions (graduate): (918) 631-2336 or (800) 882-4723
Electrical engineering: (918) 631-3270

FAX
Admissions (undergraduate): (918) 631-5003
Electrical engineering: (918) 631-3344

E-MAIL
Admissions (undergraduate): admission@utulsa.edu
Admissions (graduate): grad@utulsa.edu
Computer science: Dr. Roger Wainwright (rogerw@euler.mcs.utulsa.edu)
Electrical engineering: Dr. Heng Ming Tai (Tai@utulsa.edu)

University of Utah

www.utah.edu ☆☆☆½

Salt Lake City, UT 84112

Year established: 1850
Ownership: Public

This major public university offers degrees at all levels in computer science and electrical engineering. Evening classes, weekend study, extension courses, and distance learning are available.

Degrees Offered

UNDERGRADUATE
🔲 B.S., Computer Engineering
B.S., Computer Science
🔲 B.S., Electrical Engineering

GRADUATE
M.E., Electrical Engineering
M.S., Computer Science
M.S., Electrical Engineering
Ph.D., Computer Science
Ph.D., Electrical Engineering

Approximate Cost of Degrees

UNDERGRADUATE, RESIDENT
$15,600

UNDERGRADUATE, NONRESIDENT
$39,300

MASTER'S, RESIDENT
$5,500

MASTER'S, NONRESIDENT
$13,700

DOCTORATE, RESIDENT
$9,100

DOCTORATE, NONRESIDENT
$22,800

Admissions Guidelines

UNDERGRADUATE
High school diploma, SAT and/or ACT required

GRADUATE
Accredited bachelor's with 3.0 GPA, GRE required. GRE subject exam strongly encouraged.

Undergraduate Programs
The ABET-accredited B.S. in Computer Engineering focuses on hardware, computational mathematics, and computer science theory.

The B.S. in Computer Science focuses on theory, software engineering, and hardware-software interaction.

The ABET-accredited B.S. in Electrical Engineering represents a highly diverse and flexible curriculum.

Graduate Programs
The 30-hour Master of Engineering (M.E.) in Electrical Engineering is a professional degree designed primarily for reentry students. No thesis is required.

The 30-hour M.S. in Computer Science is a strongly research-oriented degree focusing on theory, software applications, and software engineering. A thesis is required.

The 30-hour M.S. in Electrical Engineering is a strongly research-oriented degree representing a highly diverse and highly flexible curriculum in the field. A thesis is required.

The Ph.D. programs in Computer Science and Electrical Engineering each involve a qualifying exam and a comprehensive exam in addition to the standard coursework and dissertation requirements.

Other Programs

The University of Utah also offers M.S. and Ph.D. programs in Medical Informatics. For more information, contact the department at (801) 581-4080.

Contact Information

PHONE
General information: (801) 581-7200

Admissions: (801) 581-7281
Computer science and engineering: (801) 581-8224
Electrical engineering: (801) 581-6941

FAX
Computer science and engineering: (801) 581-5843
Electrical engineering: (801) 581-5281

E-MAIL
Computer science and engineering:
info@cs.utah.edu
Electrical engineering: Dr. V. John Mathews
(mathews@ee.utah.edu)

University of Vermont   www.uvm.edu ☆☆☆

Burlington, VT 05405

Year established: 1791
Ownership: Public

This large public university offers undergraduate and graduate programs in computer science and electrical engineering. Evening classes, extension courses, and distance learning are available.

Degrees Offered

UNDERGRADUATE
B.A., Computer Science
B.S., Computer Science
B.S., Computer Science and Information Systems
🔘 B.S., Electrical Engineering

GRADUATE
M.S., Computer Science
M.S., Electrical Engineering
Ph.D., Electrical Engineering

Approximate Cost of Degrees

UNDERGRADUATE, RESIDENT
$37,200

UNDERGRADUATE, NONRESIDENT
$83,300

MASTER'S, RESIDENT
$13,900

MASTER'S, NONRESIDENT
$31,200

DOCTORATE, RESIDENT
$23,200

DOCTORATE, NONRESIDENT
$52,100

Admissions Guidelines

UNDERGRADUATE
High school diploma, SAT and/or ACT required

GRADUATE
Accredited bachelor's, GRE required

Undergraduate Programs
The major in Computer Science focuses on theory and software applications. The B.A. degree gives more weight to the liberal arts and social sciences in its general distribution requirements, while the B.S. is oriented more toward mathematics and the natural sciences.

The B.S. in Computer Science and Information Systems focuses on software applications and management information systems.

The ABET-accredited B.S. in Electrical Engineering is available with optional specializations in biomedical engineering, computer engineering, and premedical engineering.

Graduate Programs

The 33-hour M.S. in Computer Science deals mainly with theory, software applications, and hardware-software interaction. No thesis is required.

The 30-hour M.S. in Electrical Engineering is available with specializations in electromagnetics/optics/plasmas, electronic circuits and digital systems, signals and systems, and solid-state devices. The thesis requirement is waived for students who can document two years of full-time on-the-job experience in the field.

The Ph.D. in Electrical Engineering is available with specializations in electromagnetics/optics/plasmas, electronic circuits and digital systems, signals and systems, and solid-state devices. A comprehensive written examination is required in addition to the standard coursework and dissertation requirements.

Contact Information

PHONE
General information: (802) 656-3131
Admissions (undergraduate): (802) 656-3370
Admissions (graduate): (802) 656-3160
Computer science: (802) 656-3330
Electrical engineering: (802) 656-3331

FAX
Admissions (undergraduate): (802) 656-8611
Admissions (graduate): (802) 656-2699
Computer science: (802) 656-0696
Electrical engineering: (802) 656-3358

E-MAIL
Admissions (undergraduate): admissions@uvm.edu
Admissions (graduate): graduate.admissions@uvm.edu
Computer science: Computer.Science@uvm.edu
Electrical engineering: eeinfo@emba.uvm.edu

University of Virginia

www.virginia.edu ☆☆☆

Charlottesville, VA 22904

Year established: 1819
Ownership: Public

This major public university offers degrees at all levels in computer science and electrical engineering. Evening classes and extension courses are available.

Degrees Offered

UNDERGRADUATE
(ABET) B.S., Computer Engineering
B.S., Computer Science
(ABET) B.S., Electrical Engineering

GRADUATE
M.C.S.
M.S., Computer Science
M.S., Electrical Engineering
Ph.D., Computer Science
Ph.D., Electrical Engineering

Approximate Cost of Degrees

UNDERGRADUATE, RESIDENT
$20,900

UNDERGRADUATE, NONRESIDENT
$73,800

MASTER'S, RESIDENT
$9,000

MASTER'S, NONRESIDENT
$27,600

DOCTORATE, RESIDENT
$15,100

DOCTORATE, NONRESIDENT
$46,000

Admissions Guidelines

UNDERGRADUATE
High school diploma, SAT and/or ACT required

GRADUATE
Accredited bachelor's, GRE required

Undergraduate Programs

The ABET-accredited B.S. in Computer Engineering focuses on hardware-software interaction and software engineering.

The B.S. in Computer Science focuses on computational mathematics and computer science theory.

The ABET-accredited B.S. in Electrical Engineering is available with informal specializations in applied electrophysics, communication, computer engineering, control systems, digital systems, and signal processing.

Graduate Programs

The 33-hour Master of Computer Science (M.C.S.) is a professional degree primarily intended for reentry students. A project is required.

The 30-hour M.S. in Computer Science is a largely research-oriented program focusing heavily on theoretical computer science and computational mathematics. A thesis is required.

The 30-hour M.S. in Electrical Engineering is a highly flexible, research-oriented program that can be tailored to fit the interests of a diverse student body. Informal specializations are available in circuits, communications, computer system analysis, control systems, digital system design,

electrodynamics, signal and image processing, and solid-state devices. A thesis is required.

The Ph.D. programs in Computer Science and Electrical Engineering each involve a qualifying examination in addition to the standard coursework and dissertation requirements.

Contact Information

PHONE
General information: (804) 924-0311
Admissions (undergraduate): (804) 982-3200
Computer science: (804) 982-2200
Electrical engineering: (804) 924-6073

FAX
Admissions (undergraduate): (804) 924-3587
Computer science: (804) 982-2214
Electrical engineering: (804) 924-8818

E-MAIL
Admissions (undergraduate):
undergrad-admission@virginia.edu
Computer science: inquiry@cs.virginia.edu
Electrical engineering (undergraduate):
Peggy McCauley (pdm@virginia.edu)
Electrical engineering (graduate):
eegradoffice@virginia.edu

University of Washington   www.washington.edu ☆☆½

Office of Admissions
University of Washington
Schmitz Hall, Box 355840
Seattle, WA 98195-5840

Year established: 1861
Ownership: Public

This large public university offers programs at all levels in computer science and electrical engineering. Evening classes, weekend study, extension courses, and distance learning are available.

Degrees Offered

UNDERGRADUATE
ABET B.S., Computer Engineering
B.S., Computer Science
ABET B.S., Electrical Engineering

GRADUATE
M.S., Computer Science
M.S., Electrical Engineering
Ph.D., Computer Science

Ph.D., Electrical Engineering

Approximate Cost of Degrees

UNDERGRADUATE, RESIDENT
$18,600

UNDERGRADUATE, NONRESIDENT
$52,100

MASTER'S, RESIDENT
$7,400

MASTER'S, NONRESIDENT
$16,100

DOCTORATE, RESIDENT
$12,300

DOCTORATE, NONRESIDENT
$26,800

Admissions Guidelines

UNDERGRADUATE
High school diploma, SAT and/or ACT required

GRADUATE
Accredited bachelor's, GRE required

Undergraduate Programs
The ABET-accredited B.S. in Computer Engineering focuses on software engineering and hardware-software interaction.

The B.S. in Computer Science focuses on theory and software applications.

Graduate Programs
The 27-hour M.S. in Computer Science is available with informal specializations in applications, programming systems, systems, and theory. A thesis or comprehensive examination is required.

The 27-hour M.S. in Electrical Engineering primarily emphasizes electronics, digital systems, and communications. A thesis is generally required.

The Ph.D. in Computer Science is available with informal specializations in applications, programming systems, systems, and theory. A qualifying examination and a teaching assistantship are involved in addition to the standard coursework and dissertation requirements.

The Ph.D. in Electrical Engineering involves a qualifying examination and two consecutive semesters of full-time residency in addition to the standard coursework and dissertation requirements.

Contact Information

PHONE
General information: (206) 543-2100
Admissions (undergraduate): (206) 543-9686
Admissions (graduate): (206) 543-5929
Computer science/engineering: (206) 543-1695
Electrical engineering: (206) 543-6515

FAX
Computer science/engineering: (206) 543-2969
Electrical engineering: (206) 543-3842

E-MAIL
Admissions (undergraduate):
adkuwadm@u.washington.edu
Admissions (graduate): uwgrad@u.washington.edu
Computer science/engineering: Dr. Ed Lazowska
(lazowska@cs.washington.edu)
Electrical engineering: Dr. Blake Hannaford
(blake@u.washington.edu)

University of Wisconsin—Madison   www.wisc.edu ☆☆☆½

Madison, WI 53706

Year established: 1849
Ownership: Public

This large public university offers programs at all levels in computer sciences and electrical engineering with a variety of possible research and course specializations. Evening classes, weekend study, extension courses, and distance learning are available.

Degrees Offered

UNDERGRADUATE
B.S., Computer Engineering
B.S., Computer Sciences
ABET B.S., Electrical Engineering

GRADUATE
M.S., Computer Sciences
M.S., Electrical Engineering

Ph.D., Computer Sciences
Ph.D., Electrical Engineering

Approximate Cost of Degrees

UNDERGRADUATE, RESIDENT
$19,300

UNDERGRADUATE, NONRESIDENT
$56,100

Master's, Resident
$9,500

Master's, Nonresident
$28,400

Doctorate, Resident
$15,900

Doctorate, Nonresident
$47,400

Admissions Guidelines

Undergraduate
High school diploma, SAT and/or ACT required

Graduate
Accredited bachelor's, GRE required

Undergraduate Programs
The new B.S. in Computer Engineering is a mostly hardware-focused program, although students are given ample opportunity to specialize through the use of restricted electives.

The B.S. in Computer Sciences is available with informal specializations in artificial intelligence, computer architecture, foundations of computing, numerical methods, performance modeling and analysis, and systems programming.

The ABET-accredited B.S. in Electrical Engineering emphasizes electronics, digital systems, and communications. An optional computer engineering track is available.

Graduate Programs
The 30-hour M.S. in Computer Sciences is available with informal specializations in artificial intelligence, computer architecture, computer networks, database systems, distributed systems, mathematical programming, modeling and analysis of computer systems, numerical analysis, operating systems, programming languages, and theory. The program culminates in a thesis, project, or comprehensive examination.

The 30-hour M.S. in Electrical Engineering is available with informal specializations in automatic control systems, biomedical engineering, communication and signal processing, computer engineering, electromagnetic fields and waves, energy and power systems, plasmas and controlled fusion, photonics, and solid-state microelectronics. The program culminates in a thesis, project, or comprehensive examination.

The Ph.D. in Computer Sciences is available with informal specializations in artificial intelligence, computer architecture, computer networks, database systems, distributed systems, mathematical programming, modeling and analysis of computer systems, numerical analysis, operating systems, programming languages, and theory. Qualifying and preliminary examinations are required in addition to the standard coursework and dissertation components.

The Ph.D. in Electrical Engineering is available with informal specializations in automatic control systems, biomedical engineering, communication and signal processing, computer engineering, electromagnetic fields and waves, energy and power systems, plasmas and controlled fusion, photonics, and solid-state microelectronics. Qualifying and preliminary examinations are required in addition to the standard coursework and dissertation components.

Other Programs
Business-oriented B.S., M.B.A., and M.S. programs in Information Systems Analysis and Design are also available. For more information, contact the program office at (608) 262-1555.

Contact Information

Phone
Admissions (undergraduate): (608) 262-3961
Admissions (graduate): (608) 262-2433
Computer sciences: (608) 262-1204
Electrical and computer engineering: (608) 262-3840

Fax
Computer sciences: (608) 262-9777
Electrical and computer engineering: (608) 262-1267

E-mail
Admissions (undergraduate):
onwisconsin@admissions.wisc.edu
Admissions (graduate):
gradadmiss@bascom.wisc.edu
Computer sciences: cs@cs.wisc.edu
Electrical and computer engineering:
ece@engr.wisc.edu

University of Wyoming

www.uwyo.edu ☆☆☆

Laramie, WY 82071

Year established: 1886
Ownership: Public

This large public university offers programs at all levels in computer science and electrical engineering. Evening classes, weekend study, extension courses, and distance learning are available.

Degrees Offered

UNDERGRADUATE
CSAB B.S., Computer Science
ABET B.S., Electrical Engineering

GRADUATE
M.S., Computer Science
M.S., Electrical Engineering
Ph.D., Computer Science
Ph.D., Electrical Engineering

Approximate Cost of Degrees

UNDERGRADUATE, RESIDENT
$14,800

UNDERGRADUATE, NONRESIDENT
$36,300

MASTER'S, RESIDENT
$6,400

MASTER'S, NONRESIDENT
$14,400

DOCTORATE, RESIDENT
$10,700

DOCTORATE, NONRESIDENT
$24,000

Admissions Guidelines

UNDERGRADUATE
High school diploma, SAT and/or ACT required

GRADUATE
Accredited bachelor's with 3.0 GPA, GRE required

Undergraduate Programs

The CSAB-accredited B.S. in Computer Science focuses on software engineering, theory, and hardware-software interaction.

The ABET-accredited B.S. in Electrical Engineering focuses on electronics, digital systems, and electrophysics.

Graduate Programs

The 33-hour M.S. in Computer Science is available with informal concentrations in computer theory, machine intelligence, mathematical computation and modeling, and parallel computing. A thesis or research paper is required.

The 33-hour M.S. in Electrical Engineering is available with optional specializations in active circuit synthesis, analog and digital instrumentation, communication systems, control systems and robotics, energy conversion and distribution, microprocessors, power electronics, and signal processing. A thesis or research paper is required.

The Ph.D. in Computer Science is available with informal concentrations in computer theory, machine intelligence, mathematical computation and modeling, and parallel computing. A qualifying examination is required in addition to the standard coursework and dissertation components.

The Ph.D. in Electrical Engineering is available with informal concentrations in communication systems, control systems and robotics, energy conversion and distribution, power electronics, and signal processing. A qualifying examination is required in addition to the standard coursework and dissertation components.

Other Programs

A B.S. program in Management Information Systems is also available. For more information, contact the Department of Computer Science.

Contact Information

PHONE
General information: (307) 766-1121
Admissions (undergraduate): (307) 766-5160 or (800) 342-5996
Admissions (graduate): (307) 766-2287
Computer science: (307) 766-5190
Electrical engineering: (307) 766-2240

FAX
Computer science: (307) 766-4036
Electrical engineering: (307) 766-2248

E-MAIL
Computer science: cosc@uwyo.edu
Electrical engineering: ee.info@uwyo.edu

Utah State University   www.usu.edu ☆☆½

Logan, UT 84322

Year established: 1888
Ownership: Public

This large state university offers a variety of traditional programs at all levels in several major information technology fields. Evening classes, weekend study, and distance learning are available.

Degrees Offered

UNDERGRADUATE
B.A., Computer Science
CSAB B.S., Computer Science
ABET B.S., Computer Engineering
ABET B.S., Electrical Engineering

GRADUATE
M.E., Electrical Engineering
M.S., Computer Science
M.S., Electrical Engineering
E.E.
Ph.D., Computer Science
Ph.D., Electrical Engineering

Approximate Cost of Degrees

UNDERGRADUATE, RESIDENT
$13,500

UNDERGRADUATE, NONRESIDENT
$32,700

MASTER'S, RESIDENT
$5,100

MASTER'S, NONRESIDENT
$12,500

DOCTORATE, RESIDENT
$8,500

DOCTORATE, NONRESIDENT
$20,900

Admissions Guidelines

UNDERGRADUATE
High school diploma, SAT and/or ACT required

GRADUATE
Accredited bachelor's, GRE required

Undergraduate Programs

The major in Computer Science focuses largely on software engineering and theoretical computer science. The B.S. program is CSAB-accredited.

The ABET-accredited B.S. in Computer Engineering focuses largely on hardware-relevant issues.

The ABET-accredited B.S. in Electrical Engineering focuses on electronics, digital systems, and related fields. A specialization in digital and computer engineering is available.

Graduate Programs

The 30-hour Master of Engineering (M.E.) in Electrical Engineering is available with optional specializations in atmospheric and space sciences, communications, control and optimization, infrared and optical systems, microelectronics, microwaves, parallel computers and digital systems, and signal processing. No thesis is required.

The 32-hour M.S. in Computer Science is available with specializations in artificial intelligence, computer graphics, information systems, parallel and distributed computation, and software engineering. A thesis is required.

The 30-hour M.S. in Electrical Engineering culminates in a thesis, but is otherwise identical to the M.E. in Electrical Engineering (see above).

The degree of Electrical Engineer (E.E.) is a professional, post-master's credential emphasizing applied issues in the field. A project and accompanying detailed report are required.

The Ph.D. in Electrical Engineering is available with optional specializations in atmospheric and space sciences, communications, control and optimization, infrared and optical systems, micro-electronics, microwaves, parallel computers and digital systems, and signal processing. A qualifying examination is required in addition to the standard coursework and dissertation components.

Other Programs
Utah State University also offers an M.S. in Business Information Systems and Education. For more information, contact the department at (435) 797-2342.

M.S., M.Ed., Ed.S., and Ph.D. programs in Instructional Technology are also available. For more information, contact the department at (435) 797-2694.

Contact Information

PHONE
General information: (435) 797-1000
Computer science: (435) 797-2451
Electrical and computer engineering: (435) 797-2840

FAX
Computer science: (435) 797-3285
Electrical and computer engineering: (435) 797-3054

E-MAIL
Computer science: usucs@cc.usu.edu
Electrical engineering: info@ece.usu.edu

Vanderbilt University   www.vanderbilt.edu ☆☆

2201 West End Avenue
Nashville, TN 37235

Year established: 1873
Ownership: Private

This respected private university offers programs at all levels in computer science and electrical engineering. Evening classes, extension courses, co-op study, and distance learning are available.

Degrees Offered

UNDERGRADUATE
[ABET] B.S., Computer Engineering
[CSAB] B.S., Computer Science
[ABET] B.S., Electrical Engineering

GRADUATE
M.S., Computer Science
M.S., Electrical Engineering
Ph.D., Computer Science
Ph.D., Electrical Engineering

Approximate Cost of Degrees

UNDERGRADUATE
$100,300

MASTER'S
$37,700

DOCTORATE
$62,900

Admissions Guidelines

UNDERGRADUATE
High school diploma, SAT and/or ACT required

GRADUATE
Accredited bachelor's, GRE required

Undergraduate Programs
The ABET-accredited B.S. in Computer Engineering incorporates computer hardware, theory, and software engineering into a single, unified curriculum.

The CSAB-accredited B.S. in Computer Science focuses largely on theory, software applications, and programming.

The ABET-accredited B.S. in Electrical Engineering focuses mainly on electronics, digital circuits, communications, and computer engineering.

Graduate Programs
The 30-hour M.S. in Computer Science is available with optional specializations in algorithms, computational science, computational learning theory, database systems, graph algorithms, intelligent systems, machine learning, medical image processing, performance evaluation, and software engineering. No thesis is required.

The 30-hour M.S. in Electrical Engineering essentially reflects a student-defined curriculum in the field. A thesis is required.

The Ph.D. programs in Computer Science and Electrical Engineering each involve a comprehensive examination in addition to the standard coursework and dissertation requirements.

Other Programs

M.Eng. and M.S. programs in Management of Technology are also available. For more information, contact the program office at (615) 322-3479.

Contact Information

PHONE

General information: (615) 322-7311
Admissions (undergraduate): (615) 322-2561 or (800) 288-0432

Admissions (graduate): (615) 322-2651
Electrical engineering and computer science: (615) 322-2771

FAX

Electrical engineering and computer science: (615) 343-6702

E-MAIL

Admissions (undergraduate): admissions@vanderbilt.edu
Admissions (graduate): Barbara Amann (barbara.a.amann@vanderbilt.edu)

Virginia Tech (Virginia Polytechnic Institute and State University)

www.vt.edu ☆☆☆

Blacksburg, VA 24061

Year established: 1872
Ownership: Public

This large and primarily vocational university offers rigorous programs at all levels in the hottest information technology fields. Evening classes, weekend study, extension courses, and distance learning are available.

Degrees Offered

UNDERGRADUATE

(ABET) B.S., Computer Engineering
(CSAB) B.S., Computer Science
(ABET) B.S., Electrical Engineering

GRADUATE

M.I.T.
M.S., Computer Engineering
M.S., Computer Science
M.S., Electrical Engineering
Ph.D., Computer Engineering
Ph.D., Computer Science
Ph.D., Electrical Engineering

Approximate Cost of Degrees

UNDERGRADUATE, RESIDENT

$15,200

UNDERGRADUATE, NONRESIDENT

$49,100

MASTER'S, RESIDENT

$7,800

MASTER'S, NONRESIDENT

$12,200

DOCTORATE, RESIDENT

$13,100

DOCTORATE, NONRESIDENT

$20,300

Admissions Guidelines

UNDERGRADUATE

High school diploma, SAT and/or ACT required

GRADUATE

Accredited bachelor's, GRE required

Undergraduate Programs

The ABET-accredited B.S. in Computer Engineering focuses on hardware, theory, and hardware-software interaction.

The CSAB-accredited B.S. in Computer Science focuses on hardware-software interaction, programming, and theory.

The ABET-accredited B.S. in Electrical Engineering focuses on electronics, digital systems, communications, and computer engineering.

Graduate Programs

The 30-hour Master of Information Technology (M.I.T.) is available with formal specializations in business information systems, communications, computer engineering, decision support systems, networking, and software development. No thesis is required. A considerable portion of this program can be completed by distance learning.

The 30-hour M.S. in Computer Engineering is available with informal specializations in hardware and software. No thesis is required. This program can be completed off-campus through authorized extension sites.

The 30-hour M.S. in Computer Science is particularly strong in the areas of theory and hardware-software interaction. The program caps off with a thesis or comprehensive examination. Formal specializations in human-computer interaction and software engineering are currently being developed.

The 30-hour M.S. in Electrical Engineering is built around a student-defined, faculty-approved plan of study. No thesis is required. This program can be completed off-campus through authorized extension sites.

The Ph.D. programs in Computer Engineering and Electrical Engineering each require qualifying and preliminary examinations in addition to the standard coursework and dissertation components.

The Ph.D. program in Computer Science involves a qualifying examination in addition to the standard coursework and dissertation components.

Other Programs

B.S. and Ph.D. programs in Management Science and Information Technology are also available. For more information, contact the Pamplin College of Business at (540) 231-6596.

Contact Information

PHONE

General information: (540) 231-6000
Admissions (undergraduate): (540) 231-6267
Admissions (graduate): (540) 231-8306
Computer science: (540) 231-6931
Electrical and computer engineering: (540) 231-6646
Information technology: (804) 786-1604

FAX

Admissions (undergraduate): (540) 231-3242
Computer science: (540) 231-6075
Electrical and computer engineering: (540) 231-3362
Information technology: (804) 786-0590

E-MAIL

Electrical and computer engineering (graduate): gradinfo@ee.vt.edu
Information technology: IT@vt.edu

Washington State University   www.wsu.edu ☆☆½

Office of Admissions
370 Lighty Student Services Building
P.O. Box 641067
Pullman, WA 99164-1067

Year established: 1890
Ownership: Public

This major public university offers degrees at all levels in the hottest information technology fields. Evening classes, extension courses, weekend study, and distance learning are available.

Degrees Offered

UNDERGRADUATE

B.A., Computer Science
🅲🆂🅰🅱 B.S., Computer Science
B.S., Computer Engineering
🅰🅱🅴🆃 B.S., Electrical Engineering

GRADUATE

M.S., Computer Science
M.S., Electrical Engineering
Ph.D., Computer Science
Ph.D., Electrical and Computer Engineering

Approximate Cost of Degrees

UNDERGRADUATE, RESIDENT
$18,600

UNDERGRADUATE, NONRESIDENT
$46,300

MASTER'S, RESIDENT
$10,000

MASTER'S, NONRESIDENT
$22,300

DOCTORATE, RESIDENT
$16,600

DOCTORATE, NONRESIDENT
$37,200

Admissions Guidelines

UNDERGRADUATE
High school diploma, SAT and/or ACT required

GRADUATE
Accredited bachelor's, GRE required

Undergraduate Programs

The major in Computer Science focuses on computer hardware, software engineering, computational mathematics, and hardware-software interaction. The B.S. degree program is CSAB-accredited.

The new B.S. in Computer Engineering is largely hardware-focused and approaches the field from a broad, comprehensive background in electrical engineering.

The ABET-accredited B.S. in Electrical Engineering focuses on electronics, digital systems, and communications.

Graduate Programs

The 30-hour M.S. in Computer Science is a well-rounded program with notable components in theory, software engineering, and computational mathematics. A thesis or comprehensive examination is required.

The 30-hour M.S. in Electrical Engineering is available with informal specializations in computer engineering, electrophysics, energy and power systems, microelectronics, and systems. A thesis or comprehensive examination is required.

The Ph.D. in Computer Science represents a highly flexible curriculum augmented by unique study options. A qualifying examination is required in addition to the standard dissertation and coursework components.

The Ph.D. in Electrical and Computer Engineering involves a qualifying examination in addition to the standard coursework and dissertation requirements.

Contact Information

PHONE
General information: (509) 335-3564
Admissions (undergraduate): (888) 468-6978
Admissions (graduate): (509) 335-6424
Electrical engineering and computer science: (509) 335-6602

FAX
Admissions (graduate): (509) 335-1949
Electrical engineering and computer science: (509) 335-3818

E-MAIL
Admissions (undergraduate): admiss@wsu.edu
Admissions (graduate): gradsch@wsu.edu
Electrical engineering and computer science (undergraduate): Annette Cavalieri (newcoug@eecs.wsu.edu)
Electrical engineering and computer science (graduate): Ruby Young (ruby@eecs.wsu.edu)

Washington University in St. Louis
www.wustl.edu ✮✮✮

One Brookings Drive.
St. Louis, MO 63130

Year established: 1853
Ownership: Private

This large private university offers degrees at all levels in computer science and electrical engineering. Evening classes are available.

Degrees Offered

Undergraduate
B.S., Computer Engineering
B.S., Computer Science
🔘 B.S., Electrical Engineering

Graduate
M.S., Computer Science
M.S., Electrical Engineering
D.Sc., Computer Science
D.Sc., Electrical Engineering

Approximate Cost of Degrees

Undergraduate
$103,300

Master's
$38,400

Doctorate
$63,900

Admissions Guidelines

Undergraduate
High school diploma, SAT and/or ACT required

Graduate
Accredited bachelor's with 3.0 GPA, GRE required

Undergraduate Programs
The B.S. in Computer Engineering addresses computer science theory, computer hardware, software engineering, and hardware-software interaction.

The B.S. in Computer Science focuses largely on theory and software applications.

The ABET-accredited B.S. in Electrical Engineering focuses on electronics, digital systems, and communications.

Graduate Programs
The 30-hour M.S. in Computer Science is available with optional specializations in artificial intelligence, computational science, distributed systems, multimedia networking, and multimedia user interfaces. No thesis is required. An optional certificate program in networking and communications can be taken alongside this curriculum.

The 30-hour M.S. in Electrical Engineering is fairly flexible, focusing on electronics and complex digital systems in its core requirements. No thesis is required. Optional certificate programs in image science and engineering and in networking and telecommunications can be taken alongside this curriculum.

The D.Sc. in Computer Science is available with optional specializations in artificial intelligence, computational science, distributed systems, multimedia networking, and multimedia user interfaces. A qualifying examination is involved in addition to the standard coursework and dissertation requirements.

The D.Sc. involves oral and written qualifying examinations in addition to the standard coursework and dissertation requirements.

Contact Information

Phone
General information: (314) 935-5000
Admissions (undergraduate): (314) 935-6000 or (800) 638-0700
Computer science: (314) 935-6160
Electrical engineering: (314) 935-5565

Fax
Admissions (undergraduate): (314) 935-4747
Computer science: (314) 935-7302
Electrical engineering: (314) 935-7500

E-mail
Admissions (undergraduate): admissions@wustl.edu
Electrical engineering: info@ee.wustl.edu

Wayne State University

www.wayne.edu ☆☆½

Detroit, MI 48202

Year established: 1868
Ownership: Public

This large public university offers programs at all levels in the most popular information technology fields. Evening classes, weekend study, and distance learning are available.

Degrees Offered

UNDERGRADUATE
B.A., Computer Science
⊗ B.S., Computer Science
B.S., Computer Technology
⊗ B.S., Electrical Engineering
⊗ B.S.E.T., Electrical Engineering Technology

GRADUATE
M.A., Computer Science
M.S., Computer Engineering
M.S., Computer Science
M.S., Electrical Engineering
Ph.D., Computer Engineering
Ph.D., Computer Science
Ph.D., Electrical Engineering

Approximate Cost of Degrees

UNDERGRADUATE, RESIDENT
$21,500

UNDERGRADUATE, NONRESIDENT
$44,200

MASTER'S, RESIDENT
$8,800

MASTER'S, NONRESIDENT
$16,800

DOCTORATE, RESIDENT
$14,700

DOCTORATE, NONRESIDENT
$28,000

Admissions Guidelines

UNDERGRADUATE
High school diploma, SAT and/or ACT required

GRADUATE
Accredited bachelor's with 3.0 GPA, GRE required

Undergraduate Programs

The major in Computer Science focuses on theory, computational mathematics, and software applications. The B.S. program is CSAB-accredited.

The B.S. in Computer Technology primarily addresses quality control, project management, computer hardware, and computer information systems.

The ABET-accredited B.S. in Electrical Engineering represents a broad, comprehensive curriculum

in the field. A computer engineering specialization is available.

The ABET-accredited B.S. in Engineering Technology (B.S.E.T.) in Electrical Engineering Technology focuses on management and quality control issues in addition to the practical core component in applied computer engineering and electronics.

Graduate Programs

The 31-hour M.A. in Computer Science is available with formal specializations in intelligent systems and modeling/simulation/visualization, and software/information systems. The program culminates in a comprehensive examination.

The 32-hour M.S. in Computer Engineering is available with optional specializations in computer architecture and digital design, machine intelligence and applications, and parallel and distributed systems. No thesis is required.

The 33-hour M.S. in Computer Science focuses on a student-defined, faculty-approved field of specialization. A thesis is required.

The 32-hour M.S. in Electrical Engineering is available with optional specializations in biomedical systems, communication and circuits, control systems, optical engineering, and power systems. No thesis is required.

The Ph.D. in Computer Engineering is available with optional specializations in computer architecture and digital design, machine intelligence and applications, and parallel and distributed systems. A qualifying examination is involved in addition to the standard coursework and dissertation requirements.

The Ph.D. in Computer Science centers on a student-defined, faculty-approved field of specialization. A qualifying examination is involved in addition to the standard coursework and dissertation requirements.

The Ph.D. in Electrical Engineering is available with optional specializations in biomedical systems, communication and circuits, control systems, optical engineering, and power systems. A qualifying examination is required in addition to the standard coursework and dissertation components.

Other Programs

The B.B.A. program is available with an information systems management emphasis. For more information, contact the program chair at (313) 577-4842.

Contact Information

PHONE
General information: (313) 577-2424
Admissions: (313) 577-3577
Computer science: (313) 577-2477
Electrical and computer engineering: (313) 577-3920
Technology: (313) 577-0800

FAX
Engineering technology: (313) 577-1781

E-MAIL
Admissions: admissions@wayne.edu
Computer science: admissions@cs.wayne.edu

Webster University

www.webster.edu ☆☆½

470 E. Lockwood Avenue
St. Louis, MO 63119

Year established: 1915
Ownership: Private

With courses offered at more than 60 extension sites, this private liberal arts university offers undergraduate and graduate programs in computer science and related management fields. Evening classes and weekend study are also available.

Degrees Offered

UNDERGRADUATE
B.S., Computer Science

GRADUATE
M.S., Computer Science

Approximate Cost of Degrees

UNDERGRADUATE
$59,000

GRADUATE
$13,700

Admissions Guidelines

UNDERGRADUATE
High school diploma, SAT and/or ACT required

GRADUATE
Accredited bachelor's, GRE required

Undergraduate Programs

The B.S. program in Computer Science is available with optional specializations in information management and information technology. Minors are available in computer applications and Web site development.

Graduate Programs

The 36-hour M.S. in Computer Science is available with tracks emphasizing distributed systems or information systems. A project is required.

Other Programs

Both M.A. programs and M.B.A. concentrations are available in computer resources/information management and telecommunications management. For more information, contact the School of Business and Technology at (314) 968-5950.

The M.A. in Teaching is available with optional specializations in computer applications, computer studies, and instructional media technology. For more information, contact the education department at (314) 968-7490.

Contact Information

PHONE
General information: (314) 968-6900
Admissions (undergraduate): (314) 968-6991 or (800) 753-6765
Admissions (graduate): (314) 968-7100 or (800) 981-9801, extension 7100
Computer science: (314) 968-7178

FAX
Admissions (graduate): (314) 968-7116

E-MAIL
Admissions (undergraduate): admit@webster.edu
Admissions (graduate): gadmit@webster.edu
Computer science: Anna Barbara Sakurai (sakuraab@webster.edu)

West Virginia University Institute of Technology

www2.wvutech.edu ☆☆☆

Montgomery, WV 25136

Year established: 1895
Ownership: Public

This small, tech-focused public university offers undergraduate programs that address every professional nook and cranny of the information technology field. Evening classes, weekend study, extension courses, and distance learning are available.

Degrees Offered

UNDERGRADUATE
B.S., Computer Engineering
B.S., Computer Science
[ABET] B.S., Electrical Engineering
[ABET] B.S., Electronic(s) Engineering Technology

Approximate Cost of Degrees

RESIDENT
$10,500

NONRESIDENT
$19,200

Admissions Guidelines
High school diploma, 3.0 GPA or SAT and/or ACT required

Undergraduate Programs
The B.S. in Computer Engineering focuses on computer hardware, software engineering, and hardware-software interaction.

The B.S. in Computer Science is geared primarily toward hands-on study of programming and software applications, although the curriculum does involve some courses on theory.

The ABET-accredited B.S. in Electrical Engineering focuses on microprocessors, digital circuits, and power systems. The curriculum is highly flexible and allows a great deal of room for student-initiated specialization.

The ABET-accredited B.S. in Electronic(s) Engineering Technology is oriented toward the study of electronics and circuits, quality control, technology maintenance, and technology management.

Other Programs
B.S. programs in Management Information Systems and Technology Management are also available. For more information, contact the program director at (304) 442-3232.

Contact Information

PHONE
General information: (888) 554-8324
Electrical/computer engineering: (304) 442-3095
Computer science: (304) 442-3362

E-MAIL
Electrical/computer engineering: Dr. Stephen Goodman (sgoodman@wvutech.edu)
Computer science: Dr. Gary Durrett (gdurrett@wvutech.edu)

West Virginia University

www.wvu.edu ☆☆☆

Office of Admissions and Records
West Virginia University
P.O. Box 6009
Morgantown, WV 26506-6009

Year established: 1867
Ownership: Public

This major public university offers degrees at all levels in several popular information technology fields. Evening classes, weekend study, extension courses, and distance learning are available.

Degrees Offered

UNDERGRADUATE

🅰 B.S., Computer Engineering
B.S., Computer Science
🅰 B.S., Electrical Engineering

GRADUATE

M.S., Computer Science
M.S., Electrical Engineering
M.S., Software Engineering
Ph.D., Computer Science
Ph.D., Electrical Engineering

Approximate Cost of Degrees

UNDERGRADUATE, RESIDENT

$15,500

UNDERGRADUATE, NONRESIDENT

$38,000

MASTER'S, RESIDENT

$6,100

MASTER'S, NONRESIDENT

$14,700

DOCTORATE, RESIDENT

$10,100

DOCTORATE, NONRESIDENT

$24,500

Admissions Guidelines

UNDERGRADUATE

High school diploma, SAT and/or ACT required

GRADUATE

Accredited bachelor's with 2.75 GPA, GRE required

Undergraduate Programs

The ABET-accredited B.S. in Computer Engineering focuses largely on hardware issues, although a software engineering component is included.

The B.S. in Computer Science focuses on theory and software applications.

The ABET-accredited B.S. in Electrical Engineering focuses on electronics, digital systems, and communications.

Graduate Programs

The 32-hour M.S. in Computer Science focuses on theory in its core requirements, but allows a great deal of room for student specialization. A thesis or project is required.

The 32-hour M.S. in Electrical Engineering represents a broad, comprehensive curriculum in the field. No thesis is required.

The 33-hour M.S. in Software Engineering focuses on applied programming issues, hardware-software interaction, and the like. No thesis is required.

The Ph.D. programs in Computer Science and Electrical Engineering each require a qualifying examination in addition to the standard coursework and dissertation components.

Contact Information

PHONE

Admissions: (800) 344-9881
Electrical engineering and computer science: (304) 293-0405
Software engineering: (304) 293-0405

FAX

Electrical engineering and computer science: (304) 293-8602

E-MAIL

Admissions: WVUAdmissions@arc.wvu.edu
Electrical engineering and computer science: George Trapp (trapp@cs.wvu.edu)

Western Carolina University   www.wcu.edu ☆☆½

Office of Admissions
Cullowhee, NC 28723

Year established: 1889
Ownership: Public

This public university offers goal-oriented undergraduate programs well suited to traditional and nontraditional students alike. Evening classes, weekend study, extension courses, and distance learning are available.

Degrees Offered

UNDERGRADUATE

B.S., Computer Science

(ABET) B.S., Electronic(s) Engineering Technology

Approximate Cost of Degrees

RESIDENT

$11,200

NONRESIDENT

$40,300

Admissions Guidelines

High school diploma, SAT and/or ACT required

Undergraduate Programs

The B.S. in Computer Science focuses on theory, software engineering, and hardware-software interaction.

The ABET-accredited B.S. in Electronic(s) Engineering Technology focuses on computer programming and circuit design.

Other Programs

A computing-oriented B.S. in Health Information Management is offered through the Department of Health Sciences. For more information, contact the program division at (828) 227-3511.

The M.S. program in Applied Mathematics can be tailored to the field of computational mathematics. For more information, contact the Department of Mathematics and Computer Science.

Contact Information

PHONE

General information: (828) 227-7211
Admissions: (800) 928-2369
Mathematics and computer science: (828) 227-7245

FAX

Mathematics and computer science: (828) 227-7240

Western Kentucky University   www.wku.edu ☆☆½

1 Big Red Way
Bowling Green, KY 42101-3576

Year established: 1906
Ownership: Public

This small public university offers several intriguing vocational options in information technology at the undergraduate level and, at the graduate level, a top-notch program in computer science. Evening classes, weekend study, and extension courses are available.

Degrees Offered

UNDERGRADUATE

B.S., Computer Information Systems

(CSAB) B.S., Computer Science

(ABET) B.S., Electrical Engineering Technology

GRADUATE

M.S., Computer Science

Approximate Cost of Degrees

UNDERGRADUATE, RESIDENT

$14,000

UNDERGRADUATE, NONRESIDENT

$30,900

MASTER'S, RESIDENT

$5,600

MASTER'S, NONRESIDENT

$12,600

DOCTORATE, RESIDENT

$9,300

DOCTORATE, NONRESIDENT

$21,000

Admissions Guidelines

UNDERGRADUATE

High school diploma, SAT and/or ACT required

GRADUATE

Accredited bachelor's, GRE required

Undergraduate Programs

The B.S. program in Computer Information Systems focuses largely on software applications, databases, and management information systems.

The B.S. in Computer Science is available with a general track and a systems/scientific applications track. Only the latter track falls under the CSAB accreditation.

The ABET-accredited B.S. in Electrical Engineering Technology focuses on field issues relevant to electrical engineering devices such as production, maintenance, quality control, design, and project management.

Graduate Programs

The 33-hour M.S. in Computer Science focuses on advanced topics in fields such as networking, software engineering, operating systems, and theory. No thesis is required.

Other Programs

An ABET-accredited B.S. in Electromechanical Engineering Technology is also available. For more information, contact the Department of Engineering Technology.

Contact Information

PHONE

General information: (270) 745-0111
Admissions (undergraduate): (270) 745-2551
Admissions (graduate): (270) 745-5004
Computer information systems: (270) 745-5408
Computer science: (270) 745-4642
Engineering technology: (270) 745-2461

FAX

Admissions (undergraduate): (270) 745-6133
Computer information systems: (270) 745-6376
Computer science: (270) 745-6449
Engineering technology: (270) 745-5856

E-MAIL

General information: western@wku.edu
Admissions (undergraduate): admission@wku.edu
Computer information systems: cis@wku.edu
Computer science: Dr. Art Shindhelm (shindhelm@wku.edu)
Engineering technology: Dr. John P. Russell (john.russell@wku.edu)

Wichita State University

www.wichita.edu ☆☆½

1845 Fairmount
Wichita, KS 67260

Year established: 1895
Ownership: Public

This major urban university offers programs at the graduate and undergraduate levels in electrical engineering and computer science. Evening classes, weekend study, and extension courses are available.

Degrees Offered

UNDERGRADUATE

B.A., Computer Science
B.S., Computer Science
B.S., Computer Engineering
ABET B.S., Electrical Engineering

GRADUATE

M.S., Computer Science
M.S., Electrical Engineering
Ph.D., Electrical Engineering

Approximate Cost of Degrees

UNDERGRADUATE, RESIDENT
$14,700

UNDERGRADUATE, NONRESIDENT
$41,800

MASTER'S, RESIDENT
$5,900

MASTER'S, NONRESIDENT
$14,600

DOCTORATE, RESIDENT
$9,900

DOCTORATE, NONRESIDENT
$24,300

Admissions Guidelines

UNDERGRADUATE
High school diploma, SAT and/or ACT required

GRADUATE
Accredited bachelor's, GRE required

Undergraduate Programs

The major in Computer Science focuses on theory, programming, and computational mathematics.

The B.S. in Computer Engineering focuses mostly on hardware issues and hardware-software interaction.

The ABET-accredited B.S. in Electrical Engineering focuses mostly on electronics, digital systems, and communications.

Graduate Programs

The 36-hour M.S. in Computer Science focuses on programming, software applications, and software engineering. No thesis is required.

The 33-hour M.S. in Electrical Engineering culminates in a thesis, project, or comprehensive examination.

The Ph.D. in Electrical Engineering involves two batteries of written examinations in addition to the standard coursework and dissertation requirements.

Contact Information

PHONE
General information: (316) 978-3045
Admissions (undergraduate): (316) 978-3085 or (800) 362-2594
Admissions (graduate): (316) 978-3095
Computer science: (316) 978-3156
Electrical and computer engineering: (316) 978-3415

FAX
Computer science: (316) 978-3984
Electrical and computer engineering: (316) 978-3853

E-MAIL
Computer science: info@cs.twsu.edu
Electrical and computer engineering: info@ece.twsu.edu

Worcester Polytechnic Institute   www.wpi.edu ☆☆☆

100 Institute Road
Worcester, MA 01609-2280

Year established: 1865
Ownership: Private

This technology-focused private university offers degrees at all levels in several popular information technology fields. Evening classes, weekend study, extension courses, and distance learning are available.

Degrees Offered

UNDERGRADUATE
CSAB B.S., Computer Science
B.S., Computers with Applications
ABET B.S., Electrical Engineering

GRADUATE
M.S., Computer Science
M.S., Electrical and Computer Engineering
Ph.D., Computer Science
Ph.D., Electrical and Computer Engineering

Approximate Cost of Degrees

UNDERGRADUATE
$96,500

MASTER'S
$27,700

DOCTORATE
$46,200

Admissions Guidelines

UNDERGRADUATE
High school diploma, SAT and/or ACT required

GRADUATE
Accredited bachelor's, GRE required

Undergraduate Programs

The CSAB-accredited B.S. in Computer Science is available with informal specializations in design, systems, and theory. An optional track emphasizing biomedical interests is available.

The B.S. in Computers with Applications is unique in that it offers, as part of the major, a 25-hour "applications" component consisting of courses that indirectly relate in some way to applied computing.

The ABET-accredited B.S. in Electrical Engineering focuses on electronics, systems engineering, and computer engineering.

Graduate Programs

The 33-hour M.S. in Computer Science is available with informal specializations in analysis, design, systems, and theory. A thesis is required. An optional track, emphasizing computer and communication networks, is available.

The 33-hour M.S. in Electrical Engineering can be undertaken as a broad, comprehensive program addressing all major aspects of the field in a survey fashion, or it can be tailored to fit specific research interests (computer engineering, electronics, and so forth). No thesis is required. An optional track, emphasizing computer and communication networks, is available.

The Ph.D. in Computer Science involves a qualifying examination in addition to the standard coursework and dissertation requirements.

The Ph.D. in Electrical Engineering is available with formal specializations in computational fields, computer engineering, machine vision, power systems, and wireless networks. A qualifying examination is required in addition to the standard coursework and dissertation components.

Other Programs

A major in Economics and Technology is also available. For more information, contact the Department of Social Science and Policy Studies at (508) 831-5296.

A B.S. in Management Information Systems is available. The M.B.A. program is available with optional specializations in management information systems and e-commerce. M.S. programs are also available in Marketing and Technological Innovation and in Operations and Information Technology. For more information, contact the Department of Management at (508) 831-5218.

Contact Information

PHONE
General information (Worcester campus):
(508) 831-5000
General information (Waltham campus): (781) 895-1188
General information (Metro West campus):
(508) 480-9200
Admissions (undergraduate): (508) 831-5286
Admissions (graduate): (508) 831-5717
Computer science: (508) 831-5357
Electrical and computer engineering: (508) 831-5273

FAX
Computer science: (508) 831-5776

E-MAIL
Admissions (undergraduate): admissions@wpi.edu
Admissions (graduate): gao@wpi.edu
Computer science (undergraduate):
undergraduate@cs.wpi.edu
Computer science (graduate): graduate@cs.wpi.edu
Electrical and computer engineering: Dr. John Orr
(orr@ece.wpi.edu)

Wright State University

www.wright.edu ☆☆☆½

3640 Colonel Glenn Highway
Dayton, OH 45435-0001

Year established: 1967
Ownership: Public

This major state university offers programs at all levels in computer engineering, computer science, and electrical engineering. Evening classes and extension courses are available.

Degrees Offered

UNDERGRADUATE
(ABET) B.S., Computer Engineering
(CSAB) B.S., Computer Science
(ABET) B.S., Electrical Engineering

GRADUATE
M.S., Computer Engineering
M.S., Computer Science
M.S.E., Electrical Engineering
Ph.D., Computer Science and Engineering

Approximate Cost of Degrees

UNDERGRADUATE, RESIDENT
$18,700

UNDERGRADUATE, NONRESIDENT
$36,500

MASTER'S, RESIDENT
$10,700

MASTER'S, NONRESIDENT
$17,500

DOCTORATE, RESIDENT
$17,800

DOCTORATE, NONRESIDENT
$29,100

Admissions Guidelines

UNDERGRADUATE
High school diploma with 2.0 GPA, SAT and/or ACT required

GRADUATE
Accredited bachelor's with 2.7 GPA, GRE required

Undergraduate Programs
The ABET-accredited B.S. in Computer Engineering focuses largely on computer hardware, hardware-software interaction, theory, and software engineering.

The CSAB-accredited B.S. in Computer Science focuses on theory, software applications, and software engineering.

The ABET-accredited B.S. in Electrical Engineering is available with design sequences (applied concentrations) in communications, control systems, electromagnetics, electronics, and industrial design.

Graduate Programs
The 32-hour M.S. in Computer Engineering is available with informal specializations in computer engineering systems, hardware, and software engineering. No thesis is required.

The 32-hour M.S. in Computer Science is available with informal specializations in computer science theory, languages, software, and systems. No thesis is required.

The 30-hour M.S. in Engineering (M.S.E.) in Electrical Engineering is available with informal research specializations in control theory, electromagnetic simulation, information transmission systems, integrated circuit design, modeling and processing of random signals, power electronics, robotics systems, and sensor signal exploitation. No thesis is required.

The Ph.D. in Computer Science and Engineering offers particularly strong research options in the areas of computer-aided assembly planning, collaboration and cognition, intelligent systems, and vision interfaces/systems. Qualifying and candidacy examinations are required in addition to the standard coursework and dissertation components.

Other Programs
The Ph.D. in Engineering is available with a formal electrical engineering specialization. For more information, contact the electrical engineering department.

A major in Management Information Systems is also available. For more information, contact the department at (937) 775-2895.

Contact Information

PHONE
General information: (937) 775-3333
Admissions (undergraduate): (937) 775-5700 or (800) 247-1770
Admissions (graduate): (937) 775-2976 or (800) 452-4723
Computer science and engineering: (937) 775-5131
Electrical engineering: (937) 775-5037

FAX
Admissions (undergraduate): (937) 775-5795

E-MAIL
Admissions (undergraduate):
admissions@wright.edu

Computer science and engineering: cse-dept@cs.wright.edu
Electrical engineering: eedept@cs.wright.edu

Yale University   www.yale.edu ☆☆½

New Haven, CT 06520

Year established: 1701
Ownership: Private

This prestigious research-oriented Ivy League institution offers degrees at all levels in computer science and electrical engineering. Evening classes are available.

Degrees Offered

UNDERGRADUATE
B.A., Computer Science
🅒 B.S., Computer Science
🅐 B.S., Electrical Engineering

GRADUATE
M.S., Computer Science
Ph.D., Computer Science
Ph.D., Electrical Engineering

Approximate Cost of Degrees

UNDERGRADUATE
$71,000

MASTER'S
$35,800

DOCTORATE
$59,600

Admissions Guidelines

UNDERGRADUATE
High school diploma, SAT and/or ACT required

GRADUATE
Accredited bachelor's, GRE required

Undergraduate Programs
The major in Computer Science is available with informal specializations in artificial intelligence, programming languages and systems, scientific computing, and theory of computation. The B.S. pro-gram is CSAB-accredited. Joint majors in electrical engineering, mathematics, and psychology can be easily arranged.

The ABET-accredited B.S. in Electrical Engineering offers courses in a vast array of electrical engineering subdisciplines, including computer engineering, physical electronics, and communications.

Graduate Programs
The 30-hour M.S. in Computer Science is available with formal specializations in artificial intelligence, programming languages and systems, scientific computing, and theory of computation. No thesis is required. The Yale M.S. in Computer Science is considered a terminal degree; students who intend to pursue doctoral work should apply directly to the Ph.D. program.

The Ph.D. in Computer Science is available with formal specializations in artificial intelligence, programming languages and systems, scientific computing, and theory of computation. Students must pass a series of comprehensive examinations in addition to fulfilling the standard coursework and dissertation requirements.

The Ph.D. in Electrical Engineering is available with research specializations in communications, computer engineering, computer vision, control systems, microelectronics, neural networks, photonics, robot navigation, semiconductors, signal processing, and VLSI systems. Students must pass a series of comprehensive examinations in addition to fulfilling the standard coursework and dissertation requirements.

Contact Information

PHONE

General information: (203) 432-4771
Computer science: (203) 432-1246
Electrical engineering: (203) 432-4300

FAX

Computer science: (203) 432-0593
Electrical engineering: (203) 432-2797

E-MAIL

Admissions (undergraduate):
undergraduate.admissions@yale.edu
Admissions (graduate):
graduate.admissions@yale.edu
Computer science: cs-admissions@cs.yale.edu
Electrical engineering: Mary Lally
(mary.lally@yale.edu)

✱ **EXTRA!**

Alan J. Perlis, co-founder of the Computer Science department, will forever be associated with the quote "One man's constant is another man's variable." Read his complete "Epigrams on Programming" at http://www.cs.yale.edu/homes/perlis-alan/quotes.html.

PART III

Appendices

In This Part

APPENDIX A

· ·

Geographic Index:
Schools by State

Going off to college is a fine idea for many people, but for some, it just isn't practical. If you want to attend college without splitting town, here's a list of our top 199 colleges organized by state. Many of them offer night classes, weekend courses, and on-site extension programs. For details on all of these schools, see Chapter 12.

Alabama
Auburn University
University of Alabama at Birmingham
University of Alabama at Huntsville
University of Alabama at Tuscaloosa

Alaska
University of Alaska at Anchorage
University of Alaska at Fairbanks

Arizona
Arizona State University, East
University of Arizona

Arkansas
University of Arkansas
University of Arkansas at Little Rock

California
Azusa Pacific University
California Institute of Technology
California Polytechnic State University
California State University at Chico
California State University at Sacramento
Mills College
San Jose State University
Santa Clara University
Stanford University
University of California at Berkeley
University of California at Davis
University of California at Irvine
University of California at Los Angeles
University of California at San Diego
University of Southern California

Colorado
Colorado State University
National Technological University
University of Colorado
University of Denver

Connecticut
Sacred Heart University
University of Connecticut
University of New Haven
Yale University

Delaware
University of Delaware

District of Columbia
American University
Howard University

Florida
Embry-Riddle Aeronautical University
Florida Institute of Technology
Nova Southeastern University
University of Florida
University of North Florida

Georgia
Columbus State University
Georgia Institute of Technology
Southern Polytechnic State University
University of Georgia

Hawaii
University of Hawaii at Manoa

Idaho
Boise State University
University of Idaho

Illinois
DePaul University
DeVry Institutes
Illinois Institute of Technology
Loyola University in Chicago
Northwestern University
University of Chicago

Indiana
Ball State University
Indiana University/Purdue University at Indianapolis
Indiana University at Bloomington
Purdue University
University of Notre Dame

Iowa
Iowa State University
University of Iowa

Kansas
Emporia State University
Kansas State University
University of Kansas
Wichita State University

Kentucky

University of Louisville
Western Kentucky University

Louisiana

Louisiana State University
Tulane University

Maine

University of Maine

Maryland

Johns Hopkins University
University of Maryland at College Park
University of Maryland University College

Massachusetts

Boston University
Harvard University
Massachusetts Institute of Technology
Northeastern University
Smith College
Tufts University
University of Massachusetts at Amherst
University of Massachusetts at Lowell
Worcester Polytechnic Institute

Michigan

Central Michigan University
University of Michigan at Dearborn
Wayne State University

Minnesota

Minnesota State University at Mankato
St. Cloud State University
University of Minnesota at Twin Cities

Mississippi

Jackson State University
Mississippi State University

Missouri

University of Missouri
Washington University in St. Louis
Webster University

Montana

Montana State University
Montana Tech of the University of Montana
University of Montana

Nebraska

Bellevue University
Creighton University
University of Nebraska at Lincoln
University of Nebraska at Omaha

Nevada

University of Nevada at Las Vegas
University of Nevada at Reno

New Hampshire

Dartmouth College
Rivier College
University of New Hampshire

New Jersey

New Jersey Institute of Technology
Princeton University
Rutgers, the State University of New Jersey
Stevens Institute of Technology
Thomas Edison State College

New Mexico

New Mexico Highlands University
New Mexico State University
University of New Mexico

New York

Brooklyn College
Columbia University
Cornell University
Fordham University
New York Institute of Technology
New York University
Pace University
Regents College
Rensselaer Polytechnic Institute
Rochester Institute of Technology
State University of New York at Albany
State University of New York at Buffalo
State University of New York at Stony Brook
State University of New York Empire State College
Syracuse University
University of Rochester

North Carolina

Duke University
North Carolina State University
University of North Carolina at Chapel Hill
University of North Carolina at Charlotte
Western Carolina University

North Dakota
North Dakota State University
University of North Dakota

Ohio
Case Western Reserve University
Cleveland State University
Ohio State University
Ohio University
University of Cincinnati
University of Toledo
Wright State University

Oklahoma
Oklahoma State University
University of Central Oklahoma
University of Tulsa

Oregon
Oregon Graduate Institute of Science and Technology
Portland State University
University of Oregon

Pennsylvania
Bucknell University
Carnegie Mellon University
Drexel University
Lehigh University
Pennsylvania State University
Temple University
University of Pennsylvania
University of Pittsburgh

Rhode Island
Brown University
University of Rhode Island

South Carolina
Clemson University
University of South Carolina

South Dakota
South Dakota State University

Tennessee
University of Memphis
University of Tennessee
University of Tennessee Space Institute
Vanderbilt University

Texas
Lamar University
Rice University
St. Mary's University
Southern Methodist University
Texas A&M University
Texas Christian University
Texas Tech University
University of Houston
University of Houston at Clear Lake
University of North Texas
University of Texas at Arlington
University of Texas at Austin
University of Texas at Dallas
University of Texas at San Antonio

Utah
Brigham Young University
University of Utah
Utah State University

Vermont
University of Vermont

Virginia
Christopher Newport University
College of William and Mary
George Mason University
Old Dominion University
University of Virginia
Virginia Polytechnic Institute and State University

Washington
Seattle University
University of Washington
Washington State University

West Virginia
Marshall University
West Virginia University
West Virginia University Institute of Technology

Wisconsin
Marquette University
University of Wisconsin at Madison

Wyoming
University of Wyoming

APPENDIX B

Subject Index

Want an M.S. in microelectronics? An M.B.A. in e-commerce? A Ph.D. in algorithms, optimization, and combinatorics? Look no further. Here you'll find a listing of every single degree program (bachelor's, master's, engineer, and doctorate) covered in this book, sorted by subject.

Accounting Information Systems
Boise State University (B)
Central Michigan University (B)
Northwestern University (D)
Oklahoma State University (M)
Oregon Graduate Institute of Science and
    Technology (M)
San Jose State University (B)

Algorithms, Optimization, and Combinatorics
Carnegie Mellon University (D)
Georgia Institute of Technology (D)

Applied Computer Science and Computing
Azusa Pacific University (M)
Columbus State University (B, M)
Creighton University (B)
DePaul University (B, M)
Marquette University (M)
Pace University (B, D)
St. Cloud State University (B)
St. Mary's University (B)
University of Denver (B)
Worcester Polytechnic Institute (B)

Artificial Intelligence and Cognitive Neural Systems
California Institute of Technology (D)
Central Michigan University (B)
Indiana University at Bloomington (D)
Iowa State University (D)
Massachusetts Institute of Technology (B, D)
New York University (D)
Northwestern University (B, D)
Rensselaer Polytechnic Institute (M)
University of Alabama at Birmingham (D)
University of Georgia (M)
University of Pennsylvania (B)

Business Information Systems
Bellevue University (B)
Boise State University (B)
Johns Hopkins University (B)
Lehigh University (B, M)
Louisiana State University (M)
Mississippi State University (B, M, D)
Montana Tech (B)

New Mexico State University (B)
Pace University (B, M, D)
St. Cloud State University (B)
Utah State University (M)

Computational Biology
Brown University (B)
Rice University (D)
University of Pennsylvania (B)

Computational Engineering
Mississippi State University (M, D)

Computational Mathematics
Brooklyn College (B)
California Institute of Technology (D)
College of William and Mary (M, D)
George Mason University (D)
Marquette University (B, M, D)
Massachusetts Institute of Technology (D)
Princeton University (D)
Rice University (B, M, D)
Rochester Institute of Technology (B)
San Jose State University (B)
Syracuse University (M)
University of Central Oklahoma (M)
University of Memphis (M, D)
University of Rhode Island (D)
University of Tulsa (B)
Western Carolina University (M)

Computer-Aided Manufacturing and Design
Central Michigan University (B)
Purdue University (B, M)
Rice University (M)
Rochester Institute of Technology (B, M)
Temple University (D)
Thomas Edison State College (B)
University of Houston (B)

Computer Engineering
Auburn University (B, M, D)
Boston University (B, M, D)
Brigham Young University (B)
Brown University (B, M, D)
Bucknell University (B)
California Polytechnic State University (B)
California State University at Chico (B)

California State University at Sacramento (B)
Carnegie Mellon University (B, M, D)
Case Western Reserve University (B, M, D)
Christopher Newport University (B)
Clemson University (B, M, D)
Columbia University (B, M, E)
Drexel University (B)
Duke University (B, M, D)
Embry-Riddle Aeronautical University (B)
Florida Institute of Technology (B, M, D)
George Mason University (B, M, D)
Georgia Institute of Technology (B, M, D)
Illinois Institute of Technology (B, M)
Iowa State University (B, M)
Jackson State University (B)
Johns Hopkins University (B, M)
Kansas State University (B, M, D)
Lehigh University (B, M)
Louisiana State University (B, M, D)
Marquette University (B, M, D)
Massachusetts Institute of Technology (B, M, E, D)
Minnesota State University at Mankato (B)
Mississippi State University (B, M, D)
Montana State University (B, M, D)
National Technological University (M)
New Jersey Institute of Technology (B, M, D)
New Mexico State University (B, M, D)
North Carolina State University (B, M, D)
Northeastern University (M, D)
Northwestern University (B, M, D)
Ohio State University (B, M, D)
Old Dominion University (B, M, D)
Oregon Graduate Institute of Science and
     Technology (M, D)
Pennsylvania State University (B, M, D)
Portland State University (B, M, D)
Purdue University (B, M, D)
Rensselaer Polytechnic Institute (B, M, D)
Rice University (B, M, D)
Rochester Institute of Technology (B, M)
Rutgers (B)
San Jose State University (B, M)
Santa Clara University (B, M, E, D)
Smith College (B)
Southern Methodist University (B, M, D)
St. Mary's University (B)
State University of New York at Buffalo (B, M, D)
State University of New York at Stony Brook (B)
Stevens Institute of Technology (B, M, E, D)
Syracuse University (B, M, D)

Texas A&M University (B, M, D)
Texas Tech University (B)
Tufts University (B)
Tulane University (B)
University of Alabama at Huntsville (B, M, D)
University of Arizona (B, M, D)
University of Arkansas at Fayetteville (B, M, D)
University of California at Davis (B, M, D)
University of California at Irvine (B, M, D)
University of California at Los Angeles (B)
University of California at San Diego (B, M, D)
University of Cincinnati (B, M, D)
University of Colorado at Boulder (B)
University of Connecticut (B, M, D)
University of Delaware (B)
University of Denver (B, M)
University of Florida (B, M, E, D)
University of Houston (B, M, D)
University of Houston at Clear Lake (M)
University of Idaho (B, M)
University of Iowa (B, M, D)
University of Kansas (B, M)
University of Louisville (B, D)
University of Maine (B, M, D)
University of Maryland at College Park (B)
University of Massachusetts at Amherst (B, M, D)
University of Massachusetts at Lowell (B, M, D)
University of Memphis (B)
University of Michigan (B, M)
University of Minnesota at Twin Cities (B, M)
University of Missouri at Columbia (B, M, D)
University of Nebraska at Lincoln (B)
University of Nebraska at Omaha (B)
University of Nevada at Las Vegas (B)
University of Nevada at Reno (B, M, D)
University of New Mexico (B)
University of North Carolina at Charlotte (B)
University of Pennsylvania (B)
University of Pittsburgh (B)
University of Rhode Island (B)
University of South Carolina (B, M, D)
University of Southern California (B, M, D)
University of Tennessee (B)
University of Texas at Arlington (B, M, D)
University of Texas at Austin (B, M, D)
University of Texas at Dallas (B, M, D)
University of Toledo (B)
University of Utah (B)
University of Virginia (B)
University of Washington (B)

University of Wisconsin at Madison (B)
Utah State University (B)
Vanderbilt University (B)
Virginia Tech (B, M, D)
Washington State University (B, M, D)
Washington University in St. Louis (B)
Wayne State University (B, M, D)
West Virginia University at Morgantown (B)
West Virginia University Institute of Technology (B)
Wichita State University (B)
Worcester Polytechnic Institute (B, M, D)
Wright State University (B, M, D)

Computer Graphics

Arizona State University East (B)
Bellevue University (B)
Boston University (B, M)
California Polytechnic State University (B)
Carnegie Mellon University (M)
Clemson University (M)
Indiana University/Purdue University at
    Indianapolis (B, M)
Mississippi State University (M)
New Mexico Highlands University (M)
New York Institute of Technology (B)
Purdue University (B, M)
Rensselaer Polytechnic Institute (M)
San Jose State University (M)
University of Denver (B, M)
University of Florida (B, M)
University of Notre Dame (B, M, D)
University of Pennsylvania (B)

Computer Information Systems

American University (B, M)
Azusa Pacific University (B)
Ball State University (M)
Bellevue University (B, M)
Boise State University (M)
Boston University (M)
Brooklyn College (B, M)
California State University at Chico (B)
Central Michigan University (M)
Clemson University (B)
Cleveland State University (B)
Columbus State University (B)
DePaul University (B, M)
DeVry Institutes (B)
Drexel University (B, M)
Emporia State University (B)

Florida Institute of Technology (M)
George Mason University (M)
Illinois Institute of Technology (B)
Johns Hopkins University (B, M)
Kansas State University (B)
Marshall University (M)
Minnesota State University at Mankato (B)
New Jersey Institute of Technology (B, M)
New Mexico Highlands University (B)
New York University (M)
Northwestern University (B)
Nova Southeastern University (B, M, D)
Pace University (B, M)
Regents College (B)
St. Cloud State University (B)
St. Mary's University (B, M)
State University of New York at Stony Brook (B)
Stevens Institute of Technology (M)
Temple University (B, M)
Thomas Edison State College (B)
University of Arkansas at Little Rock (B)
University of Houston at Clear Lake (B, M)
University of Idaho (B)
University of Louisville (B)
University of South Carolina (B)
University of Texas at Arlington (B, M)
University of Toledo (M)
University of Vermont (B)
University of Wisconsin at Madison (B, M)
Western Kentucky University (B)

Computer Music
Johns Hopkins University (M)

Computer Networking and Distributed Systems

Boise State University (B)
Carnegie Mellon University (M)
DePaul University (M)
Illinois Institute of Technology (B)
North Carolina State University (M)
Syracuse University (M)
Texas Tech University (M)

Computer Science

American University (B, M)
Auburn University (B, M, D)
Azusa Pacific University (B)
Ball State University (B, M)
Boise State University (B, M)

Boston University (B, M)
Brigham Young University (B, M, D)
Brown University (B, M, D)
Bucknell University (B)
California Institute of Technology (B, D)
California Polytechnic State University (B, M)
California State University at Chico (B, M)
California State University at Sacramento (B, M)
Carnegie Mellon University (B, D)
Case Western Reserve University (B, M, D)
Central Michigan University (B, M)
Charter Oak State College (B)
Christopher Newport University (B, M)
Clemson University (B, M, D)
Cleveland State University (B, M)
College of William and Mary (B, M, D)
Colorado State University (B, M, D)
Columbia University (B, M, E, D)
Columbus State University (B, M)
Cornell University (B, M, D)
Creighton University (B, M)
Dartmouth College (B, M, D)
DePaul University (B, M, D)
Drexel University (B)
Duke University (B, M, D)
Embry-Riddle Aeronautical University (B)
Emporia State University (B)
Florida Institute of Technology (B, M, D)
Fordham University (B, M)
George Mason University (B, M, D)
Georgia Institute of Technology (B, M, D)
Harvard University (B, M, D)
Howard University (B, M)
Illinois Institute of Technology (B, M, D)
Indiana University at Bloomington (B, M, D)
Indiana University/Purdue University at Indianapolis (B, M)
Iowa State University (B, M, D)
Jackson State University (B, M)
Johns Hopkins University (B, M, D)
Kansas State University (B, M, D)
Lamar University (B, M)
Lehigh University (B, M, D)
Louisiana State University (B, M, D)
Loyola University in Chicago (B, M)
Marquette University (B)
Massachusetts Institute of Technology (B, M, E, D)
Mills College (B, M)
Minnesota State University at Mankato (B, M)
Mississippi State University (B, M, D)

Montana State University (B, M)
Montana Tech (B)
National Technological University (M)
New Jersey Institute of Technology (B, M, D)
New Mexico Highlands University (B, M)
New Mexico State University (B, M, D)
New York Institute of Technology (B, M)
New York University (B, M, D)
North Carolina State University (B, M, D)
North Dakota State University (B, M, D)
Northeastern University (B, M, D)
Northwestern University (D)
Nova Southeastern University (B, M, D)
Ohio State University (B, M, D)
Ohio University (B)
Oklahoma State University (B, M, D)
Old Dominion University (B, M, D)
Oregon Graduate Institute of Science and Technology (M, D)
Pace University (B, M)
Pennsylvania State University (B, M, D)
Portland State University (B, M)
Princeton University (B, M, D)
Purdue University (B, M, D)
Rensselaer Polytechnic Institute (B, M, D)
Rice University (B, M, D)
Rivier College (B, M)
Rochester Institute of Technology (B, M)
Rutgers (B, M, D)
Sacred Heart University (B, M)
San Jose State University (B, M)
Santa Clara University (B)
Seattle University (B)
Smith College (B)
South Dakota State University (B, M)
Southern Methodist University (B, M, D)
Southern Polytechnic State University (B, M)
St. Cloud State University (B, M)
St. Mary's University (B, M)
Stanford University (B, M, D)
State University of New York at Albany (B, M, D)
State University of New York at Buffalo (B, M, D)
State University of New York at Stony Brook (B, M, D)
Stevens Institute of Technology (B, M, D)
Syracuse University (B, M, D)
Temple University (B, M, D)
Texas A&M University (B, M, D)
Texas Christian University (B)
Texas Tech University (B, M, D)
Thomas Edison State College (B)

Tufts University (B, M, D)
Tulane University (B, M, D)
University of Alabama at Birmingham (B, M, D)
University of Alabama at Huntsville (B, M, D)
University of Alabama at Tuscaloosa (B, M, D)
University of Alaska at Anchorage (B)
University of Alaska at Fairbanks (B, M)
University of Arizona (B, M, D)
University of Arkansas at Fayetteville (B, M)
University of Arkansas at Little Rock (B, M)
University of California at Berkeley (B, M, D)
University of California at Davis (B, M, D)
University of California at Irvine (B, M, D)
University of California at Los Angeles (B, M, D)
University of California at San Diego (B, M, D)
University of Central Oklahoma (B, M)
University of Chicago (B, M, D)
University of Cincinnati (B, M, D)
University of Colorado at Boulder (B, M, D)
University of Connecticut (B, M, D)
University of Delaware (B, M, D)
University of Denver (B, M, D)
University of Florida (B, M, E, D)
University of Georgia (B, M, D)
University of Hawaii at Manoa (B, M, D)
University of Houston (B, M, D)
University of Houston at Clear Lake (B, M)
University of Idaho (B, M, D)
University of Iowa (B, M, D)
University of Kansas (B, M, D)
University of Louisville (B, M, D)
University of Maine (B, M, D)
University of Maryland at College Park (B, M, D)
University of Maryland University College (B)
University of Massachusetts at Amherst (B, M, D)
University of Massachusetts at Lowell (B, M, D)
University of Michigan (B, M)
University of Minnesota at Twin Cities (B, M, D)
University of Missouri at Columbia (B, M, D)
University of Montana (B, M)
University of Nebraska at Lincoln (B, M, D)
University of Nebraska at Omaha (B, M)
University of Nevada at Las Vegas (B, M, D)
University of Nevada at Reno (B, M)
University of North Dakota (B, M)
University of North Florida (B, M)
University of North Texas (B, M, D)
University of Notre Dame (B, M, D)
University of Oregon (B, M, D)
University of Pennsylvania (B, M, D)

University of Pittsburgh (B, M, D)
University of Rhode Island (B, M, D)
University of Rochester (B, D)
University of South Carolina (B, M, D)
University of Southern California (B, M, D)
University of Tennessee (B, M, D)
University of Tennessee Space Institute (M)
University of Texas at Arlington (B, M, D)
University of Texas at Austin (B, M, D)
University of Texas at Dallas (B, M, D)
University of Texas at San Antonio (B, M, D)
University of Toledo (B, M)
University of Tulsa (B, M, D)
University of Utah (B, M, D)
University of Vermont (B, M)
University of Virginia (B, M, D)
University of Washington (B, M, D)
University of Wisconsin at Madison (B, M, D)
University of Wyoming (B, M, D)
Utah State University (B, M, D)
Vanderbilt University (B, M, D)
Virginia Tech (B, M, D)
Washington State University (B, M, D)
Washington University in St. Louis (B, M, D)
Wayne State University (B, M, D)
Webster University (B, M)
West Virginia University at Morgantown (B, M, D)
West Virginia University Institute of Technology (B)
Western Carolina University (B)
Western Kentucky University (B, M)
Wichita State University (B, M)
Worcester Polytechnic Institute (B, M, D)
Wright State University (B, M, D)
Yale University (B, M, D)

Computer Systems Engineering and Administration

Arizona State University East (B, M)
Boston University (B, M, D)
Case Western Reserve University (B, M, D)
Florida Institute of Technology (M)
Howard University (B)
Illinois Institute of Technology (M)
Massachusetts Institute of Technology (M)
National Technological University (M)
Northeastern University (M)
Rensselaer Polytechnic Institute (B, M, D)
Rice University (M)
Stanford University (B)

Syracuse University (M)
University of Arkansas at Fayetteville (B)
University of Houston (M, D)
University of Houston at Clear Lake (B)
University of Maryland University College (M)
University of Massachusetts at Amherst (B)
University of New Hampshire (B, M, D)
University of New Haven (B, M)
University of New Mexico (B, M, D)
University of North Carolina at Chapel Hill (B, M, D)
University of North Carolina at Charlotte (B, M)
University of Southern California (M)

Computer Technology

Arizona State University East (B)
Central Michigan University (B)
DeVry Institutes (B)
Indiana University/Purdue University at
  Indianapolis (B)
Marshall University (B)
Mississippi State University (B)
New Jersey Institute of Technology (B)
New Mexico State University (B)
Northeastern University (B)
Old Dominion University (B)
Purdue University (B, M)
Regents College (B)
Rochester Institute of Technology (B)
Southern Polytechnic State University (B)
Thomas Edison State College (B)
University of Arkansas at Little Rock (B)
University of Houston (B)
University of Memphis (B)
University of Oregon (B)
Wayne State University (B)

E-commerce

Bellevue University (B)
Carnegie Mellon University (M)
Creighton University (M)
DePaul University (M)
Howard University (M)
Illinois Institute of Technology (M)
Loyola University in Chicago (B, M)
New Jersey Institute of Technology (B, M)
Old Dominion University (B, M)
Stevens Institute of Technology (B)
Temple University (M)
University of Maryland University College (M)
Worcester Polytechnic Institute (M)

Educational and Instructional Technology

Auburn University (M, E)
Azusa Pacific University (M)
Ball State University (M)
Boise State University (M)
California State University at Chico (B, M)
Central Michigan University (M)
Emporia State University (M)
Illinois Institute of Technology (M)
Jackson State University (M)
Mississippi State University (M, E, D)
New York Institute of Technology (M)
New York University (M, D)
Nova Southeastern University (M, E, D)
Oklahoma State University (M, D)
San Jose State University (M)
Texas A&M University (M)
University of Arkansas at Fayetteville (M)
University of Georgia (M, E, D)
University of Hawaii at Manoa (M)
University of Houston (M, D)
University of Houston at Clear Lake (M)
University of Iowa (M, D)
Utah State University (M, E, D)
Wayne State University (M)

Electrical Engineering

Auburn University (B, M, D)
Boise State University (B)
Boston University (B, M, D)
Brigham Young University (B, M, D)
Brown University (B, M, D)
Bucknell University (B, M)
California Institute of Technology (B, M, D)
California Polytechnic State University (B, M)
California State University at Chico (B, M)
California State University at Sacramento (B, M)
Carnegie Mellon University (B, M, D)
Case Western Reserve University (B, M, D)
Clemson University (B, M, D)
Cleveland State University (B, M, D)
Colorado State University (B, M, D)
Columbia University (B, M, E, D)
Cornell University (B, M, D)
Drexel University (B, M, D)
Duke University (B, M, D)
Embry-Riddle Aeronautical University (B)
Florida Institute of Technology (B, M, D)

George Mason University (B, M, D)
Georgia Institute of Technology (B, M, D)
Howard University (B, M, D)
Illinois Institute of Technology (B, M, D)
Indiana University/Purdue University at
    Indianapolis (B, M, D)
Iowa State University (B, M, D)
Johns Hopkins University (B, M, D)
Kansas State University (B, M, D)
Lamar University (B, M, D)
Lehigh University (B, M, D)
Louisiana State University (B, M, D)
Marquette University (B, M, D)
Massachusetts Institute of Technology (B, M, E, D)
Minnesota State University at Mankato (B, M)
Mississippi State University (B, M, D)
Montana State University (B, M, D)
National Technological University (M)
New Jersey Institute of Technology (B, M, D)
New Mexico State University (B, M, D)
New York Institute of Technology (B, M)
North Carolina State University (B, M, D)
North Dakota State University (B, M, D)
Northeastern University (B, M, D)
Northwestern University (B, M, D)
Ohio State University (B, M, D)
Ohio University (B, M, D)
Oklahoma State University (B, M, D)
Old Dominion University (B, M, D)
Oregon Graduate Institute of Science and
    Technology (M, D)
Pennsylvania State University (B, M, D)
Portland State University (B, M, D)
Princeton University (B, M, D)
Purdue University (B, M, D)
Rensselaer Polytechnic Institute (B, M, D)
Rochester Institute of Technology (B, M)
Rutgers (B, M, D)
San Jose State University (B, M)
Santa Clara University (B, M, E, D)
Seattle University (B)
Smith College (B)
South Dakota State University (B, M)
Southern Methodist University (B, M)
St. Cloud State University (B)
St. Mary's University (B, M)
Stanford University (B, M, E, D)
State University of New York at Buffalo (B, M, D)
State University of New York at Stony Brook (B, M, D)
Stevens Institute of Technology (B, M, E, D)

Syracuse University (B, M, D)
Temple University (B, M)
Texas A&M University (B, M, D)
Texas Christian University (B)
Texas Tech University (B, M, D)
Tufts University (B, M, D)
Tulane University (B, M, D)
University of Alabama at Birmingham (B, M, D)
University of Alabama at Huntsville (B, M, D)
University of Alabama at Tuscaloosa (B, M, D)
University of Alaska at Fairbanks (B, M, D)
University of Arizona (B, M, D)
University of Arkansas at Fayetteville (B, M, D)
University of California at Berkeley (B, M, D)
University of California at Davis (B, M, D)
University of California at Irvine (B, M, D)
University of California at Los Angeles (B, M, D)
University of California at San Diego (B, M, D)
University of Cincinnati (B, M, D)
University of Colorado at Boulder (B, M, D)
University of Connecticut (B, M, D)
University of Delaware (B, M, D)
University of Denver (B, M, D)
University of Florida (B, M, E, D)
University of Hawaii at Manoa (B, M, D)
University of Houston (B, M, D)
University of Idaho (B, M, D)
University of Iowa (B, M, D)
University of Kansas (B, M, D)
University of Louisville (B, M, D)
University of Maine (B, M, D)
University of Maryland at College Park (B, M, D)
University of Massachusetts at Amherst (B, M, D)
University of Massachusetts at Lowell (B, M, D)
University of Memphis (B, M)
University of Michigan (B, M)
University of Minnesota at Twin Cities (B, M, D)
University of Missouri at Columbia (B)
University of Nebraska at Lincoln (B, M)
University of Nebraska at Omaha (B, M)
University of Nevada at Las Vegas (B, M, D)
University of Nevada at Reno (B, M, D)
University of New Hampshire (B, M, D)
University of New Haven (B, M)
University of New Mexico (B, M, D)
University of North Carolina at Charlotte (B, M, D)
University of North Dakota (B, M)
University of North Florida (B)
University of Notre Dame (B, M, D)
University of Pennsylvania (B, M, D)

University of Pittsburgh (B, M, D)
University of Rhode Island (B, M, D)
University of Rochester (B, M, D)
University of South Carolina (B, M, D)
University of Southern California (B, M, E, D)
University of Tennessee (B, M, D)
University of Texas at Arlington (B, M, D)
University of Texas at Austin (B, M, D)
University of Texas at Dallas (B, M, D)
University of Texas at San Antonio (B, M)
University of Toledo (B, M, D)
University of Tulsa (B, M, D)
University of Utah (B, M, D)
University of Vermont (B, M, D)
University of Virginia (B, M, D)
University of Washington (B, M, D)
University of Wisconsin at Madison (B, M, D)
University of Wyoming (B, M, D)
Utah State University (B, M, E, D)
Vanderbilt University (B, M, D)
Virginia Tech (B, M, D)
Washington State University (B, M, D)
Washington University in St. Louis (B, M, D)
Wayne State University (B, M, D)
West Virginia University at Morgantown (B, M, D)
West Virginia University Institute of Technology (B)
Western Kentucky University (B)
Wichita State University (B, M, D)
Worcester Polytechnic Institute (B, M, D)
Wright State University (B, M, D)
Yale University (B, D)

Electronic(s) Engineering Technology

Arizona State University East (B, M)
Boise State University (B)
Central Michigan University (B)
DeVry Institutes (B)
Indiana University/Purdue University at
    Indianapolis (B)
Minnesota State University at Mankato (B)
New Jersey Institute of Technology (B)
New Mexico State University (B)
New York Institute of Technology (B)
Northeastern University (B)
Oklahoma State University (B)
Old Dominion University (B)
Purdue University (B, M)
Regents College (B)
Rice University (B, M, D)
Rochester Institute of Technology (B)

South Dakota State University (B)
Southern Polytechnic State University (B, M)
Temple University (B)
Texas A&M University (B)
Thomas Edison State College (B)
University of Arkansas at Little Rock (B)
University of Cincinnati (B)
University of Houston (B)
University of Maine (B)
University of Massachusetts at Lowell (B)
University of Memphis (B, M)
University of Nebraska at Omaha (B)
University of North Carolina at Charlotte (B)
University of North Texas (B, M)
University of Toledo (B)
Wayne State University (B)
West Virginia University Institute of Technology (B)
Western Carolina University (B)

Embedded Systems

University of California at Irvine (M)

Entertainment Technology

American University (M)
Carnegie Mellon University (M)

Human-Computer Interaction

Carnegie Mellon University (B, M, D)
DePaul University (B, M, D)
Georgia Institute of Technology (M)
Indiana University at Bloomington (M)

Informatics

George Mason University (D)
Indiana University at Bloomington (B)
Massachusetts Institute of Technology (M)
    [Medical Informatics]
New Jersey Institute of Technology (M, D)
    [Biomedical Informatics]
Ohio State University (B) [Health Information
    Management]
Regents College (M) [Nursing/Informatics]
Rensselaer Polytechnic Institute (M)
    [Informatics and Architecture]
University of Alabama at Birmingham (M)
    [Health Informatics]
University of Utah (M, D) [Medical Informatics]
Western Carolina University (B) [Health Information
    Management]

Information Science
Brooklyn College (B, M)
California State University at Chico (B, M)
Carnegie Mellon University (M)
Case Western Reserve University (M, D)
Christopher Newport University (B)
Cleveland State University (B, M)
Columbia University (M)
Drexel University (M)
Fordham University (B)
Indiana University/Purdue University at
    Indianapolis (M)
Kansas State University (M)
Minnesota State University at Mankato (B)
New Jersey Institute of Technology (D)
Nova Southeastern University (D)
Ohio State University (B, M, D)
Pennsylvania State University (B)
Sacred Heart University (M)
Syracuse University (B, M, D)
Temple University (D)
University of Alabama at Birmingham (M, D)
University of California at Irvine (M, D)
University of California at Los Angeles (M, D)
University of Florida (D)
University of Hawaii at Manoa (B, M, D)
University of Maryland University College (B)
University of Michigan (B, M)
University of New Haven (M)
University of North Carolina at Charlotte (B)
University of North Florida (B, M)
University of Oregon (B, M)
University of Pittsburgh (B, M, D)
University of Tennessee (M)

Information Technology
Arizona State University East (M)
Columbia University (M)
Creighton University (M)
DeVry Institutes (B)
Georgia Institute of Technology (M)
Harvard University (D)
Louisiana State University (M)
Marshall University (B)
Montana Tech (B)
Pennsylvania State University (B)
Rensselaer Polytechnic Institute (B, M, D)
Rochester Institute of Technology (B, M)
University of Arkansas at Little Rock (M)
University of Cincinnati (B, M)

University of Denver (M)
University of Maryland University College (B, M)
University of North Carolina at Charlotte (M, D)
University of Oregon (B)
Virginia Tech (M)
Worcester Polytechnic Institute (M)

Interdisciplinary Computer Science and Technology Studies
Florida Institute of Technology (M) [Aviation
    Computer Science]
Georgia Institute of Technology (M, D) [History of
    Technology]
Illinois Institute of Technology (B) [Internet
    Communication]
Massachusetts Institute of Technology (B, D)
    [Science/Technology/Society]
Massachusetts Institute of Technology (M, D)
    [Technology and Policy]
Mills College (M) [Interdisciplinary Computer
    Science]
New York University (M) [Scientific Computing]
Rensselaer Polytechnic Institute (M, D)
    [Computer-Mediated Communication]
University of Maryland University College (B)
    [Computer Studies]
Worcester Polytechnic Institute (B) [Economics
    and Technology]

Internet Law
Bellevue University (M)

Knowledge Discovery and Data Mining
Carnegie Mellon University (M)
University of California at Irvine (M)

Language Technologies
Carnegie Mellon University (M, D)

Management Information Systems
Auburn University (M)
Azusa Pacific University (B)
Bellevue University (B, M)
California State University at Chico (B, M)
California State University at Sacramento (M)
Carnegie Mellon University (M)
Case Western Reserve University (D)
Central Michigan University (B, M)
Creighton University (B, M)
DePaul University (M)

DeVry Institutes (M)
Drexel University (M)
Florida Institute of Technology (M)
Harvard University (D)
Lamar University (B)
Louisiana State University (M)
Loyola University in Chicago (B, M)
Massachusetts Institute of Technology (B, M, D)
Minnesota State University at Mankato (B)
New York Institute of Technology (M)
North Dakota State University (B)
Nova Southeastern University (M)
Ohio State University (B)
Ohio University (B)
Oklahoma State University (M)
San Jose State University (B)
State University of New York at Albany (B, M)
State University of New York at Buffalo (B)
Stevens Institute of Technology (M, D)
Temple University (M)
Texas Tech University (B, M, D)
University of Alabama at Huntsville (B, M)
University of Alabama at Tuscaloosa (B, M)
University of Alaska at Anchorage (B)
University of Arizona (B, M, D)
University of California at Berkeley (M, D)
University of Central Oklahoma (B)
University of Georgia (B)
University of Hawaii at Manoa (B)
University of Houston (B, M, D)
University of Houston at Clear Lake (B, M)
University of Maryland University College (B, M)
University of Memphis (B, M)
University of Nebraska at Omaha (B, M)
University of Pennsylvania (D)
University of Texas at Austin (B, D)
University of Wyoming (B)
Virginia Tech (B, D)
Wayne State University (B)
West Virginia University Institute of Technology (B)
Worcester Polytechnic Institute (B, M)
Wright State University (B)

Microelectronics
Arizona State University East (B, M)
Rensselaer Polytechnic Institute (M)
Rochester Institute of Technology (B, M)
University of Houston (M)
University of Southern California (M)

Pure and Applied Logic
Carnegie Mellon University (D)

Multimedia Design and Development
American University (B)
Arizona State University East (B)
Clemson University (M)
Indiana University/Purdue University at
    Indianapolis (B, M)
Massachusetts Institute of Technology (B, M, D)
New Mexico Highlands University (M)
Rensselaer Polytechnic Institute (M)
St. Cloud State University (B, M)
University of Denver (B, M)
University of Florida (B, M)
University of Pennsylvania (B)
University of Southern California (M)

Robotics
Carnegie Mellon University (M, D)
Minnesota State University at Mankato (M)
    [Mechatronics]
Rochester Institute of Technology (B)
    [Electrical/Mechanical Technology]
Western Kentucky University (B)
    [Electromechanical Technology]

Software Engineering
Auburn University (B, M)
California State University at Sacramento (M)
Carnegie Mellon University (M)
DePaul University (M)
Embry-Riddle Aeronautical University (M)
George Mason University (M)
Kansas State University (M)
National Technological University (M)
Oregon Graduate Institute of Science and
    Technology (M)
Portland State University (M)
Rochester Institute of Technology (B, M)
Santa Clara University (M)
Seattle University (M)
Southern Methodist University (M)
Southern Polytechnic State University (M)
St. Mary's University (B, M)
Texas Tech University (M)
University of Houston at Clear Lake (M)
University of Maryland University College (M)
University of Michigan (M)

University of Minnesota at Twin Cities (M)
University of Oregon (M)
University of Texas at Arlington (M)
University of Texas at Austin (M)
West Virginia University at Morgantown (M)

Software Technology

Arizona State University East (B)

Technology Education

Montana State University (B)
New Mexico Highlands University (B)
New York Institute of Technology (B)
North Carolina State University (B, M, E, D)
St. Cloud State University (B) [Computer Science
    Education]
Utah State University (M) [Business Information
    Systems and Education]
Wayne State University (M)
West Virginia University Institute of Technology (B)

Technology Management

Arizona State University East (M)
Auburn University (M)
Charter Oak State College (B)
Creighton University (M)
DeVry Institutes (B)
Drexel University (B, M)
Embry-Riddle Aeronautical University (B, M)
Georgia Institute of Technology (M)
Harvard University (D)
Lehigh University (M)
Marshall University (M)
Massachusetts Institute of Technology (M, D)
National Technological University (M)
New Jersey Institute of Technology (M)
Northeastern University (M)
Oregon Graduate Institute of Science and
    Technology (M)
Portland State University (M)
Rensselaer Polytechnic Institute (B, M)
Stevens Institute of Technology (M, D)
University of Cincinnati (B, M)
University of Maryland University College (M)

University of Texas at Austin (M)
University of Texas at San Antonio (M)
University of Tulsa (M)
Vanderbilt University (M)
Wayne State University (M)
Worcester Polytechnic Institute (M)

Telecommunications

Ball State University (B)
Boise State University (M)
Boston University (M)
California State University at Chico (B)
Carnegie Mellon University (M)
Columbia University (M)
DePaul University (M)
DeVry Institutes (B, M)
George Mason University (M)
Illinois Institute of Technology (M)
Johns Hopkins University (M)
National Technological University (M)
New Jersey Institute of Technology (B, M)
New York Institute of Technology (B)
New York University (M)
Ohio University (M)
Oklahoma State University (M)
Pace University (M)
Rivier College (B)
Rochester Institute of Technology (B)
Southern Methodist University (B, M)
Southern Polytechnic State University (B)
Stevens Institute of Technology (M, D)
Syracuse University (M)
Texas A&M University (B)
Texas Tech University (M)
University of Colorado at Boulder (M)
University of Georgia (B)
University of Maryland at College Park (M)
University of Maryland University College (M)
University of Massachusetts at Lowell (M)
University of Nebraska at Omaha (M)
University of Pennsylvania (B)
University of Pittsburgh (M)
University of Texas at Dallas (M)
Wayne State University (M)

APPENDIX C

Top Picks

Okay, so you have a pretty good idea of the degree you want. But can you fit it in your budget? And is it possible to complete it by distance learning? This appendix offers top schools in two categories: those offering a reasonably priced high-quality education and those offering degrees over the Internet. While it would, of course, be possible to further slice and dice these program in any number of ways, you will find that once you select for region (Appendix A) and subject matter (Appendix B), and concentrate only on the top schools in the country, as this book does, these are the topics of greatest interest to the majority of potential students.

Least Expensive Programs

If you're looking for a dirt-cheap IT degree, we've got you covered. Out of the 199 schools listed in Chapter 12, the programs noted in Tables C-1, C-2, and C-3 are the cheapest bachelor's, master's, and doctoral degrees available. The numbers in parentheses are the nonresident tuition figures. Remember that the costs given below (and in the listings) do not take into account room and board, travel, and other nonacademic fees.

TABLE C-1: Bachelor's Top 20

School	Estimated Tuition
Charter Oak State College	$1,300 ($1,500) and up
Thomas Edison State College	$1,400 ($1,800–2,100) and up
Regents College	$1,600 and up
State University of New York—Empire State College	$2,250 ($4,900) and up
Boise State University	$2,800–18,000 ($2,800–20,900)
Texas Tech University	$4,900 ($32,500)
Texas A&M University	$5,400 ($33,000)
Montana Tech of the University of Montana	$5,600–13,900 ($16,300–40,700)
San Jose State University	$5,700 ($37,200)
Columbus State University	$6,300–9,700 ($25,300–38,700)
Lamar University	$6,700 ($27,670)
Mississippi State University	$7,200 ($15,100)
New Mexico Highlands University	$7,500–9,300 ($9,300–30,300)
South Dakota State University	$7,700 ($8,700–24,600)
Emporia State University	$8,300 ($26,200)
Kansas State University	$8,400 ($34,800)
Southern Polytechnic State University	$8,500 ($30,200)
North Carolina State University	$8,800 ($42,900)
University of Central Oklahoma	$8,900 ($20,300)
University of Alaska at Anchorage	$9,800 ($29,400)

TABLE C-2: Master's Top 15

School	Estimated Tuition
South Dakota State University	$2,200 ($2,400–6,900)
Columbus State University	$2,200–3,300 ($8,700–13,100)
Arizona State University East	$2,200–3,800 ($9,400–12,800)
New Mexico Highlands University	$2,300–2,800 ($2,800–8,000)
North Carolina State University	$2,400 ($16,100)
Portland State University	$3,100 ($5,400)
Boise State University	$3,100–5,000 ($5,000–6,400)
Texas A&M University	$3,200 ($11,000)
Texas Tech University	$3,300 ($11,000)
San Jose State University	$3,400 ($12,200)
New Mexico State University	$3,700 ($4,000–9,000)
University of Central Oklahoma	$3,700 ($7,600)
Oklahoma State University	$3,700 ($10,500)
Southern Polytechnic State University	$3,700 ($13,500)
North Dakota State University	$3,900 ($10,300)
Louisiana State University	$4,100 ($10,300)

TABLE C-3: Doctorate Top 10

School	Estimated Tuition
North Carolina State University	$3,900 ($26,900)
Portland State University	$5,200 ($9,000)
Texas Tech University	$5,500 ($18,400)
Texas A&M University	$6,200 ($21,400)
North Dakota State University	$6,400 ($17,200)
New Mexico State University	$6,700 ($8,000–20,900)
Oklahoma State University	$7,300 ($20,900)
University of Alabama at Birmingham	$7,400 ($13,700)
Georgia Institute of Technology	$7,500 ($27,100)
University of Houston	$7,700 ($19,900)

Best Distance-Learning Programs

Want a degree, but can't relocate (or, at least, would rather not)? Here are a few programs offered by the top 199 colleges that can be completed mostly (or sometimes entirely) through distance learning. For more information on how all this works, see Chapter 8.

Auburn University
Master of Business Administration (IT concentration)
Master of Management Information Systems
Master of Science in Computer Science and Engineering
Master of Software Engineering
Doctor of Philosophy in Computer Science and Engineering

Ball State University
Master of Science in Computer Science

Bellevue University
Bachelor of Science in Business Information Systems
Bachelor of Science in E-Commerce
Bachelor of Science in Management Information Systems
Master of Business Administration (several IT concentrations)

Boise State University
Master of Science in Instructional and Performance Technology

California State University at Chico
Bachelor of Science in Computer Science
Master of Science in Computer Science

Carnegie Mellon University
Master of Software Information Technology

Charter Oak State College
Bachelor of Arts in General Studies (computer science)
Bachelor of Arts in General Studies (technology and management)
Bachelor of Science in General Studies (computer science)
Bachelor of Science in General Studies (technology and management)

Colorado State University
Master of Electrical Engineering
Master of Science in Computer Science
Master of Science in Electrical Engineering
Doctor of Philosophy in Electrical Engineering

Columbus State University
Master of Science in Applied Computer Science

Drexel University
Master of Business Administration (IT concentration)
Master of Science in Information Systems
Master of Science in Library and Information Science (digital information)

Embry-Riddle Aeronautical University
Bachelor of Science in Computer Engineering (degree completion program)

Florida Institute of Technology
Master of Science in Management (computer information systems)
Master of Science in Systems Engineering (information systems)

Howard University
Master of Business Administration (emphasis in E-commerce)

Iowa State University
Master of Science in Computer Engineering
Master of Science in Electrical Engineering

Kansas State University
Master of Science in Electrical Engineering
Master of Software Engineering

Lehigh University
Master of Science in Management of Technology

Mississippi State University

Master of Science in Computer Science
Doctor of Philosophy in Computer Science

Montana State University

Master of Science in Computer Science (Montana residents only)
Master of Project Engineering Management

Montana Tech of the University of Montana

Master of Project Engineering Management

National Technological University

Master of Science in Computer Science

New Jersey Institute of Technology

Bachelor of Science in Computer Science
Master of Business Administration (IT concentration)
Master of Science in Computer Science
Master of Science in Information Systems

Nova Southeastern University

Master of Science in Computer Information Systems
Master of Science in Computer Science
Master of Science in Management Information Systems
Doctor of Philosophy in Computer Information Systems
Doctor of Philosophy in Computer Science

Old Dominion University

Bachelor of Science in Computer Science
Bachelor of Science in Electrical Engineering

Oregon Graduate Institute of Science and Technology

Master of Science in Management of Science and Technology
Master of Software Engineering

Oregon State University

Master of Software Engineering

Portland State University

Master of Software Engineering

Regents College

Bachelor of Science in Computer Information Systems
Bachelor of Science in Computer Technology
Bachelor of Science in Electronic(s) Engineering Technology

Rensselaer Polytechnic Institute

Individualized Professional Master of Science
Master of Engineering in Electrical Engineering
Master of Business Administration (IT concentration)
Master of Science in Computer and Systems Engineering
Master of Science in Computer Science Management
Master of Science in Electrical Engineering

Southern Methodist University

Master of Science in Computer Engineering
Master of Science in Computer Science
Master of Science in Software Engineering
Master of Science in Telecommunications

Stanford University

Master of Science in Electrical Engineering
Master of Science in Computer Science (some residency required)

State University of New York Empire State College

Individualized Bachelor of Arts
Individualized Bachelor of Professional Studies
Individualized Bachelor of Science

Texas A&M University

Master of Education in Educational Technology

Texas Tech University

Master of Engineering (electrical engineering)
Master of Engineering (software engineering)
Master of Science in Software Engineering

Thomas Edison State College

Bachelor of Arts in Computer Science
Bachelor of Science in Applied Science and Technology (computer science)
Bachelor of Science in Applied Science and Technology (electrical technology)

Bachelor of Science in Applied Science and
Technology (electronics)
Bachelor of Science in Business Administration
(computer information systems)

University of Cincinnati

Bachelor of Arts in General Studies (information
technology)

University of Houston

Bachelor of Science in Technology (mechanical
technology)

University of Idaho

Master of Engineering in Computer Engineering
Master of Engineering in Electrical Engineering

University of Maryland University College

Bachelor of Arts in Computer and Information
Sciences
Bachelor of Arts in Computer Studies
Bachelor of Arts in Information Systems
Management
Bachelor of Science in Computer and Information
Sciences
Bachelor of Science in Computer Studies
Master of Science in Computer Systems Management
Bachelor of Science in Information Systems
Management
Master of Science in Management (management
information systems)
Master of Science in Technology Management
Master of Science in Telecommunications
Management
Master of Software Engineering

University of Massachusetts at Amherst

Master of Science in Electrical and Computer
Engineering

University of Nebraska at Omaha

Bachelor of General Studies (computer science)
Bachelor of Science in Electrical Engineering
Technology (degree completion)

University of Oregon

Master of Software Engineering

University of Southern California

Master of Science in Computer Engineering
Master of Science in Computer Science
Master of Science in Electrical Engineering
Master of Science in Information Sciences
Master of Science in Systems Architecture and
Engineering
Electrical Engineer (some residency required)

University of Texas at Arlington

Master of Science in Computer Science and
Engineering
Master of Science in Electrical Engineering

University of Texas at Dallas

Master of Science in Computer Science
Master of Science in Electrical Engineering

University of Texas at San Antonio

Master of Science in Management of Technology

Virginia Tech

Master of Information Technology (some residency
required)

APPENDIX D

Resources

There are literally thousands of resources available for prospective students—everything from job leads in electrophotonics to help in understanding tax breaks for students. Below, we have listed a sampling of the most helpful resources for each chapter in the book. Each of these resources will almost certainly lead you to more—through Web links, bibliographies, and the like.

Chapter 1: An Introduction to the World of IT

For getting a basic understanding of IT jobs, learning more about employment opportunities and statistics, and researching the fields that might be right for you to study, the resources below are a great start.

General Information

To find out more about IT careers, contact:

Association for Computing Machinery (ACM)

1515 Broadway
New York, NY 10036
http://www.acm.org/

Institute of Electrical and Electronics Engineers: USA

1828 L Street, NW
Suite 1202
Washington, DC 20036
http://www.ieee.org/

Web Sites

Bureau of Labor and Statistics: IT Job Descriptions

http://stats.bls.gov/oco/ocos042.htm
Excellent, in-a-nutshell descriptions that cover questions like, "What exactly does a systems analyst do?"

InfoWorld.com

http://www.infoworld.com/
Up-to-the-minute news and career information for IT professionals.

ITWorld

http://www.itworld.com/
Designed and updated for techies, by techies. A massive site dedicated to information technology both as a professional field and as a science.

Monster.com Guide to Technology Careers

http://technology.monster.com/

An excellent career resource from the excellent career people.

SolutionCentral

http://www.solutioncentral.com/

Features "roundtables" (moderated Q&A forums) hosted by such greats as Sun Microsystems co-founder Bill Joy. An excellent general introduction to the dot-com industry. As of press time, this site also includes a thriving Osborne/McGraw-Hill section (which includes a roundtable for this book hosted by one of its co-authors).

U.S. News Online: .edu Home Page

http://www.usnews.com/usnews/edu/

A large, comprehensive site (operated by the online branch of *U.S. News and World Report*) that includes the *U.S. News* rankings and general information on nearly all accredited U.S. colleges.

Books

Goff, Leslie. *Get Your IT Job and Get Ahead*. New York: Osborne/McGraw-Hill, 2000. 400 pages. $24.95. A sister book to this one, this helpful compendium deals with the nitty-gritty of job hunting and career building.

Chapter 2: Frequently Asked Questions

There are many useful resources for women, minorities, and people with learning disabilities. The books and Web sites listed here point in a number of useful and interesting directions.

Books

Dobkin, Rachel, and Shana Sippy. *Educating Ourselves: The College Woman's Handbook*. New York: Workman, 1995. 640 pages. $14.95. A frank, humorous, and immensely readable book addressing women's issues on the college campus.

Kravets, Marybeth, and Imy F. Wax. *The K&W Guide to Colleges for Students with Learning Disabilities or ADDs*. New York: Princeton Review, 2000. 737 pages. $27. Gives general tips for students with learning disabilities, lists more than 300 schools with special programs, and gives appropriate contact information for another 1,000 schools.

Web Sites

Minority Online Information Service (MOLIS)
http://www.sciencewise.com/molis/
An incredible amount of information on scholarships and other academic opportunities available to minority students.

Chapter 3: Researching and Applying to an Undergraduate Program

Researching and applying to schools is a topic amply discussed in a wide, wide range of areas. Indeed, perhaps only financial aid offers more sources of guidance and information. The books and Web sites below are some of the most useful compendia. In particular, this is an area in which the Web is extremely helpful. Many organizations are giving away highly useful facts and figures for free.

Books

Barron's Profiles of American Colleges 2000 Edition. New York: Barron's Educational Series, 1998. 1,591 pages. $25. Undergraduate profiles on more than 1,600 accredited schools.

Martz, Geoff, Kim Magloire, and Theodore Silver. *Cracking the ACT 2000–2001*. New York: Princeton Review, 2000. 388 pages. $18. A witty and down-to-earth guide to the ACT. Includes a sample test.

Peterson's Guide to Four-Year Colleges. Princeton: Peterson's, 2000. 3,264 pages + CD-ROM. $26.95. An incredibly massive guide to accredited traditional four-year colleges in the U.S.

Robinson, Adam, John Katzman, David Owen, et al. *Cracking the SAT and PSAT 2000*. New York: Princeton Review, 1999. 647 pages + CD-ROM. $29.95 for set ($18 for book without CD-ROM). Includes a vocabulary builder and other goodies. Sample tests are included.

Turlington, Shannon. *The Unofficial Guide to College Admissions*. Foster City, California: Arco-IDG, 2000. 437 pages. $16.95. Covers every aspect of the admissions process, from tests to electronic applications. The truly massive bibliography section is a must-have.

Web Sites

About.com's Guide to College Admissions

http://collegeapps.about.com/
A vast amount of information on finding and applying to the right college.

The College Planning Web Site

http://www.collegeplan.org/
A wonderful online resource that guides you step by step through the process of applying to a college.

Peterson's Online

http://www.petersons.com/
College directories and more. Probably one of the best places on the Net to look for a college.

ScholarStuff.com

http://www.scholarstuff.com/
Lots of directories and general information on the world of higher education.

Chapter 4: Researching and Applying to a Graduate School

As with undergraduate admissions, the topic of selecting, preparing for, and applying to graduate school (and taking the requisite exams) abounds with sources for guidance and information, much of it free on the Web. Take advantage of every lead offered.

Books

Asher, Donald. *Graduate Admissions Essays*. Berkeley: Ten Speed Press, 2000. 312 pages. $19.95. General information on how to write a good admissions essay, with examples.

GRE Exam 2000-2001. New York: Kaplan, 2000. 344 pages. $20. Includes a full-length practice exam.

Peterson's Computer Science and Electrical Engineering Programs 1999. Princeton: Peterson's, 1999. 788 pages. $26.95. Deals with more than 700 graduate programs in the field. Most of the book (more than 400 pages) is made up of full-page paid listings, although these listings are fairly informative (giving faculty credentials and so forth).

REA Testbuster for the GRE CAT. Piscataway, New Jersey: REA, 2000. 554 pages + CD-ROM. $34.95. An excellent, well-rounded guide for the GRE.

Still, Cathryn. *Crash Course for the GMAT.* New York: Princeton Review, 2000. 185 pages. $9.95. Want to get ready for the GMAT, but only have a week to prepare? This book just might be the answer.

Stuart, David, et al. *GRE/GMAT Math Workbook.* New York: Kaplan, 1997. 340 pages. $18. A handy, novel book dealing with the bane of many would-be graduate students: the dreaded math section.

Vlk, Suzee. *The GMAT for Dummies.* Foster City, California: IDG Books, 2000. 338 pages. $16.99. A good, well-rounded guide to the GMAT. Includes two sample tests.

Vlk, Suzee. *The GRE CAT for Dummies.* 4th ed. Foster City, California: IDG Books, 2000. 307 pages. $16.99. One of the friendliest guides to the GRE you'll find.

Warren, Rachel, ed. *The Best Graduate Programs in Engineering.* 2nd ed. New York: Princeton Review, 1998. 433 pages. $21. Excellent and very thorough profiles of 131 top engineering schools. Also covers information technology programs in non-engineering fields (such as computer science, information science, and so forth).

Web Sites

Peterson's Online

http://www.petersons.com/
College directories and more. Probably one of the best places on the Net to look for a college.

ScholarStuff.com

http://www.scholarstuff.com/
Lots of directories and general information on the world of higher education.

Chapter 6: Financial Aid Demystified

Financial aid is another area in which guidance abounds. Start out with the wealth of free information on the Net, and then delve into bookstores and libraries to fill any gaps in your knowledge.

Books

Cohen, Justin, ed. *Yale Daily News Guide to Fellowships and Grants*. New York: Kaplan, 1999. 416 pages. $25. Lists hundreds of graduate fellowships and grants sorted by school.

The Complete Scholarships Book. Naperville, Illinois: Sourcebooks, 1998. 852 pages. $22.95. Identifies more than 5,000 sources for scholarships and grants.

Kaplan, Benjamin R. *How to Go to College (Almost) for Free*. Gleneden Beach, Oregon: Waggle Dancer Books, 1999. 316 pages. $23.95. A humorous, user-friendly guide to scholarships, written by a graduate of Harvard University who took advantage of available scholarship options and attended, well, almost for free.

Peterson's Scholarships and Loans for Adult Students. Princeton: Peterson's, 2000. 398 pages. $19.95. Lists special financial aid options for adult students.

Schlachter, Gail, and R. David Weber. *Scholarships 2000*. New York: Kaplan, 1999. 584 pages. $25. Thousands of scholarships with contact information, listed generally and sorted by category. Includes some very unusual options (Yakama Tribal Association Scholarship, Western Sunbathing Association Scholarship, and so on).

Vuturo, Chris. *The Scholarship Advisor*. New York: Princeton Review, 1999. 905 pages. $25. A solid directory and excellent overall introduction to the world of scholarships. Author won $885,000 in scholarship money using the methods described in this book.

Web Sites

About.com's Guide to Financial Aid

http://financialaid.about.com/

A very thorough Web site addressing a vast array of specific financial aid options.

Families' Guide to the 1997 Tax Cuts for Education (Postsecondary)

http://www.ed.gov/updates/97918tax.html

Deals with various education-related tax incentives in a friendly, straightforward manner.

IRS Notice 97-60

http://www.irs.gov/hot/not97-60.html

Deals with IRA withdrawals and other education-related tax incentives brought about by the Taxpayer Relief Act of 1997.

Department of Veteran Affairs Education Service

http://www.gibill.va.gov/education/

An excellent site profiling educational options for military veterans and employees of the National Guard.

The SmartStudent Guide to Financial Aid

http://www.finaid.org/

Deals with scholarships, loans, grants, and other financial aid possibilities.

Chapter 7: Going Back to School As an Adult

The Net offers a lot of support and information for the older student, and there are a number of books that give guidance and the occasional pep talk. Here are some of the most helpful.

Books

Bruno, Frank. *Going Back to School: College Survival Strategies for Adult Students.* New York: Arco, 1995. $12.95. Solid strategies and a lot of hand-holding for the nervous older student returning to college. Heavy emphasis on how to learn, remembering how to study, and so forth.

Phillips, Vicky. *Never Too Late to Learn: The Adult Student's Guide to College.* New York: Princeton Review, 2000. 230 pages. $13.95. A pleasant little book that outlines (and outlines well) what adult students might expect from the college process.

Web Sites

About.com's Guide to Adult Education

http://adulted.about.com/

An excellent, well-rounded starting point for reentry students.

Back to College

http://www.back2college.com/

A broad-ranging resource that provides much, much information for reentry students. Includes a very nice section on distance-learning programs.

Directory of State Higher Education Agencies
http://www.ed.gov/offices/OPE/agencies.html
A directory of contact information (addresses, phone numbers, and Web sites) for state agencies. Often these state agencies sponsor special programs for adult students.

Chapter 8: Using the Internet to Your Advantage

If the idea of getting a degree online intrigues you, the sources below point to a number of places where you can learn more, including listings of schools that offer Internet degrees, strategies for determining whether this sort of learning is for you, and much more.

Books

Bear, John B., and Mariah P. Bear. *Bears' Guide to Earning College Degrees Nontraditionally.* 14th edition. Berkeley: Ten Speed Press, 2000. 410 pages. $29.95. Addresses nontraditional programs of every stripe (foreign and domestic, accredited and unaccredited, 100 percent online and semi-residential).

Hartman, Kenneth. *Internet Guide for College-Bound Students.* New York: The College Board, 1998. 200 pages + CD-ROM. $14.95. A little dated (two years is a long time in the Internet world), but still packed with great ideas for how to research schools online, find scholarships, and much more.

Helm, Matthew, and April Helm. *Get Your Degree Online.* New York: McGraw-Hill, 2000. 437 pages. $21.95. A very friendly, helpful book that focuses primarily (though certainly not exclusively!) on U.S. undergraduate and certificate programs.

Peterson's Guide to Distance Learning Programs 2000. 4th edition. Princeton: Peterson's, 1999. 708 pages. $26.95. Essentially a very impressive printed database of distance-learning courses, certificates, and degree programs.

Thorson, Marcie K. *Campus-Free College Degrees.* 9th edition. New York: Careers Unlimited, 2000. $27.95. Focuses on accredited U.S. distance-learning programs, addressing each one in great depth.

Web Sites

About.com's Guide to Distance Learning

http://distancelearn.about.com/

A wonderful resource for additional links, information on specific degree programs, news, and good advice.

The International Centre for Distance Learning

http://www-icdl.open.ac.uk/

Probably the most comprehensive online list of accredited non-U.S. distance-learning courses and programs in the world. You can browse the wonderfully user-friendly database or order the CD-ROM instead. Sponsored by the Open University (U.K.).

Steve Levicoff's Home Page

http://levicoff.tripod.com/

A wealth of information on portfolio (life experience) credit, individualized graduate programs, and accreditation. Also features the full text of Levicoff's book *Name It and Frame It*, which includes a helpful 72-point list for checking out questionable schools.

Chapter 9: The Importance of Accreditation

The most helpful resources for checking out a school's accreditation are the Web sites listed in this chapter. However, for a more comprehensive compendium, the book below has it all.

Books

Accredited Institutes of Post-Secondary Education. Phoenix, Arizona: Oryx Press, 2000. 735 pages. $55. A comprehensive listing of every accredited U.S. school and every U.S. candidate for accreditation.

Chapter 10: Working with Your Employer

The job resources listed under Chapter 1, above, have much of what you need to enter the workforce—job descriptions, salary ranges, classified listings, and so forth. For those serious about the union funding discussed in the chapter, however, the Web site below is a helpful resource.

Union Scholarships

http://www.aflcio.org/scholarships/index.htm
Information on union scholarships and financial aid in general.

Chapter 11: Credit for Prior Learning

Alternate methods of earning credit are often under-reported or even obscure to the schools that offer such assistance. The expanded resource listings below will help qualifying students get the credit that's coming to them.

Books

CREDIT BY EXAM

Agrawal, Om Prakesh, et al. *GRE Mathematics*. Piscataway, New Jersey: REA, 1999. 333 pages. $28.95. A useful study guide for the subject GRE in mathematics. Includes six sample examinations and a short refresher section that covers the theoretical basics.

CLEP Official Study Guide 2000. New York: The College Board, 2000. 526 pages. $18. Sample exam questions for 34 CLEP examinations, plus study tips and review materials.

Cracking the GRE Math. New York: Princeton Review, 2000. 438 pages. $16. Surveys all subject matter covered by the subject GRE in mathematics. Includes a sample test.

Cezzar, Ruknet. *GRE Computer Science*. Piscataway, New Jersey: REA, 1998. 253 pages. $22.95. Includes four sample tests with annotated answers.

Meltzer, Tom, and Paul Foglino. *Cracking the CLEP.* 4th ed. New York: Princeton Review, 2000. 448 pages. $20. Gives detailed study information and sample tests for the five general CLEP examinations, plus brief summaries and tips for the subject exams.

Regents College Examinations Official Study Guide. $18.95. The official guide to Regents College Examinations (RCEs).

CREDIT FOR MILITARY EXPERIENCE

Guide to the Evaluation of Educational Experiences in the Armed Forces. Phoenix, Arizona: Oryx Press, 1999. $35 per volume. A three-volume listing (one volume for each branch of the service) of military training programs that can be used for credit.

CREDIT FOR NON-ACADEMIC TRAINING

Guide to Educational Credit for Training Programs. Phoenix, Arizona: Oryx Press, 1999. 1,200 pages. $90. A massive listing of training programs that can be transformed into credit.

LIFE EXPERIENCE CREDIT

Lamdin, Lois, and Susan Simosko. *Earn College Credit for What You Know.* 3rd ed. Chicago: CAEL, 1997. $24.95. Details just how to design a portfolio, and lists hundreds of schools that accept life experience credit.

Mandel, Alan, and Elana Michelson. *Portfolio Development and Adult Learning Purposes and Strategies.* Chicago: CAEL, 1991. $21.50. Deals with the eight most common university approaches to granting credit for life experience.

GLOSSARY

Are you perplexed by "portfolio"? Addled by "ABET"? In this section, you'll find user-friendly explanations for dozens of terms you'll run into as you begin your search for the perfect IT degree.

ABET

The Accreditation Board for Engineering and Technology, a recognized and highly respected private accrediting agency that evaluates and accredits programs in engineering and technology fields. For more detailed information on this agency, see Chapter 9.

accreditation

A seal of approval bestowed upon a university, department, and/or specific degree program by recognized third parties, called accrediting bodies, which exist for this sole purpose. For more information on the process of accreditation, see Chapter 9.

If you are considering a U.S. program in any field, you should probably choose a program offered through a regionally accredited university.

ACE

The American Council on Education, a widely recognized organization that recommends college credit for various non-academic programs and certificates. For more information on this agency and its purpose, see Chapter 11.

ACT

American College Testing, a program offering a common entrance examination for undergraduates.

Assembler (x86)

A very low-level programming language that relies largely on memory calls and system interrupts, this would be a logical first choice for a student who wishes to specialize in hardware-software interaction.

associate's degree

A two-year diploma representing about 60 semester hours of lower-level college credit (20 courses or so), this is the credential normally offered by community and technical colleges.

bachelor's degree

The standard four-year undergraduate degree representing about 120 semester hours of lower-level college credit (40 courses or so). Students who hold this credential are referred to as college graduates.

BASIC

A programming language designed during the late 1970s to replace the complex languages that flourished at the time. Extremely popular during the 1980s (spawning such offshoots as QuickBasic and Visual Basic), BASIC no longer enjoys its former glory and primarily stays alive through its small, but vocal, following.

branch campus

An established, recognized extension site that is operated by the main (mothership) campus of a given university. The difference between a branch campus and an extension site (see below) can be fairly vague, but generally a branch campus operates as a full-time satellite facility of a main campus. In other words, it is not a hotel room rented on alternate Saturdays; it has its own address, phone number, and staff.

C, C++

Probably the most popular and widely used programming language available, this is the first choice of many professional software engineers. It is also the core programming language of most computer science and electrical engineering programs.

campus

The physical location of a college or university.

certificate

In this context, documentation that a course of study has been completed

CLEP

The College Level Examination Program. CLEP examinations are available in a variety of fields and are accepted for credit at many major universities and community colleges nationwide. For more information on CLEP and other credit-by-examination options, see Chapter 11.

COBOL

A business-oriented programming language that formed the software engineering backbone of many computer science programs during the 1980s. Although largely replaced by other programming languages, it still has a place in older computer science curricula and is the programming language of choice for many management information systems experts.

college

An institution that awards degrees, or a collection of specialized faculty in a given field (who work, in turn, for an institution that awards degrees).

We might speak of Rivier College, for instance, or we might speak of the Fuqua College of Business at Duke University. Although the difference between a college and university is not as marked as it once was, colleges generally do not award doctorates (while universities generally do).

community college

An institution that offers lower-level courses and awards two-year (associate's) degrees. Generally speaking, community colleges are equipped to address the needs of adult students; evening classes are usually available, and tuition tends to be extremely low.

co-op study

A special type of college training program that allows students to work part-time or half-time in exchange for college credit.

correspondence course

A distance-learning course where the student is allowed to mail assignments to his or her instructor rather than handing them in.

course

A program of study offered by an educational institution.

credit

Points, awarded in quarter hours or semester hours, that may be applied toward a degree or certificate.

credit by examination

Credit earned based on a single examination (or series of examinations). For more information, see Chapter 11.

CSAB

The Computing Sciences Accreditation Board, a recognized accrediting agency that accredits many traditional undergraduate programs in computer science. For more detailed information on this agency, see Chapter 9.

CSAC

The Computer Science Accreditation Commission of the Computing Sciences Accreditation Board (CSAB), a recognized vocational accreditor. The CSAC accredits undergraduate programs in computer science.

curriculum

An organized program of study.

DANTES

Defense Activity for Non-Traditional Education Support, a popular program of credit-by-examination designed originally for military personnel, but now available to civilians as well. For more information, see Chapter 11.

degree

A specific credential that documents a complex program of study. In its most traditional sense, the degree is also a title (which is why you might actually hear people occasionally referred to as M.B.A.'s, Ph.D.'s, and so forth).

diploma

A document stating that a degree, or other educational credential, has been bestowed upon a certain person for completion of a given course of study.

dissertation

An original, book-length research project undertaken by doctoral students. Sometimes the master's thesis (see below) is also referred to as a dissertation, and sometimes the dissertation is referred to as a doctoral thesis.

distance learning

Any form of study that allows students to complete all requirements remotely.

distributed learning

A program of study where students take courses from an institution in a non-campus classroom setting (with other students and, generally, an instructor).

doctorate

The highest academic degree available in the U.S. Graduates are addressed as Dr. and are generally accepted as experts in their respective fields.

EAC

The Engineering Accreditation Commission (EAC) of the Accreditation Board for Engineering and Technology (ABET), a recognized vocational accrediting body. The EAC accredits programs in engineering.

electives

Courses that fulfill no specific requirements, but contribute toward the total number of required credits for a given degree (or major). There are two types of electives: general electives, which can be in any field, and field electives (also called major electives or restricted electives), which must be in the major area of study.

engineer

A graduate-level professional degree that represents a sort of middle ground between the master's degree and the doctorate. For more information on this highly regarded credential, see Chapter 5.

external

In this context, outside of the campus. Both distance learning and distributed learning are forms of external study.

fees

Miscellaneous degree costs charged in addition to, or sometimes in lieu of, tuition (for example, an application fee).

fellowship

A grant given to graduate students who pursue research goals. These are monetary grants with stipends designed to reward achievement within a degree program. They could be teaching or research fellowships and may be quite prestigious. Scholars and students of high promise are awarded these and are given titles of "teaching fellow" or "research fellow."

financial aid

Money given to the student (or directly to the college) to defray or completely cover the cost of attendance. For more information on financial aid, see Chapter 6.

FORTRAN

This programming language was extremely popular during the 1980s and still enjoys a cult following, particularly among those interested in artificial intelligence (as FORTRAN essentially is a computer-readable form of symbolic logic).

GMAT

The Graduate Management Admissions Test, a standard graduate entrance exam for business-related degree programs.

GPA

Grade point average. The student's average grade to date as reflected on a scale from 0.0 to 4.0 (where 0.0 is an F, 1.0 is a D, 2.0 is a C, 3.0 is a B, and 4.0 is an A).

GRE

The Graduate Record Examination, a standardized entrance test for prospective graduate students. The general GRE consists of three parts and is designed to measure the prospective student's verbal skills, mathematical proficiency, and reasoning ability. Most universities require graduate students to take the general GRE or GMAT before enrolling. The subject GRE measures the student's knowledge in the respective subject area (there is, for example, a subject GRE in computer science). The subject GRE is intended to more or less represent a standard undergraduate curriculum in the respective field.

While both forms of the GRE were originally designed as entrance examinations, Charter Oak State College and Regents College will accept some subject GRE examinations for credit. For more information on this option, see Chapter 11.

HTML

Hypertext Markup Language, the current scripting format used for Web documents. Almost all computer graphic design programs include at least one course in HTML, which is generally thought to be extremely simple and fun to work with.

IT

Information technology.

Java

Developed by Sun Microsystems, this mind-blowingly portable programming language can be used to write programs that can be executed almost anywhere—on a variety of platforms, through the World Wide Web, and beyond. This is probably the hottest programming language available right now.

liberal arts

Broadly speaking, the term liberal arts refers to the humanities and, to a lesser extent, to the social sciences as well. Recent trends indicate the need for IT managers who are broadly based in training, who can hold their own in various subjects, and who are equipped to deal with a myriad of concerns and issues.

life experience (credit)

See portfolio.

Lisp

This programming language is extremely popular among artificial intelligence specialists and Unix users, but does not currently have much mainstream appeal. It is, however, an extremely flexible language well suited to scripting, data mining, language processing, and cognitive neural systems.

major

The primary field of study for a given degree—for example, the B.S in Computer Science is a B.S with a major in computer science. For a bachelor's degree, the major normally consists of 33 to 54 semester hours of coursework. It is possible to major in more than one field at the same time (such as a B.S in Computer Science and Sociology).

MCSE

This usually refers to Microsoft Certified Systems Engineer, an extremely popular form of professional certification. It can also refer to the degree of Master of Computer Science and Engineering.

minor

An optional secondary field of study for a given degree. The minor (which generally requires between 12 and 21 hours of coursework) does not generally appear on the diploma, but may appear on the transcript.

nontraditional

In this context, any form of education other than the absolutely traditional (that is, face to face in a classroom, during the day, a few times per week). For more information on nontraditional learning, see Chapter 8 (for information on distance learning) and Chapter 11 (for information on other nontraditional ways of earning credit).

nonresident

Someone who doesn't make his or her permanent home in the same state as the college. Most public universities charge higher tuition for nonresident students.

online

Over the Internet, essentially (although the term can be used to refer to any connection involving a modem). Online classes are classes where instruction takes place mostly or entirely over the Internet.

portfolio

Credit by documented life experience. For more information, see Chapter 11.

prerequisites

Courses that must be taken to qualify students for other courses (for example, students must take Intermediate Algebra before taking Calculus). Prerequisites are not carved in marble and can often be waived on a case-by-case basis.

professional degree

A degree focusing on hands-on work and related practical on-the-job issues (management, quality control, and so forth), as opposed to research-oriented degree.

quarter hour

A measure of credit based on the quarter system (in which the academic year is divided into four roughly equal parts, called quarters). The average bachelor's program involves 180 to 200 quarter hours of credit; one quarter hour is equal to two-thirds of a semester hour. *See also* semester hour.

regionally accredited
Accredited by one of the six major regional accrediting bodies. All the schools described in Chapter 12 of this book are regionally accredited. For more information on accreditation, see Chapter 9.

research-oriented degree
A degree focusing on research, publication, and academics. (As opposed to "professional degree.")

resident
Those who make their permanent home in the same state as a given college. Public universities generally charge lower rates for resident students. *See also* nonresident.

SAT
The Scholastic Aptitude Test, a common entrance examination for undergraduates. A high SAT score can almost guarantee acceptance at even the most prestigious universities.

semester hour
A measure of credit based on the semester system (in which the academic year is divided into two roughly equal parts, fall and spring). The average bachelor's program involves 120 to 135 semester hours of credit; one semester hour is equal to 1.5 quarter hours. Unless specifically described as quarter hours, all hours or credits referred to in this book are semester hours.

senior paper
A significant research paper required of students during their senior year. Also called a "senior thesis."

senior project
A significant project required of students during their senior year.

senior thesis
See senior paper.

TAC
The Technology Accreditation Commission of the Accreditation Board for Engineering and Technology (ABET), a recognized vocational accreditor. The TAC accredits programs in engineering technology.

thesis
A publishable written work addressing a research problem. At the master's level, the thesis is generally worth anywhere from four to nine semester hours of graduate-level credit and is undertaken at the end of the program. The standard master's thesis can run anywhere from 35 to 120 double-spaced pages and should represent both broad scholarship and independent thought. Some Ph.D. programs refer to the dissertation as a doctoral thesis, and some bachelor's programs refer to the senior paper as a bachelor's thesis.

transcript
A receipt of courses taken, exams passed, and other requirements fulfilled at a given university or through a given institution.

tuition
Payment required for coursework. Tuition is generally the single largest expense involved in college attendance.

undergraduate
Adjective used to describe pre-graduate degree programs (in other words, the standard college degree or two-year associate's degree) and the students who are enrolled in these programs.

university
An institution that offers courses, conducts research, and awards degrees. There's not really much difference between a college and a university these days, but the traditional definition is that a university awards doctorates while a college does not. *See also* college.

VLSI
Very Large Scale Integration, a process that involves integrating hundreds of thousands of microscopic semiconductors onto a single tiny chip.

Web development
The study of HTML scripting, Web server maintenance, security, and related areas. Specialized study in areas of professional Web development (scripting, database programming, and so forth) is often a very strong possibility.

INDEX